Azerbaijan Diary

Azerbaijan Diary

A Rogue Reporter's Adventures
in an Oil-Rich, War-Torn,
Post-Soviet Republic

Thomas Goltz

M.E. Sharpe
Armonk, New York
London, England

Library of Congress Cataloging-in-Publication Data

Goltz, Thomas.
Azerbaijan diary: a rogue reporter's adventures in an oil-rich, war-torn, post-Soviet
republic by Thomas Goltz.
p. cm.
Revised ed. of: Requiem for a would-be republic. 1994.
Includes index.
ISBN 0-7656-0243-1 (c : alk. paper)
1. Azerbaijan—History—1991– . 2. Goltz, Thomas—Journeys—Azerbaijan.
I. Goltz, Thomas. Requiem for a would-be republic. II. Title.
DK697.6.G65 1998
947.54 dc21 97-27981
CIP
Printed in the United States of America

The paper used in this publication meets the minimum requirements of
American National Standard for Information Sciences—
Permanence of Paper for Printed Library Materials,
ANSI Z 39.48-1984.

BM (c) 10   9   8   7   6   5   4   3   2   1

For Hicran

Contents

Maps appear on pages
xxvi–xxx.

Photographs follow pages
116, 154, 298, and 406

Preface

History As Contact Journalism

The original intent of this book was to tell the story of the Republic of Azerbaijan from its declaration of independence from the Soviet Union in 1991 to its decision to join the Commonwealth of Independent States in 1993. The working title of the draft manuscript, published obscurely in Istanbul in 1994, was 'Requiem for a Would-be Republic.'

The reason I selected that thoroughly depressing title was that it fit with the tenor of the times. Azerbaijan looked like it was about to fall apart, and not too many people seemed to care. It was being held up as a classic example of a 'failed state,' a place marked by such an appalling level of chaos, confusion, and self-destruction that it almost did not deserve to exist. It was not a pretty picture, but it was the way things were and it was from that eye-witness experience that the original 'Requiem' emerged. And, because the historical facts have not changed, it is that experience which remains the flesh and bones of the current work, no matter how unflattering to many of the actors within it, the author included.

The change in the title of this edition of the book, however, should speak volumes. No longer a dirge for a dead country, it is now a diary account of the rebirth, in blood and agony, of a post-Soviet republic with a future. No one can be happier than I am that the prediction implicit in that first title was at the very least premature, if not down-right wrong, and the author thus wishes to be the first to express how delighted he is that Azerbaijan *still is*.

Indeed, Azerbaijan has now taken its place on the map and in the popular imagination in a way that was almost inconceivable a few short years ago. The reason, of course, is oil. Between November 1994 and November 1997, some $30 billion in contracts have been signed between the government in Baku and a veritable alphabet soup of oil companies, all of whom (along with the governments that back them) now have a large, vested interest in insuring Azerbaijan's continued existence as an independent state and, one hopes, as a very prosperous one. A vast material difference is already evident between 'my' Baku of the bad old days, when it was impossible to find a new toilet seat, and the current boom-town on the shores of the Caspian Sea, where Mercedes dealerships are springing up like hydrocarbon-fed mushrooms.

This is not to say that everything is completely rosy. Different power factions in Moscow continue to cajole and threaten Baku by turns, while Washington both claims the Caspian as part of the new American energy future and imposes sanctions against Azerbaijan. Article 907 of the Freedom Support Act, generated by the Armenian lobby in Congress, marks the country as a political pariah, undeserving of American aid and assistance. If not resolved, the outrageous contradiction between these two positions is bound to have future repercussions—especially in light of the fact that Armenia continues to occupy some 20 percent of Azerbaijan, and nearly one in seven Azeris live as internal refugees in their own country.

The reason for this sad state of affairs, of course, was and is the ghastly eight-year war over the disputed territory of Mountainous (Nagorno) Karabakh, which resulted in over 30,000 dead (mainly Azeris) and untold misery before grinding to the no war/no peace situation that persists today. Detailing the progress of that tragedy from the Azerbaijani side of the lines is a major theme of this book, as is the intimately related rise and fall of the Popular Front government of Abulfez Elchibey.

So, too, is the amazing return to power of that amazing survivor, Heydar Aliyev. Through gutsy political realism, cynical manipulation, and just plain force of personality, Aliyev has effectively become the father of his modern country and a leader to be reckoned with in the Caucasus region, Central Asia, and the wider world.

This is an essential point, because it suggests not only the flexibility of Heydar and his ability to react to changing political circumstance, but also the dangers involved for people like myself who write about contemporary history—the old problem of 'shooting at a moving target,' as it were. Not everything is always at it seems at first blink. Political actors *do* change their attitudes, and they often do not reveal their real intent early on. In the case of Heydar Aliyev, who is still referred to as a dubious Soviet holdover in much of the Western media, the attendant distortions between perceptions and reality are vast. In an effort to try and capture this dynamic of change, I have left the bulk of the original 'Requiem' text essentially as it was, 'correcting' it with a new Epilogue. The modifications I have made to the text consist of cutting back for the sake of space and incidental editing for the sake of clarity (and ridding the text of egregious typos). The original 'Requiem' was cast as a sort of annotated diary, a journey of discovery on which the reader was invited to travel with the writer as his or her perhaps imperfect yet enthusiastic guide. I see no reason to alter that approach with hindsight.

* * *

The scholarly reader may take issue with the first-person style of writing and the virtual lack of academic-style footnotes. The reason for the paucity of reference to 'others' is that I have seen far too many examples of bad sourcing in the press and in scholarly articles on Azerbaijan to believe anything not witnessed by me (or by someone whose honesty and integrity I can vouch for). That was so when I completed the first version of this book in 1994 and remains so today.

I then called this approach and still refer to it as 'History As Contact Journalism.' If you don't get bumped around a bit (as in 'blood' sports like football and ice hockey), you have no business talking (or writing) about a place like Azerbaijan and indeed, the Caucasus as a whole. Those of us who lived through the chaos and violence of the region in the post-Soviet era are a small club of very picky people ('informational shock-troops' was how one observer put it) when it comes to differentiating fact from fiction. There was a lot of the latter floating around during the early years, and there is still a lot floating around half a decade later.

A related theme that has been carried over to the new edition is the assault on conventional wisdom, especially that which has become common in the Western media. I said it in the first preface and I will repeat it again now: the screening of sources has collapsed, and virtually anything can become 'news' (the first step to becoming 'fact') so long as it has a pedigree—no matter what that pedigree is. I can detail dozens of cases of how a non-event or factoid moves down the informational pipeline from local news sources to Reuters to the *New York Times* before being quoted in scholarly articles and now, the first generation of scholarly books on the region.

A classic example concerns Heydar Aliyev: If one is to believe a *Washington Post* report on Aliyev's visit to the Oval Office in August 1997, Heydar was a 'member of Leonid Brezhnev's Politburo,' was 'driven from office in 1991,' but then managed to 'seize power again' through a 'Moscow-inspired military coup' in 1993. There is so much wrong with this construction that I scarcely know where to begin. While Heydar was a member of the Brezhnev circle of cronies, he was first brought into the

Kremlin by Yurii Andropov. In 1991, he was not in power in Baku, but in self-imposed seclusion in Naxjivan. And as for his alleged seizure of power in 1993, this can only be described as a nasty, simplistic, and ultimately incorrect interpretation of very convoluted events. But because it was so written in the *Washington Post,* this pernicious version of the career and personal history of Heydar Aliyev (and modern Azerbaijan) has become a quotable fact. I have the arrogance to suggest to the reporters, editorial writers, and, ultimately, scholars of the period and place that they take the time to wade through this opus before furthering the promotion of 'facts' based on repetitive errors.

Lastly, I would like to end this preface on the same note that I concluded the original: a hope that a lot of readers will find the story of a rasty character from Montana wandering around Caucasian war zones sufficiently weird to command interest as an adventure, pure and simple. If the plethora of obscure names and references confuse, think of yourself as the idealistic hero of the Doonesbury comic strip who finds himself called on by the new Clinton White House to do some troubleshooting in a post-Soviet place so distant he has to call his mother to find out where it is on a map. Although probably better equipped with languages than the Doonesbury character, I was essentially that guy, boarding an aircraft bound to Baku in the summer of 1991, not even really aware of where I was going until I got there.

Thomas Goltz
Livingston, Montana
December 1997

Acknowledgments and Special Thanks

Many people helped make this book possible. First and foremost, I will thank Dr. Hicran Öge Goltz, who tolerated not only my frequent absences but my frequent excesses, too. This book is dedicated to her.

Next in line comes Peter Bird Martin, the executive director of the Crane-Rogers (ICWA) foundation, which supported me through the first years of the Azerbaijan venture. Peter convinced the ICWA trustees to accept my unilateral transfer of my 'Central Asian' fellowship to the Caucasus. I also would like to thank a number of editors who had the thankless task of dealing with me at my petulant worst. David Ignatius and Jodie Allan of the *Washington Post* are high on the list of those due thanks mixed with apologies. Ditto for 'Wild Bill' Holstein of *Business Week*.

Special thanks, too, are owed to Alexis Rowell of the BBC, another proponent of 'contact journalism,' who dragged me into places I did not want to go; Cengiz and Laura for hand-holding and ego-stroking; Elef, Nejla, Liam, Larry, Hugh, and Steve, traveling companions along the highways and byways of the Caucasus, as well as the late great Rory Peck, killed doing what the few of us do for a living. Big and Little Nana, Nata, and Nino are owed thanks for help and assistance in Tbilisi and Yerevan. Tehran would not have been Tehran without Farzin. Barry of British Petroleum and Ed of Amoco were less tight-lipped than most oilmen, and took the time to explain aspects of that vitally important subject to me, as did the late Mary Jo Klostermann of Exxon (and Shanely High School, Fargo, North Dakota). Philip Remler and Robert Finn of the American embassy in Baku were friends before they were diplomats and shared much with me that the 'hack-pack' never knew or would not learn. The same goes for Mehmet Ali Bayar of the Turkish embassy. Audrey Altstadt's support for my taking an interest in 'her' Azerbaijan was continual and deep. Thanks, too, to all the academics and institutions that had me drop by for guest lectures during the course of return visits to the United States. The 'circuit' gave me a chance to develop the ideas for this book, and discussion with experts on other, related areas (Russia, Armenia, Georgia) added depth of understanding to regional issues and nuances thereof. Robinder Bhatty of Columbia came through with moral support (and a Ph.D. dissertation subject based in part on my work) when I was convinced that no one else in this world cared about my experience. I also would like to thank my old pal Robert Scott Mason for his critical reading of the manuscript and insistence that I publish it at length and not in an abridged version. Diana Finch of the Ellen Levine Literary Agency and Patricia Kolb of M.E. Sharpe Publishers were patient far beyond the call of duty. Dan and Kathleen Kaul of the Murray Hotel in Livingston took care of me when I was seriously down and out.

Lastly, I have to thank all the citizens of Azerbaijan—including Vafa, Kubrah, Kazanfer, Niyazi, Elfrieda, Gala, Rosa, Mustafa, Yusuf, and others who opened their homes, offices and front-line lives to me during the period we shared together. There were good times, but on balance I think the bad outweighed them. Let's hope the future corrects the present to balance the past.

Prologue

In the heights above Baku, in what was formerly a festive park named after Stalin's comrade in arms, Marshal Sergei Kirov, rows of silent faces stare out from steel and glass tombstones tucked beneath a canopy of dwarf pine.

This is the *Shehidler Xiyabani*, or "Martyrs' Lane," the cemetery devoted to the memory of those killed in the cause of achieving the independence of the former Soviet Republic of Azerbaijan. It is, as it should be, a quiet and solemn place, and over the years I have found myself spending quite a bit of time there, walking the lanes and remembering. I usually lift my palms to the sky and repeat the *Fatihah* after placing a red carnation or two on the graves of friends and strangers. I am not a Muslim, but reciting the creed seems appropriate, at least for me.

The Martyrs' Lane in Baku is the second such cemetery on the same spot. The first was devoted to those who died, creating and then, defending the short-lived Azerbaijan Democratic Republic of 1918. Founded in the wake of the First World War, that republic collapsed into the waiting arms of the Bolsheviks in 1920, unable to support itself due to internal wrangling and outside meddling. The cemetery subsequently was dug up to make room for the pleasure park, and a huge statue of Kirov, the 'Lenin of the Caucasus,' was erected nearby.

The original park was reconsecrated after the last president of the Soviet Union, Mikhail Gorbachev, ordered the Soviet Army to roll on Baku to quell anti-Armenian rioting that had in fact ended a week before. The so-called pogroms had been sparked by events beginning in 1988 in Mountainous Karabakh, where local Armenians had declared their intention to secede from Azerbaijan. So emotional was the Karabakh issue and the related January 20, 1990, Baku massacre that even the Azerbaijani Communist Party was obliged to get aboard the nationalist bandwagon. To prove their patriotism, they closed a lovers' lane and rededicated the park to the memory of the victims of Black January, etching the names and images of eighty victims into a gray marble wall at the top of the park. The Kirov statue, pulled down by a hysterical crowd, was not re-erected.

But the park was large and there was always room for another grave. The first addition was a newlywed woman whose husband had been crushed by a tank on January 20. Grief-stricken, she committed suicide and was allowed to join her beloved in eternal rest. Another addition was a well-known journalist, killed in a road accident while on assignment in Karabakh later that same year. She, too, was given martyr status. Next came a local Russian paramilitary officer, or OMON, shot by a sniper while on patrol in what was known as 'Operation Ring' in 1991—a year that saw graves grow from ones and twos to fives and tens. The biggest lot were a dozen government officials, killed when their helicopter was shot down over Karabakh in November of that year.

Most of the graves, however, date from 1992, their number growing exponentially through 1993 and 1994, as the simmering Karabakh 'conflict' slowly escalated into a full-fledged, if undeclared, war. The dead are mainly men, but there is a fair percentage of women, too. A majority of tombstones have inscriptions from the Muslim holy book, the Quran, although there are also a number of stars of David and crosses marking the graves of Baku Jews and Russians. Most of the graves are decorated with at least the blue, red, and green flag of Azerbaijan, but some are more elaborate: mourning families having made flower gardens around several and placed personal totems on others—a broken guitar, a favorite childhood doll, a news clipping detailing how the fallen lived and died.

The weirdest and wickedest token in the cemetery, however, is a jar placed on the grave of a nineteen-year-old youth named Yevlak Husseinov. It contains a pickled human heart, ripped from the body of an Armenian foe, and placed on the grave by his mother. Her name is Nurjahan Husseinova. The last time I saw her, she was still a very attractive woman despite a solid row of gold teeth in her upper jaw, her rough carpenter's hands, and the fact that she had clearly gone insane with grief.

"It was such a pretty little hole," she said, describing the wound that killed her only child, in what the military refers to as 'friendly fire.' "It went in through the back of his head but came out his eye, so it didn't shatter his skull."

As the first female volunteer of the Azerbaijani national army, Nurjahan knows many of the soldiers buried in the cemetery and can describe how they were killed and where: Dashalti, Xodjali, Shusha, Lachin, Kelbajar, Agdere, and Agdam—all resonant place-names in the litany of defeat and disaster in Azerbaijan's short history as an independent state.

"The flower of the nation has been killed, and in vain," she wistfully mused during a grisly tour through the cemetery. "Sometimes I think that our real enemy is ourselves."

By the summer of 1993—not two years into independence—there was increasing evidence that Nurjahan's paranoid speculation was true: the additions to the Martyrs' Lane were not soldiers killed by Armenians or even friendly fire, but Azeris killed by other Azeris as the rage of defeat turned inward, and the oil-rich but fractious country lurched toward the paroxysm of civil war.

The issue came to a head on June 4, 1993, when government forces attempted to disarm a garrison in the country's second largest city, Ganje. The rebel group was led by a 34-year-old militiaman who refused to comply with orders from the central command. The government forces failed so miserably in dislodging the rebels that many observers suspect the entire affair was orchestrated as part of a larger conspiracy to destroy the infant democracy of Azerbaijan.

If that was the aim, then the plan nearly succeeded. Within two weeks, the militia commander, Surat Husseinov, had driven the nationalist President Abulfez Elchibey out of Baku. Two weeks later, he was nominated for the job of prime minister by Heydar Aliyev, the former KGB general and Soviet Politburo member, who had been invited back to Baku by Elchibey to help achieve some measure of stability, but who assumed the acting presidency—and thus power—the moment Elchibey fled. Husseinov's nomination as prime minister was then confirmed by a parliament that should have been, or once was, stacked with Elchibey supporters. Overnight, they had become Aliyev sycophants. Not surprisingly, Aliyev was soon elected president by an astounding majority on the promise of bringing the peace, prosperity, and victory that Elchibey had failed to deliver.

Many have compared the events in Azerbaijan in 1992 and 1993 with those in neighboring Georgia in 1991 and 1992, when President Zviad Gamsakhurdia was driven out of Tbilisi and the country was delivered into the hands of former Georgian Communist Party boss (and Soviet foreign minister) Eduard Shevardnadze. Whether by default or design, Georgia then spiraled into such chaos that many wondered whether it could survive as a state—a phenomenon that came to be referred to as 'the Georgia Syndrome.' The awful civil war in Tajikistan became the 'Tajik Variant' on this theme, while the hot summer of 1993 in Baku was called the 'Azerbaijan Example.' Political wags and post-Sovietologists can now discuss the 'Moldova Model,' the 'Crimean Complex,' and even the 'Estonian Experience,' all built on the original Georgian theme. The leitmotif in each case remained disturbingly similar: governments in former Soviet republics that wanted real independence from Moscow were riven by separatist conflicts until the population began to beg for a Soviet-style strong-man to restore order.

This was, perhaps, the saddest thing about the Georgian and Azerbaijani coups: they were unbelievably popular. And they exposed every weakness, inadequacy, and the ultimate shallowness of the democratic experiment in the post-Soviet Caucasus. In an orgy of opportunism, an unholy alliance of neo-communists, opposition parties, and even old friends of presidents Gamsakhurdia and Elchibey gave their seal of approval to the putschists—and thus tacitly agreed with the concept that anyone with 300 armed sup-porters could take over the government.

The 1993 putsch in Azerbaijan was particularly tragic because it came as no surprise at all—not even to the main victim, who had openly predicted his fate more than a year before it was effected. "The president you elect in three months will be overthrown in a year because the state we live in today is only deserving of a president who can be kept in power by force," Abulfez Elchibey said in an address to parliament. "We need to create structures that can protect a president and prevent him from turning into a dictator. If we fail to create such structures, whoever you elect as president will destroy himself or be destroyed by those nearest to him." Elchibey gave that speech three months before the elections that made him president. He was not even a candidate at the time.

Like any good prophet, Elchibey did nothing to prevent the fulfillment of his prediction. He did nothing to restructure the presidency and he did nothing in the way of forcing his 'democratic' associates to call for new, postcommunist parliamentary elections that would have bestowed demo-cratic legitimacy on his entire government—and maybe saved his regime. His failure to act created enemies out of allies and former friends and left a wide field of play for anyone interested in bringing down the Elchibey government in the spirit of establishing 'true democracy.'

That the neo-communists were delighted by the June 1993 insurrection and subsequent coup was not surprising. They had been trying to eviscerate the Elchibey government since it came to power on a wave of nationalist sentiment in June 1992. It was the performance of former allies that took many observers aback, although as one old friend put it to me, the upside of the coup was that it revealed people to be really who they were, or had been all along.

The basic criticism of the Elchibey government, however, rang true: aside from the president himself, not one official could claim any sort of mandate from the people in the usually understood sense of the word. As parliamentarians, they owed their sinecures to elections held before the collapse of the Soviet Union. As such, it is tempting to suggest that they are more tainted than any of the neo-communists, because they never fulfilled their promise of being democrats by acting like democrats and doing such things as holding elections.

It did not have to be so.

In May 1992, the 360-member, communist-dominated Supreme Soviet prorogued itself indefinitely under duress, handing legislative power over to a 50-member group calling itself the *Milli Mejlis*, or National Parliament, a group weighted on the side of the former parliamentary opposition known as the Democratic Bloc, that in turn was intimately associated with the Popular Front, which had just effected a countercoup against the former Communist Party boss and first Azerbaijani president, Ayaz Mutalibov, in order to restore the scheduling of Azerbaijan's first democratic presidential elections (and first democratic elections of any sort). Elchibey then won, with 60 percent of the vote.

The presidency was to be merely the first step. The next was for the *Mejlis* to call for new elections for the whole parliament and thus legally sweep the communist deputies into the ash heap of history, forever. But despite ample time and opportunity, the *Mejlis* never set a date for new polls. The main reason was that the leadership was afraid of losing. All too many erstwhile idealists had been seduced by little corruptions and the perks that come with power—and voters knew it.

Indeed, Azerbaijan was doubly cursed with the two greatest corrupters known to modern man: war and oil. The indecencies associated with the commercial aspects of armed conflicts are well known; the reader need only recall the character of the regimental supply master Milo Minderbinder in Joseph Heller's *Catch-22*. In Azerbaijan, individuals at the highest levels of government made good money by keeping the war going. One particularly lurid example was a commander who kept bodies in refrigerators so that he might draw his dead men's combat pay.

But the main corrupter was oil. After seventy years of Soviet exploitation and mismanagement, many thought that the Azerbaijani oil patch had gone dry. Perhaps for the sake of the country, it would have been a good thing if this had been so. But initial exploration of offshore fields in the Caspian Sea in 1991 suggested reserves in the range of four billion barrels of crude, worth over $50 billion. The prospect of dealing with this wealth overwhelmed the governments of communist President Ayaz Mutalibov and then nationalist President Elchibey. Neither could deal with the prospect of being really and truly rich and neither knew how to exact both local and international political gain from that fact. Both allowed negotiations to drag on and on while rapacious ministers, deputy ministers, and deputy-deputy ministers tried to get aboard the greasy gravy train for incidental pieces of the action before the bubble burst.

The question of how to deal with the reality of oil is also of primary importance to the current government of Heydar Aliyev. Initial indications are that Aliyev has been able to carve out at least some breathing space for himself thanks to newly acquired friends in the West and the multi-million-dollar signing bonuses they provide; but achieving and sustaining a general prosperity is another story.

The reason for this is that Azeri is also the lubricant for the great regional rivalry being played out in the Caucasus. While blessed with abundant natural resources (with seven climatic zones, allowing for the cultivation of everything from winter wheat to citrus), Azerbaijan is located smack-dab on top of one of the greatest ethnic, religious, and political fault lines in the world. It is the place where the semi-East meets the semi-West, where Russia meets Iran and Turkey, and where Orthodox Christianity abuts not simply Islam but both the Sunni and Shi'ite varieties of it. Rivalry between Moscow, Ankara, Tehran, and now Washington makes for a devil's playground indeed. Some pundits even took to calling it the 'Great Game' revived, in reference to the Anglo-Russian competition in Central Asia in the nineteenth century.

Russian interest in the Caucasus in general and Azerbaijan in particular is usually put in the context of concern about the encroachment of 'Islamic fundamentalism' in what was once referred to as the 'soft underbelly' of the Soviet Union. Given the Islamophobia prevalent in the West, many were sympathetic with the Russian position—and gave Moscow a free hand to do what it wanted, or whatever might need to be done to quell fundamentalism in places like Tajikistan, saving the people from themselves, as it were.

This level of analysis seems woefully lacking in insight and originality, not to speak of accuracy. I prefer to look at Russian interests in three broad categories: practical, strategic, and emotional. These have much less to do with concern about 'religion' than with what we usually refer to as 'imperialism,' or in the present case, 'neo-imperialism.'

Under the first rubric is the subject of borders. The frontier between Azerbaijan and Iran had been the border of Czarist Russia and then the Soviet Union for more than 170 years, and for Moscow it was easier to keep it where it was than move it. Think of the problems involved with security and smuggling if Texas were suddenly to become an independent state again.

Next come Moscow's strategic interests. Thanks to the infamous vertically integrated economy of the USSR, at the time of its break-up there were vital establishments associated with the military industry complex that suddenly found themselves in a foreign state—and the generals in Moscow did not like that at all. In Azerbaijan, one of these was a huge radar installation at Gabala that took in data from as far away as Cairo. How would the Pentagon and NASA react if Florida were to secede and start charging for, or even deny, use of Cape Kennedy?

Lastly, there was the emotional attachment many Russians felt for their colonies, like Azerbaijan, which represented the fun and sun belt for the people from the north. When Azerbaijan (and Georgia, too) became independent states, not only was all of Russia's citrus being grown 'abroad' but its beaches had just disappeared. At risk of going overboard with the comparison, think of how most Americans would feel if the Hispanic population of California were to wage a successful campaign for state independence.

Then there was Iran. In addition to whatever ideological aims the leaders of the Islamic Republic may harbor (and I think they are few and grossly exaggerated), the fact remains that until 1828, most of the territories that now make up Azerbaijan were part of Iran. Indeed, although a great deal of fuzziness exists about the numbers of self-conscious Azeris in Iran, there is little doubt that their number far exceeds the number of Azeris in Azerbaijan itself. Rather than being concerned about exporting 'fundamentalism' from the south, Iranian authorities were (and are) far more concerned about the import of Azeri nationalism from the north. One way of dealing with the issue was to embrace 'Azeriness' as a fundamental part of the Iranian ethnic and cultural landscape (which, historically speaking, Iran has every right to do) and then to contribute to instability in Baku in an ad hoc manner—by promoting events like the ritual self-mortifications associated with the Ashura ceremonies during the Muslim month of Muharram and by making 'Islamic' inroads into susceptible parts of the population, such as abject refugees and defeated soldiers.

Following the collapse of the Soviet Union in 1991, there was much speculation about Turkey's effort to carve out an area of 'special interest' in the Caucasus and Central Asia. This was usually framed in terms of its 'ethnic' and 'cultural' connections to the 'Turkish speakers' of the Soviet Union after '70 years of separation.' The reality was that one might better have spoken of 700 years of separation, and languages and cultures as 'similar' as, say, Romanian and Portuguese. Egged on by Washington, Ankara spent a lot of time and money on the dream of the coming 'Turkish Century' and a new 'Commonwealth of Turkic States' stretching from the Aegean Sea to the Great Wall of China. Little account was taken of the fact that the newly liberated 'Turks' had just (if imperfectly) become free of one Big Brother, and did not necessarily want a new Big Friend—and, as it turned out, a particularly overbearing one—so soon.

In Azerbaijan, Turkish chauvinism ran roughshod over what was arguably a much more westernized (albeit Soviet Russian–style) population than existed in Turkey itself. Precious little note was taken of the 20 percent of the population (Russians, Lezgins, Tats, Talish, Kurds, and others) who would have no interest in becoming 'Turks,' even if all the Azeris did (which they didn't).

Finally, there was Armenia—both the neighboring former Soviet republic by that name, and the Armenia of the mind, a state with far larger borders than the existing entity, and far more real for many Armenians, especially those in the diaspora. The apologists can twist this issue all they want, but for those of us who were there to see, the program was abundantly clear: the creation of Greater Armenia. The primary motor behind this tacit policy of irredentism, of course, was the collective memory of the loss of those areas of the Ottoman empire depopulated of Armenians starting in 1915. I do not want to even begin entering the subject of whether what happened was a planned genocide or 'just' spontaneous massacres of hundreds of thousands of people. But I think it appropriate to note that whatever happened to Turkish Armenians at the time, it was at the hands of the Ottoman Turks. The primary victim of the Armenian policy of gathering in ancient lands, in contrast, has not been Turkey; it has been Azerbaijan. A tempting comparison is at hand: Imagine that, seeking revenge for the attempt of the U.S. Cavalry to exterminate them, the descendants of the Lakota Sioux were to ride north and seize part of Canada, forcing all the English-speaking residents to become internal refugees. Sweet revenge indeed!

But theoretical discussion aside, one is left with the facts on the ground: as a direct result of Armenian aggression, the number of Azeris who have fled their homes now exceeds one million—something like 15 percent of the population as a whole. Nor are Azeris the only victims of Armenian irredentism. In 1988, there were around 500,000 ethnic Armenian citizens of Azerbaijan. The vast majority lived in Baku; the minority, around 150,000, lived in the Autonomous Territory of Mountainous Karabakh, also known by its Russian initials, NKAO. By 1994, there were still 150,000 Armenians in Karabakh but less than 10,000 in Baku (most being spouses in mixed marriages). The welfare of the 350,000 Armenian residents of Baku was readily sacrificed on the altar of nationalism, to provide a rationale for Karabakh's seceding from Azerbaijan and attaching itself to Armenia—along with a good-sized chunk of Azeri territory outside Karabakh that had been ethnically cleansed of Azeri Turks and Kurds for ease of incorporation.

This was and is consistently denied by the Armenian authorities in Yerevan—but so was and is everything hinting at direct Armenian involvement in the Karabakh conflict. Indeed, Armenian leaders, aided by the Armenian diaspora, have proved masters of obfuscation.

The first important victory was winning the battle for terms of reference—and the most important term of all was 'enclave.' Unless one wants to redefine the dictionary meaning of the word, in English an 'enclave' is a state or part of a state that is surrounded by another. There are not too many 'part of state' enclaves around, for the very good reason that true enclaves are usually absorbed by the states surrounding them over time. This is certainly true of the few legally recognized 'spoors' of one republic in the other during Soviet times. There were two or three of each in both Armenia and Azerbaijan, but all effectively disappeared between 1988 and 1992, along with their indigenous populations. They are still on Soviet-era maps but are difficult to spot because they were so small. Look for circles of red connected by lines around border areas and—presto!—you will see a real 'enclave.'

The territory defined in Soviet times as the Autonomous Territory of Mountainous Karabakh (NKAO) was not one of them. It was part of Azerbaijan, and even had special representational status in the Azeri parliament. Maybe it should have been left as part of Armenia back in the 1920s. Maybe its association with Azerbaijan was really a cruel joke—no, a time bomb—on the part of Stalin, a genius in the game of distract, divide, and rule. But all this is beside the point. Karabakh was not part of Armenia and still is not today: for whatever reasons, Yerevan has neither claimed the NKAO as a territory nor recognized it as a separate state. And yet, the loaded term 'enclave' persists in the literature—a tribute to editorial inertia and the success of the Armenian propaganda machine.

In terms of the sheer volume of press stories, Yerevan also won the informational battle with Baku hands down. Journalists from around the world were encouraged to go to Armenia and Karabakh to write about bad things. Armenian officials—and indeed, the population as a whole—understood the warped way the news industry works: the bleaker, the better. Sober professionals fell fool to outrageous and almost impossible exaggerations of suffering, and then reproduced it as 'copy' that was soon on its way to becoming 'fact.' A refugee would describe how the Azeris used 'Armenian heads' for soccer balls in the streets of Baku, and the quotation would find its way into print. Another would report that Azeris five miles away would train their inaccurate GRAD missiles on the flashlights and candles used by the cellar-dwellers of Stepanakert when they came out at night to draw water from wells.

I do not mean to rebuke the Armenians for this successful manipulation of the media. I would have done it too, had I been in their shoes. As the old saw has it, 'truth is always the first victim in war.' But I do rebuke the journalists and diplomats who accepted such dubious material at face value, without bothering to double-check sources or even apply logic before relaying these stories to the world.

The Azeris, in contrast, did not know how to suffer in a way that could readily find its way into the print or broadcast media. One reason was that most visiting correspondents stayed in the great whorehouse of Baku, and were wined and dined by an elite that seemed singularly disinterested in events in the rest of the country. Another was a predisposition among foreigners to find something wrong with or ridiculous about Azerbaijan. (One American journalist claimed that his translator believed Napoleon was really a Turk. An Englishman showed up with a blue jeans–clad female interpreter from St. Petersburg expecting to get a read on local Islam, and was angry at the Azeris when he did not succeed.) If they managed to get out in the countryside at all, the foreigners were likely to be accompanied by clumsy, condescending 'minders' from Baku. If their idea of a front-line tour was to hole up in a guest house sufficiently far enough away from the action to be regarded as safe, and then eat and drink the day away, no wonder so little about 'the Azeri side' of the story found its way into print (and thus into the 'Truth' pipeline).

But the biggest difference between the Armenian and Azerbaijani approach to the Karabakh conflict was that while the former was marked by an eerie and admirable national consensus that involved everyone in 'the good fight,' the latter was marked by the most open, appalling self-interest that I have ever seen. The results of this were predictable: toward the end of my stay, no one I knew believed in anyone anymore—not the president, the government, the army, or even the person next door. I would not have either, if I were them.

Nor is the process over. In late 1994, Heydar Aliyev and Surat Husseinov were locked in a convoluted power struggle that involved all the elements cited above: war and refugees, oil and greed, Moscow-meddling and the politics of personal gain. Heydar prevailed. Another contender came along in the spring of 1995—this time, Turkey's man, Ravshan Javadov. He, too, failed in his bid to unseat Aliyev. In 1996, Husseinov was extradited from Russia to Azerbaijan, joining the leadership of the Iranian-backed Islamist Party in jail on charges of coup-plotting and treason, leaving only Ayaz ('the bogieman') Mutalibov among Heydar's rivals wanted and at large.

And Elchibey? Ironically, the leader of the Popular Front who fled into self-exile in Naxjivan was 'invited' to return to Baku in November 1997, presumably to lend a fig-leaf of respectability to Heydar's version of democratic pluralism, even while hand-picked henchmen such as the erstwhile chairman of parliament, Rasul Guliyev, have thought it best to keep their distance from Heydar's wrath once they proved to be nothing much more than expendable pawns in Heydar's elaborate-if-one-man-only style of rule.

Who was, who is Heydar Aliyev? I don't know. To listen to his supporters and his detractors, he is either (a) the chief agent of post-Soviet Russian irredentism in Azerbaijan, sent in as part of a deep, dark plot to destroy the country from within, or (b) a true Azeri patriot all along, seeking the best for his shattered nation the only way he knows how.

Which is the more accurate portrait of the man? On balance, and over time, I have come to accept the latter, but after years of contact, what I can state categorically is that Heydar Aliyev is first and foremost dedicated to his own survival, no matter at whose expense. He is, was, has been, and will be everything to everyone: believing communist, KGB general, Soviet strongman, suffering dissident, local nationalist, Pan-Turkist, devout Muslim, etatist, committed free marketeer. Tomorrow he may wear Scottish kilts and claim to be a devout Roman Catholic if that is the fashion.

Yes, Heydar is the original survivor. And in many ways, this book is about him, a sort of super-unauthorized biography by someone who got quite close to the Grand Old Man but kept taking notes: me.

What I worry about is Heydar's ultimate legacy. With the help of an oil-fed cult of personality that his mentor Leonid Brezhnev would envy, Heydar has managed to establish himself as the personification of Azerbaijan—*l'état, c'est moi!*

That may serve for today. And when his Maker calls him to his reward, his subjects will no doubt rename a city or town or park after him and erect a statue or ten in his image. But some decades from now, when a new generation passes judgment on the sins of today's heroes, will they then tear down the statues and rename the towns? That is what happened to Marshal Kirov in the park across the street from the national parliament, in the place now called Martyrs' Lane.

Let it stand as an eternal memorial to and a reminder of the victims of friendly fire.

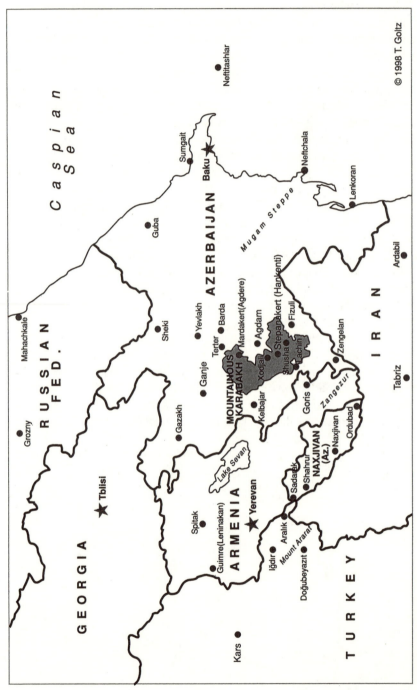

© 1998 T. Goltz

The Transcaucus.

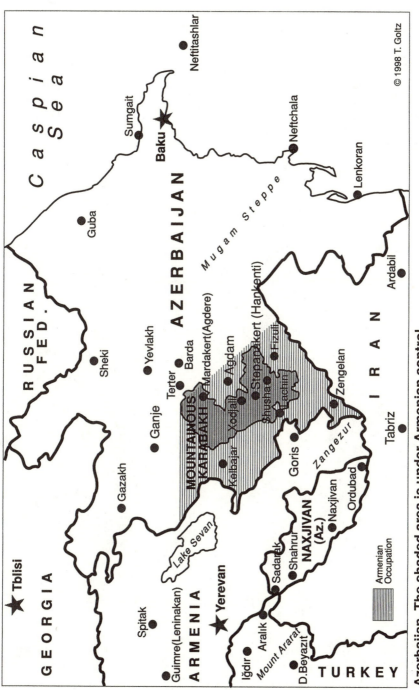

Azerbaijan. The shaded area is under Armenian control.

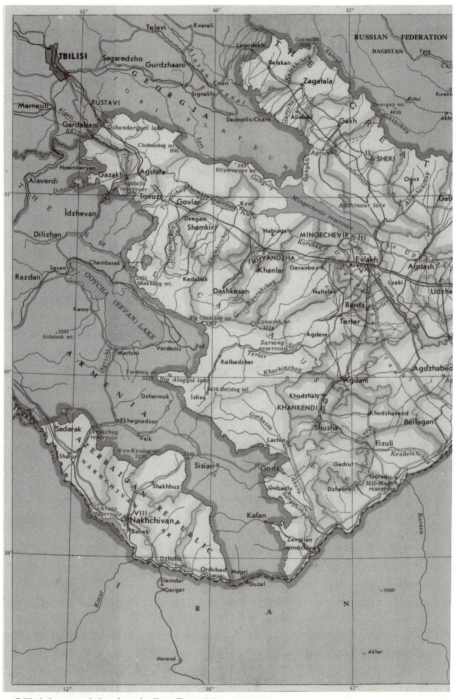

Official map of the Azerbaijan Republic, 1994.

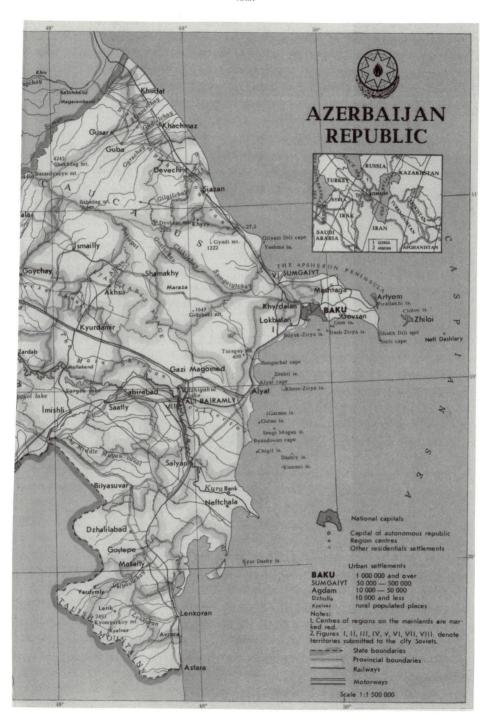

AZERBAIJAN REPUBLIC

National capitals
Capital of autonomous republic
Region centres
Other residentials settlements

Urban settlements

BAKU 1 000 000 and over
SUMGAIYT 50 000 — 500 000
Agdam 10 000 — 50 000
Dzhulfa 10 000 and less
Kyalvaz rural populated places

Notes:
1. Centres of regions on the mainlands are marked red.
2. Figures I, II, III, IV, V, VI, VII, VIII denote territories submitted to the city Soviets.

State boundaries
Provincial boundaries
Railways
Motorways

Scale 1:1 500 000

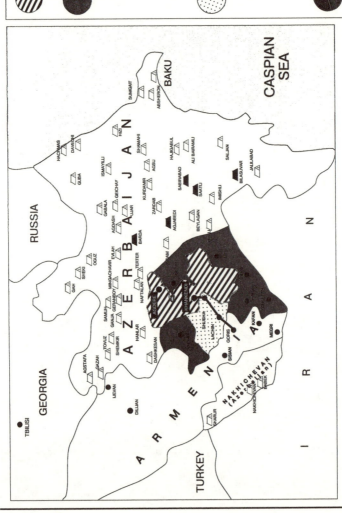

Territories of Nagorno-Karabakh region of the Azerbaijan Republic for which the Republic of Armenia demands the status of international legal party (4388 sq.km)

Azeri-populated territories which the Republic of Armenia could evacuate on condition that Nagorno-Karabakh region of the Azerbaijan Republic is given the status of international legal party.

Kelbajar region	- 1936 sq.km.
Fizuli region	- 1386 sq.km.
Qubatli region	- 802 sq.km.
Jabrail region	- 1059 sq.km.
Zangelan region	- 707 sq.km.
Agdam region	- 1093 sq.km.

total: - 6983 sq.km

Azeri-populated territories that Republic of Armenia is not willing to evacuate under the pretext of creating a corridor between the Republic of Armenia and Nagorno-Karabakh region of the Azerbaijan Republic.

Lachin region - 1835 sq.km.
(Population - 59,500 Azerbaijanians)
Shusha region - 970 sq.km.
(Population - 29,500 Azerbaijanians)

total: - 2805 sq.km.
(Population - 89,000 Azerbaijanians)

Total area of the territories of the Azerbaijan Republic occupied by armed forces of Republic of Armenia since the beginning of aggression and which undergone ethnic cleansing (population - 837 thousand) - 14167 sq.km

 Refugee camps and places of settlement

Tent camp

Official map of the situation on the ground according to the Azerbaijan Ministry of Foreign Affairs, 1994–95.

Azerbaijan Diary

Getting There Fair and Square

It was sweaty and muggy and squalid aboard the Ilyushin jet parked at Istanbul's Atatürk International Airport, and had been for hours. The air-conditioning would not be turned on until the doors were locked for take-off, and there did not seem to be much prospect of that happening any time soon.

The reason for the delay was simple. Aeroflot had grossly oversold the flight. There was nothing new in this. What was strange was that the ticket takers, stewards, and everyone involved in the boarding procedure had allowed so many extra passengers through the gate and onto the plane. They now appeared to take an almost sadistic delight in watching us climb over mountains of 'hand luggage' and then fight with each other for a place to sit.

I had paid $1,000 in cold cash for two tickets aboard this miserable flight only to discover that our assigned seats had already been claimed by others, and the interlopers would not budge. So like all the other dispossessed, we found other seats. Mine was in 'first class' at the front of the plane. The leg room was occupied by someone's garbage bag filled with cheese; the heads of my two drunken row-partners lolled on my shoulders. My wife Hicran, meanwhile, was stuffed in the back between two fat women and their screaming children—at least that is where I had last seen her several hours earlier. There was no guarantee that she was still aboard. I had already fought off a few would-be claimants to my perch—shameless men with gold-capped teeth who waved money at the stewardess to remove me. They failed for the very good reason that their ticket stubs did not match the number of my seat and I could promise the stewardess a bigger tip to let me be.

But now the threat was real: a man was thrusting a ticket stub in my face, and the number on his boarding pass did indeed correspond to the place I occupied. He was sweating and angry and became increasingly abusive when I refused to budge. Wisely and untypically, I kept my mouth shut and played dumb. The man with the ticket exploded in righteous indignation and swore at the stewardess. Then the security men pretending to be cabin crew grabbed him and threw him off the plane, tossing his hand luggage out after him.

I felt sorry for him. But I had too much at stake on this flight to Baku, the capital of the Azerbaijan Soviet Socialist Republic, to do anything about it. I had to get to Baku—even if it wasn't our destination. That was Tashkent, the capital of the Uzbek Soviet Socialist Republic, four more flight hours away in Central Asia, where I was to take up a position as an adjunct professor of history for the next two years. I was as eager to learn what I could about the Turkic-speaking societies of Central Asia as I was to teach what I had learned about modern Turkey during almost ten years as a resident foreign journalist. It seemed a fair trade, and Uzbek, I had been assured, was sufficiently close to my fluent Turkish to be picked up with ease.

The problem was that I was late—some three months late. I had been on my way from Montana to Tashkent when I took a little detour to Allied-occupied Iraqi Kurdistan. It was in the wake of the Gulf War against Saddam Hussein and I wanted to take advantage of the chaotic situation there to see some things you normally weren't allowed to see—like refugee-packed Iraqi Kurdistan, in the spring.

It had been a good time, an important time. But now our visas to Uzbekistan, acquired by hook and crook through the Soviet consulate in San Francisco, were about to expire and getting new ones seemed impossible. We had two days left. The next flight to Tashkent (via Moscow) was in three. Complicating the problem was that the entrance route was defined as being from the Bay City to Tashkent, direct. Moscow wasn't even on the visa itinerary and the Soviet authorities—this was in 1991, when there still was a USSR—were rather sticky about things like that. God knows I had tried. The day before, I stopped by the Soviet consulate in Istanbul to see about extending the Uzbekistan entry visa and including Moscow as a transit point. Rather than discovering solutions, I only encountered more problems.

"You cannot enter the USSR on these papers," the consul snarled. "A page is missing."

"That is impossible!" I said.

"Go back to San Francisco," came the reply. Then he slammed the visa window shut and announced that the consulate was closed for the day.

There seemed to be only one thing left to do: shell out the cash for two ridiculously overpriced, nonrefundable Aeroflot tickets from Istanbul to

Baku that left the next morning, and throw ourselves on the mercy of the Azeri authorities. At least we would be entering the USSR before the visas expired, even if it was the wrong point of entry. But it still looked dicey: without visas for Azerbaijan, we could not even check into a hotel.

So I picked up the phone and called my old friend Yalchin. He worked for the news agency TASS (and maybe others) at the Soviet embassy in Ankara. I always assumed him to be a spy and I always assumed that he assumed the same of me on the logic that I attributed to him, namely, that if all Soviet journalists were really spooks then all American journalists had to be, too. But we had became pals anyway and once were even featured on the same state television show about Turkey's 'image problem' abroad. This was a subject much loved by the cultural hairshirt crowd of Ankara and Istanbul. Almost every year, usually during elections when political news was banned from the airways, the state television station would trot out a couple of the few Turkish-speaking foreign journalists living in the country and let them kick around the 'image problem' subject for a few hours. The program was never of much real interest and it wasn't that year, either, aside for one element: while the rest of the guests endeavored to explain why many people in Europe and America saw Turkey through the lens of the *Midnight Express*, the famous Hollywood movie that showed the brutality of Turkish jail life as experienced by a heroic American heroin smuggler, Yalchin maintained that the Soviet Azeri people knew everything about Turkey and loved and appreciated every bit of it.

At the time, I thought it possibly a disingenuous and devious means of courting the Turkish viewing audience with Soviet cultural schmooze. But now I had to call Yalchin's bluff, hoping that he hadn't been bluffing. So I called. He answered the phone. We chatted for a while. Then I lowered the boom and I told him I was flying into his hometown, Baku, but without a visa, and needed to see a little pan-Turkic enthusiasm, as it were. I was just a bit nervous about this, given what I assumed to be his KGB connections, but I didn't know what else to do. Yalchin, for his part, tried to be generous in his assessment of my making an illegal entry into the USSR.

"You're crazy," he said. "You won't get through customs."

"We have to try."

Yalchin sighed deeply on the other end of the telephone.

"How long do you intend to stay?"

"Three or four days," I replied. "They are waiting for me in Tashkent."

"Tashkent is a dump but you'll like Baku."

"I hope so," I said.

Yalchin paused, and then spoke with a weary voice.

"If you do make it past customs, my family will be waiting for you," he said at last. "They will show you all of Azerbaijan in total freedom. That is, if you get in."

* * *

That had been Tuesday night. On Wednesday afternoon, after the last of the 'excess' passengers had been booted off the Aeroflot plane, the doors of the Ilyushin finally closed and the jet taxied out onto the runway. A hand waving to me from the back of the plane over the mountains of luggage suggested that Hicran was still on board, too. Then we were in the air, flying east over the Black Sea, then over land I assumed to be Armenia or Georgia and over water again, which I assumed to be the Caspian Sea. There was a box of someone's goodies crammed between me and the window, but I could still make out a coastline flanked by a forest of oil derricks: Baku.

We landed and taxied toward the terminal and everyone jumped up and tried to be the first off the plane, even before it came to a halt. Then the doors opened, and everyone tried to be the first to the terminal. I thought this was because everyone was hand-carrying their luggage and did not want to wait for baggage delivery. But it was soon clear that people were just acting out of line-jumping habit: not only did customs remain closed for a full hour after we were in the terminal, but in addition to more hand luggage than I had ever seen before, everyone seemed to have checked enough baggage to equip an expedition to nineteenth-century Africa. In retrospect, this was as fine an introduction to Azerbaijan as could be imagined.

While we waited in front of the customs counter, knots of men went to work beneath the belly of the aircraft, swinging out suitcases, gunny-sacks, and huge plastic bags crammed with textiles and trinkets—one could determine this due to the gathering detritus on the runway—and swigging vodka all the while. After a small mountain had collected on the tarmac, the men would then hand-load the moving mountain onto a forklift, hoist it all to the level we were at, and then hand-lift everything off the forklift, dumping it all onto a conveyor belt that led to another knot of men who then dumped each piece on yet another conveyor belt standing at a right angle to but not connected with the first, that led to the far side of the passport and customs counter, where the baggage fell in a heap. Children wailed as they watched their new toys crushed beneath tons of cheese. A man broke into tears when the new windshield to his car slid off the conveyor belt, got wedged between two unbelievably large suitcases, and then snapped under the weight of a third, fourth, and fifth monster bag. I whispered a silent prayer of gratitude that I had kept my computer and camera bags with me as hand luggage, and winced when I thought of what my professorial suits would look like; they had been packed in the same suitcase as our year's supply of toothpaste.

The immigration police finally showed up and there was an instant crush as everyone began clawing for the right to be the first through the gate. A hand-manipulated steel rod was pulled back to allow people to enter the country. Then it was shoved back in place, skewering the next person in line.

We waited at the back of the mob until we were the very last folks in the line. Then the moment of truth arrived and I walked up to the immigration counter and plunked down our passports and San Francisco–Tashkent visas.

"Your visas are no good," said the customs man, in Russian. "They are missing a page."

"We are in transit," I tried to explain, in Turkish. "And we—"

"You are from Turkey?" he asked, looking up from beneath his hat.

"Yes," I lied. "Kind of."

"My brother went to Istanbul last month. He said he could die there!"

"It is a fine city," I said, "That is why we must get to Tashkent," I added somewhat illogically.

"But why are you going there? Why not stay in Baku?"

"That's what I want to discuss with you."

"But you have no visa for Azerbaijan."

"I know, but people are expecting us."

"Your relatives?"

"In a sense."

"We are brothers!"

"We are one!"

"I can let you in."

"Please do so."

"But there is a problem, Turkish brother with the American passport."

"Please tell me, O new Azeri kinsman."

"I cannot let you back out. Your visas lack the exit page."

So that was it. The bastards in San Francisco had really locked us into Uzbekistan by forwarding the exit visa part, thus making Tashkent the only way in. I could see a whole string of problems developing, but there was really no way out at this point. I looked at Hicran.

"Let's go for it," she said.

"Punch us in," I instructed my new friend.

"*Hosh Gelmishsiz*," smiled the visa man. "Welcome!"

With that, he stamped us into the USSR, or at least the Azerbaijan SSR part of it. Getting out was pretty easy because when we left, there was no longer any USSR.

* * *

A tall man standing at the far end of customs was holding out a piece of paper with my misspelled name on it. Next to him were three others: a handsome woman in her late forties, a young man with bad teeth, and a short, fat guy who revealed a mouthful of gold when he smiled. It was Yalchin's reception committee, and they had been waiting in the airport for six hours. Still, they tried to remain enthusiastic about our arrival.

"Welcome, welcome Mister Thomas!" cried the man holding the sign. "My name is Shamil, and I am to be your guide!" Oddly, he spoke to us in Turkish, and not the sing-song dialect of Azerbaijan we had been listening to for the past eight hours on the plane (air and ground time combined).

"Hicran Hanim, I have heard so much about you!" gushed the lady, embracing and kissing my wife while introducing herself as Kubrah, Yalchin's sister-in-law. She was speaking in Azeri, with a slight Turkish twist, but understandable. Not so her son Kamran, the slight youth with bad teeth.

"*We have been eyeballing your arrival something something,*" he said. We could barely understand a word.

"We have been awaiting your arrival with great expectation," the man who called himself Shamil said, translating.

"*Kak dela!*" the pudgy gentleman shouted in Russian.

"Speak Turkish," hissed Shamil.

"I don't know Turkish," said the short, fat man.

"Then speak Azeri."

"*Ne tersiz!*" the man tried again; our Turkish-tuned ears apprehended 'What are you?' although he was merely asking after our health. It was our first full blast of the very real differences between Azeri and Turkish.

His name was Kazanfer, and we assumed him to be the bag man or driver or both. He was not. He was our host.

Rather than zipping off to a sanatorium on the shores of the Caspian Sea as promised by Yalchin, we soon found ourselves ensconced in Kazanfer's abode. It was located in a sprawling, ill-defined suburban village called Mashtagah. At first we were pretty disappointed. There were no hotels, restaurants, or anyplace even vaguely 'public' where a journalist or diplomat or spy might stop in to get a read of local sentiment. There was no place to hang out, just a series of winding dirt roads without names, leading between walled compounds with no numbers. The directions, as it were, to Kazanfer's place would be something like this: the first green metal door down the second alley on the right side after the road splits where someone had left the motorcycle sidecar with no wheels. I was always worried that someone would find a wheel for the bike and move it and then I would be lost in Mashtagah forever.

At first we felt cheated and duped and angry at Yalchin, and after the first day or two we wanted to leave. But then we started to take a look around with different eyes. Mashtagah might have been slow and sullen, but the nondescript compound walls had been put up with a specific purpose in mind: to keep prying eyes out. The reason soon became clear. Mashtagah was—and is—the center not only of the amorphous Azerbaijan mafia but also—and without any contradiction—the center of the quasi-Islamic movement. Sure, it was not the Baku we had expected. It was far more than that. We had been invited into a neighborhood where other Azerbaijanis—much less foreigners—were almost never allowed, and as a base of exploration I cannot imagine a more interesting place. Our strange collection of hosts also exposed a cross section of Azeri society that most tourists could never be privy to. I might even venture to say that it was through them that we began to get to know the country, warts and all.

First came Kazanfer. He was employed by the government as a distributor. As I understood it, he dealt in food. His salary for doing so was 300 rubles a month—about $10 at the time, the same as an unskilled laborer might receive. But Kazanfer was *rich*. And he had become so by lubricating (or milking) the rusty wheels of the socialist state: rather than perform his allotted tasks of picking up, say, five tons of white cheese from a local collective farm and bringing it to a government warehouse in downtown Baku, Kazanfer would pay for the cheese and then distribute it privately. He referred to himself as a *tujaar*, or "merchant," but in common parlance he was a black marketeer.

His home, unprepossessing when viewed from the street, was a veritable palace within. Set on about two acres of fruit trees (cherry, pomegranate, apple, pear), the estate consisted of a comfortable, two-story main house flanked by a second kitchen/den unit with an attached marble sauna and bath, separate digs for grandma, and a shack out back for Kazanfer's Russian *bakhchivan*, or gardener-cum-slave. In addition to tending to the fruit trees and weeding the large tomato, eggplant, and pepper garden, the Russian was entrusted with looking after a long, low-slung hothouse discreetly tucked behind some bushes at the far end of the compound. One day, when Kazanfer was out and the gardener deep in a vodka-induced snooze, I shimmied over to the hothouse to see what secrets it held. Easing open the door, I stepped into the humid air and discovered the horrible truth: there, staring me in the eye, were row after row of small green bulbs. *Kazanfer was one of them!* The Flower Mafia. . . .

It might sound ridiculous outside the context of the former Soviet Union, but anyone who has been to Moscow or Leningrad can tell you about the power and wealth that accrue to those who supply fresh carnations to an otherwise gray and drab communist world.

Well, Kazanfer had money, but money he couldn't very well put in the bank. So he put it in merchandise and appliances. In addition to the dozens of oriental carpets slung on the floors and hung on the walls, I counted seven television sets, four stereos, two VCRs, and an up-market fax and telephone answering machine, although curiously, there was no phone.

More fabulous was the fact that Kazanfer owned not one, but four cars: a Lada for public use and two Volgas for road trips, plus a white 1986 Mercedes-Benz 200 sedan that was kept under wraps in a garage under the house, awaiting the day when its presence on the streets of Baku would not immediately invite a visit by income-tax-fraud extortionists associated with the police or KGB. Another reason the Mercedes was not in use was that it lacked a front wheel—the whole thing. And imported rims were rather difficult to obtain even for a professional procurer like Kazanfer.

There were other toys and trinkets, too: video cameras, bicycles for the kids, an unused CD player, as well as an endless supply of export vodka, caviar, Brazilian instant coffee, real butter, and more meat than Kazanfer knew what to do with. The flock of sheep he kept in the animal section of his estate were there to be slaughtered on the occasion of the arrival of honored guests like us, or on religious holidays. And Kazanfer was religious—after his own fashion, anyway. He insisted that his two sons attend the local Persian language and Shi'ite indoctrination night school, and made substantial donations to a new mosque and minaret project in town.

Strangely, his piety did not extend to interfering with the social habits of his wife, Nazilah. She was a great, fat woman who oozed bosom out of her halter tops and force-fed us every chance she got, showing off her mouthful of gold teeth when she laughed and weeping real tears when we finally left her abode. The household was completed by Hamidah, their plump daughter, who seemed more interested in the lifestyle of a certain Turkish sex-kitten than in finishing school, and Kazanfer's huge old oak tree of a mother, who totally dominated the family despite a bad case of gout and 85 years.

Shamil was our primary babysitter. It was helpful (and initially suspicious) that he was bilingual in Azeri and Turkish. He had acquired the facility by listening to Turkish films and cassettes because he had a particular obsession: his father was an Azeri gold merchant who lived in Istanbul. A POW during World War II, Dad had chosen to join the hundred thousand Azeris from Hitler's labor camps who migrated to Turkey rather than return home and face Stalin's well-known treatment of suspected traitors. He left behind a pregnant wife and future child. Because of his father's anti-Communist sentiments, Shamil had had it pretty tough in the Azerbaijan SSR. He had been denied CP membership—and thus condemned to a life of less than optimal opportunity. One could feel his sense of having been abandoned as a youth, dreaming of the gold shop in Istanbul's Covered Bazaar while he was obliged to go through the drudgery of life in a two-room flat in an anonymous housing complex, to line up for gasoline in a petroleum-producing land, and to become the companion of anyone his boss assigned him to—in this case, us.

His boss was our official hostess, Kubrah. A physician by profession, Kubrah worked as the director of a sanatorium that specialized in naphthalene cures for various bodily ailments, including infertility. Barren women from across the USSR would come to her establishment, take the oil baths and various electric shock cures, and report back in nine months that they had just given birth to twins. The fertility business probably had more to do with couples just taking the time to procreate than in dipping themselves in a vat of hot grease, but the row of mug shots of identical kids sent to Kubrah by thankful parents were real enough, and Kubrah was rightly proud of her contribution to Soviet society.

And the Party was proud of her—to the point of elevating her to honor status in the Azerbaijan CP. Her larger-than-life picture graced the outside wall of some regional office until she removed it after the Party had dissolved itself in disgrace. Pictures of other members of the CP honor roll remained on the same outside wall until they were ripped down by nationalists later in the year. She thus saved herself the painful ignominy of having her public portrait disfigured by her eldest son—Kamran.

In many ways, he was our real guide to Azerbaijan. A skinny kid with a high voice and bad teeth, Kamran at first seemed to be just an extra, unnecessary presence in the car or at the breakfast or dinner table. He even stayed out at Kazanfer's place with us. But with time, it became apparent that Kamran had a very different agenda. Not only did he feel bound by traditional hospitality to be with us; he wanted to be with us in order to communicate a lot of information he thought we should know concerning the realities of Azerbaijan in the summer of 1991—like the coming revolution.

Given his parents' Party membership and connections, Kamran had enjoyed a privileged youth. He had studied law at Kiev, and had been able to spend his time as a draftee soldier within Azerbaijan and mainly off base, in the house of a police chief and family friend in the city of Kirovabad, which everyone called Ganje.

In another time, Kamran's destiny would have been pretty clear: get your degree, join the party, and then rise through the nomenklatura to a position of a member of the elite in the land of socialism. But something unexpected had happened that had profoundly shaken Kamran and fundamentally altered his perspective on the party, privilege, and patriotism. It was the night of January 19/20, 1990—the night that the Soviet Army rolled into Baku, and Kamran was there on the barricades when they came and killed between 100 and 200 unarmed people.

According to most contemporary press reports out of Moscow, the troops had been sent to put down anti-Armenian rioting related to events in Mountainous Karabakh, the 'autonomous territory' in western Azerbaijan populated mainly by ethnic Armenians who wanted to secede from Soviet Azerbaijan and join Soviet Armenia.

But those ugly events had been brought under control a full week earlier—leading to the paranoid, if almost universally held notion that both the anti-Armenian pogroms and the subsequent crackdown were part of a larger scheme, drawn up in Moscow, to destabilize and punish Azerbaijan. The thorny subject of the secession movement in Karabakh and the Kremlin's initial response to it would become a leitmotif of our residence in Azerbaijan, but at the time we had no idea of the significance of the Karabakh Committee, the Sumgait pogroms of February, Black January in Baku, or any of the many other related conspiracy issues in the mind of the average Azeri, although God knows we would learn.

"What happened?" we asked.

"That you have to ask just proves my point," said Kamran. "The force of the Red Army rolled on a defenseless city. We were young and old, men and women, Turks and Jews and Russians. But for the world, we were represented as a bunch of fundamentalist Shi'ite Muslim killers on the rampage against innocent Christian Armenians. *Killers?* My family hid our Armenians friends from KGB-led mobs! You have to see it within the context of the Soviet Union. We were set up to be an object lesson about the limits of glasnost by the *Tsentr*."

"The Center?" I asked, and Kamran sighed.

"As an American, and a Westerner, you will find it difficult to understand what I am about to say. But the Center is Moscow, and Moscow is the Kremlin, and the Kremlin is your beloved Mikhail Gorbachev."

Indeed. The author of Openness and Restructuring had taught a similar lesson in the limits of freedom to neighboring Georgia in 1989, and then again to the Baltic states later in 1990, when the Soviet army rolled into Lithuania. The world went wild with condemnations then. But at the time of the Baku massacre, not a single Western voice was raised in protest about the Azeris crushed beneath the Kremlin's tanks. And Kamran felt he had divined the reasons for this indifference: with no resonance group outside the country, and generally distrusted within it for their relatively affluent life-style, the Azeris were perfect targets to send a message to all others. On a local level, the result was total disillusionment with the Soviet system, and Kamran and his friends could never look at the Union, Moscow, Gorbachev, or the Party in the same light again.

Driving down the road from Mashtagah to Baku, he would tirelessly point out the roadside remembrance markers to us, naming the names of those who had fallen, and where. He also had us linger at the Martyrs' Lane, or *Shehidler Xiyabani*, in the heights above Baku. Formerly called Kirov Park in honor of Stalin's close associate Marshal Sergei Kirov, it had once been the venue for all manner of entertainment. Now it was a grave-yard dedicated to the memory of the January 20th martyrs, and all restau-rants and tea houses had been banned from the park, out of respect for the dead. The monumental statue of Kirov lay shattered at the foot of its pedes-tal overlooking Baku Bay.

In addition to the publications and literature devoted to the theme of the January 20th massacre that he pressed on us, Kamran also made us view a bootleg film documentary on the subject, replete with gruesome close-ups of crushed bodies in the streets and long, extended morgue shots and autop-sies. Here, many of the victims had been killed by 'twister' bullets the Soviet Army denies even having: an Azeri physician who had served as a (Soviet) frontline MD in Vietnam was interviewed in the program, and described how a bullet would enter the leg or foot and then corkscrew along the bone, emerging from the shoulder and leaving no hope of recovery for the victim.

"We were used as a weapons' testing ground," said Kamran in disgust.

Kamran was also the source of a lot of basic information on the main opposition organization—a group called the *Xalg Jephesi*, or Popular Front. They were the people who had taken it in the back of the neck around the time of January 20th, when most of the leadership was jailed or driven into hiding. There were some names that I knew: a tall, lanky, bearded character named Abulfez, with the odd last name of 'Elchibey,' or 'Mister Emissary.' I vaguely recalled seeing him in a Turkish television broadcast in the after-math of Black January, in which he blamed the events on the KGB. In the scant literature on Azerbaijan I had been able to pick up before the trip, I had also found mention of a few others—a young historian by the name of Etibar Mamedov, an orientalist by the name of Isa Gamberov, and then a hawk-nosed character described as the 'Lech Walesa of the Caucasus,' Nimet Panakhov, said to be involved in the labor movement when not on the run from the law.

We asked Kamran to take us around for a look and to meet some of his heroes. He bashfully declined. He had thrown away his CP card and had become a member of the Front, but his parents didn't know and he didn't want Shamil to tell them.

To make up for it, though, he took pains in helping us translate first the headlines and then the articles out of the Front news organ, a badly printed, smudgy, bi-weekly broadsheet called *Azadlig*. Most of the news was about the Front's first party congress (decisions included support for Boris Yeltsin, lifting of martial law in the country, and the rather naive and dangerous dream of reuniting Soviet and Iranian Azerbaijan) and the upcoming presidential elections. The First Secretary of the Communist Party of Azerbaijan, a slick-looking fellow by the name of Ayaz Mutalibov, was the only candidate, and the Front was calling for a boycott.

"I thought the communist boss here was whatsisname, Aliyev," Hicran said one day as we studied the papers, referring to the one name in the Azeri political spectrum that was known outside of the country: Gaidar Aliyev.

"You mean Heydar," said Kamran.

"Yeah," I said. " 'The First Turk in the Politburo'—as they called him in Turkey a few years ago. Why isn't there any news about him?"

"I don't know. I was a student then," said Kamran, vaguely. "It was a long time ago and I don't know."

The subject was dropped and did not come up again until much later.

* * *

So we started exploring Baku from our Mashtagah base—always under the friendly if watchful eyes of our hosts. Daily, we would be picked up and taken into town to be shown a sight or two before being deposited back in the safety of Mashtagah at night. There were severe limitations to this method of exploration (in retrospect, we saw precious little of the Baku we had come to see), but given the fact of our illegality in the country, we really did not have many other options.

The problem was that the city's center was rather far from our Mashtagah base, and getting there was almost painful. What separated us was a moonscape covered with old, rusting oil derricks and pumps, left like petrified birds on barren, poisoned land. This was the Azeri oil industry—and concern for the environment was clearly not on the Soviet priority list.

Oil was 'discovered' on the Apsheron peninsula in the third century B.C. by Zoroastrian fire worshippers, who built shrines around 'the eternal flames' fed by methane gas leaking from the sandy ground. One of these so-called Ateshgahs, or "Flame Palaces," had become a Soviet-style tourist trap for foreigners. It was located about half an hour north of the city's center in the village of Surakhan, and our hosts insisted that we go.

The road to the shrine was lined by a particularly dense patch of rusty rigs, many still pounding away, up and down, and leaking oil onto the ground. The Ateshgah itself was built in a Caravansaray style, with a central altar-like structure in the middle, where an eternal flame fed by underground gas burned—well, eternally. We picked up the obligatory guide and took a stroll around. Shoddy model displays depicted emaciated Zoroastrian fakirs who had traveled from as far away as India to await death near the Holy Fires. Another, less well known eternal flame was located a half-hour north of town and was far more impressive than the 'tourist-class' Ateshgah. There, an unquenchable wall of flame shot up from the primordial depths out of a naked hillside. According to Shamil, the flame appeared as a landmark on German aviation maps during World War II: despite the blackout every night, all efforts to douse the flame were in vain. When we passed by, a kebab restaurant had been set up just outside the scorch zone.

But everywhere else around Baku, the forest of antiquated rigs continued pumping like mad, and the results were ecological disaster with no hint of economic gain.

"It is the single greatest symbol of Soviet exploitation of our wealth," said Shamil, as we waited in a line of fifty cars to buy some gas. "No one has any idea of the environmental impact of leakage into the water table or even industrial diseases in the worksite or in the community. Sometimes I think they intend to pump us dry and then grant us our freedom."

After the forest of derelict derricks came another ring of blight: the rows of 'Khrushchev' highrise apartment buildings on the edge of town, whose designers should have been included in an early purge before they made their imprint on the city, but sadly were not. These were the so-called *mikroraiony*, or 'miniature-districts' that had been slapped up by socialist labor and given appealing names such as 'first,' 'fifth,' and 'eighth.' They were not prepossessing. Just beyond this double line of defenses, however, Baku revealed itself a charming, if somewhat seedy, Levantine-looking town. Along the seaside promenade, someone had been thoughtful enough to build a pleasant, tree-shaded walkway where lovers cuddled on benches, kids played snooker, and graybeards dabbled at dominoes or simply whiled away the time at one of the many boardwalk cafes. One of these establishments, built in a fairytale castle–like style with a moat, housed the chess club where World Grandmaster Gary Kasparov got his start.

All in all, I thought it reminiscent of Mediterranean cities like Alexandria, Izmir, or the Pera section of old Istanbul, and would not have been surprised to see such familiar names as C.E. Street, Sir Charles Barry, or even the ubiquitous Fossati brothers appearing as the designers of many of the nicer structures in town. Most dated from the turn of the century, when

Baku was synonymous with oil, and people like the Nobel brothers were making their fortunes and spending part of them on life's little pleasures. One handsome building on the quayside was nearly wild with wry wit, with gargoyles anointing the gables and vaguely 'oriental'-style friezes mounted along all balconies and windows. It was sad to think that the architects were probably Armenian. As the artisans of the period, they had left their mark on the city, only to have it erased in the aftermath of January 1990. The psychosis had even gone so far as to affect the local Lenin Museum on the quayside. While Vladimir Ilich was still lionized in display after display, the portraits of all Armenian participants in the revolution and government of Soviet Azerbaijan had been removed: square grease stains identified where 'heroes' of the revolution like Stepan Shaumian had once been on display. It almost went without saying that the several Armenian churches in the downtown area were boarded up and partially desecrated.

Then there was the old city, where the centerpiece (indeed, the visual symbol of Baku) was the *Giz Galesi*, or 'Maiden's Tower'—a teardrop-shaped buttress with a thin wedge of fortified wall extending out into what used to be the shallows of the port. Behind the tower, a labyrinth of small streets and lanes lined by pastel-colored houses led up to the complex of the fifteenth-century Emir of Baku, Shirvanshah. Converted into an inscription museum, it boasted gravestones bearing a peculiar mixture of animal and Quranic design; this is anathema in Islam, a religion that revels in calligraphy and rigorous geometric form as art but prohibits the use of human or animal images, to discourage the worship of idols. I tried to engage Shamil in discussion about the meaning of the peculiar mixture, but he only shrugged.

"You would never see that in a mosque in Turkey," I said.

"You know," Shamil said at last, "I have never been to a mosque."

"There's one near the Caravansary restaurant," said Kamran.

We went there. It had been turned into a rug museum.

Indeed, finding anything even vaguely 'Islamic' about downtown Baku was frustrating—and eye-opening. The closest thing to a Friday Mosque that we saw was the train depot, which was such a good replica of a mosque that we initially thought it was a place of worship converted from sacred to profane use. Closer study revealed that it had been built in 1926, but as a train depot pure and simple. The 'neo-Muslim' theme was also taken up by Stalin's architects on the quay. From a distance, one building appeared to be a *türbe*, or tomb of some pious Muslim notable; closer inspection revealed it to be a power station, and built as such.

"It's not only the mosques that the Russians destroyed," said Kamran, as we sat down for tea in the shadow of the government building located on the huge central square named after Lenin. "We have been stripped of our cultural heritage—our language, history, and culture—and had it replaced by that of our Big Brother to the North."

The looming statue of Lenin almost seemed to smile.

* * *

Having totally lost faith in the Soviet system, Kamran (like Shamil and even Kubrah) was attempting to fill the gap with something else—Azeri nationalism. For him, the symbols of this were the Azeri flag dating to the Republic of Azerbaijan of 1918–1920 and the portrait of that state's first and last president, Mamed Amin Rasulzade.

To be perfectly honest, I had never heard of the man before setting foot in Azerbaijan. But in her own preliminary, independent research, my wife Hicran had managed to pick up a little material on Rasulzade published in what might generously be called the 'right-wing' Turkish press. It was still pretty thin. A brief biographical sketch of the (failed) 'George Washington' of the country would be as follows: Born into a religious family in 1884, Mamed Amin Rasulzade began his literary and political career as a printer's apprentice in the cultural capital of the Caucasus, Tbilisi—which was then a mainly Armenian, as opposed to Georgian, town. Working for a newspaper called *Shark-i Rus* ('Eastern Russia'), he encountered and embraced the socialist movement then stirring in the Caucasus. A leading figure in the movement was a sturdy young fellow whom history now refers to Josif Stalin—a fact that few of the new Azeri nationalists liked to talk about much. Nor did they like to talk about other Bolshevik infiltrators into Rasulzade's political vehicle, the Musavat Party. One of these was Stalin's chief henchman and fellow Georgian, Lavrenti Beria.

Rasulzade's big break came in the aftermath of World War I and the collapse of Czarist Russia, when the political vacuum in the Caucasus allowed him and other Azeri nationalists to found, on May 28, 1918, the Democratic Republic of Azerbaijan—the first secular democracy in the Muslim world.

The republic lasted less than two years before the Bolsheviks moved in and Azerbaijan disappeared from the political map. First it was subsumed into the Transcaucasus Federation (in 1921, along with the other ephemeral states of Armenia and Georgia); later, under the tutelage of Rasulzade's main rival as the father of the country, Nariman Narimanov, it reemerged as the AzSSR, or Azerbaijan Soviet Socialist Republic. Narimanov was eventually replaced by Beria's police comrade in arms, Mir Jafar Baghirov, who ruled Azerbaijan until his removal on charges of treason following

Beria's fall from grace after Stalin's death in 1953. Interestingly, one of the charges against Baghirov was that he had destroyed evidence 'proving' that Beria was not a deep mole in the Musavat, but actually a double agent working for Rasulzade's party against the Bolsheviks. Baghirov was executed in 1956, and calumny was heaped on his name.

Rasulzade, meanwhile, was politically long gone. Declining Stalin's invitation to play Quisling in the new order, he was thrown in a Moscow prison for two years before managing to escape (or being allowed to escape) via Finland to Germany. There he remained throughout World War II—another aspect of his career the new nationalists did not like to talk about much—before retiring to Turkey, where he became involved in the politics of the marginal pan-Turkic movement. He died in Ankara in 1955, a broken man.

But whatever and whoever Rasulzade really was, both he and his short-lived state had become the very symbol of Azeri nationalism for a new generation. His portrait was everywhere, as was the simple red, green, and blue banner of the first Azeri Republic, with the hammer and sickle of the Soviet flag replaced by the crescent and star of Islam. The banner even hung on the facade of the parliament across from the January 20th Martyrs' Lane as well as on the interior frieze of the second floor of the Lenin Museum: the displays in this sector consisted of formerly banned publications from the 1918–1920 period, embossed in black and hung along the walls. *'Bir Kere Yukselen Bayrak Bir Daha Inmez!'* or 'The Flag Raised Once Cannot Be Lowered!' was the phrase written beneath Rasulzade's portrait. He had become the image of statehood, and the icon of yearning to be once more.

* * *

The irony was that there had never been an Azerbaijan state before our present century.

The name itself is apparently a distortion of the Greek word Atrophone, given by the successors of Alexander the Great to the region of ancient Iran known as Media, then controlled by one of Alexander's generals and inhabited by a mysterious people known as the Albans. Although they disappeared from history in the subsequent hurly-burly of the age, they continue to haunt the entire Caucasus, as each and every ethnic group now present in the region lays claim to their ancient heritage—but of that, anon.

During the centuries of Roman/Byzantine and Parthian/Sassanid (Iranian) rivalry, Azerbaijan remained the marchland—now controlled by one of the major powers, now by the other—and rarely achieved anything like independent status (although imaginative Armenian mapmakers would like to suggest that today's Azerbaijan, along with much of the Black Sea littoral and today's Turkish Anatolia, was in fact exclusively Armenian territory during much of this period).

The Byzantine/Parthian-Sassanid rivalry lasted up into the eighth century, when the region was conquered and absorbed by the new Muslim empire of the Arabs. The next masters of the land were the Turkic/Mongol tribes, who discovered the Caucasus during their great westward movement of conquest and migration in the ninth and tenth centuries. After the flow of the Mongols came their ebb, and the amorphous area by then known as 'Azerbaijan' remained a part of a greater Iranian or Turkic state or was divided into quasi-independent, Muslim principalities called *khanates*.

The defining period for Azerbaijan came in the late fifteenth century, when a Turkic-speaking warlord from the city of Ardabil in what is now northwestern Iran announced that he was the heir to imperial authority. His name was Ismael, and he styled himself Shah. Either by belief or by political expediency, he began importing clerics from the Yemen, that ever-heterodox Muslim land south of Saudi Arabia, to convert his subjects to a variant of Islam: Shi'ism.

In so doing, Shah Ismael created one of the great fault lines in the Muslim world, running from the Caucasus down to Basra, on the Gulf. In the south, it divided the Arabs; in the middle, it divided the Persians from the Kurds. In the north, the line between Sunni and Shi'ite clove a wedge between the future masters of the Muslim world, the Turks.

In the event, Shah Ismael lost—kind of. His Kizilbash troops, or 'Red Heads' as the Shi'ites were known in distinction to the Yeshilbash, or 'Green Heads' of the Sunnis, were defeated in 1517 by the Ottoman Sultan Yavuz Selim ('the Grim'), at the battle of Chaldiran, north of Lake Van in today's eastern Turkey. Technology and terror were real factors. After Selim's chain-linked cannons had ripped through Ismael's cavalry, a veritable witch-hunt began against Turkic Shi'ites of the land: a *fatwa*, or pious proclamation issued by the Mufti of Istanbul, promised paradise for any Sunni who killed a Kizilbash. The modern reader need only reflect on the death statistics associated with the almost contemporary Spanish Inquisition to imagine what followed. The result has been a deep psychosis, a hearts-and-minds passion play that is still being played out among Azeris today. In essence the question Azeris began asking themselves was: are we Turks or Shi'ites, or both—that is, Azeri?

This national schizophrenia was exploited by a third factor in the region—the nascent power of Czarist Russia. Using local Christian groups, such as the Georgians and Armenians, as a means to enter local disputes, St. Petersburg swallowed up the independent principalities of the Caucasus, one by one. The last were the Iranian border provinces of Naxjivan and Yerevan. Ceded to Russia in the 1828 Treaty of Turkmenchay, their loss effectively divided Azerbaijan—then a part of what we would today call Iran—into 'North' and 'South.' The former, now belonging to Russia, contained most of the arable land and mineral resources; the latter, now belonging to Iran, contained most of the rugged, mountainous terrain and most of the population. Strangely, perhaps, despite 150 and more years of Russian (Czarist or Soviet) domination, it was in the smaller, 'northern' Azerbaijan that a national consciousness was developed and maintained, while in the much larger and more populous southern portion of the 'country,' in Iran, ethnic consciousness appeared to have been subsumed by the majority Persian culture—be it that of Shah Ismael, Nadir Shah, Reza Pahlavi, or even the Ayatollah Khomeini.

But in the North, the question about a contemporary identity still was being asked in the same way: are we Turks, Shi'ites, or both, and thus Azeris? In the good old days of Stalinist rule, this question was probably not asked too often; and when it was, it probably received the standard reply: 'we are Soviets.' But within the contradictory context of glasnost, it was being asked again, and the answer was now two- or threefold. There were those, like Kubrah Hanim, who continued to believe in the existing system, if with some incremental changes and concessions.

Then there were those who believed in the men wearing business suits and talking about economic ties and trade: They were from Turkey, and said the Azeris were Turks. Then there were those who believed in the men wearing gowns and turbans who were teaching young men to whip themselves with chains during the Shi'ite month of passion and demanding that women return to the veil: They were from Iran. And in the summer of 1991, the battle for hearts and minds was being joined by all three.

* * *

Kazanfer and I had just finished a bottle of vodka and were watching a near-naked Turkish flick on the video when his two sons burst into the room.

"Dad," said Kazanfer's fourteen-year-old son, Rashit. "You should have seen me! *Whack! Whack!* How about a massage?"

Kazanfer looked with pride at his firstborn son.

"Granddad used to take a sword and crack his skull until it drew blood, on Ashura," he warmly related, while pouring me another shot. "Then he'd strap a loaf of bread to the cut and wake up the next morning with no headache or nothing."

"Daddy," said Rashit, "I want to go to Iran when I grow up, and become a *mullah.*"

"Great," said Kazanfer, stroking the boy's head.

"Me, too," said 12-year-old Ravshan, Kazanfer's second son.

"One cleric is enough," Kazanfer said. "You are to become a merchant, like me."

"Aww, dad . . . ." moaned Ravshan.

"*I-get-to-go-to-Iran, I-get-to-go-to-Iran,*" chanted Rashit in singsong.

The two boys had just returned from their nightly catechism lessons held in a local mosque-cum-factory designed to inculcate in them the faith of their forefathers, Shi'ite Islam. The lessons were taught by a divine from Tabriz.

"Everyone is sending their kids," Kazanfer explained, when I asked him about the Persian language lessons and Quran memorization classes. "We've been without religion so long, we've forgotten what it is all about."

As sociopolitical voyeurs, the timing of our trip could not have been better: we had accidentally stumbled into the *Ashura,* or the first ten days of the month of Muharram, the Holy Month of Atonement for the world's Shi'ite community, that celebrates the martyrdom of the Prophet Muhammad's grandson, Imam Hussein, at Karbala in the Iraqi desert 1400 years ago.

Kazanfer thought it was a good thing, too—*teach these kids religion!* But by the seventh day of Muharram ceremonies, even he was taken aback by the turn in events: his two sons were returning home at 1:00 A.M., and with self-inflicted welts on their backs. Nazilah Hanim didn't like this one bit. Nor did she like her sons telling her to put on more appropriate clothing. Their Iranian teacher said that women must be covered head to foot. 'Put on some clothes, Mom,' the two sons' eyes said when they entered the room. 'Stop showing so much skin.'

It was time to take a look-see, I said to myself, and made arrangements to tour the local religious establishments of Mashtagah. My first sortie was to the main mosque in town, the Jumaa Mesjid. Although it had functioned during the communist period, the *Akhun,* or director—a spry, friendly man by the name of Hajji Assadullah—informed me that the minaret was new, and only recently restored through community subscription.

"The communists tore down all the minarets and only allowed old men to pray," he said as we sat down on the mosque carpets for a chat. When I asked him what he had experienced in the way of repression, he was quite specific: he had learned the basics of religion from his father—secretly.

"My father would come home from work, and under the pretense of relaxing before dinner, retire to his room and close the door," Hajji Assadullah recalled. "But one day the door remained opened a crack, and I slipped in. I saw my father bending over at the waist, falling to his knees and placing his forehead on the floor and moaning a word I did not know—*Allah*."

Hajji Assadullah waited until his father was done, and then asked him what he had been doing. His father hefted him on his knee and began to cry.

"I am praying to the One God, my son," he said. "Please do not tell anyone—you don't want your father to go to jail, do you?"

Hajji Assadullah promised not to inform on his father on one condition—that his father teach him how to pray.

Learning how to pray in secret was one thing, I thought, but learning self-mortification at the end of a steel whip from Iranian tutors was something else. Delicately, I broached the subject. His answer was strange.

"The gratuitous shedding of blood is anathema in proper Islam," Hajji Assadullah said. "But however wrong, the *Taziyah* ('renewal' of the suffering of Hussein) has become a part of our cultural tradition—and it would be very difficult for us, the leaders of the newly liberated religious community, to begin forbidding aspects of expression that we disagree with so shortly after having censorship lifted on our own beliefs."

I asked Hajji Assadullah if I could attend the *Marsiyeh*, or dirge, to be held in the mosque that evening. He said fine, and I returned that night.

Evening prayers were attended by maybe one hundred believers—mainly older men and boys. At nine there were perhaps two hundred devotees; by ten they were twice that, and by eleven they numbered over a thousand.

They were young and old and in between, many with the sort of mustaches and beards usually associated with pious Islamic practice, but many others appeared to be regular Joes (or Yusufs)—cab drivers and waiters and house painters. Still others looked like merchants like Kazanfer, mid-level bureaucrats like Shamil, and students like Kamran. Many wore the black shirts and pants of Shi'ite mourning during the month of atonement; those who did not wore black armbands distributed for temporary use. All had found their way to the mosque on this weekday evening for the equivalent of vespers—only in this context, the chanting was accompanied by the slow, rhythmic cadence of men beating their breasts with their fists, remembering the suffering of Imam Hussein in the desert of Iraq:

Karbala oh! Karbala, Karbala oh! Karbala . . .

As the string of new devotees entered the mosque to perform their prayers, a rotating selection of men led the chanting of the passion of Imam Hussein: how he had begun his mission fully aware of his fate; how he had gathered his followers, how he had set off across the desert; how his horse had stopped at the spot of suffering and martyrdom; how he was met there by the cruel Yezid . . .

Karbala oh! Karbala, Karbala oh! Karbala. . . .

The men tapping their thighs were now slapping their knees, and the volume was rising.

Karbala oh! Karbala! Karbala oh! Karbala!

Again, another graybeard took over the microphone to add another sing-song element to the unfolding saga: how Yezid had come riding on his horse and demanded submission; how Hussein had declined, saying that submission was to God alone; how the faithless Yezid had threatened and how the faithful Hussein had replied: there is no Right but that of God!

The gathered slapped their thighs, chanting *Karbala oh! Karbala, Karbala oh! Karbala. . . .*

Then, at the entrance to the mosque, a thick curtain was pulled back to allow two new participants inside. They wore turbans and robes. They were mullahs from Iran. The pious mood and the self-flagellation of the penitents immediately intensified. The devotees abandoned their knees and thighs in favor of a direct beating of their breasts. The two mullahs sat and began to drink tea, tapping their knees while watching the flock slowly work themselves into a frenzy of passion.

KARBALA OH! KARBALA! KARBALA OH! KARBALA!

It was becoming a little redundant, so I asked Kazanfer's brother to take me off to another mosque—this time, the *mesjid* where Rashit and Ravshan went to Quranic night school.

Here, the atmosphere was less charged, although hardly subdued. A portrait of Imam Khomeini hung on one wall, and a blackboard with Persian/Arabic characters scrawled on it was on another. A third wall was actually a series of windows overlooking an alley, and the fourth, against which I sat, was bare, save for a makeshift *minbar*, or pulpit, and an odd-angle construction representing the *qiblah*, or the direction toward Mecca. The building—a former factory—was not aligned so as to create a natural indicator of the Kabaa along one of the walls; it was off kilter by some 15 or 20 degrees. But the local savants had made do and created their own pious weathervane, as it were, out of several bricks and a bunch of tape on the floor.

The 100-odd kids, ranging in age from around 12 to perhaps 16, seemed oblivious to such niceties as qiblah and minbar. They were swaying in a double line, facing each other, and beating themselves across the breast with their hands. At the head of the line stood a mousy-looking youth of maybe 20 years of age, dressed in black and sporting a straggly beard, correcting faulty breast-beating techniques and generally urging the young penitents on to greater feats of passion. In his hand he held a well-thumbed prayer book containing the lyrics being chanted by the group—the dirge devoted to the Martyr, Imam Hussein.

Just then, a couple of older boys standing at the fringes of the main group completed their preparatory prayers, wiped their faces with one hand (Sunni Muslims use both), and bowed to kiss the plastic blotters that were placed between their foreheads and their prayer rugs. Amen, they murmured in unison. Then one of their number went over to a corner and picked up a large bag that appeared to be rather heavy. Back in the group, he opened the sack and pulled out a tangle of chains: whips, with metal slashes attached to each handle.

Oooo! whistled the youth's companions, fondling the instruments of torture; several of the kids broke ranks and ran over for a look-see.

The passion play now started in earnest, with the leaders flogging their own backs with the iron whips, while the less devout found themselves obliged to beat their breasts with much greater blows, in poor imitation of their betters. I left the mesjid when I saw Kazanfer's kid reach for one of the whips.

The next day was the Ashura proper and the culmination of the week of passion, said to be most lively in a cemetery just north of Mashtagah, at a place called Nadiran. There were several significant mosque and tomb complexes in and around the area, but we headed straight for the main tomb, where most of the action was taking place. By the time we arrived, the familiar circles of devotees had long been beating breast with fists or whacking back with chains. Ladies formed an outer circle of undulating humanity, witnesses to the passion-play torture of their menfolk, playing the role of the Lady Zeynep, one of the few witnesses to the Karbala massacre who lived to tell the tale. . . .

Next we proceeded to the next stop on the local Shi'ite equivalent of the Stations of the Cross: the imprint that Hussein's father, the Prophet's cousin, son-in-law, and first follower, Ali, made of his gigantic foot on the shores of the Caspian Sea. The scene was decidedly sober compared to the morning's activities in the cemetery or the evening spent touring Mashtagah's mosques. Here, hundreds of folks waited patiently in line for the opportunity to enter the small, cement-block cubicle containing the size-12 boot print of Ali embedded in stone, wedding their lips to the indenture and quietly shedding tears over the unhappy fate of the prophetic family.

Finally, with the sun setting, we headed back into Baku to see just what sort of devotion was being expressed in the city center. Our goal was a large, nineteenth-century mosque with an ornamental World War II–era tank parked across the street. Folks were streaming in and out of the courtyard, where a line of young men were whipping themselves while chanting the passion of Hussein. Several of the more devoted flagellants had donned quasi–muscle shirt vestments in order to better display their scraped and scarred backs. I raised my camera to snap a picture.

The response was instantaneous. No sooner had I focused the lens than security men were at my side, demanding of me whether I had permission to record this holiest and most pious of events. I found myself ushered into the presence of the Sheikh of Islam himself.

"Sir," I began addressing the sweating, plump, bearded and berobed man, "I am a scholar from Turkey, and—"

They were the last words, save for the occasional pious epithet in Arabic, that I managed to get in for the next half-hour.

"A brother from Turkey!"

I won't bother to repeat the sermon that I received. In essence, it evolved around the death of Hussein at Karbala on this very day fourteen centuries ago and the devious plot at the bottom of all attempts to divide Sunni from Shi'ite. The Sheikh raised the level of his voice with every new verb until he was shouting point-blank into my face.

"God curse those who divide us," cried the Sheikh, a look of rage stretching and distorting his features, "In the end, we are all Muslims, praise be to the one God!"

"Amen," we whispered. "Amen."

The lecture ended an hour later. Outside, the crowds were already dispersing, and clean-up crews were sweeping the pious detritus away. Soon, aside from a single, peripatetic divine, reading palms and dispensing blessings upon a small knot of folks willing to pay for simony, the place was dead. Ashura 1991 was at an end.

* * *

We liked our hosts, and even Mashtagah, a great deal. But after a week or so of shuttling between Kazanfer's place and downtown Baku, we were starting to feel a little cramped. So one day we took a radical step and announced that we intended to travel to a place where we knew our hosts would not follow: the Autonomous Republic of Naxjivan.

"You'll be killed," said Shamil.

"Yalchin would go mad if he found out!" said Kamran.

But we were insistent, and pulled out all the stops—including Yalchin's promise that we would travel 'free and unmolested' anywhere we wanted to go. There was still a great deal of resistance to the idea, but we finally won.

There remained the problem of implementation, however. By the summer of 1991, Naxjivan seemed almost totally cut off from the rest of the country, and thus, the world: the trunk roads north, east, and west all had been severed because they passed through Armenian territory. Aeroflot flew between Naxjivan and Baku, but foreigners needed a destination-specific visa in order to purchase a plane ticket. As illegals in the country as a whole, all we could look forward to at the ticket counter would be getting arrested. Thus, we were reduced to taking the only way in—the grueling, sixteen-hour train ride from Baku to Naxjivan, which passed along the Iranian frontier under armed guard. Train travel in the Soviet Union was the one means available for getting from A to B without having your visa checked. It thus represented, for those who could stomach it, a rolling hotel to anywhere the tracks ran. The trip to Naxjivan was my first experience, and it was sobering.

Ours was a two-class sleeper that one would only find in the more remote parts of the Third World. The carriage was divided into ten open compartments with six bunks and a table in the middle. Another double row of bunks lined the aisle, adding to the sense of claustrophobia. All the bunks were filled and the air was heavy with the stench of dirty feet, unwashed socks, and urine. One reason for this was that the only ventilation was provided by shattered windows. Those, like ours, that actually had the glass in place could not be opened.

At first, the sight of the broken panes of glass gave us pause: had Armenian bullets plugged through the glass as the train chugged its way across the Armenian corridor of Zangezur which divided Naxjivan from Azerbaijan? The fact that a number of Soviet soldiers were riding shotgun on the wagons added to our unease, although in retrospect it seemed pretty clear that the windows had most likely been smashed by passengers needing a little fresh air. I was sorely tempted to do the same in the common toilet at the end of the hall, which was filthy beyond description.

So, carrying a bottle of vodka, some mineral water, and a picnic lunch, we went down to the station (which resembled a mosque), and after tearful farewells from Shamil, Kamran, and Kazanfer, boarded our second-class wagon. *Woo-woo!* the whistle sounded, and off we chugged into the night.

We did not get much sleep. Word soon spread that a couple of Turks were aboard the train, and a long line of curious folks began forming in the corridor outside our compartment. Then they started playing musical bunks within it, to the point where it became difficult to tell who our actual roommates for the night journey were. I think the other bunks belonged to: an ethnic Kurd who taught school in Lachin (a town pinched between Karabakh and Armenia); a young Azeri dentist from Moscow; an engineer from somewhere in Naxjivan; and a couple of "merchants"—i.e., black marketeers—making the run down to the border with Iran to see what sort of baubles the

Iranians might have for sale. At least those were the folks who were sleeping in the other bunks in our compartment in the morning.

All were obsessed with Turkey. Did we known this artist? Had we seen that film? Of keenest interest to all were the current activities of Ibrahim Tatlises (the Frank Sinatra/Billy Joel of Turkey). The Kurdish teacher discreetly asked whether it was true that Ibo—Ibrahim Tatlises—was, in fact, an ethnic Kurd. Upon my confirmation of this point he went mute with delight.

Finally, as the others drifted off to their bunks and into sleep, one of the merchants settled down on my bed and began to wistfully describe the beauties of communism in the days of Leonid Brezhnev and his protégé, Heydar (Gaidar) Aliyev. A worker had been able to get along on 300 rubles a month quite nicely back then, he said. Food was cheap and plentiful. Medical attention was virtually free. Housing was a problem, true, but had not been an insurmountable one: for those with the patience to wait, the state provided. In the West, the market dominated everything, forcing prices far beyond the reach of the average man. He triumphantly noted that the old system of the Soviet Union was vastly superior. I cannot say it was moving, only that it was interesting to find someone to defend the system of government discredited by nearly everyone else I had met. Then I asked what the man did for a living.

"I am a merchant," he sheepishly replied.

Thinking of Kazanfer, I laughed out loud—and the poor hypocrite slunk off to his bunk.

We woke early in the morning and flushed out our mouths with the only available liquid—the half bottle of vodka left from the night before. It was warm and strong and not the sort of way you usually want to start the day. Others, equally ill prepared for the journey, were doing the same and so we just joined in. An hour later we passed an ancient graveyard set against a steep hill; then the Araxes River valley widened out to the point where a town could be built and we pulled into the station of Julfa. Here, our Soviet Army guards, dressed in khaki uniforms and out-back slouch hats, got down from the train. The ordeal was over. Everyone was so relieved not to have been fired on by the Armenians and to be safely beyond the corridor and in territorial Naxjivan, that the platform was soon swarming with folks looking for drinking water, greasy biscuits, fatty sausage, and inevitably, more bottles of vodka. I joined a line of folks at a water fountain and managed to splash some lovely, cold and clean water on my face before reboarding for the final leg of the trip to the city of Naxjivan.

* * *

The revelry started the moment we debarked, ordered tea at the station, and took off in full, ecstatic flight when we checked into the only hotel in town—a ten-story monstrosity called the Tabriz. While waiting for the floor hostess to change our sheets and towels (she did so by rotating the filthy rags with a different set in the room next door), we descended to the restaurant and discovered that we were gods.

"Anything to eat around here? I asked.

The waiter muttered something to me in Russian.

"Look," I repeated. "If you had ears you would understand I am speaking Turkish."

The man stared at me, his jaw dropping open.

"You're from Turkey?" he finally stammered.

"Yes, from Istanbul," I lied.

"TURKEY? BY GOD THEY ARE FROM TURKEY!!!!!"

All heads in the restaurant turned, and the growing low murmur soon turned into a roar. Turks! Here, in our restaurant, in Naxjivan! Turks!

People moaned. People cried. People called their friends and relatives and begged them to come and see for themselves. The police arrived, but not to keep order; they, too, just wanted to shake hands. For the next four days, we could not pay for a meal, a taxi, or tea—and we were genuinely surprised when we were actually allowed to pay for our hotel room ourselves—albeit at the local rate of 50 rubles ($1.75) a night.

Fake Turk that I was, I found the reception interesting. But for Hicran, so used to the difficulties faced by a Turkish traveler in Europe and the standard, silly queries about the truth of *Midnight Express* in the United States, it was almost overwhelming to be so loved.

"I've never seen anything like it," she kept saying as someone else would run up and kiss her hand.

The reason for this was simple. Naxjivan was a Turkish (or Turkic) island in an Armenian sea—or at least it was so perceived by all who lived there. The very isolation of Naxjivan from the rest of Azerbaijan—and thus, the Soviet Union—had forced it to look elsewhere, and that elsewhere was its formerly hostile neighbor to the west, Turkey.

Turkey was everywhere, was everything. Pictures of the Turkish president Turgut Özal hung in shops named "Izmir," "Ankara" and "Istanbul." People talked openly and hopefully of the day when Turkey might annex Naxjivan: an obscure provision of the 1921 Kars Agreement between Moscow and Ankara (but well known and recited often in Naxjivan) allowed for Turkey to intervene if Naxjivan were threatened by a third state—namely, Armenia.

Fueling the fire of hope and salvation was a new road-and-rail project to link Naxjivan to the Turkish sub-province of Igdir, on the northern slope of Mount Ararat, at the point where a thin, 18-kilometer splinter of Turkey touches Naxjivan. The Azeris (or Naxjivanian Azeris) were furiously work-ing away on the road and bridge over the Araxes River, determined to open the border by the end of the year. It was called Sadarak.

Meanwhile, the Naxjivan Azeris were obliged to depend on their other outlet to the world—Iran. The frontier had been thrown wide open to any-one who claimed he was an ethnic Azeri merchant, and the town of Naxjivan was fairly overrun with nickel-dime salesmen sporting five-day beards, come up to Naxjivan for a weekend to flog bubble gum, matches, pens, plastic shoes, bogus brand-name cigarettes, and other amazingly cheap kitsch (most of it apparently manufactured in Pakistan) and to spend their profit on the sort of pleasures not immediately available in the Islamic Republic. In addition to a couple of boozy nights on the town, the Iranian Azeri merchants would then snap up what their Soviet Azeri cousins had to offer in the way of shoddy, Soviet-manufactured goods—Zenith cameras, children's tricycles, and ventilated accordions—before disappearing back across the frontier. It almost goes without saying that we were pestered to sell the very shirts off our backs as we wandered down the lanes of the al fresco market.

Our hotel faced the 'bazaar' in the main square and was thus the natural hostel for the itinerant merchants. We became quite friendly with two reli-gious types who rented the room next to ours (and with whom we had traded sheets and towels). They said they had been Revolutionary Guards, and detailed some of their adventures as the vanguard of the Iranian revolu-tion, but admitted to being more interested now in hawking Karachi-made imitation Chicklet bubble gum in Naxjivan than reciting the Quran. It was a little pathetic, but it was trade—and an indication of the spirit of mercantil-ism in both the Soviet Union and Islamic Iran.

* * *

If we felt mildly oppressed by the hospitality we had received in Baku, in comparison to what we enjoyed in Naxjivan, the former experience was like living in total isolation. People fought with each other for the right and delight to show us around, and our contacts ranged across the (admittedly limited) social and political spectrum of Naxjivan.

Our first guides were a pair of young family men who worked in the local government administration; we were the first Turks they had ever met, and they were determined to please. The second day was taken by the fanatically pro-Turkish fifteen-year-old son of a university professor of ar-chaeological history and current opposition Member of Parliament. The third day was spent with a bigwig in the municipal government and some sort of shopkeeper. The fourth and final day of touring was spent with a former student of archaeology who now ran a private restaurant and who claimed to be an expert on the "Albans," the mysterious people who inhabited the southern Caucasus during the gray mists of time. The only thing certain about the Albans, it seems, is that they have nothing to do with the residents of Albania, on the Adriatic coast of the Balkans, who refer to themselves as Shqiptari. . . .

The most important Alban archaeological site in Naxjivan was near "Snake Mountain"—a curiously perpendicular massif that greatly resembles Devil's Tower in Wyoming. A cleft in the summit was said to be the result of Noah's Ark scraping the submerged peak before landing atop the higher ground provided by Mount Ararat, 100 kilometers to the west. Nearby was an "Alban" church that was in use as a granary.

"Who are the Albans?" we asked our guide, the archaeologist-cum-restaurant owner, Zakir Bey.

"The Albans were the early Azeris, descendants of the Scythians, who arrived in the southern Caucasus during the gray mists of time and long before the perfidious Armenians, who now claim their heritage through a campaign of lies and disinformation," Zakir informed us. He seemed to have been waiting for the question in order to give a memorized reply.

When I pointed out that the inscriptions on the church appeared to be written in Armenian, Zakir became incensed.

"Those are later additions put on by the enemy," he stated flatly. "Look at the design of the crosses! Our forefathers disdained the ornamental use of the Swastika and Maltese-type cross on their architecture!"

The Azeri scholarly argument over the Albans could thus be summed up as this: We, the Azeris, belong right here, where we are, because we were here long before that wandering clan of thieves and liars, the Armenians, arrived to steal our native heritage.

Who knows? Maybe it is true. But it seemed a pretty obtuse effort and dangerously close to rewriting (and eradicating) history to please one's self. The point, I guess, is to establish an iron-clad claim to territory by proving one's own case of ethnic continuity—a scholarly technique that I would run into again and again in the Caucasus, where everyone was always there before anyone else of another ethnic strain.

This casual wandering through deepest Naxjivan was all very informative and interesting, but it was not the reason we had made the journey. Although we had not dared tell our Baku hosts, our goal was to meet Heydar ('Gaidar') Aliyev. But the big man remained elusive. His aides said he was in Iran, in Baku, and even in Turkey, on pressing affairs of state.

Every morning we went over to his office to secure the desired interview, but were always told that it was impossible today—maybe tomorrow. The closest we got to this myth of a man was the bust of him in the park overlooking the Araxes River. One thing, however, was pretty obvious: for all the talk about his great accomplishments, there didn't seem to be much about Naxjivan the local leader could boast about. The nearest town in Turkey, a dive called Aralik, was Paris in comparison.

We waited another day to meet Heydar, despaired, and made our plans for escape.

Leaving was easy: At the airport, we announced that we were Turks, and two passengers were thrown off the plane to make room.

* * *

Upon our return from Naxjivan, we were greeted as survivors of a harrowing ordeal by Kazanfer and his clan. But the bug of travel had begun to infect them, too—especially when we voiced an interest in taking a journey north.

"Road trip!" Nazilah Hanim fairly squealed.

"Whaddya mean, woman?" her husband, Kazanfer muttered.

"Well, you were planning on buying those five tons of cheese in Sheki, weren't you?" replied Nazilah, taking control. "We'll just come along and go visit the tomb of Imam Zade and visit with the Jones. . . ."

Firm plans were quickly put into effect. Kazanfer canceled his business trip, or doubled it with ours. At any rate, we set off together the next morning in one of Kazanfer's four vehicles—an eggshell blue, 1989 Volga sedan without a scratch on it. I called it the cruise-mobile.

"*Whee!*" cried Nazilah Hanim, as we roared through the oil-platform forest. "I haven't been out of Baku in a decade!"

"*Hmmph,*" replied Kazanfer, and pushed pedal to floor.

But the Volga didn't have much guts, and we almost crawled through the desolate landscape. The first two hours of our seven-hour cruise were tedious and depressing. Following the oil region, we entered into an equally austere and depressing landscape of low, rolling, denuded hills and plains devoid of human or animal life.

And then we started having car problems—specifically, flats. Our first happened about 100 kilometers out of Baku. Happily—or suspiciously—a local *kolkhoz* (collective farm) happened to run a tire repair shop within 100 meters of our blowout. My ever-paranoid mind drifted toward the idea of the repairmen seeding their business by laying tacks on the road, but I said nothing. During the repair pause, however, I took the opportunity to check out the other tires. They were all bald. It seemed so unlike Kazanfer to try and save money on rubber that I brought the matter up.

"Why do you think the other Volga is on blocks?" he asked. "It is easier to get a car here than new tires or even service for baldies!"

Soon, we were on the road again—although there were none of the familiar sights and blights one associates with automotive travel in the United States (or elsewhere). For starters, there were no billboards, no traffic signs, no service stations—nothing, save for an extraordinary number of electrical and communications poles lining the highway, and the rather surreal sight of 50-odd paratroopers gliding through the sky on a practice commando operation. Now, we hardly expected to find Taco Bell or the Golden Arches inviting us to take a break, but the signal dearth of any sort of enterprise was truly astounding—until you remembered that this was, of course, the Soviet Union. Advertising was not so much banned as unneeded in a land where there was one manufacturer for any given product. In a weird way, it was kind of nice (save for the electricity lines).

Finally, after some 200 miles and ten hours, we arrived at our destination—a place that appeared on all maps as Kirovabad, but which locals referred to as Ganje, the capital of the short-lived Azerbaijan Democratic Republic of 1918.

It was not a very impressive place. Dominated by a huge aluminum plant whose pollutants had killed most plant life in the vicinity, Ganje felt like a provincial town that had been subjected to too many five-year plans and production quotas over the years. If the truth be told, it was a dump.

It was also a garrison town. The streets were full of knots of young men in khaki uniforms, whiling away their time before being called on to put out the next outbreak of Azeri-Armenian violence or to march into nearby Georgia from the south, if events in that breakaway republic got out of hand.

Our accommodations for the night were in the newly acquired suburban abode of Kazanfer Bey's old pal Rashit Bey, who just happened to be the equivalent of the chief of police for Ganje and environs (and the landlord of Kamran, when the lad was doing his military service). I think it fairest to give my first impressions of Rashit: Kazanfer had disappeared somewhere and left us in the garden. Suddenly, the gate was thrown open, and in strode a broad man with quick eyes and a steady hand who saw strangers in his house.

"Hello," said Rashit, still not extending his hand but keeping it on his revolver.

"Sir," I began, "we thank you for your hospitality."

"It has not yet begun."

"If this is the extent, we are overwhelmed."

"You are welcome."

"It outdoes anything done for guests in Turkey."

"Turkey?!"

It is not to difficult to determine what happened next. Out rolled the welcome mat—*Turks had arrived!* It was time to eat unto gluttony and drink into oblivion.

While Kazanfer prepared the barbecue (the womenfolk concentrated on the salads), Rashit disappeared, and when he returned he brought back a double treat: his alcoholic brother and a bottle of *chacha*, an extremely potent, homemade mulberry brew that had the taste and elevating experience of the infamous Chinese whiskey, *Mau-Tay*. With each shot of the lighter-fluid liquid, Rashit Bey became more loquacious.

"Here we are, here! My home! Breaking bread!" he began. "We say that anyone who breaks bread and eats and drinks together must forever be friends! *Forever!* Me, you, Kazanfer, Kamran! Family, all!"

I won't even bother to try and render Rashit's brother's moaning into text-speech. This sad man, perhaps 35 years old, was obese in all the wrong areas from eating all fat and no lean and drinking like the proverbial fish. I gave him another five years before the first heart attack.

And as his brother sank into alcoholic oblivion, Rashit took control of the mulberry bottle and lectured long and liquid over a variety of subjects: eternal friendship as the meaning of life, his commitment to the integrity of the communist system by stopping criminals and profiteers from abusing the fruits of 70 years' work (sitting in a house with a garden and a fine car outside and in the presence of the master black-market man Kazanfer, this was a little hard to take, but I let it pass), and his profound and abiding love of all things Turkish.

* * *

I woke hard the following morning, my head throbbing after a mere two snorts of the mulberry misery (and a few more of standard vodka, I have to admit). Rashit was already long gone for his day's duties at a place called Chaykent, in the mountains above Ganje, on the way to Karabakh. He had given instructions for us to meet him there, after which we would all proceed to a pass on the Murov Mountains favored by the Ganje weekend crowd as a picnic place.

The climb away from the city in the plains was picturesque. Local ladies, quick to realize what visiting families and the tourist crowd needed, had set up stone-hearth bread ovens at regular intervals, flogging their delicious, home-made *pide*-style loafs to all passersby. Other picnic ingredients were also readily at hand for those who had left home without the proper makings: luscious tomatoes, piles of cucumbers, hunks of raw meat ready for spitting, and then, inevitably, liters and liters of Stoli's lesser cousin,

Russkaia Vodka. It might have been the Shi'ite holy month of atonement, but the vast majority of Azeri Muslims intended to enjoy this summer weekend like they did every weekday night: dead drunk.

Finally, after passing a series of six or seven Young Pioneer Camps—every one packed with kids playing beneath the benevolent gaze of Comrade Lenin—we approached the upper reaches of Chaykent, a long, garden town straggling along a babbling brook.

Steep alpine-style roofs punched through the canopy of grape boughs; a hundred or two or three or five hundred balconies looked unabashedly out at the sun; raspberry bushes as tall as a man stood ready to be picked; apple trees swayed under the weight of their boughs, all fed by organized sluicings from the town's common river, which remained remarkably clean.

But there was something wrong about the idyll. Among the lovely dachas, there were houses smoldering. Not from the chimneys, but from windows, broken and shattered windows. The deeper we moved into town, the stranger it became. We were here for a picnic, but the town looked like it had been bombed or involved in a battle—and a recent one.

"Stop the car," I suggested, as we rolled by one smashed building.

Kazanfer protested and tried to drive on.

"Stop the car!" I said again, and opened the door of the vehicle.

It was the post office and telephone station, or had been. Singed and burnt wires lay everywhere, tangled in a mangle of broken and splintered wood—chairs? desks? walls?

Two soldiers sauntered up as we poked around the place.

"Who the hell are you!" they demanded, pointing their guns at us.

"They are foreign friends of Rashit!" cried Kazanfer from the car.

"Let's see about that," said the men with guns, and we were escorted farther down the smoldering street, to the center of the smoldering town.

Only later did I understand that we had walked, or had been driven, into 'Operation Ring,' the police action mounted in the closing days of the Soviet Union to bring peace to the smoldering conflict in Karabakh by disarming local Armenians, even if it meant 'cleansing' them from their homes.

When I asked Rashit for details, he became belligerent and muttered about 'his boys' who had died in the recent fighting—fighting, I might add, that no one had bothered to tell us about.

"They came in by helicopter, from Armenia!" he charged. "And they were carrying American military equipment!"

The weapons, he said, had been smuggled into Armenia in the aftermath of the great earthquake of 1988. As an American, I was responsible—although as a guest, I was forgiven. . . .

Rashit still had work to do before our picnic, so while waiting, we continued to tour the smoldering town. It was thoroughly depressing, but mainly because the imagination conjured up what once was. What was it about the eastern Christians? Whether Armenian, Greek, or Nestorian, they always managed to find the most pleasant, beautiful valleys to plant their villages, towns, and even cities, while the Muslims occupied the dreary flats below.

And so it was with Chaykent. Despite several burnt-out or bombed-out houses, the sense of desertion of its original residents and the pell-mell move-in of thousands of Azeri refugees from Armenia who had been ordered to occupy the place, Chaykent, its very structure, felt *clean*. But something awful and tragic had occurred here, and recently.

I didn't have all the facts, but those that I had were enough to make me very uncomfortable: something wicked was spiraling out of control, and no one had the courage or power to try and stop it. Did the erstwhile residents of Chaykent really represent a sort of Armenian fifth column, poised and ready to take over the eastern approaches to Karabakh? Were they really supplied by helicopter from Armenia itself in order to hold out against the legitimate authorities of the land—the Azeri police? Were they really terrorist bandits, or merely half-lettered saps sucked up in the nationalistic game played by their own leadership, and obliged to defend their own homes?

And what about the refugee Azeris who had moved into Chaykent? They were all from Armenia, and they were a pretty pathetic group: just plain folks who had been swept up in events beyond their understanding and control, driven from their houses, and forced over mountain passes in the middle of winter—the familiar litany of rape and pillage and desperation and horror associated with refugees everywhere.

We continued with our programmed picnic, but the fun had gone out of it. We toasted our toasts until the host fell into incoherence, and chewed on raw, tough meat only blackened by smoke and singed by fire.

The mountain scenery was exquisite from a distance, but upon closer inspection the babbling brook was filled with trash and the quaint houses in the valleys had been gutted. We were on the northern lip of the mountains of Karabakh in the summer of 1991, and already one could discern that ineffable thing that was to come but that no one wanted to talk about. War was on its way.

* * *

And so were we. We had come to Azerbaijan for maybe two days and stayed more than two weeks that seemed like two years. Strangely, during that period we had scarcely had anything to do with the Baku that people ranted and raved about and certainly not the city that my old pal Yalchin had intended us to see. The delights of Baku? We had stumbled into something quite different, areas that few 'tourists' ever got to: the mafia suburb of Mashtagah, Nadiran Cemetery during the Ashura, and Chaykent in the mountains bordering Karabakh—not to speak about the obscure Azeri exclave of Naxjivan. It was time to push off to our real destination—Tashkent, Uzbekistan, and Soviet Central Asia; 'Baku' would have to wait for a return trip sometime in the distant future, if ever.

Kazanfer drove us to the airport and with tears in his eyes, begged us to return. We said we would try. Then he asked to change some dollars at a low rate, and we agreed.

He had been a wonderful host, all in all.

2

A Distant Coup

On the evening of August 19th, I was jamming with a band in a Tashkent nightclub located in a sauna, cranking out my rendition of 'Framed':

> *Walkin' down the street*
> *Mindin' my own affairs . . .,*
> *Then two Uzbeks grabbed me, unawares.*
> *Yo' name Tommy? An' I said, Why Sho!*
> *You be the boy we be lookin' fo!*

A birthday party of Armenians cavorted around the dance floor, while James Ruppert of the *Washington Post* did a jig with my wife. We were having such a good time that we stayed out late and didn't wake until noon the next day. It was then that we learned that we had been dancing while Rome burned.

Actually, it was Moscow, and it wasn't on fire: it was the coup of August 19th, that spelled the end of the Soviet empire.

For anyone who missed the event, it went something like this. While Mikhail Gorbachev was down in the Crimea on a much-needed vacation, a group of hard-line old communists who did not like glasnost and perestroika decided to turn back the clock and bring back the bad old days. And so they announced that Gorbachev had been incapacitated by a grave illness of an undefined sort and had handed over the reins of government to an emergency council, led by Vice President Gennadii Yanaev.

That was the official version. The unofficial version was much more complex. It started with the notion that Yanaev was more of a hard drinker than a hard-liner. The other putschists were similarly described as being a bunch of mean-spirited commie buffoons. Thank God that one man stood in their way: Boris Yeltsin! Defiantly standing atop a tank parked in front of the Russian parliament building, the White House, he let it be known that as

the democratically elected leader of Russia, he had no intention of bowing to a bunch of *putschmeisters*. A standoff ensued. The army (or
important elements of it) went over to Yeltsin, the censored press rebelled, and, after three days, the putsch collapsed. A humbled Mikhail
Gorbachev returned to a different Moscow and the terror of freedom. The
great bogeyman of western civilization, the Evil Empire, was on the ash
heap of history. The Cold War was over, and the West had won! But no
sooner had the celebration begun than other thoughts began to sink in.
Whatever else the Center had stood for, it meant continuity and control.
You could count on the Kremlin. And as the fifteen diverse republics
(and then autonomous republics and autonomous regions) that made up
the USSR started to break away, some of the same people celebrating the
demise of the Soviet Union in autumn of 1991 were becoming almost
nostalgic for it less than a year later. Of special concern to Washington
were the 'nuclear' republics of Belarus, Kazakhstan, and Ukraine. A
discreet source informed me that at a 'crisis' game session, U.S. Air
Force participants ordered SAC bombers to take out Kiev and all the
strategic missiles on Ukrainian territory—even though in the scenario,
Ukraine and the United States were not at war. The logic was that the
Ukrainian nuclear rockets only threatened the United States.

And if there was confusion about the August 19th putsch and its aftermath outside the dying USSR, there was even greater confusion within
it—and nowhere more than in the 'national' republics along Russia's long
frontier. Some leaders, like Kazakhstan president Nursultan Nazarbaev,
came out early in their support for Yeltsin and Gorbachev and thus gained
stature for being brave and democratic. While the former adjective was
certainly true, one had to wonder about the latter. Others, like Uzbekistan
president Islam Karimov, came out a little too late in their public support,
and thus gained the onus for being cowardly and undemocratic. While the
latter was true, one had to wonder about the former. Still others, like
Azerbaijan president Ayaz Mutalibov, made the mistake of publicly praising the putschists for having gotten rid of Gorbachev and then blaming their
remarks on bad translations after Gorbachev returned, proving themselves
beyond any doubt to be both cowardly and undemocratic.

Then there were the oddballs, such as Georgia's president Zviad
Gamsakhurdia. He was branded a coward and a reactionary because he said
'good riddance' when he heard about Gorbachev's (temporary) removal.
The funny thing was that he continued to say it even after Gorbachev's
(temporary) return. Gamsakhurdia, though so irascible that he managed to
alienate all his friends very quickly, was merely saying what most people in
Georgia thought about Gorbachev because of what he had done to Geor-

gia—namely, ordered the Soviet Army into the streets of Tbilisi in 1989 to crush the democratic independence movement there.

Actually, quite a few people in the old USSR had similar thoughts about Gorbachev and were not sad to see him ousted, although many were disturbed by the ousters. But with his restoration on August 21st, glasnost and perestroika were once again the next best thing to sliced black bread or maybe even a bottle of vodka, if you could find one. 'Political correctness' was *de rigueur*. Gorbachev was once more a hero and Boris Yeltsin was a god. Everyone and their mother claimed to have opposed the putschists. Everyone had been there on the barricades around the Russian White House, defending it with their naked bodies against the cruel steel of reactionary tanks.

This, of course, was a lie that stunk to high heaven. Most people had stayed at home and watched the putsch unfold and then collapse on television and were pretty indifferent about the whole thing. But everyone likes a winner, and Yeltsin had won, and so everyone had been with him there during his moment of courage, passion, and victory, standing on a tank outside parliament and manfully staring the putschists down.

Yes, it was a lie that stank to high heaven, but in late summer 1991, everything about the USSR also stank. It was like a decomposing corpse, or maybe a terminally sick patient, afflicted with leprosy. The first limbs to fall off were the Baltic states of Estonia, Lithuania, and Latvia, which declared themselves to be the free and independent states they had been before World War II. The United States, which had never formally accepted their being part of the USSR, was hesitant to bestow recognition, fearing a reaction in Moscow. Next came Ukraine, Belarus, and Moldova. They, too, announced themselves to be free and independent states, *sans* all that 'SSR' jazz. And when Russia declared itself to be *Rossiia* and independent of the USSR, well, the confusion became complete. It was almost like declaring oneself independent of oneself. As for the Union of Soviet Socialist Republics, some wags were already kicking around new names for it—like the *U.S.S.Aren't*.

* * *

I watched the breakup of the Soviet Union from the vantage point of Tashkent, Uzbekistan. It was a curious place from which to observe the process of national fragmentation and disintegration. Unlike the 'European' and Slavic republics of the USSR, which chose to interpret the moment as their first and last best chance to become free and independent, the so-called 'Muslim' republics of Central Asia were not quite so eager. 'Reluctant' is a pretty generous way to describe their attitude toward independence.

The biggest of the lot, Kazakhstan, didn't get around to making the almost proforma declaration of sovereignty until the USSR was formally dissolved and the Kazakh SSR had to be something because its previous defining features no longer existed. Leaders in Turkmenistan, Tajikistan, and Kyrghyzstan reacted in much the same way.

But my perspective was from Uzbekistan. When the dam broke, I almost expected to see Amir Timur (Tamerlane) riding out of the past at the head of legion *Basmachi* freedom fighters to wrest Central Asia away from the Russian yoke. But nothing of the sort happened. The Uzbeks were silent on August 19th and they were silent on August 20th and they were silent on August 21st. They were silent when it looked as if the reactionaries had won and they were silent when Yeltsin went out and did his High Noon act atop a tank in front of the White House and they were silent when the coup collapsed and failed and Gorbachev came back.

Then, about ten days after the coup and still with no public discussion whatsoever and without a single, solitary demonstration for or against it, Uzbekistan president and Communist Party boss Islam Karimov announced that his country was independent and sovereign, whatever that meant.

Some suggested that Karimov had selected September 1st because it was the first day of school and he wanted to peg independence day to a date that would be difficult to forget. Maybe. But the response from the Uzbek public was silence. There wasn't a word or a whisper. Where were the crowds? Where were the cries of 'freedom!' in the streets? Where were the incisive articles in the unshackled press?

What we got was independence on TV. During the three days the putsch-ists held power, Uzbek television dutifully went along with their every order. In addition to broadcasting emergency decrees, this meant running an endless cycle of symphonic concerts, cartoons, and light entertainment—a Charles Dickens movie, Donald Duck, and a flashback-style film about Genghis Khan—as well as the usual 'feature' news reporting about happy agronomist members of this or that sovkhoz or kolkhoz making new strides in cotton harvesting or watermelon hormones. There were also a couple of Novosti programs from Moscow that Soviet journalists subsequently apologized for having made—garbage news about Gorbachev's health, interviews with the putschists—that sort of thing.

Then came the Yeltsin victory, and the news began to change on the Russian language, supranational channel. First came the public apologies from reporters for not having done their duty. Then the real public catharsis began: an almost ad nauseam recounting of the coup, featuring testimony by everyone possibly associated with Yeltsin's victory, as well as live, multi-camera, moment-by-moment reportage of the state funeral afforded the three young men run over by tanks on their way to the White House. My favorite was a joint Novosti/CNN interview with Gorbachev about his own political future. The interview was live—and I mean live: viewers were treated to the entire production set up, from microphone checks in English and Russian to the on-clipping and de-clipping from Gorby's collar. I suspected the producers were trying to convince themselves and the audience that the idea of any sort of editing—not to say censorship—was out of fashion, forever, in the new Russia. We were even treated to Gorbachev stumbling away and the CNN team disassembling their equipment.

Then the Novosti team went live with another news feature: a tour of KGB headquarters in Moscow, with unshackled and vengeful reporters busting past the guards, cameras blazing. The theme was pretty clear: Glasnost might have had its limits in the bad old days of the USSR, but the citizens of post-putsch *Rossiia* were going to get the unedited, unadulterated, live, inside scoop on everything, all the time. Flipping the channel, I found Uzbekistan television still running the familiar, intelligence-insulting *schmalz* about happy agronomists and local culture, without one reference to the putsch or its aftermath. Here was someone talking about the importance of the 550th anniversary of the great national poet Alisher Navoyi; there was an interview with a factory chief who had raised the price of parking for employees as part of the embrace of the free market economy; here again was a harvester rolling through a cotton field. Then came Navoyi, again.

But on September 1st, the Uzbek media outdid itself. President Karimov made an hour-long speech in Parliament. Almost incidentally, he announced the independence of Uzbekistan. Karimov apparently liked the idea so much that he ordered the station to replay the last two minutes of the announcement of national freedom twice, in case anyone had missed the moment the first time around.

Fair enough: it was, after all, Uzbek television—and one doesn't declare national sovereignty every day. But what followed was the most mind-numbing analysis ever dreamt of by a network executive in his worst nightmare. First came a long and babbling interview with the president about how fine and nifty and neat he felt about independence and how everything would now be fine and nifty and neat because Uzbekistan was finally independent. Next in snore (sic) were four esteemed guests, answering a commentator's question of 'what do you think about independence'. The essence of their long-winded replies was that independence was nifty and neat. One of the guests, a Tajik poet and People's Artist of the USSR, got so excited that he leapt up and broke into song (about independence, I presumed). It was more than a little sad that he was mouthing the words, playback style: spontaneity still was not a desirable quality on Uzbek TV.

Another guest, an Uzbek from New Jersey whom I had met the week before along with the (ethnic Uzbek) Minister of Finance and Customs of Afghanistan, who was also on the program, came closest to actually saying something of content when he referred to all the Uzbeks in the diaspora—Afghanistan, Iran, Saudi Arabia, Turkey and the USA—who would be looking at the coming days with eagerness. There was some nervous clearing of throats, but no cutting I could discern. Then came a series of interviews with three marionette-like figures representing several of the ninety identifiable minorities in Uzbekistan: a Tatar, an Uighur, and an unidentified third party (Turkmen? Kyrghyz? the last of the Meskheti Turks? It was not clear). The three wished the Uzbek people well and stated how happy they were to participate in the glorious future of the newly independent land. Then the president's historical announcement in parliament was replayed a third time, along with the interview with Karimov. I was about to get the recycled Tajik playback singer, when I turned the channel to Moscow: more live confessions of repentant putschists and Boris Yeltsin browbeating Mikhail Gorbachev into banning the Communist Party in *Rossiia* (if not in the rest of the non-Union), thus removing Gorbachev from his only claim to gainful employment.

It must have been a real party up in Moscow. But down in Uzbekistan it was all pretty depressing—and aside from the droning nonsense on the television, totally silent. And the silence in the streets echoed through the halls of powers. One night in mid-putsch, I was drinking with a number of high-level Uzbek friends. These folks, all Communist Party members, and with money and connections and access to quality food and foreign travel, were shaken and confused. One man confessed that he wasn't really a believer in Marxism/Leninism but he had joined the party in the hope of effecting incremental change. He had always meant to resign from the party at some opportune time, and now that moment appeared to have come. . . . Another told the depressed *apparatchik* that it was madness to resign from the party that made them who they were, especially when the future remained so unclear. Another questioned why there was any talk about resignation: Karimov was thinking about renaming the party. . . .

In the end, no one did anything, and life carried on exactly as before for the very good reason that nothing, absolutely nothing (save for the offhand declaration of independence) had changed. There was one exception. In order to preserve Uzbekistan's fledgling independence, President Karimov had banned the Communist Party from activity in the security apparatus, lest the forces of reaction attempt a coup as they had in Moscow, and had placed the security apparatus under his direct control. Fine idea! But President Karimov was also the chairman of the Communist Party. . . .

No one had been sacked. No one had resigned. One didn't necessarily have to topple the obligatory statue of Lenin, as in Riga or Vilnius, but the response of the Uzbek nation to the putsch, their president's announcement of secession from the USSR, and his establishing a de facto dictatorship was so minimal that it began to seep into my thick skull that maybe, just maybe, there was something to be learned that could not easily be understood: the silence had less to do with people being powerless than being so inured to keeping their mouths shut that they had forgotten how to open them.

No, it had not been a 'good putsch' for me. One reason I had accepted the academic post was to get away from the pressures of deadline journalism for a while and do some deeper research. But how many times in a lifetime did the Soviet Union collapse? I took stock of the situation. Our living arrangements were miserable. My 'sponsors' at the University were thieves, and the Uzbeks, as a nation, were asleep. So I asked myself a simple question, and knew it was the right one to try to answer. What was happening in Azerbaijan?

The BBC reported that the 'conservative government' there, like so many 'former' Soviet republics, had declared proforma independence on August 30th. It sounded like another Uzbekistan. But after my experiences there a scant month before and a few telephone calls to our old friends, I knew it could not possibly be so. I booked a call to young Kamran, who had no time or inclination to talk but hinted broadly that Baku was boiling.

It was time to go and find out why. Taking advantage of the friendly chaos that prevailed in the wake of the failed coup, we managed to board a flight to Moscow without visas. After a few wonderful days in the capital of the new *Rossiia*, including the requisite tour of Boris Yeltsin's barricades in front of the White House, we headed south to Baku. The plan was to spend about a month in Azerbaijan and then get back to Tashkent. It was early September, and the weather was mild.

I didn't even bother to take my winter coat.

3

Friday Evening on Freedom Square

Upon our return to Azerbaijan, we checked into one of the finest hotels in the whole world. I refer to the good ship *Turkmenistan*—a Transcaspian passenger liner in semipermanent moorage in the waters of Baku bay.

Why was it so special? Well, the deck of the *Turkmenistan* afforded the very best view of the harbor area (especially from the al fresco restaurant situated between the vessel's twin smokestacks), and residents aboard the boat enjoyed immediate access to downtown. Most importantly, the *Turkmenistan* boasted the unique status of being the only hostel in Baku town where foreign folks could pay in rubles and not in dollars. For the equivalent of two bucks a day, we were immediately ensconced in the captain's quarters—a two-room suite, replete with hot, running water all the time, a refrigerator to keep fruit from rotting, and even a television (although reception left something to be desired, due to the steel superstructure).

There were, of course, certain disadvantages. The pay telephone booth back in steerage was either busy or broken. Also, our rooms were located right above the *Turkmenistan* restaurant, and the odor of charbroiled sturgeon wafting up through our portholes day and night became cloying. The most significant negative factor, though, was the other clientele. Riffraff would be the kindest way to describe them; pimps and whores would be more accurate. We had no right to be fussy. The administration was violating all sorts of laws by allowing us to stay, so it only followed that they were willing to violate all sorts of other laws, too.

Most of the pimps were local lads, and quite friendly.

"You are from *Turkey*? Turkey! We are brothers, we are one!"

Most of the lasses were Natashas—Russian or other Slavic women from the north, come down to Baku for a little fun in the sun and profit on the side.

"You are from *Turkey*? Turkey! Take me to Trabzon!"

Then there were the clients. Most of these were sex- and liquor-starved men from Iran. They were drunk most of the time and quite aggressive, especially toward Hicran, whom they assumed to be a resident professional. This case of mistaken identity could only be corrected one day at a time because most of the Iranians were only aboard the ship for the afternoon. Discussion usually took place at a midpoint along the gangplank leading up from the concrete wharf. Although it was designed for single-file traffic in one direction, the leering, drunken Iranians would try to throw their arms around Hicran when they saw her. In so doing, they not only deprived themselves of hands to hold the rope railing, but exposed themselves to her ire.

"Filth!" she would scream in her near baritone voice, stuffing an ice cream into her assailants' face. "Out of my way!" Then she would barge by, leaving the man dangling thirty feet over the cement quay. There were close calls.

Unwanted companions aside, the *Turkmenistan* was fine. And its main advantage was that it was within spitting distance of Ploshchad Lenina, the huge square with a towering statue of Vladimir Ilich that stood in front of Government House. Or rather, the statue that had stood there a mere month before: no sooner had the August 19th putsch in Moscow unraveled than the statue had come tumbling down, and the Ploshchad Lenina was renamed Azadlig Meydani—Azeri for 'Freedom Square.' Instantly, it became the natural gathering point for people when they wanted to show mass and strength. This was never clearer than on Friday night, when Baku did not talk, but shouted.

* * *

"The unemployed and retired arrive early and take seats on the cement bleachers on either side of the dais, while those with regular jobs come later and are obliged to stand. By the time the loudspeakers start blaring the Wagnerian-style Azerbaijani national anthem, thus announcing the commencement of the weekly rally, Freedom Square is packed.

"The scene is somehow familiar: Leipzig in East Germany, Prague in Czechoslovakia, and even Sofia, Bulgaria, in the late 1980s, when young democracy raised its head and old-guard regimes fell like so many dominoes.

"But the venue here is downtown Baku, capital of the newly self-proclaimed independent Republic of Azerbaijan. And if the crowd of eager listeners is a few years behind those that forced the communist regimes of eastern Europe out of office, it is still light years ahead of all the other Turkic-speaking republics that make up the southern tier of the USSR. . . ."

These were the opening paragraphs to one of my first stories out of Azerbaijan. But like many others, it was never published, probably because it did not jive with the conventional wisdom. Azerbaijan, when mentioned in the foreign media at all, was usually described by adjectives like 'conservative' (meaning 'communist') or 'Muslim' or even 'Shi'ite.' There was no reference to the real dynamic at play: almost unnoticed by the outside world, a hard core of people were trying to remove their country from Moscow's orbit and establish an independent (and, to their understanding, democratic) nation.

The prime mover in this process was the broad-based coalition of interest groups and individuals called the *Azerbaycan Xalg Jebhesi*, or Popular Front of Azerbaijan. It had its heroes and it had its martyrs—namely, those killed on the night of January 20, 1990, when Moscow sent in troops, allegedly to put down anti-Armenian riots. The real reason for the intervention, however, was to crush the Popular Front. The Front not only survived the assault, but grew. And in the wake of the abortive putsch in Moscow, it found itself representing the high ground of Azeri nationalism—and issued demands in those terms.

If on Friday the Front demanded the dissolution—and not mere renaming—of the Communist Party, on Sunday it was so. If next week the Front called for the formation of a national army—and threatened to field its own force of 10,000 volunteers if the government did not—on Monday a defense council would be created. With every perceived capitulation to an ultimatum, the crumbling government of Communist Party First Secretary-cum-President Ayaz Mutalibov became weaker. And perceiving greater weakness, the Popular Front would then up the ante once more. A shadow government had emerged—and it was a breathtaking thing to see in a society thought to be deaf, dumb, and blind.

The cast of characters on the dais was almost always the same and almost always they said the same thing: Independence! The moderator was usually Isa Gamberov, a molish-looking man with a balding pate and glasses. In September 1991 he is sporting a beard to show that he's observing the forty-day mourning period for a friend or comrade killed in the mounting conflict over Mountainous Karabakh. He is subdued, maybe even dull as he recounts the events of the previous week and reiterates standing Popular Front demands: that Azerbaijan take control over its own petroleum resources; that bribery cease; that a special meeting be held four days hence for reasons I cannot understand, and that car plate number 995573 has its blinkers on and is blocking the exit road. Oh, and that no outside nations should recognize the unilateral declaration of independence of Azerbaijan of August 30, 1991.

Say what? A nationalist movement refusing to recognize the declaration of independence of its own country? Well, yes. Because the Front has set out its own conditions of independence and wants other states not to recognize Azerbaijan until they are fulfilled. These include dissolving the current parliament and holding new and free elections monitored by international observers; affirming the right to own private property; and issuing an Azerbaijani currency. Most importantly, though, independence means rejecting Mikhail Gorbachev's new union treaty or any other attempt to keep Azerbaijan within the Soviet Union by whatever name the old empire might find for itself. Azerbaijan wants out, the Front says, and the people agree.

"Our sovereignty only exists on paper," Isa's distorted voice echoes across the square. "It is impossible to claim it as real while the keys to our economy remain in Moscow!"

"Hurrah! Hurrah!!"

Isa next introduces the poet Xalil Riza Uluturk, recently released from a one-year prison term for calling for the union of all 250 million Turks in the world. He makes the same statement now, banging his fist on the podium. The crowd applauds him politely because Uluturk seems to be missing the point: the audience wants to be united small first and think about the big picture later. They want Azerbaijan, not Pan-Turkestan. . . .

Uluturk is succeeded by a Muslim preacher whose rambling sermon ends with the Fatihah, or all-purpose Muslim expression of faith. Everyone in attendance lifts their palms heavenward, and then wipes one hand over their face. Despite this bow to religion, though, the content of his talk is pure nationalism. It is time, expounds the preacher, to march south to Iran and free their Azeri kin from the mullah-imposed chains!!

Amen, breathes the crowd, and they raise their palms heavenward again.

Isa Gamberov then reads a few announcements and messages. One is a letter from a member of a non-Turkic group known as the Talish, who live along the southern Caspian Sea coast in both Azerbaijan and Iran. The man requests that his son be allowed to go fight the good fight in Karabakh. Another letter from the southern Russian province of Dagestan concludes with a request for Front aid for the Lezgin nationalist movement there. A third telegraph brings regards from someone in Uzbekistan, a fourth from an Azeri in Ukraine.

There are a few more speakers: a woman who heads the Azerbaijan Womens' Rights Movement, the leader of the local branch of Miskhetian Turks, and even a Tat, or Mountain Jew, regretting the fact that so many of his European Jewish brethren are still trying to leave Azerbaijan for Israel. Then comes a Baku Russian from the Russian-language speakers' association *Sodruzhestvo*, or 'Solidarity.' In Russian, the name might suggest an organization for Slavs in the Near Abroad, but that is not why the man wants to speak:

"We are all children of this country!" he shouts in Russian. "And we all want the same thing—independence and freedom! We, the Russians of

Baku, demand that the ethnic designation 'Russian' be erased from our passports and replaced with the word 'Azerbaijani!' "

"SVOBODA!" the Azeri crowd roars back in Russian, 'Freedom!'

Then Isa is back behind the microphone to introduce the next speaker, clearly a crowd favorite. "Can we have a meeting without Iskender?" Gamberov asks rhetorically.

"NEVER!" the crowd shouts in response.

A small, dark, wiry man approaches the microphone. Even before he starts speaking, his right index finger is jabbing into the air in front of him like a stiletto.

"Azadlig!" bellows Iskender Hamidov.

"AZADLIG!" the crowd thunders back.

"By God," says Iskender in the twangy, vowel-distorting, consonant-spitting accent of the remote west of the country, "the deputies of the Azerbaijan Supreme Soviet are sitting at home because they don't want to work and make new laws. There are sitting at home eating and drinking but they have asked for gun permits so they can defend themselves against people just like you. And at the same time they say that we don't have the money to raise our own army. I say send those guns and those deputies to Karabakh! And if not, give me a gun and I will be the first to volunteer!!"

"AZADLIG!"

"By God, I am going to go to the Supreme Soviet with a broom in one hand and a gun in the other, and sweep the bums out—who will be the first to take the broom?"

"Sweep them into the trash can!" bellows a finely dressed matron.

"Sweep them into the ash heap of history!" responds Iskender.

"AZADLIG! AZADLIG! AZADLIG!"

The time has come to end the rally. But the Front has not yet learned how to modulate its moments properly. Or rather, the crowd (organizers say there are 100,000 here; I think one might clip a zero off that number) is still waiting for something they must have before they depart: the messenger.

A tall, thin man with a gray-speckled beard approaches the microphone. No introduction is necessary: he is Abulfez Aliev, better known as Elchibey, 'Mr. Emissary.'

"I just have a few remarks to make before you all go home," the chairman of the Popular Front says into the microphone. "First of all, remember to come to the Supreme Soviet on Monday to demand an early session so that we can then demand an early dissolution. We cannot afford to waste time."

A short discussion ensues between those in the first row and those standing on the leaders' dais about time—whether they should meet at four o'clock or five. The decision is taken that it should be five.

"The next thing I want to talk about is solidarity," says Elchibey. "Because there will be those who attempt to divide us—there always will be. We are Shi'ites and we are Sunnis, but we are all from one root." He then explains a historical detail concerning the formation of the various schools of Islamic jurisprudence, how one of the main theologians of the Sunni school of school was a student of Imam Ja'afar, whose collection of *Hadith*, or pious study of the ways and thoughts of Muhammad, forms the basis of today's Shi'ite doctrines and thus represents the essence of jurisprudence in Iran. The discussion is way over the heads of nearly everyone in the square. Soviet policy was to discourage basic knowledge of Islamic history among Muslims, reserving such dangerous discussions to a few select scholars in the universities. But Abulfez throws it out lightly and in such a way as to be totally reassuring: we are one and need not, cannot, will not be divided.

"The main reason I want to talk to you tonight, however, is about the communiqué signed by Ayaz Mutalibov and Levon Ter-Petrossian with Yeltsin and Nazarbaev," Abulfez continues, referring to the current leadership of Azerbaijan, Armenia, Russia, and Kazakhstan in one breath. The subject is on the lips (and indeed, in the hearts) of everyone present. It is Mountainous Karabakh, or more specifically, the ten-point peace accord sponsored by the presidents of the Russian Federation and Kazakhstan, aimed at bringing peace to the troubled region.

"There are serious diplomatic errors in the text that all of the government newspapers and state television have neglected to tell you about." Elchibey informs the assembled. "For example, the title of the communiqué neglects to mention just what the initiative is all about, and the preamble only refers to Karabakh, without bothering to suggest that it is within the sovereign state of Azerbaijan. Another article says that 'the law will apply.' But it does not specify whose law this is. Azeri law? Armenian law? Soviet law? Martial law? These are all serious defects in the text that are unacceptable to Azerbaijan."

Abulfez picks apart the document point by point, even down to the fact that Yeltsin and Nazarbaev signed their own names before those of the interested parties—namely, the presidents of Azerbaijan and Armenia, whose signatures appear as a mere afterthought.

"The main point is this," Abulfez says, his voice rising with emotion. "The Center now has a new name, and that is Russia—and Russia has as little right to interfere in our affairs as the Center had under Gorbachev or Stalin!"

"Yes!"

"Have they brought peace?"

"No!"

"Has the fighting ceased or even abated?"

"No!"

"The sole means of securing and protecting the territory of Azerbaijan is the immediate formation of our own army!"

"Azadlig!"

"And if the neo-communist regime refuses to create such a force within one week, we will be obliged to create our own!"

"Azadlig! Azadlig! Azadlig!"

Freedom Square goes wild. A new demand, with a deadline, has been issued. An independent army for an independent Azerbaijan!

"That is enough for tonight," says Elchibey quietly into the microphone. "Please remember to come on Monday to the Supreme Soviet. Good night."

And while the people raise their fists in silence, the Wagnerian national anthem of the 1918 Republic crackles over the PA system. Then, in groups of five and ten and twenty, they quietly disperse and go home. Another Friday night has come to an end, but the people are already anticipating the next.

* * *

Abulfez Elchibey may have been the leader of the Popular Front, but what the Front was was not quite clear. What had started as a sort of local cheering section for Gorbachev's reforms in the late 1980s had quickly attracted—or generated—a dizzying array of quasi-political parties, interest groups, self-seeking individuals, fifth columnists, and probably spies.

Front factions ranged from the Bozkurts, a local clone of the neofascist, pan-Turkic Gray Wolf movement in Turkey, led by the former police colonel, Iskender Hamidov, to the Azerbaijan Women's Rights Movement, led by the redoubtable Hanim Halilova, which was the Popular Front's answer to the Communist Party–sponsored Azerbaijan Women's Association, to which our friend Kubrah Hanim belonged. There were people from the streets, 'businessmen,' academics, journalists, and even a prison warden, Fehmin Xadjiev. One of the deputy chairmen, Arif Xadjiev, was a regional radio announcer; another, Asim Mullazade, was a psychiatrist for cosmonauts. There were the Social Democrats, or two factions of them. One was led by a lady named Leila Yunusova, who through no fault of her own, had become one of the most overquoted sources on Azerbaijan in the western media because she was quoted a few times by Moscow-based correspondents in the late Soviet period. The other SPD faction was headed by the Azeri equivalent of the Brothers Karamazov, Zardusht and Araz Alizade. Although the pair had achieved 'official' recognition of their outfit by Willi Brandt himself, they were regarded by most others in the Front as little more than government stooges, whose party represented a convenient 'opposition' to the monolithic CP. The most disturbing individual associated with the Front, however, was Nimet Panakhov, the head of the 'Free Labor Syndicate,' Turan. Styled the 'Lech Walesa of the Caucasus' by some western academics, Panakhov (later, Panahli) had a resumé that included everything from jump-starting the nationalist movement by tearing down the border posts between Naxjivan and Iran in 1989 to organizing anti-Armenian activity in Baku (and perhaps Sumgait). The weirdest charge is that he was involved in attempting to acquire nuclear-tipped torpedoes from Soviet military warehouses outside Baku. According to some sources, this was Moscow's *real* reason for mounting the January 1990 crackdown, and not any namby-pamby business about saving Armenians. Lastly, there were the independent members of the national parliament, who collected themselves together into a 22-member 'opposition' Democratic Bloc. The 'Bloc' was mistakenly viewed as identical with the Front by most 'parachute' journalists and scholars. While there was a great deal of overlapping on this point, they were not, in fact, the same. The reason for this was because the Front had boycotted the 1989 elections but allowed individual members the right to contest seats—a sort of have-your-cake-and-eat-it-too attitude that was to come back to haunt the Front, and in spades.

Still, for all intents and purposes, the Popular Front was the 'Opposition.' What they were opposed to were the policies of the 'Position,' the 350-member parliament housed in a ten-story concrete, steel and glass monstrosity built in the heights above the city. This was the venue where theoretical clarification of all manner of pressing issues was taken up and decided upon—and the news disseminated to the nation via the state television station, conveniently located across the street.

The government—that is, until its self-dissolution on September 14th, the Communist Party—tried to pretend that parliament was the throbbing heart of the nation. But the ugly building and the level of activity of its occupants were in such total contrast with the vibrancy and vision of Freedom Square that I came up with a new name for the place: the Swamp.

In it dwelled people like Prime Minister Hasan Hasanov, the Sheikh ul-Islam Allahshukur Pashazade, local KGB chief Ilhusein Husseinov, the parliamentary chairwoman (and thus vice president of the country) Elmira Kafarova, and then the personification of an old commie *apparatchik*, tall and skeletal Rahim Isazade.

A lot of people liked to refer to them (and the old Soviet elite elsewhere) as 'dinosaurs,' in the sense that they were supposedly slowly sinking into the tar pit of history like the brontosauri and pterodactyls. But I thought that 'crocodile' was a much more descriptive term. Not only did they give the appearance of snoozing in the sun (at it were), but it was clear that they retained their jaws: they were a dangerous and even vicious group of people, determined to survive and preserve what one could only call their class interest in what was, theoretically, a classless society. With a few exceptions, the crocodiles were also the directors of factories, oil-sector managers, or 'executive leaders' (mayors) of provincial towns, and should have had their plates too full to spend any time in parliament (or Baku) at all. The Sheikh ul-Islam was a classic example of this tendency of the communist state to make 'elected' leaders of appointed leaders: in addition to his role as the chief Shi'ite cleric in Azerbaijan (and the Soviet Union), Thank God Son of a General (a literal translation of Pashazade's name) was also the chief spiritual advisor for *all* Caucasus Muslims and a deputy to the Supreme Soviet in Moscow, to boot. A man of many turbans, as it were.

Not everyone in parliament was an old commie, however. Indeed, the casual visitor to any given session in the autumn of 1991 might have left with the impression that the place was filled with revolutionary firebrands. This was because despite their small numbers, the 22-man parliamentary 'opposition' totally dominated the microphones. Collectively, I called them 'the Young Turks,' and in the heady days of autumn 1991, they were a lively group indeed. In addition to the molish-looking Isa Gamberov, there was tiny and sweet Towfig Gasimov (a theoretical physicist who greatly resembled Albert Einstein), pugnacious and paranoid Rahim Gaziev (another diminutive fellow who was previously a professor of mathematics), roly-poly Tahir Karimli (a legalist with a very bad halitosis), and razor-blade Arif Xadjiev (regarded as the 'brainy Bolshevik' of the Bloc). Etibar Mamedov (an historian known locally as 'the little Napoleon') was already in the process of splitting with the Front and forming his own National Independence Party with money supplied by oil baron (and defender of the interests of the 'national bourgeoisie') Rasul Guliyev. There were others from the Bloc who had their moments on the floor, but the lion's share of assaulting the government was left up to Iskender Hamidov, a hick from the west of the country (and reportedly a Kurd) who had graduated from putting fear in the hearts of criminals to putting fear into the hearts of the neo-communist deputies in the Chamber whenever he approached a microphone. It was worthwhile attending a draft committee meeting on, say, local water rights, if Iskender was sitting in the chamber.

* * *

One classic means of weathering the storms blowing across the swamp was coopting the opposition—or even creating a phony one, for appearance's sake. In the former category was the man who served as chairman of the parliamentary opposition (the Democratic Bloc) and thus vice chairman of parliament and thus vice vice president of Azerbaijan. The position reeked of cooptation, because by definition it meant working at very close quarters with the crocodiles. But as the Democratic Bloc had made the decision to be a legal opposition, someone had to interface with the crocodiles—and that someone was Tamerlan Garayev.

A dapper man with 'family business' ties to the rich agricultural city of Agdam on the eastern fringes of Mountainous Karabakh, Tamerlan was given to hand-tailored suits and flashy ties and a taste for traveling with the presidential entourage. Although this was part of his job as the official opposition leader, there were constant whisperings that he was a little too willing to play fast and loose. Although I personally liked him, my initial read of the man was that he was the first political animal (and not 'politician') of modern, quasi-democratic Azerbaijan. He was a good speaker with a fine, baritone voice and he knew what a sound bite was. And he was totally unashamed of promoting his own 'class interest' in the cause of 'democracy.'

"We are faced with the choice of having a totalitarian elite and a democratic elite," he said, during our first meeting in the tall, ugly office block attached to the parliamentary chambers. "I prefer the latter. Legalize past theft, then tax it!"

England raped India for centuries, and the leaders of the concerns that did so later became lords and mayors, he pointed out; the same process had occurred in America with the early industrialists and oil barons.

"Our own partocrats are no worse than those people and maybe even better," he said. "Why go on a witch hunt? Let them stay here and reinvest their ill-gotten gains!"

The rich will be with you always, legally or illegally, he wanted to say. What was needed to make Azerbaijan into a Caspian Kuwait was a once-off amnesty for all the larcenies of the Soviet era.

Next, I asked Tamerlan what he thought the opposition was all about.

"The reason I chose to work with the government is that without compromise the situation in Azerbaijan would end in confrontation and bloodshed," he said, "And with violence, we will never have our freedom."

Tamerlan may have been a politician, but he had no political party. The Democratic Bloc looked like one, but was not. Nor was the Popular Front. Thus, when the Communists dissolved themselves on Saturday, September 14th, they left only one legal political party in the land—the Social Democrats, led by the two brothers, Araz and Zardusht Alizade. The Azerbaijan SDP was a curious entity. It had seemingly come from nowhere. Indeed, so obscure were the SDP finances that it was generally assumed the Alizade brothers had been 'encouraged' to set up their 'opposition' party by the Communist Party itself in order to give a fig-leaf appearance of pluralist democracy where there was none. Certainly, the Socialists never did much against the Communists; the closest thing to anti-Communist activity came when Zardusht put his name up for election during the September 8, 1991 presidential polls. While the act may have seemed quixotic and possibly even brave from a distance, on a local level all it did was give the Communist Party candidate (and acting president) Ayaz Mutalibov someone to run against in an election that was being boycotted by the real democratic forces in the country. Zardusht withdrew from the race at the last minute, lest he become tainted by collaboration.

But 'opposition' is 'opposition,' and no matter what I had heard about the brothers and their party, I thought I was obliged to check them out personally. Accordingly, I stopped by the SDP headquarters—but soon had my ears filled with such a phenomenal amount of spite, spleen, innuendo, and general nastiness against the Popular Front and Democratic Bloc that I decided that distance, and not proximity, would be my motto in dealing with them. Who knows? Maybe the brothers Alizade actually believed what they said—that Elchibey and the rest of the Front were all really KGB plants. To me, the SDP crowd seemed packed with *agents provocateurs* from top to bottom. That, or the brothers were just insane.

The hardest nut to crack in the way of making contacts was the government—meaning the Communist Party, due to the almost total identity of party and power structure in Azerbaijan (and indeed, the rest of the rapidly collapsing USSR). My initial forays were made through the utterly confused Azerbaijan Ministry of Foreign Affairs (MFA), or more specifically, its information department.

That the ministry was a mess was not a surprise. It had not existed until Azerbaijan had declared independence on August 30th, save as a sort of local prep school for future Soviet diplomats, who doubled as a 'protocol' section for the odd, visiting dignitary come down from Moscow on an obligatory tour of the fringe republics of the Soviet Union. The building said it all. Externally, the MFA was a handsome structure located downtown; but inside, it was all too evident how much importance was put on the services it rendered. Laundry lines loaded with the shirts and underwear of the adjacent building floated across the courtyard, and two bric-a-brac shops had taken root on the ground floor after the mayor of Baku had thoughtfully rented out the space to some commercially minded friends. Even if it reduced working room, having commercial space on the first floor provided the diverse crowd of plenipotentiary officials and protocol folks easy access to a daily dose of M&M chocolates and fake Marlboro cigarettes.

In the old days, life must have been pretty slow at the MFA. But with independence, the cast of characters—almost all of whom owed their sinecures to party connections or pure nepotism—was obliged to do things like draft appeals for international recognition of Azerbaijan and reluctantly issue press accreditation to foreign journalists. My number was 00001, and it was issued by Proconsul/Plenipotentiary (etc., etc.) Fakhradtin Kurbanov. He later told me that he had come under heavy pressure not to do so, lest Moscow become upset that Baku was issuing its own foreign press accreditations. Throwing caution to the winds, he signed off on the document that announced 'Tomas Qolts' to be the first registered foreign correspondent in the new Republic of Azerbaijan. Thanks again, Fakhradtin.

Still, suspicion was rife—especially for those who asked too many questions. *Why do you want to know about our oil industry? Production figures are secret. Why do you want to talk with the Foreign Minister? Our relations with foreign states* (there were no relations) *are classified.*

The interviews that the MFA did manage to set up tended to be gang-bang encounters with 'authorities' on the situation in Karabakh, 'central casting' contacts with weeping refugees and a chat with the Sheikh ul-Islam, to which local 'journalists' were also invited to attend and take pictures of. Often, it seemed that such interviews were actually designed for the local press to interview me (or maybe just to hide under my 'foreign' shirt tails and blame any untoward or awkward questions on me). After a few short weeks, I was starting to get the hang of what passed for journalism in the Azerbaijan (almost former) SSR.

* * *

The big-ticket interview remained out of reach. This was, of course, the President of newly independent Azerbaijan, Ayaz Mutalibov. He was always far too busy to talk to the press, having said all he had to say to *Pravda* last week. I was advised to find a copy and seek "Truth" there, more times than I care to relate.

Finally, after prodding the information department of the Foreign Ministry for the fifteenth time, I came up with an alternative interview with a man inside the inner circle. His card, with office and home phones, identified him simply as 'Advisor to the President.' Christ, I muttered, and went to the appointed address at the appointed time, ready for the worst.

But unlike all the other officials I previously had met with, my new high-level informant was open and talkative—even garrulous. The thought occurred to me that he was open and friendly because he was allowed to be. True, he had enjoyed plenty of contact with foreigners during his long career as a Soviet diplomat abroad, usually serving in the fuzzy category of 'cultural attaché' in embassies in Algeria, Syria, and Egypt. But there was something different about him from the start. His name was Vafa Gulizade, and we were to become dear friends.

Ironically, the meeting with Gulizade was set for Saturday, September 14th—the day the Azerbaijan Communist Party dissolved itself in accordance with President Mutalibov's 'request' that it do so. The session was closed, but was said to have been quite lively—although in the end, the Communist Party of Azerbaijan slunk off into oblivion with only three dissenting votes.

"It is just the death agony of a handful of partocrats," said Gulizade, looking out the window of his sixth-floor room in the white and brown marble executive office building. "The Azerbaijan Communist Party was a branch office of the Communist Party of the USSR, and anyone who thinks it could exist independently from the central organization has lost touch with reality."

Reality was complex and amorphous, Gulizade noted. For example, he wasn't sure where we were—in the office building of the Central Committee of the Communist Party of Azerbaijan, or in the Presidential Executive building? After Mutalibov's 'election' on the 9th of September (and his resignation from the Communist Party immediately thereafter), the old Central Committee building had de facto become the presidency, if not yet de jure. Who would protest? Mutalibov had already suspended party activity in all government offices and enterprises. Even that was a detail: the vast majority of the party's 400,000 membership had long since stopped paying dues, making it a hollow organization without funds or any real power or popular base, if it had ever really had a popular base of support to begin with. Vafa claimed he himself had only joined the party after it became clear that he could not pursue his career as an Arabist and go abroad without being a card-carrying member, and he had not paid dues for years.

And now it was gone. Party property had been nationalized by presidential decree a few days earlier, with all real estate owned by the nonentity to be divided among different governmental agencies or ministries. The presidential apparatus had rightly taken over the headquarters, in which we were sitting. The Lenin Museum had been given to the Ministry of Culture, and was already undergoing a massive overhaul: the displays I had seen in the summer were being carted off to some distant storage dump and replaced with exclusively Azerbaijani cultural fare. Even the Popular Front was a beneficiary of the decommunization of Azerbaijan: after the virtual destruction of the Front headquarters by 'unknown' thugs a week before, the president—who was committed to finding the perpetrators of the heinous crime—had found it in his heart to give the Front a new building, the headquarters of the 26 Baku Commissars region committee. The irony was that the 26 Commissars were Bolshevik martyrs killed in Turkmenistan during the rough and tumble of the 1919–1920 period. The monument dedicated to their memory, a wall with a plaque set in a downtown park, had already been effaced when I arrived in town.

The president approved of such initiatives, Gulizade continued, because he was, in his heart of hearts, a democrat. But the president was unable to communicate his vision well. He was a very shy and retiring man. But deep in his soul, he was an Azeri nationalist who had secretly waited for the day when he might become the father of his reborn country and effect a variety of sweeping, long-awaited social, economic, and political reforms.

This was no easy task—making a country where there had previously only been a party. Especially with the present situation in Mountainous Karabakh.

The president was dogged—even obsessed—with that subject, almost to the exclusion of all other interests. How could one focus on privatization when a quarter of the country was slowly but surely falling into the hands of bandit hooligans? Gulizade suspected manipulation from the bad old conservative forces of the Center, which had first neglected and then stirred up trouble in Karabakh just as they had in the Fergana Valley in Uzbekistan— all in an effort to create chaos and a climate for imposing martial law.

When I suggested that this smacked of a rather convenient conspiracy theory, Vafa replied with a question: if his theory was so outlandish, why was the Soviet army stationed in Karabakh to keep the peace 'losing' so many weapons? First it was automatic rifles, then rocket launchers; reports were coming in now about the 'disappearance' of whole armored vehicles. . . .

All in all, it was a very good interview. Sure, Vafa was a servant of the state, the point man for the shy and retiring president. But he was believable. If it was all just a snow job, it was powder. After almost two hours, I got up to leave and Vafa stood to see me out the door.

"My dear, it was a pleasure," said Vafa. "Come back to see me anytime, anytime!"

Then, almost as an afterthought, he pulled out his wallet. I thought he was going to try and bribe me into writing a puff-piece about Ayaz Mutalibov, the shy and retiring George Washington of Azerbaijan.

"No, thank you," I began to say testily, my favorable impression of the man rapidly diminishing. But Vafa had only pulled out an old photograph.

"Look at this and tell me what you see," he suggested.

It was an odd request, but I looked at the picture to indulge him.

Four young men, most likely university students, were posing together in a flower garden, with the taller two in the back, resting their arms on the shoulders of their shorter comrades, squatting in front.

"Let me guess," I said, pointing to one of the shorter lads in the picture. "That's you."

"You've got a good eye," said Vafa. "But do you know who that is?"

I studied the old photograph again, and thought I saw something familiar about the taller, thinner youth behind Vafa.

"Is it Mutalibov?" I ventured.

Vafa laughed, and then a nostalgic, almost bittersweet smile passed over his face.

"No," he said. "Guess again."

"I give up."

"It's Abulfez Aliev."

"Who?"

"Elchibey."

* * *

The taxi drove me by the building twice because I couldn't believe the description of our meeting place was right: the old schoolhouse just down from the statue of Nariman Narimanov, the great rival of Rasulzade who delivered the first Azerbaijan republic to the Bolsheviks and thus earned himself a monument and boulevard named after him.

Finding the statue was easy. Finding the school was not. It looked more like an apartment in the South Bronx, ready for bulldozing. The windows, at least on the first floor, were boarded up, and a small mountain of trash was piled outside the main door. It was hard to believe that this was the headquarters of the Popular Front of Azerbaijan, the guys who were conducting a creeping coup that was about to overthrow a well-entrenched neocommunist government and attendant bureaucracy. Fat chance.

"What do you want?" a sleepy guard asked. I said I wanted to speak with Abulfez.

"He's on the second floor," said the scowler.

I made my way to the stairs via a corridor flanked on both sides by what I assumed to be classrooms. There was something wrong. The place was not just dilapidated. It had been completely trashed. The doors to the rooms hung by one hinge, usually with the sort of holes a fire ax or metal-toed boot make when they connect with thin plywood. Windows were broken, and glass lay everywhere. In the classrooms, shattered bits of chairs and desks were here and there, dismembered, the way chairs and desks get when you throw them around for awhile.

The stairway up to the second floor was a continuation of the mess in the corridor and the rooms. The level of destruction eased off when I got to the landing. Here sat a group of unshaven men, idling away the time. They were sitting beneath a poster depicting a gray wolf howling from within a crescent moon—the Bozkurt symbol. Two of the men were bruised about the face. One had his arm in a sling. I asked what had happened.

"The Repentance Society," said one.

I said I had never heard of this group before.

"They are Mutalibov's goons," someone was thoughtful enough to explain. "They say they are Muslim fundamentalists but they are really KGB."

"Oh," I said.

I still had a lot to learn about Azerbaijan, but I was already an hour late to my appointment, so I excused myself and asked directions to Abulfez.

"He's in there," someone yawned, nodding to the door on the right.

It was open, so in I went.

"Sorry I'm late," I said to the bearded man behind the desk. "I meant to call but—"

"It's all right," Elchibey interrupted me with a wave of the hand. "Besides, the phones don't work anyway."

Thus began my first interview with Abulfez Elchibey—the tall, thin, bearded philosopher-king of the Popular Front, an organization whose headquarters looked like a dump in the South Bronx, a place where the telephones didn't work for the very good reason that no one had bothered to pay the bills. It was strange, in retrospect, to think that one year later we would be flying together toward Moscow to meet Boris Yeltsin and sign the first bilateral agreement between Russia and Azerbaijan. Actually, I was just along for the ride. Elchibey did the signing, because by then he was president of Azerbaijan. Stranger still is to reflect on the situation in Azerbaijan a year after that, when Abulfez had been driven from power and replaced by someone quite different—but now I'm getting ahead of the story.

* * *

"Democracy is a child of Europe, and it is now rolling over the world like a wave," Elchibey said, trying hard to adapt his native Naxjivan Azeri to Anatolian Turkish for the benefit of my understanding. "It is wholly natural that the first countries in the Soviet Union to be affected were those in the Baltics—those closest to democratic Europe. The last will be Central Asia. But Azerbaijan is a special case, partly because of geography, partly because of our history. We were a colony of a European power—and were thus kept in contact with European ideas while other neighboring states were not. Also, we had an independent state for two years, starting in 1918—the first secular republic in the Muslim world."

For the first half hour, my notebook contained less notes of an interview with the usual give and take than scribbled memos of a rambling monologue that leapt from subject to subject. Still, it was a pleasure listening to this man, 'Mister Emissary,' whose life seemed to be the sum of contradictions of life on the fringe of the now former Soviet Union.*

Born Abulfez Aliev in 1938, Elchibey was a native of Naxjivan, the obscure exclave of Azerbaijan, separated from the rest of the country by Armenia, that has consistently given the country its national leadership.

After university studies in Orientalism, Abulfez joined the Communist Party and landed a job as a Russian-Arabic translator at the Soviet-funded Aswan Dam project in Egypt. Who knows? Maybe it was Nasser's vision of secular Arab nationalism, or even a reading of the literature concerning the *Wafd* ("The Mission"), the anti-colonial, Egyptian nationalist party of the past, that inspired him, but upon his return to Baku to lecture on Islam at the university's Orientalism faculty, something had changed in Abulfez Aliev. He could no longer look at the world through the Russian-dominated Soviet lens; he had started looking at the world through the narrower, nationalist lens—and he didn't like what he saw. For one thing, it didn't make much sense to him that he, an Azeri professor, lecturing to Azeri students, should be obliged to speak Russian. So he made the audacious suggestion that Azeri be elevated to the level of Russian as a means of instruction in the high schools and universities of the country, for which he was thrown out of the Communist Party, dismissed from his position, and put on trial on charges of anti-Soviet agitation and the catchall crime of Pan-Turkism. Found guilty, he was sentenced to 18 months of hard labor in a quarry, where his daily task was to load some 900 building blocks weighing between 30 and 35 kilograms each onto trucks.

"The essential problem with the Soviet system is that it wanted slaves, but ones it could work to death," he said in his staccato, Naxjivan delivery. "Compare this with the treatment of the Africans brought as slaves to the United States. Of course, one must condemn the very fact of slavery—but for better or for worse, the owners of the slaves in America cared for their

---

*Remarkably, a scan of the available literature on Azerbaijan in the late 1980s reveals almost no references to the name Abulfez Aliev/Elchibey, while the names of Isa Gamberov, Etibar Mamedov, Nimet Panakhov, and Leila Yunusova are constantly cited as 'the Young Turks' of the new nationalism.

property to the point of insisting on stronger slaves breeding with one another. Anyone who doubts this only has to look at American sports teams: most of the athletes are black. Here, though, the authorities made the people slaves but wanted them to wither and die. Rather than just kill them, the system slowly works its slaves to death."

Upon his release from the local *gulag*, Elchibey was unable to return to teaching, due to his dangerous views. But the system that declared unemployment illegal had to find him work, and it assigned him a position archiving Persian and Arabic manuscripts at a desk in a back room of the Academy of Science—a perfect place to keep an activist from talking to anyone. These might have been the days of detente between the USA and the USSR, but for a solitary dissident figure in a distant Soviet republic they were very lonely years indeed. It was not until the rise of Mikhail Gorbachev and the concepts of glasnost and perestroika that other, younger critical voices began to come of age in Azerbaijan and eventually coalesced into the Popular Front.

"We are not a political party but a movement," Elchibey tried to explain. "The Popular Front will exist until there is real democracy in Azerbaijan; after that, its mission accomplished, it is wholly likely that the Popular Front will dissolve."

The Popular Front had publicly condemned Iraq on day one of the invasion of Kuwait, just as it had publicly condemned the August 19th putsch in Moscow. Although Abulfez was no admirer of Mikhail Gorbachev after the Soviet president sent the Red Army into Baku, support was a matter of principle. "We condemned the putsch on general principle, because we are a democratic organization and the putschists were clearly against democracy," said Abulfez. "But as for Gorbachev, his actions in Baku, Tbilisi, and Vilnius have proven without a shadow of a doubt that he, too, is anything but a democrat."

The process of democratization of Azerbaijan and the rest of the former USSR would no doubt last years, even given optimal conditions for learning. And the situation in Azerbaijan, at least, was hardly optimal. The communists—or whatever one wanted to call that interest group, now that they had dissolved themselves and changed stripes—were desperately trying to cling to power. Abulfez ran down the familiar litany of crimes he lay at the door of the ruling Communist Party. The most recent was the declaration of independence announced by Azerbaijan CP boss Ayaz Mutalibov right after the abortive putsch in Moscow of August 19th, which had been approved almost unanimously by parliament. Abulfez dismissed all this as total nonsense, pointing out that a similar, almost 'unanimous' majority in the communist-dominated Supreme Soviet had voted for continued association with the rest of the USSR a few months before. He also pointed out that so long as Azerbaijan—or any other 'newly independent' former Soviet republic—lacked such basic attributes of statehood as control over its own resources and territory, it could not claim to be a real state. There were no Azeri banks, currency, or army. The government was relying on Moscow to solve the growing problem in Karabakh. Accordingly, Mutalibov's declaration of "independence" was an insult to the memory of the heroic founders of the short-lived republic of 1918. . . .

Adding insult to injury, Mutalibov had then gone forward with direct presidential elections—elections in which he was the only candidate. For months, the Front had called on the public to boycott the polls on the grounds that they were to be conducted in an atmosphere of martial law. Then, on August 23rd, thugs attacked on the Front headquarters—smashing windows, kicking in doors, and breaking heads, including that of Elchibey, who was hospitalized. Despite the Front's boycott, the 'elections' were duly held. The results were hardly a surprise: a whopping 98 percent approval of the sole candidate, Mutalibov—figures that recalled the sort of elections held during the halcyon days of Communist Party rule.

We wandered into other areas of common interest—Turkism versus Azerism, Shi'ism versus Sunnism, and then drifted into Sufism, or Islamic mysticism. Abulfez was enamored of the great Sufi-inspired Azeri/Persian poets of the past like Nizami, and references to their works were sprinkled throughout his speech. Along with his Old Testament–like looks, this suggested to many outsiders that he was one of the much-feared, Iranian-inspired, Islamic fundamentalists allegedly trying to strip power away from the secular, democratic, westward-looking regime of the Azerbaijan Communist Party. But it was a portrait of the founder of modern Turkey, Mustafa Kemal Atatürk (along with a smaller picture of the ultra-pan-Turkist Alparslan Türkesh), and not that of Imam Khomeini, that hung in his office; he also wore a buttonhole pin with Atatürk's likeness on his lapel.

Iran was a particular black spot on Elchibey's political map—he accused the Islamic Republic of attempting to influence developments in Azerbaijan and to keep the country dependent on Moscow. All such efforts would ultimately backfire, he said. It was only as recently as the nineteenth century that Azerbaijan was divided between Czarist Russia and Iran. Yearning for reunion was natural, and the realization of that dream inevitable.

In recent years, contacts had been reestablished through the opening up of a 45-kilometer-wide strip of passport-free border area to facilitate visits between Azeri families split by the frontier. One result of this was that an increasing number of fundamentalist southern Azeris, connected with the

Iranian regime, were appearing in 'northern' Azerbaijan, hoping to fill the philosophic void left by the demise of Marxism-Leninism with the ideology of the Islamic Republic. While this was a real danger, Elchibey maintained that there was a flip side: Iran was inadvertently importing Azerbaijani nationalism as those same Iranian Azeris returned from their sojourns north, tainted by the vision of a unified, secular, and democratic Azerbaijan.

"Union between south and north Azerbaijan cannot be effected immediately but will be determined by the flow of history," said Elchibey. "Iran is just as much a heterogeneous empire as Russia and is thus doomed to fall apart if democratic reforms and voluntary confederation do not occur. Religion cannot hold a state together for long. Nationalism spelled the end of the Christian empire-states of the West and it will spell the end of the Muslim states of the East. When it does, it will be impossible to foresee how many countries will emerge from the rubble."

One interesting aspect of this was the (northern) Azerbaijani program to reintroduce the Latin-based alphabet pioneered in the early 1920s—several years before the Republic of Turkey converted its script from the Arabic-based Ottoman. The demand that Azerbaijan do so had been part of the Popular Front platform for some time, although the organization seemed to accept the government's more gradual approach: the transition should start with advertisements, shop signs, the names of newspapers, and then articles; no overnight crash course, please. . . .

But Tehran had made known its unhappiness at even this incremental attitude toward language change.

"I remember once when a *mullah* from Tehran told me that our accepting the Latin alphabet was tantamount to accepting Christianity and that we had to return to the alphabet of Islam, Arabic, or at least stick to Cyrillic," Elchibey recalled. "I pointed out that Arabic is the stepchild of Aramaic and Hebrew and goes all the way back to Phoenician and can in no wise be described as inherently 'holy' or 'Islamic,' and that if there is such a thing as a 'Christian' alphabet, it is Cyrillic because it was created by priests to teach the Slavs, whereas Latin was created by pagans. It just serves to underline how boneheaded the clerics can be, and therein lies the danger."

Finally, I touched on the subject that motored modern Azeri nationalism—the situation in the disputed territory of Mountainous Karabakh. Abulfez was categorical in his views.

"Armenians have been living in Azerbaijan for centuries, and as full citizens of the state—just like Kurds, Lezgins, Tats, and Talish," exclaimed Elchibey. "Let them continue to live here as equal citizens before the law—but they must obey the laws of the state. No country would demand any less!"

As for the Armenian claim to land in Mountainous Karabakh, Abulfez compared it with Iraq's claim to Kuwait—a historical claim had been thrown up to cover a blatant land-grab.

I ventured to ask Elchibey about a solution to the Karabakh crisis. His reply was curious. The German-speaking, French provinces of Alsace-Lorraine had been the cause of dreadful wars in Europe, Elchibey noted, but Europe had managed to mature beyond narrow, nationalistic thinking. Look at what was happening now—the states of the European Community were voluntarily ceding elements of their sovereignty to a greater whole! Why couldn't the same thing happen in Caucasia? More unites Azeris, Armenians, and Georgians than separates them. Let the EC be a model for a voluntary federation, a common Caucasian home. . . .

The interview came to an end. There would be many more in the future, and I have to say that they have all begun to blur together. But this I remember with clear distinction: I left the schoolhouse feeling optimistic about the future—perhaps because I had less than a perfect perception about the weight of the past.

* * *

There was one other major personality left to cover in my initial survey of the political Who Is/Was Who in Azerbaijan—the Man from Naxjivan, Heydar Ali Rzaogli Aliyev.

Heydar's home was Naxjivan—the tiny Azeri 'autonomous republic' separated from the rest of the country by a large slab of inimical Armenia but connected to the world by a sliver of Turkey and a slice of Iran. It was not a large arena for a man who, with his cronies, had once ruled the USSR.

Heydar was a man with a past—a long one. A former KGB general and first secretary of the Communist Party of the Azerbaijan SSR, in 1982 he had been elevated to the dizzying heights of the Politburo—the Kremlin inner circle. Heydar was a Brezhnev man—and that was not the thing to be during the heady days of glasnost and perestroika in the mid-1980s. Rudely booted out of power in 1987 by Mikhail Gorbachev for his unrepentant ways (and the persistent rumor that he was the biggest Soviet mafia 'don' of them all), Heydar did not just fade away—he disappeared. When he resurfaced in 1990, in the wake of the January 20th Baku massacre, he was dressed as pan-Turkish nationalist democrat and political martyr. Many people regarded this transition with more than a little suspicion—and no one more than the late-communist elite in Baku associated with Ayaz Mutalibov.

No one I spoke with in Baku had any idea of what Heydar was up to.

Most did not even want to know. Even raising the subject of Heydar Aliyev made a lot of people very uncomfortable. This made contacting him problematic, because unless I wanted to subject myself to that awful Night Train to Naxjivan again, I needed a visa to get there—and no one at the Foreign Ministry was obliging.

"Why do you want to see *him*?" squealed a self-inflated little Azeri pork-pie by the name of Parvin, when I asked about getting the requisite visa.

"Because it is my job," I answered.

"Sure it is!" said Parvin, with that flicker to his eyes and edge to his smile that I long ago had learned meant 'I Know Who You Are Really'— that is, a spy.

I was about to throw up my hands and get on the train, when another man at the ministry intervened.

"Give me your passport," said Araz Azimov. "Just tell me what he has to say."

"I'll let you listen to the tape," I said, and caught the next plane.

* * *

It was a brittle, windy Sunday morning and a crowd of several thousand men and perhaps five women had gathered in Independence Square to listen to the leaders of the local chapter of the Popular Front. The subjects were familiar: condemnation of Armenian designs on Karabakh; proclamation of PF commitment to the democratic process; heavy, personal criticism of the government of President Ayaz Mutalibov on all counts; and an emphatic rejection of ever being part of what was once known as the Soviet Union.

And from the second story of the government building flanking the square, an elderly gentleman with tremors in his left hand and the slow blinking, green eyes of a crocodile turned away from the window, and smiled.

"They will start chanting my name now," said Heydar Aliyev.

The crowd outside reacted as if on cue.

Ali-ev! Ali-ev! Ali-ev!

A cult of personality was not in the making; it was made: Heydar Aliyev was, had become, would be and remain, the very essence of Azeri nationalism. And now he was a democrat, to boot.

Change was not new to Heydar Aliyev. He had been, was and would be many things. In addition to his recent guise as the personification of Turkicness (sic) in the collapsing Soviet Union, he has been many other things: KGB general, Communist Party boss, Politburo member, and first deputy premier of the USSR. As such, his detractors suggested that Aliyev was less interested in fathering a country than in exacting revenge on old enemies, and that the best thing he could do for Azerbaijan would be to return to the obscurity of exile in Moscow and leave the fledgling republic alone.

He clearly had no intention of doing so. Heydar had been playing politics so long that he literally had nothing better to do with the rest of his life. And he had been playing a long time. Born in Naxjivan in 1923 (some say his birthplace was actually Armenia), Aliyev joined the NKVD, a precursor of the KGB, while still in his teens and rose with incredible alacrity at the height of the Stalin Terror, achieving the rank of general before he was 30 (some even say when he was 21). His duties during the Great Patriotic War included leading a *Smersh* battalion—the folks responsible for publicly executing enough deserters to keep others from fleeing the front lines.

No one knows for sure what Heydar was involved in during the Cold War. The unwritten list was long, and rumors rife. Some say he was the man designated to run 'Red' Azerbaijan, when Stalin ordered his men into northwestern Iran in 1945. Others say he was the head of a destabilizing operation among the Kurds of Turkey in the early 1960s. The plan was allegedly code-named 'Operation Light Eyes' in reference to the color of Heydar's peepers. Without access to KGB archives, no one could know for sure if Heydar really had been connected to those Soviet enterprises—or others in Syria, Lebanon, and Egypt. But in 1969, possibly as a reward for spy successes he had coordinated (or—if we are to believe an expert on the Soviet 'mafia,' Arkady Vaksberg—thanks to outright bribes), Leonid Brezhnev elevated Heydar Aliyev to the chairmanship of the Communist Party of Azerbaijan.

The stories of Aliyev's sycophancy are legion, and range from the record number of times Heydar mentioned Brezhnev's name in a one-hour speech (146, I believe) to the cost of a 15-point diamond ring, signifying the fifteen Soviet republics revolving around the Sun of Brezhnev. In return for such obeisance, Heydar allegedly received free rein to rule Azerbaijan as he saw fit for fourteen long years. An 'ascetic' dictator, Heydar was less interested in personal wealth than in personal power. After crushing local mafias in well-reported campaigns, he then allowed his own men to amass incredible fortunes through the control of the oil, caviar, fruit, cotton, tourism, and even flower mafias.

Then, in 1982, Leonid Brezhnev passed away and the Soviet spymaster Yuri Andropov was chosen as the new head of the Communist Party of the USSR. Some say that Heydar's name was already in the pipeline and that Yuri Andropov took him in not to rock the boat (or maybe to get him out of Azerbaijan). Others maintain that Heydar was really Andropov's man from the beginning, and that when the spymaster began looking around for people to help regenerate the Soviet Union, he relied on his friends from the security apparatus—people like Heydar Aliyev, Eduard Shevardnadze, and Mikhail Gorbachev.

"I didn't want to go, but Andropov was insistent because he wanted to have his own people there and I was one of his people," Aliyev explained as we sat down to chat. "So I started work in Moscow in early 1983 as a member of the Politburo—the highest body in the land, made up of ten people drawn from the communist parties of the Soviet Union."

It was a time of great change in Moscow. But rather than the changes being expressed socially or politically, they were mainly expressed in funerals. Brezhnev was dead and buried. One short year later, Andropov was also gone, replaced by a sick and dying Konstantin Chernenko. Then within a year, Chernenko passed away, and Kremlinologists scurried back to the official pictures of last year's celebration of the October Revolution and the May Day parade on Red Square, trying to divine from the protocol order of who was standing where, who might be the next in line to lead the USSR. Almost as interesting as who the next Politburo chief would be was the question of his age: Viktor Grishin, aged 71? Andrei Gromyko, aged 76? Or maybe Nikolai Tikhonov, aged 80? The inner circle seemed all to be octogenarians.

Then, in March of 1985—and far more quickly than any of the Soviet watchers predicted—the Kremlin inner circle selected a surprisingly young and almost unknown member as general secretary of the Communist Party: Mikhail Sergeevich Gorbachev, a man once described as having a nice smile but steel teeth.

Gorbachev brought a new style to the Kremlin—and two new concepts that were soon to become catchwords of the late 1980s: *glasnost' i perestroika*—'openness' and 'restructuring.'

The idea that *Gorbachev* coined those phrases made Heydar Aliyev see red.

"It wasn't Gorbachev who came up with those notions," snarled Aliyev. "The entire process began under Andropov. I was one of Andropov's men and I participated in the preparation and realization of his ideals. But then Andropov became ill and as a result the process was stalled. Then he died. Chernenko was sick even at the time of his election, and he didn't want to go down the road laid out by Andropov. Gorbachev, along with the rest of us in the Politburo, then attempted to revitalize Andropov's ideas. But it didn't happen all at once. Take a look at Gorbachev's address at the April 23rd Central Committee Plenum! There is no serious proposal in it at all about perestroika. Not even the word."

Aliyev said that power started going to Gorbachev's head about a year after his selection as general secretary.

"He started violating the collegial principle of leadership," Aliyev explained to me, as if I were intimately familiar with the inner workings of the Kremlin. "He started acting on his own. He didn't like disagreement. He knew everything, was wiser, more clever, more farsighted than everyone around him. The result was that mistakes were made. The most fundamental of these was about the national question. You are a witness to what an extent the national question has damaged the Soviet Union. It has torn it apart. Take the crisis in Karabakh. He could not understand that the issue of Karabakh would have enormous ramifications for the entire Soviet Union. He couldn't understand. I was the leader of Azerbaijan for fourteen years and as such was also the leader of Karabakh. I was often there and had good relations with the local Armenians. Had Gorbachev asked at the time about Karabakh, I would have explained the realities of the situation to him. But he didn't ask because he wanted to give Karabakh to Armenia."

So Aliyev fought with Gorbachev over mistakes in the Center's policy about the ethnic question and about Karabakh, and Gorbachev fought back by cutting Aliyev out of the loop and cutting others out of the loop as well. Those so cut out were branded as reactionary hard-liners, the people standing in the way of glasnost and perestroika and the development of better relations with the United States and the West.

Heydar Aliyev was said to be one of them.

He resigned his positions in the Politburo in 1987, or was fired; it depends on which way you look at it.

And then a campaign of calumny against him began.

In the Moscow press, and then the world press, the name 'Gaidar Aliyev' became synonymous with corruption and abuse of privilege. Heydar tolerated it all, like a late-Soviet-style Job. He stayed out of the public eye, refusing to reply. And he started thinking about things he had never thought about before. He started thinking about his country, and his people. From being a Soviet internationalist, he started becoming a nationalist.

"My ideas had changed," he said, concerning his period of self-exile. "Even had I stayed on in the Politburo, it would have been impossible to achieve any political objectives with Gorbachev. So I made the decision to be among the people and the democratic movement, working for the real independence of the Azeri Turkish people. But the conditions weren't suitable. I was unable to return to Azerbaijan because the leaders of Azerbaijan were Gorbachev's slaves. They were people that I had trained, people that I had brought up through the ranks, but they had all become Gorbachev's slaves. That was the character of our Soviet Communist Party and its apparatus."

So Heydar stayed in Moscow, a man out of favor (and thus without friends), a simple pensioner. Then came the night of January 20, 1990, when Aliyev's former colleagues in the Politburo ordered tanks into Baku.

"It was the KGB," said Heydar flatly. "It was the Moscow KGB and the Azerbaijan KGB. And the entire leadership of Azerbaijan. They were all involved in the attacks on the Armenians in Baku on January 12, 13, and 14 and then again on January 20th, when Azerbaijan was attacked by the Soviet army. It was all in accordance with the plan prepared by Moscow with the complicity of the Azeri leadership—Abdulrahman Vezirov* and Ayaz Mutalibov. They were in on it, too. Mutalibov now says it was Vezirov's responsibility and that he knew nothing about it. But up until today, nothing has been done to apprehend the criminals responsible for the events of January 1990. Mutalibov wants it kept secret because his hand is right in there along with all the rest."

On January 21, 1990, Heydar Aliyev began his comeback from the political wilderness at a meeting in Moscow, where he demanded an accounting of the slaughter the day before and announced his intention to return to Baku—the capital city of the Soviet republic that he had led for fourteen years but had not seen for eight.

"I wanted to go to Baku but they wouldn't let me," said Aliyev. "The leadership made it clear that I was not welcome and would not be allowed. I was followed. My telephone was tapped. The KGB made my life miserable."

But Heydar Aliyev was determined to return.

"I called my sister to tell her I was coming on a certain day. The word spread that I was coming and people started to organize a sort of reception committee. One of them was an old friend of mine, a publisher by the name of Ejdar Hambabayev. He called me and said that all sorts of writers and other figures of the opposition were going to meet me at the airport. Then the Azerbaijan KGB started calling to tell me not to come. They had been tapping the phone. I didn't pay them any mind. It had been eight years since I had been back in Baku, and I was determined to go. Then, the evening of the day I had spoken with Hambabayev, somebody shot and killed him. Terrorism. It was clear that they were trying to frighten me: if I went to Baku, they would kill me, too. But I was still determined. So I bought another ticket and of course they knew about it right away. This time Mutalibov called me on the telephone and begged me not to come to Baku, saying that the situation was very tense and that my arrival would only

---

*The Russified Gorbachev-designate who preceded Mutalibov as head of the Azerbaijan Communist Party. He was forced to resign after Black January.

make it worse. I demanded to know why I shouldn't come—I am Azeri, I lived in Baku. He requested that I not do so and I replied that I would return. Then he asked me to wait and said that he would come to Moscow to talk. So I waited, and he came to Moscow, but he didn't bother to call. So I bought another ticket and went."

There are those that say a million people came out to meet him. Given the Azeri tendency toward hyperbole, one might reasonably take one or maybe even two zeros off—but in a Baku under martial law, 10,000 was still a lot of people. There were quite a few others who did not want Heydar back home at all, including most of the 350-member *Ali Sovyet*, or Azerbaijan parliament. Heydar went to address the representatives of the nation—and was openly mocked by the Mutalibov crowd, who called him a man of the past.

Humiliated, Heydar went home to his native Naxjivan. According to Aliyev, some 80,000 people came out to greet the native son. Not bad, for a place where only 300,000 people live. Heydar made a stump speech calling for the real independence of Azerbaijan from the USSR and the exposure of the criminals involved in the January 20th events. The people of Naxjivan liked this a great deal. They liked it so much that they wanted him to lead them. The new Naxjivan parliament needed a chairman, a person who would double as president of the Autonomous Republic and thus become, according to the constitution of Azerbaijan, the deputy speaker of the Azerbaijani Supreme Soviet in Baku—the vice vice president, as it were.

The people pleaded with Heydar to take the job. Thrice he refused. Caesar on the Lupercal couldn't have done better. The fourth time the people demanded, Heydar accepted.* It was clear that if he did not, there would be chaos in the land. So Heydar reluctantly accepted the job. It was not because he was ambitious. He had no further ambitions. He had ruled Azerbaijan for 14 years and served on the Politburo for five. He had seen it all and did not need to see any more. He had returned to his native Naxjivan in its hour of need, and that was all.

"After I left the Communist Party in 1990, I resolved never to join another party. After I returned to Azerbaijan against the will of the party, Mutalibov said he was going to form a commission of inquiry and then to fine me! I laughed, because the biggest fine one could serve to a party member was dismissal. But I was already out. How could they fine me after that?"

---

*Armenian President Levon Ter-Petrossian was the first—and last—foreign dignitary to call and congratulate him. It was nice to have another democrat in the neighborhood.

I asked about Heydar's relations with the 'other' Aliev in Azerbaijan—
Popular Front chairman Abulfez Elchibey. Elchibey's term in jail in 1975
and 1976—on charges of fomenting pan-Turkic sentiments and Azeri nationalism, positions that seemed close to what Heydar said he was now up
to himself—coincided with the very zenith of Heydar's power.

"Listen," Heydar snapped. "I have never met Abulfez or even seen him. I
was the leader of the Azerbaijan Communist Party then. It was the KGB
that was responsible for his arrest and imprisonment. I don't know everybody in the KGB. I was the leader of the party at the time. And Abulfez
himself knows that I had no part in the matter."

Heydar had nothing against the Popular Front. He had even appointed
two of its local leaders as his assistants. Nor did he have anything against
the communists—at least not against those without sin.

"But I will have no truck with those who wish to suffocate or strangle the
people's movement," he declared emphatically. "Take Mutalibov. I have
nothing personal against him, but he is a worm, two-faced, a liar. He has
filled the parliament with his partocrats, 85 percent of them are communists
and many of them are filthy people indeed. I know them. I raised them all
through the ranks. There is no question in my mind where I stand in relation
to them."

Their most recent offense, he said, was ramming through legislation that
lowered the maximum age for a president to 65—thus disqualifying Heydar
as a potential candidate in the recent elections. It was a gratuitous insult,
because Heydar had had no intention of running for the post. He had come
home to be among the people because he was from the people and had
always been.

"When I was the leader of Azerbaijan, I pursued the policies of the
Communist Party because I was the general secretary of that party and
because I was a communist," Heydar stressed. "And I was a real communist. A believing communist. One who believed in the idea of communism.
I had a very close connection to the people. I wasn't just somebody sitting
back in his office directing things, I was out there with the people, working
for the people. I was close to the people then, and as result, my rapport with
the people now is very good. Even when I was working in the KGB, doing
secret work, I had a network of relationships that kept me in contact with
writers, artists, and professors. My closeness with the people was nothing
new. I tried to live the communist ideal. I have no house or business and I
have no trade and I never took any bribes, although I could have taken
plenty. The bribe-takers now rule in Baku. They have everything. I have
nothing. I am a victim, a victim of communism."

He sure looked like one, sitting in his sister's apartment over breakfast the next day, a place he sardonically called his 'palace.' It was on the third floor of a Khrushchev-style apartment complex, a two-room apartment with an extra room made out of the balcony, and with the toilet separated from the sink by a wall. Heydar shared it with his sister, her husband, and their three kids. It was a long way from the sort of place most retired Politburo members live in, much less the president of country, or even quasi-country. The place was so dumpy that it was strange. Wasn't there even a temporary guest house for the president? It seemed Heydar was atoning for past sins, living the life of a Sufi mendicant to prove some point. There was only one other person in the political arena who lived with his relatives in very modest circumstances: Abulfez Elchibey.

There were other similarities too, like Heydar's pushing the issue of changing the characters Azeri is written in from Cyrillic to Latin, hoisting the nationalist flag above Naxjivan while it was still illegal in Azerbaijan, and even banning Soviet holidays like the October Revolution in favor of Azeri ones before Baku did. It almost seemed that Heydar Aliyev's Naxjivan was coopting the most potent symbols of Azeri nationalism, symbols developed by the Popular Front.

A thought occurred to me that I tried to dismiss as paranoia, pure and simple: the old spymaster, CP boss, and Politburo member was playing a very long game indeed. It was about power, power that he needed and craved, and power he would take at all costs. Heydar was building his base for a comeback, and not even the Grim Reaper himself would stand in his way.

* * *

It was time to leave Naxjivan, but the problem was finding a way out. There was a plane, but it was so overbooked that I decided not to fly. It wasn't just the tons of baggage in the aisles or the people sitting on top of the bags or the man dressed in the purple silk suit bribing the hostesses to crunch five passengers into a two-person seat. It was the three people camping in the toilet that caused me to abandon my seat on the plane moments before takeoff.

The train, for all I already knew about it, seemed an imminently more reasonable mode of transportation. Accordingly, I went to the station, and after a good amount of elbowing gray-bearded elders out of the way, I finally got up to the counter and got a ticket. There was still an hour to kill, so I went back into town to find some food at a dirty shack that served as a restaurant. Sadly, the cook announced he was out of hot food. Happily, he did happen to have some *Rindfleisch* and *Kaese* and *Blutwurst* cold cuts on special. I couldn't believe my good fortune! Food, here, in Naxjivan, and all nicely and neatly packed in a take-away box!

Then the coin dropped. The chow in question was German Army combat rations that I had tasted before, in Iraqi Kurdistan. While not as imaginative as the French front-line grub, they were far superior to the Meals Ready to Eat (MREs) of the American forces involved in the Gulf War against Saddam. The question was how they had ended up here, as ersatz food in a filthy restaurant shack in Naxjivan. Then I remembered. The night before, seven semi-trailer trucks leased by the Turkish Red Crescent Society had reached Naxjivan by crossing the semi-completed Sederek Bridge in order to deliver 126 tons of desperately needed Turkish food aid. I had attended the welcoming banquet, and been witness to the touching moment when the prime minister of Naxjivan, with tears in his eyes and vodka on his breath, had kissed each and every Turkish truck driver in gratitude for their bravery and selflessness in delivering the aid. He also suggested an exchange of brides.

But the aid that had been delivered amid such pomp and ceremony was not Turkish at all. It was—at least in part—German Army rations, donated to the Kurds of northern Iraq. Although I was very grateful on a personal basis, I had two questions: what was the German aid doing in Naxjivan, and how had it managed to make it from government storage depots to be on sale in the restaurant in less than twenty-four hours?

The answers were pretty simple. Although there were plenty of "Made in Turkey" goods that could have been shipped as symbolic aid to Naxjivan, the authorities in Ankara had decided to save a few kopeks and send materials that had managed to fall off a truck on its way to Iraq. As for how the aid had ended up in the restaurant—and not in the hovels of those who needed it—the answer was equally clear. The authorities in Naxjivan—*the* authority in Naxjivan—was flogging the aid on the market. It was not a very reassuring indication of how Heydar Aliyev ran a country—but when I thought about it, nothing I had seen in Naxjivan really suggested a firm hand or crisis imagination in anything.

I returned to the station and boarded the train, but my bunk was already claimed and I had to opt for the steward's berth against a fee. It was a good thing I paid, because when we got back to Baku about sixteen hours later I learned that the second train had not made it: the Armenians, in retaliation for the Azeri blockade of Karabakh, had decided to effect a blockade against Naxjivan, and ours was the last train to or from Naxjivan for a very long time.

4

Karabakh: The Black Garden

Captain Sergei Nikolaevich Shukrin poked the butt of his assault rifle in my ribs and pointed in the direction of a roadside memorial bedecked with flowers.

"Look," he shouted over the engine roar of the Soviet-style armored personnel carrier, called a BTR. "That's where another of our boys bought it."

The slab bore an impression of a man in uniform, but we were driving too fast to identify the name and Commander Sergei did not want to stop for fear of more snipers. After a relatively quiet 22-year career as a soldier in the OMON, or forces of the Ministry of the Interior of the Soviet Union, the last three years had brought him to nearly all of the ethnic hot-spots that had flared up in the wake of Mikhail Gorbachev's policies of glasnost and perestroika: the Fergana Valley in Uzbekistan, in 1989; Tbilisi, Georgia, later that same year; the Baku riots of 1990; and now, in 1991, the inter-communal violence in Mountainous Karabakh.[1]

"Step on it, Andrei," Sergei shouted to the BTR driver, and we roared through the outskirts of Stepanakert toward our destination—a hamlet called Imarat Garvant, located North of the Sarsank Reservoir. Suspected Armenian gunmen had torched houses and killed an old lady in the town the night before, and we were to inspect the claims, allegations, and damages.

It was supposedly a dangerous trip, but I was so relieved to have escaped the embrace of my Azeri hosts that I had insisted on riding atop the BTR with Commander Sergei in order to see something of the disputed territory and the longest-running ethnic conflict in the lands that were the USSR. Since February 1988, when the Karabakh Armenians declared their intention to secede from Azerbaijan, something like a thousand people had been killed. This number was often thought to be exaggerated, because in the early days of the conflict, combatants fought with fists and knives and pistols. Folks felt they had an arsenal when they carried a shotgun and a bandoleer full of shells. The acquisition of a Kalashnikov was a major escalation in the local arms race.

But with the slow breakup of the Soviet Union and the parallel breakup of the Soviet Army in the autumn of 1991, the nature of the Karabakh conflict changed. Molotov cocktails and the 'heavy' artillery of the conflict—the *Alazan*, a two-pound explosive on a booster rocket shaft used for seeding clouds and making rain—were replaced by RPGs, or rocket-propelled grenades, stolen or purchased from deserting soldiers. Next came the introduction of BTRs, either on rent or loan from corrupt garrison commanders in the field. GRAD multiple missile launching units came next, followed by older and then newer model tanks and eventually attack helicopters and jet bombers. Not surprisingly, casualties spiraled with each upward escalation of the means of making war.

But during my first visit to Karabakh, in the autumn of 1991, it was still an LIC, or low-intensity conflict, fought more in the realm of propaganda and the press than in Karabakh itself. Because the Azeris were getting tired of the world hearing only the Armenian version of events, the newly established Foreign Ministry organized a helicopter trip to the region to show a handful of foreign journalists their side of the story.

Our destination was Shusha, the 'impregnable' fortress town built in and around an ancient citadel overlooking the Karabakh capital, Stepanakert. Our host was Vagif Jafarov, the chief Communist Party functionary in the territory. Jafarov was pleasant enough and genuinely tried to please by stuffing us with food and plying us with alcohol, but his idea of showing the reality of Karabakh was to subject us to endless, triple language (Russian, Turkish, English) lecture/interviews in his office, still decked out with the diverse accoutrements of the USSR—busts of Lenin, certificates of appreciation from the Supreme Soviet in Moscow, and other bits of Soviet-style iconography.

"So, where's the action?" I asked Jafarov, or something to that effect. His response was to show us weaponry seized from Armenian militants—shotguns, the odd Kalashnikov, and a couple of the much-feared Alazan rain rockets. As an afterthought, he also invited us to interview three Armenian captives in the local jail.

At least that allowed us to have a look around Shusha, a place usually described by the Azeris as being the great font of their national culture, the birthplace of poets and heroes of the past. True, there were chunks of ancient ramparts sticking out here and there—but it was hardly a place to write home about. The heights above the town were dominated by a Soviet-style 'sanitarium,' or four-story cement structure of only negative architectural interest. It was filled with Azeri refugees from Stepanakert and a few Ahiska Turk families from the Fergana Valley in Uzbekistan. Downtown was a single street that had a gaudy Friday mosque and mediocre meat and vegetable market at one end and a couple of bad restaurants at the other, near the standard, ugly, Soviet-style local administration building. The most interesting building in town was a large, forlorn-looking church, built by the erstwhile Armenian residents of Shusha, who were nowhere in evidence anymore.

When asked about this, Vagif Jafarov became defensive and insisted that the church could not be Armenian, because there were no Armenians in Shusha or Karabakh. The church was a cultural heirloom of the mysterious Albans, he said. They had transmogrified themselves into the Uigdins, one of the many small ethnic groups in Azerbaijan—but they certainly were not, could not be Armenians. If we were so interested—which was in itself deeply suspect—he could show us any number of studies conducted by any number of eminent Azeri scholars proving the point that Karabakh was, had always been, Azeri—or at least Alban.*

It was at this point that Commander Sergei Shukrin burst into the room to announce that an attack had been reported in the north of the territory. I jumped at the chance to get out of Shusha, and suggested to Jafarov that if he really wanted the western press to understand the dynamics of the conflict, he would send me on the mission with Commander Sergei. Reluctantly, he agreed—and I clambered aboard the BTR.

* * *

The main, north-south highway from Stepanakert to a town called Xodjali was eerily vacant of traffic, save for the occasional fellow BTR on daylight patrol. So was the main, east-west road to the Azeri city of Agdam, just outside Karabakh proper. So was the road leading northward from there back into Karabakh via the Armenian town of Mardakert. There, we left the tarmac road and proceeded north and then west over dirt and gravel roads cut into the cliffs of the Sarsank Reservoir, and it was here that we saw the first concrete signs of recent conflict. Rounding a sharp curve, we ran over two gaping holes in the road. Next to one was a caked pool of blood—the spot where the 27th Soviet soldier had hit the big one while on patrol the night before. Cables led from the holes into the roadside bush: homemade mines.

The dead soldier had been with the 5430th unit of the Krasnoyarsk regi-

---

*Some scholars, such as Sergei Arutiunov, agree with the Azeri argument that the 'Karabakhians' are the Armenized descendants of the Albans. Others, such as Richard Hovannisian, beg to differ. Ultimately, this is a moot point because whatever the genetic truth may be, the 'Karabakhians' feel themselves to be Armenians—and probably more so than any other Armenian group, anywhere.

ment, stationed outside the nearby village of Umudlu, which means 'Hope' in Azeri. It was our next stop. There, we tried to collect information from the garrison commander about local security. There were some 300 troops milling around their compound, idling away the hours by lifting weights, smoking, and talking about their own respective homelands—Russia, Ukraine, Kazakhstan. Six BTRs were parked inside the fence, and I had to wonder why we had been subjected to a four-hour cross-country trip when these guys were within 30 minutes of our destination. I asked the commander of the Umudlu garrison about that; he told me he had no orders to do anything.

We pushed on, and passed through another Armenian town called Zeyle, at which point the security boys atop our BTR went locked and loaded. I asked Commander Sergei about the concern. He replied that a BTR from Umudlu had been ambushed in the town a few weeks before by a mass of women and children. They surrounded the vehicle and took 12 soldiers hostage for a week. Then they released them, stripped of their weapons, including the BTR. I waved at the women in the streets of Zeyle and they waved back. But I was left with a very unsettling idea: somewhere in the town, someone was hiding a fully loaded BTR.

Women and children stealing an all-terrain, armored vehicle? It didn't make any sense until you cracked the code language of the corrupt Russian military: there had been no hijacking or hostage taking at all. The soldiers of Umudlu had gone AWOL and sold everything they had to the partisans. After all, the Soviet Union was busting up and no one really cared about anything but going home and with as much money as you could get out of locals in exchange for your side arms, rifles, boots, and even armored personnel carriers. It was the beginning of a tradition that might be summed up as this: in the Russian army, everything was for sale—a fact that was contributing mightily to the escalation of ethnic conflicts everywhere, from Moldova in the west to Tajikistan in the east.

Finally and mercifully, we arrived in Imarat Garvant. It was a sprawling, not unpleasant agricultural village set in a wooded area north of the reservoir. It was also the base of another indifferent garrison of troops from the Soviet Ministry of the Interior, or MVD. Once again, their concerns seemed to be weight lifting and card playing. They had done nothing when the local Azeris were attacked the night before, because, as the commander noted, they had not received orders to do anything. We asked where the burnt houses were, and the troops were kind enough to direct us down a cow path to a point where the Azeri town kissed the contiguous Armenian village of Chapar across a stream.

In another time and place I would have thought about casting flies for trout. But not here and not now. There were a dozen brick and wood houses lining a muddy lane; four were still smoldering; one was still on fire.

A rustic-looking character came running out of the first smoldering house upon our approach. He identified himself as Mahmud Mirzaev, and said he was the owner. I asked his age. He said he was 52; he looked more like 70.

"It was Heno, Heno Asiriyan!" wailed Mirzaev, pointing across the brook to the closest Armenian house in Chapar. Then he described how a gang of eight Armenians had attacked at around five o'clock the previous evening. He and his family had managed to escape via a window and hide in the orchard as they watched their neighbor torch their house. The As-iriyan household had once been the first place the Mirzaevs would look to if a chicken had gone astray. So much for the claim by Azeris in Baku and Armenians in Yerevan that the intercommunal dirty work was being carried out by volunteers from afar: in Imarat Garvant, it was former neighbors who were in deadly combat.

The identity of Heno and the nature of the conflict was confirmed by the next neighbor, a schoolteacher by the name of Valida Kafarova. She had returned to her house to collect bedding and a few personal effects; her four-room structure had miraculously not caught on fire during the attack, although the interior walls had been raked by automatic fire and there were burn marks on the wooden stairs where the attackers had placed some burning embers.

"It was Heno and Limberk and Vladik and Agop," said Kafarova, naming four of the attackers. She knew them all from school.

I studied the Asiriyan house. It was across the ravine, maybe 100 yards away. Dad was working in the garden, but wouldn't look in our direction. Maybe it pained him to see five burning houses just like his on the wrong side of the stream. Maybe he was glad. I wondered if Heno was there, hiding in the wine cellar or sitting in the outhouse. I also wondered why Commander Sergei and his security team didn't drive the BTR across the stream and interview the suspect: "Where were you last night at 02:34 A.M.?"—basic police work; that sort of thing. I asked Commander Sergei about this, and he smiled weakly. His orders, he said, were restricted to taking pictures and picking up evidence like spent shell casings. He had no authority to interrogate or arrest anyone. Or inclination. It was only a month after the failed coup in Moscow that meant the beginning of the end of the Soviet Union. The boys were understandably not very keen on getting involved in a local ethnic squabble between two groups of people distrusted and disliked throughout the rest of the USSR, especially when the soldiers instinctively knew there wouldn't be a USSR much longer. Why bother to do anything but your minimal duty? Keep score on the conflict by taking pictures of torched houses and listing the names of corpses—and then go home again.

And that is what we did: snap pictures of the buildings by the stream and pick up spent bullet casings. Then we moved on to the last two houses torched the night before. One had become the crematorium of a 96-year-old blind woman by the name of Zeynep Alieva. Her dog, still chained to a post outside the front door, lay cringing and whimpering beneath a defoliated bush, its hair singed crisp. The dead woman's son was raking the ashes for bone fragments, weeping softly.

As we prepared to leave, I noticed a truck parked next to an unscathed farmhouse nearby. The family was throwing all their earthly possessions in the back—mattresses, blankets, chairs, pots and pans, and even, if I remember correctly, a stove. They were afraid they might be next and they had no faith in either the future or the Soviet troops stationed in town. The garrison had done nothing to stop Heno Asiriyan the night before and would do nothing to stop him and his gang tonight, they knew.

So we left Imarat Garvant, but rather than trace our way back through Karabakh proper, Commander Sergei ordered the BTR driver to take us on an eight-hour detour along twisting mountain roads through a place called Kelbajar, a sliver of Azerbaijan dividing Karabakh from Armenia. The idea was to avoid freshly laid mines on the road we had come down during the day. We stopped twice for directions, once at Kelbajar town, and then again at a place called Lachin. Strangely, everyone there spoke Kurdish, not Azeri.

It was too cold to stay outside the BTR, but riding inside was torture. First I tried to conjugate Russian verbs, but the roar of the engine prevented such mental gymnastics. Then I studied the interior design of the BTR for efficiency and found it poor: whenever I turned my head, I would painfully knock it against the ammunition boxes or other military hardware strapped to the rough metal walls. Then I tried fantasy, and imagined myself to be a Russian soldier bumping over the roads of the Wakhan corridor in Afghanistan, waiting for the *mujahideen* to pull the plug. Finally, I resigned myself to mindlessly stare at the Samantha Fox decals with which the driver had decorated his cab, recalling adolescent sex to pass the time and stay awake, lest in dozing I smash my head on a turret structure again.

We arrived back at Fortress Shusha at four o'clock in the morning and the news that awaited us was not happy. There had been another attack across the stream in Imarat Garvant, this time with several dead. I wondered who they were—Mr. Mirzaev? Mrs. Kafarova? And I wondered if I knew who had done it. Heno and Levon and Gaik? Sergei and the BTR inspection team would have to return in the morning to take new notes.

"I did not serve in Afghanistan," said Commander Sergei wearily. "But I cannot imagine that it could be worse than this. There, we were foreigners, but this is the *rodina*, the homeland, and we are allowing it to be torn apart."

He was not talking about Azerbaijan. Commander Sergei was still thinking in terms of the USSR. It would not be around much longer, and the growing conflict in Karabakh had something to do with that.

* * *

The historical claims and counterclaims in the Karabakh conflict are so complex and contradictory that the writer will take the radical step and leap over more than two thousand years of disputed history and start in our present century. It does not seem productive to analyze dialectical differences and establish the construction dates of ancient monasteries, as Armenian scholars and their foreign parrots do in order to 'prove' almost eternal ownership of the region. Nor does it seem productive to deconstruct the inhabitants and pour them into a different ethnic mold, as Azerbaijan scholars attempt to do.

No, far too much time and paper—and now blood—has been wasted in waltzing around a central fact: whatever its previous history, at the time of the collapse of the Czarist Russian empire in 1917, the territory now known as Mountainous Karabakh was mainly inhabited by individuals who identified themselves as Armenians and who lived a communal life as Armenians in a marchland claimed by both the new states of Armenia and Azerbaijan, and over which they soon engaged in war.

Perhaps it would have been best if that process had been allowed to continue until one side admitted defeat. But the issue was left unresolved when both states, more interested in fighting each other than preserving their new independence, collapsed in the face of the Bolshevik takeover of 1920. Then Nariman Narimanov, the new communist Azeri leader, 'gave' Karabakh to Armenia as an act of 'socialist solidarity.' Faced with a public reaction, he retracted the decision and put the status of Karabakh on the table with the great division of spoils of the *Kafburo*, or Caucasus Bureau, headed by Joseph Stalin. The man later described as 'the breaker of nations' decided to keep Karabakh in limbo by giving the region the same special 'ethnic reservation' status afforded such territories as 'Red Kurdistan,' Abkhazia and Ajaria within the context of the Transcaucasian Federation. When the three major states of the region—Armenia, Azerbaijan, and Stalin's native Georgia—were recreated as republics of the Soviet Union in the 1930s, Karabakh was tied into the administration in Azerbaijan.

Was this a good or bad idea? I don't know because I was not there. Are the Hispanics of Texas and southern California worse off because they ended up in the United States rather than Mexico? Some would say yes, and others, no. Are the German-speakers of Strasbourg better off in France than they would have been in Germany? Several wars have been fought over the issue, but today all seems calm and everybody happy. Aside from islands, there are not too many ethnically and culturally homogeneous countries in the world. And most countries—or at least, most peoples—have left ethnic spoors elsewhere. On a theoretical level, it is by no means unusual that this is the case with both Armenia and Azerbaijan. And on a practical level, it seemed to have worked for almost seventy years.

The reason for this is simple. From 1920 until the mid-1980s, the hand of the Center was so dominant in local affairs that the theoretical status of all the states or their constituent parts throughout the Soviet Union was a moot point. They were all more a part of the Soviet Union than anything else. Was there a de-culturization campaign against the Karabakh Armenians? I am sure there was—just as there was a de-culturization campaign against the Azeris, to the point where Azeri as a language was demoted from the official tongue of the country to a kitchen language, written in an imposed script. This is a central fact ignored by most Armenian scholars and their apologists, who endlessly cite stories of the regional government in Baku conducting an anti-Christian, anti-Armenian campaign to de-ethnicize Karabakh. But how could 'Baku' effect such a policy while Azerbaijan itself was subjected to an anti-Muslim, anti-Azeri campaign from Moscow? Did the authorities destroy churches and monasteries and rough up priests? They probably did—just as they destroyed mosques and *medreses* and planted KGB *mullahs* (and rabbis and lamas and everyone else) in religious communities, too. The point is that everyone in the USSR, from the titular people of each republic to each and every one of the minority groups scattered throughout the land, were subjected to the same program of (communist) Russification and Sovietification. Everyone was in the same prison, only in different cells.

The warden kept a tight grip for almost seventy years, and everyone—Azeris, Armenians, Georgians, Abkhazians, Ossetians, and even Chechens—were officially happy. Perhaps they really were—at least in comparison to the misery that has descended on all today. I don't know and cannot say because I was not there in the 1960s, 1970s, and 1980s to see for myself, and I find most memoirs and information about the period just a little suspect because of the famous level of control during the heyday of the Communist Party of the Union of Soviet Socialist Republics—or the tendentious reports penned by those opposed to it.

Then came glasnost and perestroika, and things began to change.*

In 1987, an advisor to the new Communist Party chief Mikhail Gorbachev floated the idea that the Autonomous Territory of Mountainous Karabakh should be disassociated from the Azerbaijan SSR and attached to the Armenian SSR. Whether this was just or unjust is not the point: the hint at a new policy toward Karabakh was like blowing on embers. They began to smolder, and then burst into flame. There were demonstrations in Stepanakert and there were demonstrations in Yerevan, most organized by the 'Karabakh Committee,' which somehow grew out of the Armenian Green movement. Concern for environmental destruction was seamlessly translated into political action aimed at righting perceived historical wrongs. Instead of shouting 'Save Lake Sevan,' the cry became the same as that of the Palestinians in Israel, the Kurds in Turkey and Iraq, the Muslims and Serbs of Bosnia, the Greek and Turkish Cypriots of Cyprus, the French-speakers of Quebec, the native peoples of Hawaii, and for all I know, the Ainu of Japan: *Self-determination!*

It is an attractive concept, and even enshrined by Woodrow Wilson in his Fourteen Points as a basic human right. But self-determination, with a few notable exceptions, has almost always meant a war of secession—and thus the violation of the equally hallowed concept of the territorial integrity of existing states, as enshrined in the charter of the United Nations.

Still, pursuing the dream of self-determination is how states are made. Sometimes they win—like the United States of America, Algeria, and Bangladesh. Sometimes they lose—like the Confederate States of America, East Timor, and Biafra. Sometimes they only fight with words and ballots before splitting, like the Czech Republic and Slovakia. Other times they fight until they reach a (temporary) compromise and end up half and half, like Ireland or Korea. And still other times, they achieve temporary independence in anticipation of absorption by a neighboring state, like Texas—which was then part of the sovereign state of Mexico.

In February 1988, the Armenian citizens of Karabakh held a referendum about formally petitioning the Politburo in Moscow to re-associate the then-NKAO with Armenia, in line with a resolution adopted by the parliament in Yerevan that reserved seats in the national parliament for deputies from Karabakh. Not surprisingly, Azerbaijan did not like this at all, and protested vigorously. What is surprising is that Baku continued to put such faith in the Center to right perceived wrongs, and that its protests should have been framed in such servile, banal, and Lenin-licking tones.

---

*For Gorbachev's version of events and his role in the growing problem, see pp. 333–340 in his *Memoirs* (New York: Doubleday, 1996).

Meanwhile, there were more pro-*Anschluss* demonstrations in Yerevan and Stepanakert and anti-secessionist demonstrations by local Azeris in other parts of Karabakh. Tensions continued to mount when thousands of ethnic Azeris and Kurds living in Armenia began packing their possessions and leaving, either because they were 'encouraged' to do so by Armenian nationalists or simply because they saw the omens and decided to leave of their own accord. This subject—of who began ethnically cleansing whom first—is a matter of extremely 'spirited' discussion to this day.

Azeris and Kurds, among them many mixed, Azeri-Armenian couples, also began leaving their homes in the Karabakh capital, Stepanakert. Once again, the question of whether this was due to a general fear of the future or thanks to more 'active' measures on the part of Armenian nationalists is a matter of the most bitter dispute. The refugees settled in the nearby Azeri towns Xodjali or Shusha, or went (or were sent) to places like the Caspian Sea industrial wasteland city of Sumgait, north of Baku.

There, on February 27–28, 1988, they went on an anti-Armenian rampage. While gangs armed with knives and police batons roamed the city, looking for victims according to prepared lists, pre-set photographers on roof tops captured all of the violence: gang rapes, butchery, and all. Some forty local Armenians—others say hundreds—who had nothing to do with the Karabakh business were killed. Virtually all others were obliged to flee or take refuge in the houses of their Azeri neighbors. The circumstances surrounding the Sumgait pogrom remain shrouded in wild conspiracy claims. While Armenians say that it was just a taste of things to come, Azeris say it was a KGB plot hatched by agent provocateurs to ratchet up the intercommunal violence. If that was the aim, it was a massive success: the word 'Sumgait' has become a symbol of native Azeri madness and hatred toward all things Armenian.

Events rapidly spiraled out of control. In response to the Sumgait pogroms, Armenia began evicting all the remaining Muslim Azeri and Kurdish population from its territory. The refugees soon swamped Baku, like a tinderbox ready to be lit.

The explosion came in early January 1990, when after a month of strikes and protests and nationalist meetings designed to get the government in Baku to do something about the deteriorating situation in Karabakh, the refugees—prompted by whom?—began seeking their own form of redress. Homeless and hungry, they chose the easiest target at hand: the 300,000-strong, mainly Russified and assimilated Armenian community in Baku. When the smoke cleared on the 14th, scores of Armenians had been killed and virtually all the Armenian population of Baku—twice the number of

Armenians in Karabakh—had fled, sacrificed on the altar of nationalism. For Azeris, the rumor of conspiracy became hard fact a week later. On the night of January 19th, Soviet tanks rolled on the Azeri capital to pacify a city that was already quiet. Up to 200 were killed. Azeri ultra-nationalism joined Armenian ultra-nationalism as an ideology based in hatred of the other. The reason could be given in two words: Mountainous Karabakh—the Black Garden.

* * *

So we toured the Black Garden, and did not like what we saw: terrified Azeris, cocky Armenians, and indifferent Russians. Then, as we were preparing to leave Shusha, news came that two men were on their way to make peace and harmony out of the fragmented mess: Russian Federation president Boris Yeltsin and Kazakhstan president Nursultan Nazarbaev, fresh from their great victory against the August 19th putschists in Moscow.

Most observers sat back and marveled. Why would Yeltsin, a man certainly on a political roll, put his prestige on the line by claiming to be able to do something about the no-win situation in Karabakh? Nazarbaev's interest was more explicable: in addition to fulfilling his dual role as a liberal (ex-)Communist and token 'Muslim' to appease Azeri sectarian fears, his presence served to underline the fact that neither he nor Yeltsin wanted any similar border disputes between their own countries: there are as many Russians in Kazakhstan as Kazakhs, and most of them live in regions bordering the Russian Federation. Calls by Russian nationalists like Alexander Solzhenitsyn for 'union' with these territories had (and have) the potential for a replay, on a much larger (and potentially nuclear) scale of the situation between Azerbaijan and Armenia over Karabakh.

The two leaders were flying in the next day to announce a new peace plan, so once more we wrested ourselves free of the Azeri authorities in Shusha and went to meet them at the airport town of Xodjali, the dumpy little town we had passed through aboard the BTR on our way to Imarat Garvant, and began our wait.

Xodjali was inside the Azeri blockade against Karabakh, sort of an Azeri enclave within an Armenian enclave (to use all the wrong terms). And like the Armenian towns in the bigger 'enclave,' it didn't have any electricity. Actually, it did not have much of anything. It was a dump. Still, the guest house was no worse than our accommodations in Shusha on most counts, and far better on one: the toilets worked.

We waited and waited, shuttling between the guest house and the airfield. But Boris Yeltsin did not come. To kill more time, I asked the commander of airport security, a big, swaggering Azeri named Alef Khadjiev, to show me the rest of the town.

There wasn't much to see, and 'town' was an odd way to describe Xodjali. It didn't have many of the features one usually associates with an incorporated, urban entity but was more like a series of rural neighborhoods defined by mud or gravel roads cutting between two-story houses with toilets set in little gardens out back. A miasmic river and several other seasonally dry canals also crept through the place. There were knots of waddling white geese, but no trees.

But Khadjiev had other things to show me. One item was an ornamental cannon he said he had captured (he said he had twenty others like it) from the Armenians. This may have been true, because there was a similar cannon in every agricultural town in the area. They had once been used to catapult 'Alazan' rockets into the clouds to seed for rain, but were now used to catapult missiles on the enemy. Forty Alazan rockets had been shot at Xodjali the week before, Alef said, although the destruction seemed to be limited to a couple of holes in roofs and water pipes, plus the occasional gouge in the ground. He showed me a couple of houses so hit and he showed me some gouges. It was difficult to get that excited about the destructive force of the Alazan. It was a joke unless it hit you.

When evening fell on Xodjali and Boris Yeltsin still hadn't come, Alef came around to the guest house and invited me and a couple of others out to dinner. We were hungry and cold, so we said sure. We got in a couple of other cars and drove in convoy down a valley to Agdam, the nearest big town inside Azerbaijan proper. It was only about 10 miles away, but it was across the invisible Armenian lines. We were very angry when we learned where we were going because it meant we were driving over dangerous roads at night. We demanded that we return to Xodjali and eat there, even though there was no food. Alef Khadjiev laughed and refused to take us back. It was irritating and infuriating. But by the time we got to Agdam we understood why we had come: there was electricity and there was food and there was booze. We sat in a brightly lit room and packed ourselves with food and loaded ourselves with drink and listened to all the toasts, making a few ourselves.

"To peace!" crowed the director of the Xodjali airport, a big fat guy who was becoming particularly drunk. "And if they don't want peace on our terms—then, Bang! Bang! Hahahaha!"

The short and stocky but by no means fat director of Yeltsin's pre-security team stayed pretty sober, and uttered solemn words: "Here we are, from a host of nations, breaking bread and salt. . . ."

The producer of an Australian television team, calling in his translator, uttered the usual clichés. "The first casualty of war, they say, is the truth. . . ."

My wife, Hicran, was coaxed to her feet, and let the Azeris have it with both barrels: "You all say we Turks and you Azeris are brothers (or sisters), and this is a beautiful thing," she intoned. "But that does not mean that you must share our hate and that we must share yours—No! The Armenians that you are now talking about killing are your citizens, too, and have their rights! Let us drink to real peace between countries, but not to the emotional pan-Turkic nonsense I hear every day from people who have never seen or experienced the contradictions of my own country!"

It was not a popular toast.

Then we ate on and drank on, and our hosts ate and drank more than we did. It got to the point that we were more concerned about their driving us back than about being ambushed. It is one thing to die in a hail of gunfire and quite another to depart this valley of tears stupidly in a car wreck. But our concern only made our hosts more determined to drink even more and prove their prowess at the wheel while loaded. It was similar to my memories of high school drinking bouts. The difference was that in Azerbaijan they started drinking vodka very young and had built up a real physical tolerance to the stuff. It isn't so strange to watch some guy defeat two bottles and remain on his feet, even though he had become brain-dead. People not used to drinking so much just pass out, but people who have gone through this sort of training just get very, very drunk and very, very scary.

We were so scared that we refused to get into the cars. This changed the real drunks from being too friendly to being very hurt and angry and belligerent. But we were insistent—that is, we became selective about which drunks we would ride with. This made the drunks we would not ride with even more belligerent. So when we returned up the road along the Gorgor river valley to Xodjali in the car driven by one of the lesser drunks, one of the humiliated drunks stopped his empty car in the middle of the highway and started shooting his pistol to show he was a man. It was, of course, the overweight director of the airport.

"Hahaha! *BANG BANG!!*" he crowed, and shot.

It is lucky no one shot back, because we later learned that the fireworks display was staged in a place called Askeron, which was an Armenian stronghold and a place fond of shooting anything that moved—including the population of Xodjali, as it fled down the same road a few months later.

"Let's go," Alef Khadjiev quietly said, after the drunk packed in his pistol, fumbled for his keys, and veered down the road. He was not happy with the show at all.

* * *

We waited around for Boris the next day, too. Then we despaired and left Xodjali for Baku aboard a plane sent to pick up some bigwig. We thought it was good luck, but it was bad timing. Quite literally upon our arrival in Baku, a long line of big black ZIL and Volga limousines roared into the VIP section of the airport: from a safe distance maintained by security personnel, we watched the Azerbaijani leader, Ayaz Mutalibov, kiss Boris Yeltsin and Nursultan Nazarbaev good-bye as the two men and their retinue boarded the Aeroflot plane. It was now bound for Ganje, the main Azeri city north of Karabakh, whence the delegation would make its way to Stepanakert by helicopter the next day. Our effort to break through the security perimeter and board the plane was in vain, so we missed the party the next day. The essence is this: damning diplomatic niceties, Yeltsin had managed to bring together the leaders of Armenia and Azerbaijan as well as the respective communities in Karabakh, and made them sign a loosely worded protocol aimed at establishing first a cease-fire and then a permanent peace.

It did no such thing. Within days of its signing, the Ten-Point Peace Plan was a dead letter, the first of many that would not hold for over three years in the growing vortex of Karabakh. Eventually, the accumulated weight of these documents would bring down Mutalibov and deliver the country into the control of the Popular Front and Abulfez Elchibey's subsequent military and diplomatic failure to secure Azeri aims would lead to the destruction of his government and the restoration of Heydar Aliyev, who, in turn, would throw more men into the military meat grinder than all previous governments combined. Not three years into independence, the casualties had risen to 20,000 killed, 100,000 wounded, and over 1,000,000 displaced.

But I am getting ahead of the story.

Note

1. The Soviet/Russian designation for Karabakh lives on in press and scholarly reports that use 'Nagorno-Karabakh' or even via the acronym 'NKAO,' which translates to the 'Autonomous Territory of Mountainous Karabakh.' Both uses are ridiculous, because there is a perfectly good word in English to replace the Russian adjective 'Nagorno,' namely, 'Mountainous.' Likewise, the usual formula 'disputed enclave' will not be used in this book. An enclave is a state or part of a state completely surrounded by another state—and aside from the brief few months between the Karabakh Armenians' declaration of independence on January 6, 1992, and the establishment of the so-called 'Lachin Corridor' on May 5th of that year, that connected Karabakh to Armenia, Karabakh has no claim to being an enclave because it was and is (a) part of Azerbaijan, (b) an independent state with multiple border partners, or (c) part of and connected to Armenia. That being said, Karabakh is nothing if not disputed. Located about five hours west of Baku by road (or about one hour by helicopter), the kidney-shaped and Connecticut-sized (4,800 square meter) region is called either *Daghlig* or *Yukari Garabagh* by the Azeris, which translate respectively to

'Mountainous' and 'Upper' Karabakh. The inference is that there is also a 'lower' Karabakh—the flatlands to the immediate north, south, and east of Karabakh proper. Armenians vacillate between calling the area *Lernayin Gharabaghi Hanrapetutyun* ('Republic of Mountainous Karabagh') or simply *'Artsakh,'* its (Armenian) historical name. Likewise, the Armenians call the capital of the NKAO/DG/RMK *Stepanakert*; the Azeris call it *Hankenti*. The Armenian town of *Martakert* is called *Agdere* by the Azeris. Sometimes it is a mere vowel that separates the two language-designates of a town. The Azeris call the ancient capital of the region *Shusha*; the Armenians call it *Shushi*. The ill-fated town of *Xodjali* (Azeri) is called *Xodjalu* by the Armenians. To avoid confusion, the author will stick to the names *used by the majority of citizens of any given locale at the time he was there*. This will serve to offend everyone equally.

5

Home Sweet Baku

Meanwhile, back on the Good Ship *Turkmenistan*, things were souring.

The incredibly friendly staff were starting to become too friendly. Rather than asking us everyday whether we wanted to sell this or that item of clothing, they had simply got in the habit of assuming everything we had was for sale, that their credit was good and that collection of the debt would happen at some future date.

That was the way we chose to look at it, because otherwise we would have been obliged to call them thieves. First it was the socks; then it was a couple of T-shirts; then a sweater. We finally drew the line when the big-ticket items started to disappear—like my $500 camera, $20 shortwave radio, and $2 belt. This last was a particularly desirable item because decent belts were hard to come by in Baku, and to this day I suspect that the camera and radio were only grabbed as an afterthought. We reported this to the management. They suggested that we lost or misplaced the equipment on a park bench. Then we called in the cops, who grilled us for hours before calling in the management, who then blamed us for bringing temptation to the boat. The cops agreed.

Yes, the welcome mat was wearing thin. Worse, winter was starting to come on and the *Turkmenistan* wallowed when there was a bit of wind, making for seasick nights. Also, the neighborhood—it was the docks and never really that nice to begin with—was seriously starting to go to seed. First it was the body found in the bushes along the Lovers' Lane promenade, not two minutes from our gangplank. Then there were more reports of muggings in and around the bumper car and ferris wheel rides, as well as rumors of untoward doings atop the public billiard tables after midnight. Not only was Hicran tired of being assaulted by Iranians who thought she was a hooker, she was increasingly irritated about having her bags sliced open in the streets nearby, where razor-equipped pickpockets plied their silent trade. It was high time to move.

The problem was where to move to. Aside from a handful of Indian and Arab students living in dormitories and a few consular officials from Turkey and Iran who were obliged to sleep in their hotel room offices, there were no foreigners living in Baku. People simply did not know how to deal with the idea of renting an apartment. Through 'good contacts' like our friends Kubrah and Kazanfer, we would be introduced to someone willing to rent out an abode and then ask the price.

"Two thousand dollars," the owner would say without shame. Jaws—ours—would drop. A year? No, a month.

"You would be paying $3,000 a month in the Intourist hotel," the owner would explain. "$2,000 a month is a deal."

This was theoretically true. A hundred bucks a night for a room with a broken toilet in the Intourist chain was the walk-in rate for foreigners. That this price had become the measure for apartment rentals was really not that strange, because no one had ever rented an apartment to a foreigner before. Part of this had to do with the Soviet system: the government provided everyone with housing, and if the government was not providing housing, then something was wrong with us—which was right, because we were still, in fact, illegal aliens in the land.

It was getting pretty depressing, to the point where I had to ask myself what we were doing hanging around a Baku that clearly didn't want us to be there. Maybe the Azerbaijan mission was finished. There were other options—for example, returning to Tashkent.

With a heavy heart and a sense of failure, I went off to the Aeroflot office to see about tickets to Uzbekistan. After waiting in line for an hour, I finally got to the ticket counter, stooping so as to peer into the tiny window to book a flight. The ticket agent informed me I couldn't buy tickets in rubles but had to pay in exorbitant dollars, and that there were no tickets anyway for three weeks and that she was closed for an extended lunch break and that I should return tomorrow or in three weeks, but with a gift, if I knew what she meant. Then she slammed down the window, nearly taking off my fingers.

I returned to the boat to find Hicran packing our things.

"He came back," she said, visibly excited.

"Who? The Iranian you wanted me to throw overboard?"

"No!"

"The thief who stole my camera?"

"No!"

"Who then?"

"Fuat the cop."

"Who the hell is that?"

"The guy with the apartment."

"Oh," I said, vaguely remembering the man who had tried to hit us up for two grand a month. "What does he want now, only fifteen hundred?"

"No. He said he was sorry because he didn't understand the value of the dollar against the ruble."

"So?"

"So, he said we could have it for one hundred a month."

"It must be a dump," I said with finality.

She pulled out a book about architecture in Baku she had picked up, flipping to a page that introduced the classic, turn-of-the-century-style oil-baron-type residence.

"That's it," she said, jabbing a slender finger at a handsome, vine-draped structure called 'The Bankers' Building.'

"Nice place," I said, admiringly, "Did we get the basement?"

"We got the third floor," she said. "Half of it is ours."

Well, not quite. Only a third of it was. But that was more than enough. And amazingly, it had not been 'communized.' We had seen a few examples of so-called 'socialist' use of space, where the original architectural proportions of formerly handsome apartments had been altered to a considerable degree: rather than having a normal vertical/horizontal ratio of, say, 2/3, the addition of a few new walls could change this to ratio of 2/2 or even 2/1.5—thus making an elevator shaft out of a living room. Shared kitchens and even bathrooms were common. Not in our new abode, thank God. From the arched street entrance to the winding stairwell to the high, molded ceilings, parquet floors, and French doors leading to a raised study, it seemed to have been designed for a senior clerk at Rothschild's or one of the Nobel brothers while on his way up the slippery slope of the early petroleum industry. In addition to a master bedroom, guest bedroom, small kitchen, and full bathroom, there was a spacious living room with double windows overlooking the pleasant, triangular Akhundova Park. A chunk of plaster had fallen out of the ceiling, exposing the ribbing, and the wallpaper—a huge poster of an impossibly idyllic mountain scene—was not to everyone's taste. But at least we'd gotten that and not the velvet Elvis posters we had seen in other places. It was, finally, a prince of an apartment and would have been one anywhere. It almost shouted 'Baku.' The local movie industry liked the place so much that they shot a scene or two there every year—and it was ours for a hundred bucks a month.

* * *

We adjusted to life as residents of Baku and lived, more or less, like all our neighbors. One major difference, of course, was that due to the rapid collapse of the ruble against the dollar in late 1991, we were flush with cash at any given time. The sad truth though, was that there was nothing to buy. The exception was caviar. We lived on the stuff, often going through a kilogram a week. It was much easier to get than the condiments that go with it—like butter, and sometimes bread.

Household necessities, however, remained problematic. Lightbulbs could not be found at any price. Plastic buckets were also rather scarce. While the ordinary home owner or tenant in the United States or Europe might not think much about the lowly bucket, it was an essential element of urban life in Baku due to the very erratic water supply. Usually, we only got on line every third day and then in the middle of the night, obliging us to set the alarm and then start cleaning dishes and clothes and filling every old vodka bottle and pan in the house to create a reserve. Then one day, while browsing around a shop that specialized in such things as real coffee, cigarettes, foreign beer and chocolates, I discovered something even more exotic: ten-gallon plastic buckets. I bought three instantly. No sooner was I on the street than I was mobbed by people demanding to know where I had found the treasure.

We never got into the Soviet habit of standing around in lines, waiting for hours in front of a government store with limited stocks. To be perfectly honest, I am not sure how many Soviet citizens actually participated in this activity, which became the cliché image of the failure of communism on television sets throughout the capitalist world. Most of the lines you saw were the kind you saw anywhere else: people with time on their hands who had heard about cheaper goods here than there and were looking for a deal. We shopped in the opposite direction—that is, we walked around with massive amounts of cash in order to make instant purchases at the many private *Komisyon* shops, even then springing up like mushrooms all over town. You never knew what you might find between the leather jackets and rolls of imported wallpaper. Twelve-ounce packs of real orange juice, made in Greek Cyprus? Buy ten! German-made Coca-Cola? Snap up five! Estonian cheddar cheese? *Buy a ten-kilo brick, now!* Georgian wine was more problematic, because it came in gallon glass jugs and was a little heavy to lug around, especially if you were on your way to a press conference.

Other items we would find on the shelves were strange: complete desktop computers and facsimile and automatic answering machines, selling far below the normal cost anywhere else in the world. This was a little perplexing. At first, I assumed the presence of the electronics on the local market was a political act aimed at giving the population the impression of modernity and prosperity. Few locals had the means to plop down $1,000 cash (in rubles) for the 40 megawatt desktop Epson printer combo or even

$300 for a Murata Fax. Or did they? Because inventory was moving. It was almost impossible to prove, but all traces kept on leading back to a central idea: there was a lot more money around than anyone imagined, and that all statistics about wages and disposal income were lies.

A lot of this secret prosperity had to do with trickle-down economics controlled by that murky group of people known in the lands of every former Soviet republic as 'the Mafia.' The label never seemed to be exactly accurate, because this entrepreneurial class would have been known simply as 'businessmen' anywhere else in the world. But the cultural prohibition against profit-making was so strong that most of these characters, whether legally or illegally engaged in economic activity, acted like criminals out of sheer habit. A true confession: we were glad they were there.

* * *

The main joy of long-term residency in Baku was the equally exhilarating and frustrating experience of exploring terrain cognita without a map.

But explaining my discoveries to the world was problematic at best. I may have been the first foreign correspondent to take up reporting from Azerbaijan, but support was patchy. Most editors I had worked with in Turkey were very reluctant about taking in any copy from what was, in theory, part of their Moscow bureau's patch. The reason was concern about offending their reporters there, the editors explained—even though those same reporters seldom, if ever, came down to Baku, and picked up most of their news from such 'independent' (and thus theoretically 'reliable') Russian agencies as InterTass, the renamed Soviet news agency TASS.

The main problem, however, was local communications. Some said the Baku telephone system was the worst in the former USSR. One cited reason was that the telecommunications exchange had been situated next to an old wheat depot, and legions of rats had chewed through the telephone cables when they ran out of chaff. When water accumulated in the basement, the system short-circuited.

And water was accumulating all the time, thanks to the slow rise of the Caspian Sea. This was an ecological enigma if ever there was one. The Caspian, the world's largest lake, has risen more than six feet over the past three decades. Some say this is due to periodic tectonic movement beneath the seabed, and that after a certain point the waters will recede once more— and concerned environmentalists will wring their hands about how to bring the water table back up. Others say that the rise of the Caspian is connected to the dramatic drop of the water level in the Aral Sea in Central Asia which has somehow sprung a subterranean 'leak.' In conspiracy-prone Baku, there is also a third theory: the nefarious Russians have opened dams on the Volga in order to flood the oil-wells and coastal installations in Azerbaijan and Iran. Whatever the cause or causes, the fact remains that the rising waters are playing havoc with existing infrastructure and the environment.

It goes without saying that communication with the world via international calls (or even calls to Moscow) was frustrating in the extreme. The idea of using a fax or modem was simply insane. Thus, I was obliged to consider another, outdated option in the communications world—the lowly telex. The logical place to find said facility was at the offices of 'colleagues' in the local press. The best-nameless, 'independent' news agency recommended by the foreign ministry was located on the fifth or sixth floor of a steel and glass building, where most of the other offices had something to do with Soviet-style joint ventures. The boss was a short, stocky lady known and respected throughout the land as the doyenne of 'the new journalism.' I introduced myself and said I wanted to establish a professional relationship.

"Great! Wonderful!" came the reply. "At last, a western journalist who will tell our side of the story, and not merely regurgitate the lies of the perfidious Armenians!"

Then came the anxious query.

"By the way, whom do you work for?"

I showed a letter of introduction from the *Washington Post.* She breathed a sigh of relief.

"Thank God it's not the *Christian Science Monitor,* the *Boston Globe,* the *Philadelphia Inquirer,* the *Baltimore Sun* or the *New York Times!*"

It seemed the agency churned out vital copy to these and other newspapers based in Moscow and it would not be proper to help a rival. . . .

I asked to see a sample of the copy sent out on the agency wire. It was unintelligible. I then asked how much the service cost subscribers. None of them had actually paid anything yet, but they would be charged, *err,* a thousand dollars a year after they learned of the value of the service. They were now receiving it for free, whether they wanted it or not.

It was a strange way to do business—churning out the same news 100 times on the telex, and hoping for the best. But there seemed to be some potential. The office was large and filled with empty desks and owned a couple of misfiring telephones. But thanks to the all-important telex line, it was de facto a press center. Accordingly, I made the agency an offer the boss couldn't refuse. In exchange for access to the telex, I would assist in the editing of the English-language copy, reorganize the office, and pull in paying clients.

Great, wonderful! Yes!!

As a professional observer, I noted that there was a 20-megabyte computer and dot matrix printer gathering dust in a corner. I set the system on an idle desk, thinking that it might be used for a little word processing as well as a tool to bring the employees into the electronic era. (I had earlier noted that the agency's writers and translators wrote their copy by hand before giving it to the telex operator.)

Great, wonderful! Yes!!

The next day, the computer and printer were back in their dusty corner. The message was clear: whoever really owned the system thought a little computer knowledge a dangerous thing.

The real struggle, for the ancient telex, was yet to be joined, however. Like all telex machines in Baku, it had a double function Cyrillic/Latin keyboard that made copy-punching a hunt-and-peck hell. 'P' was either 'p' or 'r'; 'H' was either 'h' or 'n'; 'Y' was either 'y' or 'u'; 'D' was either 'd' or 'b'; and 'B' was either 'b' or 'v'. It all depended on which side of any given key your eye first fell on or which function button you had previously punched. This was so frustrating that I almost immediately gave up trying to cut my own copy. Also, my sitting at the machine meant that I was, by definition, keeping it busy and thus interfering in the flow of non-news to the non-subscribers. Then I noticed a second telex machine in another dusty corner.

"Why don't you use one machine to punch the tape and one to send it?" I inquired.

"Because we only have one line," came the reply.

"Silly dears," I pointed out. "You don't need a line to punch a tape, only to send it!"

I cleared off one of the tea tables, set the second telex machine on it, and showed the staff how one machine might be used to cut a tape while the other machine was used for transmission. The next day the second telex was back in its place on the floor. A collective decision had been made that a telex was of no use unless it had a line.

The last straw came on the third or fourth day, following the announcement in parliament on October 10th that Azerbaijan was to set up its own army. This was news—but not of the kind that the agency wanted to transmit.

"It is a state secret," said the boss.

"What do you mean? It was a public announcement! Your reporter was there, too!"

"Our sponsor does not want us to transmit this news," she said.

"Who is your sponsor?"

"That is none of your business."

It was time to find a different local partner.

The story was always the same with the other 'independent' news agencies (there were quite a few). They either closed at exactly six o'clock or were so busy sending their own copy (to non-subscribers) that I could never get time on a telex machine to file. Clearly, there was only one solution: I needed my own.

But this was still the Soviet Union, or kind of—and even while the public communications systems of places like Moscow and St. Petersburg had been thrown wide open (usually as satellite phone joint ventures between western telecom companies and the KGB), in provincial places like Azerbaijan, even the lowly telex was still regarded as a technological tool that inimical unknowns would only abuse. Access had to be controlled. The reason for this, I assumed, was based on a desire to learn what the foreigners were up to. The Ministry of Communications and the KGB were the most natural of marriages. I was wrong. Whomever the Communications folks were really working with, it soon became abundantly clear that truth and/or information were not what they sought. It was money.

The venue for the shakedown was the top floor of the telephone and telex exchange building down the street from the ministry, a place where I had already wasted many hours trying to book calls to Tashkent, Moscow, London, and the world. Curiously, most of the coin-operated machines in the building were of the gambling variety. Somebody in the ministry had given somebody else the right to set up a row of one-armed bandits smack-dab in the middle of the Baku telephone exchange. I suspected that the jingle-jangle of coin dropping in and out of 1980-model Las Vegas electronic boxes somehow had to have a negative effect on quality of line to Kiev or Rostov-on-Don, but could not be sure.

My appointment was with a woman named Nayilah Hanim. She was five feet tall, weighed 150 pounds, and had dyed red hair and gold teeth across her upper jaw. Our conversation went something like this:

"What a delight to meet a foreign journalist among us! With your pen, the Truth about our country will finally be known in the inner circle of your government! . . ."

"I do not work for the government."

". . . Truly, there is an information blockade that must be broken! The cursed Armenians have infiltrated newsrooms everywhere and arranged things so that only their agents report on our country, purveying nothing but lies to the world."

"I serve the truth, ma'am, I am its slave."

"God praise you! Now, let me show you our equipment."

"I am eager to see it."

We proceeded down a corridor to the musical clickity-clack of a dozen telexes in action.

"This is our intake room. . . ."

Clickity-click-clack-clack

". . . And this is our out-going room. . . ."

Clickity-click-clack-clack

". . . and these are our employees, at your beck and call, day and night!"

Clickity-click-clack-clack

This sounded almost too good to be true.

"Well!" Nayilah Hanim declared. "Now you've seen our operation. Let's go have some tea and talk about our contract. . . ."

"I am eager to see its terms."

"Let's see here . . . the client agrees to *da ta da* and *da ta da* . . . the client further more agrees to *tum tum tum* . . . Ah! here is the important part—the cost!"

"Please advise me."

"Each minute of the telex is 100 rubles. . . ."

I made a quick calculation: it came to about fifty cents a minute at the Black Market rate of exchange. This was high, but still not really exorbitant. Nayilah Hanim went on.

". . . And each minute the typists type is an additional 100 rubles. . . ."

That brought us up to about a dollar a minute—it was getting steep.

". . . And each minute of waiting for an international line, no matter what the cause of the delay might be, is also 100 rubles. . . ."

I didn't like the implications of this open-ended charge at all—but I was not in a position to complain.

"The contract, ma'am!"

"*Pozhaluista!*" she said in Russian. 'If you please!'

She handed me the contract, and I extended my pen toward it.

"Oh, my dear boy," Nayilah Hanim thoughtfully said. "There is one other small detail."

"What could that be?"

"The rates we are speaking of are, of course, pro-rated in the exchange rate of dollars against the ruble of the day."

This was not good news: the legal price of the ruble against the dollar was around 50 to one, while the street rate (no one liked the words 'Black Market') was half that, or 100 to one. Nayilah Hanim had just doubled the cost of doing business.

"That's steep," said I.

"Yes, but it's not a problem for your government," smiled Nayilah.

"I don't work for the government."

"I know, I know. . . ."

I re-did my computations. Even at the official rate, we were still talking about the range of two or three bucks a minute. It was high, but I figured it was still worth it.

"Ma'am," I said again. "The contract!"

"*Pozhaluista!*" she repeated, shoving the document across her desk.

I studied it another moment.

"Ma'am, a query."

"I beg of thee, ask."

"We have spoken of the diverse rates and charges. . . ."

"Yes. . . ."

"And have agreed that I shall pay in pro-rated dollars."

"Yes. . . ."

"But you neglected to tell me from which of the three legal rates of exchange I am to pay in—the official, the commercial, or the tourist; I do not even mention the Black Market. . . ."

"Yes. . . ."

"Well, it says here in black and white that the rubles to which we agreed shall be charged according to the official rate of exchange!"

"Of course it's the official rate! We are the government!"

"Truly, ma'am, the costs of purveying the Truth are great! But for my love of Veracity, I might despair!"

"I beg your pardon?"

"Let me explain," said I. "Neglecting the curiously open-ended commitment for the client to pay for 'waiting time' as well as the punching of the telex tape by one of your girls—I crave your indulgence for any error of understanding due to my faulty command of your tongue!—it means here that each minute of telex time is to cost fifty dollars!"

"So? Your government has lots of money."

"Ma'am," I said at last. "It is time for me to take my leave."

I still did not hold it against Nayilah Hanim personally. It was government policy. But when I stood and extended my hand to say good-bye, I understood exactly what was happening.

"Okay, okay," she said, her voice changing from officiously friendly to condescendingly cunning. "The official rate is high. I agree, it's high! Fifty dollars a minute, hey! . . . But those are the rates imposed by our foreign-exchange commission, over which we have no control. But if you promise not to tell another soul, I can give you a break. I think we can settle on the commercial rate. . . ."

"No, thanks," I said, and started for the door.

"Why not?"

"That is still twenty dollars per minute line time, plus your unknown extras. No one in the world pays such outlandish rates. We have nothing to talk about. Thank you for your time."

"Sit down," Nayilah Hanim commanded.

"No."

"Look, buster, are you trying to bargain with me? The Iraqi consulate pays us the official rate! The Iranian consulate pays us the official rate! I give you the commercial rate and you complain and try to nickel-and-dime me! And you are still trying to bargain! This is no bazaar!"

"Not at all, ma'am," my hand on the doorknob. "I know that this office is not the bazaar. It is extortion! Let the government of Saddam Hussein pay for your summerhouse!"

"Hey, sit down!" Nayilah Hanim almost pleaded, her fish about to flop free. "I was only kidding, okay? You've made your point! Let's cut a deal! I'll give you half price on the commercial rate!"

"Madam, you disgust me."

"A quarter! What do you expect, the tourist rate?"

"Let all the news about Azerbaijan be reported from Armenia!"

I didn't catch what else Nayilah of the telex office had to say, because I was already on my way down the stairs toward the street. I was tempted to report her to the Minister of Communications, but it was just as well that I didn't. He was the biggest crook of them all.

* * *

There was a silver lining about my problem with getting information out: it left me plenty of time to get information in—that is, to study Azerbaijani society at leisure, and from multiple sources, meaning new friends. Initially, I tried to get by with Turkish—which worked well with the Popular Front crowd but was less welcomed by others in the country, who remained deeply suspicious of getting rid of one Big Brother only to get saddled with another. Accordingly, I began making a concerted effort to convert the Anatolian Turkish I spoke to Azerbaijani, which opened up many more doors, especially among such groups as the Lezgins, Talish, and Tats, who, although not native speakers of Azeri, felt themselves to be Azerbaijanis, not 'Turks.'

Finally, I decided to bite the bullet and start learning Russian—and with that effort, I cracked open a society I had previously known of but neglected without knowing it: the 'Soviets.' My guide to this special little corner of the USSR—later to be referred to by the term 'the Near Abroad'—was none other than my Russian teacher, Elfrieda.

A taskmaster of the old school, Elfrieda started skipping her own classes as director of the Language Academy to teach us her language. And that was Russian. She loved Russian as a language and as a culture—and for her that meant Soviet culture, the culture of the 'big country' that was collapsing around her ears. Yes, Elfrieda was a Soviet—the nationality that wasn't supposed to be. Half Azeri, half Russian (father/mother respectively), she was first married to an Azeri Kurd who had studied in East Berlin. Her kids were thus one-quarter Russian, one-quarter Azeri Turk and half Azeri Kurd, although there was a good possibility that there was a touch of the dreaded Armenian tar brush in the genetic mixture, too. After a divorce, she had married a German/Ukrainian/Russian judo instructor named Valerii, who had no apparent hours of work or interests save picking olives from the neglected tress lining streets and avenues throughout the city until he became the driver-cum-chaperon of the second foreign correspondent to take up residence in Baku, my future sidekick, Laura Le Cornu.

But back to Elfrieda. With independence, like all the other 'Soviets' in Azerbaijan, she was asked to shift her loyalties from the big country to the small—the equivalent of demanding that a 'German/Irish' American renounce his or her earlier, composite identity as an 'American' and embrace one or both of his or her ethnic strains. Elfrieda didn't like that choice one bit. Perhaps this was the reason that she was so given over to the concept of the conspiracy. Every time we read a newspaper (Elfrieda insisted that the newspapers we read were always Moscow-based publications; her local news came exclusively through the grapevine), Elfrieda was reading between the lines. Sometimes, the plots got so convoluted that I thought she was trying to plant (dis)information. The thought that she might be (at least former) KGB occurred to me a few times. On a general level, her position as head of an institute devoted to teaching future foreign leaders how to speak and love Russian made her a natural contact for those who wanted to control foreigners. Her previous students included the Israeli politician Iliya Zimtzov and the President of Angola, Eduardu Dush Santush.

And she took an almost obsessive attitude about teaching me the terms I needed to express my opinions about contemporary events—and thus became immediately privy to what I thought about who was in the power structure and who said what at an interview or press conference. Maybe she was just a good teacher: as any student of foreign languages knows, the essence of learning is to allow oneself to become a child again and then grow back into one's more sophisticated self with the aid of one's instructor. And Elfrieda was mine.

It was through Elfrieda that we were introduced to the most obscure group of 'Soviets' still living in Azerbaijan: the Armenians. As recently as

1988, there had been as many as 500,000, arguably one of the most concentrated (if Russified) Armenian communities in the world. Remarkably, despite the pogroms, expulsions, and growing war over Karabakh, in 1991 some 10,000 Armenians remained. Most were part of mixed marriages—Armenian/Russian, Armenian/Jewish or, primarily, Armenian/Azeri, and they and their children had made the decision to stay in Azerbaijan when all the others had left.

Like other Russian speakers, they were 'Soviets' by mentality—meaning that they still clung to the idea of the 'big country' of many nationalities. But unlike the others, who might count on Russia (or some other state) to look after their general interests, the remaining Armenians had no one but their immediate families to aid them when things started getting rough. And as the war over Karabakh grew, things started getting rough indeed: the Baku Armenians became a pool from which one could acquire hostages in exchange for one's own lost loved ones.

The matter touched us in a personal way, because among our many friends and acquaintances built up over the year, we had a number of mixed couples as friends. The closest of the lot were Elchin and Gala, whom we referred to playfully as our local 'culture vultures' due to their obsession with the remaining traces of 'high' Soviet culture in Baku. There was not an art opening, concert, ballet, or opera that they did not attend; it lent their lives a little normalcy, and recollected the days when Baku was a multi-cultural city, a place where well-dressed, cultured people would finish an evening at the opera with a late-night stroll along the promenade.

But in the autumn of 1991 the pedestrian zones were empty, and Elchin and Gala were running scared. To keep would-be abductors guessing, Gala stayed with different friends every night, while Elchin stayed at home lest thieves break in. More worrisome was what to do with their two teenage sons. Although they carried Elchin's name and spoke Azeri without an accent, they were potential targets, too.

"You jump every time someone knocks on the door," said Elchin. "But the people we are worried about don't knock. They just kick in the door, put a bag over your head, and take you away."

There had been enough instances of sudden disappearances of friends and relatives to justify their fears: not only was Gala an Armenian, but Elchin's sister was married to one. Almost by definition, most of their friends and relatives were also mixed pairs. Most of these, including Gala's brother, had left Azerbaijan. Going elsewhere in the former USSR was problematic, however. Would-be migrants needed travel documents—and the very act of applying for a passport could be dangerous. The low-level clerk sitting across the desk might have a relative in need of an easy hostage. And even if one managed to come up with documents, there was almost nowhere to go. Moscow and St. Petersburg in Russia were the destinations of choice, but the authorities there were proving reluctant to house the growing mass of ethnic Russians who were trying to 'return' after several generations in the colonial republics, and had little time or sympathy for ethnic refugees from the Caucasus. Some couples had gone to Central Asia, but only to join the local Russians there in worrying about the future.

Curiously, Armenia itself was seldom the first choice of refugees—even for couples who were both Armenian. And for the Azeri/Armenian couples, it was not even the last choice; it was an impossibility. Whatever mixed Azeri/Armenian couples had lived there before had fled in the wake of the first upsurge of ethnic violence in 1988.

Now xenophobia had come home to roost in Azerbaijan and there were roving gangs whose goal was to find and take Armenian hostages for exchange. As might be imagined in such an atmosphere, there were quite a few close calls of mistaken identity. We even heard about an old man who had been seized by a gang in the market. They thought he was Armenian because of his accent, but released him when he proved himself a Jew by dint of circumcision.

"It's not just the gangs," said Elchin one night. "We know of cases of men giving away their Armenian sister-in-law while the husband stands by in terror. We also know of cases where the neighbors have chased away would-be abductors. We don't know of any case of police preventing an abduction."

Despite the threat, Elchin and Gala did not want to leave Baku—and certainly not for an unknown future in the United States, which was the destination all other would-be refugees (including hundreds of local Russians) were struggling to get to.

"Our life is here and we want to stay," said Gala one night after the opera. She was familiar with the various criteria governing refugee status in the United States—legitimate fear of persecution due to race, religion, or ethnic background—and knew that she qualified on every one. "What can we do in the United States? Wash dishes and join a refugee culture club?"

Meanwhile, the couple continued to play cat-and-mouse with potential abductors while attempting to maintain some semblance of their normal life as 'culture vultures.' A week would not go by without Elchin or Gala calling to tell us about a production of *Köroghlu* or *Leila and Majnun* down at the rebuilt opera house or a jazz concert in the al fresco symphony hall, with proceeds to be devoted to refugee families from Karabakh. Then we would all walk home together through the deserted streets, first dropping Gala off at her most recent abode for the night, and then Elchin at his.

* * *

Then there was Nana. She was our maid. I am still not sure what winds sent her our way, but I suspect that it was someone in the Turkish embassy who had fired her for drinking on the job but still felt suffi- ciently warm toward the creature that they thought of giving her another chance—with us. I am still not sure what 'nationality' she was. She claimed to be Russian, but had weird—almost wicked—green, almond- shaped eyes that were more typical of . . . well, I am not sure. A Tatar? No; she was Christian. A Georgian? She denied it. The one thing we knew with certainty about Nana—and this seemed to confirm her Russianness in a sad way—was that she was an alcoholic. Frequently, she was so drunk that she was dangerous. But when she wasn't snor- keled, she was great. Although she was working as our maid, her profes- sion was as an extrasensory physician. I didn't understand exactly what this meant until I was back in the USA and saw advertisements calling for extrasensory specialists from the (ex-)Soviet Union to come and do their thing for ten thousand dollars a month. Most of the available posi- tions were in southern California.

Feeling hungover and blue? Nana would blow on your eyes. Got a funny, knotty feeling in your knees? Nana was there to wave her hands over the default, creating some sort of vacuum. Kink in the neck? The traditional cure was a quick twist. . . . And on top of all these delights, we got the most excellent bargain-shopper in the realm. Nana combined competence in mar- ketplace Azeri with the penny-pinching attitude only Russians can own. She was proud and delighted when she shaved five cents off the price for a kilo of beef, and even prouder when she could report to us that she had told some rapacious bastard in the bazaar to get screwed because he wanted ten cents a kilo for lemons, and not nine.

"You will starve us to death to save our money," Hicran once shouted at our physician/maid after Nana returned from the market emptyhanded, with one of her (daily) status reports about inflation.

She was just too weird, too devoted, too penny-pinching, too drunk, too—*Russian*! She liked to buy me *sala* (bacon fat to eat raw with bread), but snitched from the booze cabinet, if and when she didn't mistakenly (and drunkenly) mix good single malt or *raki* or tequila with water. We almost fired her four times, but always relented and brought her back: we could not imagine life without a knock on the door at exactly eleven o'clock, fol- lowed by '*Dobroe utro*,' or 'good morning,' in Russian.

Then one Monday morning the telephone rang at ten, and Nana's daugh- ter was on the other end, wailing and babbling.

"Nana won't come to your house today or tomorrow or ever again," she said. "And I need all the money you owe her."

Nana had quit, permanently. After finishing up the dishes and ironing and making me a last borscht soup, she had gone home, got blitzed and drowned in her own puke in a small metal tub set on the kitchen floor in her filthy, one-room tenement apartment. When we went to sort out her things and make arrangements for her funeral, it was the first time we had ever been to her house. It was a world away from our place. It was real life in Baku for most Russians.

* * *

In the meantime, we had a fine new house and it was the holiday season. As a house-opening party, we invited old and new friends and neighbors to a Thanksgiving supper. The guest list included our landlord, Fuat, and his mother, Aliyah; our original hosts, Kubrah and Kamran; Elfrieda and her husband, Valerii; Vafa Gulizade and his half-Russian wife, Leila; Gala and Elchin; Niyazi Ibrahimov of the Popular Front; Dilshot and Fahrettin, a pair of fanatically pro-Elchibey, East Berlin–trained Germanologists; their son Vugar, a former *spetnaz* paratrooper in Estonia, and his Lezgin buddy, Elchin; our Ahiska pal, Ibrahim; Suat, the director of the new national airlines, AZAL; Kameran, a local publisher and his spouse; a Jewish computer expert named Felix and his attractive bride, and Araz Azimov of the infant foreign ministry. The preferred language of the evening was Russian.

Acquiring the requisite bird was the biggest problem. Although Nana managed to secure a small but tasty *indiushka* (turkey) on the poultry market, I was obliged to supplement it with a large rooster that was actually much tastier than the gobbler. The dressing was the kind that grandma used to make—dried breadcrumbs ground by hand, onions, assorted spur-of-the-moment seasoning (oregano only existed as tea), chestnuts, walnuts, almonds and raisins. Sadly, there was no cranberry sauce or sweet potatoes or anything resembling corn or wild rice. Someone thoughtfully brought over a gallon of Georgian wine, relieving us of the obligation to punch shots of vodka all evening, and after a few glasses I felt moved to relate the story of the first Thanksgiving, throwing in a postscript on the fate of the hosts at the hands of the guests. It might have seemed childish or even dumb until one considers that I was probably the first American any of the guests had ever met, and there was much cultural explaining to do. Then Suat sang Georgian church songs in a splendid tenor voice; Elchin and Gala related the details of how they met and married; Araz showed us his wounds from Afghanistan—and there was even more cultural explaining to do. Looking around the room, I was almost overwhelmed. The guests were a microcosm of a strange and little understood society: Old commies, neo-commies, pan-Turkists, Popular Frontists, Soviets, Russians, Azeri-Azeris, Muslim 'minorities,' an Armenian (or two), and us.

"To Azerbaijan—and its two new friends!" Elfrieda said, as a last great toast.

"*Za Azerbaidzhana!*" I echoed, raising a glass.

Yes—*To Azerbaijan*! Within two months of landing back in Baku, we had established ourselves as a sort of honorary consulate/foreign press club/general *Treffpunkt* and had become privy to the public and private details of everything from Azerbaijan's future communications network to its political relations with the outside world. The reason was simple: we were actually living in Baku, and everyone else was merely passing through.

6

A Reborn Republic

Our main activity in the late autumn of 1991 was watching foreign states decide whether there really was an independent entity called Azerbaijan.

True, most of the fifteen republics that made up the USSR had declared themselves independent (or at least 'sovereign') in the wake of the August 19th abortive putsch, but there still was a USSR. And, although he was a very lame duck, Mikhail Gorbachev was still its president. Few foreign states wanted to offend him by jumping the gun and recognizing what he did not—namely, that he was president of a concept in history.

This put any number of countries in a diplomatic jam. And, as regarded Azerbaijan, no one was in a bigger pickle than Turkey. While the Mutalibov government (and much of the population) craved Turkish recognition, Moscow let Ankara know that Russia was less than enthusiastic about 'the coming Turkish century' in its backyard. More to the point, Ankara had spent a lot of time and money setting up a huge barter agreement in the USSR whereby Turkish construction companies were building everything from spas to shoe factories in exchange for Soviet raw materials and natural gas, and Ankara didn't want to provoke Moscow's ire by indulging two-bit dictators of new states that claimed independence but really didn't mean it.

But there was very great pressure from Turkic nationalists in Turkey and in Azerbaijan for Ankara to do just that. Time and again, Turkish officials had to reiterate their country's intention to be 'the first state' to recognize Azerbaijan—but only when the time was right. And as Ankara prevaricated, the level of anticipation in Baku rose. There were no less than three false announcements that Turkey had indeed recognized Azerbaijan—and made by such figures as Prime Minister Hasan Hasanov and opposition deputy Towfig Gasimov. This put local Turkish diplomats in a bind: they had to explain that Turkey really was very determined to be the first country to recognize Azerbaijani independence—but not yet.

Finally, in early November 1991, the last act of outgoing Turkish Prime

Minister Mesut Yilmaz was to recognize Azerbaijan as a sovereign state. Normally stoic men wept for joy, and Turkish flags were on every street corner. Even the Popular Front got aboard the band wagon, its former position of nonrecognition-until-we-have-our-own-money, army, and new parliament conveniently forgotten.

Then the Turks moved in big time. Advisors were sent to advise on everything from privatization to religion. This was a little odd, given the fact that Turkey was overwhelmingly Sunni Muslim while Azerbaijan was mainly (if really only theoretically) Shi'ite; but no matter. Credits were issued to firms to redo the water and communications grid, and thousands of Azeri students were invited to Turkish universities. Turkish television was soon being broadcast into Azerbaijan and Central Asia so that Azeri (and Turkmen and Uzbek and Kyrgyz and Kazakh) viewers could take a look at the world through a 'turquoise' view-finder. Another plan was to gift the Azeri government with thousands of Turkish-key typewriters to assist in the transformation from Cyrillic to Latin characters, and thus seduce the Azeri 'dialect' away from certain orthographic symbols not found in Turkish, like X, Q, and upside-down E.

These grand pan-Turkic plans needed someone to implement them, and the man of the moment was Mehmet Ali Bayar, a young Turkish diplomat on his first tour of duty anywhere. Even if only half the story of his activities is true, I think it fair to say that from the lowly post of third secretary of the Turkish embassy he almost ran Azerbaijan—and apparently never slept. When Mehmet Ali and his wife Ayça announced that they would soon be having 'company,' the first response among his friends was mocking disbelief that he had found time to become a father.

Bayar remained almost unique among the official Turks in Baku. As an employee in a ministry known among the international press for its timidity and vexing habit of obfuscation, he was always—always!—a source of news. Until the arrival of American and then European diplomats in Baku, he was the 'western diplomatic source' quoted in 'deep background' press dispatches—a delicious irony for a Turk. Sadly, as time progressed he was increasingly reduced to shuttling to and from the airport as part of the obsessive Turkish protocol to deal with the growing number of highly connected Turkish carpetbaggers arriving aboard the weekly and then biweekly Istanbul Express, determined to discover the newly opened 'Turkic East.'

The Iranians were another story. The breakup of the Soviet Union arguably had a greater impact on the Islamic Republic than any other country. Tehran was deeply confused. Suddenly, instead of one monolithic neighbor to the north—the Soviet Union—it found itself having contiguous land or sea borders with five new countries (Armenia, Azerbaijan, Russia,

Kazakhstan, Turkmenistan), and two autonomous republics (Naxjivan and Daghestan), as well as two other countries (Uzbekistan and Tajikistan) that were very close geographically and culturally, even if they had no actual frontier abutting on Iran. Now Iran would have to re-negotiate economic cooperation agreements with all those states, work out new security guarantees, and generally try and promote (and protect) its own interests in the region.

The most problematic of all these new countries for Iran was Azerbaijan. The dilemma was ethnic; there were more Azeris living south of the Araxes River—in Iran—than north of it, and it was feared that modern, ethnic-based nationalism might infect them. Faced with Azerbaijan's independence and its move toward Turkey's embrace, Iran had to do something. So in December, the Islamic Republic sent foreign minister Dr. Ali Akbar Velayati to Baku—but not in his capacity as foreign minister. Rather, he came in the guise of a scholarly participant in a symposium on the great Azeri/Persian poet, Nizami. The ruse allowed him to duck the recognition issue while promising Azerbaijanis the world, in terms of economic aid—trains, roads, planes, ships, oil imports, and even a new bank—if and when mutual ties were established.

"The Azeri people know that the Iranian people have had the Azeri people in their hearts for 170 years—that is the important thing," cooed Dr. Velayati at a press briefing I attended. To some ears, this seemed to be less political prevarication than veiled irredentism—because 170 years ago Azerbaijan was a part of Iran.

The point was not missed at Baku University, where students (many of them female—and none wearing the veil) gave it to the Iranian VIP with both barrels after his scholarly presentation on the delights of Nizami's poetry.

"Why is Iran dragging its feet on the recognition issue?" one coed demanded. Dr. Velayati's answer was that Iran was waiting for the results of the December 31st referendum on independence, when the people of Azerbaijan would decide for themselves on the issue. Less than a year before, he pointed out, the majority of the citizens of Azerbaijan had voted in a similar referendum to stay in the Soviet Union—and the people might so vote again. . . .

This may have been diplomatically correct—why recognize a country that could vote itself out of existence a month later?—but it was not politically expedient. The crowd started whistling and making cat calls, and a very irritated Dr. Velayati cut short his talk and departed, much to the joy of the pan-Turkic secularists and to the chagrin of the fundamentalist fringe. Turkey, apparently, had won round one of the new Great Game—

the putative struggle between Tehran and Ankara for the hearts and minds of Azerbaijan and Central Asia—before the mullahs had even been able to field their team.

Then there began a constant stream of Third (mainly Muslim) World diplomats stationed in Moscow, who took to flying down to Baku to announce their recognition of Azerbaijani independence. Nightly we were treated to half the government standing on the airport tarmac, waving at departing guests from countries traditionally friendly to Azerbaijan, such as Ghana, Sri Lanka, and even Cameroon.

I like to claim a little credit for this. One night, when I was down in the Foreign Ministry trying to get a residency permit, I discovered the Protocol Section working on the English translation of a document they had been tasked with delivering to the parliaments and heads of state of every nation on earth. It was entitled *The Appeal of the Azerbaijani Supreme Soviet to the Nations of the World*, and it was a masterpiece of diplomatic rhetorical excess run amok. It was clear that without a little editing, most of the kings, queens, emirs, emperors, presidents, and premiers the Appeal was being sent to wouldn't understand what they were being asked to do—namely, to recognize Azerbaijan as a sovereign state. I decided to help. The first thing was to confirm that the message to be conveyed by the Appeal was indeed designed to invite recognition. My protocol pals informed me that this was indeed the intention, or sufficiently close to the point that I was able to proceed. Accordingly, I reduced the number of rhetorical Whereupons, Observings, and Notings by half and *Presto!*—once sent, the document resulted in the recognition of the Azerbaijan Republic by almost everyone in the world.

Headlines in the state-controlled newspapers soon read: *Korea* [which one not specified] *Becomes Fourth Sovereign State to Recognize Azerbaijani Statehood! Sixth and Seventh Members of International Community To Make Ties—Egypt and Algeria! Latvia Tenth Country! Ukrainian Rep Meets with President and Vows Friendship and Cooperation! Italy Fifteenth Foreign State to Send Congratulations!*

The Greeks tried to sneak in a Trojan Horse by coupling their recognition of Azerbaijan with Azeri recognition of (Greek) Cyprus—a real dig at Turkey, which was about to sponsor Azerbaijan's application to join the U.N. The French went even further: the bearer of diplomatic recognition was Dr. Bernard Kouchner, Minister for Humanitarian Affairs—and one of the loudest supporters of the cause of the Karabakh Armenians. London, too, sent in a great friend and sponsor of Karabakh separatism, Baroness Caroline Cox, although I don't think the Azeris understood the point. The United Kingdom chose, for the time being, anyway, to project the British presence via another BP—British Petroleum. The establishment of relations between the UK and Azerbaijan would wait until March 1992, to be announced by deputy Minister of Foreign Affairs Douglas Hogg, at which point the delightful Harold Formstone took up residence as the Queen's representative.

My big failure was extending the recognition franchise to the homeland—my homeland. The United States played hard to get. You might even say that thanks to the efforts of certain lobby groups in the United States, Washington had changed the goalposts. The defining moment came during a speech at Princeton delivered by Secretary of State James Baker III about the future of United States relations with the 'Newly Independent States' (of the former USSR). While skipping merrily over such thriving democracies as Kazakhstan and Belarus, Baker singled out Azerbaijan and Georgia as undeserving of American recognition until they accepted a long list of conditions that Washington had not bothered to ask many other countries to fulfill before bestowing diplomatic recognition. These ranged from a written commitment that Azerbaijan would not develop nuclear or other weapons of mass destruction to a pledge that Azerbaijan would subscribe to international norms governing human rights and the inviolability of borders both external and internal. There were also subclauses about establishing a pluralistic democracy based on the rule of law, committing to move rapidly toward a market economy open to foreign investment and letting the Peace Corps and other U.S. institutions operate in Azerbaijan. All in all, they amounted to the blacklisting of Azerbaijan.

"Look at this crap!" said an angry and depressed Vafa Gulizade, shoving the list of conditions across his desk toward me. "What would you do?"

I studied the conditions and then gave him my opinion. I said that he, or his president or whoever was responsible, should close his eyes and hold his nose and sign off every one of the items, immediately.

"Put it behind you," I advised the advisor to the president of the new Republic of Azerbaijan. "Get recognition and worry about the details later."

Without an American embassy or consular office in Baku, it was quite natural for people like Gulizade to seek my advice on matters of American policy—a subject in which, of course, I had no competency whatsoever. But as the only American around (aside from a few odd oilmen) I didn't think it overstepping the bounds of decorum too much to take up the diplomatic slack while Washington got its act together.

"You know what the difference is between us, my dear?" sighed Vafa, fingering the document containing the State Department's demands. "Azerbaijan has become your hobby, but it is my life."

Then he signed off on the American conditions and sent them off.

* * *

It still took the State Department a few months to hang out their diplomatic shingle on a door in the old Intourist Hotel, and when they did, it started a peculiar game of musical embassies: the Americans took over the rooms vacated by the Turks, who had been working in the same cramped quarters until they managed to graduate to their beautiful embassy building downtown. Then, after the American operation had so expanded that it was moved to an entire upper floor, the same rooms on the second floor that were first occupied by the Turks and then the Americans were taken over by the Russians after they, too, finally got around to recognizing Azerbaijan as an independent state.

Then something strange and wonderful and totally unexpected happened. The State Department, known for sending Japanese-speakers to Peru and Spanish language specialists to Zambia, finally got one right. They assigned two old friends of mine to staff the new office: Philip Remler and Robert Finn. Both had served tours in Turkey and were not only fluent in Turkish in the usual, order-a-kebab way, but were Ottoman scholars to boot.

I had last seen Philip in Iraqi Kurdistan, wandering around as a sort of U.S. liaison with a government not recognized by the United States—i.e., the shaky coalition that had been stitched together between Massoud Barzani's KDP and Jalal Talabani's PUK. Philip had subsequently been posted to Moscow and had just started cracking the 'nationalities question' when the Soviet Union fell apart. Because competent staff was needed on the periphery, he was sent down to Baku—a fact that he bitterly resented, at first. Like many Soviet citizens, he felt he had just lost the Big Country in the center for a small one on the fringes.

Robert had been involved in the Great Kurdish Relief Effort, tasked with coordinating the dozens of nongovernment organizations (NGOs) and do-gooder individuals hanging around the squalid refugee camps of the Turco-Iraqi frontier. Most of these folks were determined to blame Turkey as much as Saddam Hussein for the plight of the cuddly Kurds, on the general principle that Turks hate Kurds and thus want them to suffer, and it fell to Robert to crack heads, keep the record straight and—despite the whining and wailing of the NGOs—keep the aid flowing to where it was needed most. After returning to the tedium of a desk job in D.C., he was only too happy to hear about the prospect of opening an embassy in Baku: it was exactly the sort of absolute hardship post that he delighted in. Besides, his dog Bobo had yet to travel to what was once the Soviet Union.

So Remler and Finn, along with the usual motley crew of communicators and general service people, showed up to make an embassy in a Baku hotel room, totally open and exposed to any would-be refugee, KGB-phobic paranoid, or wandering drunk who might take a wrong turn after getting off the elevator. And when the Stars and Stripes were duly raised, I got Robert to sign off on a document that formally relieved me of my status as the Unofficial, Uninvited, and Maybe Unwelcome Consul General of the State of Montana, and confirmed the transfer of my nonauthority to the legitimate representatives of the government of the United States of America. My short, fake diplomatic career was over, and the level of access I had previously enjoyed took an immediate plunge. As the song says, it was fun while it lasted.

* * *

Beyond the issue of recognition and the speculation about who would become the major cultural influence in Azerbaijan, there was a more fundamental question—whether the country would be allowed to survive as an independent state.

In October, the government announced that it would be forming a 'national army' separate from the Soviet/Russian units still stationed in the country. But President Mutalibov could not seem to decide whether he wanted a real army or an elite presidential guard to defend him from the Popular Front—even while every Azeri village in Karabakh was being evacuated.

Then the first big blow fell. On November 20th, a helicopter carrying 23 passengers and crew was shot down over Karabakh, killing all aboard. The dead included two high-ranking Azeri government officials, Vagif Jafarov, my host in Shusha, and the pleasant presidential spokesman, Osman Mirzaev. A number of Russian and Kazakh observers associated with the Yeltsin/Nazarbaev Ten-Point Plan also died that day, and with them, the Peace Plan.

The response to the tragedy was so queer that one immediately entered the soft sands of conspiracy. First came the reports on Moscow television that the chopper had crashed into a mountain due to low visibility. But November 20th was a sunny day and the helicopter went down in an area of Karabakh where there were no mountains. Next, Russian television (and then the BBC) quoted President Ayaz Mutalibov as accusing Armenia of shooting down the helicopter; he had said nothing of the sort. But Armenia reacted by saying that Azerbaijan's contention of Armenian complicity was tantamount to a declaration of war—or so Russian television announced. After that, the mis-, dis-, and noninformation network went into high gear. In a report on the BBC, a correspondent from Reuters who had traveled with Armenian partisans operating in the region related how the fighters had set up a heavy machine gun to pepper a tank with hot lead. Although the tank was standing still, the reporter related, the Armenians had been unable to hit it. (Why someone would shoot at a tank with a machine gun was beyond my comprehension, as was the reason why a tank under attack would remain immobile—but no matter.) The reporter then extrapolated from the Armenians' inability to hit a sitting-duck tank that they could not possibly have shot down a moving helicopter in the air. If this was reducto ad absurdum, the reporter then outdid himself by stringing together several disparate pieces of information to create a unique whole: reminding listeners that Ayaz Mutalibov was one of the few Soviet leaders who supported the August 19th putsch against Gorbachev and that the communists had made 'common cause' with the Popular Front of Azerbaijan over the issue of Karabakh, the reporter then took a quantum leap and suggested that it was most likely the Azeris had shot down the bird themselves in an attempt to whip up anti-Armenian hysteria. *Say what?*

But the conspiracy-prone Azeris were not far behind, and the rumor mill was working overtime. There had been a shoot-out between the Azeris, Russians, and Kazakhs aboard the chopper, resulting in the crash; the helicopter was not shot down, but had landed in a field, at which point all the passengers were butchered by the KGB; a mysterious second helicopter had blasted the first out of the sky. . . .

My own gut feeling was that the perpetrators were most probably a straight-shooting group of Armenian partisans in Karabakh who managed to hit their mark. There was nothing odd or strange about this at all: the Armenians had been shooting at all symbols of Azeri domination for some time, and picking off a helicopter on the wing would have been not only natural, but desirable. Backing up this assumption was the distribution of fuel and machine parts on the ground at the crash site, which suggested a midair explosion; bullet holes in the fuselage suggested that the explosion was caused by ground fire hitting a fuel tank. Although badly burned, all corpses were recovered and identified; the 'missing' eight had been sent back home.

But even if it was as simple as that, the most disturbing part of the helicopter business was the growing evidence that dark forces were indeed at work—if not involved in downing it, then at least in disseminating disinformation that could only ratchet the conflict up another notch. The *Center*—that faceless, formless thing in Moscow that was supposed to have died along with the Communist Party after the abortive coup and the much proclaimed Second Russian Revolution and the rebirth of freedom and democracy in Mother

Russia, was alive and well out here on the fringes of the Evil Empire, extinguishing lives like playthings.

Get back in line, it was saying. *I can affect you.*

In Baku, everyone believed in the reality of the unseen hand cynically manipulating events—and to a degree that was difficult to comprehend for anyone who had not been so manipulated before.

One result of the tragedy was political. The 350-member parliament was prorogued, replaced by a 50-member *Milli Shura*, or 'National Council,' made up of 25 deputies chosen by the government and another 25 chosen by the Democratic Bloc, the quasi opposition in parliament. The even split represented a theoretical balance of power and interest that made up for the 'shortcomings' of the last parliamentary elections, which had been quasi-boycotted by the Popular Front.

But even this measure was controversial. Because their power was truncated, some neocommunists whispered that it was the Front/Opposition that was responsible for downing the helicopter. The Popular Front, meanwhile, went so far as to cancel its weekly Friday night rallies. The rationale was that it would be too easy for Moscow to cause an incident and then, as it had in January 1990, proceed to invite itself in to restore order.

Not all heeded the order. While the rational leadership tried to keep things in line (by such actions as stopping unarmed volunteers from entering Karabakh for a little free-lance ravaging of Armenian villages), the irrational fringe mounted provocative demonstrations that begged for countermeasures. One such show of force was an attack on the new Defense Ministry in the former KGB clubhouse downtown. The incident was defused when the mob was invited to join the regular army. Two days later, the first 200 men of the newly formed Azerbaijan national army took their solemn oaths at a ceremony at Martyrs' Lane and then shipped off to the front. It seemed almost impossible that Armenia would not respond in kind.

This was incredibly depressing, a horrible déjà vu come true. The year was 1918. Under the protective umbrella of the Entente powers' occupation of the Caucasus and the removal of the dead hand of czarist Russia, three mini-states came into being: the ancient countries of Georgia and Armenia, and then, on May 28, 1918, the brand-new Republic of Azerbaijan. All were destroyed within two and a half years, as the (Bolshevik) Russians manipulated internal faction against faction and each state against the other.

The first to collapse was Azerbaijan, with the government of Mamed Amin Rasulzade literally handing the communists the keys to the government before running away into exile. The Dashnaksutyun government of Armenia cheered the collapse of their Azeri enemies only to discover that their great protector had the same thing in mind for them: after sealing a deal with the Kemalist Turks, Lenin's legions marched in and drove the Armenian nationalists to the hills and then exile. Georgia, with a Menshevik government, managed to hold out until 1921, when native son Josef Stalin lowered the boom and initiated a reign of terror in his homeland. The three short-lived states were then crunched into a Transcaucasus Federation, with Moscow making arbitrary adjustments to the internal and external borders of the new entity and thus sowing the seeds of future discord and revitalizing the old saw 'divide and rule.'

Curiously, I had just finished reading a lovely little novel entitled *Ali and Nino*. Written anonymously by someone using the pen-name Kurban Said, the story is a *Romeo and Juliet* romance between an Azeri lad and a Georgian girl caught up in the hurly-burly of the Caucasus during and just after World War I. Much of the courting occurs in the Karabakh town of Shusha, with the assistance of an Armenian, who after seeking a union of the Caucasus peoples, finally decides that it is hopeless working with the Azeris and makes an attempt to elope with Nino in order to save her. He is caught and killed by Ali, who then is obliged to flee into exile in the mountains of Daghestan, where he is protected by the descendants of the Chechen hero, Sheikh Shamil. After the Armenians are driven out of Baku by the Turkish general Nuri Pasha, Ali returns—only to be forced to flee, along with Nino, to a strangely familiar, 'fundamentalist' Iran. Cultural differences begin to emerge, and Ali even finds himself participating as a penitent in the Ashura. Then the English expeditionary Dunster Force arrives in Baku, and Ali and Nino return to participate in the establishment of a western-looking government. Alas! The story is by no means over—the infant Republic is attacked from within, and then collapses into the hands of Bolshevik railway workers and vengeful Armenians. Ali dies defending a bridge in Ganje, the capital, while Nino flees to Georgia.

Romantic schlock? It was not a bad effort at writing a 'modern' historical novel of the region fifty years before current events began to unfold.* So similar were the themes and issues in the book to the reality of the

---

*Others think so, too. Partially due to my efforts at promoting the book in Azerbaijan, and those of Alexis Rowell of promoting it in Georgia, *Ali and Nino* soon became a 'cult' book among Caucasus folks themselves. Professor Alexander Rondeli of Tbilisi State's International Affairs division has made the novel mandatory reading for his students.

post-Soviet Caucasus—the communal rivalry between Azeris, Armenians, and Georgians; the dark hand of colonial Russia; Caspian oil; and even the Iranian/Turkish rivalry—that I started looking into the possibility of writing an updated scenario and making a film.

Then life started to mimic art, and the house of cards we were living in began to crumble.

The venue was Karabakh.

Our neighborhood in Baku. Formerly a private residence, this building became the State Wedding Palace. (T. Goltz)

Vista of Baku from Shehidler Xiyanbani, Martyrs' Lane. (T. Goltz)

Oil derricks stretch into the distance at Neftitashlar, "Oily Rocks." (O. Litvin)

Baku's religious leaders, including the Sheikh ul Islam, the Patriarch of the Russian Orthodox Church, and leaders of the Ashkenazy and Sephardic Jewish communities. (T. Goltz)

A Popular Front rally in Lenin Square, renamed Freedom Square. (O. Litvin)

Army Day in Baku, October 10, 1992. (T. Goltz)

In the Martyrs' Lane cemetery, overlooking Baku.

Caviar pirates. Overharvesting threatens the Caspian's famed sturgeon with extinction.

7

Xodjali

February 26, 1992 seemed like a regular working day. Iranian Foreign Minister Ali Akbar Velayati was back in town to finally bestow diplomatic recognition on Azerbaijan, as well as to respond to American Secretary of State James Baker III's recent comments about the growing threat of Iranian influence in the Caucasus and Central Asia.

It was not the Islamic Republic of Iran that posed a threat to the region, remarked the wiry Iranian emissary, but the United States of America. In addition to being the country responsible for continued bloodshed throughout the world, America was actively fomenting conflict in Karabakh. The Islamic Republic, in contrast, was a country interested in peace between nations and peoples. To that end, Dr. Velayati had brought a peace plan for the increasingly bloody and senseless conflict in Karabakh—and one that both Armenia and Azerbaijan had agreed to sign. He himself planned to visit Karabakh the next day.

This was newsworthy, and I was getting ready to file a story on the subject to the *Washington Post* when Hicran came rushing into my work room. She had been on the telephone with the information section of the Popular Front, and had some very distressing news: sources in Agdam were reporting a stream of Azeri refugees from Karabakh filling the streets of the city, fleeing a massive attack.

There had been many exaggerated reports about the conflict from both sides, and perhaps this was just another, but I thought it best to start working the phone. Strangely, no one in government answered. Perhaps they were all at the Gulistan complex, having dinner with the Iranian delegation. So I waited for a while, and then started calling people at home. Around midnight, I got through to Vafa Gulizade.

"Sorry for calling so late," I apologized. "But what about this rumor—"

"I can't talk about it," said Vafa, cutting me off and hanging up.

A sense of unease filled my gut. Vafa was usually polite to a fault.

Perhaps he'd been asleep? I decided to call again, but the number stayed busy for the next half hour. Maybe he left it off the hook, I thought, and made one last effort and the call rang through.

"Vafa," I said, apologizing again. "What is going on?"

"Something very terrible has happened," he groaned.

"What?" I demanded.

"There has been a massacre," he said.

"Where?"

"In Karabakh, a town called Xodjali," he said, and then he hung up the phone again.

Xodjali.

I had been there before. Twice, in fact. The first time was in September, when we had staked out the airport waiting for Boris Yeltsin to come through. The last time had been a month before, in January 1992.

By then the only way to get to Xodjali was by helicopter because the Armenians had severed the road link to Agdam. I remembered that little adventure all too well. Doubting the many reports from the Armenian side that the Azeris were massively armed and that their helicopters were 'buzzing' Armenian villages in the territory for fun and terror, I had traveled out to Agdam with Hugh Pope then of the (London) *Independent* to chat with refugees about their situation.

Refugees were easy to find at Agdam. They were all over the place. The heaviest concentration was at the local airfield for the simple reason that many of the refugees didn't want to be refugees anymore: they were going back to their homes in Xodjali. Their pride had silenced their better sense. One was a 35-year-old mother of four by the name of Zumrut Ezova. When I asked why she was returning, she said it was better 'to die in Karabakh' than beg in the streets of Agdam.

"Why can't the government open the road?" shouted Zumrut in my ear over the roar of the nearby chopper's engines. "Why are they making us fly in like ducks, waiting to get shot?"

I didn't have an answer.

Then someone was lurching toward me from across the airfield. It was Alef Khadjiev, the commander of airport security at Xodjali and the gentleman who had saved us from the Agdam drunks during the Yeltsin visit three months before. He had been pretty chipper then, but despite his broad smile for me, it was no longer time for fun and games. I asked him what the situation was in his hometown.

"Come on," said Khadjiev. "Let's go to Xodjali—then you can see for yourself, and write the truth if you dare."

Behind him stood a MI-8 helicopter, its blades slowly turning. A mass of

refugees were clawing their way aboard. The chopper was already dangerously overloaded with humanity and foodstuffs, and waiting on the tarmac
was even more luggage, including a rusted 70mm cannon and assorted
boxes of ammunition.

"I'm not going," said Pope, "I've got a wife and kids."

The rotor began to twirl faster, and I had to decide quickly.

"See you later," I said, wondering if I ever would.

I got aboard, one of more than 50 people on a craft designed for 24, in
addition to the various munitions and provisions.

I thought to myself: *There is still time to get off.*

Then it was too late. With a lurch, we lifted off the ground and my
stomach smashed through my ears. I could see Pope waving at me while
walking away from the field, and wished I was with him on terra firma.

The MI-8 corkscrewed up to its flight altitude of 3,500 feet—high enough to
sail over the Askeron Gap to Xodjali and avoid Armenian ground fire. Two
dozen helicopters had been hit over the past two months, including the one
filled with officials in November, as well as another 'bird' a week before. The
machine we were flying in had picked up a round through the fuel tank the
week before, the flight engineer told me. It was lucky that fuel was low and the
bullet came in high. This was all very reassuring to learn as we plugged
through the Askeron Gap, bucking headwinds and sleet.

Through breaks in the cloud cover I could see trucks and automobiles
driving the roads below—Armenian machines, fueled by gas and diesel
brought in via their own air bridge from Armenia (or purchased from Azeri
war profiteers).

Finally and mercifully, after a trip that seemed to take hours but really
only lasted maybe 20 minutes, we began our corkscrew descent to the
Xodjali airfield. No one who has not been aboard such a flight can appreciate what I felt when the wheels touched ground.

I am alive! I wanted to shout, but thought it most appropriate to stay cool
and act like I did such things twice a day.

"How do you feel?" Alef Khadjiev asked.

"*Normal'no,*" I lied in Russian, cool as cake.

Meanwhile, the chopper was mobbed by residents—some coming to
greet loved ones who had returned; others trying to be the first aboard the
helicopter when it went back up and out. All were there to get the most
recent news from the rest of Azerbaijan: newspapers, gossip, rumors. The
reason for the excitement was pretty obvious: there were no working
phones in Xodjali, no working anything—no electricity, no heating oil, and
no running water. The only link with the outside world was the helicopter—
and those were under threat with each run.

The isolation of the place became all too apparent as night fell. I joined Khadjiev and some of his men in the makeshift mess hall of the tiny garrison, and while we dined on Soviet army SPAM with raw onions and stale bread to flickering candlelight, he gave me what might be called a front-line briefing.

The situation was bad and getting worse, a depressed Khadjiev told me. The Armenians had taken all the outlying villages, one by one, over the past three months. Only two towns remained in Azeri hands: Xodjali and Shusha, and the road between them was cut. While I knew the situation was deteriorating, I had no idea it was so bad.

"It is because you believe what they say in Baku," Alef chortled. "We have been utterly sold out."

Baku could open the road to Agdam in a day if the government wanted to, he said. He now believed the government actually wanted the Karabakh business to simmer on, to distract public attention while the elite continued to plunder the country.

"If you write that and say I said it, I'll deny it," he said. "But it's true."

The sixty men under his command lacked both the weapons and training to defend the straggling perimeter, he told me. The only Azeri soldiers worth their salt were four veterans from the war in Afghanistan. The rest were greenhorns. If the Armenians shot off one round, they would answer with a barrage of fire and waste half their precious ammunition.

So it was that night: I was awakened from sleep by a distant burst of fire coming from the direction of a neighboring Armenian town called Laraguk. The Armenian sniper fire was returned with at least 100 rounds from the Azeri side.

The firefight continued sporadically until dawn, making it impossible to sleep. No one knew when the Armenians would make their final push to take the town; everyone knew that some night they would. Xodjali controlled the Stepanakert airport and was clearly a major objective for the Armenians. I thought to myself: I would take it, if I were them. But what would the residents do when they did?

In the morning, people were just standing around—literally. There was not a single tea shop or restaurant to idle away the time, so people just stood in small knots in the mud and gravel streets, waiting. Waiting for what? The only person I saw actually do something was a very fat girl who worked as a sales clerk in the fabric shop where there was nothing to sell. I first saw her waddling to work at nine in the morning; I next saw her in a video, lying dead on the ground with a pile of others—but that was later.

We whiled away the morning around the airport, waiting. A photographer from an Azeri news agency happened to be around, so the soldiers put on a show, rolling out of their bunkers and running behind an old BTR, recently acquired from some Russian deserter. It was the only mechanized weaponry I saw in the hands of the Azeris in Xodjali.[1]

'These guys are going to die,' I said to myself. 'And I do not want to die with them just because they think war is theater.' Alef Khadjiev seemed to agree. We sat together in silence, watching his men run hither and yon, brave looks carved on their physiognomies for the sake of the camera. I felt sick and refused to take a picture or write a note.

Finally, around noon, I heard the tell-tale whine of a chopper moving high over the Gap. *Thank God!* I silently crowed, but tried to look indifferent. I made my way toward the airfield, and arrived just in time to see the overloaded bird disgorge its cargo of food, weapons, and returning refugees. One kid got off with a canary in a cage, or maybe he was getting on. I cannot say for sure. When those getting on seemed to be more than those getting off, I tried to get on myself. I didn't care that the chopper was carrying twice or three times its weight limit, nor did I mind that part of that weight was a corpse—one of Khadjiev's boys picked off by a sniper the night before. I wondered if we had had Soviet-style SPAM dinner together, but thought it impolite to pull back the death-sheet and stare.

The engines gunned and whined, and we lifted with a lurch—but this time I was not afraid of the flight. I just wanted *out*. We climbed and climbed, corkscrewing high into the sky and blowing over the Askeron Gap at 3,500 feet with tailwinds. Maybe we took ground fire; I do not know. But this I did: I would never go back to Xodjali again.

There was no need for vows. The last helicopter flight into the surrounded town was on February 13th. The last food, save for locally grown potatoes, ran out on the 21st. The clock was ticking quickly toward doom. It struck on the night of February 26—the anniversary of the massacre of Armenians at Sumgait in 1988.

* * *

We were in the car at seven and drove as quickly as we could across the monotonous flats of central Azerbaijan.* Brown cotton fields stretched to the horizon in all directions, and men stood along the roadside waving dead ducks at us as we roared by, hoping for a sale.

We stopped for gas at a town named Terter and asked the local mayor

---

*In addition to myself, the group consisted of Hicran, Elif Kaban of Reuters, and my own personal 'Tonto' in this and many subsequent front-line adventures, photographer Oleg Litvin.

what was happening in Agdam. He said he didn't know anything. We stopped again, in a town called Barda, and took a moment to inquire about events and rumors. Clueless looks greeted us.

We were starting to think that the whole thing was a colossal bum steer when we arrived in Agdam and drove into the middle of town, looking for a bite to eat. It was there that we ran into the refugees.

There were ten, then twenty, then hundreds of screaming, wailing residents of Xodjali. Many recognized me because of my previous visits to the town. They clutched at my clothes, babbling out the names of their dead relatives and friends, and dragged me to the morgue attached to the main mosque in town to show me the bodies of their relatives.

At first we found it hard to believe what the survivors were saying: the Armenians had surrounded Xodjali and delivered an ultimatum—get out or die. Then came a babble of details of the last days, many concerning Commander Alef Khadjiev.

Sensing doom, Alef had begged the government to bring in choppers to save at least some of the noncombatants, but Baku had done nothing. Then, on the night of February 25th, Armenian *fedayeen* hit the town from three sides. The fourth had been left open, creating a funnel through which refugees might flee. Alef gave the order to evacuate: the fighting men would run interference along the hillside of the Gorgor River valley, while the women and children and graybeards escaped below. Groping their way through the night under fire, by the morning of February 26th, the refugees made it to the outskirts of a village called Naxjivanli, on the cusp of Karabakh. They crossed a road and began working their way downhill toward the forward lines and the city of Agdam, only some six miles away via the Azeri outpost at Shelli. It was there, in the hillocks and within sight of safety, that something horrible awaited them: a gauntlet of lead and fire.

"They just shot and shot and shot," wailed a woman named Raisha Aslanova. She said her husband and a son-in-law were killed in front of her and that her daughter was missing.

Scores, hundreds, possibly a thousand were slaughtered in a turkey shoot of civilians and their handful of defenders. Aside from counting every body, there was no way to tell how many were dead—and most of the bodies remained out of reach, in the no-man's-land between the lines that had become a killing zone and a picnic site for crows.

One thousand dead in one night? It seemed impossible. But when we began cross-referencing, the wild claims about the extent of the killing began to look all too true. The local religious leader in Agdam, Imam Sadik Sadikov, broke down in tears as he tallied the names of the registered dead on an abacus. There were 477 that day, a number that did not include those missing and presumed dead, nor those victims whose entire families had been wiped out and thus had no one to register them as dead before God. The number 477 represented only the number of confirmed dead by survivors who had made it to Agdam and were physically able to fulfill, however imperfectly, the Muslim practice of burying the dead within 24 hours.

Elif Kaban of Reuters was stunned into giddiness. My wife Hicran was paralyzed. Photographer Oleg Litvin fell into a catatonic state and would only shoot pictures when I threw him at the subject: corpses, graves, and wailing women who were gouging their cheeks with their nails. Yes, it required stomach, but it was time to work, to report: a massacre had occurred, and the world had to know.

We scoured the town, making repeated stops at the hospital, morgue, and growing graveyards, out to the ends of the defensive perimeter for horrible spot-interviews with straggling survivors as they stumbled in, and then back to the hospital to check on new wounded and then back to the morgue to watch truckloads of bodies being brought in for identification and ritual washing before burial. I looked for familiar faces, and thought I saw some people I knew: one corpse was identified as that of a young veterinarian who had been shot through the eye point-blank. I tried to remember if I had known or been introduced to such a man in Xodjali, but could not be sure. Other bodies, stiffened by rigor mortis, seemed to speak of execution: arms were thrown up, as if in permanent surrender. A number of heads lacked hair, as if the corpses had been scalped. It was not a pretty sight.

Toward late afternoon, someone mentioned that a military helicopter on loan from the Russian garrison at Ganje would be making a flight over the killing fields, and so we traveled out to the airport. There was no flight, but there I found old friends.

"*Tomas*," a man in military uniform gasped, and grabbed me in an embrace, and wept. "*Nash Nachal'nik. . . .*"

I recognized him as one of Alef Khadjiev's boys, tall, skinny man named Asif who had been in the KGB before volunteering for duty in Karabakh. He was speaking in Russian, babbling—but only one word got through the tears: the commander. . . .

A few other survivors from the Xodjali garrison stumbled over and seized me. Of the forty-odd men under Alef Khadjiev's command, only ten were left alive. Dirty, exhausted, and exuding what can only be described as survivor's guilt, they pieced together the awful night and next day—and the death of their commander, Alef Khadjiev. He was killed by a bullet to the brain while defending the women and children. Most of the women and children died anyway.

* * *

Toward evening, we returned to the government guesthouse in the middle of town to look for a telephone, and there we met a drained and exhausted Tamerlan Garayev. A native of Agdam, the deputy speaker of parliament was one of the few government officials of any sort I saw there. He was interrogating two Turkmen deserters from the Stepanakert-based 366th Motorized Infantry Brigade of the Russian Interior Ministry forces. They had taken refuge in Xodjali a week before. The last piece of the tragic puzzle suddenly dropped into place: it was not only the Armenians who had assaulted the doomed town, but the Russians.

"Talk, talk!" said Tamerlan, as the two men stared at us.

"We ran away because the Armenian and Russian officers beat us because we were Muslims," one of the pair, a man named Agamuhammad Mutif related. "We just wanted to go home to Turkmenistan."

"Then what happened?" Tamerlan demanded.

"Then they attacked the town," said the other. "We recognized vehicles from our unit."

I thought of Commander Sergei Shukrin, and wondered if he had been involved.

The two fled along with everyone else in the town, and were helping a group of women and children through the mountains when they were discovered by the Armenians and 366th.

"They opened fire and at least twelve were killed in our group alone," Mutif related. "After that, we just ran and ran."

A Russian-backed assault by Armenians on an Azeri town, resulting in up to one thousand dead?[2] This was news. But it was at this point that things started becoming very strange. No one seemed very interested in the story we had stumbled on. Apparently, the idea that the roles of the good guys and bad guys had been reversed was too much: Armenians slaughtering Azeris?

"You are suggesting that more people have died in one attack in Karabakh than the total number we have reported killed over the past four years?" said the BBC's Moscow correspondent when I tipped him on the slaughter. "That's impossible."

"Take a look at Reuters!"

"There's nothing on the wire."

Indeed. While Elif Kaban was churning out copy on her portable telex, nothing was appearing on the wires. Someone was either spiking her copy, or was rolling it into larger, anodyne regional reports of 'conflicting allegations'. The BBC stayed silent for three days, without so much as an 'alleged' or 'reported.'

To be fair, the government and press in Baku didn't exactly support our reporting. While we were off in Agdam trying to get out the news, the presidential spokesman was claiming that Xodjali's scrappy defenders had beaten back an Armenian attack and suffered only two dead. Just a regular night in Mountainous Karabakh.

We knew differently, but it was the three of us against the Azerbaijani state lie machine.

Finally, I got a line through to the Moscow bureau of the *Washington Post* and said I wanted to file a story. The staffers there were too busy to take a dictation but reluctantly patched me through to the foreign desk in Washington when I insisted. I used 477 as the number of dead, as religiously reported to Imam Sadikov, and was dragged over the coals by editors: where did I get this number from, when Baku was still reporting that only two had died? Had I seen all the bodies? What about a little balance? The Armenians were reporting a 'massive Azeri offensive.' Why wasn't that in my report?

I was about to answer that this bit of information was not in my report for the very good reason that it had not happened, when the first *Kristal* missile crashed into Agdam, about a mile a away from the government guesthouse I was calling from. Then came others; and when one crashed into the building next door and blew out all the windows in our downtown *dacha*, we thought it best to get off the phone and into the basement before we were blown to smithereens.

After about an hour of huddling under mattresses, we came up for air and decided it was probably a good idea to leave Agdam. So did about 50,000 other people, and we discovered ourselves in the middle of a mass exodus of trucks, cars, horses, and people on bicycles, all trying to flee eastward.

* * *

I broke the story about the Xodjali massacre with a February 27 world exclusive on an inside page in the *Washington Post*.[3] This was followed by a 'European' front page of the London *Sunday Times*. By then, the international hack-pack had started parachuting in to count the bodies and confirm that something awful had happened. The first western reporter to actually get out into the killing fields and perform the grisly task of checking documents on the dead was Anatol Lieven of the London *Times*. His companion was the late Rory Peck of *Frontline News*, another cool professional and friend.

Others performed less well. One reporter from Agence France Press arrived in Agdam the night we left and found the city 'quiet,' apparently having confused the silence that followed the missile-induced exodus of 50,000 people with peacefulness. Still another, while a guest at my house, abused the confidence of Vafa Gulizade by grossly misquoting him. At the height of the crisis, Douglas Kennedy, son of Robert, showed up with a KGB-minder/translator from St. Petersburg, and thought he might do a little poking around. After I convinced him that his translator would probably get killed by a mob, Kennedy took my advice and hired my two 'kids,' Vugar and Elchin, and then failed to pay them.

The government of Azerbaijan, meanwhile, had performed a complete about-face on the issue. The same people who had remained unavailable during the early days of the crisis were suddenly asking me to provide the phone numbers of foreign correspondents in Moscow whom they could invite down, at government expense, to report on the massacre.[4]

I did not react very well. I almost physically assaulted the presidential press secretary, Rasim Agaev, and publicly accused him of lying. The spokesman was not pleased and began a rumor that I was an Armenian spy sent to Xodjali to ferret out 'military secrets' during my January visit to the doomed town. I was temporarily detained, thanks to that charge, and started to slide into a very bad mood. For the record, the man who interrogated me was Mahir Javadov, brother of Ravshan Javadov, a name that would figure large in subsequent political developments.

When I was released, I went downtown and found myself sitting around a commercial shop with a bunch of black marketeers, vaguely waiting for rubles to arrive in exchange for my dollars, when the whole thing hit me and hit me hard.

The evening streets were still filled with smiling shoppers, apparently oblivious or even indifferent to the fate of the citizens of Xodjali. It was the same men in leather jackets and the same women with far too much rouge on their cheeks and they were all smiling and laughing and parading and I have to say I hated them all. Maybe they didn't know what I did. Maybe they knew but didn't care lest it drive them insane.

I canceled the dollar deal, walked out of the shop and wandered the streets. I think it rained, but I cannot be sure. I wandered and wandered, unable to stop anywhere or see or talk to anyone for hours and hours.

"Ha ha," someone cackled, as they turned on the key to their car.

"Ho ho," someone else chortled as they lurched out of a *Komisyon* shop, bottle of Finnish vodka under the arm.

I wanted to slash tires, smash noses, burn houses—do something, and violently. But I did nothing but wander the streets and avoid humanity. It was better like that. When I got home, I sat down and poured myself a long drink and drank it, and Hicran asked me where I'd been.

"Xodjali," someone said, in a voice I didn't know.

I was there with the ghosts in a dumpy town with no food to speak of or water to wash and all the people I knew or had known there were dead, dead, dead, and I just started to cry and cry and cry.

* * *

There weren't too many bodies. Most were still in the hills, waiting for the higher temperatures of spring and for rot to set in. Some, the few, were being spaded into the shallow ground of the growing Martyrs' Cemetery across from the parliament building in Baku. One of those was Alef Khadjiev. I liked to think of him as a friend because we had consumed a few drinks together. A jocular cop with a big swagger and smile, Alef had managed to galvanize the Xodjali community around him in the belief that despite the odds and an almost total lack of support from Baku they could hang on and survive. But now Alef Khadjiev was dead. He had bought a bullet through the brain and after rotting for a week in the mountains of the Black Garden his body was bought for 100 liters of gasoline and then brought back to Baku to be buried with military honors.

Despite the proximity of the parliament across the street, no one from the government came to the funeral, and maybe that was out of good taste, because had they been there, whispering eulogies about courage and fortitude, Alef, the hero and then martyr of Xodjali, might have broken free of the bonds of death and climbed out of his grave and strangled the hypocrites with his own cold hands. He was that sort of guy.

But they weren't there, and the funeral procession was small because Alef was a native of Xodjali and all or at least most of the would-be mourners were either dead or had become refugees and had to be brought to Baku by truck or bus or train for the last rites.

The exception was Alef's widow, Gala, a chubby Russian girl with a hint of a mustache who lived in Baku. We had met in Agdam in the aftermath of the massacre and she refused to believe that her husband was dead. Aside from an overwhelming sense of grief, she was frightened out of her wits, wondering how she could live without him.

"I'm just a Russian, a Russian!" she cried. "And now everyone looks at me with hatred!"

I gave her my telephone number in Baku and told her to call if there was anything I could do. She called a few days later, babbling into the phone.

"*Tomas*," she wailed. "Alef is here."

At first I thought a miracle of mistaken identity had occurred and that Alef was still alive. But Gala was only calling to tell me that Alef's remains had been recovered in an exchange with the Armenians for several dozen gallons of gasoline, and then had been shipped to Baku for burial. It was tough for me to understand her Russian on the telephone, and probably a lot tougher for her to have to pick up the phone at all. But she stayed coherent long enough to give me her address and the time of the funeral procession. I went, not knowing what to expect: A week-old cadaver in the living room? Mutilated like others? Scalped like some? I got in a taxi and traveled through a wasteland of hissing, blue- and pink-belching pipes of the oil refining area of Baku, driving over streets that seemingly had never seen repair. We drove and drove, and it was a drive through an utterly depressing landscape, the sort that no one ever sees or admits to having seen: broken, diseased, and bad. It was a symbol of the rapacity and ugliness of Azerbaijan. How can you allow people to live and die like this?

Complicating my dark mood was the fact that the Azeri taxi driver only wanted to make jokes, and in Russian. I told him what I thought. I told him I was going to attend the funeral of my friend, Alef Khadjiev, Martyr of Karabakh, and that all the people of Baku were greedy cowards and that only the good men died and the filth remained behind. He agreed, refusing to take money for the ride. It was his contribution to national defense, or something.

I got out of the taxi in front of a series of high-rise, Soviet-style buildings. Walking through the mourners, I saw people I knew or at least recognized, and embraced them. Then I saw Gala. She was standing in back of a truck carrying the flag-draped coffin, holding the hand of her smiling child, who was still oblivious to what had happened to her father. I said something stupid like 'be strong.' I tried to plant a hand-extended kiss on the coffin perched on the back of the truck, but I couldn't reach it, and decided against climbing up on the truck, and just waited for the procession to proceed.

There were plenty of people crying. Everyone but me. My eyes were dry; I don't know why. Then someone somewhere, responsible for formalities, gave the word, and the column started out toward the Martyrs' Cemetery in the heights above Baku. The funeral train in was the same as my journey out, although the route was different: another broken road leading through another industrial wasteland. It was Alef's route to anywhere, nowhere, death.

We arrived at the Shehidler Xiyabani, or Martyrs' Lane Cemetery, the place where victims of the Soviet army crackdown on January 20, 1990, were buried in a long line along a granite wall shaded by dwarf cypress trees and pine. I had visited the cemetery before and I have visited it since, but it was different this time. I wasn't there as a journalist covering the event or even a political/cultural tourist. I was there as a mourner for Alef

Khadjiev, the most recent addition to the second tier of graves, where the dates of death are different from those in the first row. There was no third row, yet, but it was a place that would continue to grow.

Alef's was the 127th grave, a hole in the ground surrounded by freshly dug earth. His casket was lifted down from the truck, and I joined the pallbearers as they hoisted it on their shoulders and brought Alef's remains down the line, as a local man of religion recited the *Fatiha*, or Muslim creed of faith. This seemed odd because I was not sure that Alef was actually a Muslim except in the formal sense of the word. He never expressed anything approaching piety to me, and he was a drinking man. He didn't smoke, and that was really odd, because Azeris usually smoke all the time, even at funerals. Another strange thing about Alef was that he didn't like Turks. He once told me that he had found too many 'Made in Turkey' labels in the trash cans of Stepanakert to believe in any pan-Turkic ideal.

I was thinking thoughts like these because I was remembering, which is what you are supposed to do when you put bodies in the ground. Alef Khadjiev was the first of a whole string of people I knew who died violently over the next few years, so he got more thought than most.

Alef's wife, Gala, and her Russian relatives were confused by the ritual placement of the body, the pious incantations, and the fact that the week-old corpse had to be lifted out of the casket to be put in the hole dug in the muddy ground. They put the body in. An honor guard clicked heels, slapped dummy slugs in their Kalashnikovs, and let off three volleys. The empty shells fell clattering on the granite walkway. I picked up one and put it in my pocket. Then the family and intimate friends began covering the body with dirt and the wailing really began. Women scratched their cheeks and men sobbed last regards. I was invited to say something into the grave, but declined. I had quite a bit to say but I didn't want to say it, even in a language no one would understand. Cultural differences and all. I would do it differently today.

Then another, larger funeral procession started moving down Martyrs' Row. They were heading for the shallow grave next to Alef's. It was the corner spot and the next corpse would start a new row, even then being dug among the dwarf cypress trees in anticipation of the next to die in that horrible place called Karabakh. More young men would soon lie here, and their numbers would soon exceed all those killed at Xodjali, and the events of February 25–26, 1992, would soon become just a detail, just another grim statistic in the ongoing litany of death and destruction in Karabakh, the Black Garden.

I swore I would remember Alef and all the others, whose names I never knew but whose faces were etched on my memory forever.

Yes, I would remember Xodjali.

It was a dump. But now it was dead.

Notes

1. Armenians would later justify taking out Xodjali because it was a 'major military base' used to mount rocket attacks on Stepanakert. This charge can be dismissed as propaganda. The main Azeri base was up in Shusha, the 'impregnable fortress' over-looking Stepanakert. Hicran had traveled there in late December and found the place an armed camp under the command of Popular Front member Rahim Gaziev. Morale was high because Gaziev had brought up some 'secret weapons': GRAD multiple missile launchers, which he subsequently used to rain indiscriminate death and destruction down on Stepanakert from the heights.

2. After three days of denials that anything at all untoward had happened in Xodjali, the government picked up this emotionally inflated number as 'fact.' Later, the head of the commission of investigation into the massacre gave me the still 'provisional' number of 688 confirmed dead and buried, with 400 more left unaccounted for. This provisional number was unofficially confirmed by the Agdam-based representative of the International Committee for the Red Cross on the basis of the number of body bags supplied by the ICRC. Of the recovered dead, autopsies were performed on 187, revealing all manner of barbarity—severed penises, breasts, etc. Armenian sources, meanwhile, consistently maintain that 'only' 200 died—most of whom were allegedly caught in crossfire when Azeri troops from Agdam allegedly sallied forth in a counterattack—that is, the Azeris killed their own. Most recently—and most outrageously—in 1997, the Armenian Foreign Ministry cited a Human Rights Watch/Helsinki report on Karabakh, and claimed that the HRW/H fact-finders had discovered evidence of this allegation. The response from Jeri Laber of the HRW/H was to demand an immediate retraction and apology from the Armenian Foreign Ministry, because nothing in the HRW/H report even vaguely hinted at the Azeris killing their own.

3. Due to bad communication and my own churlishness, I started bad-mouthing the foreign editor David Ignatius and the rest of the *Post* foreign desk for 'eviscerating' my copy, and announced I would no longer write for them. Certain writers and researchers of a pan-Turkic persuasion began lionizing me for my 'principled resignation.' Hogwash. Months later, when I received tear sheets of my several files over this period, I discovered to my deepest chagrin that David and his team had run virtually every word I had filed. For the record, then: I screwed up, and David Ignatius had the courage to run with a story many others would not touch.

4. The government also began churning out pamphlets and picture books on Xodjali, replete with the most gruesome images imaginable to use as 'press packs' for visiting dignitaries. The publications were so badly produced that they became counterproductive. When in Yerevan, I stopped in the Foreign Ministry information section and discovered a stack of the Azeri literature on Xodjali on display. When I asked why the Armenians were passing it around, the response spoke volumes about the Azer-prop effort: 'We keep these on hand to show visitors,' smirked the information clerk.

8

Slithering in the Swamp

The Xodjali catastrophe of February 26–27, 1992 joined the Baku Massacre of January 19–20, 1990 as one of the two most resonant dates on the nationalist calendar of Azerbaijan. There would be others in the future, too, but the result always seemed to be the same: rather than forge unity in the face of tragedy, political adversaries began charging each other with short-term political gain based on treason. *Satkinlig*, or 'selloutness,' rapidly became the standard political libel thrown around by one and all.

The first victim of the backlash was the president of Azerbaijan, Ayaz Mutalibov.

Mutalibov had never been a particularly popular leader, and it was difficult to describe him as 'legitimate' in the usual sense of the word. Like most of the Communist Party bosses in the republics of the USSR, he had neatly turned the position of general secretary of the local branch of the Communist Party into the presidency when it looked expedient to do so, confirming his position by means of tainted elections. He was corrupt, but only in the way all other Communist Party leaders were. In Azerbaijan, that meant using his position and knowledge of the oil industry to salt away private savings and create slush funds. He also allegedly was given to a certain amount of vice, like having nubile young girls clip his toenails down in the "bear's cave" lounge in the presidential guesthouse.

But Mutalibov's main fault was that in a society where image is all, he did not project the *look* of authority. He sported dandified hairdos and wore white suits. On the street, many referred to him derisively as 'Missus Ayaz.' Even his advisors scorned him.

"Did he say anything really dumb?" asked Vafa Gulizade after he had arranged an interview for me in December.

"I don't think so," I replied. "Just nothing very interesting."

"Good," Vafa had said, turning on a television to create anti-bug static. "I have spent the last year trying to explain away his idiotic mistakes."

131

Mutalibov's biggest mistake was his pathetic response of 'not knowing' about Xodjali for three long days. At the height of the Xodjali crisis, he called the Turkish embassy for help—the new, presidential Mercedes was lacking a spare tire and the carpool staff had ordered the wrong size rim. Could Ankara send one, ASAP?

Then, in the face of the growing public reaction to the official silence, he became desperate and came very close to calling in the remnants of the (now former) Soviet army based in Azerbaijan to save his regime. Semi-secret meetings were held between the president and Nikolai Popov, the commander of the 4th Army. Mutalibov wanted joint command.

The Popular Front, meanwhile, was doing all in its power to keep people from demonstrating. Given the involvement of the 366th Motorized Infantry in the Xodjali slaughter, local Russians were thought to be natural targets for hot-heads—or natural targets for agents provocateurs. *Stay indoors*, the Front advised local Russians, *stay out of harm's way*.

But the Front was not a monolithic organization—and not all its members subscribed to the policy promoted by the leadership. One of these was the Azerbaijan Writers' Association, a group that included many university professors and other 'intellectuals.' They initiated their own, silent protest vigil in front of the presidential building, gathering at noon every day to stand in the street while one man waved an Azeri flag and another held up a single, simple sign: *Istifa*, it read, 'Resign.' There were no quotable speeches because there were no speeches at all. The silent demonstrators just stood there. The first gathering attracted around 200 people; the second day, 300; by the third day, the crowd had only grown to 500—still less than the number of people allegedly killed at Xodjali. Like the proportionately small crowds that defended Boris Yeltsin's White House in Moscow in August 1991, they would have been pathetic if they had not ultimately been so effective.*

* * *

Elsewhere there was movement afoot, too. On March 3rd, the *Milli Shura*, or National Council, called for an emergency meeting of the full Supreme Soviet, which had been in suspension since early December.

During its brief life, the Council had tried to function as an alternative parliament, but had to satisfy itself as acting as a limited break or even just ineffectual irritant on the autocratic presidency. When the Council at-

---

*With hindsight, it was of note that the Azerbaijan Writers' Association was a group with a very special patron: Heydar Aliyev.

tempted to push through critical legislation—ranging from the removal of (former) Soviet troops stationed in Azerbaijan to the formation of a national army and the readoption of the Latin-based script for modern Azeri—Mutalibov might go along with the principle, but he consistently reneged on implementation. And when the Council challenged Mutalibov on fundamental issues like the signing of treaties aimed at bringing Azerbaijan into the new Commonwealth of Independent States, Mutalibov merely shrugged and claimed executive prerogative.

Still, the Council did have a function: its presence and composition gave Azerbaijan the appearance of enjoying the accouterments of democratic pluralism, but with little or none of the substance. Ironically, the most effective, independent act performed by the Council was its self-dissolution, when it called the full parliament back into emergency session. The opposition deputies hoped to use the wave of popular discontent against Mutalibov as the means to have him legally dismissed, and to dissolve the all-powerful presidential apparatus. The progovernment members of the Council, meanwhile, saw the reconvention of the full parliament as a window of opportunity to ram through a legal endorsement of Mutalibov's signing Azerbaijan on as a 'founding member' of the CIS, with all that this decision implied: common currency, common defense, and ultimately, common political culture with the rest of the rump Soviet Union. Almost incidental to the special convocation was the subject of Xodjali.

* * *

The *Shehidler Xiyabani*, or Martyrs' Lane cemetery, is located diagonally across a large traffic circle from the Ali Sovyet, or parliament. The rows of graves in the park, accessed by granite walkways, are as simple and moving as the ten-story parliament building is unattractive. One is made of dashed dreams and the other of cement. And on March 3, 1992, those who walked the halls of parliament were quite different people than those found walking through Martyrs' Lane. Gone were the two- and three-day growths of beard found on chin and cheek and the shabby clothes and permanently un-buffed shoes of the average Azeri. In parliament, the men sported tailor-made suits, wore Gucci shoes, were cleanly shaved and always enveloped in a bubble of cologne. The lady deputies were rotund matrons dressed in satins and silks and wearing high-heeled pumps—painted dolls whose hair was done twice a day. The special session seemed less an occasion to boldly confront the national disaster at hand than to sun on the legislative log, glad-hand friends and colleagues not seen since the last session, and discuss new business deals and recent vacations.

Still, there was business to attend to. The main item on the morning agenda was to find a fall guy. In this case, it was a fall gal: the Chairwoman of Parliament, Mrs. Elmira Kafarova. No sooner had the session begun than she tendered her resignation 'due to poor health,' and it was immediately accepted by the floor. But Elmira did not look sickly, and losing the post did not seem to overly upset her. During the recess she laughed and smiled with colleagues, as if nothing had happened. From all appearances, Kafarova assumed there was a resign-today/return-tomorrow game plan under way. And with good reason. She had been obliged to resign in September 1991, in the wake of massive public protest and indignation over her remarks, accidentally carried live on TV, that the opposition were nothing but "drunks and dope addicts." After the ruckus over her ill-chosen words had died down, she managed to walk right back into her old post.

The new—and apparently, temporary—chairman was the rector of the medical faculty of Baku University, Dr. Yagub 'Dollar' Mamedov. A Mutalibov crony, 'Dollar' Mamedov had earned the nickname due to his reputation for lowering university entrance standards for a fee. It was assumed that he would stand aside when the crisis was over and allow business to proceed as usual in the Swamp. Xodjali, it seemed, had been forgotten.

Or almost. In addition to the handful of Popular Front–affiliated deputies from the Democratic Bloc, there was a surprise guest: Elman Mahmedov, the mayor of Xodjali. We had met before, in September, and I remembered Elman as being a live wire. But now he was in semi-shock, unable to comprehend that 30 members of his family had perished while he had survived the death-run through the mountains. He had been invited to address parliament. But Elman wanted something else.

"The film," he said. "They won't show the film."

"What film?" I asked, but I already knew.

Jengiz Mustafayev, Azerbaijan's star roving newsman, had forced his way aboard a military helicopter that was flying over the killing zone and shot footage of bodies scattered across a shallow ravine. This was the film that Mayor Mamedov wanted shown to the chamber as a 'curtain raiser' for the general discussion of the tragedy, but the motion to do so had been overruled on 'procedural grounds.'

But word of the film (like everything that occurred in the chamber) had leaked outside, and the crowd of protesters was growing.

"Show the film! Show the film!" shouted the crowd, audible even through the thick, tinted glass of parliament.

Maybe it was Dollar Yagub's introductory concession to the opposition in order to establish a proper working relationship. Maybe he was just buckling under pressure, or trying to humor everyone. Maybe he wanted to put off discussion of the rest of the agenda—the status of the presidency, the status of the National Council, the status of the army, the status of refugees—for as long as possible. Maybe he really wanted to see the film himself. Who knows? But when the deputies returned to the chamber after a lunch break, and the opposition again demanded that the film be screened, Chairman Dollar Yagub Mamedov accepted.

The lights dimmed, and the four voting screens lit up to act as video monitors. The first frames of the film started rolling—and the next ten minutes changed the history of the country. Mustafayev's camera, pointed out a port-hole of the chopper, was picking up a number of objects on the ground below. It was difficult to tell exactly what the objects were. Unintelligible talk was mixed with more motor noise. Then the helicopter landed and the door opened and over the loud whining roar of the engines, Jengiz let out a terrible cry.

"*Oh God,*" he said as the lens focused on the objects we had seen from the sky, "*Oh God! Oh God! Oh God!*"

A literal wake of stiff, dead bodies trailed back into Karabakh. Many, including women and children, had their hands raised above their heads as if shot after having surrendered. Others were mutilated, with fingers cut off and eyes gouged out by knives. Some were apparently scalped. Still crying, Jengiz had enough presence of mind to pan to the horizon, which was covered with lumps and bumps of stuff that were once living beings, as inanimate as their pathetic belongings, among which the corpses lay. Jengiz added a few more close-ups, and then a few parting shots of hysterical Azeri men loading twisted bodies on the chopper.

Then the film was over. But the reaction had just begun: groans and sighs and whispers welled up from the chamber floor as the magnitude of the event began to penetrate the thick protective scales of the crocodile deputies. They were sobbing, chilled by the gruesome, force-fed footage of the mutilated, rotting corpses in the killing fields. Something big had broken and there was no going back. Elmira Kafarova might have thought of her resignation as temporary earlier in the day, but not now. New scapegoats were needed and heads had to roll.

Istifa! chanted the crowd outside, *Istifa!*

* * *

After a recess, Ayaz Mutalibov asked to take the floor. He wasn't looking good. His eyes were puffy and his usual blow-dry hairdo looked ruffled. They said he hadn't slept much over the past few days, but he looked more like a man who had gone on a five-day drunk. He didn't look or act presidential. And once he got behind the podium, he did not sound very executive. He rambled.

Several key points emerged from his long monologue, however: in the aftermath of the failed, August 19th coup in Moscow, Russia had become the new substitute for the Center. That same Russia was pursuing a pro-Armenian policy because Azerbaijan had not ratified either the economic or the political treaties of the CIS. Azerbaijan would lose Karabakh if it did not now sign the upcoming treaty on a unified command for CIS troops and integrate its inchoate army into that command structure. Local forces should be limited to a national guard, which would serve at the president's command. Mutalibov had scarcely mentioned Xodjali. And in light of growing evidence that elements of the Soviet/CIS forces had participated in the massacre, his suggestion that Azerbaijan should make an alliance with the killers was insane. Even loyalist deputies sat in stunned silence. Ayaz had lost his mind.*

The first to take the floor after Mutalibov's delivery was Rahim Gaziev, limping up to the microphone clad in camouflage togs with a pistol strapped to his side. He was just back from Shusha, which he was credited with having saved from Xodjali's fate. There was nothing in Mutalibov's address that even vaguely addressed the situation at hand, said Rahim. Not one culprit had been named. And as for the future of the army, a universal mobilization was needed—and not the mass demob. . . . Other opposition deputies followed Gaziev to the microphones, all playing variations on the central theme: Mutalibov had to go. Iskender Hamidov reminded the chamber that Mutalibov had come to power as a result of the January 1990 bloodbath and was appointed the head of the Communist Party of Azerbaijan by Moscow in order to implement its program. He bore personal responsibility for Xodjali, and should resign. . . . Towfig Gasimov charged Mutalibov with violating the constitution by hampering the building of the Azerbaijan National Army. The deputies, he reminded the assembly, had passed the Law on the Armed Forces and also the Law on the Protection of the Borders. Therefore, Mutalibov should be impeached according to Article 121/7 of the basic law of the land. . . . Etibar Mamedov went further, calling Mutalibov a traitor for even suggesting that Azerbaijan join its army to the unified force that had so recently slaughtered Azeri citizens. On

---

*Six months later, from his Moscow exile, Mutalibov would exculpate the Russians and the Armenians by claiming that the real perpetrators of the Xodjali massacre were militiamen associated with the Popular Front. Not surprisingly, the charge found very wide coverage in the Armenian press.

behalf of the Democratic Bloc, he then voiced a draft resolution demanding Mutalibov's resignation and called for a floor vote.

'Dollar' Yagub denied the motion and called for a recess. The Democratic Bloc deputies protested but were overruled. Reprieved for the moment, the crocodile deputies went out into the vestibule to smoke—and there they discovered a disconcerting fact: the parliament had been surrounded by thousands of people, and the noses of the protesters' shock troops—namely, the members of the Azerbaijan Women's Rights Association, led by the redoubtable Hanim Halilova—were literally rubbing up against the lobby windows.

Istifa! Istifa! chanted the ladies, banging their fists on the glass. Then two of the plates cracked. Then they broke, scattering shattered glass all over the vestibule floor. *Istifa! Istifa!* bellowed the matrons, now with no glass muffler to lessen the volume of their chant. The Azeri Amazons were terrifying—and the crocodile deputies ran for their lives, back into the chamber, with the ladies in hot pursuit. Front-associated deputies quickly intervened before a lynching could take place, and prevailed upon the crowd to return to their street-side vigil.

Back in the chamber, the debate over Mutalibov's fate resumed. The opposition once again voiced its demand for his immediate resignation; the government continued to stonewall. As the night ground on, Mutalibov was once more prevailed upon to make an appearance and voice his attitude toward the calls for his resignation. His lame remarks only fueled speculation that the president had become unbalanced: apologizing for past mistakes, Mutalibov promised to redistribute cabinet posts and include several opposition personalities in key positions. In the next breath he threatened a crackdown. The call was taken up from a very strange quarter—Araz Alizade, the head of the Social Democratic Party of Azerbaijan and a nominal member of the noncommunist Democratic Bloc. He called on Mutalibov to declare a state of emergency, prohibit the activities of political parties, and suspend parliament for six months. It all seemed like a done deal. Russian garrison troops had taken up positions in the back of the parliament, awaiting the order to assault the citizens gathered in front.

This announcement unleashed the full fury of the opposition deputies, who were now joined by a large number of (former) Communist Party deputies in protesting any intervention. Discovering his name on the request for intervention, 'Dollar' Yagub Mamedov declared that a forger was in the house, and immediately resigned, demanding that the Soviet troops return to their barracks. He had been the chairman of parliament for 12 hours. Exhausted and having reached another impasse, the session was suspended at 2:00 A.M. Most of the deputies slept in their chairs, because the parliament remained surrounded by protesters who refused to go home despite the early March chill.

* * *

The Russian soldiers disappeared during the night, and 'Dollar' Mamedov called the parliamentary session to order early Friday morning. His 'resignation' in anger over the forging of his name on the plea for Russian intervention the day before had not been voted on, so he was still legally the chairman. As soon as a quorum was established inside, the unofficial 'delegates' who had spent the night on the steps outside began their own session. There was only one subject they were interested in, and they phrased it in terms of an ultimatum: the president had to resign by noon, or they would storm the building.

The message was relayed to Mutalibov, and he said he needed some time to think about it. Noon came and went; the deadline was extended to 14:00 hours. That hour came and went, and still there was no official announcement about Mutalibov's plans. The crowd then sent in another ultimatum. The seriousness of the threat was brought home by another window-smashing spree; this time it was the plate-glass replacement windows that had been slapped up the night before. Once again, the deputies of the Democratic Bloc begged the crowd for patience. The president was reportedly suffering from high blood pressure and could not return to the chamber to work out the modalities of his resignation.

Then Hanim Halilova, backed by her militant matrons, launched her own attack. Shaming local KGB guards who tried to prevent her from entering the parliament lobby, she managed to create a breach, and the Azeri Amazons poured into the vestibule area. The assault on the inner chamber, though, was to be her own.

'Resign, you worm!' roared Hanim, breaking through the last line of defense and penetrating the inner chamber in her quest to wring Mutalibov's neck. 'You have been playing sick for hours, damn you! Just tender your resignation and go!' She was dragged from the chamber before she could find her target, however, and was then returned to the vigil on the steps, to the applause of the protesters.

The exhausted and despondent deputies could only imagine what would happen next. Then suddenly, there was movement from behind the scribes' desk, a door was flung open, and a phalanx of political personalities led by Prime Minister Hasan Hasanov emerged from the inner sanctum of parliament. In their midst was Mutalibov, looking pale and ghostly and walking like a man condemned. He stumbled up to the podium and looked at the microphone like it was a weird guillotine. Then he spoke, asking for silence. It was 6:00 P.M.

"Mistakes have been made and the People demand that I go," he said, lips trembling. "I thus ask that the deputies of this high body accept my resignation."

Ayaz Niyazioghli Mutalibov had skulked off into history 'forever,' becoming the first neocommunist leader in the post-Soviet age to quit. For his services to the nation, he was granted a 10,000-ruble monthly stipend for life. The cash value was about $100 at the time but only worth about $20 a year later and $5 a year after that; it might have seemed small, but it was twice that given Mikhail Gorbachev when he resigned as head of the USSR. In addition, Mutalibov was given a country vacation house, a ten-man security detachment, and a car. Most importantly, he was granted immunity from prosecution—a clause that would come back to haunt many of the people so delighted to see him go.

* * *

The Popular Front had the neocommunists down for the count. But as believers in due legal process, they had to abide by the constitution and what it said about succession to the presidency when that office was vacated by death or resignation—and what the law said was that the chairman of parliament would become acting head of state until a new president was elected within three months. This clause automatically made 'Dollar' Mamedov the temporary, legal head of the country—a state of affairs that surprised no one more than Yagub Mamedov himself.

While the Front accepted this as a temporary expedient, it made no secret of its own agenda: rather than new *presidential* elections, it wanted new *parliamentary* elections. The reason for this was that only the parliament could go about the task of drafting a new, postcommunist constitution, and what the Front wanted to do was draft a basic law that would radically redistribute power away from the executive branch of government and toward the legislature. The problem was that so long as the current full parliament remained sitting, it was dominated by people who owed their sinecures to the (now defunct) General Secretariat of the Communist Party/Presidency, and it was unlikely that they would call for early parliamentary elections that would spell the end of their power.

This sort of political stasis was a common problem for all the emerging republics of the former Soviet Union—whether Russia, Azerbaijan, Moldova, or Armenia. The structure of government inherited by all was based on the concept of the supremacy of the Central Committee of the all-Union Communist Party, that is, the Politburo, and when that structure collapsed, it left an immense power vacuum on the local level.

Previously, when the Kremlin spoke, its words were to be implemented by the local representatives of the central government—i.e., the staff apparatus of the General Secretariat of the (local) Communist Party, or *apparat*. Although at the time of the collapse of the Soviet Union most if not all of the CP bosses in the republics were 'ethnics,' there was no question about where their allegiances lay—they were Moscow proxies whose only dream was to be elevated to membership in the central, inner circle. If a local 'ethnic' got uppity for any reason, there was also someone around to remind him who was really boss: the Second Secretary in every local Communist Party was inevitably a Russian or Slav in good standing with the party, and usually responsible for ideological affairs.

Parallel to the *apparat* was another local institution designed to look like government, but which really only served as a grooming house for future CP bosses. This was the Council of Ministers. Although members held titles like 'minister of agriculture' and 'minister of industry' and 'minister of forestry,' their tasks were redundant because a similar, more powerful position already existed in the local *apparat* (as well as in Moscow).

The very bottom rung of the local power structure was parliament. Both the Supreme Soviet in Moscow and the local legislature of any given republic were bodies that only met once or twice a year in a pro-forma manner to rubber-stamp decisions already made above. In the fading days of the USSR, following the first 'multi-party' parliamentary elections in 1989, it also served as a sort of pressure release valve: dissidents and opposition types could blow all the steam they wanted, often on live TV, but power was still very clearly in the hands of the all-Union Communist Party.

But with the collapse of the Center, the declarations of independence of the republics and the dissolution of both supranational and local Communist Parties, everyone moved one or two notches up the chain of command. With a few notable exceptions, local CP bosses became national presidents and the *apparat* became the de facto executive branch of government, inheriting all CP property after the various local Communist Parties were closed, dissolved or renamed. Then the (local) Council of Ministers began acting (or play acting) like a presidential cabinet, replete with foreign and defense minister posts. The most dramatic change, however, happened in the (local) Supreme Soviets. First they officially renamed themselves (Duma, Ali Sovyet, etc.), then they decided to start functioning like real-life houses of representatives.

The problem was that most of the representatives in question had been elected to the local parliaments during the communist period, when vote rigging was the norm. And beyond the question of democratic legitimacy was the question of power. Because unlike the *apparat*-cum-presidency (which at least had an institutional memory of implementing policy), the Council of Ministers and the Parliament had been nothing more than showpieces during the days of the Soviet Union. But in every former Soviet republic that had experienced a democratic/nationalist reform or revolution—including, pre-eminently, Russia itself—the parliament became the repository for neo-communists determined to preserve their privileges and torpedo further change. Time and again, after effecting victories against the dead weight of the old system, the 'democrats' (or better, 'reformers') were to see their very 'liberalism' turned against them by those who, claiming to be the preservers of the constitutional order, were able to reverse or at least freeze change. The 'democratic' forces could not root them out, because—well, because the democratic forces had to act like democrats.

The exception to this caution about the rule of law was Boris Yeltsin, who literally blasted the standing parliament out of the Russian White House in October 1993. To its shame, the West—and especially the United States—applauded Yeltsin's heavy-handed tactic as necessary to oust the communists and preserve 'democracy' in Russia. It was no irony that when the political logjam was due to be broken there by new parliamentary elections, in December 1993, the 'democratic' reformers ended near the bottom of the electoral heap, with the majority of the population voting for either neocommunists or protofascists to represent their interests.

* * *

About a week after the Mutalibov resignation, the evening news concluded with a shrill, half-hour monologue delivered by a peculiar-looking man with soulful eyes and a salt-and-pepper beard. The stranger ranted about Russian manipulation of the conflict in Karabakh, rambled about the need to establish a national currency and banking system, and ended his delivery with a call to forcibly retire anyone currently working in government who was over 45 years of age. They could no longer change, and the times they were a-changin', the bearded man explained.

Viewers who did not recognize the speaker could have been forgiven, because relatively few people in Azerbaijan had actually ever seen him before. He was Abulfez Elchibey, the leader of the Popular Front. And up until March 1992, he had been an official nonperson.

Even if the performance left much to be desired in terms of broadcast quality, the very fact that the Front leader had been on television was an

event of significance. Someone in power had allowed him there. That someone was the Prime Minister, Hasan Hasanov, a former communist functionary who had recently started to dress in nationalistic attire.

Like everyone else in the *apparat*, Hasanov had worked his way up
through the CP by the tried-and-true method of sucking very hard. But once
he neared the top, things started to go sour—especially when he was
obliged to work under Mutalibov. Those in the know said that there was a
great personal animosity between them; some said this was because
Hasanov thought he should have been given the position of general secretary of the Azerbaijan Communist Party following Abdulrahman Vezirov's
removal in January 1990, but that Moscow had given the nod to Mutalibov
because of Hasanov's 'nationalist' tendencies (and general testiness).

Now, with Mutalibov gone and the confused and pliable 'Dollar'
Mamedov installed as acting president, Hasanov was invited to form his
first government (as opposed to having his government assigned him). Before doing this, he discreetly sought a meeting with Elchibey to bring the
Front into a coalition government of national unity.

The life of secrets is short. I was told of the meeting between Hasanov
and Elchibey by an impeccable source, and then decided to ask Hasanov
about details. The venue was a press conference with British Deputy Foreign
Minister Douglas Hogg, who was in town to open up diplomatic relations.

"Sir," I asked Hasanov after he had acknowledged my raised hand.
"Could you comment on reports that you have met with Abulfez Elchibey,
and if true, what you spoke about?"

Hasanov went white with anger, and sputtered that the press conference
was about Azerbaijan's relations with the United Kingdom, and not local
politics. But by the end of the press conference, Hasanov had changed his
mind and decided to butter his bread on both sides.

"I would like to respond to your question about my meetings with
Elchibey," he said, half an hour after I had asked the question. "Abulfez is a
highly respected political personality, and we have entered into discussion
with him about forming a government of national reconciliation and unity."

Hogg had no idea what Hasanov was talking about, but the news was a
bombshell in Azerbaijan. Within a week, a protocol was signed: in return
for the Front's entering into a coalition government, Hasanov was to appoint three Front-member deputies to the key posts. One was the new
Minister of Defense, Rahim Gaziev.

On March 28th, 'Dollar' Yagub Mamedov called for parliament to reconvene to discuss the future status of the presidency. The session was to
have been pro forma: the Front had conditioned its participation in Prime
Minister Hasanov's national unity government on the postponement of the

presidential elections, and the government had agreed. Still cleaving to the letter of the law, the Front noted that the constitutional clause governing elections would thus have to be changed. The only way to do this was to reconvene the parliament and vote on it, and the government had done just that.

It seemed almost too easy: the neocommunists had fled without a fight; the Front had won. But you would scarcely have noticed this, looking at the deputies gathering in parliament on March 28th. To be sure, Democratic Bloc members such as Tamerlan Garayev, Iskender Hamidov, Isa Gamberov, and Towfig Gasimov were not looking exactly blue. But the vast majority of the neocommunist crocodiles—Sinan Alizade, the head of the Azerbaijan oil industry, Sheikh ul Islam Allahshukur Pashazade, and even my bête noire—presidential spokesman Rasim Agaev—were scurrying around, glad-handing each other and wearing curious smiles painted on their faces.

The main issue on the morning agenda was the creation of a national army outside the command and control structure of the new Commonwealth of Independent States. The idea had first mooted six months before and was brought into law on October 10th. But aside from the government announcing that the old KGB office building and recreation club in downtown Baku would house the new national Ministry of Defense, very little had been done on an organizational level to insure the creation of a credible force. Many of the parliamentarians, I knew, had actively or tacitly tried to retard the creation of the army because it represented the final exit from the former Soviet Union which they still cleaved to in their hearts. But everyone in the chamber seemed to have always been behind the idea of a national army. Speaker after speaker, including the new acting president, Dr. Yaqub Mamedov, made withering attacks on the former government for neglecting its development.

"We all saw it coming, not just Xodjali but all the other villages in Karabakh, as the Armenians took them one by one," said the new Defense Minister, Rahim Gaziev, in a keynote address that drew applause even from members of the old, communist elite. "I am not here today to accuse anyone by name, but you know you are all responsible for the disastrous situation of today. We have no army at present. We called for 20,000 volunteers, but in real terms we have less than 5,000. The borders are weak, and even towns under attack have not bothered to fortify positions. There is no plan, no sense of tactics, no idea of what equipment is available or even who knows how to use it. This is the truth, and the people need to know it! To build up an army takes years, and we are presently at war."

Gaziev then called on the parliament to declare a state of emergency and to close down places of entertainment at nine o'clock at night so that the whole nation might 'understand' the conditions at the front. He also harshly attacked his predecessors for looting the military till, and demanded that the local militia groups be 'liquidated' and that all weapons be registered with the Ministry of Defense, lest Azerbaijan devolve into a new Lebanon. Another way of looking at Gaziev's motives might be that he wanted to liquidate all the militia groups that he (or his associates) did not control. 'Dollar' Yaqub Mamedov praised Gaziev's speech and promised that parliament would pass all the laws and measures he deemed necessary. He also made the rhetorical wish that the Karabakh conflict might still be solved through peaceful means, but that the moral and material resources of the nation had to be marshaled lest peace negotiations fail.

Following a long lunch break, the session resumed in the mid-afternoon to deal with the matter of refugee support as well as defining exactly what one needed to do, or have done, to become a Hero of Azerbaijan. Most agreed that a basic criteria was that you should have died for your country, but there was some debate on this point. Given the circumstances and the alleged reason for the parliamentary session—to vote on postponing the presidential elections and proroguing the 350-seat parliament in lieu of the 50-man National Council—there seemed to be a lot of time devoted to peripheral issues. Stranger still, it was the crocodiles who were doing most of the talking—and in a fairly organized manner.

"They're stalling," I whispered to Mehmet Ali Bayar of the Turkish embassy. There was a word for it that I had once learned in high school civics but couldn't remember.

"It's called a 'filibuster,' " he reminded me.

That is exactly what it was: droning, nonsensical chatter about incidentals, designed to exhaust one's opponents, to bore them to death. And as the day wore into evening and then into night, the Democratic Bloc deputies slowly but surely got so sick of the debate that they left the chamber, singly and in pairs, to go into the hallway and smoke. Some of the delegates were moving toward the cloakroom, assuming that discussion of the elections clearly would not be raised at this late hour and would wait for the next day.

I was heading toward the exit myself when someone on the second floor gave a shout to one of the Democratic Bloc deputies below. With an explosion of profanity billowing out of their mouths along with the last puff of smoke, the deputies in the lobby were suddenly fighting with each other to be first back into the chamber.

"What happened?" I asked Isa Gamberov as he pushed past a guard.

"They're voting without us!" he swore.

Indeed they were.

'Dollar' Mamedov, upon seeing the Bloc deputies depart the chamber in boredom over a discussion of what really constituted the definition of Hero of Azerbaijan, had tabled a motion to vote on the matter of dissolving the presidential apparatus.

This may have seemed a mere procedural detail to most observers. To others, it might have occurred that this subject was not what had been agreed upon among Mamedov, Hasan Hasanov, and Abulfez Elchibey the day before as an appropriate topic of debate. To others still more skilled in the niceties of parliamentary debate, the very question, as posed, whether there should or should not be a presidency, was more than splitting hairs, but also was an issue over which the majority of deputies could only vote 'no.' Logic dictated that an initial 'nay' would precipitate a series of other 'no' votes against postponing the elections. There was no other way to explain it than as a double cross, and of the cheapest kind.

"Know that you are now responsible for all that happens as a result of this travesty," Democratic Bloc member Arif Xadjiev shouted, moments before the voting.

Iskender Hamidov was so apoplectic that he couldn't speak, and was actually being restrained from attacking some smiling crocodile across the floor by—I could scarcely believe my eyes—Abulfez Elchibey himself.

I didn't know and never learned whether he had been invited to attend the session, or whether someone had just let him in through the back door. But there he was in the parliamentary dress-circle, holding down Hamidov lest the Front chairman's personal Doberman go through with the murder on his mind.

The result of the voting was predictable: of the 262 parliamentarians (a quorum was 240) who registered, 207 voted against the motion to dissolve the presidential apparatus while 35 voted for it. Twenty voters either abstained or had their ballots invalidated. Next came the motion to suspend the presidency during the election campaign leading up to the June 7th polls; of 263 deputies registered, 191 voted against while 54 voted for the resolution. Another 18 either abstained or had invalid votes.

The crocodiles could scarcely conceal their glee. They had effected a bold-faced double cross—and they had gotten away with it.

Then something very strange happened. So confident were they of their control of the reins of state, the neocommunist leadership invited Abulfez to address the august body. It was almost—no, it was—an insult. Amazingly, Abulfez accepted.

"Esteemed ladies and gentlemen!" Elchibey began in his familiar, Naxjivani-staccato speech. "This is not the first time that I have been deceived. I once said I might be deceived twice but I won't forgive anyone who means to deceive me three times. I now regret having accepted the proposal of Premier Hasan Hasanov and Chairman of Parliament Yaqub Mamedov to participate in a coalition government. This game you are playing is very insulting, and I don't know how I will respond to the 80,000 rank-and-file members of the Popular Front when they ask me what happened. Because we have been deceived. . . .

"Now you are in a rush to elect a new president—elect him! But the president you elect in three months will be overthrown in a year. And this is natural. Because today the state that we live in is only deserving of a president who can be kept in power by force, and the people will be forced to overthrow that force.

"What is the alternative? We need to create structures that can protect a president and prevent him from turning into a dictator. This requires institutions. Power can be divided into legislative and executive branches with an independent judiciary supervising the first two branches. Everybody must obey the Court, including the president. Everyone has a right in such a society to bring an action against anyone, even the president. Otherwise no one will fear anyone and least of all the law.

"If we fail to create such counter-balancing structures, whoever you elect as president will destroy himself or be destroyed by those nearest to him because there is no institutional structure to prevent all this. . . .

"We are not adamant about the abolition of the presidency. Our concern is its monopoly of power. Share it. Give some to the judiciary, some to the cabinet of ministers, some to the parliament! But after 70 years of domination by Moscow, we know very well what the presidency means: control and manipulation from above. . . .

"The Xodjali tragedy was effected by the empire's KGB. We possess the facts that the first rallies and strikes in Hankenti (Stepanakert) were organized by the deputy chairman of the all-Union KGB. It was the KGB that organized the first rallies in Yerevan. Even here in Baku they managed to organize a few meetings. Suspecting nothing, we all participated in them. . . .

"We are being hit from two sides: Moscow does everything possible, including pitting different groups of our population against each other in order to prevent us from creating a truly independent state. Then, when we manage to agree and meet each other halfway, they organize something in Karabakh and border areas to distract our attention and create chaos. . . .

"The empire that brought so many tragedies to us is seeking to thrust its hand in anew. To prevent this, we should first reform our National Security Ministry. We believe in our defense minister. We believe that the Interior Ministry can and should be reformed. But as for National Security, it should be reorganized completely. Once we are sure we can defend ourselves—then, and only then, will we be able to speak about elections and other matters. My time is over by two minutes. Excuse me. Thank you."

Polite applause and a sigh of relief rose from the swamp as Abulfez returned to his chair in the chamber. Yagub Mamedov tapped his microphone and damned Elchibey with faint praise, describing him as a great man and thinker whom he greatly respected, especially about his thoughts concerning so many incredibly interesting and important matters. Now, however, it was time to move on to other pressing and incredibly important matters—like voting on the election laws and how much money should be budgeted for the campaign.

A couple of motions were brought forward from the crocodile section of the floor, and the microphones were opened to comments before pro forma voting commenced. As usual, the handful of deputies from the Democratic Bloc began to line up at the microphones, and the crocodiles got ready to put in their earplugs and sleep through whatever rhetorical attack was made on them. Why not? It was late at night after a long day—so why not let the disconsolate losers have their say?

The red light was blinking on the microphone in the center aisle, and Iskender Hamidov was given the nod to speak.

"Yaqub *Muallem*," Iskender muttered hoarsely, referring to the acting president by the honorific title of 'teacher,' and thus subtly reminding everyone of Mamedov's position as rector of the Baku Medical Institute. "There really is no point in discussing or even voting on the new election laws and the commission and campaign budget business, as you have suggested we do. It is late, and we want to go home. You can conduct the elections any way you see fit—but please, don't waste any more money from the treasury on the matter. You have already taken enough over the years and can fund the campaign yourself. Thank you."

Silence filled the chamber. Then a gurgling grew into a sputtering and then a roaring as Yagub Mamedov rose to his feet, blood drained from his face, his jaw working into a howl.

"You . . . you . . . you!" sputtered the acting president of the country. "I refuse to accept such abuse! I . . . I . . . I quit!"

Equating word with reaction, nothing made sense. But Hamidov had apparently hit a raw nerve: Mamedov's alleged penchant for accepting bribes from students.

Pandemonium broke loose in the chamber as Mamedov stumbled off, exiting stage right. Some crocodiles went running after him, while others tried to claw their way toward Hamidov to gouge his eyes out. Members of the Democratic Bloc and the VIP part of the audience, including Abulfez, rushed to Hamidov's aid.

Then someone realized that Mamedov's microphone was still on. Rather than turn it off, there was a fight over who might use it for broadcasting. At the end of a brief tussle, the thin, gaunt form of a man in a uniform emerged: KGB chairman Il Hussein Husseinov.

"*Order! Order! Order!*" he shouted in Russian into the microphone, a two-inch sheet of ice on his voice. Like well-trained schoolboys hearing the voice of the principal, most in the chamber turned toward him. "I demand that Iskender Hamidov be brought to trial before the nation for his slander and calumny against the head of government!" he said, his voice rising. "This is a scandal of unprecedented proportions and—"

Whistles and catcalls from the gallery drowned out his voice.

"Hey, this isn't Moscow!"

"Speak in Azeri, spook!"

"I demand that—" Husseinov began again. . . .

He got no further.

Azer-bai-jan!! came a chorus of singing voices, *AZER-BAI-JAN!!*

Husseinov put up token resistance, but then gave up the microphone. He returned to his seat, shouting and cursing and pointing at the deputies, who continued to taunt him. Then Elchibey had the microphone but someone turned off the sound and there was no making out what he had to say, at least from up in the gallery, anyway. There were more howls and catcalls and general pandemonium, and then Elchibey and several of the Democratic Bloc deputies disappeared in the direction of 'Dollar' Mamedov's stage-right exit. After several more minutes of ebb and flow around the floor, the stage doors were thrown open again. A procession of actors emerged, with Yagub Mamedov in the middle.

"Hey, 'Dollar!' " someone in the gallery shouted. "I thought you resigned!"

"Twice!" cried someone else, resulting in titters of laughter.

Mamedov refused to acknowledge the catcalls, and resumed the discussion of several other items on the agenda, acting for all the world as if nothing had even happened and he had been there all the while. Then the KGB team in charge of parliamentary security entered the gallery and instructed all the journalists and other voyeurs to leave.

Without a huddle and without any communication, the normally docile Azeri press corps refused to do so—and had to be escorted out one by one by the goon squad assigned the task.

The session continued in secrecy deep into the night. No one knew the details, but we all knew this: something remarkable had happened, to which no one could put a name.

9

Of Militias and Mamed the Mule

Rahim Gaziev, the new minister of defense, promised to bring right all setbacks in Karabakh by building up a national army. But doing so meant acquiring competent men. This was easier said than done.

A major source of soldiers (and officers) was the rapidly dissolving Soviet army, and Gaziev called for all those currently serving in that organization to return to serve the motherland. Azeris started coming 'home' from near and far.

One such volunteer was Yusuf Agaev, a Soviet-trained criminologist from Kazakhstan who took on the position of military prosecutor for Karabakh. This was an almost impossible job: in addition to having to deal with every Armenian 'crime' in the territory, Yusuf also had to deal with every Azeri 'crime' in the conflict zone, ranging from desertion to profiteering and hostage taking.

Another volunteer was Colonel Nejmettin Sadikov, an Azeri officer from the neighboring Russian republic of Daghestan. He seemed to be more typical of the new volunteers than Yusuf Agaev, because Colonel Sadikov could barely speak a word of Azeri. Also, his ability to command was a little dubious. Tacit Soviet policy had been to put Muslims into construction and not combat battalions. Thus, Azeri 'veterans' might know how to build a bridge over a river but not how to drive a tank across it.

A second element in the security scene were the paramilitary gendarmes, or OMON units, associated with the Ministry of the Interior. Although trained to use weapons, here, too, there was the danger of split loyalties: many of the soldier-cops were members of Iskender Hamidov's pan-Turkic *Bozkurt* society. Chief among these men was Ravshan Javadov, later to gain fame as the leader of the so-called 'Turkish Coup' attempt against Heydar Aliyev, in March 1995. Others seemed beholden to Moscow.

The main forces involved in early fighting in and around Karabakh, however, were the militia groups.

While the word 'militia' may once have had a romantic resonance for Americans who associated the word with Paul Revere and the Minutemen, in post-Soviet Azerbaijan (and elsewhere) the concept had decidedly different connotations. In essence, 'militia' meant private army, usually made up of men divided by partisanship, regionalism, and often murderous jealousy.

In Azerbaijan there were different types of militias under the general rubric. The Lachin, Fizuli, and Gubatli 'brigades,' for example, often seemed to be composed more of extended families than soldiers. One former Popular Front man by the name of Aliekber Humbatov established what was known as the 'Talish Brigade' after its headquarters in the southeastern Caspian city of Lenkoran, more than 300 miles away from anything resembling 'the front.'

The best-known militia was a group then known alternatively as the 'Ganje Brigade' or the 'Surats,' after their financier, a shy and retiring young director of the state wool combine, Surat Husseinov. There was even a 'university' brigade associated with Etibar Mamedov of the National Independence Party, said to be made up of hotheads from the history department of Baku State. To tell the truth, I never saw a trace of them on or near the front, although Etibar's party headquarters always seemed to have an abundance of armed guards.

The militia that I was most familiar with, however, was based outside of Agdam, and led by a former sculptor named '*Katir* Mamed,' or Mamed the Mule. I had first heard of him through Imam Sadik Sadikov, the administrator of the Agdam Mosque and Morgue complex, when I traveled out to Agdam to check out a story concerning an Armenian hostage named Lev Vaganovich Ovakov-Leonov (Leoniyan), an octogenarian set-designer with 'national artist' status in (Soviet) Azerbaijan. Leonov had been picked up in Baku by unknown individuals and dragged off to Agdam to be exchanged for the elderly father of a well-known Azeri judge. I thought I might ask my old friend Imam Sadikov if he had heard anything about the incident. I found him washing a batch of Azeri corpses that had just arrived as part of some sort of exchange.

"So what about the hostages?" I asked the Imam.

"Better ask Yaqub Mamedov," Imam Sadikov said, pulling off the surgeon's mask he wore to cut down the stench and to stop from gagging.

"Yaqub Mamedov?" I naively asked. "The acting president?"

The Imam cackled the cackle of someone who had seen too much.

"Oh, no," the cleric answered. "*Katir* Mamed—the Mule."

"Who's that?" I asked.

"You'll find him out in the old graveyard."

"Digging graves?"

"No, no—we only bury our people in the new cemetery. The Mule lives in the old one."

* * *

As the fog settled over the old Muslim cemetery outside Agdam and the rattle of small arms, punctured by the occasional artillery blast, echoed through the rolling hills east of Karabakh, '*Katir*' Mamedov smiled.

A short man with thick curly hair and a full gray beard that framed a face so far beyond red that it looked purple, the 42-year-old Mamedov said he had once been a sculptor and a father of four but he had abandoned his chisel for a Kalashnikov and had adopted a new family—600 armed men. They called themselves the '*Mudafah Shahinlar*,' or Defense Falcons, but I preferred to call them the 'Mules' because of their leader. 'The Ghouls' might have been the best sobriquet, given the location of their HQ.

The Mules' self-appointed task was to defend the perimeter of Agdam from further Armenian encroachments. The forward position was at the end of the cemetery and less than 100 meters from the most forward Armenian positions that protected the eastern approach to Karabakh. It was called Post 19. Beyond it was the enemy, and the Mule said he looked forward to the day when his men would go beyond the Post and start to reconquer all the territory that had been lost, eradicating every last Armenian from Karabakh in the process, no matter how long it took. Generations, even.

"The population of Azerbaijan is seven million and pushing on eight, and the Armenians are only two and a half million," the Mule computed. "They can kill half of us and we still will outnumber them two to one. You understand? They can't win."

The Mule did not believe in cease-fires—except those that he made himself with the commander of the Armenian *fedayeen* forces on the far side of the line, with whom he had gone to school. They had a lot of contact, the Mule said, and he hoped to kill his old schoolyard pal someday soon.

"All that peace talk is empty talk because it is talk between empty people in Baku and Yerevan," said the Mule. "*This* is the front—the *Jebhe*. *This* is where brave men fight and die."

And Falcons had been dying. The group had developed a reputation for free-lance assaults on fortified Armenian positions without a great deal of depth to their attacks. They blamed their setbacks on a lack of coordination with the national army, although they refused to coordinate with it in general principle. There was an almost palpable belief in the equal evil of the enemy without and the enemy within.

"We have war on two fronts," said the Mule over a meal in the Falcon cemetery mess hall. "We will win both."

When I asked what he meant by that, he smiled darkly. "Think about it," he said. "We have been fighting for four long years. There is a very good reason why we haven't won yet. The sell-outs, the traitors within."

This independent attitude was starting to attract the attention of well-meaning patriots—including the shadowy Azeri 'mafia.' In addition to uniforms, provisions, and light arms, the Mule's troops possessed three T-54 tanks and a number of armored personnel carriers—all apparently purchased from departing (former) Soviet units, and paid for by invisible supporters. I was treated to a training session for operators of a new, heavy-caliber anti-aircraft gun that had just been donated by a Baku 'merchant.' Along with equipment, the number of Falcons was growing. In addition to a wide assortment of Azeris, the Mule's brigade had managed to attract a curious crowd of outlaw volunteers: half Azeri/Russian construction workers from Baku, a Pan-Islamic fighter from Tajikistan, and even a baby-faced Ukrainian whom Commander Yaqub referred to as his 'lost son'—a psychic replacement for his own boy who was killed in an Armenian missile attack on Agdam earlier in the conflict. Perhaps the best way to describe the foreign component was 'mercenaries,' but the term didn't quite fit; psycho-killer seemed better.

"If I killed Armenians at home, they'd throw me in jail," said Yuri, the baby-faced Ukrainian. The Mule gave him a big kiss.

Despite an official cease-fire, the Falcons were gearing up for the next round of war. Baku and Yerevan might make as many cease-fires and agreements as they liked, said the Mule, but so long as he did not agree to the terms or purpose of the peace, his men would fight on.

After another year and a half of free-lance assaults and an active trade in bodies, Mamed the Mule was tricked into coming to Baku, where he was arrested on suspicion of treason and collaborating with the enemy—i.e., making deals to withdraw so the Armenian commander on the other side might claim a victory or two without losing too many men, in return for the same favor to enhance his own reputation. The arresting agent was my friend, Yusuf Agaev.

Murder was another charge. There had been too many 'accidental' deaths of other commanders in and around Agdam to chalk up to chance. One alleged victim was the popular commander of the Popular Front office in Agdam, Allahverdi Bagirov, whose jeep ran over a rather-too-well placed mine in a sector under the Mule's control. The suspicion was that the Mule was knocking off anyone who got too close to his secret source of income: corpses. When Yusuf Agaev arrested the Mule, he had one of his men check around the Mule's headquarters. During the search, they opened some cold storage tanks, inside of which were a dozen bodies of young Azeri soldiers, being kept on ice while the Mule continued to draw their combat pay.

But that was much later. In early 1992, the Mule was one of the few heroes Azerbaijan could claim and volunteers swarmed to his graveyard HQ to join up. The militant mood of prospective martyrdom had even begun to infect Azeri women, who were serving not just in the kitchen but on the front lines.

"Don't you dare suggest that I cannot do the job you think you can," shouted a woman recruit named Nurjahan Husseinova at a male comrade in arms at Post 19. "Where were you during Dashalti? Where were you during the battle of Askeron? Have you even seen a corpse before or had someone in your sights? You say you have just returned. That means you ran away."

The new recruit had suggested that Nurjahan's honor might be violated if she were to fall into enemy hands, but the 38-year-old mother's only concern was for the honor of her child.

"The law says that you have to be twenty years of age to join up," she said, putting away her mascara kit inside the pouch that held her hand grenades. "But my son is only nineteen and I don't know if they will take him."

Thanks to his mother's connections, Yevlak Husseinov did manage to enlist even though he was underage. After basic training, he was shipped off to the front with his mates—and killed during his first mission. There was no cause for heroics, because he was killed by what they call 'friendly fire.' I know all this because I got to know Nurjahan quite well. I even wrote a song about her, which I delivered as we stood at her son's grave in Martyrs' Lane a year later.

It went to a 'rap' mode, with the 'u' and '/' denoting down/up beats, respectively. I will spare the reader the entire song, save for this:

She was a rust-haired vet'ren	u / u / / / u
And me a balding hack	u / u / / u
Her job was offing Dashnaks	u / u / / / u
I led the pundit pack	u / u / / u
The site of our strange try-st	u / u / u / u
Occurred at Post 19	u / u / / u
A shell-shocked bunker	u / u / u
on the front	/ u /
Where thinking was obscene	u / u u u /

Chorus:

It was no fun war	u u u / - u
It was no good war	u u u / - u
It was death	u u /
and amputation all around --	u / u / u / u
It was no fun war	u u u / - u
It was no good war	u u u / - u
Just another dirty place	u u / u / u /
to get mowed down --	u / / u

I called the little ditty "Ballad of a War Groupie."

I guess I was starting to become one.

I certainly had not planned on dealing with so much death and destruction when I arrived in Azerbaijan.

It was time for a break.

A joint Azeri-Russian inspection team on patrol in Mountainous Karabakh. The man in the upper left holds an 'Alazan' rocket. (T. Goltz)

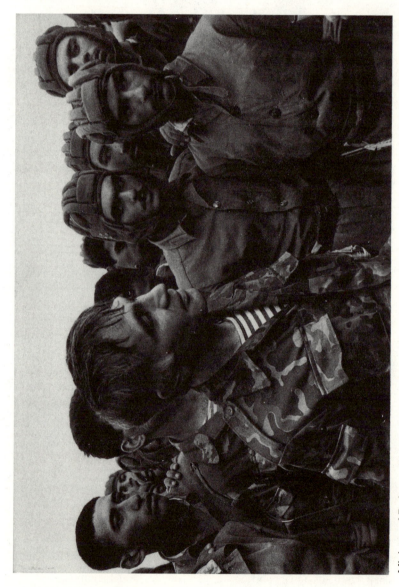

Minister of Defense Rahim Gaziev with tank troops. (O. Litvin)

Alef Khadjiev, commander of the defense forces in Xodjali. (T. Goltz)

Yaqub Mamedov, aka 'Mamed the Mule,' at his Agdam base. (O. Litvin)

Alef Khadjiev, 1953-1992. (T. Goltz)

Outside the Agdam morgue, awaiting the arrival of more bodies from Xodjali. (O. Litvin)

10

A Diversion Through the Islamic Republic of Iran

I was hanging around Post 19, looking through the evening mist and wondering when the most recent Iran-brokered cease-fire would collapse. It had been arranged in order to allow United Nations Special Envoy Cyrus Vance a chance to explore the possibility of UN mediation in the Karabakh conflict parallel to his efforts to bring peace to Bosnia-Herzegovina.

"I saw everything I could possibly need to see," Vance told me as he climbed out of the Russian Army BTR that had brought him in and out of Karabakh. "Stepanakert is in an awful state. The Karabakh Armenians say they want peace like everybody else. The seven-day cease-fire made by the Iranians is a positive step forward."

As soon as he left, the sharp rattle and crack of gunfire was already starting to reverberate through the hillocks between Agdam and Askeron. I was ready to find a phone and declare the cease-fire broken when in the distance, two lights appeared on the Armenian side of the lines, moving toward us through no-man's-land. The vehicle blinked its lights as it approached Post 19 and then eased to a halt as the militia men lowered their guns at the windows. As their chief interrogated the driver, I stuck my head in the back window.

"Hello!" said one of six men crammed in the back, in English.

"Hi," I replied. "Who are you?"

"I am Hakbin," said the man, still draped in shadow in the back seat. "I am the head of the delegation of the Islamic Republic of Iran that arranged today's cease-fire."

"Pleased to meet you," I said, introducing myself. I wanted to chat, but it was absurd to think that an interview could be conducted in such circumstances. The small arms fire was being joined by the heavier thump of 70mm cannon rounds as the last vestiges of the cease-fire broke down.

"Gotta go!" said Hakbin. "Look me up at the embassy!"

When I got back to Baku, I duly went over to the Iranian embassy, where

I met two bearded men wearing Islamic-style collarless shirts, coming down the steps I was walking up. One was the fellow with whom I had conducted the brief backseat chat outside Agdam. Once again he was too busy to talk, although he was friendly.

"Look me up when you get to Tehran," he said. "And when you come I will provide you with all sorts of information."

"That's why I am here," I said. "I need a visa."

"We must telex Tehran about this first," said Hakbin. "Come tomorrow for your visa."

This was too optimistic. But after a week of pestering him, the consul asked for my passport and stamped in a visa to the Islamic Republic of Iran. I am sure he gave me the visa just to get rid of me. I had one week to get there and one week to stay. I was about to become the First American Tourist in the Islamic Republic of Iran—or so I like to think.

* * *

The driver managed to effect a daring, no doubt illegal, and certainly dangerous turn off Enqelab Avenue into another four-lane street, and I asked him what they called it.

"*Vali Asr Khiyabani*," he said, the Avenue of the Prince of the Age—one of the many names usually associated with the Imam Khomeini. "But its real name is Pahlavi Avenue. Ahh, those were the good old days. You should have been here in Tehran then."

It was difficult to imagine that things could be much better than right now. My perspective had been warped by over a year in the former USSR, because what I saw seemed like commercial heaven. Up and down the street were rows and rows of shops selling everything under the sun: cars, motorcycles, computers, machine tools, fashion clothes for men and women, and then, most prominently, dozens and dozens of fresh fruit juice stands: bananas, kiwis, strawberries, carrots, and oranges—a burst of colors and potential tastes that I had not dreamed of in months.

After checking into a room in a small hotel, I called an Iranian-Azeri-American acquaintance whom I had met in Baku. Farzin was very surprised to hear I was in Tehran, but pleased. My suggestion that we get together sometime over the next few days was instantly turned into an immediate link up; he had to show me his town. Along with him was his brother Afshin who had not seen an American in ten years.

We piled into Afshin's beat-up vehicle and began a merry, motorized tour, swerving between traffic lanes and coming so close to mowing down pedestrians that I was literally hiding my face in my hands. I had been warned about driving in Tehran but was now experiencing it firsthand: it was *Inshallah* driving—God planned all crashes, and men were merely his agents. The only reason that there were not more accidents is that there were so many traffic jams, and cars couldn't get up enough speed to do real damage.

We headed north, uphill, into an area called Darband—a pedestrian zone of tea shops, restaurants and juice stands running along either side of a babbling mountain stream. Both the tea houses and restaurants were 'traditional' in the sense that they combined both old and new: dozens of young couples, enjoying the evening air while sitting atop piles of cushions and carpets and nibbling on fava beans, ice creams and sherbets, an assortment of pistachios and other nuts, and chocolates, and sipping diverse soft drinks: a bootleg Coca-Cola, Seven-Up, various Schweppes, and even an 'Islamic' (alcohol-free) beer.

Aside from the headscarves (*hijab*) and raincoats (*manto*) worn by all women, it could have been Istanbul, Athens, or Rome. But it was Tehran. Where were the mullahs and revolutionary guards ready to throw you in some hellish prison for glancing at a woman or daring to smile?

"No one who has not been here can believe it," said Farzin. "This place is in the throes of change. The mullahs are on their way out. No one listens to them anymore." It was all pretty difficult to quantify, he admitted, because there was so much reading between the lines required: the way the ladies wore their *hijabs* pulled back daringly to reveal locks of hair; the fact that most men were clean shaven or sporting bushy mustaches—both contrary to the style of beard prescribed for pious men by the Prophet of God.

"There was a Frank Sinatra musical on television last night," Farzin said, almost breathlessly. "Can you imagine? *Frank Sinatra*, singing decadent songs on Iranian TV! *Someone* made the decision to air it! *Who? Why?*" In April 1992, there was already a name for it: the "Tehran Spring."

* * *

We started our tour of town in the university area. There were a lot of bookstores and other shops catering to the student crowd. There was, of course, a lot of Islamic stuff. But most of the titles seemed to be what one would expect to find in a university area: law books, medical and engineering texts, and all sorts of literature—originals and translations of Western authors like Hemingway, Sartre, Goethe, and Cervantes, plus originals and translations of Persian classics like Omar Khayyam and Ferdowsi.

I was a little wary at first of revealing myself to be the first American tourist in the country in a decade, and hid beneath the fiction that I was from Baku. But Farzin took an almost perverse delight in informing our various interlocutors that I was from the USA, so that he could register attitudes for his own research about the changing face of Iran—and the result was universal delight at my presence in the country. Conveniently, Farzin also served as a sounding board for my own casual study of head-counting Azeris in Tehran. They were everywhere. After initially and naturally speaking to people in Persian before *Turki*, Farzin followed my lead and pretended he was from Baku. We never experienced a linguistic dead end once.

"*Fars kalmadi*," Farzin said. "There are no Persians left."

Eventually, we ended up at Maydan-i Khomeini (Imam Khomeini Circle), where the Tehran telephone exchange was located. Like many strategic structures in Tehran, it had been hit by a SCUD missile during the 1980–1988 war with Iraq and virtually destroyed. But now it had been slapped back up like new. The only trace of the devastation was a large park flanking the exchange building, where some other structure that urban renewal could not salvage had once stood. Farzin assured me that many of the new 'green' areas in town were the result of a creative—and cheap—response to war-related blight. Curiously, there was no trace of the human carnage of the eight-year war in Tehran: cripples were nowhere to be seen; most had been tucked away in low-profile jobs like the telephone exchange.

Finally, we arrived at our planned destination—the labyrinth of the Tehran Bazaar. It was here among the wealthy, religiously inclined (and mainly Azeri) merchants that Khomeini received the necessary financial support to pull off his revolution. The vehicle for collecting cash is called *khums*, a special tithe for the Shi'ite clerical leadership that is not practiced among Sunni Muslims. Symbols of Shi'ism were everywhere—but there was also a lot of kitsch on sale using the American flag as a design emblem. And despite the ubiquitous portraits of Imam Khomeini glowering from every wall and post, everyone we met was absolutely thrilled to meet an American—me.

The bazaar was a wonderful, dusty-musty, noisy rabbit-warren organized into discrete service sections that all purveyed the same sort of goods: scores of shoe shops down one lane, utensils and kitchen implements concentrated in another, fabrics here and plastics there. Warehouses were filled to bursting with cases of Iranian-made Seven-Up and Pepsi-Cola, twelve-packs of mango chutney from India, Nescafé from Switzerland, cornflakes from Germany, olive oil from Turkey, and even the odd bottle of Louisiana Hot Sauce. It was difficult to resist snap-purchases right then and there, but I realized that if I started buying I would be soon be weighed down with a ton of stuff that I craved, so I limited myself to a few luxury purchases like razor blades and shaving cream and a bag of pistachios.

Extricating ourselves from the bazaar, we wound our way back up Vali

Asr (former Pahlavi) Avenue north to take a look at the New Town, and stopped in a number of upmarket boutiques to see what was available. Almost everything, and all of it ultimately 'un-Islamic' in the understood sense.

In the entry to an arcade devoted to stereo equipment, a young man was selling disco tapes, advertising his wares with the aid of a streetside ghetto-blaster. True, most were instrumentals and rather far from Donna Summers's orgasmic disco songs, and the volume was not as high as one would expect at similar music outlets in Istanbul or even Baku, but the point was that the salesman was breaking the law by advertising sin, in the Islamic sense—and just didn't care.

Visually, this subtle change was expressed most clearly by the dress code for women and the way they were violating it. In principle—or at least according to the Western cliché about fundamentalist Iran—women should be covered from head to foot in the *chador*, the all-enveloping black sack that defends their honor by preventing the eyes of unrelated men from wandering too freely—and thus also protects the fidelity of the men.

But while some women were wearing the *chador*, most had rejected it in favor of a fashion *hijab/manto* combination—or kerchief and 'Islamic rain-coat.' Now, faking it with a kerchief is easy enough—but even the *manto* was undergoing a 'fashion' transformation. *Manto* came in a variety of colors, fabrics, and cuts designed with braids and tassels. . . . If not designed by The United Colors of Benetton, the *manto* was almost sexy in several of its permutations. And what was worn beneath it was hardly a secret: the ladies' shops are literally packed with the most up-to-date lingerie, form-fitting T-shirts and blue jeans, spiked heels, and jewelry, presenting the bizarre spectacle of presumably pious ladies window shopping for frivolous panties in downtown Tehran, oblivious or indifferent to the presence of a muddled young clerical student of downcast eye who was wandering by.

We stopped into a juice stand (run by Azeris, of course) and then again for a quick snack in the IranMac restaurant, set up exactly like that place of the Golden Arches. Down the street was the Tehran headquarters of IBM—Iran Business Machines. From there we proceeded through a large, pleasant botanical park where Farzin had courted girlfriends in bygone days. The young couples were still there, sitting on the grass between the trees and whispering sweet nothings to each other. It could have been Central Park, but for the graffiti: *"Bad Hijab or No Hijab (is) the source of all prostitution!"* But girls were walking under the pious proclamations with their headscarves pulled back to reveal frosted hair and even bits of naked ear; and the only thing hiding their eye shadow was their fashionable sunglasses.

From the top of the park, we turned downhill again, dodging traffic down the former Roosevelt Boulevard to the grounds of the huge, abandoned American Embassy compound, where the notorious hostage-taking took place in 1979. The Revolutionary Guards who took over the place had created a Center for the Den of Espionage at the entrance to the embassy, but interest in the reconstruction of shredded American documents had so waned that there was no one even attending the agit-prop stand. The guard on the embassy wall above didn't mind my taking a few pictures and even posing for one. I asked to be given a tour of the grounds, but the guard politely said no because the 'ambassador is not in residence.' I didn't press the issue.

Then we stopped in for coffee at an espresso bar owned by a designer (not Bijan) who spent ten months of the year attending the design whims of the Hollywood elite but came back to Tehran for the other two in order to relax. Quiet jazz was playing on the sound system, and a couple of pretty girls were smoking cigarettes while sipping cappuccinos in a corner, almost as though they were waiting for someone to walk over and ask them what they thought about the latest Bergman film. If it hadn't been for the *hijabs* we could have been in the East Village in New York.

* * *

Farzin and Afshin picked me up at 6:30 A.M. sharp for the drive to the *Behesht-e Zahra*, the vast cemetery south of Tehran where hundreds of thousands of dead from the Iran-Iraq War lie buried. It is also where Imam Khomeini has taken his final rest and is thus a very holy place. His mosque, said to be built to the exact volume specifications of the huge Prophet's place of communal prayer in Medina, Saudi Arabia (also designed to hold tens of thousands), was large but not really very imaginative or imposing. It consisted of a gilded dome above the Imam's tomb, two gilded minarets, and two dormitory structures off to either side of the entrance. But the most striking feature of the Khomeini complex was its incompleteness. Air ducts were exposed beneath absent ceiling paneling, the internal columns stood without pedestals or heads and wires sprouted out of walls. The only finished part of the structure was the Imam's tomb, in the center, located behind a steel grating beneath the central dome—and all after three years of 'day-and-night' construction.

Another striking feature was that the mosque was virtually empty—a fact exaggerated by unused capacity. There were perhaps five hundred people in the mosque at the time of my visit that Friday morning. It looked like a coliseum whose home team had been having a bad season and couldn't attract a crowd. Most of the pilgrims in the mosque tended to be of the bootless variety: peasants and soldiers and even greengrocery truckers who were using the mosque as a free hotel, snoozing in small knots near the outer walls. It had already taken on the lingering odor of socks and sweaty feet exposed to the air when removed from shoes: mosque-musk, I call it. I was starting to understand why Afshin had pulled out a steering-wheel lock for his car after we pulled into the parking lot. Even in this holy precinct, there were plenty of thieves. . . .

In the center of the mosque a couple dozen believers, mainly women, were saying their prayers at the eastern side of the crypt—thus keeping Khomeini between themselves and the Holy City of Mecca—while another score were circumambulating the tomb and kissing the grill work in different places. I pushed a small donation through the grill, the bill fluttering down to join a small pile of others near the sarcophagus: a neon light bulb, perhaps, or maybe a small bag of two-penny nails for the roof.

From the Imam's mosque we proceeded to the real object of our pilgrimage—the *Behesht-e Zahra*, a sprawling cemetery area devoted to the memory of those fallen in the Path of God during the eight-year war between Saddam Hussein and the Imam. Actually, the *Behesht-e Zahra* was founded during the time of the Shah, leading to a famous remark by Khomeini that it was the only public work made by the Shah that was actually for the people. Typically, the people of Tehran had turned the gratuitous venom back on the Imam by noting that if true, Khomeini had greatly expanded on the theme: the majority of the graves were those belonging to the military men—either the professional soldiers who chose to stay and fight for the Islamic Republic or the masses of volunteers—some only thirteen years old—who made up the famous human waves that washed into Saddam's defensive positions to be mowed down, row after row. Additionally, there were tombstones dating to the anti-Shah street protests of 1978 and 1979, the graves of political leaders assassinated by the *Mujahideen-i Khalq* after the establishment of the Islamic Republic as well as a couple of hundred graves of nameless Kurds gassed by Saddam Hussein at Halabja, in northern Iraq, in 1988. There was also a pathetic section of unmarked and desecrated graves of the Mujahideen, whose bodies were allowed in the cemetery but whose memory had been effaced.

But it was the war martyrs' graves that caught the eye. There were so many. The graves were marked by flagstones, where the name, age, place of death, and other pertinent information were carved, along with a pious epithet or verse from the Quran. Above this stood curious, box-like edifices made of glass and aluminum that usually contained a picture of the dead man (or woman) plus personal mementos—flowers, beads, a miniature

Quran, a picture of the Imam or a lesser imam (frequently posing with the deceased in pictures strangely reminiscent of Santa Claus with a child at a department store). Most of the tombstone display cases came in two or three standard sizes, and were clearly state issues—like the flags that fluttered above them. Those graves dating to 1981 or 1982 had more variety, presumably because the death-edifice industry was not ready to serve them. There were so very many. Here and there, family members and friends gathered to remember the fallen. They washed the flagstones with bottles of rosewater, swishing the crusted dust out of the stone; sometimes they sprinkled grains or placed fruit and vegetables on the stones, or made small, silent picnics with those who were no longer there. There were so very, very many.

* * *

It was getting on toward noon and the commencement of the second part of our mourning: the annual march of local Armenians marking the Day of Remembrance of the Armenian Genocide, April 24, 1915. When we arrived near the main Armenian church, there were already ten thousand marchers wending their way through downtown Tehran, shouting well-rehearsed chants called out by parade marshals from portable megaphones.

Not surprisingly, most were variations on the theme of 'Down with Fascist Turkey!' But there were several other banners and chants of note— like 'Death To America!' and 'When Palestine Is, There Will Be No Israel!' It was not clear whether the Armenians had been instructed to carry such banners as a condition for holding their march, or whether they had felt that they should, as a gesture of friendship and loyalty to the regime. Whatever the case, it left Farzin and Afshin seething.

"It is not the marching—let them march!—it is the hypocrisy that makes me mad," Farzin hissed. "The Armenians in Los Angeles are probably carrying anti-Iran banners along with their American flags and the Armenians in Israel are chanting 'Down with the PLO.' "

Farzin and Afshin were not alone in their anger. The night before, after dropping me at the hotel, Farzin had run into a number of his ethnic kinsmen who were busy ripping down the posters announcing the march. After establishing his ethnic bonafides, Farzin asked them what they were up to. The group of youths described themselves as part of a quasi-underground Azeri culture club that had decided to go beyond reading poetry and take some action. They had asked for permission to hold a rally in commemoration of the victims of Xodjali but had been denied; now, they were doing the only thing in their power to balance the pro-Armenian bias of their government. Now one of them had found us in front of the United Nations building on Argentina Square, where the march and rally had ended. We ducked into a nearby Pizza Hut for a bite to eat and began to chat.

"They have a right to march, but so do we," said Burhan, the young man from the Azeri Culture Club. "Let them march about April 24, 1915, but we also have the right to march about the massacre in Xodjali of February 26th. We are second-class citizens here. We have not only been deprived of our cultural identity as Turks, but do not even enjoy the same rights as these Christians who are killing our brothers in Karabakh." If the government didn't wake up, he said, the next action planned by the group was to turn in Armenian moonshine makers. The suspicion was that the profits from the illegal manufacture and sale of booze were being funneled to the Armenians of Karabakh to buy guns. The plan was for the Azeris to take control over the alcohol trade themselves and send the profits to their brethren. When I inquired about the propriety of making alcohol in the Islamic Republic for good Muslims like the Azeris, Burhan merely laughed: the decision by the mullahs to deny them the right to march was the last straw. The mullahs had proven themselves traitors to Islam by siding with the Christians, and they were not to be listened to anymore.

"I wouldn't have believed it a year ago," said Farzin, shaking his head. "The mullahs are so dumb—and it is all because of Karabakh. It is going to rip this country apart."

* * *

I devoted the next day to officialdom—namely, a chat with the young official in the Foreign Ministry whom I had first met at Post 19 outside of Agdam—Hakbin.

He was very glad to see me and I think the reason was that Hakbin knew that I knew that he was a very brave man. A dapper man in his early or mid-30s, he deported himself with an almost haughty, holier-than-thou attitude that was at the same time neither aggressive nor unfriendly. He spoke an incredibly slow, precise, and considered English, but was capable of chuckling at the occasional joke. He had studied mathematics and computer science in London, but had abandoned his studies to return to Iran and volunteer for duty on the Iraqi front. He was, in a sense, exactly the sort of representative of the Islamic Republic you always wanted to buttonhole at a cocktail party but never could because the Iranians do not attend cocktail parties. But there I was in his office, less a journalist than a guest and 'brother from the front.'

Ineluctably, the conversation turned toward a discussion of the much-touted Turkish/Iranian 'rivalry' for the hearts and minds of the Turkic-speaking 'Muslim' states of the former USSR. My host denied any rivalry existed, because Iran wasn't playing the same game as Turkey. If there was any race, it should be compared to the story of the tortoise and the hare. The Turks were investing all sorts of money in television, the press, and high-profile visits in an effort to dominate the new republics, Hakbin said. But this was a short-term policy that would explode in their faces when the local cultures decided to define their own place in the sun. The Turks were likely to lose a lot of money—and respect—when that happened. Iran's policy, in contrast, was one based on regional stability and allowing the new republics to make up their own minds about where their interests and identities lay. There was no competition in this, it wasn't a zero-sum game: Iran had things to offer and Turkey had things to offer; so did Pakistan, and even Afghanistan, once it recovered from its decade-long civil war. Let the Azeris and the Central Asians come and take a look and decide for themselves what they wanted to take from Iran's material, moral, and political culture, Hakbin said. Iran wasn't beating people over the head with this ideology or that. What you see is what you get.

Hakbin said that he had already seen the positive development of this policy among (northern) Azeris who had visited Tehran. He said his government explained to them the difference between Iran's incrementalist, what-you-see-is-what-you-get policy and the grand promises of eternal friendship and fraternity between the Turkic peoples, now being made in Ankara. The Azeri guests had walked away wary of Turkey's intentions and convinced of Tehran's good deeds. The soft-spread of influence was also happening on a very human level due to a new border regime that allowed families split by the frontier to visit the other side with minimal control. There had been more than 300 marriages this year between Azeris from north and south, said Hakbin. Do you see the same human relationships between the Turks and the Muslims of Azerbaijan?

All in all, it was pretty clear that Hakbin assumed that the tortoise was winning the race already; in the instance of the mixed marriages, it was also pretty clear that he believed that the 'Iranian' component would prevail over the 'Azeri' component. My impression, in contrast, was that such unions meant an incremental 'infection' of Azeriness into Iran: in the south, Iranian/Islamic consciousness was at a nadir, while in the north, Azeri/Turkish national consciousness was at a zenith because of the crisis over Karabakh.

And the vehicle for this reverse cultural penetration was language—Azeri 'Turkish.' Turkey, of course, was capitalizing on the idea that modern Turkish is close enough to make an impact on the average Turkic speaker of the new republics of Central Asia, although I had to agree with my host that Ankara's famous media blitz of the region might backfire due to local resentment over the level of sheer arrogance involved in Ankara dictating what is and what is not standard 'Turkic.' But Iran literally had its tongue tied. Persian was about as useful in Central Asia and Azerbaijan as Latin is in London: people might respect you for your cultural and intellectual acumen, but it didn't help much when you wanted to order fish and chips or belly-up to a bar, as it were.

But Iran did have its own Turkic language card to play—and with potentially far more resonance in Central Asia and Azerbaijan than Anatolian Turkish. This was, of course 'Turki,' or more specifically, 'southern' Azeri. Not only was it almost identical to the Azeri spoken in Baku, but because of substantial Persian accretions, 'southern' Azeri also was much closer to the Central Asian Turkic tongues, which were thoroughly permeated with Persian phrases and constructions. Tehran was still reluctant to play the Azeri card because of domestic political considerations: while tolerant of Azeri as a 'folk' language—there were a few newspapers and the odd collection of poems printed in Azeri—Tehran was not ready to promote the tongue to the level of a proper language to be studied in schools and used for broadcasting, lest it become a vehicle for separatist tendencies. It was, I thought, a familiar nationalist paranoia, similar to that in Turkey about the Kurds: in both instances, the groups in question were not and could not be regarded as a 'minority,' because they were such an essential part of the state. But while tempting, the comparison did not hold up well in the light of day. The Iranian ambassador to Baku, for example, was an 'ethnic' Azeri; so were most of the staff. Tehran had no problem with them conducting official business in Azeri and not Persian. In the Turkish foreign service, an 'ethnic' Kurd might get some mileage out of dropping hints about his background in liberal, western European countries, but would be professionally lynched if he were to go around speaking Kurdish in Ankara. It was almost a scandal when Turgut Özal implied that he, too, might have 'some Kurdish blood.' In Iran, however, the situation was quite different. Hakbin detailed the identities of other prominent Azeris: President Khameni was an Azeri; so was Hakbin's boss.

"Dr. Velayati?" I asked.

"No," smiled Hakbin. "My wife."

Finally, we touched on the war over Mountainous Karabakh and Iran's mediation efforts.

"That's no war," he chuckled. "You have no idea what war is."

I had forgotten: Hakbin was a veteran of the Iran-Iraq bloodbath, one of those nameless young men who wore the martyr's black band as they charged at Iraqi positions. But for the grace of Allah, he might have been lying in the *Behesht-e Zahra* with the others I had visited the day before.

"Excuse me," Hakbin said suddenly, springing to his feet. "We were so wrapped up in talk that I forgot my prayers!"

He rushed down the hall to wash his feet and returned with his shoes removed. Then he reached for the classified advertising section of a local newspaper, and taking advantage of an arrow painted on the ceiling to mark a *qibla*, he pointed the Used Cars and Household Goods section of the paper toward Mecca.

"I have found a new use for these," he said with a wry grin, as he readied to make his first *riqah*, or prostration. "Most people just throw them away."

* * *

My real destination was Iranian Azerbaijan—the extreme northwest of the country, bordered by Armenia and Azerbaijan in the north and Turkey in the west. The plan was to go to Tabriz, but there was another important stop along the way: Ardabil, the hometown of Shah Ismael, the founder of the Safavid dynasty, who made Shi'ism the state religion of Iran.

With a few notable exceptions, it was mainly the non-Arab converts to Islam who embraced the doctrine of Shi'ism. In addition to the poor and dispossessed, it was also a favorite cult of the freebooters and marchland warriors of the medieval Muslim age—i.e., the Turkic tribes of the Iranian and Anatolian plateau, so recently converted from shamanic beliefs. And it was here that Shah Ismael, writing under the pen name of Shah Khatai, got his start, composing campfire songs in Azeri Turkic that focused on rhythmic reminders of the names of the imams and the imagery of martyrdom and its counterpart, heroism.

> *Sanma daim yürüya düshmani*
> *Bir gün olur növbet ona da gala*
> *Bashindadir altun taji*
> *Budur erenler me'raci*
> *Kiskindir yolun qilichi*
> *Qalsin könül, yol qalmasin!*

> (Do not think of the enemy ever-advancing
> One day his turn, too, shall come
> Golden crown upon his head
> This is the heroes' path to heaven
> The road is steep
> Take heart! And let the journey continue.)

The deciding and defining moment for 'modern' Shi'ism (and thus, Iran) came when Ismael began importing Shi'ite clerics from the Yemen to solidify that brand of Islam in the realms over which he held sway—and possibly to expand those realms westward. This was a direct challenge to the Ottoman Sultan Yavuz Selim ('The Grim'), who feared losing the vast tracts of eastern Anatolia to Ismael and his Shi'ite/Ja'afari heresy. The Ottomans and the Safavids were soon on a collision course over who and what the pre-eminent power in the medieval Muslim world would be: a Shi'ite Turkic dynasty with pretensions of reviving glories of ancient Iran, or a Sunni Turkic dynasty ensconced in the New Rome. One might regard the decades of war that followed as a replay of the ancient enmity between Alexander and the Achamenians, Rome and Parthia, or Byzantium and the Sassanids—or maybe most simply, between East and West; a conflict in which the sectarian Shi'ite-Sunni factor was but a new permutation on a very ancient theme.

And here I was, at the font—the unprepossessing agricultural city of Ardabil, Ismael's hometown and final resting place. As soon as I arrived, I asked to be brought to the mosque and burial complex where Ismael, his family, and the leading cleric of the day, Sheikh Safi (whence the name of the dynasty, the Safavids) were entombed beneath a wealth of blue tile and a honeycomb ceiling of painted, if peeling, wood. Curiously, the tomb complex seemed more a neglected, provincial museum than a living, throbbing place of pilgrimage—although I gather that Ardabil is quite lively during the first ten days of the month of *Muharram*, when pious Shi'ite Muslims beat their breasts and whip themselves in remembrance of the martyrdom of Imam Hussein.

* * *

It was snowing the morning I left Ardabil by bus, and the date was April 30th. The ride westward was uneventful—a long, tedious crawl across the high plains that stretch from the Caspian Sea to the Aegean—a landscape identical to that in eastern Anatolia: cold, treeless steppe.

We passed through shabby villages with no names—or villages that were at least so indistinguishable from one another that they could have been the same place, passed twice. Muddy lanes and adobe-brick houses, clustered around the remnants of some half-destroyed Islamic monument or other—the sort of places that fill you with indifference until you are about 2,000 miles away and you read about the place in someone else's book, and then want to get back, but can't. Finally, we gained the main East-West, Trans-European-Asian highway, and turned north and there, in the distance, was Tabriz.

Tabriz has been a great trading city since (as they say) the dawn of time—and certainly since the time of the tenth-century Seljuk Empire. More to the point, the city's vast, vaulted market is one of the few traditional Middle East markets that has been left unsullied by tourist kitsch and unimproved by undue decoration and reconstruction.

A web of small and large commercial establishments fed by dozens of warehouses that are in turn fed by hundreds of tiny workshops on the furthest fringes, the Tabriz bazaar preserved all the elements of the 'oriental' market place in a lovely, organic whole. . . . Here was the winding, ventilated vaulted lane where some 100 shops were devoted to the sale of milk products—cottage cream, cheese, yogurt—with additional shops selling related items like raisins and honey to break up the monotony. There was another lane, where another 40 or 50 shops dealt only in dry grocery goods, like 10 different types of rice and grains and 20 different dried legumes and nuts and flours. There was, of course, a vast butcher's section where, in addition to the usual chops and cuts of raw animal, dozens of specialized shops answered the need of connoisseurs of goat's eyeball, steer's lymph gland, and young ram testicle. And that was just the edible part of the market, making up less than 25 percent of the fabulous whole. There was the tin pot alley and the plastic shoe street and the textile lane, all structurally identical but functionally quite different. You could find any product at any stage of development. Shoes? For the finished item, take the first right hand turn from the heart of the market, stoop through the small door into the vaulted lane, and take your pick of half a mile of almost identical stands boasting almost identical wares. What about wholesale? Just keep on moving down the line, toward the edge of the bazaar, where the shops got bigger and the lights got dimmer and where, as opposed to a hundred different types of shoes on display, the counters only carried three. You need it more basic than that, like soles or heels or the leather uppers themselves? Leave the vaulted part of the bazaar and cross the street into the labyrinth of narrow lanes and cul-de-sacs beside it, and find yourself within the supplier side of the local shoe trade; beyond that (or often mixed in among the wholesale heel and sole shops) were the cottage industry stands where the products were glued and hammered together before your eyes. There was a beauty in the intricate web of relationships—especially after suffering through a command economy in collapse in the former Soviet Union.

* * *

That night, I went and blew my head off with three bowls of Shirazi tobacco in a hubbly-bubbly pipe. I had not smoked a waterpipe in a long time, and with very good reason: the anticipation of exactly the kind of headache that such hyperventilation uniquely produces. But there was no getting out of it. At the bazaar's closing time, I spotted a row of men honking on their *hookahs*, took a picture, and then was commanded to sit down to take a pipe. The first was obligatory; the second was not. And by the time the attendant came around a third time, I was just smoking and changing table partners and making new pals.

My fellow smokers were regulars at the shop and came from a number of different niches of Tabriz society. One worked in the retail end of the huge shoemaker section of the bazaar and had seen me prowling around there earlier in the day. Another was a driver. A third was a chicken salesman. Nearby were a couple of students who were studying a text written in Cyrillic, trying to enunciate the words with the hookah mouthpiece clamped between their teeth. When I inquired about the text they were working on, I discovered that it was the epic *Dede Korkut* ('Grandfather Korkut's Story'), the 'Beowulf' of the Turkic world. They wanted to study medicine in Baku and assumed that (northern) Azeri would be the language of instruction, and were boning up on Cyrillic through a familiar medium.

The lads asked what they might bring as gifts. I began with a short list that grew into a long list: bananas, cinnamon, office stuff (tape, paper clips, tacks), coffee, butter, shoes that fit, switch blade knives, material to make suits, linen shirts, pistachios, even packs of condoms replete with the picture of the prophet Muhammad to give religious sanction to birth control. Then I decided to reduce the list to one easy item that would be sure to make lifelong friends: the five-kilogram cones of sugar known as *kaant* in Azeri. I tried to explain to my unbelieving listeners that you couldn't get sugar in Azerbaijan, not even the powdered stuff. Your cousins chew bad candy with their tea, I said. They wouldn't, couldn't believe me.

Finally, hours later, head spinning and lungs aching, I finally managed to break free and returned to the hotel. I would need all of my wits about me on the morrow, but from the feeling in my head, I had none left. The need for my wits was pretty straightforward: it would be Friday, the Muslim Sabbath, and I had decided to become a fake Muslim and attend prayers in the city's main mosque, to try and gauge religious sentiment where it should be strongest.

* * *

The walls around Tabriz's *Jumaa Mesjid*, or Friday Mosque, were festooned with the usual portraits of the Ayatullah and the usual, pious graffiti and obligatory anti-American banners. Nothing odd about that. What was strange was that it was guarded by men with automatic rifles. After identifying myself as a Turk from Azerbaijan by means of an ID written in Cyrillic, I was subjected to a quick frisk before being asked to walk through a metal detector. Pretty heavy security for a mosque, I thought.

The mosque was not prepossessing. In fact, it was little more than a huge, covered parking lot with *minbar* and *qibla* tacked on as an afterthought. Structurally, the only part of interest was a huge, imposing wall made of baked brick located just outside the area of prayer. The roof and the other three walls were missing, and apparently had been missing for some time—like a few centuries. Who built it? I asked one of the Revolutionary guards accompanying me on my tour. Shah Abbas, came the reply—conforming with the cliché that any structure of unknown provenance in Iran was built by that ruler.

Returning to the gallery, I learned that I was an hour early for prayers. In addition to having to wait in the cold, I was marginally unnerved by this news because it suggested that I didn't know when the pious prayed. I remarked that I had come early because of the time difference between Turkey and Iran.

"Yes, brother," said some religious character. "Two brothers from Turkey have made the same error. Here they come now."

Oh-oh, I said to myself: Exposure as a fake Turk and fake Muslim. They do nasty things to people for playing with the Truth, like kill them on charges like 'apostasy.'

Quickly and imperfectly changing from Azeri to Turkish, I hailed the two well met and entered into a burst of non-informational fog about myself, stressing the fact that I was living in Baku and working as a writer and strongly and repeatedly alluding to the fact that it was my wife who was the Turk and that I was a mere, imperfect, and recent devotee of obscure heritage. The point was to keep talking and get them and myself out of the mosque and beyond the reach of the revolutionary guards manning the metal detector before any real slip happened. I succeeded, and once on the street, I suggested that we have tea somewhere before the prayers.

The pair, a little confused about the sudden friendliness from a stranger, agreed. And as we walked along, our conversation turned toward the 'homeland,' Turkey. Where were our (royal we) religious and linguistic brothers from in the Republic? The pious pair announced that they were from the eastern Turkish town of Malatya. I breathed a deep sigh of relief. *They were Kurds*, and the room for duplicity had just been expanded by a factor of five. Immediately, I found myself slipping back into the Azeri of the North, a dialect that would confuse and amaze the pair of cautious

Kurdish Turks (or Turkish Kurds) and allow me all the leeway I could possibly want.

We arrived at the tea shop where I had blown out my lungs the night before and were joined by four men.

"Hello," they asked. "Are you guys from Turkey?" One Kurd muttered 'yes.' This was true enough geographically speaking, but given their background, the pair were very suddenly on the slippery slope of traveling incognito—just like me. The second, looking at his watch, suggested we return to the mosque.

The four Azeris nearly cackled.

"Are you kidding?" they said. "You're going there to listen to those boneheads?"

"Aren't you a Muslim?" asked one of the Kurds.

"No, no," said one of the quartet, "at least not your kind of Muslim. If I pray, I pray at home, but I don't even do that."

"Never in a mosque," said a guy with a proud mustache. "The mullahs wouldn't let me if I wanted to. . . ."

"Why not?" asked the first Kurd, disturbed.

"See this?" asked the Azeri, pointing to the full *Schnurrbart* covering his upper lip. "This means that I don't want anything to do with them."

"Why don't you cut it in accordance with the Ways of the Prophet?" asked the second Kurd, referring to the *Hadith* that suggests that believers trim their facial hair in the way that the two Kurds trimmed theirs.

"I want to show the rag heads that I want nothing to do with them," came the response, and all the Azeris chuckled.

"Look around! You'll see that most of the people in town feel the same way. You should have been here during the Shah's time. Things were good then, cheap. . . . Those were the days. . . ."

The Kurds looked at each other and bit their lips. But not the four Azeris. They wanted to talk about the Black Sea city of Trabzon, and the delicious babes there. It was embarrassing. The Azeris wanted to learn about the fun spots of Turkey and the Kurds of Turkey wouldn't tell them where to find them, and the Kurds wanted the Azeris to go pray with them and they only laughed at the idea. Visibly disturbed at finding such sin in the land of Islam, the Kurds finally turned away. I walked with them toward the Friday Mosque, but left them with some lame excuse at the door, reluctant to follow them inside. Far more people were walking away from the mosque than approaching it and even those who seemed to be moving in the direction of the mosque were not entering. Why then, I asked myself, should I attend? Maybe if the mosque had been beautiful or even enclosed or had just provided me with a wall to rest against, I might have gone in again. But the Tabriz Friday mosque was a covered parking lot with all the aesthetics one associates with parking lots, and there were no walls to rest against, and the people were not even going themselves.

* * *

My last stop in Iranian Azerbaijan was Torkoman (Turkmanchay), the place where the Russians dictated the peace of 1828 to the crumbling Qadjar dynasty of Iran, splitting the amorphous thing known as Azerbaijan in two. Not stopping in Turkmanchay, for a budding Azeri-specialist, would be rather like a Civil War buff not visiting Gettysburg.

Sprawling down the slope of a hill, with sturdy houses set up every which way, Turkmanchay was not a pretty or quaint town but I did not expect it to be so. Save for a main, rutted and muddy road that dissolved into a footpath about halfway through the town, there were no streets. Downtown consisted of a couple of dry-goods stores that seemed fairly well stocked, two camera shops and a tea house that had a minor interest in collecting or selling carpets. There was also a sort of fast-food stand near the tea house; when we stopped in to chat, a sausage sandwich with all the condiments magically appeared for both the driver and myself. Judging from a conversation with one of the lads in the tea house, the place had just been incorporated as a dsitrict seat: for the first time, Turkmanchay was to have its own representative in the national parliament, and was plastered with election posters, as well as a good number of other posters advocating a national literacy campaign. It was also a friendly place, and rather than it being difficult finding informants, they found me.

'Rus! Rus!' chanted a third of the 100 kids who instantly gathered around, the moment I got out of the car, assuming I was Russian. 'Turk! Turk!' another third cried, contesting the judgment of their peers, suggesting I was from Turkey. The other third decided I was from Shu'awiyah ('Communism'), which could mean that I was Russian or Azeri or Bulgarian.

I inquired about the Treaty of 1828, and someone remembered that there was something related to that event in the morgue, which was attached to the local mosque. After negotiating a series of very muddy lanes, with the attendant crowd growing with every step, we arrived at the mosque to meet even more people. Word had spread that a foreigner of some sort had descended on Turkmanchay (the first time since 1828?), and everybody wanted to get in on the act. The imam cut short his prayers, produced a large ring of keys and led me and a group of attendants into the morgue to see The Historic Remains.

Happily, the morgue was not a cold-storage holding tank for corpses but a kind of junk space between the back wall of the mosque and the back wall of an almost adjacent house. It was here that the imam stored his burial biers when not in use. The junk space was also cluttered with other debris of the usual, uninteresting variety: broken chairs, tables and shattered bottles. But in the middle of the heap were The Remains—an old weathered stone about the size and shape of a mountain goat, replete with head and horns.

"See!" crowed my guides. "See!"

It was pretty clear to me that they didn't know what they were looking at, even if I did: The Remains were nothing more nor less than an ancient *Akkoyun* funerary stele, the carved rock anthropomorphisms that one associates with the medieval Turkic tribe known as the White Sheep. It had nothing to do with the Persian-Russian peace treaty whatsoever and I had to wonder just how much history my interlocutors had been exposed to in school. The inscription on the tombstone was almost totally effaced, so I asked for a bucket of water to splash on it in the hope of increasing the contrast and being able to read something off it. In vain.

"Why do you keep the thing here?" I asked the imam. He said he was afraid that if he put it in front of the mosque, the authorities might take it away to a museum or locals might destroy it. There had been another stone stele just like it, but local youths (and here the imam swung his suspicious eyes around the crowd of youths surrounding me) had believed it filled with gold, and smashed it open one night.

"There's gold in that one, too," said a youth.

"Was there any in the first?" I asked the kid.

"No," he replied. "It was solid rock."

"So is this," I pronounced with finality, possibly having preserved the tombstone for another generation.

The discussion about the merits of my theory went back and forth for awhile, until I announced that I had had enough of hanging around the claustrophobic mosque morgue-cum-junk yard. I asked if anybody knew about other remnants or physical hints of past, especially those connected with 1828.

"Well," said someone. "There is the Russian girl."

"Take me to her," I said, not knowing what this could mean.

We flooded out of the mosque on to the muddy lane that served as the street, and scarcely had we turned the corner than we ran into a most peculiar sight: the Russian girl. Lady, really. Grandma, if truth be told.

She was at least 60 years of age and withered as a prune. But she wore no *hijab* or *manto*, and by her white hair and piercing blue eyes I knew that in her youth she was probably a looker, and a blonde one at that.

"*Kak dela?*" I asked in Russian. "How are things?"

"*Otlichno,*" she replied, "fine." It was as if having a chat *po russkii* in the middle of a crowd of fifty Azeris in Turkmanchay was an everyday occurrence. I apologized for my less than perfect Russian, and suggested we turn to Azeri, but her mind was in Russian-lock and she would speak no other language with me.

"Are you from Moscow?" she asked.

"No, from Baku—or actually, Montana," I replied.

"How nice," she responded.

"Well," I asked. "Where are you from?"

"Moscow."

"Well," I continued, "when did you get here?"

"Oh, in the 1930s sometime," she replied. "My father, Vasili, was a *kulak*, a rich peasant you know, and Stalin had it in for him, so he came here. One of my sisters got to Texas, and I don't know where she is and a brother died in the USSR. You know anybody in Texas?"

"A few people," I said.

"Well, if you see Jena, tell her hello."

"Sure, I will," I decided to humor her. "And who shall I say the regards come from?"

"Maryam Pakomova Gorbachova, née Marusa," she said, wife of Rahmatullah Yakubzade, and mother of five kids: one daughter in Canada, one in Mashhad; one son in Turkmanchay, another boy in Isfahan and a third in Shiraz. But I was still stuck on the name.

"*Gorbacheva?*" I asked. "Any relation to Mikhail?"

"Of course," answered the Russian girl. "We are cousins. My father and his father are brothers, or were before they died. . . ."

Gorby's cousin camped in Turkmanchay? Stranger than fiction, if true!

I wanted to pursue the matter further, but there was a veritable swarm of well-meaning people trying to direct my attention to this or that Historic Remnant in town or across the valley. Too many, in fact. So I fought my way through the crowd to the tea shop. Once again, it was a friendly crowd, although a little more controlled and less unruly than in the muddy streets.

"What do you guys do around here?" I asked. Agriculture, most said. Is it all right out there on the farm? Not bad, not bad, came the replies. There were the standard complaints that one hears from farmers all over the world but on the whole the coffeehouse crowd seemed content. They had their own land, they stressed again and again (the assumption being that I, hailing from *Shu'awiyah*, or "Land of Communismness" was ignorant of such things) and got to grow what they wanted and could sell that wherever they wanted for whatever price the market would bear. But usually, they just sold their crop to the middlemen from Tabriz, who screwed them. Familiar farmer talk.

Then I had an idea.

"Excuse me guys," I said. "I have a question."

"Shoot," they said, gathering around the table.

"Who are you?"

Huh? came the collective reply.

"I mean, how do you define yourselves to yourselves?"

Still confused looks.

"Let me give you a couple of categories," I said. "If you rate yourself, how would you? First Azeri? Turk? Muslim? Iranian?"

I know that my sociological study left much to be desired, especially the very casual method of surveying—but a crush of replies came rolling forth.

"Azeri Turk," said the first. "Turk," said the second. "Muslim," said the third. "Human being," one clever character quipped, and chuckled. "Muslim," "Turk," "Muslim Turk," "Azeri," "Azeri Turk," the remainder replied. Not one of them had said "Iranian," and I asked why.

"Iran," spat one farmer. "Iran is for the mullahs, and we don't want anything to do with those thieves anymore."

* * *

I left Tabriz in the early morning and traveled west toward the Turkish town of Dogubeyazit. It was cold and over certain stretches it snowed. Then it cleared and we drove through Maku and Bazergan between fine vistas of treeless steppe and distant mountains. Kurdish kids—for this area of both Turkey and Iran is populated by Kurds—hung around the edges of the road, selling cheap Iranian petrol and oil. I remembered other times when I had been on the Turkish side of the frontier, looking into Iran from across the Turkish half of the jointly controlled building, when the idea of walking across the line seemed dangerous or impossible. Now, stepping through the joint customs house on the frontier, I knew that such notions were totally foolish. The Turkish officials hadn't stamped Yankee papers in a while and asked how I liked Iran.

"Just fine," I said, and with no irony.

In the old days, Dogubeyazit was the very end of the world. But now, it seemed a connecting link to somewhere again—Iran. And there had been a lot of changes since the last time I had been there. There were automatic telephones. There was even credit card banking. I drew a bunch of badly needed dollars on VISA from a local bank. After a pit stop in the bar of the Ararat Hotel, I worked my way around Mount Ararat to the town of Igdir on the north slope, and the as yet officially open border at Sadarak, into Naxjivan.

I slept between clean sheets that I knew I would not find the next day, and went shopping for things like bananas, lamp chops, red lentils, cracked wheat, and long-grained rice and other exotic foods you can't get in Azerbaijan.

"You will be the first foreigner to cross the bridge, if it is still there in the morning," said a customs officer I met in my hotel bar that night. I asked him what he meant by the remark. He said something about the war between Armenia and Naxjivan. No, I corrected him, he meant the war over Karabakh. No, he insisted, he meant Naxjivan. There had been fighting not five kilometers from the bridge.

Great. Turkey had just re-signed the 1921 Treaty of Kars with Heydar Aliyev that supposedly gave Ankara the 'right of intervention' if Naxjivan were under threat. That meant war, and theoretically, not just between Turkey and Armenia but between Turkey and Armenia's ally, Russia. It was almost too crazy to consider. But when I got to the bridge, there were plumes of smoke rising on the far side, and I could hear the distant burp of artillery fire, although it was not clear who was shooting at what.

Welcome home.

11

Riding the Roller Coaster

The Shahrur hospital stunk of iodine, fresh blood, and urine. Doctors and nurses hauled patients into surgery rooms and removed shrapnel with a cool professionalism and efficiency that were highly impressive, given the state of the hospital and the fact that there were no anesthetics. I watched as one physician scraped a disinfected Q-tip along a half-inch crease traversing the top of a young man's head, cleaning out the filth that follows hot lead. He was going to have a scar, but he was a fortunate lad: another half-inch lower, and the bullet would have torn his cranium apart.

The doctor reported that there were four dead that day, including one fellow-doctor shot by a sniper as he tried to rescue a wounded soldier. Another casualty was a woman whose car had been blown up by an incoming artillery round while she was traveling to the front to look for her son. The other two deaths were combatants. There were also forty seriously wounded, soldiers and civilians. The town of Sadarak, with a population of 15,000, had been evacuated.

I went over to the mayor's office and asked him to call Heydar Aliyev. Heydar answered the phone himself. The situation was critical, but not out of hand, he said. Then he told me to get to Naxjivan city to see him right away, because he was giving a little press conference.

Heydar looked much the same as the last time I had seen him—identical, in fact. He was wearing the same dark blue suit and dark blue tie and his blue-green eyes were still steady to the point of staring. In addition to the bank of telephones and diverse paper detritus of leadership on his desk, I noticed a Quran, in Turkish. That was new, anyway. He said he had been on the line with Armenian president Levon Ter-Petrossian every day of the current crisis. He had called for an immediate cease-fire and for the creation of a commission to determine who had shot first. In the meanwhile, he had put all the armed forces in the territory under the strictest discipline. They were to hold their fire unless absolutely necessary, and he demanded that

Ter-Petrossian do the same for forces in Armenia. But Ter-Petrossian seemed to be playing games. He said he did not control the forces engaged at Sadarak. While this was a familiar argument from Yerevan about the Armenian fighters in Karabakh, the Armenian lines facing Sadarak were a mere 30 kilometers from Yerevan and the forces there were using heavy artillery. Moreover, the guns were positioned right behind a Russian border post, making it impossible for the Naxjivani forces to try and take them out lest they start shelling Russians.

Heydar said he was left with two explanations, and neither was very comforting: either Ter-Petrossian was lying and using the excuse of 'no control' to further his own larger plan, or he was telling the truth and admitting that he was not in control of his own country. Aliyev said he suspected the latter, and that the Armenians involved in the conflict were members of the Dashnaksutun Party, whose aggressive policies had often 'embarrassed' Ter-Petrossian in the past. Heydar, too, had difficulty reining in the hotheads in the local chapter of the Popular Front. He let the inference dangle that the current trouble was being made by the Russians, just to stir the ethnic pot.

"What is your message to Ankara about intervention in accordance with the Kars Agreement?" asked a Turkish correspondent in the room with us, referring to an obscure reference in the 1921 treaty between the Turkish nationalists and the Bolsheviks that supposedly allowed Turkey the right of intervention in Naxjivan if the province were attacked by a third force—that is, Armenia.

"Let Turkey fulfill its commitments," said Heydar. "Let Turkey keep its word."

While the Turkish correspondent scribbled down the quote, I sat there with my jaw dropping to my knees. Heydar had just openly asked that the Turks go up against not just the Armenians, but the Russians, since Yerevan had a defense pact with Moscow. And given Turkey's membership in NATO, that could mean World War III.

* * *

After a meal of cold meat, warm vodka, and weed salad at an eatery set in a gravel pit, I checked into the squalid, eight-story rat hole known as the Tabriz Hotel. I was remembered by one and all. Celebrity did not change the service, however, and I was happy enough that the elevator got me to within a couple of decks of my seventh-floor suite, and that the man already occupying my room was not averse to letting me crash on the couch.

In the morning, I woke to the odor of dirty socks and smelly feet. My roommate had already left. There was no water, so I brushed my teeth with vodka, spitting into the street from the balcony, lacking the courage to even open the door to the latrine. Then I grabbed my kit and walked down the seven flights of stairs to the ground floor to go over to Aliyev's office. Heydar wasn't in but had left a message for me to come over to his 'palace' for breakfast—the dumpy, three-room, third-story apartment the former Politburo member shared with his sister, brother-in-law, and three children. I went over and had breakfast with him—tea and marmalade and cheese, with fresh bread. Then the phone rang—the red one, I believe—and Heydar answered it. He was soon frothing at the mouth.

"What the hell do you mean, there's a demonstration?" he demanded. "Don't you know there are no demonstrations around here unless I say so?"

Breakfast was canceled, and we were soon racing back over to his office, where we were met by Heydar's aide-de-camp, a short, pudgy guy who just happened to be his brother-in-law.

"Mister President" (Heydar liked his titles kept straight), muttered the brother-in-law aide-de-camp, "It's the people, they want to see you. . . ."

"It's those pimps from the Popular Front, you mean."

"No sir, Mister President, it's the people of Shahrur. . . ."

"Okay, okay. . . ." said Heydar.

We went back downstairs to his official car to make the journey to Shahrur. A crowd had already gathered outside. I am not sure whether it was to show devotion and support or simply because there wasn't much else to do in Naxjivan other than hang out and watch the native-son-made-good enter and leave his office twice a day. Heydar smiled and waved at the crowd while hissing under his breath to the brother-in-law.

"Where's the car?"

"Sir, the driver. . . ."

"I asked where the car is. It's not here."

"Sir, the driver. . . ."

"I asked where the car is."

"It's not here."

"The car is not here?"

"No."

"The president's car isn't here when he needs it?"

"No, sir, the driver, he—"

"My car is not here when I want it?"

"The driver, sir, he—"

"IT'S NOT HERE?"

For a quick, fleeting moment, I had the opportunity to see the old Heydar Aliyev—Communist Party boss, KGB general, Soviet Politburo member—

better known by the Russian pronunciation of his name, *Gaidar*. He was back in Moscow, at the Kremlin, in 1982 or 1983, a place and a time when there was no waiting, ever, and everything worked, always. It was a place and time he had relished and now wanted to re-live and re-create. But he was not in Moscow. He was not even in Baku. He was here in the backwater of Naxjivan, where nothing really worked most of the time and where the driver of the president's Volga sedan, we learned, was using it as a taxi to ferry friends and relatives around because no other cars had any gas. I have never seen anyone so livid with rage. Heydar Aliyev was speechless.

"Take my car," said the Minister of the Interior, opening the door to his Volga and trying to calm the boss. Still seething, Heydar got in, and the car disappeared in a cloud of blue smoke and dust while the crowd clapped madly. Some minutes later, another car appeared—the prez-mobile, I presumed—and the Minister of the Interior of Naxjivan and I jumped in it to roar down the road after Heydar. We were really pushing it, honking combines and tractors and the odd military vehicle off the road, making the 100-kilometer journey in record time. We passed Heydar about half way. Plowing our way through the crowds gathered on the *meydan*, or city square, we pulled up in front of a makeshift podium set on the back of a flatbed truck.

"Heydar! Heydar! Heydar!" the crowd chanted. Folks were visibly disappointed to see it was just me and the Minister of the Interior. Then the second car rolled in, a smiling Aliyev emerged and the crowd went wild.

HEY-DAR! HEY-DAR! HEY-DAR! they roared.

From my position atop the truck, I watched as Heydar started moving through the crowd. The square was already packed with upwards of 5,000 people—half the town, maybe more. And Heydar was in his element, pressing the flesh, kissing babies, and generally acting like a politician on the hustings. It was the more impressive because this was actually one of those rarest of occasions: a spontaneous demonstration.

Or at least so it seemed. A gaunt young man sporting a full dark beard was standing next to me atop the flatbed truck. I had seen him somewhere before, in Baku maybe.

"How are you doing?" I queried.

The gaunt young man shot me a nasty look, as if I had discovered something I should not have, and then turned away. Then it occurred to me who he was: Nimet Panakhov, the famous 'free labor' leader and nationalist/provocateur. What was he doing here, and now? There was no time for discussion or speculation, because the next instant, Heydar Aliyev was on the podium. The crowd went wild.

Hey-DAR Hey-DAR AL-I-EV! AL-I-EV!

Heydar raised his hands for silence.

"Dear people of Shahrur," he began. "I have come because you demanded to see me!"

Hey-DAR Hey-DAR AL-I-EV! AL-I-EV!

"Dear people, I have come to see you because you demanded to see me, but I have to say that I do not know what this meeting is about or who organized this meeting."

AL-I-EV! AL-I-EV!

"I ask you to be silent! I said I do not know who organized this meeting and I do not support this meeting or any other meeting because in this time of crisis we have no time for meetings. They are unnecessary. But because you have called me here, I have come."

HEYDAR! HEYDAR AL-I-EV!

"I told you to be quiet!"

Silence.

"I have spoken with Armenian president Ter-Petrossian. . . ."

"Booo!"

"SILENCE, I SAID!"

Silence.

"I have spoken with Armenian president Ter-Petrossian, and we have agreed to find and punish whoever was responsible for violating the peace near Sadarak. If it was an Azeri formation that fired first, I will make them pay ten times! The reason for this, dear citizens of Naxjivan, is that there are those who wish to expand the war in Karabakh to include Naxjivan. We do not need this war. I say again, *we do not need this war!* And I say to you that we do not need demonstrations of this or any other sort. I beg of you, go to your homes, go to your jobs! Go home!"

"But Comrade Heydar—" came a voice from the crowd.

"DON'T INTERRUPT ME!"

Utter silence.

"But now that you're here, I have a few words to say. As you know, there are to be elections in Azerbaijan on June 7th, following the resignation of the partocrat traitor, Mutalibov. . . ."

"Boo! . . ."

"And as you know, the partocrats were so afraid of me returning to power that they changed the laws to say that I am too old to become president again."

"No! No!"

"They say I am too old!"

"NO!"

"But I am happy among my people in Naxjivan, among you I feel reborn. . . ."

"Heydar, Heydar Al-i-ev!"

"So go to your homes and remain at peace! But on the day of election, should your hearts be moved to tell the people in Baku what you think of their dirty, filthy tricks—"

"Yes! Yes!"

". . . then I give you my allowance to write my name on the ballot in protest against the filth that run the country and the disaster they have imposed on us all."

"HEYDAR HEYDAR AL-I-EV! HEYDAR HEYDAR AL-I-EV!"

Pretty slick, I thought: in ten minutes of public oration, Heydar had not only managed to defame Mutalibov and his old Communist cronies, but the Popular Front as well. And rather than play public spoilsport and declare a boycott of the elections, he was announcing a write-in campaign. And every vote cast for the old fox would be tossed in the 'invalid' category, thus working against the absolute majority needed by any candidate and opening up the possibility of parliament having to choose the next president—like himself. Heydar had just set a timebomb beneath the first free elections in Azerbaijani history. Not bad for a man who had turned seventy years old that very day. Yes indeed, I said to myself: the old boy is playing for keeps. After Shahrur, nothing—absolutely nothing—surprised me politically over the next year. And Heydar knew I knew. Thereafter, in meetings in Naxjivan, Ankara, Istanbul, and last of all, Baku, he began to exercise a unique self-discipline in contact with me: I had seen too much.

* * *

Rather than return with Heydar and his entourage to Naxjivan city, I decided to take a poke around Sadarak and the front, represented by a series of three-story administrative buildings that served as the Naxjivani Defense Forces' HQ. An ambulance was running the gauntlet to pick up a few bodies, so I got in for the ride. I was soon sorry for this decision: although flanked by trees, the road ran straight toward the main Armenian frontier command post and anything moving down it was a sitting duck in a bowling alley.

Happily, no one shot at us as we made the approach, and I was soon ensconced in the Azeri command center, located in a basement. Maps and radios were thrown helter-skelter over crates and boxes of ammunition. Then the radio started to crackle.

"It's the Russian border garrison," the commander explained, referring to the noise on the squawkbox. "They pass on Armenian movement and signal traffic to us."

The Armenians, reported the Russians, were preparing an evening barrage. *Great*, I thought. One well-placed round on the command center, and the magazine we were sitting in would blow us all to kingdom come. But nothing came. We waited and we waited, and even had a last meal—a portion of Slim-Fast noodles that someone had thoughtfully donated to some starving people somewhere else but that had ended up here. Finally, after a half-hour that seemed an eternity, I decided that I had spent enough time in the basement magazine with the boys. Emerging from the HQ, I took a quick poke around the area and then departed with the same ambulance I had come in. This time, we swerved our way down the arrow-straight road, frequently driving into the ditch to further defy anyone behind us who thought they could get a freebee shot at our rear.

We pulled into the field hospital, the place where the young doctor who had been killed the day before had worked. There were wounded and refugees and general gloom and I decided to wait for the anticipated barrage to begin. And wait and wait. After two hours I realized that I was almost disappointed that the cease-fire was holding.

War warps the mind. It also makes one almost pathologically suspicious: if the Armenians were not attacking, then why had the Russian garrison been telling the Naxjivanis that they were about to do so? It was almost an invitation to preventive interdiction—exactly the sort of thing that would have demolished the cease-fire and led to another round of war.

But the cease-fire held, and a jeep was going back to Naxjivan city and I managed to hitch a ride. With the driver, we were eight. This was good, because despite turning off the motor to coast down any sort of hill or declivity to preserve fuel, we still ran out of gas some five kilometers out of town and were obliged to push the jeep. After about a kilometer, another car stopped and gave us enough fumes to get into town.

It was night and I was tired and there was no electricity at the Tabriz Hotel, and I couldn't face the prospect of stumbling up seven flights of stairs to my abominable room of the night before, so I managed to pull a few strings and get a room at the government guesthouse. Usually, it was filled with shady Turkish 'businessmen' ripping off anything of value in Naxjivan in the name of pan-Turkic solidarity, but the rumor of war had driven most away. There was a room free and I took it. It was clean and I slept like a stone.

In the morning, I tuned in my radio to the BBC. There was some mention of Naxjivan and Armenia, Turkey's threat to intervene, Moscow's response and the implications thereof—World War III, and all that. But

following that news there was a special program on Mountainous Karabakh—the usual story of besieged Christians fighting with shotguns against
Shi'ite Muslim fanatics armed with top-of-the-line-tanks.

But wait! There was actually a news peg. The Azeris had been shelling
Stepanakert's airport and damaging the runway, the speaker related, quoting
Armenian defense sources. Stepanakert's airport? *That was Xodjali!* Then
came another piece of news that confirmed that something big was up: an
urgent meeting between Armenia and Azerbaijan had been set for the next
day, May 7th, in Tehran, to arrange a new cease-fire.

Shelling in Naxjivan? An Azeri 'attack' on Karabakh? Calls for an urgent cease-fire? You didn't have to be a seer to know what it all meant.
Another Armenian assault was imminent. And I knew where: Shusha, the
'impregnable fortress' in the heights above Stepanakert. It was the only
Azeri-held place left in Karabakh, and had been used as a base for launching GRAD missiles on neighborhoods in Stepanakert, forcing the population to live like rats in a basement and giving the Armenian military a
perfect excuse to take the place out. Living under GRAD attacks was not
much fun, and the well-oiled Armenian propaganda machine was really
able to milk this one. One article that appeared in the *New York Times*
quoted a resident who described how the citizens of Stepanakert were
obliged to sneak out at night to fill water buckets and how the Azeris would
train their GRAD missiles at the candles and flashlights used to negotiate
the way from the basement to the well and back. This was total nonsense.
Not only is the GRAD highly inaccurate, but the gunners were five kilometers away—hardly in a position to spot candles. Such details were meaning-
less at the moment, however: Shusha, I knew, was doomed.

* * *

I returned to Baku that same day aboard a dangerously overloaded Yak-40
jet carrying twice as many humans as it was supposed to, as well as lots of
luggage that clearly didn't belong on board. It was close-your-eyes and fly
time, and I was almost relieved when the pilot asked anyone who could
move among the crates and baggage cluttering the aisle to shift toward the
back so that he could lift the nose and land.

My first stop was the Turkish embassy, to tell Mehmet Ali Bayar about
what I had seen in Naxjivan and warn him to take anything Aliyev said with
a grain of salt. It was my own little gesture aimed at preventing World War
III. Then I went home to discover that my phone had been cut all the time I
had been away. I ran down to the communications ministry to demand that
the line be restored so I could function as a journalist and tell the world the

unadulterated truth, et cetera. It was starting to get old, but the deputy minister was obliging and promised to re-open the line.

Almost incidentally, I asked whether he had heard anything from Shusha. The man stared at me. The telephone and radio link had gone dead earlier in the day but the ministry had picked up some radio traffic from the area, he said. It was all in Armenian. Then he shuddered and broke down.

Fortress Shusha had fallen, and almost without a fight.

* * *

Unlike the three-day silence at the fall of Xodjali, however, the fact that Shusha was gone was known throughout the country by nightfall. In addition to the 'official' accounts of the disaster, the rumor mill was churning out incredible stories. Fifth-columnists had doped the defenders before the fight and snipped detonation cables in minefields; most of the soldiers defending it were pulled out right before the Armenian militiamen began their long-expected assault; the defending armored vehicle's gas tanks had been tainted by water; there were still Armenians living secretly in the town, passing signals . . . All of this was reduced to an increasingly common phrase: like Xodjali before it, Shusha had been 'sold' for political gain.

The first public salvo was delivered by Acting President Yaqub ('Dollar') Mamedov, who called Defense Minister Rahim Gaziev a traitor. Not only had his army been unable to defend Shusha, Mamedov noted, but suspiciously like the Mutalibov government at the time of Xodjali, the Defense Ministry initially had denied that the city had fallen. This was not so, said Mamedov. With a heavy heart, he was obliged to relay the unspeakable truth: Shusha had been infested on Friday, the 7th of May. Casualties were high and the disaster complete. Beyond complete! 'Dollar' Mamedov did not want to point fingers, but the fact remained that Rahim Gaziev had been lying to him personally and lying to the nation collectively about the status of the town for three long days. Mamedov had repeatedly tried to contact the defense minister to get an expert assessment of the situation to distinguish between rumor and fact—but in vain. The last thing he heard was that Gaziev had gone to Moscow. . . .

This was an amazing suggestion. The defense minister, Rahim Gaziev, member of the Popular Front and the Lion of Shusha, accused of being a stooge of the Russians? It was so incredible that it almost seemed true. The program ran twice that night.

Gaziev replied the next night with his own televised announcement. He was not in Moscow, but with the men on the front who were fighting for the country—unlike other cowards in the Defense Ministry and in the presidential apparatus whom he could name. He would soon return to the capital to sort out exactly who had 'sold out' Shusha. He ended his interview with a vow not only to retake the fallen city but to root out the 'traitors in Baku' who had sullied his name. The roller coaster ride had begun, with Mamedov and Gaziev as the proxy players and the television studio the proxy venue.

Across the street at the Supreme Soviet, meanwhile, the pro-Iranian 'Repentance Society' had defied the ban on protest demonstrations and set up a tent and soup kitchens on the steps of the parliament, and were shouting *Allah ul-Akbar!* (God is Great!) on the hour, every hour, in order to restore the nation to the Islamic faith of its forefathers, and incidentally, President Mutalibov to his rightful place in power. When not chanting, the Repenters occupied themselves with threatening anyone who walked in or out of the parliament building, demanding that Acting President Yaqub Mamedov reconvene the full parliament and dissolve the National Council.

But if the steps of parliament were the loudest venue for remonstration and protest, the most sentient site was right across the street at the *Shehidler Xiyabani*. Here, grim-faced, bearded friends of those fallen at Shusha were paying final tribute to their comrades in arms and asking themselves why the war was going so badly. In addition to the pro-forma honor guard whose task it was to let off a volley of blanks after bodies were laid in graves, the veterans would let off multiple rounds of their own weapons, simulating the fusillade of enemy fire that had killed their comrades. One such emotional burial was that of Albert Marum, a Baku Jew whose feats of bravery as a volunteer fighter in Shusha made him one of the most popular soldiers in the theater. His funeral, attended by hundreds of soldiers and friends, was an odd mixture of Shi'ite Muslim *Taziyeh* and Sephardic Jewish *Kaddish*. The rattle of live fire released from the weapons of those present sent casual observers scurrying for cover. Many thought the long-expected civil war had just broken out. It had not, but it was clearly only a matter of time. Skirmishes in the side streets already could be heard over the weekend of May 8 and 9: the late-night rattle of small arms fire and the thump of grenades in a distant alley.

* * *

Parliament reconvened on May 14th, on the pretext of hearing the preliminary report by the Xodjali Disaster Commission. The press was excluded from the hall but allowed to view the proceedings via an in-house television channel in a second-floor room usually used for press conferences. The acoustics in the room were bad, but the gist of the discussion was clear: a whitewash of Ayaz Mutalibov's role in the national disaster. . . .

Well, asked one crocodile deputy rhetorically, if Mutalibov was not responsible for Xodjali, then should not parliament reconsider its decision of
March 6th regarding his resignation? Speakers got up and expanded on this
idea, but it was all just so much talk, because the number of deputies in the
session did not represent a quorum—meaning that of the 360 deputies, 240
had to be in attendance before anything they did had legality. I was about to
walk out the door and have a smoke when there was a sudden commotion in
the chamber, and everyone in the press room jumped up and crowded
around the TV.

"Good God!" someone shouted. *"It's him!"*

I turned around and elbowed my way through the throng. Indeed, there
on the screen was the electronic image of a dapper man with a puffed-up
hairdo, taking a seat in the first row while smiling and waving to old
friends: *Ayaz* ... Someone then raised a motion to be voted on: retracting
the March 6th resignation.

"They can't!" someone in the gallery shouted.

"They are!" someone shouted back.

And then they did. We knew it by the shy smile that spread across
Mutalibov's face. He was looking cool, calm, and collected, a poker player
who knew he was playing with a stacked deck. We knew it by the way he
got up from his deputy's chair and began to move toward the dais. We
knew it from the cheers in the background and the joyous crocodiles who
mobbed Mutalibov on his way to the chair at the head of parliament. We
knew it by the handshakes and kisses being showered upon him: Hajji
Abdul, the leader of the Repentance Society, was the first of the lot.

"Thank you, thank you," Mutalibov was saying over the speaker system.
"It's like being elected president for a third time."

"You were never elected once before!" screeched some legalist in the
television room.

But it didn't make any difference. Ayaz Mutalibov had just been restored
to power by his old, rubber-stamp parliament, sitting without quorum. And
now he was announcing his new agenda for the country. The concept of
democracy, he noted, was getting out of hand. It was thus time to rein it in
by banning all political activities and imposing martial law. It went without
saying that the presidential elections scheduled to take place for June 7th
were canceled: they had been set to replace the void he had left behind; with
his return, the void was filled. He would now rule with an iron hand.

"If the country needs a dictator to save it from disaster, *I am that man!*"

Thunderous applause crackled over the speaker system in the television
room. Then Ayaz got to the real point of the matter: although Azerbaijan
had the greatest respect for former Soviet republics like Ukraine and

Moldova that were trying to break free of the Russian yoke once and for all, Azerbaijan was in a different situation. It was time to make peace with Russia by signing on, immediately, as a full member of the Commonwealth of Independent States. As it happened, there was to be a meeting in Tashkent the next day, and Ayaz had every intention of going there and putting his signature on every document he could get his hands on.

Great applause greeted this suggestion; it was time to bring Azerbaijan out of the cold and back into the post-Soviet fold. Thundering applause followed Mutalibov as he withdrew into an inner chamber of the parliament, and we rushed out to catch the crocodiles as they burst forth from the chamber, flush with the success of their parliamentary putsch.

"It is a great day," Sheik-ul Islam Islam Allahshukur Pashazade exclaimed. "The country has a leader again!"

"The criminal traitors responsible for the March 6th putsch must be put on trial for their crimes against the state!" demanded the head of the Social Democratic Party, Araz Alizade.

"I think I'm going to puke," said a voice at my side. It was Mehmet Ali Bayar. "These people have just announced civil war."

"Who gets to fire the first shot?" asked Philip Remler, standing nearby.

"Let's take a look at the Front defenses," I suggested.

On the way down the hill we passed the crowd of Repentance Society members, now rapturously chanting their pious battle cry while taking credit for Mutalibov's return.

"God is Great!" crowed Hajji Abdul. "We saw how Imam Khomeini managed to oust the Shah of Iran through his belief in Almighty God, and now we have effected our ends through similar faith! *Allah ul-Akbar!*"

* * *

Several hundred people had gathered outside the Front's headquarters when we arrived. But inside it was virtually deserted. Of identifiable leaders, we could only find Towfig Gasimov, the wiry Democratic Bloc MP and Albert Einstein look-alike. He said he was heading a skeleton staff in order to maintain communication with the 'democratic' forces of the outside world until the building was stormed. He was greatly relieved to see Philip and Mehmet Ali, as they were the representatives of the said 'democratic forces' he meant to contact, and the telephone wasn't working too well. . . . The two diplomats did their official listening, pledged their respective countries' moral support, and assured Gasimov that both the United States and Turkey would take up a joint position of protest in the event of an attack on the Front headquarters. Mehmet Ali went so far as to promise safe haven for families of Front leaders in the new Turkish embassy complex across from 26 Commissars Park, and said that Turkey would be ready to offer asylum if necessary. The belief that Turkey was taking sides in the showdown was underlined by the action of some anonymous pan-Turkic enthusiasts who had acquired a huge Turkish flag and draped it from the roof of the Front HQ. Someone else had gone further. They had set up a public address system on the second-story balcony. In between messages from the leadership, they broadcast the theme song of the day—a rousing Ottoman Janissary marching tune, or *mehter*, that mixed piety with martial prowess and neatly co-opted the Islamic pretensions of Mutalibov's Repentance Society:

> *Allah ul-Akbar! Allah ul-Akbar!*
> *Ordumuz daima olsun muzaf-far!*
>
> (God is Great! God is Great!
> Victory is our army's fate!)

And the people were responding: within the space of the half hour we had been inside the building, the number of Front supporters had grown from several hundred to over a thousand—and supporters were still streaming in from all sides of the park. More to the point, armed, uniformed men had taken up positions on the roof and upper balconies of the Front HQ. A number of them were using radio packs to relay information about what they saw to invisible others posted in the 26 Commissars Park across the street as well as on nearby street corners. The question of who the army would side with didn't even have to be asked; the only question was how much of it could disengage and get to Baku before the night was through.

Part of that question was answered as I walked away through the growing throng. A cheer rose at the far end of the park that soon turned into a roar, and beneath the whistles and cries of *Bravo!* I could make out the distinctive, mechanical smokers' cough of a heavy diesel engine and the uniquely ominous clank of metal tread on cement. The Front had just procured its first piece of armor and was parking it in the garage for future use.

* * *

It was a long day and a long night, May 14th, although it was probably longer for Mehmet Ali than for me, and certainly longest of all for the Front leadership. The 26 Commissars Park was packed with thousands of people, some dangling from the trees. They were young and old, men and women, rich and poor: they were the people who had been supporting the Popular

Front from the beginning. I knew many, either from the Friday night rallies or from totally different contexts: here was the 60-year-old owner of the good ship *Turkmenistan*, waving a miniature Azerbaijan flag; there was a guy who supplied me with coffee from a certain *Komisyon* shop; there was the local hacker who had once tinkered with my laptop when it was on the fritz; there was the flashy young film director I had met in Naxjivan. Those were the acquaintances, people whose names I could not remember if I had ever learned them. Then there were the others: Kamran and his mother, Kubrah Hanim, the decorated former Communist Party member determined to stay with her wayward son until dawn or until the tanks rolled—whichever came first. There was Elmira, a feisty correspondent for the opposition press, who had often helped Hicran with certain issues, and Dilshot, the talkative mother of Vugar, one of our interpreter 'kids.'

Inside the building there were more old pals: Pasha, a huge, baby-faced teddy bear of a fellow who organized Pan-Turkic conferences throughout the lands of the former USSR, now holding watch over the door, a Kalashnikov slung across his beefy back; Javdat, a Russified Azeri reporter for some Moscow news agency or other, terrified about what was going on but determined to be part of the action. Standing next to him was Niyazi Ibrahimov, the deputy chairman of the Front and director of its information department and an intimate of Abulfez, coat draped over his shoulders like a cape, almost advertising the shoulder holster under his right arm.

The personification of cool and calm, however, was Fehmin Hadjiev, a balding former prison warden now decked out in uniform and a stiff-brim cap that made him look like a member of the Gestapo—and indeed, he was calling himself the 'Military Commissar of Baku.'

"Any developments?" I asked him.

"Everything's in order," he said, a smile spread over his lips.

Meanwhile, speakers appeared on the balcony and were issuing status reports to the crowd. There were messages of goodwill and solidarity from other nationalist movements in other parts of the former USSR and the world. Even the Grand Old Man of Naxjivan, Heydar Aliyev, had sent a statement of support against the 'illegal putsch' by the traitor, Mutalibov. For entertainment, somebody put the microphone to the television as Mutalibov reiterated his words about being 'the right man to be dictator,' resulting in howls of laughter from the crowd. Then, after another blast of the Janissary marching tune to get the crowd on its feet, a familiar voice came crackling over the speakers: Abulfez Elchibey, come out from underground.

"My dear fellow citizens," Elchibey began, "I do not need to tell you what happened today in parliament. There was a coup, an illegal overriding of the constitution of Azerbaijan. It will not stand! We have begun a journey down a difficult road. But we will not turn back! Independence or death!"

AZADLIG! bellowed the crowd, *AZADLIG!*

"Our message is this," Elchibey continued. "If Citizen Mutalibov does not vacate the presidential palace by two o'clock in the afternoon of Friday May 15th, we'll be obliged to throw him out ourselves!"

An ultimatum—and the crowd went wild! But I had a few questions: the Front might be able to defend its headquarters with the bodies of its supporters backed up by a little bit of armor, but to threaten an attack? But mine was not to wonder why, merely to file the facts. Accordingly, I rushed back to my house and managed to get a call through to a newspaper.

"Any bodies yet?" the editor asked.

"No, but they have issued an ultimatum and—"

"Let's wait until the streets are flowing in blood," said the editor, who is best left nameless. "Then file. Lots of color, remember."

I was no sooner finished slamming down the phone in disgust than a bomb exploded somewhere outside the building. Then someone was knocking at the door. It was Vafa Gulizade.

"I have a message for you to deliver to the Front," he said, face drawn tight. "You must tell them that we, the government of Azerbaijan, today received a note from the governments of the United States and Turkey that they do not recognize the Mutalibov restoration as legal and that any moves against the people of Azerbaijan will result in reexamining bilateral relations between the respective governments."

It was a little odd being asked to be a conduit for this sort of information, but if Vafa thought it was so important, it was clear that I had to deliver the message. Presumably, it would bring the Front some cheer, knowing that at least a couple of countries refused to recognize Mutalibov. More importantly, perhaps, it meant that the very sending of the message meant that Vafa had finally jumped ship—and I had to wonder how many other members of the old elite were having second thoughts about Mutalibov's return as well.

Dodging roadblocks, I returned to the Front HQ and then managed to work my way through security to the second floor. The man I was looking for was Niyazi Ibrahimov, the deputy chairman of the Front and director of its information department and an intimate of Abulfez. I found him and told him, without comment, what Vafa had to say about the official American and Turkish attitudes about a crackdown.

"Gulizade told you to tell me that?"

"Yes."

"Why?"

"I don't know."

A smile spread over his grim countenance.

"They're cracking," he said, and hurried off to report the message to an emergency council of Front leaders, meeting in a back room of the building. It was around three in the morning, and even if the Front planned on staying up all night, it was high time for me to go home and catch some rest before the next day's showdown. But even in bed, adrenaline and the constant shooting in the side streets kept me awake until dawn.

* * *

May 15th was a sticky spring day along the shores of the Caspian Sea. I found my way blocked—not by riot police but by crowds of shoppers who seemed singularly oblivious to the fact that their nation was about to lurch headlong into civil war. The *Komisyon* shops were doing a brisk business. Ladies were having their hair done and nails manicured. Men sat around in tea shops playing dominoes and rereading newspapers. Perhaps most civil wars, and maybe even most wars, are like that: people cope with the pending insanity by cleaving to normalcy. It's only when they write the histories that it seems as if everybody dropped everything to rush off to the front to stay there until the ultimate victory or defeat as bombs continuously fell.

Before going down to the Front HQ, I decided to check out the brown-and-white granite, twelve-story presidential building down the street from my house. Here, a less lunatic mood prevailed: that is, hundreds of armed men were gathering in anticipation of the threatened attack. They, at least, were taking the ultimatum to 'Citizen Mutalibov' seriously. Most were regular policemen armed with assault rifles. But they were also backed by their own collection of armor; in the inner courtyard of the building, I counted four BTRs and two T-54 tanks, their engines rattling on low idle. More disturbing than the presence of the armor was the identity of the crews—I had met them out in Agdam: Mamed the Mule's men. One of these characters was a half Russian/half Azeri psychopath by the name of Vagif. I hailed him as he passed by.

"Vagif," I cried. "How's tricks?"

"Great," he said.

"Where's the Mule?"

"He's coming tomorrow with more men," said Vagif, and sauntered away.

In the middle of the crowd of cops, I saw someone else I knew: our landlord, Fuat. A tremendously nice guy with a body of steel, he was a captain in the plainclothes police. Today, though, he dressed out in body armor and was carrying a sniper rifle.

"This thing will end in blood," he said. "I can't see any other way out."
It was noon, and the clock was ticking toward the deadline.

* * *

The atmosphere at the edges of the 26 Commissars Park was electrically charged and became all the more pulsating as one approached the Front HQ. It was so densely packed that it was difficult to make headway through the crowd to the entrance and equally difficult to get through the door, especially because normal discourse was impossible with the PA system blasting out the Janissary marching tune, which everyone by now was singing.

> *Allah ul-Akbar! Allah ul-Akbar!*
> *Ordumuz daima olsun muzaf-far!*

I managed to fight my way through the mass and inside, and then upstairs to the second floor, forcing my way through knots of heavily armed men into the foyer of Elchibey's office. In a corner of the room I saw Mehmet Ali Bayar, huddling with Iskender Hamidov, the diminutive sparkplug of the Popular Front and the terror of parliament. He had disappeared the day before, and most assumed that he had gone underground. But hiding was not Iskender's style. He might have been out of sight, but he had been busy.

"They are going to do it," said Bayar after the conference ended. Mehmet Ali looked totally drained—and well he should have, after not having slept for forty hours.

"What do you mean?"

"After you left last night they had another conference."

"Yes?"

"And they were about to back out. Only Iskender wanted to go through with it. I told the rest that they had to do it, that this was their only chance, that they'd all be in jail today if they didn't march. Then I told them that Turkey had received assurances from Moscow that Russia would not interfere, that it was Azerbaijan's internal affair."

"So?"

"There was no such cable."

"I see—"

"I've got to stop them!"

"It's not your burden—"

"No! Let them march, but let them get it legally and diplomatically right before they do!"

And then he was forcing his way through to Elchibey's inner chamber.

The clock showed a quarter to two, and it was ticking ever closer. I smoked one cigarette and then lit another. Then it was two o'clock, and then five after the hour. The deadline had come and gone, but there was no order to march, only the constant blaring of the *Mehter* tune. Then the doors to Elchibey's inner sanctum flew open and a stern but smiling Elchibey, wearing an overcoat to hide his body armor, marched out, in the middle of a phalanx of guards, to the balcony. I grabbed Mehmet Ali to ask him what had happened.

"They needed an appeal, a last appeal," he said. "I just dictated it to them and told them to deliver it to me and the Americans and to Yaqub Mamedov before they marched." Mehmet Ali wasn't running on thin ice, he was sprinting.

Out on the balcony, someone had turned off the *mehter* marching music while a young man read off points from a piece of paper—the one Bayar had just dictated.

". . . Having exhausted the patience of the nation . . . Noting the illegal seizure of power . . . Regretting the necessity to use force to restore the constitutional order disrupted on May 14th . . . Calling on the democratic forces of the world. . . ."

It was the usual rigmarole that appeals and manifestos are made of when revolutionaries throw the dice—only this time, the handwriting was Mehmet Ali's. It was now a quarter to three, and with a lurch, Abulfez Elchibey, almost buried under a dozen bodyguards with radios strapped to their backs and wired by earphones to one another, took the microphone to deliver the final word to the troops and the nation before they departed on their journey. A sustained, deafening roar welled up from the street, obliterating almost everything he had to say save for the last few words of a very familiar note: "The road is long and difficult, but we know our path is true! LIBERTY OR DEATH!"

AZADLIG! AZADLIG! AZADLIG!!

I thought he had just given the marching orders, and I'd begun to fight my way down to the street when another thunderous roar came rolling over the crowd.

BOZKURT! BOZKURT! BOZKURT!

It was Iskender Hamidov, the 'Gray Wolf.' I swear he was looking at his watch, and counting. Then Iskender said something into the microphone that was indistinguishable from everything else around: the roar of the crowd shouting his name, the roar of the war machines in the back of the Front HQ, and the roar of the march being cranked out of the PA speakers, now blasting at an ear-splitting decibel level:

Allah ul-Akbar! Allah ul-Akbar!
Ordumuz daima olsun muzaf-far!

And then the steel doors barring the Front's parking lot from prying eyes were thrown open and the first armored vehicles rumbled out, metal treads grinding up the curbs and digging into the early summer–soft asphalt of the streets. A BTR, then two, then a truck filled with men with rifles and rocket launchers; another BTR, a mobile anti-aircraft gun, the truck crammed with jubilant soldiers blowing kisses to the crowd and the crowd blowing kisses back; then the first tank, then the second—as if from nowhere, Iskender had come up with fighting men and armor. An entire armored column was moving out and instantly was joined by thousands and thousands of citizens, marching away to make revolution or die.

* * *

I bounded up the stairs of our apartment building to our flat on the third floor, where I found my sidekick Laura Le Cornu and Hicran. The former was terrified and reluctant to put her head outside and the latter just back from the Front HQ by a different route, and chomping at the bit.

"They marched," said Hicran. "Let's get over to the presidential apparatus building."

It was a quarter after three when we arrived, but the building was not in flames. The cops surrounding the place twiddled their thumbs; the only action we could see was a couple of secretaries leaving with boxes of personal artifacts via the back door. I approached a knot of cops and asked how things were going.

"Fine, fine," they answered.

Was Ayaz in the building? I asked.

The cops weren't sure, but a few minutes before, a man from the Iranian embassy had come by with official congratulations on Mutalibov's restoration, so they assumed he was. Why shouldn't he be? It was the presidential building, and he was the president!

Were the cops aware that the army of the people and the Popular Front was at this very moment marching on them?

One of them looked at his watch and smiled.

"They said they were going to attack at two, but it's after three thirty now," he smiled. "They are all talk and no action."

"We know what to do with them if they are stupid enough to come," said another, patting his weapon.

"They've gone home with their tails between their legs," chuckled a third derisively. Then there was a sound from down below the apparatus building that wiped the smiles off all their faces: the long, multiple blast of automatic weapon fire, coming from somewhere behind the symphony hall.

"Here goes," said one cop, going locked and loaded with his Kalashnikov. A similar agitation gripped the crowd of security men on the street below and on the grand steps leading up to the main entrance of the building. Our landlord, Fuat, was standing in the middle of the group in front of the building. He looked up and I caught his eye and he nodded grimly, then jerked his head to the side. Get out of the way, he was trying to say.

Another blast of automatic fire in the distance brought all the muzzles of all the police rifles into the air. It didn't seem a particularly good idea to be standing at either end of the funnel where the firefight was to be conducted, and so I grabbed Hicran and pulled her back toward a small park to the rear of the apparatus building. It was filed with policemen and other security personnel, positioned to guard the flank in case the Front army came that way.

Another blast of distant fire erupted from somewhere in front of the building and riveted attention there. A command car came screeching up and an officer jumped out and started shouting at a knot of cops sitting on a bench, apparently trying to dispatch them from the rear to the front. Some of the men didn't want to go and the officer was about to strike one of them when suddenly he paused, hand cocked to slap, and looked up.

On the hill behind us, someone had let off a long and leisurely blast of automatic fire. Then there was another burst. Silence for a moment, and then all hell broke loose as hundreds of automatic weapons, rocket launchers, and heavy machine guns roared.

"It's the parliament!" someone wailed. "They've hit the parliament!"

Suddenly, it all clicked into focus: the preliminary shooting in front of the presidential building had been a diversion. Iskender's main column had marched on the parliament and television station on the hill. The cops were defending the wrong point. And as the thump of cannon and tank rounds echoed down from whatever battle was happening up above, chaos and confusion began to grip the security forces below. They could do nothing until they abandoned the defense of the presidential building and made their own uphill assault. Making mincemeat out of the Front as it marched along a grand avenue was one thing; committing suicide was another—and to gauge by the sound and fury of Iskender's army in action, that was exactly what an uphill assault would be.

Adding to the growing chaos among the rank and file was the attitude of the scores of ordinary citizens of the neighborhood who had been caught out in the streets nearby when the maelstrom began. Like us, they were reluctant to leave the sheltering row of buildings between them and the battle in the heights above. But they now saw a target to take out their rage and frustration on: the police force guarding the presidential apparatus.

"Look what you have brought us to!" wailed one distraught man, jumping up from his place of safety and lashing out at three policemen with his fists. "What, whom are you defending!"

"You dogs, you dogs!" swore an elderly lady, sitting behind a wall with grocery bags strewn around her, and spitting at any security man in range.

It was time to file a story about the assault, if I could get a line out.

"Let's go," I said to Hicran. "Maybe Laura has got a line through."

"You go," she replied, "I'll stay here."

"Let's go together, now."

"No."

"Please."

"No."

I saw it coming—a domestic spat on a public street in a city in the midst of revolution. I wanted no part of it.

"Okay," I reluctantly agreed. "You stay right here. I will be back in five minutes."

I ran the 200 or 500 yards to the house and charged in.

"What's happening?" asked Laura. She was white as a sheet.

"Civil war," I succinctly replied. "Get a line out?"

"No. Where's Hicran?"

"Down the street. She wouldn't come."

We tried to get an operator for a few minutes, but it was pretty clear that someone had snipped the lines. So I gave up and ran back to where Hicran had been hiding. She was gone.

"Where's Hicran?" I demanded of Elmira, our local journalist who had been huddling nearby in a gutter. She could only sob and point in the general direction of the parliament.

"She's gone up the hill?" I asked incredulously.

Actually, I shouldn't have been that surprised at my wife's disappearance. I was starting to learn that she was drawn to the sound and smell of gunfire and just had to be part of the action—even if the action was jumping into an inferno. I am not known as a cautious fellow, but there was only one thing to do—and it was the last thing I wanted: follow her up the hill.

Shit, I said to myself. *Why does she do this to me?*

The gunfire was only coming in bursts every step I took, and then there was an eerie silence.

All that was left to do now was count the corpses and determine who had won.

* * *

There were plenty of bodies on the parliamentary steps, and all were very much alive. My wife Hicran was one of them, and she was dancing with some soldier with a carnation in the barrel of his gun, just one of thousands of jubilantly cheering people. Another was my old pal from Post 19, Nurjahan Husseinova, literally ecstatic about the 'conquest' and kissing everyone who came within range—including the American defense attaché.

For all the shooting, there were not many dead bodies. Of the Front forces, one volunteer had had the bad luck to fall off his transport and be crushed beneath its wheels. The losses on the side of the defenders who had taken up positions in parliament and in the upper floors of the Moscow Hotel across the street from it were never announced; triangulation of events would suggest that those killed were less than a dozen.

And to believe official reports, there were only three wounded. One was Iskender Hamidov, shot in the arm as he marched at the head of the column. But one thing was perfectly clear: Iskender's strategy of hitting the parliament, and hard, was a total success. Not only had it terrified the men guarding the presidential apparatus into abandoning their positions without firing a shot, but it had prevented the bloodbath that everyone in the country had anticipated. There were some, including Philip Remler, who found the level of casualties so incredibly low that they wrote it up to incompetence.

"That amount of gunfire and you come up with only three wounded and one killed by mistake?" he said incredulously as we walked the steps of the shattered parliament building.

But that is what happened. It was a miracle, and from the expressions on the faces of the stream of civilians parading up to see the symbol of success, the shattered glass and cement of the parliament, you knew that they knew it had been one, too.

They'd had a revolution, and no one got hurt, almost.

12

Coup Redux

The next stage of the revolution was to legitimize the countercoup, and the Front took great pains to frame the events of May 14th and 15th as an illegal attempt by Mutalibov to circumvent the constitution of the country. The Front had merely restored constitutional order by turning back the clock to two-thirty on the afternoon of May 14th. There had been only 229 deputies in parliament at the time of the Mutalibov 'restoration.' That was not enough for a quorum; ergo, everything that had happened in parliament on May 14 was null and void.

This obsession with constitutional legalism resulted in some rather obtuse formulas. Yaqub ('Dollar') Mamedov, for example, was thus still legally the chairman of parliament, and as such, acting president. Thrice he submitted his resignation to the deputies of the Democratic Bloc and thrice the Bloc refused to accept it. According to the constitution, a majority of the necessary quorum of two-thirds of the parliament had to vote in the affirmative to accept his resignation. 'Dollar' Yaqub was thus stuck with a job he did not want until the required number of deputies could be gathered.

The resignation session was duly set for three in the afternoon of May 18th, but was suspended an hour later because there were still less than 200 deputies in the chamber. The rest were in hiding. Meanwhile, some 10,000 triumphantly angry people had gathered on the steps of parliament, waiting for news about Citizen Mutalibov. There were about as many theories about his whereabouts as there were interlocutors: he had been spirited away via a Russian helicopter from a nearby air base after having sneaked through the streets in cross-mufti; he had been allowed to drive to the airport and board a flight to Iran; he was in Mashtagah, rallying his Repentance Society supporters for the next round of civil war; he was dead of a KGB-induced heart attack in a Moscow hospital; he was nursing his wounds in his Baku dacha, soon to be accepted back into the political fold. . . .

"He's here, downstairs!" said a friend in a conspiratorial tone, leading me into the parliamentary latrine. Some wag had placed pictures of Mutalibov in each of the six marble urinals.

At four in the afternoon, a new roll was called. But the requisite number of deputies for a quorum was still lacking. Another roll was called at five and then again at six. Still no quorum. But with each registration, the numbers increased: the Front and its supporters were literally hunting down deputies in hiding and dragging them to parliament. Once inside, there was no way out: the crowd was there to insure that no one left until a quorum was established, and a legal stamp put on the countercoup.

At around a quarter after six, a buzz started to pass around the foyer: a few late arrivals had pushed the session numbers over the top. Instantly, there was a crush on the doors to the chamber, with deputies and VIP visitors flashing badges to the security guards for clearance. A cheer from the gallery and the chamber rose when it was announced that 255 deputies were present. No matter what else happened in this late-night session, it was going to be sealed with the stamp of constitutional legality.

The first vote concerned 'Dollar' Mamedov's request to resign his office. The first attempt to do so failed due to some obscure procedural reason (or maybe just to drag out the humiliating scene a few more minutes). The next two ballots also failed because there was no quorum: although 255 deputies were present, only 238 and then 234 had voted. This was a bad omen. A fourth roll call garnered 243 registered deputies, however, of whom 221 accepted Mamedov's resignation as chairman of the parliament and acting president of Azerbaijan. 'Dollar' Yaqub was not present to note the moment.

The next step was to find a new chairman. The valedictorian poet Bakhtiar Vahabzade asked for the floor. Immediately, he launched into an unctuous rhapsody of praise for a man the deputies 'all knew and respected,' a man of 'pristine integrity' who, despite his 'young years' had proven himself 'intellectually, morally, and patriotically capable' of assuming the difficult roll of chairman of the Supreme Soviet of Azerbaijan in these trying times. . . . I turned around and took a picture of Isa Gamberov while he was still mortal. He flicked me a sardonic smile that seemed to say 'I know it's dumb, you know it's dumb, but these are the little cultural holdovers from the past that we must make allowances for.'

It took a while for Vahabzade to get around to mentioning Isa by name, and when he did, Isa issued a look of mock surprise. Then he rose and walked to the floor and declared himself stunned and honored to be nominated. The tasks of chairman of the Supreme Soviet of the Republic of Azerbaijan were many, and a challenge to the best of men, he said. Still, if his colleagues believed him up to the task, he would submit to their judgment and try and perform to the best of his abilities, to help guide the lawmakers in their difficult duty of leading the nation to true and real independence.

The floor was then opened to proforma questioning of the candidate on his views on various subjects. The first of these pertained to Isa's attitude about the May 14th coup and May 15th countercoup. Isa replied that while the events of May 14th were certainly a coup, May 15th was not. The Popular Front had the chance to seize power, but had not. The rule of law must obtain and the constitution must be respected—including the need to hold the presidential election on June 7th.

The next question concerned Mountainous Karabakh. Isa's answer was succinct: the first task of the government was to secure Baku; after that, it would be time to deal with Karabakh.

The third individual to pose a question announced that he did not have one, but rather wished to express his views on a certain subject of great importance.

"Then I am sitting down," said Isa, and did so. He was easily bored with stupid questions, but positively detested the sort of rambling rhetorical queries that Azeri politicians (and journalists) were so given to.

It was now time for the vote. But before the ballots were punched in, someone asked if there were other candidates for the post of chairman to be considered.

"No," said Tamerlan Garayev, acting as chairman. "No one else has been nominated." Nervous laughter echoed through the chamber.

"Well," said the spoilsport. "What about Heydar Aliyev?"

This was clearly not part of the evening's pre-programming.

"If Heydar Aliyev had the slightest interest in taking a position in our parliament, he would be here right now," growled Arif Xadjiev. "But he is not; which means he is not interested; which means it is ridiculous to even think of nominating him!"

But the neo-commies had found a chink in the wall: suddenly it was they who were being open and pluralistic and—the word almost stuck in the throat—democratic. How could one exclude or overlook any individual simply because he was not able to be present when momentous decisions were being made? Why all the fuss? Why all the fear? Why not just call and ask the man if he were interested in the job?

Indeed, there was no reason not to consider the Grand Old Man of Naxjivan for the post. But Heydar as chairman meant Heydar as acting president, and the legality of 'acting' was enough for the old fox to impose a state of emergency until the end of his days. If it was scraping the bucket-bottom by the neo-commies, the prospect of a resurrected Heydar was their one, last remaining hope of a new lease on political life: Heydar was not the

Front. And now that Heydar's name was being bandied about, he had become a factor: excluding him from the proceedings would only make his shadow loom even larger.

The Front tried to push the voting through anyway.

"All in favor of Isa Gamberov, the unopposed, single candidate for chairman of parliament, say aye," the acting chairman intoned.

The deputies duly punched in their registration cards. The scoreboards flashed the result a moment later, and the atmosphere inside the chamber rapidly soured: 221 had voted and 3 against. That was 224 votes; no quorum.

"Who are the traitors here who sit in this session but refuse to vote?" screamed Iskender Hamidov. "You may have your immunity today, but you will pay for this treason the minute after the next election!"

"Neo-Bolshevik filth!" someone howled back.

The situation was deteriorating rapidly. There were spoilers out in the audience, at least twenty of them, determined to turn the tables on the Front at its moment of constitutional glory. There was only one thing to do: call a recess before a fist fight broke out on the floor. And while the majority of deputies filed out to the foyer, a select delegation retired to an antechamber to try and raise Heydar on the telephone, to see what he thought about competing with Isa for the job of chairman of parliament.

"Heydar won't have anything to do with this idiocy," said Isa, when I found him chain-smoking by the door. "He knows that any collaboration with the Communists is the political kiss of death."

This was a very hopeful interpretation. More likely, I thought, it was Heydar himself who had put the worm in the wine. Across the cigarette haze in the foyer, I noticed my old friend, the Naxjivani Minister of the Interior.

"Let's get out and get some air," I suggested. No sooner were we through the frame of the door (the glass was blasted out on the 15th) than we were surrounded by Front militiamen.

"Where do you think you're going, creep?" spewed forth a truck-wide man whose voice I knew from somewhere. It was Pasha, the baby-faced pan-Turkic Hulk. Recognizing me, he became apologetic and allowed us to continue our alfresco stroll unmolested.

"Where is Aliyev in all this?" I asked, as we looked over the sea of seething people in the square between us and the shimmering Caspian, beyond.

"Heydar is a patriot," said the Minister carefully. "Please note that he declared the Mutalibov restoration illegal and threw his support behind the Front."

"But he doesn't like the Front at all."

"That's just the point," said the Minister. "Heydar hates Mutalibov and his crowd as only a deposed king can hate a usurper. Anything else is to be preferred. He won't go for their stupid gambit."

We fell silent for a moment or two, and then we went back to the shattered door to re-enter the parliament. After being frisked by Pasha and his gun-happy crew, we were allowed to re-enter the building. The buzzer sounded, and we shuffled back into the chamber to listen to the contact delegation's report.

Heydar had refused to answer the phone.

"We tried and tried," said the spokesman of the telephone contact committee. "But his aides said he was 'too busy'."

To prove their point, the contact committee had filmed themselves while on the phone, and they were kind enough to play the video for the rest of us. Relieved laughter and even guffaws sounded around the chamber, especially from the bench where Isa Gamberov sat.

I had different thoughts on the matter. *Heydar.* The old fox—he was playing it both ways. By dealing with the issue through surrogates and not directly refusing the nomination himself, he was leaving the door of denial ajar. He would snub yesterday's Yes-men, and stay clean in deepest darkest Naxjivan, waiting for the moment to make his next move. You had to give credit where credit was due: there was no one who knew how to play politics like Heydar.

* * *

There were no other nominations to the chairmanship and voting proceeded without further interruption. There was only one possible result. Of the 244 deputies in parliament (it was never explained what had happened to the 255 present a few hours before), 241 voted for Isa Gamberov as the new chairman of parliament. Two votes were against and one disqualified or indifferent. There was more relief than joy when the numbers were tallied. Another legal hurdle had been leapt, and the 35-year-old Isa had become not only the first non-Communist president of Azerbaijan but also the youngest president (even if just 'acting') in his young nation's history. His reign was to be short: three weeks.

"Let's not waste time on acceptance-speech nonsense," Isa said for his acceptance speech, and took his place on the dais. "I nominate Tamerlan Garayev as deputy chairman. Anybody object?"

Silence.

"Good," said Isa, turning to Tamerlan. "Change your chair from my left to my right." Garayev did so, graduating from vice deputy chairman to deputy chairman. "Now, let's get down to work."

Then came the third and last hurdle: the appointment of a new Council of Ministers—the government. First came the security portfolios, and there were no surprises there: Iskender ('Bozkurt') Hamidov was the new Minister of the Interior, and Rahim Gaziyev was re-appointed to the post of Minister of Defense. Next, Towfig Gasimov was appointed Minister of Foreign Affairs. Sabit Bagirov was to take over the sensitive job of chairman of the state oil company, SOCAR.

So far, so good. But as Isa began reading off the names of the other prospective ministers, we were all dumbstruck: they were crocodiles, to a man. In fact, they were the exact same people who had previously held the posts! True, the portfolios were restricted to economic matters of which the Front and Bloc deputies knew precious little. But the mere prospect of bringing the same people back into power who had just been thrown out created an immediate fall-out among old friends. Etibar Mamedov, for one, declared the whole thing a travesty that he would have nothing to do with and announced that he and his supporters among the 'national bourgeoisie' were going into 'constructive opposition.' He would not taint himself or his National Independence Party by associating with the old regime, which is exactly what the Front was doing!

"They won't even have time to set up their staffs before a new government is formed," cackled Towfig Gasimov, taking a chair next to Philip, Hicran, Mehmet Ali, and me. He was looking and acting a little punchy, and as events turned out, talking just a tad prematurely.

The ministers were voted on and accepted. Then Isa floored the motion that all knew was coming: the self-dissolution of parliament and the bestowal of authority on the National Council—the fifty-person body that had been acting in lieu of the parliament for the past six months. It had been a long day, and we all expected this pro forma procedure to be over with quickly. But the neo-commies choked on it.

"How can you call yourself democrats when you are destroying the democratically elected parliament and replacing it with a 50-member Bolshevik clique?" demanded Rahim Isazade, in his weird, lisping Ganje accent. "This is a travesty!"

"Let's vote," said Gamberov, not willing to even listen to the point, and deputies went about the task of registering their voting cards. Then the tallies appeared on the twin voting scoreboards: 171 deputies had voted for and 48 had voted against dissolution. Once again, the total number was less than the necessary quorum.

Isa rolled his eyes.

"Perhaps there has been some misunderstanding," he said. He rephrased the language of the motion and called for a second vote. Again it failed to pass due to a lack of a quorum. Exasperated, Isa threw the floor open to discussion and a line of neo-commies appeared at the microphones. All picked up the antidemocratic theme and began a long, bitter criticism of the 'totalitarian nature' of the National Council. It was unclear which audience the speakers were performing for—history, perhaps?—but in their political death throes, they had turned into the epitome of democratic pluralists. It would have been almost funny if the clock were not ticking toward one in the morning.

But some folks in the Front were tired and wanted the charade of democratic pluralism over sooner than later.

"Let's end this piece of theater," said Iskender Hamidov, seizing a microphone planted in the middle of the commie deputies. "If you vote against the motion, it will mean that we have to stay all night, and I'm tired and want to go home and I have a lot of police work to do tomorrow. . . ."

Arif Xadjiev put it a little more bluntly.

"Perhaps there are some deputies here from the provinces who have not been in Baku for the past few days and who do not understand the situation," he said ominously. "Let me explain: There has been a revolution by the Popular Front. We are in control of the country—and there are thousands of people outside who are fed up with your games and who will not let you leave this building until you come to your senses. *So vote like we say!*"

Tahir Aliev, the interim Interior Minister, pulled out his KGB-issue machine pistol, cocked it so that all could hear, and then asked Isa for the voting registrar.

Deputy chairman Tamerlan Garayev took the floor for a last appeal before the third vote.

"I beg you, stop playing politics," he said wearily. "Your children are watching, your grandchildren are watching, the world is watching. For a show of unity, for the nation: vote for this bill so that we may all go home!"

Again the scoreboard flashed a total of 255 members registering their attendance. There was a quorum. The ticker then went through its electronic calculations. Of the 255 deputies, 244 said 'yes.' Parliament had just voted itself into the void. 'Indefinitely prorogued,' I think, is the legal term. A sufficient number of deputies applauded the moment to make it look good, but it would have been a lot finer if it had not been a vote taken under duress. It would also have been a lot finer if the parliament had voted for new elections. That was always a subject to be discussed tomorrow, and tomorrow never came.

* * *

Amid all the celebration of the popular victory, there was one very sour note. The Armenians had taken advantage of the chaos in Baku to effect a long-stated goal: the creation of a 'humanitarian' corridor linking Karabakh to Armenia itself. Not only was the timing obvious, but so was the place: Lachin, a mainly Kurdish-populated town located at the narrowest point between Karabakh and Armenia.

If any further proof were needed of impending attack, two news items served to seal the case: on May 16th, Russian state television ran a bulletin, quoting Armenian defense ministry sources, that spoke of a 'massive, one-thousand-man,' uphill Azeri assault on the 'Armenian' town of Shusha. The second piece of evidence was the simultaneous announcement that the Azeris and Armenians, within the context of the Commission on Security and Cooperation in Europe (CSCE), had agreed to meet and talk peace in the Belarusian capital of Minsk. For anyone who had been following the Karabakh conflict, the announcement of a 'peace conference' meant only one thing: the Karabakh Armenians, allegedly operating outside the control of Yerevan, were preparing themselves for another fait accompli.

The attack on Lachin began on May 17th. What Azeri military units were still there ran away, followed quickly by the local Kurdish population. A film clip shot by Jenghiz Mustafayev showed soldiers hiding their weapons beneath bedding piled atop flatbed carts and trucks. Lachin was then given over to looting and then burned; stragglers were slaughtered. The late, great Rory Peck of *Frontline News* was with the first lot of Armenian looters to pass through the newly opened 'humanitarian corridor' to Karabakh from the Armenian city of Goris.

"I asked Armenian soldiers what they were doing with the captives," he related to me. "They would smile and draw their knives over their throats. They didn't care if the people were Azeris or Kurds. To the Armenians, they were Muslims, and fit for slaughter."

Another source, an Estonian journalist who went by the odd Armenianized pen-name of Yuri Malumiyan, was in the Armenian Ministry of Defense press office when the decision to take Lachin was taken, and related the discussion to me. " 'How do we justify it?' someone asked. 'Use the Kurdish angle,' someone replied. 'It won't stick,' another said. 'But it will confuse the issue for a few days, and that is all we need.' "

And so it happened. Lachin was attacked, and taken. Once more, the government of Armenia maintained that it had nothing to do with the assault and conquest. The forces involved were 'solely Karabakh Armenians' opening up a 'humanitarian corridor' while aiding local Kurds in revolt. The new myth was awe-inspiring in its audacity. It was an internationally accepted cliché that Turks instinctively oppress Kurds and that Kurds are always revolting against their oppressors. The events in Lachin appeared to be just one more example of this old story of Turco-Kurdish enmity, but with a twist: the selfless, oft-victimized Armenians had thrown caution to the wind and had supported innocent Kurds against vicious Turks!

The ruse worked: the international community hesitated to form an opinion, while fact finders were sent to the region to see if the Armenian version of events was true. And when they got to the frontier, they actually found some Kurdish-speaking people who confirmed the story of the Kurdish uprising. The problem was that the individuals who met with the fact finders were not Muslim Kurds, but Kurdish-speaking Yezidis, or Zoroastrians. More to the point, they were not even native to the Lachin area at all, but citizens of Armenia who had been shipped into the area after its conquest.

If there was still any question about what happened to all the Kurds of the Lachin area, it was answered for me a few days later in a rather personal way: a stream of refugees began arriving in the courtyard of our building. The reason for this was that the Lachin Friendship Society was located in the basement. Almost overnight, the club was transformed from a place where one could look for old pals to a venue where one could seek lost relatives and friends or even volunteer for the Lachin Brigade. They were men and women, old and young, and came from every level of society—taxi drivers, schoolteachers, former *kolkhoz* agricultural workers, and professionals. Sadder still was the fact that almost half of the refugees said they were Kurds from Armenia who had been thrown out along with the Azeris in 1988, in the first round of conflict between Armenia and Azerbaijan. Far from being the beneficiaries of the Armenian action, these poor souls had now been expelled from their homes not once but twice by the people who claimed to be their liberators.

Within a week of the original announcement of the 'Kurdish revolt' in the Lachin region, the Kurdish theme was quietly dropped. It would reappear some ten months later, during the siege and conquest of the neighboring Kurdish-populated Azeri province of Kelbajar. Then, once again, Yerevan would trot out the 'Kurds in revolt' formula for international consumption while chopping off another chunk of Azerbaijan, ethnically cleansing some 60,000 Kurds in the process. The remarkable thing about all this was the total indifference of Kurd-lovers throughout the world—and of most of the world's Kurds as well.

* * *

There was another area of the country where Baku's control was tenuous at best: Naxjivan, the abode of the Grand Old Man, Heydar Aliyev.

No one really knew how to deal with Heydar. When I asked the new acting President Gamberov about Heydar during an interview at the presidential palace, he dodged the issue.

"The issue of Heydar Aliyev is complex," said Isa. "Naxjivan is too narrow a venue for a man of his stature, and we just hope that he will be able to cooperate with the new government."

There was talk of offering him a ministry—the most likely choice was the KGB, for old times' sake. Others thought that giving him the job of prime minister might be the way to accommodate him. Sending him off as an ambassador somewhere was another possibility. But the one thing the constitution-conscious Front government was not going to do to please Heydar was change the election law to allow him to compete in the upcoming elections.

"He is too old to be a candidate," said Isa Gamberov's chief aide, Niyazi Ibrahimov, referring to a clause in the Azerbaijani constitution, adopted during the heady days of Gorbachev's glasnost, that set the upward limit for chief executives anywhere in the (former) USSR at age 65. Heydar Aliyev had just turned 70.

This effort to freeze the Old Man from Naxjivan out of the democratic process would come back to haunt everyone associated with it, because despite his years and his reduction in power and status from that of CPSU Politburo member to that of 'president' of a territory of some 350,000 people, Heydar was not about to retire. If anything, his instinct for the political moment—and political revenge—appeared to be getting better with time. And he chose the moment for making his presence felt with inspiration. At the moment of the Popular Front's greatest triumph, he stole Nation Day.

* * *

The presidential Tupolev seemed to hang in the air, swaying back and forth in mild turbulence created by the wind currents around the peak of Snake Mountain, Naxjivan. Then it banked to the right again and flew along the Araxes River toward the denuded cone of Mount Ararat, hung in the air, banked, and flew back along the Araxes toward Snake Mountain once more. I was beginning to memorize the details of Naxjivani geography from the air. I was also starting to get dizzy, and a little worried.

"He is not going to let us land," said Mehmet Ali Bayar, who had now joined me in chain smoking our nerves away.

"Oh, he will eventually," someone aboard the aircraft said. "He just wants to make sure we realize who we are—and who he is."

'He' was Heydar Aliyev. 'We' were the government of Azerbaijan—everyone from the chairman of parliament (and acting president) Isa Gamberov to the minister of aviation and, for all I knew, agriculture and tourism, too. The date was May 28, 1992, the 74th anniversary of the declaration of the Democratic Republic Azerbaijan of 1918. As a nationalist movement, the Popular Front government had intended to make the most out of the occasion, and planned a flag-waving, bugle-blowing, poetry-reading celebration in Ganje, the capital of the first republic.

But then Heydar Aliyev struck. Ignoring an invitation to attend the Ganje festivities, he had decided to throw his own, rival party: the confirmed guest list included a "Who's Who" of the government and political elite of Turkey; the occasion was the opening of the Bridge of Hope across the Araxes river at Sadarak—the crucial link between Turkey and the greater 'Turkic' world to the east, and the first step in the dawning of the promised 'Turkic' twenty-first century.

Few in Turkey—or probably the world—noticed that the date set by Heydar Aliyev for this emotional moment just happened to be the same as that set for the commemoration of Azerbaijan's independence and statehood. Fewer still were aware that the new government of the Popular Front now had to hastily cancel the Ganje celebrations and crash the party in Naxjivan. Fewer still were aware of the dynamics between the Popular Front and Heydar—namely, that this first meeting between the new and the old was to take place on Heydar's turf and according to his terms. The first lesson, it seemed, was to learn humility in his presence—and that extended 1,000 feet over his head.

* * *

After about half an hour's wait, ground control at Naxjivan airport finally gave us permission to land. It went without saying that the usual protocols afforded dignitaries were going to be totally neglected. The welcoming committee consisted of my old pal, the Naxjivani minister of the interior, and a few sour cops. The VIP transportation was a series of dilapidated buses. It was incredibly humiliating, but the Heydar show had just started.

After arriving in town, Isa and his entourage marched up the stairs to Heydar's office. But Heydar was not there—and no one knew were he was. While we waited for Heydar to show up, his smirking assistants announced that breakfast was available downstairs. Having nothing better to do, the government of the Republic of Azerbaijan duly got up and marched into a small, closed building in back of the presidential chamber, where a long table had been set with white cheese, cottage cream, honey, and bread.

It was quite a spread, given the usual fare available in Naxjivan. But looking around at all the armed men in the garden with us, I did not feel like sitting at the table. The only thing I could think about was the infamous day in Egypt when the Ottoman Viceroy, Muhammad Ali, invited the Mamluk warlords to his Cairo Citadel for a peacemaking dinner, and excused himself from the room at the moment his henchmen arrived to slaughter the Mamluks, one and all.

'He wouldn't . . . ,' I said to myself, got up from the table on some pretext, and went into the garden.

Finally, Acting President Isa got angry. Leaving the knot of functionaries behind, he went off to have a chat with the local chapter of the Popular Front. No sooner was he gone than a black Volga turned a corner and pulled up in front of the building.

Hey-DAR! Hey-DAR! AL-I-EV!! cheered the familiar crowds that gathered in front of the Naxjivan presidential building at all times, Hey-DAR! Hey-DAR! AL-I-EV!!

As Heydar emerged from the back seat, the line of former communist functionaries who were now included in Isa's government almost snapped to attention, taut smiles stretched across their faces.

"Afyettin . . . ," said the grand old man from Naxjivan, stroking the jowly face of the new assistant deputy chairman of parliament, who was rumored to be Heydar's bastard son.

"Abbas," he cooed, as a fifty-year-old man tried to kiss his hand, "How's your wife Fatma and your boy Alijan?"

"My Ilham," he said to another trembling leaf of more than 200 pounds, stuffed into a tailor-made suit. "We haven't seen you in a few years. You've put on weight."

It was quite a scene, watching their hopeful expressions as Heydar went down the line as if on an inspection tour. All were his former assistants, but so corrupt or desperate that once they had dumped Heydar for Mutalibov, they had scrupulously avoided all contact with him for the past several years. And it wasn't even as if he had come back. They had come to him. They were political dwarfs in his presence, and knew it. Heydar turned and waved to the crowd and once more received their applause, and then went into his office building. He did not snap his fingers, but he might have, for the way the men in line jumped like schoolboys and followed him inside for a less public chat about old times and maybe new ones.

"What a man, what a leader!" sighed a short, dark man with frog-like features who was standing next to me on the steps to Heydar's office. "There is only one Heydar Aliyev!"

The man looked familiar, but I could not place him.

* * *

The clock struck twelve. Suddenly, a caravan of half-polished official cars and a lot of bruised private vehicles was nosing its way through the thickened crowd in front Heydar's office to wheel us to the airport. I didn't think there were so many cars (or gasoline to power them) in all of Naxjivan, but there were even more on the tarmac: rickety buses, more banged up cars, and even flatbed trucks, all trying to ram their way ahead of the next. It was, I swear, the first traffic jam in Naxjivani history.

And the airport was packed. Front and center was a line of perhaps a hundred or so Naxjivani maidens decked out in national costume and carrying trays of oranges, while another line of Naxjivani lads also dressed in national attire stood nearby, carrying placards bearing very youthful resemblances of several Turkic heroes: the founder and first president of Turkey, Mustafa Kemal Atatürk; the founder and first president of Azerbaijan, Mahmed Amin Rasulzade; current Turkish premier Süleyman Demirel; current Turkish president (and Demirel archrival) Turgut Özal; and then, of course, multiple likenesses of the native son in his prime—Heydar Aliyev. . . .

Soon, the jet-engine droning of an airplane could be heard in the distance, and the crowd, as one, looked to the west. First it was a speck in the sky, then a bug, and then finally one could make out the shape of an Airbus passenger jet with the red tail markings of Turkish Airlines. The crowd roared and surged forward as one to greet the plane as its wheels and flaps descended for landing.

I am not sure what the security arrangements were supposed to have been. Maybe there never was a plan. But it was perfectly evident that if there had been one, it was totally useless now. The crowd was an animal with only one instinct: get as close to the runway as possible. The airbus touched down, and there was an instant crush to get out to the end of the red carpet someone had thoughtfully rolled out toward a point in the middle of the field. The plane taxied and came to a halt somewhere else. The crowd followed it, and when the doors swung open, a deep sigh of collective disappointment was heard. The aircraft contained only hangers-on, such as the entire domestic and foreign press community in Turkey, businessmen, and flunkies. Süleyman Demirel, the prime minister of Turkey, was not on board.

Then a second, smaller aircraft appeared in the western sky. It circled the airport and then majestically descended to the tarmac: the Gulf Stream jet of Prime Minister Süleyman Demirel and his inner circle. Once again there was a crush to get out to the end of the red carpet. This time, Heydar and Isa's security detail (they had bumped into each other and exchanged a few civil words on the tarmac) managed to hold back the crowd to some degree, forming an empty pocket at the end of the stairs now being shoved up to the Gulf Stream door. The airlock opened, and there was Demirel, waving his trademark fedora and descending the stairs into Heydar's embrace. A hundred still cameras clicked and video cameras whirred, recording the historic moment. *Demirel and Aliyev, together, at last!*

Watching the two of them as best I could through the swaying crush of humanity, I reflected on how wildly different and yet similar they were, and where and when their paths might previously have crossed. There were persistent rumors that Aliyev's rise to power in the Azerbaijani and Soviet security apparatuses was predicated on the success of a KGB operation code named 'Blue Eyes,' designed to destabilize several Demirel governments in the 1960s and early 1970s by inciting unrest among the Kurds. All one had to do was look at Heydar's unblinking crocodile eyes to understand whence the operation had taken its name. And here they were, orchestrating a pan-Turkic party under the shadow of Mount Ararat. Times change.

The Chairman of the Azerbaijan Supreme Soviet and Acting President of the Republic of Azerbaijan, Isa Gamberov, meanwhile, was no longer visible. A Turkish Television cameraman had elbowed Isa to the ground for having the gall to stand in the way of Demirel and Aliyev.

"Do you know who you just knocked down?" I said, grabbing the cameraman.

"Can't you see I'm working," he spat back.

I helped Isa to his feet, and he smiled a tight smile that said it all: stay cool—it is going to be a long, hot day.

Starting with welcoming ceremonies under the cloudless sky on the shadeless runway, I spent the rest of the afternoon either packed in slow-moving buses with no air-conditioning or trekking by foot through the three miles of gridlock on either side of the Sadarak Bridge to an open field on the Turkish side, where a massive rally of more than 50,000 people was taking place. While the politicians sat in relative comfort beneath an awning, the mass of exhausted and sunstruck people stood under the full blast of the late-May sun. Some clever Turks had brought in cases of cold Pepsi to sell for about a buck a piece. As this represented almost a week's wages (if one even had a job), the poor celebrants from Naxjivan were thus obliged to drink warm water brought across the bridge in plastic jugs.

Then there were the speeches—endless, and almost all the same.

"Dear Azerbaijani Turks, dear Naxjivani Turks!" cried Demirel. "We are here to tell you that you are not alone! The Bridge of Hope across the Araxes River of Despair we open today is the first step in opening a road from the Aegean Sea to China!"

Then Heydar spoke, and then Deputy Premier Inönü spoke, and then that fellow who was tagging along, Gamberov, or whatever his name was, spoke, too. None of the speakers, however fulsome their words about Turkic unity, wanted to address the obvious and unspeakable truth: the road east from Turkey across the Bridge of Hope over the River of Despair to Baku and beyond to China was still and would remain a dead-end street until Armenia decided to open a toll gate across Zangezur—and that didn't look like it would happen any time soon.

Not that many of those attending the crazy festivities that hot day in late May were thinking so subtly—possibly with the exception of Heydar Aliyev. Face flushed with sunburn and excitement, voice raspy from his tenth speech of the day, he was even upstaging that veteran stump-speaker and political survivor, Süleyman Demirel—and Demirel didn't seem to mind.

And Heydar was still capable of quite a few tricks. Subtly, steadily, Heydar stressed his own independence by differentiating between Azerbaijan and Naxjivan. The dignitaries from Turkey echoed his words, oblivious of the impact. The thankless task of reminding the crowd that Naxjivan was part of Azerbaijan was left to Isa Gamberov. Few of those present—especially the Turks—seemed to understand that point. Isa was furious but was obliged to silently steam.

"The important thing is, a president of Azerbaijan came to Naxjivan," he told me as we made our way back to Naxjivan city at the end of the long, hot day. "Other aspects of the visit will have to be evaluated over time."

Finally, after several more rallies in Naxjivan town and the second traffic jam in Naxjivan's history, we were all back on the tarmac in front of the pathetic shell of Naxjivan airport and Demirel was climbing aboard his Gulf Stream, waving his fedora at the adoring throng. The pressure door closed and the jet taxied to the runway and lifted off into the sky for the westward journey home.

"*Vsë!*" sighed one of the Naxjivani maidens to another, as they dropped their wave-exhausted arms. "It's over!" She was speaking Russian.

Meanwhile, two men and their retinues were left standing on the tarmac, each wondering what to do with the other.

"It is time to transfer authority from old shoulders like mine to the younger generation," Aliyev cordially said to Gamberov.

"Your long years of leadership are a great source of inspiration for us," replied Gamberov with apparent respect.

Our Tupelov pulled up, and the Baku delegation re-boarded. I was the last up the ramp, and turned to Heydar to say good-bye.

"Why not come to Baku with us?" I asked playfully, indicating the way up the stairs and into the plane. Heydar stared at me.

"Not yet," he said, and turned away.

13

From Ballots to Bullets

For all intents and purposes, Abulfez Elchibey was already president of Azerbaijan when the country held its first free elections on June 7, 1992. The Popular Front chairman had moved into the executive building and was participating in every decision made by the Gamberov interim government.

"Abulfez thinks I like it so much here that I will declare a state of emergency and suspend the elections," Gamberov joked shortly before the polls were held.

Still, it was a strange election. Rallies and meetings had been disallowed due to security concerns, so there was no 'campaign' per se. The real battle for votes was conducted on television, but in a very stilted way. Each of the candidates was given an hour to meet the nation, live. The format included 15 minutes for the candidate to present his views as he saw fit, and then 45 minutes to field questions on a call-in basis. It was almost *Larry King, Live!* in Azerbaijan, save for a few cultural details.

Elchibey, running under his legal name of Abulfez Aliev, was the first to appear. In a cool and realistic assessment of the situation in the country, he reiterated the message he had been delivering for years. The country had to take on all the attributes of statehood, from maintaining its own borders to establishing its own currency. While Azerbaijan needed to develop bilateral ties with its neighbors, he categorically rejected the idea of inclusion in the Commonwealth of Independent States. Karabakh was an integral and inseparable part of Azerbaijan, a place where citizens of many different ethnic backgrounds might live in peace while obeying the laws of the land. He expressed hope that mediation by international bodies such as the CSCE, NATO, and the United Nations would help achieve a peaceful solution to the Karabakh conflict and keep it from turning into a full-fledged war with neighboring Armenia; Azerbaijan had to be prepared for this, however, and thus needed an army.

When questions began, Elchibey fielded them with candor. Someone asked why the economic situation remained so bleak and why foreign investors remained so few. Elchibey replied that western investors were reluctant to do business because of the perception of instability in the country, a state of affairs that would end once a new, legitimate regime was in power. Someone else called in to ask about state economic policy, and Elchibey's response was blunt: There is no state economic policy today because there is no state, he said. Azerbaijan was emerging from the anarchy of the collapse of the Soviet Union and had to start from scratch. Then, when asked how he felt about the inclusion of members of the old Communist elite in the current government, Elchibey waxed Lincolnesque and stressed that there was room for cooperation with anyone in the country who wished to build the Azerbaijan of the future. Now was the time for unity, and not division.

The other six candidates qualified as a motley crew, and none really had much to say.

First, there was the Deputy Chairman of Parliament, Tamerlan Garayev. That he was a candidate at all was peculiar, because as a Front member Garayev was supposed to support Front candidate Elchibey. He was unable to define his motives for running, aside from some vague notion of 'keeping the process honest' and providing 'constructive opposition.'

Etibar Mamedov, the chairman of the National Independence Party group, was an even stranger contender. Within days of announcing his candidacy, the 'Little Napoleon' revoked it—but then withheld his 'official' withdrawal until the last week of the campaign, in order to use television and radio time devoted to presidential candidates to foul the electoral process.

Equally strange was the continued candidacy of 'Dollar' Yaqub Mamedov. Despite the onus attached to his participation in the aborted Mutalibov operation, he had decided to stay in the race to the bitter end.

Bringing up the rear in the field of six were a pair of vanity candidates whom no one ever heard of before or after the polls: Rafig Abdullayev and Ilyas Ismailov. They had nothing to say for themselves.

Then, at the last moment, a seventh candidate announced his intention to contest the elections: Nizami Suleymanov, an obscure academic whose claim to fame was his having invented a unique water filter that looked like a can with two plastic antennas sticking out. Because he was last in line alphabetically, Suleymanov was also the last to speak on TV. We tuned in more out of a sense of completion than real interest.

It promised to be entertaining, anyway. For starters, Nizami disagreed with the other candidates about the state of the country. Azerbaijan was rich, very rich. True, it had been looted by previous regimes, but the country's resources remained such, that rather than raise the price of bread and other essential goods in accordance with market economy reforms promoted by the other candidates, a Nizami government would actually slash the price of a whole range of goods—bread, butter, and meat were just a few commodities that would be reduced in price by 1,000 percent. The inventor had other ideas, too: it was time to use Azerbaijan's oil wealth to put all government employees on world-level dollar salaries. As for the thorny problem of Karabakh, Nizami had a secret plan that was guaranteed to liberate the territory within three months—and without the loss of life or limb of another Azeri national.

It was, to dip into American political metaphor, an anti–Ross Perot performance: rather than asking the populace to 'look under the hood' of cars coming off the line at General Motors, Nizami was asking everyone to look in the display window of the nearest Mercedes dealership, pick the car of their choice, and send the state the bill.

I didn't take it very seriously until the next day, when I conducted a quick straw poll among the usual 'typical' types who go into straw polls: taxi drivers, telephone operators, and the underemployed one found hanging around street corners and cafes.

The response was sobering. No one mentioned anything about independence or statehood or foreign investment or cultural ideology or the rule of law and democratic pluralism or anything else that Elchibey had spoken about. Nizami was the name on everyone's lips. One man rubbed his hands and put it like this: "I want butter."

* * *

Compounding the problem of Nizami's sudden surge in popularity was the Front government's response to it. Rather than confront the issue directly and explain why Nizami's quick fix to all the worldly woes of Azerbaijan was just a pack of lies, the Elchibey inner circle merely chuckled. But as the promise of free butter and meat and cheap bread and gasoline began to resonate through the land, the reaction of Abulfez and his inner circle moved from humor to anger. The glorious democratic moment they had all been waiting for, when a responsible public could choose the future of the nation, was being hijacked by a pied piper! It was beyond outrageous and insulting; it was utterly disappointing.

And then, two days before the election, the Front blinked. Another live, three-hour debate between the candidates had been scheduled to take place at the television studios on Friday, June 5th. Etibar Mamedov had by this time officially withdrawn. But of the remaining six, only five showed. Elchibey's chair was empty.

The other candidates waited for a decent period of time, and then the moderator began the program. The first candidate to take the microphone was Tamerlan Garayev. His remarks were succinct: for the sake of the nation, he was withdrawing his candidacy and throwing his support to Elchibey. Then he walked out of the studio, leaving the moderators, audience, and other candidates flabbergasted—and angry. Still they waited for the man of the moment—Abulfez Elchibey. He never showed up.

Quite naturally, this became a subject that Nizami capitalized on during the debate between the remaining four candidates—Dollar Yaqub, Abdullayev, Ismailov, and himself. But center stage belonged to Nizami. Elchibey's refusal to participate in the forum was proof positive that he was not the great democrat he claimed to be, the inventor said. It also proved his fear of going nose to nose with Nizami over economic matters, and was also an open insult to the viewers and the public. During the course of the three-hour program, he had the chance to repeat these charges again and again.

Elchibey's response came a day later. On June 6th, he held his own press conference at the Popular Front HQ. It was carried live on state television and it featured only one man: Abulfez Elchibey. Not only was it outrageously arrogant, it was also illegal, because all electoral 'propaganda' was to have ceased at midnight on the evening of the 5th. As such, it was a crystal clear abuse of the would-be independence of the media.

And Elchibey's performance did not reassure. He was shrill, even belligerent—especially in answering questions about Nizami. The other pundits kept ducking the question, so it fell to me to ask why he had not been at the debate—and where he had been instead.

"I have no time to deal with Nizami's nonsense," said Elchibey with a snort. "And as for where I was, I was over at the KGB. . . ."

The idea of Elchibey hanging around the KGB after midnight was so ironic that it drew howls of laughter from the crowd. But it also left a gnawing question: what right did Elchibey have to assume that he would win the elections the next day? After listening to two hours of blather, I left for a cigarette and found Hugh Pope.

"Is he drunk?" asked Pope.

"It's not very pretty, is it," I replied.

"I hope he wins tomorrow," said Hugh.

"Why?"

"Because if he doesn't, it sounds like he'll win anyway."

It was not a comforting thought.

* * *

The polls opened early Sunday morning. As the official international monitors spread out over the city and countryside, I chose two nearby polling stations as my unofficial control points—#7 at the Baku Academy of Sciences, and #8 at a nearby school. After inspecting voter registration forms and interviewing the polling station monitors, I went outside and waited for voters to emerge in order to conduct what they call an informal exit poll.

This was more difficult than it sounds. First I had to stop people and then explain what I was trying to do—namely, invade the privacy of the voting booth. Not only had my interlocutors never had free elections before, but they had never had snoopy foreigners going around asking how they had voted.

By noon, however, I had managed to collect data from 80 voters. They seemed to be a pretty good cross-section of the neighborhood: mainly middle- to upper-class Azeris, but with a strong mixture of Russians and Jews. If truth be told, it looked like natural Mutalibov turf, and I was surprised to learn that something more than 50 percent of those I managed to interview said they had voted for Elchibey. Suleymanov claimed around 25 percent, while the remaining 25 percent was split among the three other official candidates; those who allowed themselves to be interviewed but declined to identify who they voted for; and those who openly admitted that they had cast their vote for a name that was conspicuous by its absence on the ballots: Heydar Aliyev.

At noon, I took a break to join a casual group of official and unofficial observers for lunch at the Caravansary Restaurant to compare notes. The voting patterns were pretty much the same. One issue, though, was the matter of 'block voting' in more down-market neighborhoods. Michael Ochs of the Helsinki Commission opined that this tendency, for one family member to vote for part or all of the clan, was certainly illegal, but would have been more disturbing if it had not been so innocent. He had discovered one man carrying five passports: his own, his wife's, his daughter's, his mother's, and finally, that of his younger brother, who was a war invalid. The block voting seemed to be spread out across the spectrum and reflected the overall patterns. We decided to note the phenomenon but not to cry foul.

The biggest question, however, was whether the elections would legally stick. A quorum of the nation's approximately 3.9 million potential voters—including the Armenians of Mountainous Karabakh—was 50 percent plus one. If a quorum were not established, new elections had to be held after two months. Alternatively, if a quorum were established and no candidate gathered more than 50 percent of the total, a runoff had to be held after three weeks.

Audrey Altstadt, the world's leading scholar on Azerbaijan, happened to be in town doing some research and joined us for lunch. She came out with a distressing statistic: it was generally held in scholarly circles that less than 30 percent of all potential voters ever really cast their ballots in (Soviet) Azerbaijani elections. More distressing still was the possibility that if no quorum were established in the first and second rounds, the full parliament could then choose an acting president—and one not subject to the various regulations of candidates for the job. Only one name came to mind: Heydar Aliyev. Pieces were starting to fall into place, but I still had not figured out the puzzle.

Fortified with caviar and champagne, we fanned out across the city and its suburbs again to try and get a second reading on trends or simply to remind the polling station workers that they were being watched. My last destination was Mashtagah, a place known for its mixture of politics, religion, and commerce. In local parlance, that meant Mutalibov, his Repentance Society, and the Azeri mafia. But once again, voting patterns largely fit those of downtown Baku: about 50 percent for Elchibey, 25 percent for Suleymanov, and 25 percent for others, including candidates with no names and protest ballots. Block voting was very widespread here, but seemingly spread over the general voting pattern. One individual even announced that he—and thus his entire family—was boycotting the elections because a local poll station worker had refused him his right to vote for all.

"There is a real clash between the spirit and the letter of the election law," said Audrey Altstadt. "Preventing heads of traditional families from a vote for all is close to disenfranchisement, because many people won't vote any other way."

There was one reassuring aspect of our controlling the polls at Mashtagah. Of 4,868 registered voters at the two stations we had controlled, 3,971 had cast ballots by the time we left. By our statistics, that was over 81 percent participation in Mashtagah; if those numbers were reflected nationwide, the elections had passed the hurdle of the initial quorum. The next question was who the 81 percent had voted for.

* * *

I had made arrangements to monitor the ballot box opening and counting at station #7, in the Academy of Sciences. After the polls closed, the station master signaled to a policeman to go and bar the door, and the local monitors picked up the locked ballot boxes, unlocked them, and spilled the ballots out on a long table around which sat six designated ballot counters. Then the monitors sat down behind the counters and began to monitor as the counters made stacks of ballots according to candidate, with a separate stack of ballots that the counters deemed disqualified. The process was completed after an hour or so, and the numbers were read out and noted by the station master, who then asked the monitors if they wished to personally check any or all of the stacks. None did. Then all the individual stacks were collected into larger units, separated according to candidate with a separate category for disqualified ballots, and then counted again. The station master then asked the monitors again if they wished to check any or all stacks. Once again, they declined. The total percentages at Polling Station #7 were as follows: Abulfez (Elchibey) Aliev had received 56 percent, followed by Nizami Suleymanov with 32 percent. The third largest category was that of disqualified ballots—8 percent. Rafig Abdullayev followed with 3 percent and Yaqub Mamedov with 1 percent. Ilyas Ismaelov had not received one vote at voting station #7.

For the record, I then asked each local monitor if they had any qualms or complaints. All expressed their complete satisfaction and trust in the results. Then they asked me what I thought about the first free and fair elections in Azerbaijan. I replied that aside from a few instances of block voting in Mashtagah, I was well pleased and very impressed with the civilized manner in which the polls were conducted. Then I personally thanked them for inviting me in to help monitor the counting. There would be those who would charge fraud, I told them, and their allowing me to witness the actual counting procedure would help refute such charges. To underline the point, I related the details about an encounter I had with two men in front of the polling station.

"They told me that Nizami would get 90 percent of the vote but that the Front would put in a fix to prevent his victory," I said. "So I showed them the results of my exit polls that suggested that Nizami was only getting about 30 percent, to prove that their claim of a fixed election did not appear to have any basis in fact."

The poll station attendants then put the ballots in a sealed container, signed a document that listed the official results, and Polling Station #7 at the Academy of Sciences was closed. In theory, it would not be used as a voting station for a presidential election for another five years.

* * *

We had stocked in a good amount of vodka, caviar, bread, and butter, as well as party-type snacks, in anticipation of a traditional all-night election watch around our television. While waiting for the early returns, we compiled our own preliminary results drawn from the information collected at the various voting stations monitored by the dozen or so people staying in or passing through our abode. Altogether, our collective, unscientific results suggested that total participation ran at around 70 percent—well over the 50.1 percent needed to make the election results valid. Of this, Abulfez seemed to be collecting around 60 percent against Nizami's 30 percent, with the remaining 10 percent scattered to the four winds. Still, we were only dealing with a tiny fraction of the potential vote, and so before filing any stories we thought it best to wait for a larger, more official picture.

Around midnight, the head of the electoral commission of Azerbaijan, Jafar Veliev, appeared on television with an announcement: the chairman of the Popular Front, Abulfez Elchibey, had made an unofficial estimate of the election results. According to Elchibey, he had received around 65 percent of the vote, with Nizami Suleymanov receiving around 30 percent.

Although those results tallied more or less with our estimates, we found it more than a little odd that the head of the election commission would quote one of the candidates about unofficial results, and then not even bother to back up the claim with anything resembling statistics. Well, we said to ourselves, perhaps it was merely a mistake, and hard numbers would soon be forthcoming. It was not to be. Instead of being the first of a series of announcements, it was also the last: Veliev signed off with the remark that in accordance with the constitution, the official results would be ready in ten days.

Ten days? We were dumbfounded. From all appearances, the elections had been run in a free and fair manner and Elchibey had apparently won by a substantial margin. But here was the election commission, known for its previous corruption, literally throwing the results into doubt by its indifference to processing the numbers in a rapid and forthright manner—and with the apparent collusion of the would-be winner. It was beyond political sabotage. It was almost political suicide.

Michael Ochs of the U.S. Congressional Helsinki Commission spelled out the problem from his perspective. He was leaving the next day, and had to come up with something more definitive than Abulfez Elchibey declaring provisional victory through the mouth of Jafar Veliev. So we made a plan. If these guys didn't know how to run a post-election wrap-up, we would teach them.

In the morning, Ochs and I managed to reach Jafar Veliev at his office in the electoral commission. We thanked Veliev for receiving us during this important and hectic period, but said we felt obliged to take some of his valuable time to note the dearth of any preliminary results. It was, well, irregular.

"What's irregular to you is a matter of indifference to me," said Veliev. "The constitution states quite clearly that I am not obliged to announce anything until ten days after the election."

The country was large; there was war. One needed time to collect and check and double check. We listened to this smoke for awhile, and then Ochs rammed home the point in less than completely diplomatic terms: without an immediate, public announcement of preliminary results, most the world would start to suspect that the elections in Azerbaijan had been a fraud.

"But that is a scandal!" squealed Veliev.

"So is sitting on the ballots for ten days," Ochs replied.

Silence filled the room as Veliev glared at us.

"We have a recommendation," said Ochs. "It is that you hold an immediate press conference, preferably with international observers who monitored the process, and give us some numbers."

A seething Veliev reached for some papers on his desk and then spat out a couple of numbers: 79 percent of all potential voters had voted; 55.1 percent had cast their ballots for Elchibey, and 29 percent for Suleymanov. He did not bother to tell us whether this was final, professional, local, or national.

"Mister Veliev," Ochs repeated. "The point is not to tell us, but the public."

We were not surprised when three hours later, the Chairman of the Electoral Commission of the Republic of Azerbaijan, Mr. Jafar Veliev, held a press conference to announce unofficial preliminary results of the presidential elections held the day before.

The press conference was mind-numbingly bad. It consisted of a very sour Veliev announcing the same numbers he had recited under duress to Ochs and me earlier in the day: 79 percent participation, 55.1 percent of the ballots for Abulfez and 29 percent for Nizami.

"Are these the final results?" someone asked.

"No," snapped Veliev. "Officials are still counting."

"Then what percentage of the vote are the preliminary results based on?" I asked.

"You ask too many questions," he snapped.

"That is what a press conference is for!" I shouted back.

Happily, the assistant chairman of the electoral commission, Asim Mullahzade, intervened and announced that the percentages just delivered to the press were derived from 325 wards in eight districts in the region of Baku, where of 453,738 potential voters, 338,057 citizens had cast ballots. Once again, the numbers sounded right even if the attitude of those delivering them seemed wrong.

There was one last task to be performed before putting the elections to bed, hopefully forever: contact the main loser, Nizami Suleymanov. Whatever else, he had run a phenomenal campaign. A total unknown collecting something like 30 percent of the vote! Even his detractors had to admit that it had been an impressive performance. I called his office to solicit his views.

"I'd like to speak with Mister Nizami, please."

"Who are you?"

"A foreign correspondent for the—"

"FRAUD!! THE ELECTIONS! HIJACKED! STOLEN!"

The man himself was on the phone, it seemed.

Nizami was appealing to the world. He had contacted the American and Turkish embassies, but both were indifferent to his plight: they were in bed with the Popular Front. . . . To reveal this and other crimes, he was going to hold a press conference to expose the election-rigging crimes of the neo-Bolshevik Popular Front!

The last thing I needed at this point was overexposure to a sore loser, but professionalism overruled prudence and I agreed to meet Nizami to see the evidence he claimed to possess. I was soon walking into Nizami's institute on the outskirts of town. He leapt up from behind his desk to embrace me like an old friend and comrade when I entered.

"For the sake of freedom and democracy, you must tell the world about this travesty!" he wailed, tears in his eyes.

I was stunned. Not with the theatrics; I had expected as much. I was stunned because we had met before. The date was May 28th, and the venue was Naxjivan in front of Heydar Aliyev's office. He was the frog face! And as I looked around the room, I realized that I knew about half of the Nizami supporters sitting there—and all within the context of Naxjivan and Heydar Aliyev. The old fox: Nizami was Heydar's stalking horse!

I pretended to be taking notes as Nizami filled my ear with vicious, anti-Elchibey innuendo. I desperately waited for a convenient moment to escape, but it never came. When my special, exclusive interview came to an end, Nizami invited me—no, forced me, for the sake of democracy and truth—to attend his scheduled press conference.

The venue was a special acoustical dome. I don't know if it was Nizami's design, but the structure allowed some two hundred people to speak to each other across the thirty-meter diameter as if they were having a private conversation with someone three feet away. There was no need to bellow or shout or use a microphone. The effect was nearly hypnotically intimate and soothing. In my instance, however, it was almost torture. There was no escape from Nizami's voice, floating, or ping-ponging, or reverberating across the acoustical tiles of the dome, reiterating his charges of massive fraud and a hijacked election and producing his evidence.

"Here are five ballots cast by dead people for Abulfez," chuckled Nizami, waving some papers in the air. "And here are another ten ballots made out to the same name—all had been cast for Abulfez!" (Actually, the exclamation point I just included in the text was not there in his speech; there was no need to raise one's voice at all in the dome.) "They will tell you that Abulfez received 65 percent of the vote and that we received 25 percent," cooed Nizami. "This is a lot better than the old days, when the electoral commission would announce that candidates received 99 percent of the vote. That's progress! Now they try and lie in a reasonable manner."

Individual chuckles bounced around the dome.

"But I will tell you the truth. According to our sources, we collected 90 percent of the vote. Even in Naxjivan, Abulfez's home district, we know we got 90 percent. But they will tell you that they got 65 percent and we got 25 percent."

The most damning chunk of evidence, however, was a stack of 90 ballots cast for Nizami that had been removed from a certain Baku polling station and thrown in the trash. A friendly monitor had been thoughtful enough to bring this to Nizami's attention. He invited the monitor to come forward and present the evidence.

Once again I was stunned: it was a woman monitor at the Academy of Sciences polling station, #7, where I myself had controlled the counting.

"Yes," she said. "What Nizami said is true. There was massive fraud at the polling station at the Academy of Sciences. Why, our friend the foreign correspondent was a witness to this himself. His estimate is that 90 percent of the ballots cast were for Nizami but that corrupt officials cooked the results into something quite different." Everyone in the room turned, ready to hear me vouch for the horrible truth about the corrupt events at voting station #7.

"I never said anything like that or saw anything like that!" I sputtered.

"But you told us!" came the ghostly voice, ricocheting off the dome.

"I said no such thing!"

I was suddenly having an argument with thirty different people, but no one wanted to listen to a word I had to say. That was not why I had been invited.

"Thank you, thank you," said Nizami who now wanted to move on to an analysis of the election. The reason that the Front had been compelled to stoop so low was perfectly evident, Nizami said: they had no support, and they knew that the people knew that he was the only man who could change Azerbaijan. Even Yagub Mamedov, on the day before the election, had realized this, and calling Nizami, had informed him that he had thrown all his support to him. Still, mistakes had been made, and Nizami hoped his supporters would forgive him. For example, he had grossly overestimated the cost of bread and meat and butter in his economic plan, and this might have cost him some votes. And as for his secret solution to the problem of Mountainous Karabakh, well, he now felt obliged to reveal a few key points. He had many friends in Moscow, in the highest levels of government and industry. These friends, who feared and loathed the Popular Front, had expressed a keen interest to supply him, personally, with a number of attack helicopters via Iran. They were to be flown by Russian mercenaries. The fighting on the ground, too, would be conducted by foreign troops, because the sad truth was that the Azeri youth were not accustomed to fighting. He estimated that his Clean-Out-Karabakh campaign could be effected in 90 days.

Then Nizami got down to the meat of the matter. He didn't want to dwell on the past, but the future.

". . . and if the people demand that I lead the struggle against the neo-Bolshevik dictatorship that has stolen our victory by force and falsification, I am ready," Suleymanov said in an ordinary speaking voice.

"Yes, we want you to do that," the crowd calmly replied.

"My first act as president will be to invite the *Aksakal* to join me here in Baku to lead us all," said Nizami.

"Good idea," said the crowd.

I wanted to scream.

The *Aksakal*—the 'White Beard,' or Wise Leader.

In Azerbaijan, there was only one such: Heydar Aliyev.

The Man from Naxjivan had just announced that he was still in the game by calling the validity of the elections he could not contest into doubt.

You had to give credit where credit was due. The biggest crocodile of them all was still in the swamp, eyes blending into the surface, waiting for the goats to walk by.

* * *

Perhaps it was a good thing that Nizami claimed to have won the election with 90 percent of the vote. If he had cast his protest in a more reasonable manner—such as maintaining that both he and Abulfez had taken 45 percent each—he could have created a much bigger problem. He had managed to tarnish the polls, but his outrageous claims made them easy to dismiss.

Thus, despite the continued coyness of the Electoral Commission about issuing official results, by the evening of June 8, 1992, Abulfez Aliyev Elchibey became the president-apparent of Azerbaijan. On June 13th, he was announced the official winner. On June 18th, draped in the blue, green, and red national flag, he took the oath of office in the shell-scarred parliament, kissing the Quran at the end of the proceedings.

I was not around for either the official announcement of Elchibey's victory or for his swearing in, having departed on the evening of the 12th for a scheduled speaking tour in the United States. In preparation for the trip, I had asked to speak to president-apparent Elchibey. The old access was already becoming difficult—the growing crowd of diplomats, oilmen, and assorted sycophants all had preferential meeting and greeting rights, it seemed. Then, around eleven o'clock on the evening of June 10th, the telephone rang. It was Vafa Gulizade.

"I am sorry to call you so late," he said. "And I hope you have not been drinking too much. The president wants to see you."

I ate a chunk of garlic and brewed some coffee, and then walked down the street to the presidential building, hung around Vafa's office for another hour, and then, at midnight, stood up to congratulate Abulfez when he walked into the room.

It was less a formal interview than a meeting between old friends, and so I decided to focus on the personal, intimate details of Elchibey's life rather than on the usual cliché-eliciting questions I might have asked. One of the first was why he still lived with his brother and his family. The reason for this, Abulfez replied, was a mixture of convenience, tradition, and moral principle: when he had returned from Egypt in the early 1970s, he had a chance to get his own apartment, but he had become so outraged at the treatment given a tubercular old widow waiting in line ahead of him at the housing authority that he had forsworn the right. He had also rejected his second opportunity to get his own home: upon his release from prison in 1976, the KGB had offered to 'assist' him in finding housing, with the implication that their intervention would be in exchange for future favors.

"They worked like that, you know," he reflected. "They would try and get into your life by using the thin edge of a wedge, and after that, you were theirs."

So Elchibey continued to live with his brother, and didn't really like the idea of moving out and into the presidential residence. It was too far from his family and friends. The closest of these were a Jewish family who lived in the apartment next door and had given him great support throughout the years. They were thinking about emigrating to Israel; Elchibey was trying to convince them to stay and participate in the creation of the new nation.

That task was immense, and Elchibey was under no illusions. One could talk about a free-market economy on a theoretical level, but the reality was that the country was already run by a mafia-economy—and breaking that would require time. Another major issue was how to fill the moral void left in the wake of the collapse of communism, without allowing people to fall into the trap of religious bigotry and extremism—as in Iran.

In a way, it was his last chance to whack away at the Islamic Republic without creating an international incident: while the remarks of a president are usually equated with policy, he still was not officially the head of state.

"The state-controlled media in Iran call me a Zionist agent because I favor development of ties with Israel," he chuckled. "And they call the Popular Front an atheist organization—all in an effort to defame us in the eyes of the people of Iran as well among people in Azerbaijan they feel might be susceptible to such slander. And the reason is clear: because we call for the democratization of Iran. Despite the existence of an independent state of Armenia, Iran is supporting 140,000 Armenians who want to establish their own state in our country, while at the same time 20 million Azeris in southern Azerbaijan are unable to open up their own schools. Can you imagine the repression involved? And at the same time Iran says it wants to mediate in the Karabakh conflict! Let it focus on its own problems! Don't expect blood from one wound and water from another."

I reminded him of his speech in parliament on March 28th, when he had condemned the 'crocodiles' for their decision to go ahead with presidential elections during a time of crisis, and his prediction that whoever was elected would be deposed within six months simply because of the sickness of the system.

"I have thought about that speech for some time," said Abulfez. "The point was less the need to abolish the presidency than the need to create a system wherein absolute power does not rest in the presidential apparatus. The president must be responsible to the parliament, and not the other way around. That is why we need three separate bodies, controlling each other: the executive, the legislature, and an independent judiciary."

It seemed a little thin to me, but I let it pass.

"We are nearing the end of a long and difficult journey—the creation and preservation of a truly independent state of Azerbaijan," he continued. "That is my mission. I may die tomorrow, or I may die today, but the main thing is a truly free and independent Azerbaijan. The idea terrifies the dictatorships in the region, and therein lies the danger. If we can have five months of peace, free of the war with Armenia, our economy will start to develop and then you will see the democratic movement begin in both southern Azerbaijan and Central Asia. It will be impossible to stop this movement."

Finally, with the clock moving past one in the morning, I brought up the stickiest subject of all: Karabakh, and what approach the Elchibey administration would take to heal this gaping wound in the middle of the national psyche. Had not the Armenians succeeded in establishing, by fait accompli, a quasi independent state in Karabakh that his government would simply have to live with? Elchibey meditated on this for a moment, and then gave me what I only later understood to be a Delphic response.

"If the world wants to think about faits accomplis, let us look at the matter of Karabakh in the following manner," he said. "Let us assume that Azerbaijan goes so far as to recognize Karabakh as an independent state or even as part of Armenia. Good. Then we devote all our resources to create a great army, and one day overrun not only Karabakh but Armenia and announce our own fait accompli. If you let one fait accompli stand, why not the next? Where does it end? We are a member of the United Nations and subscribe to its tenets. Armenia is also a member of the U.N. and says it subscribes to the same tenets. If this is so, the question has to be asked: why is Armenia invading the territory of an independent state? If it comes to force, we will wait—and then, when we are ready, we will give our own answer in kind."

* * *

The answer was given on June 12th, when the Azeri national army, spearheaded by Iskender Hamidov's Bozkurt Brigade and OMON units of the police, launched a massive offensive across the entire north of Mountainous Karabakh. Or so it was reported on CNN, sourcing Yerevan, as I sat in an Istanbul hotel room, in transit to the United States.

I laughed. The concept of an Azeri attack was an oxymoron. It was axiomatic that when the Armenians declared themselves on the defensive, the exact opposite was the case. What about Xodjali, Shusha, and now, so recently, Lachin? The big question was where they would attack—Agdam, Fizuli, or Kelbajar?

But this time the Armenians were right.

At the height of the chaos of the coup and countercoup of mid-May, Azerbaijan and all the other republics of the former USSR had met in Tashkent to sign an additional protocol to the Conventional Forces in Europe (CFE) Agreement governing the force levels allowed to members of the (former) Warsaw Pact and NATO. The details were arcane, but the essence was that Warsaw Pact weaponry had to be moved—and the Tashkent protocol provided for just that. In exchange for the former Soviet republics assuming a share of the collective USSR foreign debt, they received part of the army. In the case of Armenia and Azerbaijan, that meant an army apiece: 220 battle tanks, 220 BTRs and BMPs, 220 other pieces of mechanized weaponry such as GRAD missile launchers and field artillery, plus 100 combat aircraft, ranging from MiG–24s to attack helicopters.

And the equipment was almost immediately available. In addition to Europe, the other major front in the Cold War was between the Caucasus republics of the USSR and Turkey and Iran. Accordingly, the Kremlin devoted significant resources to this particular theater—the 4th and 7th armies. In concrete terms, this meant that both Armenia and Azerbaijan, like two wayward nephews of a rich, childless uncle, were to become heirs to all the nonnuclear, conventional weaponry stationed on their territory.

The local arms race in Karabakh that had begun with pistols and shot-guns had not just escalated, it was about to go through the roof.

Azerbaijan struck first.

14

An Army Stumbles Forward

The outgoing Azeri artillery in the wheat field behind the reservoir thunders in the distance like deadly timpani while the incoming Armenian mortar rounds from behind the ridge come whistling in like evil piccolos. Between is the staccato cough and sputter of high-caliber machine gun and other, smaller arms fire, crashing through the canopy of trees.

. . . *Brrrit-tit-tit, Brrrit-tit-tat!*

VTWWWWEEE! . . . VBROOOMMB!

It is a satanic cacophony, and it is all too near.

Then something big erupts from behind the trees to the right and I am eating dirt between the front wheels of a truck while Mustafa my guide laughs. An ecologist with expertise in Caspian Sea pollution in better times, he has learned many things about the front that I have not—like the difference between incoming and outgoing rounds. He is also laughing because not only do I not know when to duck, I don't know where: the truck I am under is a portable ammunition dump, loaded high with boxes of shells and self-propelled grenades. It is a necessary load because an army travels more on its ammo than on its stomach. But it is not what one wants to get caught hiding beneath when it gets hit by incoming fire.

And I am not alone as the object of Mustafa's mirth. There, under the truck with me, are about a dozen greenhorn recruits from the Baku Automobile Police Inspectors Group who have just joined us at this part of the mountainous front. Like me, they have crawled under the truck rather than seek shelter in the leaves and twigs of the nearest ditch.

Then Mustafa is diving into a ditch and I try to flop in after him as a deafening explosion smacks into the embankment behind us, maybe 100 yards to the left. Another shell bursts 75 yards to the right, and then a third maybe 50 yards to the left again.

"They know where we are," he says, smile wiped from his face. "They are working a coordinate grid pattern and are finding the range. It's going to get nasty now."

Great.

It was August 1992, a time of year when most of my pals in Montana were off fly-fishing and working the barbecue. But here I was, back in Azerbaijan, doing my duty—recording the death and destruction of the great Azeri offensive in northern Karabakh. Since launching the offensive on June 12th, the Azeris had allegedly rolled back all the Armenian gains over the past year, at great human cost. Armenian sources were talking about figures like 20,000 dead on their side alone. This was clearly an exaggeration; but because the Azeris had not allowed any outside observers anywhere near the front, there was no way of knowing for sure. Nor was there any independent confirmation of the Azeri claim that they actually controlled the northern third of the disputed territory. The only source of information was the so-called 'Analytical Department of the Press Office of the Ministry of National Defense,' which broadcast new gains every night on national television.

The week before, the said department announced that the national defense forces had taken the key town of Mekhmana, south of the Sarsank reservoir. That is why I am here on this particular stretch of mountain road in northern Karabakh. Pulling every string in the government I could, I finally managed to convince the authorities to let me into the combat zone to see the aftermath of the battle.

Maybe the ministry actually believed that their army had taken Mekhmana. But the evidence at hand—a battle blowing up around me—would suggest differently. More to the point, I may be the first foreigner (mercenaries aside) allowed up to the front Azeri lines since the army began its offensive, but I don't want to be the first foreigner (mercenaries aside) to buy the red badge of stupidity in this seesaw campaign to control Karabakh.

Vbam-BRAM!

Another missile whistles in and smashes somewhere nearby, bringing me back to the specific present and the task of eating dirt again. The greenhorns are also flat on the ground. My ears are ringing, so I can't tell if anyone is moaning, wounded, dying, or dead, or whether they are just hunkered down next to the ammo dump.

I think it is time to go. The main thing is to get away from the ammunition dump before it blows. I jog down the road toward an armored personnel carrier they call a BTR. It has four solid rubber wheels and carries a 70mm gun in a dwarf turret. Actually, there are two BTRs standing there by the side of the road and they are made of metal and look strong. They would be more reassuring if there were someone manning the guns or manning the steering column so that we might drive away at full speed if need be, but there isn't anybody behind the wheel or the guns—just two empty, armed steel boxes parked by the side of the road. I kind of hunch down next to the huge rubber wheel of one of the beasts and try to make it look like I am only leaning up against it. Two of the greenhorn soldiers who were huddling next to the ammunition death-dump truck follow me over to the BTRs. They, too, are trying to look casual. One asks for a smoke, and I pass him an Astara. It is the local equivalent to a Lucky Strike Straight—a World War II sort of smoke, strong and unfiltered, the kind Audie Murphy would have smoked if he had been an Azeri grunt and if he had smoked. The other guy asks for a light, and I try to oblige him, but the matches are damp from sweat and my hands are shaking.

"Are you afraid?" one asks with a grin. I am about to punch him in the nose when another mortar shell comes in and leaves us sprawling on the ground. We all laugh when we realize we have survived. We are all scared shitless.

"Why don't you get inside the BTR," one suggests. "It is safer than out here." I decline the invitation, saying I feel better outside, where I can move. Another mortar shell crashes in, very close, and I climb into one of the twin sphincter-like apertures in the back of the machine while my new friends climb in the other. Once inside, they pretend it was my idea to get in the BTR in the first place and that they are to keep me company inside the steel coffin out of a sense of duty and courtesy. I pull out cigarettes and this time succeed in lighting my own and start smoking, filling the cramped interior with blue haze. They want to talk, but all I can do is think. Specifically, I wonder what happens when a mortar round connects with two-inch steel. Does it bounce off and leave us laughing, or does it penetrate and kill us instantly, or does it do something in between, leaving me permanently deaf? I had spent a lot of time and effort learning a bunch of foreign languages and it would be a pity to put them on low volume forever just because I decided to be a war correspondent in the wrong time and place.

VTRRRRRREEEE. . . . . . !

That one rocks the BTR and brings me back to the present. Then there are voices outside, speaking staccato Azeri, and someone is prying open the steel-trap door on the back of the BTR. It is Mustafa from the Defense Ministry. I think he wants to get in and try to make room, but he reaches in and drags me out, and we are running toward the staff car that served as our transport up into this little corner of hell.

We get in, but it won't start. And it is parked in the wrong direction. We will have to push it in a curve out into the road in order to turn it around. These guys have brought me up to the very front lines to get my head shot off, and now I am supposed to push their damned car around so they can jump-start it on a downhill roll, hopefully before the next mortar round blows us to smithereens. *No way.*

There is an ambulance down the road that is already pointed in the right direction and ready to go. I make a break and sprint to the ambulance and get in, leaving Mustafa behind. The better part of valor and all that. Another mortar round comes crashing in behind us, but we are already spinning through the first hairpin turn and going downhill, fast. The ambulance lurches on two wheels, narrowly avoiding a T-72 battle tank roaring uphill, and skids in a half donut, almost going off the road. A transport truck carrying 50 grim-faced vets comes screaming around the down-side curve and lurches to a halt in front of us, while a VAZ staff car comes roaring down behind us, the driver leaning on the horn. We are blocking the road, and I get out to take a picture.

"What the fuck do you think you are doing!" screams a heavy-set man from the back seat of the VAZ. I start to explain that I am a correspondent and that I—

"A journalist?!" the man howls. "You're not supposed to be here! Where is your damn permission!"

My papers, of course, are with Mustafa. It goes without saying that I am supposed to be with him. That's what guides and permission papers are for when you are a foreigner in a war zone, especially if you like taking pictures of military equipment. Other people might reasonably ask what you are doing there and start saying nasty things about you, like you might be a spy. They do nasty things to suspected spies in war zones when they think you might be responsible for the deaths of their comrades and friends. I am about to respond to the question of permission by explaining that I abandoned my escort several moments before in an act of cowardice, when suddenly we are all ducking, although I am still not sure why.

"They're coming!" wails the heavy-set man. "Let's go!"

The ambulance is already gone and I have no other choice but to get into the second staff car or face the wrath of the advancing Armenian army alone. I choose the former.

"Drive, drive!" screams the rotund major from the back seat. The man sitting next to him—squeezed is a better word—is wearing epaulets on his uniform. He smiles and incongruously greets me in German: *Alles klar?*

We are careening down the mountain road, over craters dug by yesterday's mine implosions and today's missile explosions, and competing with upcoming troop transports.

TWRRRR!

By now, we all know the familiar whistle of an incoming mortar round, and everyone instinctively crouches lower in his seat, holds his breath and prays. Everyone, that is, except for the German-speaking major.

Twrrrrr!

There is no impact.

Twrrrrr!

The German-speaking major laughs and whistles again.

"You shit," says the other major, and chuckles. Everyone else in the staff car laughs.

"You fuck," says the guy crammed next to me. "I thought it was right on top of us."

Twrrrrr! One of the two other guys crammed into the back seat mocks the mortar, and everybody breaks out into a belly-aching laugh of relief.

Twrrrrr! Now it is the driver's turn to pick up the whistle. Everyone laughs again. We are off the mountain road and out of range and are thus feeling safe and foolish for having been so afraid in the first place. The only antidote for this state of affairs is to start spinning epic battle sagas to compensate for our lack of wounds. By the time we have reached the destroyed city of Agdere in the lowlands, the fat major is describing our battle to me as if the others had not even been with him, including illegal me.

We pull up to the police station in the bombed-out town that fell a week before and are met as heroes. The chubby security man continues regaling everyone with his tales of derring-do. Everyone listens attentively and with the respect afforded new veterans of the good fight until the transport I abandoned to jump in the ambulance that led me to the VAZ pulls up in front of the station. Mustafa is okay as is everyone else in the car, but the passenger window is smashed and there are four bullet holes in the door opening to the seat where I should have been sitting.

Just what the hell are you doing here, I ask myself, do you even know where the hell you are? As if to answer my question, another truck filled with volunteers comes wheeling by, heading back up the road to mortar ridge to join the firefight and start adding new blood to the river of sadness spilled in the birthing of this young country.

"*Azerbaijan!*" the green soldiers cry as the truck disappears in its own, self-generated cloud of dust. "*Azerbaijan!*"

* * *

I had been under fire before, but never like that first day on the Mardakert front. The funny thing was that it had taken a lot of effort to almost get killed. After breakfast in Baku, I had flown by helicopter over the barren wasteland of the Azerbaijani steppe, putting down at the airport outside the small city of Yevlakh and proceeding from there by car to the front-line town of Terter for lunch at the regional military headquarters and a briefing by the local commander, Colonel Nejmettin Sadikov. He was an ethnic Azeri from the Russian 'autonomous republic' of Daghestan, and was one of the former Soviet officers who had heeded Rahim Gaziev's call to 'return' to Azerbaijan and serve his ethnic kin. The problem was that he spoke virtually no Azeri, so his headquarters had a distinctly Russian flavor. That was the language we were obliged to communicate in, anyway.

Things were not as rosy as projected in Baku, Sadikov said. The Armenian positions in the heights above the Sarsank reservoir were proving rather difficult to crack. His suspicion was that a number of Russian *Spetsnaz*, or Special Forces troops on loan from Moscow—or maybe just mercenaries were responsible for the problem. Sadikov then kindly offered to equip Mustafa and myself and two photographers, Oleg Litvin and Xalid Askerov, with weapons from the Terter arsenal. Mustafa, Oleg, and Xalid took Kalashnikovs and a couple of hand grenades; I was offered a pistol, but remembered something about the bad mixture of weapons and journalism in Vietnam, and declined the gun. We jumped into a VAZ military jeep and proceeded toward the front—and thus began my career as a 'war correspondent.' In previous encounters with organized violence and crisis, I had just kind of stumbled into the middle of it all. Now, I was specifically risking my life in order to take notes on the progress of an armed action, that is, war.

The most disconcerting thing about it all was that upon my return from the front-line tour, not one newspaper or magazine I was associated with was interested in any reporting whatsoever. Interestingly enough, my personal frustration put me into complete agreement with the Armenians on this issue. To this day, the Armenians are bitter about 'world indifference' to the events of the summer of 1992, and the fact that no reporting was done on the Azeri offensive. Not so. There was mine; it merely remained unpublished. The reason, I suspect, was Bosnia. Ethnic wars begin to resemble one another after a while, and the conflict in the former Yugoslavia put Karabakh on the back burner, editorially speaking.

* * *

Our destination was the town of Imrat Garvant, the little hamlet north of the Sarsank reservoir where Captain Sergei Shukrin of the Soviet Interior Ministry (MVD) forces at Shusha had brought me to inspect a house where an old Azeri lady had been burned to death by her Armenian neighbors. That trip, made atop an MVD armored personnel carrier, had occurred less than a year before. Now I was traveling in a jeep called a VAZ, courtesy of the Azerbaijani Ministry of Defense. How quickly things changed.

The late summer landscape was just as I remembered it: a paved road flanked by ripening wheat north of the Sarsank reservoir, then followed by an increasingly rough dirt track among juniper and pines around the shimmering blue water of the man-made lake.

The strangest thing of all was the fact that there were no people. A year before, there was fear, but still some semblance of normal life in the towns and villages I had passed through. Now there was no normal life at all, only soldiers running up and down the roads and batteries of cannons tucked between the trees. Still, it was easy to forget that this was a war zone until you focused on the details: farmhouses and outbuildings of the Armenian settlements along the road, scarred by burn marks around the windows or punctured with gaping holes in the walls where a tank shell or GRAD missile had connected, blowing out the interior. In the courtyards and barns, disabled tricycle tractors and miniature harvesters lay twisted into weird shapes and sizes, most beyond any possible use but scrap metal.

All along the roadside, too, lay the detritus of ruined lives: suitcases crushed by tank treads, dropped where refugees decided to dump their possessions and run; black-and-white family and school photographs, fluttering in the wind and pinned by one last staple to a shattered frame. It was all too clear that the Armenian civilian population had not been evacuated when the Azeri offensive began. It would be easy to call the Armenians murderously irresponsible for having left civilians as a front-line buffer in a war zone—if you didn't remember that the Azeris had done exactly the same thing at Xodjali and elsewhere. Were all these people so callous to their own kin, or just totally indifferent to the lives of others? What were the civilians doing in Xodjali and Shusha when they fell? What were they doing here?

Not surprisingly, the closer we got to the proper front, the more military rubble we encountered. Scattered piles of ammunition boxes that had carried larger shells and self-propelled grenades and oversized sardine tins that once contained smaller caliber rounds were as common as Pepsi cans along an American highway circa 1965. Then came the shattered tanks and APCs, gutted VAZ staff cars and burned troop trucks, lining the roads, marking the spot where someone had put up stiff resistance. As in every war, both sides would have their heroes—the guys now buried six feet beneath the earth.

As we made our way down to the northern lip of the reservoir, the landscape subtly changed from undulating wheat fields to one of wooded hills and steep ravines, reminiscent of the Blue Ridge Mountains or the Berkshires, perhaps. We passed the spot where a year before Sergei Shukrin's BTR had stopped to inspect the hole in the road where the 27th Soviet soldier had bought the big one. Wire services and newspapers were still using the formula 'Over a thousand dead during three years of ethnic conflict,' if they talked about Karabakh at all. Now the number of soldiers killed in one month of action was in the thousands—and who could say about the civilians?

We drove down to the dam that created the blue ribbon of the Sarsank Reservoir and drove over the road crossing it. The water was mountain blue. In any other setting, the sandy banks would have been lined with sunbathers and the road packed with Sunday picnicers. But not now, not here. We were the only traffic to be seen, and turned the exposed corners of the road at high speed lest someone take a well aimed shot. On several occasions, we came close to pitching off the side of the dirt road into the waters below.

Finally, we arrived at Umudlu—the Azeri town called 'Hope,' which I had passed through a year before. It appeared to be the same town, but with one notable difference: there were no people there. It was time for a stretch, so while Mustafa and Oleg went about picking raspberries from the gardens of the abandoned houses, I watched an artillery duel in progress on the far side of the reservoir. An explosion, sometimes two or three or four, would erupt from some distant location to my left; a second or two later, a plume of smoke and dust would eject into the air among the hazy green trees across the waters; the sound of the explosion would reach us after another three or four seconds, and the concussion of the blast after about five, reverberating across the reservoir.

"Don't stand there," said the solitary guard at the bombed-out security post in the middle of town. "Their snipers are good."

"Thanks," I said. I couldn't imagine anyone under the barrage I was watching would bother to train a sniper scope on such a distant object as me, and I remained where I was, watching shells explode in silent white plumes on the far shore of the man-made lake.

"Hungry?" It was Mustafa, standing at my side, his camouflage cap filled with berries, offering me some.

"No, thanks," I said, having no appetite for anything.

"They say they have sent commandos across by rubber boats to cut the road," he said, chewing a handful of fruit. "I don't think we should go on to Garvant until they clear them."

Commandos in rubber dinghies; plums of silent smoke marking death on the far side of the reservoir; the rattle of distant, indistinct weaponry echoing across the water: *War....*

* * *

We spent the night in the local hospital, in the newly 'liberated' town of Mardakert. My lice-filled bed was in a ward for trauma patients, but all were gone. The town had been reduced to a pile of rubble, an urban quarry for looters who were pillaging anything of value left. Most of these scalpers were Azeris from Karabakh, themselves made refugees at an earlier stage in the conflict. They regarded it as their right to take back what was taken from them. Not only did the soldiers and military police in the area do nothing to stop them, but they seemed to be involved in the looting business as well. Tanker trucks were portaging out quantities of wine and cognac from the shattered distilleries of the region. I was told that the profit was to go to the Azeri war orphan and widows fund, but suspected that it was more likely that sales would be in the hands of the 'national bourgeoisie.'

In the morning, we went over to the local security office. A quarter of the second floor was missing, destroyed when a GRAD missile slammed in during an aborted counteroffensive by the Armenians a week before. As if to guard against the possibility of the Armenians retaking the town, the priority of the authorities had been to rename it, as if in erasing a name, they might erase a memory: henceforth, Mardakert was to be known as Agdere. To underline the change, two new traffic signs had been prepared—one announcing that one was entering the renamed city, and the other announcing that one was leaving it. Lolling about in front of the Agdere police station were a group of about 50 Bozkurt security personnel associated with the Ministry of the Interior. I recognized some of the 'Wolves' from mid-May, when they spearheaded the countercoup against Mutalibov; others knew me from Shusha and Xodjali; still others from Agdam. One was an occasional doubles partner of mine from a tennis club in Baku.

Over a lunch of kebab and salad, washed down with Armenian *chacha*, or potent mulberry spirits, we had the chance to catch up on old friends in different times and places. It was almost old home week, except for the palpable smell of death and imminent destruction in the air. By the next day, we all knew, many of them also would have joined the growing list of the fallen, and our meeting over lunch in the recently renamed town of Agdere was as much a farewell as it was a reunion.

After lunch, we pushed on toward the south side of the Sarsank reservoir, along a road that had been denied us that morning due to the intense shelling from the Armenian positions above. It was a sphincter-cinching drive down a winding tunnel of dense bushes and trees; while the underbrush protected us from detection from spotters in the hills above, the nature of the road was perfect for a partisan ambush, and our unaccompanied VAZ staff car appeared to be a perfect target. Not one sentry had been posted.

Finally, rounding a corner, we ran into the Sadikov Brigade, camped beneath the pine trees on either side of the road. It was an exquisite setting—an alcove in a pine forest, the sounds of a thousand men softened by the inch-deep blanket of fallen needles on the forest floor, the sun setting across the shimmering reservoir, visible through a narrow window carved by nature in the trees. The young soldiers swarmed around our VAZ and destroyed the reverie. They were kids, mainly, cannon fodder, and they knew it. And they were visibly disappointed when they discovered that rather than being senior officers with information about the coming battle plan, to advance or to retreat, the staff car contained only war voyeurs—Mustafa, Oleg, Xalid, and me.

"We have no orders, we have no working tanks, and the GRAD truck is empty," wailed one young man, "They are sending us into battle with slingshots!"

Back up on the ridge, meanwhile, the road was crowded with a dozen pieces of working armor—two battle tanks, a number of BTRs, and a couple of BMP mobile guns—as well as hundreds of men in battle gear. Most were Bozkurts, and they saluted us and each other with the curious Bozkurt greeting—the index and small finger of the right hand extended, with thumb and middle fingers pinched together to create a shadow theater *canus lupus*—for all the world, a "hook 'em horns" salute given by fans at a Texas football game.

Many of the Wolves were dressed in the black jumpsuits and equipped with radios, rolls of high-caliber shells, sniper rifles, and long, wicked-looking Bowie knives. These special forces units were to spearhead the night-fighting on Armenian positions above. Among them were a number of men from the Baku Road Inspectors group, including my tennis partner. He sheepishly raised his Bozkurt salute when I approached.

"It's quite a change from the club in Baku," he said, and then disappeared beneath the forest canopy.

On the road back to Mardakert, we stopped at a knot of cannons firing like crazy into the southern distance. The chief gunner was stripped to the waste and blackened by powder burns and smoke stains. He called me over as his men loaded another shell and powder pack into the big gun. New coordinates had just come in from an invisible spotter overlooking the Armenian lines. After the gunner had modulated the range, he offered me the cord tied to the trigger. I declined. He shrugged his shoulders and then gave the cord a yank.

The concussion nearly knocked me on my back, and by the time my ears stopped ringing, the forward spotter had been able to radio in a new report. The gun had just bagged a tank some fifteen miles away. The entire artillery crew went wild with jubilation. I shuddered at the thought that the potshot might have been mine.

* * *

We drove back down the winding, deserted road to Mardakert/Agdere with our lights out and then proceeded back to Terter for the night. A rumor had passed around that Abulfez Elchibey would make a lightning visit to the front the next day, and I thought it a good idea to be there. We had a sloppy meal at the HQ mess and then checked into the only hotel in town. It was filthy beyond description—although Mustafa maintained that in the bad old days of the USSR, it was the most reasonable hostel in the area. The landlady was accommodating. After assigning us a room already occupied by an exhausted soldier, she became very apologetic and ejected the interloper. Then she gave me a glass of wine from a large jug to make up for the offense. I nearly gagged after the first gulp, sure that I had been poisoned by lighter fluid.

"Sorry, wrong bottle," she said, after taking a sniff herself. "This is the stuff the Armenians use as a starter for cognac."

I continued drinking, licking the edge of the glass rather than sipping the 180–proof stuff in the vain hope that having lighter fluid in my system might ward off fleas.

* * *

There was a commotion in town the next morning: the presidential procession, no doubt. But instead of Elchibey we discovered a truck full of Bozkurts in a very evil mood.

"I want to find that fucking commander and fuck him good," slurred one young man I recognized from the Bozkurt group on the ridge road the evening before.

"What did you say about the colonel?" queried one of the HQ guards, tightening his grip on his Kalashnikov.

"I said I'll fuck him and I'll fuck you, too," screamed the Bozkurt into the guard's face. "The fucker can't even coordinate two fucking companies, much less two brigades!"

"Cool out, cool out," another Bozkurt came up and separated the two. The security guard moved back toward the entrance of the HQ and whispered a few words into his radio while the battle-scarred Bozkurt stumbled down the street, muttering darkly while cleaning his fingernails with his Bowie knife.

The rest of the group remained sitting on the curb outside the HQ, exhausted and broken. Some were crying; others were gawking around in a daze. I offered one a cigarette.

"What happened?" I gently asked.

The man pointed at his mouth and his ears.

"What happened?" I repeated.

Again, he pointed to his mouth and ears.

"Speak Azeri," I said, a little irritated by the stupid pantomimes people put on when they assume you can't speak their language, even when you are.

Once again, the soldier pointed to his mouth and ears, but with a pained and twisted expression on his face.

"He can't talk and he can't hear," another soldier squatting nearby said.

"What do you mean?" I asked.

"Bombs," he told me. "Our bombs."

Concussion, and by 'friendly fire.' I tried to piece it all together and came up with the following: it had been a bad night on the front, a very bad night indeed. The Bozkurt group had gotten within fifteen meters of enemy lines and were ready for a breakthrough; but rather than send in supportive armor, someone had called in the field artillery. The company had been ripped apart by its own supportive guns at its moment of triumph and martial glory. No one knew the total number of casualties yet, because the survivors had only managed to extricate 16 Bozkurts with concussions and three bodies. I thought about my tennis partner from Baku and I thought of the tank-killing cannoneer. Friendly fire, indeed.

* * *

The caravan of bullet-proof Mercedes 500s and lesser Volga limousines rolled into town a half-hour later, carrying not only the president but the prime minister and a host of other high officials. It was a strange entourage for Elchibey, I thought. He had been elected three months before on the promise of removing Azerbaijan from the Russian sphere of influence and solving the problem of Karabakh once and for all. But after his election, he had increasingly surrounded himself—or had been surrounded—with many members of the old elite. And although certainly appropriate for a president, it was a little odd to see the tall, lanky, bearded Elchibey step out of a luxury Mercedes.

"Look, there's Surat!" said Mustafa, nudging me in the ribs and nodding toward a knot of men. He was referring to the great patriot and 'generalissimo' of the war effort, Surat Husseinov, a man whose legend had spread far and wide but who kept such a low profile that I was not sure to which man Mustafa was referring.

"Which one?" I asked, priming my camera.

"The one to the . . . ah, now he is behind the others," said Mustafa.

The legend surrounding Surat Husseinov was that he came from an old Azeri family of a religious bent and that he was a descendant of the Prophet Muhammad himself. Through native intelligence, he had managed to amass great wealth while director of the state wool combine at Yevlakh. Then, although he had no military background himself, he had been touched by the wand of selfless patriotism and had donated his personal fortune to building up his own army, to help in the liberation of Karabakh from the perfidious Armenians. To honor his success and as a mark of deep appreciation, the government had not only bestowed the rank of colonel in the new Azerbaijani army upon Surat but had coupled that with the honorific title of 'national hero,' an award usually reserved for those killed in battle.

Meanwhile, the militia he had built up had been renamed the 104th battalion. So famous were its exploits on the front, that desertion from other, less successful units to the 104th's main base at the city of Ganje had become a problem. So, too, was the 104th's reluctance to fully integrate into the control and command structure of the national army—but few were going to argue with success at this point. That would come later, when Surat was revealed to be a deep agent of Russian military intelligence, built up by Moscow in order to destroy the Azerbaijani security forces from within.

I got a premonition of this during the course of the briefing Elchibey received from Colonel Sadikov and other commanders. I was too far away to understand what was being said, but at a certain point Elchibey got to his feet and began to upbraid the military men.

"What do you mean, they don't know?" he shouted. "What are generals for? What are colonels for? What are captains for? Get that son of a bitch on the radio right now and tell him we need to know!"

I could only speculate about what the problem was, but it seemed that some vital order was not being carried out and no one knew why.

After receiving the briefing, Elchibey walked over to the local theater to give a pep talk to the population. He started by praising Iskender Hamidov and Surat Husseinov as well as all those involved in the battle for Karabakh, noting that the people of Azerbaijan were earning the right to the country through their courage and their blood. He then compared the progress of the war to that of World War II, when the Russians had to dig deep within themselves as a nation to overcome a sense of inferiority in the face of German arms, but once overcome, how they became an unstoppable force. Then he told the gathered people that he was deeply grateful to them for not having run away during the ugly, depressing days of the spring and early summer—unlike the civilian population of other parts of the country affected by the war.

"The flood of refugees in our country has been the greatest disaster to befall us in the course of the Karabakh crisis," he intoned. "Not only does it seed chaos and confusion in the land, but it is also a destroyer of Azerbaijan's most precious asset—the family."

He detailed the tragedy of various groups of refugees, focusing especially on those from Lachin. Then he dipped into humor, relating the request of a resident of Baku who wanted assistance in getting his two daughters out of the town lest the Armenians defile them when they reached Baku. The audience chuckled as if on cue.

Elchibey touched on all his familiar themes, reiterating his call to create a state based on law, noting that independence is not complete without democracy, and that democracy means discussion and consensus. The people should not be surprised or worried by arguments and fights in parliament and public accusations—that was the nature of politics. He spoke about Russian imperialism and Iranian fundamentalism and about the problems of transition to a free market economy. There were a dozen other subjects and themes and it was hard to keep pace with them all—even Elchibey couldn't. In the midst of the stream of consciousness, the president paused, and the hiatus grew.

"I forgot what I was saying," Elchibey admitted, after a good half minute of silence. Then he dropped the bomb.

"Oh, yes," he said at last. "We have signed a cease-fire agreement with Armenia, effective tomorrow."

The room, turned into a sauna by the number of people packed inside it, went stone silent.

"What's your problem?" asked Elchibey defensively. "You lived side by side with the Armenians for years. Did you never sit and drink tea with them?"

Then he opened the floor to questions.

A father had lost his son two weeks before, but the body still had not been delivered for ritual washing and burial. Elchibey was deeply sympathetic but informed the grieving father that without mechanisms for exchanging prisoners and bodies, it was impossible to expect the country to stop the war just to collect the corpse of his son.

A young man complained about delayed payment or nonpayment of salaries to soldiers. There were lots of guys just like him.

"What do you mean, 'lots'?" asked Elchibey sharply. "Do you mean 10, 20, or 500? Who are you talking about?"

"Well, lots," the man muttered weakly.

"Just tell me about your own case," said the president. "What unit are you in?"

The young man stuttered and sputtered, and if I understood the line of questioning correctly, the result was that Elchibey had just discovered a very vocal deserter.

He fielded questions left and right: people wanted to know why the government was raising the price of bread; why the Popular Front was in bed with old communists; why the government officials drove around in big cars; when the war would finally end. The most difficult question concerned the negotiations with Armenia and the future status of Karabakh. What did the president exactly mean by his remarks about peace talks with Armenia? Was he preparing to give Karabakh away? Elchibey once more carefully went over the provisions of the cease-fire, saying that while it pertained to the border between Azerbaijan and Armenia, Karabakh was regarded as an internal affair of Azerbaijan. Within that context the government was willing to give those Armenians who chose to continue to stay some form of cultural autonomy. If they wanted to open a movie house that showed films in Armenian, he said, they were welcome to do so.

This was not a popular idea among the population of a frontline city, but I regarded it as almost a stroke of political genius for Elchibey to announce this caveat here, in Terter, among the troops and families who had lost the most, rather than simply issuing a statement in Baku for international consumption.

The town meeting ended, and I waved to Elchibey. He stopped to say hello, noting that he was a little surprised to see me at the front. It was always fine seeing Elchibey. He might be president and all but I liked him personally and worried about when some idiot would blow his head off. Then the caravan of Mercedes 500s and Volga sedans departed from Terter, and about 20 kilometers out of town, a farm truck darted out from a cross road, and the lead car smashed into it, injuring a number of security guards. People talked about an assassination conspiracy for a few days, but then speculation disappeared.

Mustafa and I, meanwhile, were already on our way out of Terter by another road, heading back to Agdere. I wanted to check out the maverick group working the war—the brigade of Yaqub Mamedov ('The Mule'), the sculptor-turned-mafia-financed-militiaman in Agdam, who like Surat Husseinov, had recently and imperfectly folded his private militia into the national army. He was said to be nearby.

* * *

The highway south from Agdere was a cratered mess, an obstacle course further complicated by the series of cement barriers the Armenians had thrown up as part of their defensive perimeter. These were now shattered, and four-foot-square chunks of cement lay this way and that across the road, waiting for the day that someone might think about clearing them.

We turned right at an Azeri town called Papravend and drove toward the mountains. The road deteriorated with each passing meter until it disappeared into a ribbon of dust three inches thick that disguised whatever might be beneath—potholes, tire-ripping metal, or mines. It was the most frighteningly exposed road I have traveled in combat zones, before or since.

We knew we had re-entered the disputed territory when we drove over the decomposing corpses of swine in the road; confirming the change in geography was a lone, bullet-riddled road sign announcing that beyond was 'Artsakh'—Karabakh, in Armenian. Our VAZ began to fill with the odor of nameless dread. But no one wanted to be the first to admit that they were afraid, so no one said anything, and we just drove on. Then we turned a blind corner and almost ran into the back of an oil tanker blocking the road. Its back wheels had been blown off and the chassis was slanted back into two gaping holes: mines.

"I don't like this road," said Mustafa. "Let's go back."

I didn't have any problem with his suggestion.

The Mule brigade had humped forward across this rising, exposed terrain, hauling tanks and transports and everything else they could get their hands on toward their part of the front, and were continuing to resupply catch-as-catch-can. Fording a small stream in a pitched declivity, we discovered the road blocked by a multi-nippled, two-ton device that had fallen from a truck. It was clearly a powerful weapon, but I couldn't make any sense of it and finally was obliged to ask just what the thing was. The two 18-year-old vets trying to lug the thing back onto their truck looked at me as if I were an idiot. It's the wing-pod cannon of a MiG–24 jet fighter, they said, doesn't everybody cannibalize weapons systems from crashed jets?

Some miles beyond the gully, past a number of blown BTRs and BMP mobile guns, we finally reached the normal tarmac road connecting Agdere to the up-mountain towns of Gulyatak and Janyatak. The lower, Agdere end was off-limits because of mines, and the upper end beyond Janyatak was off-limits because of the enemy, although it was unclear where either side's control began or ended. So that is where we went.

At Janyatak, we found a mechanic cannibalizing the treads of a tank that had taken a turret shot, grafting them onto another tank that had sprung a mine. We asked where the road to Gulyatak might be. He pointed us in the direction of a couple of looter trucks that were moving down a side road, and suggested we follow them. We did so, eating the dust of the strange convoy as it proceeded up toward the goodies. One by one, the vultures peeled off to abandoned Armenian farmhouses to see what they could find, and eventually we were alone again. I missed the scavengers when they were gone. So long as they were driving ahead of us on the road, they would be clearing the mines.

Gulyatak was a postcard-perfect town nestled in a ravine between two sharply defined, wooded hills. The upper part of the town was on fire as we entered it, and sporadic shooting echoed from the heights around it. We were some five miles from the defensive perimeter of Mekhmana as the crow flies, and within easy range of whatever the Armenians had there to interdict the Mule brigade's supply line—the road we had just come up.

Several Muleteers were patrolling the upper town when we arrived, and they would not let us go any further without the specific permission of their commander, the Mule himself, Yaqub Mamedov. The writ of the sculptor-turned-militiaman apparently overran that of the authorities in Baku in these parts, and we did not want to push our luck with a man who was rumored to have such a nasty temper that 'accidents' often befell those who had the temerity to question his authority. But we were guests who had come from afar, and the Muleteers were obliged to extend basic courtesies and were happy to tell me about their conquest of the town and what they were facing now.

"Look at the defensive possibilities!" crowed one Mule, an insane look painted on his face. He explained how he and thirty other commandos had come over the southeastern hills and stormed the town, taking it almost without casualties. "The Armenians ran away almost without a fight—and these are the guys whom we believed to be supermen a year ago!"

The difference between Gulyatak and Mekhmana, the Muleteers explained, was that the latter was defended by Russian mercenaries, who were a far harder nut to crack. I asked how they knew the difference. Through a convoluted reasoning process, one tried to explain.

"The Russians have been trained in extreme conditions and live on nothing and can tolerate anything. You can bomb their trenches for a week, but when you bring up a tank, they will run out and throw their shirts over the view port. No view port, and the tank is useless. An Armenian would never think of doing that, and neither would we."

I tried to explain that while the logic was interesting, it was hardly proof of Russian mercenary involvement. Mustafa decided to interpret.

"We need bodies—*find me bodies!*" he demanded.[1]

* * *

We left the Mules at Gulyatak and returned down the dust road to the main track back to Agdere. The MiG wing cannon device was gone, dragged up to some sector on the front where it might find optimum use. At Agdere, we stopped for gas at a local depot, where troop transports and tanks were also lining up for fuel. The men were cocky. Morale was high. The push for Mekhmana was on. Once more we followed the troopers up to mortar ridge, and there we waited as companies disappeared beneath the canopy and tanks pushed down narrow logging roads. In the distance, the monotonous thump of the field artillery began pouring long-distance death on the enemy, hopefully not hitting any more of their own. Plumes of smoke and dust rose on the far hillside a full five seconds before I could hear the explosion. From somewhere deep within the beautiful pine forest, a tank was firing at something at close range, with virtually no hiatus between the shot and its impact: *Vbroom-Vrang!*

Then, with an alacrity that is difficult to describe, the sounds of death and destruction merged into the satanic roar of heavy machine gun fire crashing through the trees that was answered or maybe augmented by the sputtering of scores of Kalashnikovs firing on full automatic. Two armies— teachers, grease monkeys, farmers—were closing on each other.

Mustafa asked if I wanted to try the northern road above the reservoir again and check out the third Azeri brigade, working its way east from Kelbajar, which was now shelling Kochegot and Drombon from the west. That way, he said, we could get to Imarat Garvant as initially planned.

I said I didn't need to see anymore because there was nothing new to see: It was all a bad dream turned worse, turned nightmare, turned real. No one could have imagined this a year ago, when neighbors were still fighting each other with knives and pistols. As we returned down the shell-battered and mine-gouged road from mortar ridge to Mardakert to Terter and then to Baku, troop trucks were trundling up the highway all the way.

Fresh troops. Fresh blood. Fresh bodies to be used as fertilizer in the Black Garden of their dreams.

"*Azerbaijan!*" they called as they passed us by, "*Azerbaijan!*"

Note

1. About a week after my tour, Mustafa got his wish: Kurdish villagers in the trans-Karabakh province of Kelbajar managed to capture six Russian soldiers as they were making their way overland from Karabakh back to their base in Armenia. Put on display to reporters in Baku, the six admitted that they had been recruited at a Russian 7th Army base in Armenia and 'allowed' to go to Karabakh as a company by their commander, picking up a per diem of 5,000 rubles with an additional 7,000 for each Azeri tank they destroyed—about $20 and $35, respectively. This might seem ridiculously low by world mercenary standards, but it was a princely sum in the former USSR, given the large pool of unemployed Russian youths during the painful transition to the market economy. More interesting was the fact that the six men—more pathetic kids than supermen, if truth be told—had been AWOL for over one year but were only listed

as such by the Russian Military Prosecutor after they had been condemned to death in Azerbaijan—at which point Moscow demanded their extradition. Hoping to placate Moscow, Heydar Aliyev sought a parliamentary pardon for the men in the summer of 1993, at which point the six were sent home. I had mixed feelings about it. They were far too young for any sort of death, especially death in a noose; but if they were dumb enough to kill for a living, maybe they were dumb enough to die for one. It is hard to have sympathy with guys who would slit your throat for no better reason than to pocket the equivalent of twenty bucks to blow on vodka and cheap whores.

15

Alla Turca

The summer and autumn of 1992 were the halcyon days of Abulfez Elchibey and his Popular Front–based regime. Baku and the rest of the country continued to glow with pride in achieving independence from the USSR. Lest there be any doubt about future intentions of involvement with the Moscow-centric world, in early October, parliament voted to formally reject inclusion in Russia's slap-dash alternative to the USSR, the Commonwealth of Independent States.

Still, while it was hoped that the great bear to the north had slunk off into terminal hibernation, the nationalist government in Baku thought it best to explain to the Russians what Azerbaijan really meant by independence. Accordingly, on October 11th, President Elchibey and a large retinue of Front-connected bureaucrats and Mutalibov-era apparatchiks who had survived the nationalist purging of the summer traveled to Moscow to lay the foundation of a new era in Azeri-Russian ties.

One of the most significant passengers aboard the presidential jet was Minister of Defense, Rahim Gaziev, who was to meet with Russian Minister of Defense Pavel Grachev concerning arms supplies. About halfway through the three-hour flight, Rahim wandered back to the press section of the plane, plopped himself down in a chair, and began to extol his own greatness as a military commander. After about half an hour, he was interrupted by his press secretary, Leila Yunusova, who started to fuss about Rahim and insist he take his medicine. It was the first time I had been made aware that Rahim had what might be called nerve-related health problems.

Waiting for us at the airport was a long motorcade of ZILs, Volgas, and other cars, and we were whisked toward the Kremlin gates, running red lights all the way. I was starting to think that being part of an official delegation was a fine thing, until Hicran and I, being the only non-Azeris in the group, started getting iced out of the formal activities, such as actually meeting Boris Yeltsin.

More galling still was getting charged the 'international' (dollar) rates at the Azeri mission's guesthouse. It was also sobering and very instructive to see many of our brave 'nationalist' pals turn into Soviet-style, self-conscious hicks from the Caucasus when in the Big Town. Many switched to speaking Russian among themselves, almost as a conscious attempt to blend in better. Say what they would about the need for independence from Moscow when in Baku, it was clear that the bright lights of Moscow still represented a very attractive scene.

Happily, at least one man continued to hold the Azeri banner high—the president. At the requisite press conference following the diverse meetings and agreement signing sessions, Abulfez insisted on speaking in Azeri—although he was not above correcting his translator when dissatisfied with the nuance of certain phrases as reproduced in Russian.* He only deigned to go into the colonial language once—when an Armenian correspondent kept on rattling on about the death and destruction in Karabakh.

"It is not only the Armenians who have suffered in this conflict," he finally snapped in Russian. "Please think about all the dead and wounded among the people of Azerbaijan, too!"

The summit meeting ended after two days, and the Azeri delegation returned to Baku in triumph. I did not return with them, ducking down to Tashkent to pick up my winter coat instead. It had been a full year since I had been in Uzbekistan, but the place was still engaged in its post-Soviet snooze. I was very glad to leave and return to the action in Azerbaijan.

* * *

Back in Baku, many of the foreign states that had formally established diplomatic ties with Azerbaijan had begun setting up embassies. Noting this might seem a little odd—*of course* countries with diplomatic relations would have reciprocal embassies! But at the time, doing so was unique in the lands of the former Soviet Union: most foreign nations continued to 'monitor' events in such places as Uzbekistan, Georgia, and Moldova from their perch in Moscow.

But because of its independent political line, Azerbaijan was different— and distant capitals started finding money to fund diplomats and monitor political and economic developments firsthand. The result was that only one year after the breakup of the Soviet Union, Azerbaijan could actually lay claim to a foreign diplomatic community. In addition to the Turks, Ameri-

---

*This insistence on speaking Azeri, both in Moscow and in Baku, later resulted in the ridiculous assertion that Abulfez could not speak decent Russian.

cans, Iranians, and Iraqis, there were the French, Germans, Chinese, Pakistanis, and, officially in March 1992, even the Russians themselves. Israel, Greece, and Egypt were soon to follow.

The reason for all the new interest was oil. Even before the embassies, western oil companies involved in bidding on the great Caspian Oil Sweepstakes had begun moving to Baku. Amoco, UNOCAL, and Pennzoil were some of the first to make the move, and they were soon followed by a veritable alphabet soup of hydrocarbon seekers—McDermott, Ponder and RAMCO which later claimed to have been the very first.

For us 'locals,' however, all the new foreign activity in town had a downside: the price of doing business in Azerbaijan. When a landlord asked $1,000 a month for a three-room flat with a view and two years' advance payment, the oilmen (and then diplomats) would simply plop the money down on the table. With our flat costing a tenth of that, we were not really surprised when our landlord informed us that he would not renew our lease. We offered to double the rent—but to no avail. Fuat said he needed time to renovate our flat on Akhundov square place for his family—transparent code language for his wanting to doll up the place for some petroleum executives. Finding a new abode became an increasingly vexing problem in the newly inflated environment.

* * *

The majority of the foreigners in town, however, were not oil executives but Turks. They were suddenly everywhere—and Mehmet Ali Bayar's office in the newly refurbished Turkish embassy became a veritable swinging door for all manner of parliamentarians, academics, human-rights observers, preachers, ultranationalist howlers, nickel-and-dime businessmen, fly-by-night artists and carpetbaggers. The reason was simple: Azerbaijan was the major link in Ankara's new policy of cultural and economic expansion into Central Asia, and Elchibey and his government were to be cultivated at all costs.

Abulfez's first visit abroad was to Istanbul, as part of the Black Sea Economic Conference. He first declined to go because Armenian President Levon Ter-Petrossian was also in attendance, but was eventually convinced by the Turkish ambassador to Baku, Altan Kahramanoglu, of the necessity of appearing at international fora.

"Actually, his refusal to go had less to do with Ter-Petrossian being there than with his being shy and unsure of himself," Altan Bey later told me. Elchibey's reluctance also had a bit to do with his vow that his first trip outside of Azerbaijan would be to Tabriz—the 'traditional' capital of 'greater' Azerbaijan in northwestern Iran. Perhaps he might have been able to fulfill this promise as a common citizen, but as president of a very nationalist regime with tacit claims to 'southern' Azerbaijan, the idea that the Iranian authorities would invite Elchibey to Tabriz was, frankly, insane. Yassir Arafat would have had a better welcome in Tel Aviv prior to the Palestinian-Israeli accords.

So it was to Turkey he went, and the Turks duly showered honors on their man in Baku. Elchibey was almost overwhelmed with all the doctoral degrees, speeches, and applause he received. Indeed, judging by an insider story told me by his confidant Niyazi Ibrahimov, it was too much. Unable to stand the constant courting, Elchibey escaped from the luxury hotel in which he was staying along with Ibrahimov. Ditching their security guards, they hailed a taxi and prowled the City of the Sultans until dawn, ending up on the lawn of the Ciragan Palace Hotel overlooking the Istanbul Bosphorus. *"What a town! What a night!"* Abulfez blurted to his deputy.

And the wining and dining soon paid off. In an explicitly political deal, Abulfez informed the foreign oil companies vying for drilling rights in the Caspian Sea that the Turkish State Oil Company, TPAO, would be given a minority share in any future consortium of western firms granted a license to exploit offshore reserves.

Of far greater importance was the matter of how to get the Azeri oil to international markets—that is, where to build a new export pipeline. Azerbaijan's preference for the route, Abulfez announced, was to have it cross eastern Anatolia to the Mediterranean terminal of Ceyhun/Yumurtalik.

Tremors of excitement rolled through Turkey's construction industry: *a billion-dollar job, and it's ours!* The state, too, was very much pleased: in addition to the political goodwill generated by fully employed laborers (and hoteliers, caterers, grocers) there would be direct transit revenues accruing not only from Azeri but also Kazakh, Turkmen, and maybe even Russian oil. And if—Ankara hardly dared dream it could be true—the United Nations lifted the export sanctions against Iraq and allowed Baghdad to start pumping crude from Kerkuk, the literal flood of crude would demand even greater storage and refining facilities. Turkey, a country lacking any major hydrocarbon deposits itself, would perforce become a major oil hub.

There were some logistical problems to be overcome. According to Azeri thinking, the pipeline should make a 40-kilometer detour south through Iran before re-emerging in Naxjivan, whence it would once more travel south and west, to Yumurtalik in Turkey. The detour through Iran, however, was problematic: not only were the American firms interested in the project unable to get political risk insurance for any venture in the Islamic Republic, but Washington was adamant to the point of threatening lawsuits against violators that no American business have anything to do with the terrorist state.

The Americans and the Turks had another idea. Geographically, the shortest route from Baku to Yumurtalik went straight west—over Armenia. The Azeris were thunderstruck. *Build our economic lifeline across enemy territory? Open ourselves to blackmail and sabotage?* Are you mad?

But Washington and Ankara were insistent. The 'Armenia option' was not only doable but desirable. Under pressure, Elchibey allowed for the so-called 'peace pipeline' option as a possibility, but subject to numerous conditions and demands concerning Karabakh. None of these translated very well when explained to the public, especially by the increasingly vociferous opposition press: Elchibey was ready to 'sell' Karabakh to the Armenians simply for the sake of oil revenues, and to provide jobs to the enemy state while so doing. The perception grew like an unattended cancer in the Azeri body politic, and was to become one of the main reasons behind Elchibey's eventual downfall.

* * *

By the late autumn of 1992, other things were starting to backfire as well—not the least of which was the 'Turkification' of Azerbaijan.

Emerging from the ruins of the Soviet Union, Azerbaijan was struggling to find or define its identity. Unlike neighboring Georgia and Armenia, which both enjoyed claims to ancient culture via their respective churches, the Azeris were a 'new' people. Ethnically, they were an amalgam of Turkish and Persian blood laid on top of small, extant islands of older peoples, while culturally they were a mixture of Sunni and Shi'ite Islam, with a good dose of Russianism injected for good measure. While fascinating in an anthropological sense, the very newness (and relative complexity) of the Azeri identity left it open to manipulation by three outside powers: Turkey, by dint of the strong pull of language; Iran, due to geographic, cultural, and religious proximity; and Russia, which could project itself as the 'traditional' economic partner as well as protector of the diverse non-Turkic/Shi'ite elements in society, ranging from local Russians to minority groups such as the Jews, Kurds, Lezgins, Talish, and Tats.

There was no secret about where Abulfez Elchibey hung his hat. He and his Popular Front entourage envisioned a very intimate relationship with Ankara. This open espousal of Turkey as the political and cultural icon to be emulated almost naturally led to the charge that Elchibey was a 'Pan-Turkist,' or believer in a larger, unified 'Turkic' world stretching from the Aegean Sea in the west to the Great Wall of China in the east.

But this was not so. If anything, Abulfez was an 'Atatürkist,' or student of the life of Mustafa Kemal (Atatürk), the man who founded the modern Republic of Turkey from the ruins of the Ottoman Empire.

For many both inside and outside Turkey, Atatürk remains a controversial figure. He developed his own personality cult and ran roughshod over centuries-old traditions. His attitude toward Islam was best expressed by his decision to strip the veil off women and force men to wear hats with brims. He also changed the Turkish alphabet from the Ottoman script, with all its Islamic associations, to a Latin-based set of characters.

In the minds of most pro-Atatürk scholars, his greatest achievement was forging a new national identity for the plethora of ethnic groups that made up the majority, Muslim segment of the Ottoman Empire—Albanians, Abkhaz, and Arabs, to name but a few. The new man was a '*Türk*,' a word elevated from being a sneering reference to members of seminomadic tribes to a national identity—whence the famously vague epithet about being 'proud to call himself a Turk,' literally carved in mountains across the Anatolian landscape.

But Azerbaijan was not Turkey in the 1920s—or even in the 1990s. The former was a colony of a large empire that managed to break free when that empire collapsed, while the latter was a rump empire itself. If there was a parallel to be made, it was between the breakup of the Ottoman Empire and the collapse of the Soviet Union and subsequent efforts to rebuild the core state. Indeed, if Elchibey wanted to look for historical models for Azerbaijan, he might have done better to regard the fate of the Armenians, Kurds, and Greeks in Kemalist Anatolia. Similar to Azerbaijan's effort to break with the Russian/Soviet past, all of these little peoples likewise had attempted to set up independent states on the Ottoman periphery when they thought the center was too weak to stop them—and all were crushed when the main state revived. It was not an attractive paradigm for Azerbaijan or any of the other 'newly independent states' faced with resurgent Russian nationalism in the post-Soviet period, but one that went a long way toward explaining many subsequent developments.

There were other philosophical problems in Abulfez's reliance on the Atatürk model to forge a 'Turkic' identity for Azerbaijan. The main one was that with the exception of a few months in 1917, when the redoubtable Ottoman general Nuri Pasha occupied Baku, the territory of Azerbaijan had never been part of either the Ottoman Empire or the Republic of Turkey, and thus had no real claim of being inhabited by 'Turks' as understood anywhere but in right-wing circles in Turkey.

Objectively speaking, the people living in Azerbaijan and Turkey were not identical and did not speak an identical language. Stressing that difference had been Moscow's policy during the long years of the Soviet Union. The inhabitants of Azerbaijan had officially been tagged Tatars, Muslims, Azeris—anything but 'Turks.'

But the politics of the Popular Front was based on the *rejection* of Soviet ideology, root and branch. And because it was Moscow that had declared the people of Azerbaijan 'Azeris' and their language 'Azerbaijani,' those terms were suspect. With a nationalist government in power, it was time to correct the errors of the past.

First came the rejection of the Cyrillic alphabet imposed on Azerbaijan in 1939 and the restoration of a Latin-based script. Although often described in the Russian (and Western) media as Azerbaijan's 'adoption' of the 'Turkish alphabet,' nothing could be farther from the truth: the characters, replete with the letters X, Q, and upside-down E—that make a Turkey Turk shudder just to look at, much less to hear them—were pioneered by 'Europeanized' Muslims of the Russian empire and officially adopted by the new Communist government of Azerbaijan in the early 1920s. That is, the Azeris were printing newspapers and books in a Latin script while Atatürk was still writing in the Persian/Arabic script of Ottoman Turkish. Another way of saying this is that it was Turkey, in 1928, that adopted the Azeri alphabet—and not vice versa.[1]

Exactly *because* it was so 'Azeri' (as opposed to 'Turkish'), the public's reaction to the formal readoption of the Latin script was massively positive. Sometimes, enthusiasm seemed to get out of hand—such as the spelling of my name on my press card. Following a ferocious parliamentary debate about whether to adopt the letter 'Q' as opposed to 'G' (or 'K'), as well as an 'upside-down E' in lieu of 'umlaut A,' with all the attendant backroom lobbying and horse-trading one associates with the workings of the United States Congress, the Azeri traditionalists carried the day, the Turkophile modernists slunk home in defeat—and I officially became 'Tomas Qolts.'

I was not the only one to have his name changed. It suddenly became fashionable among nationalists to drop the Russian patronymic *'ov'* ('son of') from the family name in favor of the Azeri equivalents like *'ogli,'* *'zade,'* *'li'* or just dropping the patronymic altogether. Isa Gamberov thus became Isa Gambar.

This was easy enough. But complicating the situation was the removal of the need to transliterate from Russian, where certain letters do not exist—such as the letters 'H' and 'J.' *Dzhamal Gusseinov* thus became *Jamal Husseinli* or *Jemal Husseinzade* or even *Jemil Husseinogli*. Further complicating the mess was the tendency of Turks (or foreign journalists, scholars, and diplomats based in Turkey) to 'Turkify' Azeri names without reference to the Azeri script. Elchibey's Foreign Minister Towfig Gasimov became *Towfig Qasimov* and then *Tevfik Kesimoglu*, and Popular Front Deputy Chairman (and shadow Secretary of State) *Eli Garimov* became *Ali Kerimli*. Down in Naxjivan dwelled one *Haydar Alioglu. . . .*

Quite different was the reaction to the move to redefine the national language. The proposal, brought forward by Parliamentary Chairman Isa Gambarov (later Gambar), would change the name of the state language from *'Azerbaijan Dili'* (Azerbaijani language) to *'Türk Dili,'* or 'Turkic language.' Linguistically, this was ridiculous—rather like renaming Russian 'Slavic' or French 'Latin.' But politically, it was a disaster: the subtle difference between 'Turkic' and 'Turkish' was lost on most people both inside and outside the country, and led to the belief that the Popular Front had renamed the national language as 'Turkish,' which it had not. But the charge stuck and became part of the growing package of 'evidence' that Elchibey's infatuation with things Turkish meant the eradication of local culture.

"Today our language is changed to Turkish (sic), tomorrow they will call us all Turks, and next we will be declared to be a province of Turkey!" charged Araz Alizade on the day the language was officially renamed. Although Araz and his brother Zardusht were regarded as little more than stooges of Moscow, his words had resonance for the newly created 'minorities' in the country, many of whom regarded the move as the first stage of a larger plan to disenfranchise them in the name of pan-Turkism.

Abulfez attempted to assuage such fears by issuing a presidential decree guaranteeing the cultural rights of all groups that had ever existed in Azerbaijan—including the descendants of the Medes and the mysterious Albans. While it may have been one of the most remarkably specific human-rights documents ever issued, it still missed the essential point: the government was creating divisions where none had existed previously.

Still, Azeri was close to Turkish. Disregarding minor grammatical differences and including 'Islamisms' retained in Azeri that had been officially rejected by Atatürk's famous Turkish Language Institute, my personal calculation was that there was about 80 percent identity between the two languages, with the missing 20 percent on the Azeri side of the ledger being Russian and Persian loan words, and English, French and Arabic loan words on the Turkish side.

But even within the large percentage of words that were 'identical' there were a whopping number of 'false friends.' My favorite was the word *sümük*. In Azeri, it means 'bone,' like the object you find in stews and soups; in Turkish, it means 'snot,' like the stuff children remove from their noses. Another word that caused consternation among visiting Turks was *jenayet.* In Azeri, it is the generic word for 'crime.' In Turkish, it means 'murder.' Strung together, such apparent cognates were loaded with possible misunderstanding. At risk of boring the non-Turkic/Azeri reader, a few more examples might be given:

"*Machina o agach'in dalinda sakhla, ve dusherim.*"

In Azeri, that sentence means: 'Stop the car after that tree, and I will get out.' But the Turkish ear hears: 'Hide the machine in the branches of that tree, and I will fall down.'

On the Karabakh front, things would become even more problematic because of all the Russian military terms used by the Azeris, which Turks had never heard before, even as 'false friends' or cognates.

"*Pervaya Liniya'dan indi gayitdim. Gradlar göyden yaghish kimi yagirdi. Ve kahbadaki rayonda onlarin Voyeni Texnikasina gorduk. Ruslari oxshadi. BTR-adeen, BMP-dva, ve hatta T-sevset-dva! Sonra, pluminotlar ve minamyotlar. Kackinlar çöla firladiler. Tajavükârlar bizim yahshi ushaklirimiz hamasini kesiplar. Özüm shahid oldum.*"

The Azeri means: "Listen. I just returned from the front lines. Anti-infantry multiple rockets were dropping from the sky like hail. Then we saw their military hardware coming through the administrative district in front of us. They resembled Russians (using) older generation APCs, newer self-propelled guns, and even a T-72 battle tank. Then came the heavy machine gun and mortar fire. Refugees were fleeing into the fields, while the aggressor was killing all our fine young men! I saw it all."

The Turkish ear would hear this: "Hang an ear! I registered (?) an Indian from (incomprehensible something). Thermal degrees fell like rain from the blue. Then, in the rude (something) we saw their (something) technical. Stroking Russians. BTR-intellectual. United Nations P-something. And even (incomprehensible) T-something. Then came the plural something and the plural something. The sprinters flew in the desert. The raping individuals cut all our good children. I am a martyr."

* * *

The symbol of Pan-Turkism in Azerbaijan (and indeed, the rest of the 'Turkic' world) was and is the *bozkurt*, or gray wolf. The lineage of the totem is traced back to the mists of time in the depths of Central Asia, when the proto-Turkic tribes, lost in the Ergenekon valley and facing death by starvation and cold, espied and then followed a lone *Canis lupus* through the only pass and were thus saved from collective destruction.

After the proto-Turks encountered the Arabs, Persians, and Islam, the *bozkurt* was slowly replaced by other motifs in keeping with the official

Muslim ban on using human and animal designs. But as a symbol, it was never completely forgotten, and it even vied with the traditional Islamic/Ottoman star and crescent for pride of place on the flag of Republican Turkey. That idea was finally nixed by Mustafa Kemal, who allegedly said something like 'I don't want any damned animal on our banner!'

In Azerbaijan, the man most intimately associated with Pan-Turkism and 'bozkurtness' was Elchibey's fiery Minister of the Interior, Iskender Hamidov. Bozkurt was the name of his political party. It was the name of his police-based militia. It was the name of his newspaper. Iskender even kept a stuffed gray wolf in his office as a totem, and he would pose for pictures, patting its head. His followers saluted each other with a 'hook 'em, horns!' salute—the index and little fingers extended into 'wolf ears,' with the thumb and two middle fingers forming the wolf's snout—that would have passed perfectly at a Texas Longhorns football game.

All this devotion to the wolf totem with its pan-Turkic associations drove visiting Turkish intellectuals wild, and with good reason: in Turkey, the Bozkurt movement was intimately associated with the National Action Party of Alparslan Türkesh. During the bloody politics of the 1970s, the Turkish Bozkurts were responsible for the murder of leftist and liberal university professors, journalists and others who disagreed with their ultra-nationalist, anti-Communist vision for Turkey.

After the Turkish military putsch of September 12, 1980, the National Action Party was banned and many Bozkurts were rounded up and sent to prison. But throughout the 1980s and 1990s, the Bozkurts were alleged to enjoy special 'protection' by subsequent civilian governments in Ankara in exchange for their performing extragovernmental actions—such as the assassination of Kurdish dissidents in the Turkish southeast.

Most of this was dismissed as left-wing paranoia until November 1996, when a bizarre car crash outside the town of Susurluk in western Turkey revealed the true depth of collusion between the state, the Turkish security services and the Bozkurt movement. Killed in the crash were the chief of police of Istanbul, formerly in charge of developing 'special teams' (read: death squads) in the Kurdish southeast, a former beauty queen known to hang out with mobsters and a certain Abdullah Catli, a notorious Bozkurt who had 'escaped' from prison in 1979. Catli had been on Interpol's 'most wanted' list ever since, but seems to have enjoyed such a cozy relationship with the security services that they provided him with diplomatic passports to travel on and 'cold' weapons to kill with.

It is unclear whether the Azeri chapter of the Bozkurts was aware of this aspect of the Turkish Bozkurts or even the personal history of Mr. Türkesh. What they did know—and what so few liberal Turks wished to appreciate—

was that Türkesh had been virtually the sole voice of outside support for native 'Turkic' culture in the lands of the USSR before it became fashionable for Istanbul businessmen and academics to travel east to rediscover their roots. Whatever his motives (anticommunism, mainly), Türkesh was thus revered by many in Azerbaijan and even Central Asia. And the Turkish Bozkurts loved Iskender for his loving Türkesh, and loved him the more for his law-and-order ways.

"I bring greetings of the *Bashbug* to you, O! Iskender Hamidov!" bellowed Türkesh's son Tugrul at a '*Türk Ocak*,' or 'Turkish Hearth' meeting in December 1992.* "O! keeper of the fire and the flame! The enemies within and the enemies without—even in Turkey!—say you are terrorizing the population! But let us ask who is afraid of Iskender Hamidov? Thieves, whores, and traitors, that's who!"

Iskender's rise began in the aftermath of his successful countercoup in May. After having slept off the accumulated exhaustion of the heady days of May 14th and 15th, he was appointed acting minister of the interior, with immediate effect. His name alone should have been enough to put the fear of God into the dark forces of the night (or even the shadowy forces of the day). Iskender Hamidov simply would not tolerate anything resembling chaos in the city he had just conquered. He said he would restore order, and he did so. And those who chose to test his rhetoric soon discovered that his writ was as good as his word: Iskender, though a great believer in security, made no pretense about being a great believer in democracy. He was the sword of the nation, and the usual rules no longer applied. He was everywhere, all the time: closing down a *Komisyon* shop that had declined to contribute to the police defense fund 'tax' (he correctly assumed that anyone with the money to open a *Komisyon* shop was 'mafia' and thus had acquired their capital illegally from somewhere); next, moving on to a 'sting' operation in the Kubinka slum area of town, where tons of illegal caviar were being flogged alongside any sort of gun you could ever want; and then hunting down and arresting Hajji Abdul and other members of the Repentance Society, allegedly after a hand-to-hand fight in my old neighborhood of Mashtagah. I even ran into him twice in three nights in our neighborhood, looking into a stray grenade explosion outside the Iranian embassy and then again slapping up half a dozen cops caught trying to shake down drivers while manning roadblocks.

"*Boz-KURT! Boz-KURT!*" Iskender's fans would chant when they saw him prowling the streets in his new, ministerial Mercedes. The diminutive

---

*Bashbug translates neatly to 'Führer.'

Hamidov would emerge from the car, flash the in-house 'hook 'em horns!' salute—and then let loose with a torrent of invective against the enemy of the day, be it Ayaz Mutalibov ('I will hang him!'), Etibar Mamedov ('the KGB plant!') or Heydar Aliyev ('I will put a bullet through his brain!').

Then Iskender allowed power to go to his head. First, he announced that he was going as the head of an official delegation to Bill Clinton's inauguration ceremony after acquiring a generic invitation from a Washington law firm. When news of the faux pas leaked out, he was ridiculed right and left by the opposition press. Next came an unfavorable story about his family in the organ of the Social Democratic Party, which so provoked his ire that he drove over to the editorial offices and punched out the staff. A protest visit to his office by another offending journalist resulted in Iskender pistol-whipping the man. Whatever the man's offense (or possibly, provocation) it seemed a bit unfair: one could not fight back against the minister of the interior in his office, no matter how many blows received.

Iskender's last political sin was to claim to be in possession of two tactical nuclear missiles, which he threatened to use against Yerevan unless Armenia capitulated in the Karabakh conflict. It was a stupid, empty threat—but by using it, Iskender Hamidov, the Bozkurt, had gone too far, and Elchibey was obliged to dump him. No one was sadder than his many supporters in the Turkish Bozkurt movement, who had been fleecing the country since the day Iskender had assumed office.

But once again, I am getting ahead of the story.

Note

1. According to Professor Peter Golden of Rutgers University, Mustafa Kemal was influenced by a theoretical book on the subject of a new alphabet for (Ottoman) Turkish when serving as military attaché to the embassy in Bulgaria. In the course of an Internet discussion on the subject, Prof. Golden wrote: "The question of going over to a Latin script system was first raised in the 19th century by the famous Azerbaijani author Mirza Feth Ali Akhundzade (1812–1878). Mustafa Kemal Atatürk was already interested in these questions during the First World War. He came upon Nemeth's *Tuerkische Grammatik,* which was in the possession of a second lieutenant named Hagop Martayan (an Armenian from Istanbul, subsequently better known as A. Dilacar, one of the leading figures of the Turk Dil Kurumu, or Turkish Language Institute). Nemeth's transcription system became one of the sources of the Republican Turkish alphabet and was so honored by the TDK. A brief account of this event can be found in A. Dilacar, "Prof. J. Nemeth's Role in the Turkish Alphabet and Language Reform," in *Hungaro-Turcica: Studies in Honour of Julius Nemeth*, Gy. Kaldy-Nagy, ed. (Budapest, 1976), pp. 351–356 and in the biography by Kaya Turkay of Dilacar Bey (as he was invariably called when I was studying at Ankara University in the 1960s): *A. Dilacar* (Ankara, 1982), pp. 45ff."

16

Of War—and Oil

BAKU, AZERBAIJAN: The former Soviet republic of Azerbaijan today (Friday) marked the first anniversary of the formation of its armed forces, vowing to solve the crisis in the disputed territory of Nagorno Karabakh with force if no political solution is found.

As foreign dignitaries and a crowd of thousands watched, the elements of the Azeri services paraded by the review stand in downtown Baku. In addition to the phalanxes of marching soldiers, slow-moving artillery pieces and tanks clanked across *Azadlig Meydani*, or Freedom Square, to the martial delight of the crowd.

"Let the presence of our army serve notice to our enemies of our resolve to defend our independence and the integrity of our state," declared President Abulfez Elchibey. "We have no territorial claims on anyone. But if need be, we will end this war in the three months!"

Attracting particular attention was a formation fly-by of MiG-24s, SU-25 fighter bombers and Crocodile attack helicopters that make up the new Azeri air-force. The show of strength culminated with airborne commandos parachuting into the square to delirious applause, while several ships in Baku Bay let off salvos. . . .

That was a story I wrote on October 9, 1992. But like most of my dispatches, it was never filed that fateful autumn. Editors were not interested in 'anniversaries.' Space was tight; there were the U.S. elections; there was the Middle East, South Africa, and of course, there was Bosnia. There was always Bosnia.

Azerbaijan's Army Day celebration may have been a perfect example of the weird processes of nation building and social deconstruction happening in the former Soviet Union's backyard, but the *timing* was off. The details would only become important when it was too late to explain how and why something happened the way it did.

Like losing a war when you appeared to be winning. Here was a country locked in an undeclared war and losing hundreds of men a day; but then, to mark an anniversary, someone had decided to pull the tanks and troops off the front lines, drill them in the art of marching down a main street, had them so march—and then shipped them back out to the front.

The queer thing was that none of the chaos and confusion that I had witnessed on the front was in evidence among the snappy troops on display. And with good reason: it was a rented army—and navy—that was on parade. The pilots of the jets thundering overhead were Russians, Ukrainians, or Tartars on temporary 'loan' to Azerbaijan, as were the parachuting commandos. If half the tanks and APCs and mobile guns that crunched across Freedom Square had been on the front, the war would have been over in September, August, or even July.

But it was still grinding on. Cease-fires came and cease-fires went. All were broken within hours, with Baku and Yerevan accusing the other side of unverifiable violations. One reason was that the Azeris said cease-fires only pertained to the border between Azerbaijan and Armenia and did not include Karabakh, which was an internal affair; Armenia always maintained that the term 'zone of conflict' contained both the border areas as well as Karabakh. Explaining this to editors took time. The details were always changing while the story always seemed to be the same—no wonder so few papers were interested.

One constantly changing constant was what we in the field referred to as the 'Russian Factor.' Again, my editors might be forgiven for tearing their hair out, because the Russians in my reports were forever changing sides. First they were fighting with the Armenians and then they were fighting with the Azeris, and then they were fighting for both. It must have seemed confusing. Russians fighting Russians? It didn't make much sense until one reflected on the history of mercenary warfare: who was Xenophon but a Greek fighting other Greeks?

And the problem was that it was true. The six Russian mercenaries from the Russian 7th Army in Armenia whom the Azeris had picked up in Karabakh had been paid to take out tanks driven by their comrades in the pay of the Azeris, specifically, Surat Husseinov's 104th Division in Ganje. Despite the wealth of circumstantial detail suggesting that the knowledge of (and thus tacit permission to) Russian soldiers fighting on both sides went all the way up to the highest levels of government in Moscow, most western journalists and scholars tended to dismiss such men as 'rogue soldiers,' pure and simple. The Russian military, like Russia, was too busy trying to survive to get involved in messy operations on the former Soviet rim, the theory went. Few wanted to consider the idea that destabilization of the newly independent states was actually part of an ad hoc policy mounted by the Russian defense establishment in order to allow the warring parties to bleed themselves dry, come begging to Moscow to solve their problems—and thus allow Russia to reassert its 'traditional sphere of influence' in the Caucasus and elsewhere.

But for those of us on the ground, by the winter of 1992–1993, a distinct pattern of Russian behavior was starting to emerge in many of the former Soviet republics on the rim: Moscow would sow chaos and confusion by arming governments and rebels, alternate favoritism to lull everyone into believing they had a special relationship with 'the Center'—and then break them all. It was true in Georgia, Moldova, Tajikistan, and in the late fall of 1992, Azerbaijan. Like Georgia before it, Azerbaijan was being led down this primrose path—and believing that every step led toward victory. So optimistic was the Azeri leadership, that Elchibey had begun to condition the continued presence of Armenians in Karabakh on the return of refugee Azeris to Armenia.

"The subject of the Armenians of Karabakh and the Azeri refugees from Armenia is a special case," Elchibey told me in an interview marking his first 100 days in office. "Parity is necessary for numbers as well as for special rights for the two communities. If Armenia accepts one Azeri in their old homes in Zangezur, we will accept one Armenian in Karabakh. If they accept 100, we will accept 100. If they are willing to give cultural autonomy, we are also willing to do the same. If they give political autonomy to their Azeris, we will give political autonomy to our Armenians. As for other Armenians and ethnic groups within Azerbaijan, let anyone come and live as equals."

While this idea might have been interesting from a demographic point of view, the fact remained that all the Azeris in Zangezur (and elsewhere) in Armenia had been driven out by 1989—and it was hard to imagine that any of them would care to go back any time soon. Elchibey's formula was, in effect, an announcement of the eviction of all the Karabakh Armenians—a task he clearly believed the national army capable of doing.

To believe the 'free' press in Baku, this was true. The story of the week in mid-October was that the Azeris had established control over the southern Karabakh city of Martuni. The Defense Ministry had announced that its troops had entered the strategic town when the Armenians, after suffering hundreds of casualties, had withdrawn. The information about Armenian losses came from eavesdropping on military frequencies used by the Armenians. . . .

The reality was just a little bit different. The Azeris had indeed entered the town—but they had walked into a trap. Scores were slaughtered before they withdrew—only that part was not reported.

"We entered an empty town," admitted a depressed Vafa Gulizade over drinks one night. "Then we got pounded by the Armenian position and had to withdraw with heavy losses. The rest is just a lie."

Even when the Azeris admitted to getting 'hit,' they usually got it wrong—and for a reason. Around the same time as the (non-reported) Martuni debacle, the official media announced that Armenian aircraft had 'terror-bombed' the town of Fizuli, just south of Karabakh. If true, this was news because it would have marked a real escalation: the Karabakh Armenians had no air force, and an Armenian air strike—especially against civilian targets in Azerbaijan—would have shattered the myth of Armenian noninvolvement in the conflict. I tried to check it out with the spokesperson of the Ministry of Defense, Leila Yunusova. Her response was a bombshell from the blue.

"No, it was not the Armenians," Yunusova said, lowering her gaze. "It was our own planes that dropped the bombs."

Everything, of course, is possible in war, and much larger and deadlier mistakes have been made (and covered up). But the identities of the pilots—Russians—in the context of the ebb and flow of imperial irredentism in Moscow gave me pause: this was 'friendly fire' of a highly suspicious kind. Indeed, it seemed more like a hidden hand, purposefully escalating the war.

But such concerns seemed far away on the first anniversary of Army Day, and especially at the grand reception at the Gulistan complex. Everybody who was anybody was there—from the Sheikh ul-Islam, Allahshukur Pashazade, to the Minister of Defense, Rahim Gaziev, a baby-lamb Papaz atop his head, despite the heat. At the head of the banquet table was the man of the moment—President Abulfez Elchibey, looking utterly lost. As the obsequious waiters brought around the usual lukewarm kebabs, sturgeon steak and then lukewarm rice and sliced lamb, the master of ceremonies introduced the usual cultural fare: Daghestan Knife Dancers, child prodigy singers and belly dancers. Between performances, the band played Azeri dance music at a volume so loud that it prevented any sort of intelligible conversation at the tables, possibly by design.

A regular night at the Gulistan; I had forgotten how fun it could be.

Finally, it was time for the speeches. They were all long and sloshy, suggesting that far too much vodka had been consumed by too many, and reeking of belligerence. Elchibey's bellicose keynote was made more pathetic by the applause it collected from every table in the cavernous room: he spoke about how having an army insured peace through mutual fear, citing the example of MAD (Mutually Assured Destruction) as the element in international relations doctrine that had kept the world free of an East/West nuclear holocaust. He was babbling, but the audience of crocodiles, Popular Front hangers-on, Pan-Turkic dreamers and obsequious journalists hung on every word.

The evening ended with a fireworks display and a rousing rendition of the Azerbaijan Army's marching song, with Abulfez Elchibey, vodka glass in hand, leading the sing-along chorus:

Forward, Ho! Forward, Ho!
Azerbaijani soldiers, Go!
Never retreat, No! Never retreat!
We are too strong to taste defeat!

* * *

Armies cost money—lots of it. But they make money, too. War, as they say, is good business. And in post-Soviet Azerbaijan, it was very good business indeed.

No final accounting will probably ever be made about how much was skimmed from the state coffers as purchasing agents went about acquiring soldiers' uniforms, winter boots, and personal weaponry—not to speak of the requisite jeeps, trucks, APCs, GRAD launcher systems, tanks, helicopters, and planes—and all the fuel to keep those machines running. But skimming there was—and of the sort that would make Milo Minderbinder of *Catch-22* fame blush with shame.

Pure rapacity explained a great deal about the strange 'connections' the Azeris were making in order to keep up a steady supply of weapons for the war effort. While all the hardware they could possibly want was being produced right next door in Russia (or in Ukraine), purchasing junkets often led agents through London and elsewhere in Europe, where prices for, say, anti-tank RPG rounds were 10 times higher than in Moscow. The logic of such inflated shopping sprees was evident: the middlemen, working on a ten percent cut of money spent, wanted to keep prices as high as possible. After all, ten percent of 100 is ten, while ten percent of 1000 is one hundred.

In one instance I know of, a cohort of Azeris were brought to Israel by a Slovenian middleman to check out the latest in Kevlar body armor. While Kevlar is pretty good at resisting point-blank fire from a low-caliber pistol like a .22, it is not much good at stopping a high-velocity bullet. To stop that sort of slug, Kevlar vests are reinforced with shock plates—which makes them both heavier and far more expensive than the basic Kevlar jacket favored by paranoid Wall Street executives. The purchasing agent in question ordered up a batch of jackets for the shelf price—but decided not to buy the plates. Too expensive, he said. The Israeli salesman tried to explain again that the vests were almost useless without them, but the Azeri middleman/purchasing agent was insistent: he had no need of the expensive plates and would take the vests without them.

"It doesn't take a genius to figure out why he didn't want the plates," the Slovenian told me one night in a smoky Baku bar.

"Try me," I said.

"Because he was going to charge the government the full price and pocket the difference!"

The penny, as they say, fell in the box.

* * *

And where did the money squandered on war come from? In Azerbaijan, there was an easy answer: oil.

Baku was the world's first oil town—and vast fortunes were made out of the sweet, light crude lifted around the city at the turn of the century. The largesse of the period was still evident in the handsome residential buildings in the central city—as well as in the oil swamps and literal forests of rusty derricks in today's suburbs.

But oil was, and remains, less a blessing than a curse. It fueled the economy of the briefly independent Democratic Republic of Azerbaijan of 1918–1920, but it was oil field workers who joined the Bolshevik revolt to force Azerbaijan into the new Soviet Union. An early agitator was a young man from Georgia, who went by the code name of 'Koba.' He is better known to history as Josef Stalin.

During World War II, the Baku oil fields were regarded as such a prize that the city and its primary industry were spared bombardment by the German Luftwaffe in the hopes that the German army might capture it intact. They failed—and lost the war at least partially due to running out of diesel fuel for their tanks.

If the Nazis were unable to pump Baku crude, the Soviets made up for it. By the 1960s and early 1970s, the onshore landscape was littered with rusting derricks, and offshore platforms were pumping more crude into the water than into the leaky underwater pipes. By the 1980s, Azerbaijan was relegated by the Soviet Ministry of Energy to the status of a has-been area for oil, with new Soviet (and foreign) investment directed toward the vast fields in the permafrost regions of western Siberia.

But the breakup of the Soviet Union in 1991 radically changed perceptions. At first tentatively, and then with growing interest, western oil firms such as Amoco and British Petroleum came to Baku to conduct their own studies in three offshore fields. These revealed that rather than being exhausted, Azerbaijan was potentially a 'second Kuwait.' Other hydrocarbon pools both on and off shore were equally promising.

With a growing awareness that it was sitting on incredible wealth, first the Mutalibov government and then that of Elchibey crept forward toward a deal. But concern that western techniques in exploiting oil reserves included duping and exploiting greenhorn governments gave both leaders pause—with the result that there was always yet another round of negotiations to be held before a 'final agreement' could be signed. . . . As the money spent on hotels, translators, trips abroad, and other 'sweeteners' started to reach skyward, many of the western oilmen began wondering if the Azeris really understood what oil exploration was all about—or whether they really wanted a deal.

"Whether in Kazakhstan, Russia, or Azerbaijan, the story is the same," Amoco's Baku representative, Ed Lake, told me one night. "The officials we have to work with are precisely the people who have a vested interest in keeping things exactly how they are, because that is how they got rich in the first place. Want to talk about the public good? Take another guess. Our logic means nothing here."

That logic, Lake informed me, was the theory that every dollar pumped into the oil sector attracts another three dollars of investment in related sectors—hotels, restaurants, travel agencies, and shoe shops. It is not the revenues from the oil, he said, but the investment that makes the difference. "If we spend ten, forty arrive—that is enough to transform this country into a little paradise. Everyone wins. But that is not the way it works here."

'Dithering' was the kindest thing oilmen had to say about the Azeri tendency to delay. 'Salami tactics,' or playing one suitor off against the other was another complaint. 'Attempted extortion' was still another. But as the months passed, it began to occur to me that there was another reason for the continued delay in contract signing. The moment the western firms made a capital investment in the oil sector, they would also take a capital interest in making sure that it ran as smoothly as possible—and that would mean an end to 'leakage.'

Just how much crude and refined oil was being systematically siphoned from the existing offshore and onshore wells and refineries was and is not known, but the amount is believed to be massive. One of the first local oilmen I met in Baku was the director of 'Baku Invest,' an Azeri/German joint venture that had its headquarters, oddly enough, in the 'old' KGB club downtown. Baku Invest, the director explained, made 'patriotic profits' by cleaning up the oil swamps outside of town and then selling what they had culled on the international spot market. But western oilmen familiar with the firm scoffed at the idea.

"Patriotic, planned pillaging," chortled one, explaining how the system worked: the internal, Soviet price for diesel fuel refined in Baku was $2 a ton, while on the international market it was around $150. The government overstated its needs for energy and then had Baku Invest pull its tankers up to the 28th Party Refinery to spirit away the 'spill' for sale on the spot market. Some of the loot associated with the greasy gravy train returned to the national economy in a Ronald Reaganesque 'trickle-down' manner: well-connected folks went into import/export business. This provided jobs (and won their loyalty) for hundreds of people, ranging from travelers to Istanbul and Dubai to purchase textiles and electronics to clerks in the newly opened kiosks around town, filled with everything from Snickers bars to VCRs (and lots of imported beer and vodka).

On a micro level, everyone was happy. There were jobs and goods to buy with money so earned. But on a macro level, it was all a one-off disaster of the highest magnitude. It was all for today, with nothing for tomorrow.

"For 70 years, they have been told things will get better next year if they are patient and everyone works together," another frustrated oilman said. "They no longer believe it. They just want what they can get their hands on, now."

The weirdest example of how this national corruption affected the country was the experience of the Houston-based Pennzoil. Seeking to improve its chances of getting a lucrative development contract, Pennzoil executives hit on a new and theoretically attractive ploy: lend-lease a $100 million natural gas compression plant to Azerbaijan to capture natural gas vented from Oily Rocks, a surreal city of rusty pipes and collapsing platforms built on stilts in the middle of the Caspian. Due to the Soviet technique of creating economic dependencies between the former republics, Azerbaijan purchased most of its natural gas from Turkmenistan—even while blowing off the equivalent of $50 million a year of its own resource. In the future, Azerbaijan would be able to use its own natural gas, and for free. Moreover, Azerbaijan would not spend one dime in building the plant: the project cost was to be rolled into an eventual exploration deal to be signed at a later date. It was a win/win situation.

The nine custom-built compressors were assembled in Texas and shipped across the Atlantic and through the Mediterranean to the Black Sea, and arrived in Azerbaijan via Volga River barges—only to languish for months on the docks in Baku because a sufficiently healthy incentive was not given to the official in charge of barges to bring the equipment to its final destination at Oily Rocks. Still, after further delays (partially due to the theft of $60,000 worth of wrenches and other tools from the site), the Pennzoil equipment, replete with computerized unit control stations, was finally put in place—but remained off-line because the underwater pipes to the mainland have not yet been laid to completion. Meanwhile, the natural gas continued to get blown into the air at the rate of $165,000 a day. The problem was that Pennzoil had forgotten one small detail: no one in government had any incentive to get the free gas project on line because a 10 percent kickback on nothing is nothing.

"The project is unique in the annals of the oil industry," Pennzoil vice president Tom Hickox told me with a sardonic smile. "They blow 165 million cubic feet of gas into the air every day. In Texas we call that money."

Another frustrated Pennzoil man put it a lot plainer.

"Sometimes, in my most cynical and gloomy moments, I think that nothing will happen until the existing infrastructure collapses so totally that there is nothing left to steal."

* * *

Then there is the unsavory story about the highly combustible mixture of war, oil, and greed in Azerbaijan.

It is a complex tale, drawing in such diverse elements as Afghan *mujahideen* mercenaries, American military trainers, Iran-Contra figures and even the owner of a toy store in my hometown of Livingston, Montana. Throw in a 'sting' operation aimed at potential nuclear weapons smugglers, and you have the basic elements of the little adventure known in some circles as MEGA Oil.

It all started in the late autumn of 1991, when the local representative of a major American oil company called and asked me out for a drink. I will call him Pond.

"Pond here," the oilman announced himself. "I need to talk to you."

"Come by the consulate," I said, referring to my home, which was still known as the quasi American embassy in Baku.

"No, the walls have ears—you had better come down here."

'Down here' was the Old Intourist Hotel, a black granite structure on the shores of the Caspian that was regarded as the best hostel in town. Compared with the others, such as the Azerbaijan or Apsheron—the twin rat holes that reeked of urine and fried sturgeon—this was true enough. But the Old Intourist also left much to be desired in terms of creature comforts, service, and clientele. The sauna, for example, was essentially a hot whorehouse, somehow connected with 'valuta,' or the hard-currency bar in the basement, where knots of 'Natashas' hung around, looking for an overpriced score.

No, I did not particularly like hanging out at the Old Intourist. But Pond must have had his reasons for asking to see me. So I put on my coat and trundled on down, my route leading past the Iranian consulate to the Baku Soviet metro and the symphony building, and then down the wide boulevard toward the crumbling wreck that passed for the oil ministry building. Like everything in Baku, it was in some stage of prolonged, Soviet-style decay and looked much better at night than during the day: the crumbling facade and shattered tile work and broken windows shut over with cardboard were hidden, in part, once shadows turned to night.

After a 20-minute meander through the dark streets, I arrived at the hotel and proceeded to the 'Ho Bar' in the basement. That was our name for the place where the whores hung out. It may not have been original but it certainly was appropriate.

"Hi, honey," said Myra, a thin but attractive brunette, as she slid into the booth next to me. "Got some time to spend?"

"Thanks, darling," I replied, patting her properly.

Myra was, or had been, a geologist during Soviet times, but had discovered she could make a lot more money letting the diverse foreign oilmen now descending on Baku do their drilling on her. She also was thought to draw a second income from the KGB in Moscow, after she was discovered chatting on a mobile phone in the toilet.

"Change your mind, and you know where I am," she cooed, and moved across to the far end of the bar where a knot of new oilmen were seated. They were Americans by their accents and attitude: they were making a tin castle out of beer cans. Myra tipped it over, and everyone laughed; I had not seen them before.

The beer was warm, but I sipped at it while waiting for Pond. He appeared after a few minutes, and slid into the booth next to mine.

"Hey, good to see you," he said, feigning surprise. "What brings you down here at this hour of night?"

"Just felt like a bump," I said. We kept up the banter about our coincidental meeting for some minutes, and then said our good-byes.

"Hey, stop by some time and share some of my peanut butter," he said. "Just got a new supply."

"Great. Tomorrow?"

"Why not?"

I left first, and Pond met me on the oil-stained Caspian quay near the looming sports complex moments later.

"You see those guys at the far end of the bar?" Pond asked.

"Yeah—the most recent arrivals in the great Azeri oil sweepstakes."

"Only in a manner of speaking." said Pond. "I have been talking to them, and none know the difference between a dipstick and a donut."

"So who are they?"

"They say the represent a new company in town, but one no one in the industry has ever heard of it before."

"What's the name?"

"MEGA Oil."

"So who are they if not oilmen?"

"I don't know," said Pond. "But the consortium seems to be made up of about five or six small companies with addresses in Georgia, Florida, and other Dixie states where Special Forces guys like to retire."

"What does that mean?"

"I mean MEGA Oil is a front for something, and I don't know quite what. But it stinks, and as far as I can tell, all the little companies involved got their start during the glory days of Iran-Contra."

"Ollie North and all that?"

"General Secord just checked out of the hotel last night."

* * *

General Richard Secord, he of Iran-Contra fame during the late Reagan presidency, had flown into Baku as the guest of Ponder International, an Alice, Texas–based wildcat 'service' company specializing in what oilmen call the 'rope, dope, and smoke.' That is, they were involved in the nitty-gritty of the industry, performing necessary tasks like 'fishing' lost tools out of on- and offshore wells and perforating the pipes that went down those wells in order to let the oil seep in and thus be pumped back up. But in addition to what contracts Ponder wanted to sign in and around the Azeri oil patch, it had apparently agreed to act as a the 'legitimate' front for whatever General Secord was up to outside the oil patch.

Traveling with Secord was another retired American military man, for-mer Air Force Brigadier General Harry ('Heini') Aderholt, a name well known in circles that deal with Vietnam-era POWs and MIAs. General Aderholt, it seems, was obsessed with tracking down the very last American (or remains thereof) from that war. A few years earlier, he had made contact with the Moscow-based Soviet Peace Committee—a curious organization that was allegedly funded by donations from concerned Soviet citizens but was more likely a KGB front. The quid pro quo was that SPC would use their good offices in Hanoi to release missing Americans, while the Ad-erholt group would use their contacts in Afghanistan to release Soviet POWs there. In the event, the Soviet side of the project failed to track down any Americans, while the Americans succeeded in getting several Russians released by the Afghan *mujahideen*. The individual responsible for making the various contacts leading to the release of the Soviet POWs was a gentle-man from Marietta, Georgia, named Gary Best.

Further POW release plans required further financing, and this is where MEGA Oil came in: it would raise money by reworking some of 35,000 derelict oil wells in the USSR, then use its portion of the profits to continue Aderholt's philanthropic search. The most promising patch was in newly independent Azerbaijan, where 100 years of erratic, inefficient Soviet-style production had left literal forests of creaking, rusting derricks trying to leach the last drops of oil from ancient subterranean oil fields. The initial survey of the country also revealed another sector where the Azeris needed help.

"The Azerbaijani army, or what passed for one, was being torn apart by the Armenians in Karabakh, mainly due to a lack of training," Aderholt explained to me much later. "I told the government (of President Ayaz Mutalibov) that they should make an official request to the United States for a mobile training team. I also told them they would not get it, but that it was best to have an official request on record. Then I told them to start shopping around the private sector for advisors to do the same thing."

To that end, Aderholt had an idea: with the help of his old comrade in arms, General Secord, he offered to train 5,000 Azeri troops for rapid deployment missions. The price tag was to be $10 million, with a special emergency medical evacuation program thrown in gratis.

General Aderholt still insists that the military assistance program was to be regarded on its own merits and had nothing to do with MEGA Oil's project to increase the productivity of old oil wells, although a portion of the profits were still to be funneled into the POW release project. But the coincidental identity of most if not all of the players in the two projects stands out, especially that of General Secord—and Gary Best.

Negotiations were problematic due to the high level of confusion and corruption in newly independent Azerbaijan. Once, a deal seemed to be at hand—until it was discovered that the $10 million allocated for the training program had 'disappeared' somewhere between the presidential office and the ministry of defense. General Secord, for his part, said that Mutalibov could not make up his mind whether he wanted to build up a national army to do battle with the Armenians, or concentrate on creating a presidential guard to protect him from domestic opponents, like the Popular Front. The final straw for Secord and Aderholt came when someone in the Mutalibov government suggested that MEGA use its contacts in Afghanistan to recruit a mercenary force to fight in Karabakh. The idea was anathema to the originators of the 'force multiplier' idea.

"The point was to train young, patriotic Azeris to be able to defend their country," General Aderholt told me. "The last thing they needed was a bunch of mercenaries to fight their war for them. So we left."

But Gary Best stayed on—and it is at this point that the story of MEGA Oil and MEGA Military becomes truly complex. No sooner was Ayaz Mutalibov gone and Yagub 'Dollar' Mamedov installed as acting president, than MEGA Oil started to receive 'services' from the Azerbaijan security departments. For example, when Ponder International first brought oil-rig reworking equipment to the country, they landed at a military airport where the usual customs formalities (and even passport control) were dispensed with.

"We thought it was a little odd, but we just wanted to believe that it was due to Gary Best's good contacts," Ponder President, Joe Ponder, told me during a drunken evening at the 'Podval,' or 'Basement Bar,' run by a couple of entrepreneurial Turks a few years later. "It was just the start of a lot of funny business with Gary Best."

Other "funny business" included the arrival of planes on the military airstrip that had nothing to do with Ponder's project, as well as the surreptitious arrival of other American "oilmen" who, once again, didn't know much about petroleum. Many of the strangers stayed in a complex managed by the Interior Ministry just north of the capital, fueling speculation at the time that the new republic of Azerbaijan had done a deal with the CIA, trading off the use of its territory for covert activities against neighboring Iran in exchange for "protection" from Russia.

Years later, I met one of the men involved in this action in another smoky bar in my hometown of Livingston, Montana. Known to his pals as 'Special Friend,' this real-life Rambo had served in Iraqi Kurdistan after the Gulf War against Saddam Hussein, before receiving a rather special, don't-ask-too-many-questions assignment. His mission? Set up a new airline in Azerbaijan—with a little help from Ed Dearborne of Air America fame.

"We brought in a lot of interesting things—brown bags filled with cash for certain members of the government—that sort of thing," the Special Friend told me over drinks in the Owl Bar in Livingston. "But our real mission was false flag, that is, we were to act wild and crazy and attract weirdoes who might be interested in selling us some loose nuclear weapons."

Still, the official cover of the operation was to train pilots, and the Special Friend took his job seriously. "I interpreted 'training' literally, and we brought the Azeris to Texas and gave them the full treatment."

This was a good thing, because when instructor and students returned to Baku, they discovered that the clients had a new assignment for the new airline—picking up hundreds of Mujahideen mercenaries from Afghanistan.

"It was a night landing on a dirt road in the mountains," said Special Friend. "Not a bad trick, considering we were flying a 707."

Meanwhile, Ponder was becoming more and more concerned about its 'partners.' One reason was a letter faxed to Ponder's office from a man named Bob Fletcher, who claimed to have known Best since 1985, when the latter bought out his toy store in Atlanta, Georgia—and then used the Barbie and Ken doll boxes to ship weapons in as part of the Iran-Contra deal (and maybe to import dope back into the USA).

'Gary Best, along with a few generals, used my toy company as a covert front for their illegal and immoral acts of mercenary actions, death squad training, weapons sales and drug operations,' Fletcher wrote. 'These guys do these operations all the time ... and are fully covered by the U.S. government at the highest levels!'

"Who is this nut case?" I asked Joe Ponder.

"Well, Ah sure hope he is a cracker," a very worried Ponder drawled. "'Cuz if he ain't nuts, Ah'm in bigger shit than I could flush in a Texas outhouse."

I looked at the bottom of the fax; the name 'Fletcher' meant nothing to me. Then I looked at the top, where the return telephone number was printed: I could scarcely believe my eyes. Fletcher was faxing Baku from my hometown, Livingston, Montana.

I called some friends to have him checked out.

'Oh, *him* . . .' was the usual response.

Throughout Montana, it seemed, Bob Fletcher was regarded as a paranoid kook, a man who saw 'Soviet' tanks trundling down roads late at night and predicted the imminent takeover of the Land of the Free and Home of the Brave by a diabolical cabal associated with the Trilateral Commission. After the Oklahoma City bombing of April 1995, Fletcher fled Livingston and moved to Noxon, the home turf of the Montana Militia. There, he became their effective spokesman and was found and featured by an intrepid reporter of the *New Yorker* magazine as the very personification of right-wing paranoia, in a long story published in the summer of 1995.*

Meanwhile, back in Baku, the new U.S. Ambassador Richard Miles—a former Marine known in diplomatic circles as the only American ambassador whose son is a cop—was quietly putting pressure on the government to show MEGA and Gary Best the door.

"I had him thrown out of the country—twice, in fact," Miles told me when the subject of Gary Best came up. "I don't know what else anybody expects of me."

---

*The *New Yorker* writer included one vague reference to Gary Best but did not pursue the issue. A pity, as they say—because while Fletcher may have had certain problems connecting with reality, there is no doubt that he properly identified the main players in Iran-Contra and those involved in MEGA Oil long before anyone else, and apparently had reason to fear because he was a man who knew too much.

But Best kept coming back, and each time he returned, the MEGA project looked less like having anything to do with oil, and everything with military training and mercenaries. And Best started using his new muscle to get back at some of his former partners. Backed by about a dozen armed men in military uniforms, he broke into Ponder's headquarters and seized a satellite telephone and other electronic equipment at gunpoint, and threatened to return to take other oil sector–related provisions.

"I have never been so scared in my life," said a partner of Ponder's who happened to be in the office at the time.

Ponder later made an official complaint to the government of Azerbaijan, asked the FBI to investigate, and filed suit against Best and MEGA Oil in a Texas court for $13 million in MEGA-related losses.

This hardly deterred Gary Best. The mystery airlifts between Kabul and Baku increased, and Baku was soon swamped with the detritus of the Russian-Afghan war. Despite official denials of their presence, the Afghanis were instantly recognizable due to their tribal garb and beards (both around the front as well as in Baku tea shops and even bars). The '*muj*' may have been highly motivated guerrilla fighters against the Red Army in their homeland, but fighting someone else's war for money was a different story: they distinguished themselves more through insubordination than as disciplined fighters. On several occasions, local Russian draftees (or Azeris with light hair and blue eyes) had to be removed from sectors dominated by the Afghanis, lest the *muj* kill them out of general principle.

Best's main focus, however, was to duplicate the Secord/Aderholt 'force multiplier' project. Using Secord's name to gain connections in the obscure world of military experts for hire, Best brought several dozen Americans with special forces backgrounds, including smoke jumping forest-fire fighters who had successfully trained Iran-Contra guerrillas in the fine art of jumping into hellholes, or deep penetration operations behind the enemy lines. The smoke jumpers were also from Montana—Missoula, in this case.

The core group to be trained, it seems, were the remaining elements of the so-called 'university' brigade associated with Etibar Mamedov, which had been trained by the Turks but was disbanded after one of the many disasters in Karabakh.

Finding one of the trainers was the tricky part. But one night, as I was sipping a beer with Joe Ponder at the Podval bar, the oilman nodded across the bar at a thin, hard-looking man sitting by himself. I sauntered over and introduced myself, expecting to be told to get lost. To my surprise, the man actually engaged in conversation. The reason was pretty simple: he was bitterly critical of Best, and maybe just a little lonely. He also had heard of me and knew I was not just a parachute journalist looking for a snap story. So we talked, but on the grounds of total anonymity.

"You ever want to talk again, give me a call," I said and gave him my card. A month later, the telephone rang.

"This is Rex McIntrye," said the voice on the other end of the phone. "We met in a bar. I think I'd like to have another drink and talk about mutually interesting issues."

Rex was running, and he wanted to talk. This time on the record. After all, he had already been debriefed by the State Department and was planning on making a date with the FBI to tell everything he knew about Gary Best, so why not me, too?

"The core group came from a small circle of professionals with previous U.S. government contracts in places like Afghanistan and Iraq," Rex explained. "But the real professionals got out quickly because the mission was not being accomplished. Those that stayed behind were men who may have been Special Forces on paper but who had no field experience." He said that of around 35 men contracted for the training operation, only a handful remained. Broken promises about working conditions was one reason many had left. Best reportedly seized 'everything from passports to peanut butter' from one group of arriving trainers. Fudging on payment—or simply the siphoning of the cash earmarked for the project—was another. According to Rex, a total of $12 million was paid into the MEGA project—the original budget of $10 million, plus $2 million going to Defense Minister Rahim Gaziev as a 'bonus.'

Rex didn't know if Best received the entire payment at the start of the training project, or merely a portion thereof. But while Best appeared flush with cash most of the time, he was strangely reluctant to disburse the promised salaries to his trainers—or even to provide the sort of equipment required for the Azeri elite force they were training. Rex didn't know how much direct involvement Best had in procurement, but the supply of the war materials for the commando units was a part of the original Aderholt/Secord proposal, and I assumed it to have been a part of Best's tender, too. This was the most shocking part of the story: in addition to being improperly trained, many of the Azeri elite groups were issued dysfunctional equipment, such as bulletproof vests with no titanium insert plates and antitank rockets that were designed for practice. Rex himself was witness to one assault by the Azeris on entrenched Armenian positions. In one engagement, a unit hit an Armenian tank with 20 RPGs before being forced to retreat when they discovered the cause: they had been issued practice rounds.

"Blanks are a lot cheaper than real RPGs, and the middleman can keep the difference," Rex pointed out.

So stunningly ineffective was the MEGA project, that there was a growing suspicion among the trainers and the Azeris that the level of disorganization and corruption associated with the project may even have been planned. My new pal, Rex, for one, said that due to the Aderholt/Secord connection, he originally assumed the MEGA project had some sort of CIA connection or at least sanction. But after his involvement with the project, he—and other men previously associated with Best, ranging from Aderholt to *Soldier of Fortune* publisher Bob Browne—said they did not dismiss the suggestion that Best may have been 'turned' by the Russian security services.

"The Gary Best story brings to mind the case of Frank Terpil," Browne told me, referring to the 'rogue' CIA operative who worked for Muammar Ghadhafi in the mid-1980s.

The evidence for KGB involvement in the MEGA project was thin but tantalizing, and mainly predicated on the notion that it takes real effort and determination to arrive at such an abject failure in achieving stated goals—arranging Azeri defeat rather than victory.

"A KGB connection answers more questions than it raises," said Rex. "And if Gary Best turns out to be KGB, he has got big problems with those of us whom he managed to involve in this ugly scam—like a contract on his head."

That is, if anyone can touch him.

In the spring of 1996, I got a call from the CIA. The officer got straight to the point.

"What do you know about Ponder International?" she asked.

"Why do you ask?"

"We've got a report that says that customs police in Baku have found a barrel of fissionable nuclear material at the airport with Ponder's logo on it."

"Gary Best," I muttered.

"That is what we thought, too."

Silence.

"By the way, there's a guy over at the Treasury Department who would like to talk to you."

"Sure, let him call."

He did. We arranged a meeting in D.C. We met and we talked. And at the end of our little chitchat about illegal military training, smuggled nuclear weapons, Montana smoke jumpers, and Afghan mujahideen, I decided to ask the T-man a question.

"How does this guy survive?"

"Best?"

"Yeah."

The T-man sat silently for a moment, looking toward the distant Washington monument through his Ray-Ban sunglasses.

"I don't know," he replied at last.

"Friends on high?" I probed.

"That is what I am worried about."

17

Corruption in the Ranks

Pork barrel politics and petty corruption have been with us since the first municipal council held by primordial man, and they were not new to Azerbaijan. But the change of regime from Mutalibov's neocommunists to Elchibey's protonationalists also seemed to mean that 'competent corruption' was exchanged for 'incompetent graft.' At times it even seemed the new bureaucrats knew they were looting on borrowed time and were determined to squirrel away as much as possible, now.

There were exceptions. One was Sabit Bagirov, the head of the national oil company, SOCAR. An intimate of Elchibey, Bagirov was regarded as incompetent, which really meant that he was so squeaky clean that he actually put what he regarded as the national interest before personal profit. You could tell just by looking at his office in the no doubt once lovely, but now totally down-at-the-heel SOCAR headquarters on Neftjiler Prospekti, or Oilmen's Boulevard. The stairs were cracked, paint and wallpaper peeled away in large slabs, and the elevator did not always work. Apparently, Sabit thought it more important to devote the limited resources at his disposal to pay the bloated staff than fix up anything fancy for himself.

On the other side of the spectrum was Panakh Husseinov, whose activities so managed to discredit the Elchibey regime that one is tempted to label him an agent provocateur—although he was probably just greedy.

Husseinov was a short, stocky fellow with no neck who looked almost Neanderthal. He was often likened to a real-life version of Sabak Sabakov in Mikhail Bulgakov's once-banned Soviet novel, *Heart of a Dog*. He was also known as 'The Watermelon Merchant' because he used to sell fruit and vegetables in the market before getting involved in opposition politics in the late 1980s. His official biography had it that he had earned a degree in economics from Moscow State University—or was about to have earned it when destiny and patriotism called him back to serve and save the motherland. Whatever the truth, the rumors and stories started the moment he assumed the position of state secretary in the presidential apparatus, where Panakh found himself ideally placed to regulate contact with the president and to openly and massively use his position to amass personal wealth. He was soon known as the man who drove 'a white Mercedes during black times.'

Panakh's purview was wide ranging. First, he focused on the sale of favors to individuals interested in owning basements and storefronts to conduct a little '*al-ver*', or petty commerce. Next, he moved into the more lucrative business of supplying the world with cut-rate caviar—the second 'black gold' culled from the Caspian Sea.

I had enjoyed plenty of contact with the caviar mafia at the retail end— one always had one's special connections in the Kubinka district of town, where jars of sturgeon roe could be got for a song. With the rise of Panakh, this source started to dry up, so I decided to try to get a little closer to the industry. I arranged a visit to the largest processing plant in the country, in a dumpy little town called Neftchala.

It was not a pretty trip. Local youths whispered to me that they had become virtually indentured serfs, obliged to cull sturgeon from the river day and night—or be shipped off to the Karabakh front. Meanwhile, their owner, a huge flabby sack of a man with the title of Director of the Tagayev Caviar Works, maintained that due to a rise in the Caspian, the Kura River had been blocked off by mud deltas, preventing the sturgeon from moving upstream to spawn.

The logic was simple: no sturgeon equaled no caviar. But factory workers were busy packing the black goo in shallow glass jars for export, and the factory manager—who allegedly had purchased his position from Panakh— drove a Mercedes. Something did not add up, and it was time to look elsewhere.

Then late one winter's day, when no one in their right mind would be swimming, I went out to a Caspian beach north of Baku to see what I could see. I did not wait long, and I did not wait in vain. Within an hour, I spotted a tractor racing down the beach, pulling a boat trailer. Poachers, I said to myself.

The notion was confirmed moments later, when a large wooden skiff powered by two outboard motors appeared on the waves, heading quickly toward the tractor rig waiting on shore. The boat hit the shallows; the tractor backed the trailer into the water; and with a slick, practiced maneuver, the boat slid over the rollers and was lashed down and pulled from the water and onto the beach. I ran over to see what was inside.

There was no surprise; I found a mass of dead fish. There were sturgeon of all sizes and types—beluga, osetra, and sevruga as well as a bastard type of sturgeon known as *jop*, all slashed open for their famous roe. Perhaps 100 pounds of gray goo, worth maybe $20,000, had been dumped indiscriminately into a large and dirty bucket.

"Democracy is a great thing," said one of the fishermen, as he held up a two-meter beluga, then out of season. "We can fish anytime we want, where we want, and can keep the whole catch."

Then a swarm of cars roared down the beach toward us, trunks open. Within minutes, the fish were crammed in among spare tires and tool kits, destined to become kebab steaks in restaurants across the Caucasus. The filthy bucket of caviar disappeared into a white Mercedes; although I cannot swear to it, I believe it was that belonging to the State Secretary, Panakh Husseinov.*

* * *

With the most salient ideological features of the Popular Front on public display being Iskender's Pan-Turkic howling and Panakh's capital accumulation, it was hardly surprising that other, competitive ideologies began to appear.

The field was so open that it became confusing trying to keep all the new political parties (or at least political associations) straight. By late 1992 there were no less than 30—some of significance, many of none. I believe the contemporary term for this used among political scientists is 'elephantitis of democracy,' with all that the phrase implies.

Some of the new 'parties' had been around for the past year—even if they remained one-man shows and existed only on paper. Tamerlan Garayev's True Path Party was a good example of this sort of fictitious entity. Others, such as Isa Gambar's New Equality (Musavat) and Etibar Mamedov's National Independence Party, had headquarters and membership lists, the former claiming to be the 'main' governmental party and the latter the 'main' opposition, even though neither had existed at the time of the last parliamentary elections, which had been held in Soviet times. That honor was owned if not actively claimed by the Social Democratic Party of

---

*Panakh was also interested in oil, where potential profits far outreached those associated with caviar. In anticipation of the June 1993 state visit by President Elchibey to London to finalize a deal with British Petroleum, Panakh threatened to scuttle the visit unless he was flown to London first on a reconnaissance trip that included a guided shopping tour of Harrod's, at BP expense. It was his last blast before being removed from office.

the brothers Alizade, or potentially, the newly reformed Communist Party of Azerbaijan (which also seemed to be a one-man show).

The most interesting new political party on the scene in late 1992 was the Islamic Party. It was no secret who was behind its development: the ideological and financial support for the group all came from the Islamic Republic of Iran.

After a limping start in the much touted Turco-Iranian rivalry for influence in Azerbaijan (and Central Asia), by late 1992 the Islamic Republic was making increasingly resonant inroads through the astute use of diplomats, businessmen, and clergy, as it embarked on an ethnic 'outreach' program.

This was a very interesting development. While the Turks were refusing to make the first concession to Azeri culture and language, the Iranians had literally filled their embassy with a staff of Iranian Azeris (or Azeris from Iran) who were able to talk straight up with their 'brothers' from the Azerbaijan Republic—and as Azeris, not as 'Turks.'

A couple of days after the founding of an 'Islamic Party,' the Iranian ambassador gave a two-hour press conference/chat followed by a two-hour reception/snack for local pundits, to explain Iran's position in the Caucasus.

It was quite a performance. Starting with an invocation of the name of God, and orchestrating quite a few pious epithets of '*Allah!*' and '*Ya Salaam!*' when he mentioned such names as Khomeini, Khamenei, and Rafsanjani, the ambassador proceeded to fill ears with the beauties and progress made by Iran, the country that dared go it alone in the face of the world—and survive.

Iran felt for Azerbaijan, the ambassador intoned. After all, they had been one—*one!*—until the Russians had ripped northern Azerbaijan away from its roots in 1828. Now, God willing, as Azerbaijan attempted to break free of the Russian and Soviet yoke, the Islamic Republic was ready to assist its Azeri brethren with all manner of aid and development programs, ranging from the supply of natural gas to heat the offices of the newsmen to throwing open the doors of hospitals in Iran to treat wounded soldiers from Karabakh. Still, there were problems.

"You say we should support you against the Armenians because you are Muslims and they are not," the ambassador said. "We do support you—we do! But what distinguishes you from the infidel enemy? Both you and the Armenians drink like fish, eat pork, and—forgive me my words!—fornicate all day. By all public indications, you are not Muslims at all—and are thus undeserving of our aid (although for the love of Allah we will aid you anyway) until you return to the faith."

And when a local journalist asked about the reported 'rivalry' between

Turkey and Iran for the hearts and souls of the Azeris, the ambassador was ready with a reply made for quotation.

"I am not a *rekabetchi* but a *refahetchi!*" the ambassador declared, playing on the words 'rival' and 'philanthropist.' "Let Turkey help its Muslim brethren in Azerbaijan—but in more ways than bringing in beer and wine and—God forgive me!—taking your women!"

"Ya Salaam!" echoed the crowd.

* * *

Fomenting distrust and dislike toward the overbearing Turk was a theme quietly taken up by another recent diplomatic addition to the Baku scene: the Russian ambassador. It had taken Moscow awhile to actually send in an ambassador after having formally established diplomatic relations, but when they did, they sent in a real winner: Valter Shonia.

More than being a Russian, Shonia was an 'ethnic' Soviet—half Georgian and half Russian. He was multilingual in a number of 'sensitive' languages, including Turkish: he had previously been the head of the political section at the (former) Soviet embassy in Ankara. If Shonia's institutional connections during his time in Turkey were suspect, in Baku they became perfectly clear: he had been entrusted with a very delicate mission—to wean the Azeris away from the Turks and back into the (post) Soviet fold.

The thin edge of this program was playing off the growing anti-Turkish feelings among the cultural vanguard, the Russified artists, writers, and academicians known as the 'intelligentsia.' Valter Shonia managed to accomplish this slow subversion with consummate skill. At dinner parties and receptions and other special little events, he reminded people of the protected life they had once led in the Soviet period, knowing that many yearned for the same now.

The government left itself wide open to this velvet assault: as part of its campaign of 'Azerification' (or 'Frontification') of the state bureaucracy, perfectly capable administrators and cadres from the Soviet period were summarily axed and replaced by politically correct fools from the Popular Front.

The first cry of alarm came from my Russian teacher, Elfrieda: her job as director of the Russian Language Institute for Foreigners was hanging by a thread because she refused to matriculate a couple of well-connected Turkish students. They had failed the qualifying exams (in Russian) for the very good reason that they refused to study, but had paid someone 'up there' to get the grades—and good ones. Accordingly, a man had come by to give her an offer she could not refuse: if she did not pass the kids, she would be regarded as anti-Turkish (pro-Russian) and dismissed.

Next on the block among our personal friends was Kubrah Hanim, our original host in Baku, who resigned her position as director of the main sanitarium after her would-be successor threatened her with a fraudulent case of corruption. "I have my honor," said Kubrah. "I will not contest such filth." Her son Kamran, who had benefited from his Popular Front connections to get a job in the Ministry of Foreign Trade (although he knew nothing about the subject), was heartbroken but unable to lift his protests beyond his immediate circle of friends.

If Russified Azeris like Elfrieda and Kubrah Hanim had problems, local Russians were particularly hard hit. Although many exaggerated their sufferings to foreign ears, there was no question that their dominant role in society had changed. The major issue was the requirement that those working for the state speak Azeri. While theoretically reasonable, the implementation left something to be desired: Russian cleaning maids and busboys in hotels, which were still state-owned, were being evicted from their jobs.

"We should try and understand the reasons for the new nationalism, but we should not pretend that the ugly incidents to those who are not ethnic Azeris are not happening," said Robert Finn of the American embassy one night. It was impossible not to agree.

* * *

And there were other opposition heroes in the making, too. In mid-December, members of the Social Democratic Party were detained for some ten hours after trying to mount a demonstration protesting the decision of the National Parliament to change the name of the official state language from 'Azerbaijani' to 'Turkic.' Two days later, they were back in the news after one of the party's leaders attempted to enter Karabakh to work out details of an exchange of prisoners of war with the representatives of the self-declared 'Republic of Mountainous Gharabakh.' The Defense Ministry called the foray a provocation and detained them all.

Nothing could have suited the Social Democratic Party chairman Araz Alizade better. At a press conference, while he howled about the 'neo-Bolshevik regime,' I scanned the room. It was packed full of well-dressed people in fur coats and beaver caps. Few of the individuals were from the press; most seemed to be from that murky group known collectively as 'the intelligentsia'. As part of a clearly orchestrated plan, strangers got up to give witness to the truth of Alizade's words. I left in disgust when a 'soldier' who just happened to be in town got up to describe how the government was 'selling' towns and villages to the Armenian foe.

The brothers Alizade had ulterior motives for trying to destabilize the regime. But their words and actions had resonance for one simple and compelling reason: the Elchibey government had made little progress on the promised political or economic reforms in its half-year in power. Nor could it, in a democratic, consensus-based way, until a new parliament had been elected to draft, argue, and pass laws.

Chairman Isa Gambar had repeatedly promised new elections—but the promise remained unfulfilled due to 'technical' problems in passing an election law. The biggest hitch seemed to be that Gambar's New Equality Party, a Popular Front spinoff named after Rasulzade's original Musavat, was rapidly losing support and could no longer assume a parliamentary majority if and when elections were held.

Meanwhile, the unshackled press was having a field day with the subject of the alleged lack of democracy in the land. This may seem like an oxymoron—how can the press enjoy a lack of democracy? Well, in Azerbaijan there may not have been a properly elected parliament, but there was no censorship, either. More to the point, there was no sense of editorial responsibility or even restraint.

Every political group, it seemed, had their own newspaper, which they used not to inform but to smear and libel everyone else on the political spectrum. Broadsides at Elchibey, Gambar, and other leading members of the Front government usually included the charges that they were Russian, Turkish, or even Armenian agents, possessed vile personal habits, and were even remiss about basic hygiene.

One piece in the pro-Aliyevist *Yeni Azerbaijan* was a story on Elchibey's behavior while in prison in the mid-1970s. The president was described by a former cellmate as a cowardly, sniveling dupe, ready to cooperate with the authorities in any way to make life more bearable for himself. The former cellmate was identified only as a 'former' KGB operative.

All this might have been just so much bad news of a manageable proportion, but for one very important factor: Heydar Aliyev.

Quietly operating from his Naxjivan base, Heydar was fast becoming the personification of everything the Popular Front government was not: poverty, piety, and perseverance.

It was an open secret that Heydar was orchestrating something, but it was not clear exactly what. Like a master chess player, he took his time to push his pawns forward.

The first oblique move had been his refusal to answer the phone when asked if he were interested in the job of chairman of parliament. The Front leaders had laughed at the time—but few wanted to ask the real question: who had put the man who made the motion up to the job of ruining the Front's victory party in the first place? Then there had been the hijacking of

Independence Day, with the concomitant snubbing and humiliation of Isa Gambar. The phenomenon of Nizami Suleymanov in the presidential polls spoke for itself—he was Heydar's stalking horse, thrown in the list to cast doubt on the legitimacy of Elchibey's victory.

Over the summer, when support for Abulfez Elchibey was at its peak, Heydar lay low. But in the fall of 1992, new signals began coming out of Naxjivan. In order to establish a firm and official toehold in mainland Azerbaijan, Heydar founded his own political vehicle—the New Azerbaijan Party—with branch offices everywhere in the country.

The old fox also created a parallel social group—the Azerbaijan Philanthropic Society. By sheerest coincidence, its acronym was the same as the Popular Front's: now there would be two AXC organizations to choose from.

Then there was Heydar's quiet usurping of Elchibey's 'special' relationship with the Turks. Elchibey might have tickled that part of Turkish society that delighted in such symbols as the howling wolf, but Heydar knew how to manipulate more sophisticated Turkish concepts—especially those having to do with 'statesmanship.' Not only was he the 'first Turk in the Politburo,' but he was also the first 'outside' Turk to actively participate in internal Turkish affairs: he invited himself to and was received in administrative meetings with the governors of the eastern provinces of Turkey, acting, for all the world, as if Naxjivan were a province of Turkey—or a separate state. Heydar signed energy and trade agreements with Iran and Turkey, and even began issuing stamps made in his own likeness. When Baku announced that it was extending its writ by sending in a new Minister of the Interior to Naxjivan, Heydar quickly turned the tables and declared the effort 'an attempted putsch,' and sent the new minister and the local chapter of the Popular Front packing.

By early 1993, Heydar had clearly become a force to be reckoned with, and slowly but surely a growing number of western oil company executives, diplomats, and scholars began making the pilgrimage to the Autonomous Republic to pay homage to the Grand Old Man.

One particularly galling incident was when Heydar managed to cadge a batch of humanitarian aid from his 'good friend' Bill Clinton, in quasi-violation of the ban on government-to-government assistance to Azerbaijan as specified in the infamous Article 907 of the Freedom Support Act.

The delivery of the aid package, brought to Naxjivan by Robert Finn, underlined the ideas that Naxjivan was somehow 'different' from the rest of the country and that Heydar was not 'government' at all, but a sort of ensconced opposition.

Worse still for Baku, in soliciting the American aid for Naxjivan, Heydar had agreed to the queer terms that it would be delivered via Yerevan, while a like amount of food and medical supplies would be delivered to Karabakh via Baku—thus tacitly suggesting that the status of Karabakh and Naxjivan vis-à-vis Azerbaijan and Armenia were identical.

The re-emergence of Heydar was all the more phenomenal because he managed to make his presence felt even though he was never in Baku. There were a few false sightings, such as during the funeral of one of his brothers; people waited for hours in the street outside his sibling's house, hoping that Heydar would show up for the last rites—but in vain.

In early 1993, Heydar condescended to pass through the capital. He was on his way to Moscow for a medical 'checkup,' and the government managed to prevail upon him to have a meeting with Elchibey. During their conversation, the increasingly beleaguered president offered Aliyev the position of prime minister in a government of national unity. Heydar declined.

"I told him that Azerbaijan is a democracy, but there have been no new parliamentary elections," Heydar informed me after his meeting with Elchibey. "As a democrat, I cannot accept a position by decree. It is time to let the people speak—hold elections and then appoint the leader of the most popular party as prime minister!"

The venue of our meeting was almost surreal—the temporary U.S. embassy on the second floor of the Old Intourist Hotel, where Heydar had popped up to discuss modalities of getting American aid to Naxjivan. Heydar had let it be known when he was going to be there, and almost immediately, the embassy-in-the-hotel was flooded with members of the public and press.

Hijacking Robert Finn's office for a 'spontaneous' press conference, Heydar sallied forth, lecturing and laughing and fielding questions right and left. He wanted to thank his friend Bill Clinton for his concern about the situation in Naxjivan, and he wanted to thank his good friend Ambassador Dick Miles for his intervention and he especially wanted to praise the efforts of his very special friend Robert Finn for traveling to Naxjivan and giving such attention to the needs of the people. He smiled, laughed, and schmoozed like a man who had every reason to be relaxed—and not because the doctors had given him a clean bill of health. He did not look like a man who needed to see a doctor in Moscow at all.

Interestingly, Boris Yeltsin had just announced the so-called 'Monrovskii Doctrine' that claimed the right of Russian intervention in the lands of the former Soviet Union to curb chaos and despair, and I asked Heydar about how he felt about this. He dodged the question several times, but finally answered it in the following manner:

"Russia had an interest in the Caucasus yesterday, has one today and will have one tomorrow," he delphically replied.

"What does that mean for independent Azerbaijan?" I asked.

"You figure it out," he said, calling the meeting to an end. It was time to meet with new members of the New Azerbaijan Party before he departed for Naxjivan again.

I ran into Robert Finn in the hallway of the hotel, clutching his pug Bobo. He had left his office when the press had barged in, but was typically reserved in his fury. He knew when he was being used, even if few others knew or cared.

"Why aren't you in your office, listening?" I asked.

"One old dog is enough for me," said Robert.

Bobo wanted to bark, but only drooled on the frayed carpet.

* * *

Finn's frustration was understandable. Despite having the best staff of any of the embassies in Baku, American impact on the new political and economic society emerging in Azerbaijan was hobbled from the beginning by politics back home.

While Peace Corps volunteers coached Uzbeks on how to play baseball and the international branch of the AFL-CIO taught eager Kazakhs about trade unions, Azerbaijan, with far better 'democratic' credentials than most post-Soviet states, had become an off-limits area for American influence.

The reason for this was quite simple: the Armenian lobby in Washington had pulled out all the stops to pass a caveat to the Freedom Support Act for the former Soviet Republics, and had succeeded in having Azerbaijan declared a pariah. According to Section 907 of the bill, "United States assistance . . . may not be provided to the government of Azerbaijan until the President determines, and so reports to the Congress, that the Government of Azerbaijan is taking demonstrable steps to cease all blockades and other offensive uses of force against Armenia and Nagorno Karabakh."

From the vantage point of Baku, this meant that Azerbaijan was obliged to feed, clothe, and give fuel to those aiding the individuals determined to secede from the state, and not resist the secession to boot. It would be impossible for any government in Baku to comply with such conditions, which were tantamount to, say, excluding Spain or England from NATO and the EC until Madrid and London stopped resisting Basque and Catholic separatists.

"Forget about A.I.D. or cultural exchange programs," said a frustrated Robert Finn. "We couldn't even get the money to send someone to a 'Conference on Tolerance'."

The irony was that the economic and social aid that was banned was exactly what might have promoted real pluralistic democracy in the state, while its absence, from both a physical and a psychological standpoint, forced the increasingly isolated Elchibey regime toward greater authoritarianism in order to survive.

18

Rumblings of Dissent

The paradox was that according to all outward appearances, Baku was booming. New shops were opening by the day, and the streets clogged with foreign cars. But beneath the veneer of oil deal–induced prosperity, things were rapidly going from bad to worse. There may have been art exhibit openings to attend and an increasing number of diplomatic receptions to go to, but it was all so much slow dancing in the dark.

In this case, the blind partner was the rest of the country, and particularly that in or around Karabakh. Cease-fires came and cease-fires went, along with a whole series of international negotiators, all determined to bring an end to the conflict. But each visit and contact and brokered peace deal seemed to end in renewed fighting that brought further gains to the Armenians and further losses to the Azeris.

A visitor to Baku, however, might have been forgiven for remaining oblivious to this aspect of the war. The Elchibey government, like the Mutalibov government before it, had banned bad news.

Increasingly, what we got instead were images of the President meeting foreign dignitaries (mainly visiting Turks), pictures of the Minister of Culture opening yet another art exhibit (of mainly state-sanctioned artists), and endless invitations from either the protocol section of the information department of the Foreign Ministry to attend this briefing or that photo opportunity with a visiting U.S. Congressman from Texas or a knot of MPs flown in by British Petroleum (BP).

As for the real situation in Karabakh, there was no news at all save for the mind-boggling propaganda churned out by the so-called Analytical Section of the Information Department of the Ministry of National Defense and Security. All attempts to get permission to travel to the front were now rebuffed.

There were rumors, however—some based on fact, others on fancy. A new friend of ours, Yusuf Agayev, the chief military prosecutor for

Karabakh, would periodically show up at our house in order—there is no other expression—to chill out. Yusuf would not talk much; but it was clear that he felt more relaxed at our place than wandering down the streets of Baku, watching draft dodgers zoom around in new cars.

Other 'old friends' from the front would also check in—people we knew from Shusha, Lachin, and Xodjali. After an initial show of braggadocio, all would inevitably settle in and give us the goods after a second or third drink: there was a total lack of coordination in the field; local commanders were 'selling' villages to the Armenians; soldiers were being forcibly 'recruited' from bus stations, and sent to the front with one or two days' 'training,' only to be slaughtered the first week out.

Then one day, a number of families carrying wooden coffins mounted a vigil in front of the presidential building. They were protesting the new government restriction of new burials in the *Shehidler Xiyabani*, or Martyrs' Lane Cemetery, to 'national heroes'—and those dead whose families had enough influence at the Ministry of Defense to have the restriction waived no matter how their kin had died. The pathetic knot of hicks from the front-line area were driven away by police using rubber night sticks. If reported in the local press at all, the incident was referred to as a 'provocation.'

There was another provocation on the December 31st anniversary of International Azerbaijan Day. The date marked the day in 1989 when the self-styled 'independent' labor union leader Nimet Panakhov and some friends had ripped down the barbed-wire fences along the Soviet-Iranian frontier in Naxjivan. A rally had been organized by the Elchibey government to mark the occasion, which was to be held on the vast expanse of *Azadlig Meydani*, the former Lenin Square, in the center of Baku. Then, at the last moment, the government had canceled the rally, for fear that it would be hijacked by Nimet himself, now out of political favor, and turned into an antigovernment demonstration.

The irony was that Nimet had organized two other meetings on *Azadlig Meydani* earlier in the fall that had been abysmal failures. In late November, the first had been successfully hijacked by the government. The second, marking the real anniversary of his tearing down of the fences between Iran and Naxjivan, December 4th, had attracted no more than several hundred people.

But the authorities didn't like Nimet's linking his own protests to the pan-Azeri Solidarity Day, and thus they revoked permission for the third demonstration. To reenforce the point, they put up three lines of police barricades to keep people away from the square—and then tried to pretend that everything was normal.

Many citizens came anyway, either to show support for Panakhov, to celebrate Azeri solidarity—or to register their displeasure with the government for not trusting them to use their own brains.

"We simply want to exercise our right as citizens of a free and independent country to walk across the square," said one of two well-dressed, middle-aged women who had managed to talk their way through the first two lines of police. They were stopped just short of the empty square by another group of security men who said it was off limits because of 'maneuvers.'

The two well-dressed ladies then decided to up the ante.

"The government is sending untrained 18-year-old boys out to the front," said one. "But here you trained gunmen are guarding an empty square."

The cops didn't like that argument, but they didn't take it out on the ladies. One beefy guy actually folded, and offered to walk them across the square and back.

"There you go," he said. "You have walked across the square—now go home."

It was cold; there was no demonstration or rally; it was New Year's Eve, and I had a turkey to cook for some guests. I decided to take the cop's advice, and started to go.

But when I reached the last line of police—or the first, depending on how you look at it—I noticed a handful of people moving in my direction, toward the square.

Maybe they were locals, trying to take a shortcut home; maybe they were hard-core agents provocateurs—I do not know and will never be able to say. Suddenly, voices were raised; as suddenly, a man had thrown his arms in the air, and was instantly surrounded by five policemen. One threw a punch into the man's face; someone else tried to restrain the cop, and was dropped to his knees by another lawman with a kick in the groin.

I did the only thing I could in the situation: I primed my camera, raised it discreetly to chest level, and began to record whatever was breaking out. I got off two shots before four cops were on top of me, trying to twist my arms into a hammerlock while reaching for the camera.

"You idiots!" I shouted, breaking free of the two pudgy men trying to pin my arms. "I will have your asses!"

One brought up his truncheon to whack me.

"Touch me, and I will not only report this to the world, but to Iskender, your boss!"

My evoking the name of the Bozkurt gave them pause, and my captors grudgingly bundled me away into a nearby squad car, having to be satisfied with some good pushing and shoving but no real rough stuff. I should have been grateful that I managed to keep hold of my camera—but I was furious.

"Do You Know Who I Am!" I shouted. "Do You Know Who I Am!"*

As the only foreigner arrested—detained is perhaps the more accurate word—I was separated from the rest of the crowd of those to be incarcerated and trundled off to an upstairs room. The sign on the door said it was occupied by one Colonel Guliyev. He was a small, rat-faced man, and when he snarled at me to show him my identity papers, I snarled right back, telling him to call the presidential apparatus to find out who I was.

"Ask for Vafa Gulizade," I spat. "He's my guest tonight for dinner."

The colonel dialed the number I gave him. But it was New Year's Eve, and Vafa was not in his office—and I did not have his home number on me.

"You are good friends, huh?" smiled the colonel.

"Then I better call my wife and tell her to cancel our New Year's party," I muttered.

"Go right ahead," said the colonel, and dialed the number I dictated.

To my delight and surprise, it was not Hicran but Philip Remler who answered the phone. I quickly explained the situation.

"Let me talk to that colonel," said Philip. I knew what he was going to say. He was going to say that in addition to being an American citizen, etc., etc., the detainee was a friend not only of Chief Advisor Gulizade but Minister of the Interior Iskender as well as the President of the Republic himself. Philip must have said exactly that, because the colonel started looking nervous and began clipping and unclipping a leather gun strap to his service revolver.

"And who are you?" he asked in Russian, just a little off balance.

I heard Philip shouting down the far end of the telephone, while nearer, I heard the colonel say 'Da . . . da . . . da.' I think he was being threatened with an international incident, but I cannot be sure.

The colonel hung up the phone without giving it back to me, called for the pair of thug-cops to come in, and had one of them take dictation in Russian for a statement for me to sign. I decided to press my luck.

"I sign nothing until these creatures not only apologize to me for their behavior, but until they write their apology into the statement itself!"

This did not sit well with anyone in the room but me, and a shouting match ensued which threatened to come to blows when the colonel told me it was time to go.

---

*If the cops did not know the identity of the egomaniac in their hands, others certainly did: my 'arrest' not only made the Armenia and Moscow press, but was even reported by the Committee to Protect Journalists—and I did not do the reporting. My interpretation is that someone found it useful as to broadcast my detention as proof of how undemocratic and generally awful Azerbaijan could be. . . .

We walked into the room next door to drop off the still-unsigned deposition, the arresting officer trailing behind, and found the room filled with other people who had been picked up for trying to go to the demonstration that had been canceled.

"Javdat!" I said, spotting a meek reporter who sometimes worked in the Popular Front information section. "What are you doing here? And Hamid and Elkhan, too!"

I started taking down names and numbers and statements from the detained about what had happened, and the colonel did not like that at all. He liked it so little that he seemed to forget about my unsigned deposition entirely, and concentrated on getting me back out of the room filled with detainees, and downstairs. There was another large batch of folks in custody there, too—another twenty people were waiting to be arraigned. By this time I was getting cocky, and I started taking down more names. The colonel didn't like that, either, and escorted me to the door.

"What about my deposition?" I cried, as two or three other cops tried to force me out of the station. "You have no right to get rid of me until you have recorded that you arrested me!!"

Someone got an elbow under mine, or maybe an arm; someone else pried my fingers from the door—and I was free, if reluctantly.

"Let me in, you bastards!" I shouted, banging on the barricaded door. "Let me back in!"

There probably was plenty of humor in the moment, but I saw none of it.

* * *

The police station was not far from the headquarters of the Popular Front HQ. There I found Niyazi Ibrahimov, who had recently resigned as presidential spokesman because he didn't like the turn things were taking—such as Iskender Hamidov's security excesses, Panakh Husseinov's corruption, or even the cancellation of demonstrations. I told him about the arrests and several Popular Front people I had seen in detention, and that they needed his help.

"Shit," said Niyazi, and put his head in his hands.

We went back to the station but the cops wouldn't let Niyazi into the arraignment room or detention center to see anybody. Maybe it was because they remembered me.

"You have got to call the president," I said. "He has to know what they are doing in his name."

"If I call him now I will explode," Ibrahimov replied.

We got back in his car and drove up the hill to parliament. I had no idea what he thought he could do there. But Niyazi went in, and I waited; and when he returned after half an hour, he told me that he had seen Isa Gambar, and that Isa had promised everyone's release.

"When?" I asked.

"I don't know," Niyazi replied.

We drove back down the hill in silence.

"This is just the beginning," Niyazi said at last. "And we have started the counterrevolution ourselves through stupidity."

* * *

The next public protest was on January 20th, the third anniversary of the Baku Massacre—and the most resonant date on the calendar year in Azerbaijan.

The 'official' mourning was an impressive and solemn occasion: an all-day dirge held by the religious leadership of the Muslim, Jewish, and Orthodox Christian communities in the Martyrs' Lane. Up to a million people walked through the cemetery, planting red carnations on the graves set among the trees.

Then, in the evening, a select group of people were invited to a requiem concert held in the Republican Theater: choirs of all the nationalities living in Azerbaijan—Azeris, Kurds, Lezgins, Talish, Jews, Russians, and even Georgians—singing their native dirges in front of an austere but moving stage set: a black highway, splattered with red, symbolizing the Baku streets down which the Soviet army had rolled that night.

It was tremendously beautiful and tremendously moving. There was no applause; there was meant to be none.

But there had been applause in the afternoon, and all for Nimet Panakhov, still held incommunicado three weeks after his arrest—along with that of 1,000 others, including me, on December 31st.

The occasion was a midday rally on Freedom Square. After a few warm-up speeches, a well-barbered and dapper Elchibey mounted the podium to address the crowd.

"On that black day in our nation's history," Elchibey intoned, "the people of Azerbaijan became victims of the . . ."

"FREE NIMET! FREE NIMET!!" came catcalls from below.

". . . faced with the wrath of the oppressive Soviet system . . ."

"NIMET! NIMET!! NIMET!!!"

The interruptions continued throughout Elchibey's speech, until finally the ex–dissident leader-cum-president gave in.

"I, too, want Nimet to be with us, especially today. . . ."

"Then let him go!" came the jibes. "Aren't you the president?"

". . . and he will be released."

"WHEN?!"

". . . after the necessary . . ."

"Yooooooo!!!!"

Elchibey's words were drowned in hisses and boos.

The counterrevolution had begun.

* * *

There is a postscript about the colonel who had booked me on Azerbaijan Solidarity Day, and then threw me out of his police station.

One fine evening in late January, Philip Remler, Robert Finn, and I were down at the so-called 'Ho Bar' in the basement of the Old Intourist, getting smashed on imitation Scotch and warm beer, and warding off whores. Philip left, and Robert and I went over to his house for a nightcap.

Along the way, we stumbled on a large semitrailer parked in front of a basement. Military cadets were busy off-loading hundreds of boxes. We took a peek at the labels, and discovered that the freight was chocolate bars. We chuckled at this example of the little corruptions, and went our way.

An hour or two later, I stumbled out of Robert's apartment—only to discover the truck still in place and the military cadets still hard at work. They were getting toward the back of the container, and in addition to the boxes of chocolates, I could see German-made space heaters, a couple of refrigerators, and other white goods. I assumed they were either stolen or brought into the country with no customs tax. Once again, I chuckled and started for home.

Then, suddenly, a police car came roaring up to the truck. What fun, said I to myself, and stayed in the shadows to watch.

"What do you think you're doing!" screamed an officer at one of the cadets.

"Off-loading, sir," said the cadets, snapping to attention.

"We'll see about that!" said the officer, and disappeared into the basement.

A moment later, a second car, a Mercedes, came screeching to a halt near the truck.

"What happened?" squealed the driver.

"Cops," said one of the cadet/porters.

"Oh, no!" wailed the man, and disappeared down the basement stairs the police had gone down before.

The cadet/porters waited for order and I waited for action—but no one reemerged. Let's take a look-see, I said to myself, and trotted down the stairs into the basement, to find myself walking through a labyrinth of boxed goods piled to the ceiling. Most contained chocolate bars. I proceeded further, and at the end of the chocolate corridor, I arrived at what I assumed to be an office door.

What fun! I thought, Busting a deal between cops and robbers!

I was a little drunk, I admit.

Without bothering to knock, I opened the door and walked in. A dozen confused and inimical eyes stared at me. I guess I should be grateful that I was not shot on sight.

"Hi," I said. "What are you boys up to tonight?"

There was no response, so I plopped down in a chair across from a small man with a ratty face whose eyes wore a particularly malignant expression. I extended my hand, which he did not take—and with a rush of excitement and horror, I realized that I knew the man from somewhere, but I could not for the life of me remember the context. The Karabakh front? A diplomatic reception? An alfresco shop in the bazaar? There was only one thing to do: brazen my way out of the mess.

"Hi!" I said again, friendly-like.

The man just sat there, playing with a pocket calculator and looking away.

"Hi!!" I said in a louder voice.

Again, rat-face was silent—and I was getting angry. I went over and plunked my elbows down on his desk like I owned it.

"I remember you. Why don't you remember me?"

His silence only made me more furious.

"YOU DON'T KNOW WHO I AM?" I shouted.

This time he nodded, although he remained silent—just like the other three men in the room. I think they were stunned, too.

"Nothing like old pals," I said, lighting a cigarette. I flicked an ash on the floor and took my leave, stomping on as many boxes of chocolate as I could on my way out. Who was he? *Who was he?*

I got home but couldn't sleep.

Then suddenly, it dawned on me with an awful splendor: *It was my colonel,* the man who had booked me after the Solidarity Day non-rally on New Year's Eve, now sitting sans uniform in a room full of illegal chocolates.

I laughed aloud, and Hicran woke and asked me why I was ruining her sleep.

"It's him!" I cackled. "It was him!!"

"Go to sleep," she said.

But I couldn't. It was the casualness and ubiquitousness of it all. Corruption was everywhere, everywhere! And no one cared. . . .

The colonel. . . .

Perhaps it was unfair to focus on him. He was just unlucky enough to be the guy who had detained me once upon a time; otherwise, the deal down in that basement would not have been of any interest at all. His nickel-and-dime chocolate operation was nothing compared to the activities of the others. In addition to the cops who used their patrol cars as pimpmobiles, there were other security men who openly admitted dealing in dope across the Iranian frontier. There was the growing trade in stolen Mercedes sedans, some with bullet holes in the doors, that could be removed from the Interpol computer net for an additional $500 added to the purchase price. There were the international fly-by-night artists, my favorite being Bernd Thompson, the ex–East German secret police agent-cum-telecommunications man, who along with the minister of communications had set up a 'private' satellite service designed to gouge the oilmen (and, rumor had it, eavesdrop on their traffic, with confidential information culled from faxes and recorded phone calls sold to the highest bidder).

Indeed, everyone was trying to make an extra buck and to exploit the collapsing system in any way they could. So, let the colonel make a few bucks on the side, using his cadets as porters!

My problem was that I kept running into him—and always in somewhat compromising situations. Once, when I was escorting some friends back to their hotel in an ambulance that we had appropriated as a taxi, a squad car pulled us over, looking for a little I-Will-Look-The-Other-Way-This-Time grease. I got out to explain the situation and found myself face to face with 'my' colonel, again. He jumped back into his car and sped away.

Another time, at a reception hosted at the unspeakable Gulistan, I saw him hovering in the back of the hall, near the service corridor used by the waiters and busboys. I got up from my table to go and say hello, but once again he thought it best to disappear down the corridor into the kitchen. I guess the man just didn't like me.

Philip Remler turned the various episodes into a Raymond Chandler–style report for the State Department, entitled *'Quis Custodiet Custodes'* (although I prefer to think of it as "The Man Who Knew Too Much"). It was a limited official use cable, but because it was about me, he thought I might get a kick out of it, and showed it to me.

"They're going to kill you, you know," he said.

I guess that was supposed to be flattering, or a joke.

In Stepanakert, Russian president Boris Yeltsin (third from left) and Kazakh president Nursultan Nazarbaev (third from right) announce a 10-point peace plan for Karabakh. (O. Litvin)

Azerbaijan's president Ayaz Mutalibov (center), with U.S. secretary of state James Baker III (left), who visited Baku in January 1992 to discuss Washington's conditions for establishing official diplomatic relations with Azerbaijan. (O. Litvin)

Heydar Aliyev, out of favor in Moscow and Baku, bides his time at home in Naxjivan. (T. Goltz)

Popular Front leader Abulfez Elchibey issues an ultimatum to "citizen" Ayaz Mutalibov to vacate the presidential palace. (T. Goltz)

Iskender Hamidov's "Bozkurt" (Gray Wolf) militia moves out of Popular Front headquarters to take over parliament. (T. Goltz)

After taking the oath of office, Abulfez Elchibey touches his head to the Quran given to him by Sheikh ul Islam Allahshukur Pashazade. (O. Litvin)

Elchibey addresses the crowd on Army Day. Towfig Gasimov is third from the left; to Elchibey's left are Iskender Hamidov, Isa Gambar, and Panakh Husseinov. (T. Goltz)

Surat Husseinov orders his men to march on Baku and oust Elchibey.
(T. Goltz)

Heydar Aliyev, newly elected chairman of the parliament, escorts President Elchibey to a waiting Mercedes, effectively delivering him into obscurity and exile in Naxjivan. On Elchibey's left is Afyettin Jalilov. (T. Goltz)

Acting President Heydar Aliyev with his new prime minister, Surat Husseinov, at his left; at his right is Vafa Gulizade. (O. Litvin)

Heydar Aliyev during his oath-taking ceremony as president of the republic, October 10, 1993. (T. Goltz)

19

The Snow Job

The snow fields began on the far side of the border, as if Stalin had decided to demarcate the frontier exactly at that place where the rugged, forested beauty of his native Georgia stopped, leaving the cold, denuded plateau to the Armenians.

"Better eat now," said my new friend Alexis Rowell, pulling the white NEVA up to the Georgian-Armenian border post. "It is probably going to be the last hot food we will have for a week."

Alexis was the BBC's correspondent in the Caucasus, and the first foreign correspondent to take up residency in the neighboring republic of Georgia. Azerbaijan was part of his new beat, and he had looked me up in Baku in mid-January during a summit between Elchibey and the Georgian leader, Eduard Shevardnadze. We had become instant friends—it was nice to have another madman in the neighborhood. Then Alexis issued a challenge.

"Tommy," he said. "Don't you think it is time for you to take a look-see at Armenia? The last time I was there, you were a regular subject of conversation."

I was only too aware of what the Armenians were saying about me. In the summer of 1992, for example, I had participated in a U.S. Congressional hearing in Washington, D.C. about 'Recent Events in Azerbaijan.' The session rapidly deteriorated into an unseemly mudslinging match between me and members of the Armenian Assembly of America, who had packed the hall. The tone was set by one Van Krikorian, who took the floor to 'ask a question for the record'—and then proceeded to dump calumny and slander on me in a theatrical presentation that culminated in his claim that I had fabricated the Xodjali massacre, which he said 'never happened.'

"I am disgusted to see you here," Krikorian said, making a cowardly egress from the room under cover of the applause of those assembled before I could respond.[1]

Other friends tuned in to the Armenian grapevine went so far as to warn me never to go to Armenia, lest I be killed.

"They really hate your guts there," said a Ph.D. candidate pal researching militia groups in the Caucasus. "Stay away."

But Alexis was insistent.

"How can you pretend to expertise on the subject of Karabakh and the Caucasus when you have only seen one side of the conflict?" he asked rhetorically.

This was the argument I had been hoping he would not raise. So, with more trepidation than reluctance, I agreed to go along. My only caveat was that we travel in a sort of convoy of other visiting journalists—safety in numbers, and all that. Alexis saw the wisdom of this, and made arrangements for us to link up with a number of Moscow-based correspondents. We would all meet in the Georgian capital, Tbilisi, and then travel down to Yerevan in a caravan of cars.

My security concerns alleviated in part, I flew to Tbilisi and was met by Alexis and his translator, Nana Talakvadze, at the airport.

"Let's go!" he said.

"Where are the others?"

"Umm, they all canceled."

"Canceled?"

"Yeah, they said they were afraid to drive down the bandit highway after the last killing."

Alexis was referring to the road between Tbilisi and Yerevan, where roving bands of Georgian brigands had the nasty habit of intercepting lone vehicles for fun and profit. That, however, was the least of my worries. I wanted to cancel, but Alexis was insistent.

"Why should the Armenians be interested in the presence of a Turkish agent doubling as an Azeri spy?" he chuckled. "Seriously, all you have to do is sit in the back and keep quiet if and when we are stopped. And no one is going to stop us."

This cavalier attitude had gotten Alexis through a lot of checkpoints where lesser correspondents feared to go. My honor was on the line; I could not bail out.

"I am in your hands," I said at last. "But I would prefer not to die."

Thus we set out from Tbilisi in a car crowded with gas canisters, bread, and too many people. In addition to Alexis's translator Nana, I had enlisted her sister Nata as my own, personal interface/buffer with the Armenian world. She was actually a Spanish-Russian translator, with limited English—but in a pinch, she was tasked with distracting the authorities by rattling away in Spanish and referring to me as Juan Carlos, the name of a correspondent from *El Pais*. In addition to the four of us, Alexis added a fifth person to the NEVA: a half-Georgian/half-Russian would-be driver-*cum*-cameraman whose presence made things more than a little cozy but added to my sense of security. For good measure, I acquired a brimless felt hat favored by the Georgian hill people known as 'Svanies' as a sort of disguise. To all appearances, or at least from a distance, we were a NEVA full of Georgians driving down the road with a BBC sticker on the car.

That is what the Armenian border guards apparently thought. They did not bother to check anything. The adrenaline coursing through my veins subsided as they raised the iron gate and waved us through.

"Welcome to hell frozen over," chortled Alexis, and pushed the gas pedal to the floor.

* * *

It was late January 1993—and the word 'Armenia' meant bleakness, wretchedness, and suffering. According to all the reports, there was no food, no gas for transportation, and no fuel for heating or industry, which had come to a standstill. People were cutting down the trees in the botanical garden, Reuters had reported. The *European* ran a front-page story on packs of starving dogs attacking their starving owners. Other press and radio reports followed the same tone: Armenia, the smallest of the former Soviet republics and arguably the most isolated, was on the verge of national catastrophe—and all because of a blockade mounted by Azerbaijan.

We were no sooner inside the country than we ran into the first teams of fuel-hunters. Slogging about in the snow by the side of the road, men and boys were hacking down trees, leaving long rows of ugly stubs behind them as they went.

Our first stop was at the town of Spitak, the epicenter of the great earthquake of December 1988, when 35,000 were killed as shoddily constructed apartment buildings came crashing down on the occupants. A tour of the local cemetery was sobering: row upon row of black granite tombstones were inscribed with the images of the victims, often five family members to a grave. Engraved stone watches recorded the exact time of the earthquake.

One side effect of the tragedy was the arrival of millions of dollars of international aid for the reconstruction of housing. All along the road to and from Spitak was evidence of a massive project to create what might best be termed modern, structurally sound apartment buildings—and with a touch of style. The Swiss- and Finnish-sponsored sections could have been transplanted into a suburb anywhere in either of those two countries.

Sadly, the same was true of the 'Ukrainian' section, which resembled the sort of public housing one saw everywhere in the former USSR—exactly the sort of buildings that had come crashing down in the earthquake.

Due to the difficulties of building in winter, coupled with electricity shortages, however, most of the construction works seemed to be in hibernation. Scores of cranes stood idle, and there was no visible activity on the sites. Four years after the earthquake, victims continued living in temporary shelters, or even just the container crates used to bring in material. The steel boxes had been converted into what increasingly seemed to be permanent abodes.

We stopped in one such area, where we discovered row upon row of tubular dwellings set in what looked to be a parking lot in the middle of nowhere. Knocking on the nearest door, we were received by a spindly old lady with a pronounced mustache. She invited us inside from the cold. It was not much warmer within.

"What happened?" I asked, referring, of course, to the earthquake.

"I don't know," she replied, baking some *levash* bread over a twig fire. "I wasn't here then—I am from Yerevan."

Nor were most of the other residents in this section of relief housing, it seemed: most were Armenian refugees from Baku. We asked our hosts to introduce us to one such, and soon a not unattractive, small woman with some sort of eyelid disease appeared.

"Why did you leave?" I asked, referring to the pogroms of January 1990.

"Well, I was living very peaceably in Baku with all my friends—ah, my friends! There was Yuri and Marisa and Vlado and Dilshot. . . ."

I scribbled down notes, and was going to ask a second question. But she just kept babbling, on and on and increasingly without any context.

". . . Ah, yes! And the black dog, a puppy, really, that used to jump and run whenever mama, sweet mama, would turn on the radio to that program, that program, what was that program? before rolling out the dough and then the other one, too. . . ."

We put away our notebooks. The woman was mad, really insane. The only question worth asking was what had unhinged her, but she was incapable of answering that. On our way to the car, we ran into another group of women carrying plastic buckets to the nearest source of drinking water. One was a big strapping blonde from Ukraine. She was wearing cast-off gym warmup slacks, and informed us she had volunteered for the earthquake relief effort and then got stuck in one of the tubular huts when her government refused to pay her way home.

"Such is life," she said with resignation.

Another was a refugee from Azerbaijan, who said she had worked in Heydar Aliyev's famous air-conditioning plant until driven from her home, job, and city in 1990.

"Ah, Baku," she sighed. "Once we hoped that our dislocation would only be temporary, but now we have given up all hope. The last years have been poison—poison."

On the other end of Spitak we stopped in at a series of houses that resembled Swiss chalets. Here, the atmosphere was quite different. Children played on the swings set in a snow-covered playground, and when doors opened, the sound of music came pouring forth from stereos and radios. The chalets were built to accommodate the Finnish nationals involved in the earthquake relief effort and were hardly typical of emergency housing. Most importantly, the Finns had left a generator behind, and the dwellings had electricity, heat, and running water.

We knocked on a door at random, and were immediately ushered inside by the occupant. His name was Oganetz Hovanisyan. Instantly, the table was cleared and then piled high with the family's food stocks—delicious pickles, cheese, a meaty stew, *levash* bread, and of course, Armenian brandy.

"We are ashamed that we cannot offer you more," said Hovanisyan. "You have saved our lives—and we have nothing to give!"

He and his wife were from Spitak—and had been there on that fateful morning when the earth shook its great shaking, and their world came crashing down. The family had lost a daughter. By Spitak standards, they had been spared.

"At first we thought it was the Azeris, setting off a huge bomb," Hovanisyan related. "Only later did we realize it was something far more devastating."

I asked why he thought it was the Azeris, when all the local Muslims had been driven out of the region almost a year before the catastrophe. Ten miles in from the border, we had come across a large Muslim cemetery. The dates on the tombstones suggested that the last burials had taken place in 1987 and early 1988, suggesting clearly that all local Azeris had left long before the earthquake struck.

"We thought there might still be a few around—agents provocateurs, you know," said Oganetz.

When I asked how relations were with the Azeris before the expulsions, he winced.

"Good, good—I mean, we really didn't have much to do with them, you know. They were farmers, and we were not."

Did he have any friends among them?

"Well—no," he said. "They were Turks, after all—and we can never forgive or forget what they did to us in 1915. And now, of course, the Turco-Azeri blockade. . . ."

* * *

A snowstorm was kicking up and light was fading, so we thought it best to try and cross the Spitak Pass to Yerevan before it got too dark. Fortified with a last toast of the delicious local brandy, we set off again, driving over a uniform landscape of white fields, studded by tree-stumps and jagged boulders. Soon, even that definition was lost as blowing snow reduced our vision to the tunnel of road immediately in front of us.

Then, with a start, there was a man standing in the way, waving his hands for us to stop. We did so, only then noticing the outline of a large semitrailer parked nearby.

"*Hgymph!*" the man said, apparently in Armenian.

"*Benzin nyetu,*" said Alexis in Russian, assuming the man was looking for fuel.

The man continued to twist his mouth and touch his ears. Another daft or mad Armenian, wandering around in the snow?

"Let me try," I offered, and addressed the man *in Turkish.*

"Thank God!" he cried. "Someone at last to talk to! I am lost! Is this the road to Istanbul?"

"Well, in a manner of speaking," I said, describing the route up to Georgia, and then back into Turkey via the Batumi/Sarp border gate.

"Thanks, thanks!" said the truck driver, and put his rig in first gear.

"*Turkish?*" exclaimed a flabbergasted Alexis. "This is *Armenia,* for God's sake!"

I explained that as a trained observer, I had looked at the license plates on his truck and had noted that the vehicle was registered in Istanbul.

"What was he doing here?"

"Dropping off a load of chocolates, cigarettes, and preserves," I replied.

"But what about the blockade?"

Yes, indeed, I asked myself rhetorically, what about 'the blockade'?

* * *

That Armenia had not been reduced to surviving on sugar-jolts from Turkish chocolates became even more apparent when we finally pulled into Yerevan and checked into our rooms at the Hotel Armenia. It was dark and cold, and we had to feel our way up the darkened stairwell to the sixth floor by hand-held candles. We were hungry and went to the second-floor restaurant. It was closed, although a number of people were dancing in the semi-dark to the music of a three-piece band, whose electric instruments were powered by a small, noisy generator.

"The blockade," explained the manager. Then he suggested we go over to a place known locally as 'the Mafia' to try our luck there.

"They're open when everyone else is not, and have the best food in town," he said.

It sounded like a wild-goose chase, but soon we found ourselves parking in front of a series of buildings that fit the description he had given.

"Is this the *Mafia?*" Alexis asked the armed doorman of one of the three buildings.

"Yes, it is," came the reply.

We were ushered inside and soon ensconced behind a table sagging under the weight of plates and bottles. Service was provided by almost obsequious waiters, who would only smile when we asked how they managed to acquire caviar and sturgeon steak from Baku. There was also a pleasant duet of wandering minstrels, playing traditional Armenian and 'international' tunes on the guitar and violin. It was, without exaggeration, the very best meal I had enjoyed in almost two years of living in the former Soviet Union.

The restaurant was so oddly wonderful that we felt obliged to inquire more closely into the source of all the providence. The manager, a round-faced character by the name of Sarkis, broke away from a birthday party he had thrown for himself to explain. A wealthy, influential but best anonymous Armenian from the diaspora had taken over the buildings from the museum trust, Sarkis told us, in order to cater to the needs of the growing number of diplomats, aid workers, and foreign journalists in town. There had been some mutterings that the ostentatious service was not in keeping with the spirit of the current crisis, but a suggested curtailment of service had been scotched due to the protests of the foreign clientele, who had become dependent on the restaurant for relief from the suffering they reported to be all around them.

It was easy to understand why the foreigners had protested. It was a great place, and Sarkis was a fine host.

"I am like Scarface, the man in the movie—it is a movie about my life!" he cackled, whipping out a pistol and pointing it at the band for emphasis. "*Bang Bang! Hahahah!* It is my birthday, you will forgive me! Please come back, soon!"

We did forgive him, and came back often. Every day, in fact.

* * *

We devoted the next day to an initial assessment of the situation in Yerevan. The thing that struck us immediately was that contrary to the reports we had been reading about all the trees having been hacked down by desperate people seeking fuel, most were standing. Perhaps residents wanted to chop down the oak, walnut, and plane trees lining the boulevards and parks downtown, but doing so made no sense: without installing a woodburning stove, replete with stovepipe shot out the window, apartment dwellers had no use for such fuel—and most people in Yerevan lived in apartment buildings.

A prowl around the outskirts of town, where folks lived in individual houses, revealed a different story: there, people were indeed cutting down branches and whole trees and carting them home on sleds. But in Yerevan itself, the very structure of the city preserved the trees on the boulevards and in parks, and the idea that all had been felled was a gross exaggeration.

This was small consolation for most residents of Yerevan, however, who had been reduced to shuffling around their homes in greatcoats with candles in their pockets. Cooking hot food at home was another problem, because most ovens and stoves in Armenia were fed by a natural gas line from Turkmenistan and Kazakhstan that passed through Azerbaijan—and the Azeris had cut it off as they had the trains, roads, and electrical lines that passed to Armenia across their territory.

Kerosene heaters and the requisite fuel to burn in them was thus an important part of the huge aid package being pumped into Armenia by the United States. U.S. Embassy officials were proud to say that the total aid package for fiscal 1992–1993 was to be $312 million, the largest per capita assistance for any former Soviet Republic, and after Israel, the largest U.S. per capita aid package in the world. None of it was supposedly usable in the war effort in Karabakh in any way. But when we asked about 'controls' on the donated kerosene—namely, what insured that the fuel was not being misdirected into diesel-burning tanks and APCs, the USAID official in question assured us that the tender had been issued for a type of kerosene that made conversion into machine use impossible. Ever cynical, Alexis scoffed at this one, and explained to the diplomat that a Japanese-made converter was already in use in Karabakh to effect exactly that process. Had the diplomat ever been to Karabakh to see for himself?

Alas, no. The United States regarded Karabakh as part of Azerbaijan; it would be a violation of protocol for him to go there. Accordingly, the staff of the U.S. Embassy in Yerevan was obliged to rely on their Armenian interlocutors for all its information on developments there—and they had every reason to believe that they were not being lied to.

Perversely, the embassy staff actually seemed to like all the suffering around them, or at least liked to advertise it. To give us an inkling of the dire state of affairs in Armenia, one diplomat set up a meeting with a research institute conducting a study on the loss of body mass—in other words, starvation.

We went over at the appointed time and met a chubby fellow by the name of Professor Vladimir Davidiants, project director of a joint venture between the United States Center for Disease Control and the Armenian National Institute of Health. With the aid of charts and figures, Davidiants explained how he had been able to compute, through a voluntary cohort of 100 pensioners, that a typical retiree had lost 10 percent of his or her body mass over the past six months due to a general lack of food and mild hypothermia, both due to the Turco-Azeri blockade.

The numbers were impressive. But when we asked the director about comparative loss of body mass in other countries of people of a similar age, he was obliged to admit that he had not bothered to collect such data. I then asked him how much body mass he had lost as a result of the blockade. Davidiants was not amused, but got on the scale and made the various calculations, next inviting me to do the same. We were both sufficiently far from shriveling not to worry about starvation in the immediate future.

* * *

That evening (at the Mafia restaurant, of course) we ran into the author of the story in the *European* about the starving packs of dogs attacking their former owners. Earlier that day, we informed the writer, we had seen the curious sight of several proud pet owners walking their handsome animals on leashes—a coincidental contradiction to his story, it would appear. The journalist cringed in shame and blamed the story on his editors. "I didn't write the lead, or even the second graph!" he whined. "But they attributed all that dog stuff to me!"

We studied his original story and compared it with that printed. True enough, he had not used the starving dogs in the lead. But there was a lot of other, very dubious material in his copy that made the starving dogs fit right into the bleak picture. The most dramatic was a statistic, attributed to the Red Cross, that up to 50,000 people would perish over the winter as a direct result of cold and hunger deriving from 'the blockade.' But we had met the director of the International Committee of the Red Cross during the course of the day, and he had categorically denied that his organization had anything to do with the number quoted in the story.

The source, it turned out, was the *European* correspondent's constant companion—a gentleman associated with the local office of the French Red Cross, named Jean-Pierre Masiyan. He was actually sitting across the table from us, going into a slow boil. We asked him how he had come up with the grim statistic. His response was a sneer: he was, by profession, a statistician, and knew how to quantify such things better than we did.

* * *

The next day, we took up the theme of hospitals, and specifically, the subject of power to light operating theaters. Curiously, there was no problem with this at the two hospitals we visited because they both had generators. The staff said that all other hospitals and clinics in Yerevan were equally supplied. The director of Clinical Hospital #3, Mrs. Isabella Papayan, said that the main problem was the supply of food and the acquisition of specialized cardiovascular medicines and antibiotics. Food was a problem because the hospital, as a state institution, could not purchase from the bazaar; it had to be supplied from state-run stores, which were mainly empty. As for medicines, Mrs. Papayan said that she 'waited every day for Turkey to break the blockade.' She was apparently unaware that a snack shop specializing in the usual assortment of chocolates, cigarettes, and soft drinks imported from Turkey had been set up in the outpatient lounge, replacing the pharmacy.

A similar state of affairs prevailed at another clinic responsible for the health of the 20,000 employees of 24 factories in Yerevan's industrial zone, seven of which dealt in chemicals.* One of these factories was Narit Chemical, allegedly the largest producer of resins in the former USSR. It was also a long-time target of the Armenian Green Movement, due to the high level of pollution it produced.

Ironically, the Green Movement gave rise to the Karabakh Committee, which in turn gave impetus to the conflict with Azerbaijan, itself resulting in the embargo that in turn was held responsible for the alleged closure of Armenian factories, including Narit.

But the director of the industrial park's clinic, Dr. Emil Nadjarian, said Narit and all of the 23 other factories in the industrial zone were working, although staffed only by skeleton crews due to the shortage of electricity and raw materials.

---

*'No Soviet missile flew without Armenian help', is a claim made in Yerevan. Not only did the Republic make computer chips, but it also specialized in refining the essence of chrysanthemum, which allegedly has unique coolant qualities vital in rocket fuel. One begins to understand the importance of Armenia to the Russians when one compares the traditional Azeri contribution to the Soviet economy: carnation flowers and air-conditioners.

But the very fact of the crisis was giving rise to silver-lining solutions. Armenia's economic planners were getting out of the cul-de-sac of manufacturing heavy industrial products that no one wanted, and developing the sort of energy-efficient, high value–added stuff that would integrate Armenia into the world economy. None of the 'high-tech' plants suffered from a want of electricity or material; it was dinosaurs like Narit Chemical that were being deprived because they had no place on the map of the future. Like many of the other factories in the industrial park, Narit was not being kept alive—it was being allowed to die.

There was a similar silver lining to the gasoline crisis in the country. To believe press reports, not one car was on the streets, because Baku had cut off petrol and diesel supplies. That was why we had packed four twenty-liter gas cans in the back of our car and suffered mild fume-induced nausea all the way from Tbilisi. But once in Yerevan, we discovered gasoline tankers parked at every street corner, doing brisk business. Prices were about twice that for fuel in Tbilisi and ten times that in Baku, but it did not seem to prevent motorists from filling up. Motorists were thus undergoing a sort of 'shock-therapy' adjustment to world gasoline prices—a state of affairs that would have resulted in riots in Azerbaijan.

Indeed, so low were fuel prices in Azerbaijan and so high in Armenia that the rumor the Azeri mafia was making a killing out of the trade seemed more than plausible—it was very probably true. Indeed, about two weeks after our trip, a colleague from the AFP made a journey down the bandit highway from Tbilisi to Yerevan with a caravan of gasoline tankers. When he asked his driver where the fuel was coming from, he laughed and said 'Baku.'

Still, the subject of power was of great urgency. The Armenians might learn to live like modern troglodytes on their two hours of power every day, but the crisis went far beyond that. Time and time again, we were told about the looming ecological disaster awaiting Lake Sevan, the source of most of Armenia's hydropower, if overuse continued. According to Energy Ministry officials, the lake had dropped by 18 meters (50 feet) over the past 30 years due to over-depletion. An island, on which a monastery stood, had become a peninsula.*

---

*Weather conditions prevented us from going out to Lake Sevan at the time, but a year later I traveled to Lake Sevan with Liam McDowell of the Associated Press. According to our quick, visual calculations, if Sevan were to be refilled to its original volume, the lake would inundate all roads, railway tracks, and towns along the shore. As for the causeway connecting the (former) island with the mainland, it would be submerged, too—but not the tops of the trees lining it, which were more than 50 feet high.

To address this crisis, President Levon Ter-Petrossian announced that despite the considerable risks, he had ordered the reactivation of the Metsamor nuclear power station. Located 37 kilometers outside of the capital, and virtually straddling a major fault line in the crust of the earth, the 800-megawatt Metsamor station had once supplied 40 percent of Armenia's power needs. It was shut down in 1988, two years after the Chernobyl explosion, and kept closed after the great earthquake later that same year. International experts agreed that reactivating the plant was highly undesirable.

To take a closer look, we drove south and then west down a highway that was alternately lined by shops selling the usual consumer products from Turkey and men hacking down trees and eventually arrived at the telltale funnels.

The plant did not generate much confidence. There were cracks in the walls and ceiling and the building's security doors were held together with twine. In one of his more brilliant BBC radio 'packages', Alexis recorded the following for broadcast: 'I am inside a nuclear plant where the doors are held shut by string. . . .'

But there seemed to be more manipulation than madness in Ter-Petrossian's nuclear plans. Namely, it seemed to be a pretty effective means of blackmailing neighboring Turkey: supply us with electricity from your own grid, and we will not cover your country with nuclear ash when our reactor blows up in the next earthquake. Although perhaps a sound policy, there was a nasty twist: if Turkey were forced to supply energy to Armenia in order to keep the plant turned off, it was as good a way as any to destroy Ankara's relations with Azerbaijan. There was already heavy American pressure on Ankara to reopen land links and airspace to Armenia in order to allow refugee relief to arrive—and the mere rumor that Turkey was doing so drove the Azeris wild.

In the meanwhile, Armenia (or individual Armenians) were supplying Turkey (or individual Turks) with a wide range of 'export' items, from medicines to meat.

For a country allegedly on the brink of mass starvation and hypothermia, this was a very strange development. But the facts were clear: for the first time in 70 years (and unlike other citizens of the former Soviet Union), Armenians were able to travel across the Turkish frontier without visas. And they were doing so at the rate of at least 400 a week aboard a special weekly train from Leninakan (Gümre, in Armenian) to the eastern Turkish city of Kars. There my friend Philip Remler had discovered a lively 'Armenian' market that specialized in 'privatized' humanitarian aid, ranging from baby food to blankets. The U.S. embassy in Yerevan suppressed his report because it was so contrary to conventional wisdom.

Trade in animals had also sprung up on the compelling logic of supply and demand: a sheep cost around $15 in Armenia, but fetched around $150 in Turkey; a steer (or cow) was double those prices. The authorities might attempt to crack down, but business was business. The head of state security (KGB) at the town of Oktober'an on the Turkish frontier told us that his men had apprehended 350 head of cattle during the first week of a state of emergency that had been imposed to interdict the growing export trade of meat-on-the-hoof across the border.

Happily, the authorities had achieved some measure of success in interdicting the illegal animals, and the results were showing up in the streets of Yerevan: in addition to the meat one could eat at the 'Mafia' restaurants, any number of sidewalk grills had sprung up on major avenues, and we were able to eat delicious mutton and pork chops at a number of select stands. A single 'shish,' or steel cooking blade run through cubed flesh, cost around a dollar, or more than an average daily wage. But people were lining up, defying the mathematics of official salary and apparent spending power.

Yerevan's several large markets were also crowded with customers. In addition to all the dairy products one could ask for and piles of the pita-like Armenia bread, there was an abundance of locally cured pastrami, Abkhazian tangerines, and even 'winter grapes', as well as the usual selection of potatoes, cabbages, carrots, and other tubers. In a word, it was not a starving city—although many clearly wanted to give that impression.

"Come here, come here, take my picture!" an elderly woman shouted at me, grabbing me by the sleeve and posing in front of a batch of miserable goods she had lined up on the street for sale.

"Come here, come here," another old man would demand, leading me down a side street to show me a state bread shop. "You have to come back to this place in the morning to watch us line up for bread!"

What did it all mean? Why was everyone so uniformly happy to tell us how bad things were? Had they been programmed, or had everyone in the country somehow instinctively 'felt' the need to use a certain vocabulary to express it?

In a weird way, everyone seemed eager not only to accept the miserable state of affairs brought on by the war, but to advertise it—without mentioning the war itself. Although no official would say this, we were left with the lingering sense that the government had succeeded in making the war touch everybody, that is, they had managed to put the country and its citizens into a war economy and a war psychology—war footing, in a word. The fact that foreigners could be duped into believing the place was falling apart—and thus moved to send in massive aid—was certainly a plus. But the main thing was much closer to home: through deprivation and war, the Armenians were becoming a nation again. The national icon was no longer Mount Ararat or even the stark, gray granite memorial commemorating the Victims of the Ottoman Genocide.

It was the overcoat and the candle, commemorating Karabakh.

* * *

Those who did not agree with this process were muted. This was driven home to me the second or third day in town. Tired of waiting for the hotel's electrical grid to come on, I hit the snowy, slushy streets in search of a cafe with a generator or even a woodburning stove to brew my morning coffee.

Most were closed, but I finally found one in the basement that was "open" in the sense that it was not closed, although the salon was so dark and bleak that it was difficult to tell where the tables ended and the chairs began. It was run by an attractive woman named Lena, and after she brewed up a couple of cups, she invited me into the office where she and several of her friends were sitting, rubbing their hands in front of the small stove. Inevitably, the conversation focused on the cutting down of trees, the lack of gas, and the other trials Armenia was undergoing.

"It's horrible, horrible," said Lena. "And it is all due to the blockade."

"What do you expect?" asked a man named Gaik, filling a glass with homemade schnapps to stay warm. "We are at war."

This was not the first time that my interlocutors privately accepted what their government so adamantly refused to concede, namely, that most states at war do not conduct normal trade with the enemy. But it was the first time that it provoked the sort of response we heard from Lena.

"Karabakh!" she spat angrily, "Karabakh! It is all a pack of lies! They lived like kings there, but then they decided to make a war and drag us into it, too."

This was a curious attitude, and so I warily pursued it. How, I asked, through my 'fence,' Nata, did she know the Karabakh Armenians lived like kings?

"Because we went there on vacations!"

"From here?"

"No!" she said, looking at me like I was an idiot. "From Baku!"

"Really? When did you leave?"

"In 1990, with everyone else."

"You must be very happy to have gotten out. . . ."

"Happy? Here?" Lena almost wailed. "We had everything there! It was an international place—Armenians, Azeris, Jews, Russians, everyone! And now look at us! I'd go back in a minute if I had the chance! Maybe you won't believe this, but I speak better Azeri than Armenian."

I decided to roll the dice, and changed languages.

"*Nejesiz?*" I asked her in Azeri, "How are you?"

"*Yahshi,*" she replied, dumbfounded, "Fine."

And then, to the amazement of the three or four other characters sitting around the office, we launched into a long conversation about Baku: how and why and when she had made the decision to leave, and *all in Azeri*. It ended with her promising to introduce me to two friends of hers the next day who would tell me more: an Armenian woman married to an Azeri man, one of several mixed couples she knew about who had decided to live a discreet life in Yerevan as opposed to Baku.

This was dynamite, because however ridiculous the ultranationalist Armenians' claim that all Armenians had left Azerbaijan, the Azeris made the same claim about how the Armenians had expelled every last Azeri from Armenia. Here, at last, was some evidence to the contrary.

"*Saghol,*" I said, thanking her, when we eventually left.

"*Saghol,*" Lena replied, with a great smile on her face.

But when I returned at the appointed time the next day, Lena had changed her mind as well as her mood—or had had it changed for her.

"We're closed," she said, opening the door a crack before shutting it again without further explanation.

* * *

There were other meetings, interviews, and observations, but none of any great import and certainly none that changed the general picture: Yerevan was cold and grim, but the reason the country found itself in that uncomfortable state of affairs was because it was pursuing a war with a neighboring state that sat atop its traditional transport lines and energy arteries. It was hardly reasonable to expect Azerbaijan to conduct "business as usual" with Armenia so long as guns were firing.

But time and again, when I pressed my interlocutors, all would finally admit that the war was worthwhile. As for the pending national catastrophe due to the 'blockade,' most shyly (and slyly) admitted that beyond the real misery that people endured, the idea of suffering made for great propaganda.

Yes, the *blockade*—that was not. Although trade and communications with Azerbaijan had been (imperfectly) interdicted for the very good reason that the two countries were in a virtual state of war, the road and rail links between Armenia and Georgia (and Iran) were open, as were air links between Yerevan and anywhere in the world that Armenians might choose to fly—Moscow, Beirut, Paris, and even L.A.

No, there was no blockade—unless, of course one wished to alter the meaning of the word. Armenia suffered from an *embargo* placed upon it by a non-friendly neighboring state—Azerbaijan—because Armenia was involved in a rather large land-grab, undertaken by means of violence and war. It baffled common sense to try and understand why Baku should *have* to trade with the enemy, supplying it with gas for its tanks and food for its soldiers, but this was the attitude being taken by most of the world or at least the United States.

* * *

To get a better read on the war, we dropped in the offices of the Dashnaksutyun News Service. The agency was a natural draw for foreign correspondents because it provided a battery of computers, a data bank, and satellite fax transmission for quick relay of information to the world.

Providing information on Karabakh was clearly very high on the agenda, but it was not the sole province of the agency's activities. Internal Armenian politics was also fully addressed: the news service was tied into the main opposition political party, known as the Armenian Revolutionary Federation, or ARF.

The ARF/Dashnaksutyun ('Dashnaks' for short) has a long history. Founded in 1890, the Dashnaks alternatively cooperated with and rebelled against both the Sultan and the czar, depending on which approach would secure greater gains for the ultimate goal of an independent state of Armenia.

It was the Dashnaks, in the main, who led the Armenian resistance in the Ottoman East during World War I and who set up the short-lived Armenian Republic of 1918–1920. They were made very non-grata once the Bolsheviks took over for the very good reason that they represented Armenian nationalism and were, by definition, opposed to Soviet-style internationalism. Suppressed or expelled from Soviet Armenia, the Dashnaks became the most visible and resonant anti-Communist opposition group in the Armenian diaspora for the next seventy years. They were especially strong in Beirut, Marseilles, and Los Angeles.

With the collapse of the Soviet Union, the Dashnaks emerged from under ground. A flood of national feeling, much focused on Karabakh, plus a torrent of diaspora money allowed them to reassert their influence in Armenia as never before. Why, then, were they not in power?

According to the director of the news service, unofficial polls suggested that if snap parliamentary elections were held, the Dashnaks would capture some 25 percent of the vote and thus take 40 percent of the seats. The

Liberal Democrats—the other 'traditional' political party in Armenia, set up in 1889—would collect something along the same lines. President Ter-Petrossian's Armenian National Movement would get less than 5 percent, he said.

There was something familiar about all this number-crunching of polling data mixed with badmouthing of the elected leader. Indeed, when other 'opposition' figures began telling us what they thought of President Ter-Petrossian, I almost felt like I was back in Baku, listening to Nimet Panakhov rant and rave about Elchibey being a sell-out, hypocrite—and worse.[2]

"Ter-Petrossian pretended to be following an absolutist position on *Artsakh* (Karabakh) to gain power, but now he is letting us (the Dashnaks) bleed ourselves dry because it suits his evil political goals!" charged some nameless, wild-eyed character who strolled into the ARF news office for an instant interview.

Connected with this notion that Ter-Petrossian was keeping the noble Dashnaks 'busy' in Karabakh was the charge that his inner circle were intimately involved—no, identical—with the hydra-headed Armenian mafia, including Svo Raf. He was a notorious Armenian gangster whose two main capos were—surprise!— Azeris.*

Still others accused Ter-Petrossian of being a closet communist. His father, they said ominously, had been 'very high' (some said Secretary) of the Syrian Communist Party (others said Lebanese). It followed from this that the president was most likely a KGB plant, developed and tooled by Moscow to destroy the country from within and make it utterly dependent on Russia. As I say, if one just changed the names, the paranoid opposition assessment of Ter-Petrossian could have been transferred to any country in the Caucasus (or maybe even every country in the former Warsaw Pact).

One main detractor was Parour Harikian, leader of the Union of National Self-Determination (and garrison commander of the key town of Goris, that overlooked the 'Lachin Corridor' to Karabakh). After a long prison term on charges of fomenting nationalism when it was not yet fashionable to do so,

---

*After being arrested in Moscow sometime in 1993 and thrown into "The Place That Has No Name," Svo Raf was disemboweled by his roommates with a dull knife because he refused to help out on the clean-up detail in his cell—or so the story goes. His funeral in Yerevan in early 1994 literally turned the lights on in the city. Either under threat or through bribery, the dreary Armenian capital was illuminated for a week to allow Svo Raf's friends and business associates to show due respect. They came from America, Lebanon, Europe (France, mainly), India, Ethiopia, and various former Soviet Republics—including, of course, Azerbaijan.

Harikian emerged from jail to become one of Ter-Petrossian's shrillest critics. He told us that the presidential elections that brought Ter-Petrossian to power were rigged and that Ter-Petrossian was now using the police and security apparatus to sustain his autocratic rule in classic, old communist fashion.

According to Harikian, he had organized an anti–Ter-Petrossian demonstration that was attended by over 100,000 people. The mob almost got out of hand and was only dissuaded from attacking the presidential building by the intervention of Harikian and his cohorts from the UNSD—who had organized the rally in the first place.

We met Harikian at a much smaller demonstration in Opera Square, attended by at most 1,000 people. Still, those gathered were intensely interested in what he had to say. In addition to reiterating his position on Karabakh—he supported the right of self-determination, followed by recognition of the Republic of Mountainous Gharabakh as a separate state—his speech consisted of maligning Ter-Petrossian and accusing him of diverse crimes against democracy. Armenia, said Harikian, needed 'the rule of law instead of the rule of personalities.'

But if Harikian was not happy with Ter-Petrossian, not everybody was happy with Harikian. After the demonstration I ran into some disgruntled religious fundamentalists, Armenian Apostolic style, parading around with a white cloth banner emblazoned with a red cross. The banner, they said, was made from the vestments Jesus wore and had descended to them 'from heaven' so that they might raise it over the 'Christian tanks' in Karabakh. Harikian had declined the token, and the furious men now lumped him into the same category of the condemned as that godless, Levantine KGB agent and Moscow toady, Levon Ter-Petrossian, predicting that after the latter was lynched for his sins against God and the Nation, it would be time to do the same for the former.

The president, meanwhile, remained aloof and inaccessible. We tried to apply for an interview through the executive office, and then through the Ministry of Foreign Affairs. Hours would go by, and then word would come back that the president had no time for us.

The wait was not exactly in vain, however: the walls of the foreign ministry press office were decorated with maps of Armenian states at different points of history, and well worth study. A three-part series of maps (385–536, 536–591 and 591–653 A.D.) showed medieval Armenia in various stages of glory and expansion, reaching at its zenith the Greater Armenia that stretched from the shores of the Caspian Sea almost to the eastern Mediterranean. Most interesting was a poster/map combination of the Republic of Mountainous Gharabakh (RMGh). The former was a flag designed to look like it had been ripped in two by a chain saw: the two-thirds on the left was Armenia while the other third on the right symbolized the detached state of Mountainous Gharabakh. Closer inspection of the RMGh map revealed that large swaths of Azerbaijan had been designated 'areas of traditional Armenian settlement outside the RMGh' in red ink. In addition to the highland province of Kelbajar, pinched between the RMGh and Armenia in the north, these included the Gubatli, Fizuli, Jibrail, and Zengelan provinces, to the south of Karabakh, as well as the lowland farming areas around Agdam, Barda, and Terter, to the east of the RMGh. The city of Ganje, to the north, was just outside this zone. When we asked if this 'red-line' zone represented areas claimed by Armenia, the answer was, of course, that Armenia had no claims to any of Azerbaijan at all, and that all of the maps were merely 'cultural.'

Far more talkative were officials of the Armenian Ministry of Defense, although one had to wonder what their words were worth: despite the overwhelming firsthand evidence that thousands of Armenia Armenians were engaged in the war for Karabakh, including Defense Minister Vazgin Manukiyan, the ministry was still adamant that it had no troops or tanks in the theater at all. Armenia was merely an 'interested observer' in the fate of the Karabakh Defense Forces.

"The Karabakh Defense Forces are made up of 95 percent Karabakhians. The remaining 5 percent are Armenian volunteers with family connections in Karabakh," Defense Ministry spokesman Aram Dooliyan coolly told us at a briefing. "We, as the Armenian Ministry of Defense, have no control over any of them."

Nor was the Defense Ministry involved in the supply of weapons or petroleum or any other military supplies to Karabakh, said Dooliyan. Karabakh was, or was almost, an independent state, and any and all military equipment there was either purchased by Karabakhians on the international market or donated by Armenians from the diaspora, he said. Dooliyan did allow, however, that there might be some foreign soldiers in the theater. Why, Armenia itself had solicited 'specialists' from other republics of the Commonwealth of Independent States to help it build up the Armenian army—so it logically followed that the Karabakhians might have a similar policy of recruiting foreign soldiers as well. The Azeris, in any case, were doing the same: two pilots, one a Ukrainian and the other a Russian, had been captured alive after their planes had been shot down over Karabakh, and they confessed to taking the mercenary work for a cool $5,000 a month.

No, the Armenian Ministry of Defense had only one task: to protect the Republic of Armenia. By that he meant from cross-border incursions from Azerbaijan, and Dooliyan said there had been many. Azerbaijan was currently occupying the Armenian enclave of Krasnaselsk and the country would fight to regain its territory if negotiations failed.*

Armenia, Dooliyan stressed, had no territorial ambitions—not in the area around Lachin nor around Kelbajar, the two Azeri provinces to the west of Karabakh. Armenia was satisfied that both had been neutralized after the recent, spectacular gains by the Karabakh forces in the northern theater.

I had heard propaganda before, but this business about 'spectacular' Armenian gains in the northern theater was a bit much, and I said so.

"Perhaps you have been out of touch with events for a while," smiled Dooliyan smugly. "There has been a coup attempt in Baku."

Alexis and I went bolt upright. A coup attempt in Baku, and us not there?

"The government in Baku dismissed the Minister of the Interior, Ragim Gaziev for general incompetence and corruption," he informed us. "He then tried to take over the television station, but failed."

"And Gusseinov?" I asked, referring to Surat Husseinov according to the Russian pronunciation of his name.

"He has been sacked as well," Dooliyan smiled serenely.

Rahim and Surat gone, due to a failed coup attempt? The war front in chaos?

Dooliyan purred on.

"We continue to hope for a lasting cease-fire and a peaceful solution to the Karabakh conflict," he cooed. "But there is no sign from the Azerbaijani side that they want this. It is clear that Azerbaijan regards Karabakh as its territory. . . . A pity, because the only realistic solution to the conflict is for Azerbaijan to accept the independence of Mountainous Karabakh. This is the only way to lead to good relations between all three states. . . ."

The rest of the shmoozing was lost on both Alexis and me.

It was time to hightail it back to Azerbaijan, but how?—Via the bandit highway, again.

* * *

We decided to leave the next morning at the break of day. This was fortunate, because it gave us a chance to participate in one last event: a press conference and reception by Massachusetts's junior Congressman, Joseph Kennedy. Arriving with an entourage of 56 journalists, Congressman Kennedy was given a whirlwind, 24-hour tour of the city that left an indelible impression on him.

---

*This was one of the several true 'enclaves' in the area—a part of Armenia, located just north of Karabakh, surrounded by Azerbaijan. He disallowed any comparison with several Azerbaijani enclaves inside Armenia: the residents had simply 'left' in 1988 and 1989, along with the Azeri minority of Armenia proper.

It was no fault of Armenia's, he said, that it was "cut off from the rest of the world" by the Azerbaijani/Turkish blockade. He had stopped through Ankara on his way to Armenia and made it clear to President Turgut Özal that Turkey "must accept the responsibilities that go along with regional leadership," whether transshipping massive amounts of aid to Armenia suited Turkey's interests or not.

"I have never seen such human suffering," he said at a candlelit, over-coats-only press conference/cocktail held at the Armenian Assembly of America's offices over at the Ministry of Agriculture. "The pungent odor of the ending of life in the hospitals and orphanages filled with refugees from Baku I visited will stay with me always."

It was excellent theater, and he said a lot of other quotable things. But it stank to high heaven. It went without saying that the ex-Congressman's hosts did not take him to the Mafia restaurant but rather to someplace sufficiently cold and nasty that he would get the right idea about local conditions. Nor did they take Kennedy to Hospital Clinic #3, preferring, I imagine, to show him some hospital that was obliged to use candles in the operating room. As for his visit with refugees, his hosts most certainly did not introduce him to Lena, the lady in my favorite coffee shop. And the last thing they wanted to promote, I am sure, was the idea that whatever deprivations Armenia was experiencing were the result of its territorial ambitions on a neighboring state—i.e., that the Azeri blockade/embargo against Armenia was directly connected to Yerevan's participation in and promotion of the war in Karabakh.

I thought it inappropriate to ask Congressman Kennedy about all this in front of his hosts. But I did ask him if he intended to take a trip to Baku any time soon, to take a look 'at the other side.' No, he said, there was a lot of work on the Hill. This trip to Armenia was pretty exceptional, and mainly in response to pleas from his constituents in Watertown, Massachusetts.

Then I asked him a personal question.

"Is Douglas Kennedy your brother or your cousin?"

"Dougie is my brother," answered the Congressman, with the sort of shit-eating grin that older brothers reserve for their maybe wayward, younger siblings. "Why do you ask?"

"He spent some time at my house in Baku," said I. "Give him my regards."

"Sure," said Kennedy. "He told some pretty wild stories about that trip. What's your name again?"

When I told him, all the people from the Armenian Assembly of America standing around and listening to our discourse sucked in their breath—but maybe I was just imagining things. It was, I have to admit, the first time I had spoken my full name during the trip. Paranoia, perhaps.

Then the cold cocktail party broke up, and Kennedy and entourage went out to the airport while we went back over to the Mafia restaurant for a last taste of sturgeon steak, kebabs, caviar and the rest of the whole nine yards. He would have his memories of Yerevan, and we would have ours.

Inevitably, we were joined by the usual crowd: whining diplomats, A.I.D workers, and Red Cross relief personnel. Among our table companions was also Mr. Statistics, Jean-Pierre Masiyan of the French Red Cross, and his constant companion and propaganda vehicle, the correspondent from the *European*. We ate and drank and danced and then went back to the sixth floor of the Hotel Armenia and drank cognac by candlelight in our cold but clean rooms, trying to assess our experience and to put our impressions into some context.

"They are really impressive liars," mused Alexis.

"They are totally without shame," said our Georgian translator, Nana, as we set off the next morning, heading north across the snowbound landscape.

Our progress was halted for an hour or so by a line of cars behind a snow grader. The driver refused to budge until properly 'tipped' for having performed his state-appointed task of pushing some 20 meters of deep snow off the road to let us pass. Once he'd been dealt with, we continued wending our way through long and tedious snowfields until we arrived once again in Spitak, where the denuded snowfields began melting into gray-green winter pastures and forests.

It was indeed time to get back to Baku and find out just what the hell was going on.

Rahim Gaziev dismissed? Surat Husseinov stripped of his glory? Kelbajar pacified? Perhaps it was all part of the relentless Armenian disinformation campaign. . . .

At the border, we cheered as we passed the last of a line of two dozen petro-tankers that were lined up at the Armenian checkpoint, and continued laughing as we entered the banditland of southern Georgia.

The snow job was over, at last.

Notes

1. All this is to be found in the official OSCE/Helsinki Commission transcript of the hearing, dated June 21, 1992. There is more, however. Krikorian then wrote a letter of protest to the Commission, reiterating his 'disgust' at seeing me given 'a forum' to disseminate my 'extreme views.' I was unqualified to say anything of value on Karabakh/Azerbaijan because I was, among other things, 'a convert to Islam,' 'married to a Turk,' and a 'personal friend' of Abulfez Elchibey's. To their credit, the Commission's reply to this calumny pointed out that even if true, my alleged religious, familial, and fraternal associations should not disqualify me—lest the Helsinki Commis-

sion disqualify testimony from anyone who was Christian, married to an Armenian, or associated with Armenia in any way. Later, one AAA member, Danny Beylian, made a point of apologizing for Kirkorian's attempt at defamation.

2. The paranoid predictions of the ARF came home to roost in 1995, when, in anticipation of parliamentary elections, Ter-Petrossian banned the ARF, charging the organization with extortion, drug running, and treason. The elections, which unsurprisingly resulted in an ANM victory, were described by international observers with the interesting formula of having been 'free but not fair' (or possibly 'fair but not free,' as if it makes a difference). The 1996 presidential elections only confirmed this: all but the most devoted apologists for the Ter-Petrossian regime say the president hijacked the elections.

20

Kelbajar

SSKREEEeee! . . .

It was another GRAD missile screeching in, and everyone on the helicopter landing pad dove for cover that was not there. Some things were instinctive.

KRVROM! VROM VROm VRom Vrom vrom vro vr. . . .

The echo reverberated down the canyon in undulating waves. Then it was silent again, and everyone on the ledge called the Kelbajar got to their feet and wondered if the next missile would strike a little closer. There was not much to do, even if it did.

The GRAD is not a very accurate weapon. Rather, it is designed to instill fear and panic. It whistles and screams and screeches through the sky before smashing home, wherever that is, and keeps you hunkered down and very frightened. It was doing a good job of doing that right now: there were about two or three hundred people on the landing pad, and we were all hunkered down and very frightened indeed.

The only reason no one ran away was because there was nowhere to go except up. The only way to do that was to get on a helicopter. That was how I had gotten into this rat-hole, killing zone called Kelbajar, and I was cursing myself for having done so. I wanted to get back up and out very badly.

The night before, a GRAD had blown up the house where I was staying. If it had been a 152mm shell or a 500-pound aerial bomb, I probably wouldn't be around to tell the story. But it was only a GRAD and so everyone in the house was able to escape, tumbling over burning chairs and mattresses into the garden, glad we had only been hit by a GRAD and not something else.

This was, of course, of small consolation for the owner. His name was Shamil Askerov, and he was the curator of the local museum and an authority on the Kurds of Kelbajar and Azerbaijan because he was one—a Kurd, that is. So were most of the people living in and around Kelbajar. He was so outraged at what was happening to his town that he wept.

"Forty Armenians—and they take Kelbajar!" he wailed. He was using the number 40 rhetorically, in the sense of '40 days and 40 nights,' 'Ali Baba and the 40 thieves' and even the 40-day period of mourning in Shi'ite Islam. Ironically, from what I have been able to patch together in the aftermath of the Armenian assault, the real number of attackers was not much higher.

Shamil's son Xalid, who worked as a cameraman for Reuters, tried to calm his father. But it wasn't much use. It was not the loss of the refrigerator or television that upset Shamil so much, or even the loss of the family pictures or the autographed portrait of Mullah Mustafa Barzani that hung on the wall. That in itself was a tremendously resonant keepsake for a Kurd. I did not ask if it was really so—why underline the point of pain?—but I wanted to think the autographed portrait had been hand delivered by the spiritual father of Kurdish nationalism himself, the mullah, during the course of his Great Retreat from Iraqi Kurdistan to the Soviet Union in the 1960s. Why not?

Shamil was not weeping about the loss of the Barzani portrait or autograph. He was weeping for his books. All thirty thousand of them. They might have been dog-eared, badly printed, and maybe not even very interesting to anyone else, but they were Shamil's pride and joy. He had even made his own card catalogue to guide the odd visitor through the collection. It was nicely and neatly organized into thematic sections like History (Ancient), History (Modern), Local Lore, Geology, Geography, Fiction, and Politics. There were lots of standard, mass-produced titles about Soviet culture, along with works of the sort of minority language poetry and literature and obscure language dictionaries that only state sponsorship such as that of the late USSR could create: Russian-Kurdish-Azeri, Armeno-Georgian, and even a Lezgin-Talish-Russian phrase book, if I remember correctly.

I was given a tour of the shelves by flashlight the night before it all went up in smoke, and uttered appropriate 'ooos' and 'aahhs' when an interesting, odd, or familiar volume showed up on the shelves. I was tempted now to ask Shamil if I could take a few books out on loan. But he was distraught, and the request seemed too disingenuous: borrow a book tonight because tomorrow it won't be here anyway? No, asking for anything would have been too much like asking our host to give up hope, even though we knew that when the moment came to ask or plead that Shamil part with this or that particular book so that it might still be saved, it would be too late. The unspoken hope was that when Kelbajar fell and the house got looted, the man who looted it would be a bibliophile and not just a looter and burner plain and simple. He would be a man, I wanted to think, who would claim the library as his own and then protect it as his own—just like the other looters who would claim the refrigerator, chairs, rugs, and pots and pans would protect their booty as their own.

That was the unspoken idea, anyway, as we sat around the table that last night and drank the last bottle of vodka that was in the refrigerator that didn't work because there was no electricity and ate the remaining fruit preserves in the pantry. That was dinner. There were big bags of rice and dried beans in storage, but we couldn't cook them because there was no running water, because it ran on an electric pump, and no gas for the stove, because that had been cut some time before. I guess we could have lit a fire outside, but that seemed like a pretty stupid idea when the enemy was looking for anything in the dark to train their weapons on. So we just sat around and drank in the dark and talked about everything else but the inevitable—such as the destruction of the library.

That moment came near dawn while we were asleep in the living room, snuggling between thick, lice-ridden mattresses and thick, lice-infested blankets. The room was redolent with the uniquely pungent odor of dirty socks and unwashed feet, and resonant with the undulating rasp of five snoring men. I heard it and awoke, or I awoke and heard it.

sskKREEE! . . .

There was no time to duck or cough, only to seize my boots used as a pillow and hope the roof didn't cave in before I made it to the door or the window or through the hole in the wall that had just opened before my eyes.

KvVROMP!

"Where's the old guy," someone asked of Shamil as the house started to burn and blaze.

"In the library," said someone else.

One or two or maybe all four of us went back in and made our way through the detritus and smoldering rubble. We found our host sitting among his thirty thousand books, most of which had pitched from their shelves, dictionaries mixed with poetry and geology and local lore, all scattered on the floor.

"I want to die!" cried Shamil. "Let me die with my life!"

Some of the books were already starting to smolder, and it didn't seem like a very good time to argue about the merits of dying just because one aspect of one's life's work was about to go up in smoke. But Shamil said he would not, could not, leave without his books. Someone, maybe me, was about to try and reason with him when the next GRAD came crashing into the house. Actually, it crashed into the garden, where we had all been standing a few moments before, hitting close enough to the outhouse to scatter shit and shrapnel all over everything outside and make us very glad that we were inside when the thing hit. Getting killed by shit and shrapnel—what a way to die.

There was no time for reflection, however. GRADs were shot in clusters, and if we had picked up two, there would soon be a third and then a fourth and maybe more. Someone grabbed the crying old librarian by one arm and someone else grabbed him by the other arm, and we dragged him out into the morning, out past the outhouse and the garden and into the street.

ssskKREE . . . KVROMP!!

The house was ablaze now, but we were running down the road toward the heliport. We passed soldiers stripping off their uniforms and pulling on civilian clothes that didn't fit, stray dogs sniffing at trash and whimpering at every passing human, looking for their master. There were suitcases discarded all along the road, plastic sacks filled with clothes someone had belatedly deemed unnecessary, and lots of other junk: pots and pans, baby strollers, broken TVs.

Then another GRAD came slicing in, and we were eating dirt again, and I was wondering what in God's name I was doing here in a place called Kelbajar and how in God's name I was going to get out.

* * *

Actually, I knew perfectly well why I was in Kelbajar. I had asked for it—or at least not resisted the idea sufficiently to be able to complain a great deal about the outcome.

When I had returned to Baku from Armenia, the immediate crisis caused by Rahim Gaziev's and Surat Husseinov's joint dismissal seemed to be over. The details, however, remained murky. What I was able to stitch together was that on the night of February 8th, Iskender Hamidov was on State TV, possibly to announce Gaziev's removal from office on charges very close to treason. In the middle of the live broadcast, Gaziev and a cohort of men had attempted to take over the station.

The government's response to Gaziev's action was to label it an 'attempted coup.' Although removed from office, Rahim was not even detained. To see a man accused of treason sulking around the streets was very strange indeed. More serious was the game played by Surat Husseinov, who had been dismissed as the 'generalissimo' at the same time that Rahim lost his job. His response to demotion was to pull his 709th brigade off the line—and retire to the headquarters of the Russian 104th division in Ganje.

The result of this insubordination was not long in coming. Almost immediately, the Armenians launched a great winter offensive against the

Azeri positions, and bloodspots like Janyatak, Mekhmana, and Dromboi fell like dominoes. The Azerbaijani army suffered more casualties in retreat than when it was advancing. While I was in Armenia, Hicran had gone off on another of her one-woman, illegal tours of the collapsing front just in time to watch the Azeris pull back from the area around the Sarsank reservoir in chaos and confusion.

"It was not very pretty," she said with unusual understatement.

(The tour was by courtesy of Fehmin Hadjiev, the former prison warden–cum–Baku Commissar. After May 14–15, he had been rewarded with the position of commander of the Daxili Kurshunlar, or 'Internal Forces'—an army of policemen with heavy weapons. Fehmin had no authority to let Hicran into an area that should have been under the control of the General Staff, but he was an old friend and made certain allowances. In Hicran's case, he provided her with a seat in the sidecar of a three-wheel motorcycle, and off she went.)

Queerly, then, there almost seemed to be a sense of relief in Baku in the face of the debacle on the front. Perhaps this was due to what one might call the 'Sadat Syndrome,' as when the late Egyptian President claimed victory in the 1973 October War by dint of having proven to the nation and the world that his army could mount an attack, even if then obliged to retreat. If it had taken the horrific and miserable sacrifice of hundreds if not thousands of young men to arrive at this conclusion, it was worth it because the bloody reality would bring both sides to the negotiating table. According to this logic, it was time to bury the dead and let international mediators to do their thing.

Or so thought Baku.

Then, on March 31st, the telephone rang. It was Arif Aliev, Elchibey's new press spokesman. I assumed he was inviting me to yet another photo opportunity with yet another departing dignitary at the airport.

"Arif," I said. "I told you I do not have time for that sort of nonsense."

"No, no," he said wearily, "I am not calling to invite you to distract you from your very important work of opening a bar."

"OK, you heard about that," I replied, irritated that anyone in government had heard of my get-rich-quick-off-the-oilmen scheme. "Then what do you want?"

"The Armenians have launched a new offensive."

"Says who?"

"I say so, as the press spokesman of the President."

"You know my rule, Arif—if I don't see it, I don't write it."

"You tell me about it every time I talk to you," he said.

That was true—I must have been rather difficult to deal with at times.

"Get to the point. Why are you calling?"

"I am telling you we have arranged a helicopter to take the press to the front to see it all!"

"What part of the front," I asked, mocking him. "Ganje? Fizuli, or maybe this time Baku?" It was a standing joke that 'the front' now meant a visit to a restaurant in a town sufficiently far from the action so that one's overly inquisitive minder would not feel afraid.

"No, Thomas—this is not like before."

"Well, where do you want to send me?"

"To Kelbajar."

A sick feeling began to fill my gut.

Kelbajar—the province that extended like a finger in a vice between Karabakh and Armenia. With access restricted to a logging road over a 12,000-foot pass over the Murov Mountains, it had been under virtual blockade for a month and was the obvious place where the Armenians would pursue the war next. That day had apparently arrived.

Kelbajar. Arif was right. This was no invitation to go see the front lines for an hour or two and then proceed to the rear. It was an invitation to drop into hell. And after all my prima donna antics about having to be an eyewitness before writing anything about the war, there was no way I could decline.

Still, I tried to do just that, cloaking my anxiety in terms of a need for more information. Accordingly, I started calling around to friends in high places to get a better read of the situation. Everyone seemed to be otherwise occupied with affairs of state—like that all-important discussion in parliament about the price of champagne.

Then Arif called again.

"The helicopter leaves in one hour—are you going to be on it or not?"

"Tell the pilot to wait," I said. "I need to make a few more calls to editors."

I packed my bags and told Hicran where I was going. She wailed and shrieked and demanded the right to come along, too. I said no, muttering something about life insurance that we didn't have to support children we had not made, and the need for being rational at moments like this. She ran out of the house, tearing her hair. Through the door walked my sidekick, Laura Le Cornu, the American correspondent I had encouraged to set up shop in Baku.

"Come with me as far as the taxi stand," I asked her.

"Why?"

"I've got a bad feeling about this one and I want to dictate something."

"A will?"

"Yeah," I said, not having thought about it in those terms. "A last will and testament."

Laura took down the various notes before I jumped in a taxi to take me to the heliport at the edge of town. There I found my old pal Mustafa, the ecologist-cum-guide from the Defense Ministry Information Department, with whom I had traveled when the Azeri army was lurching forward in the summer. He was not looking very happy himself.

"Where are the locals?" I asked, referring to the Azeri press.

"They are afraid to go," Mustafa replied.

It seemed the only other journalist in the group was a religious Turk who wrote for a newspaper called *Zaman*, which had the habit of calling me a spy. What fun.

"Mustafa," I said as I got aboard the bird, "I don't like this."

"Neither do I," he replied.

We got aboard the Mi-8 chopper and were airborne, flying north and west over awful gray tundra for an hour before putting down at Agdam, where we picked up a dozen or so greenhorn soldiers and some ammunition. I did not like this at all.

"They told me this was a press trip, not one to bring in reenforcements!" I shouted at Mustafa after we were airborne again. He shrugged.

Our next stop was Yevlak, where Arif Aliev had told me that we would change the Mi-8 for a Cobra, or armored helicopter. But there was no Cobra to be seen on the tarmac, only dozens of other Mi-8's, coming in to off-load knots of weeping and stunned refugees before taking off again. Mustafa offered no explanations, and none were needed. A disaster of magnitude was unfolding before our eyes. We were looking at the pathetic survivors coughed out of the vortex into which we were diving.

"Where's the armored bird?" I asked, referring to the Cobra that was supposed to protect me.

"This is our transport," said Mustafa, indicating the Mi-8 we had come in on.

I stood on the tarmac and took another good look at the helicopter. It was a duck, and dripping oil. Worse, there were soldiers on board, reenforcements, making it a legitimate target to shoot down if there ever was one.

"Shit," I said to myself, but aloud.

"Are you coming?" Mustafa asked.

I had to be insane to say yes.

"This is the last time," I said, and got back on.

The pilot gunned the engine, the rotors began to whirl, and we were once more airborne. We climbed and climbed and then moved west, skirting the familiar landscape of northern Karabakh from what I hoped was a missile-safe distance. Then we climbed some more, and the air grew thinner and the cabin grew colder. There was snow on the ground below, and jagged peaks ahead: the Murov Mountains. We drifted over them, and the pilots started to take what seemed to be evasive action, banking and dropping and lifting. I could see plumes of smoke rising from the valley floor. Then we descended into a canyon, and after a long, low swoop through a narrow gorge, we were suddenly hovering over Kelbajar.

Something beyond any fear I had ever felt was tugging at my guts, but I came up with a formula to defeat it. I said to myself: you have had a good run at this thing called life, so don't feel too blue if it is over soon. You are dead until you get out of this mess you have let yourself into.

I didn't hear the gunfire until I got out of the aircraft—and then it was too late to get back in.

* * *

The first day had been chaos, the night hell, and now, at noon on the second day, the situation did not look promising at all.

We had missed two helicopters that morning after running away from Shamil's house, and they had been the last two we had seen. Now, in addition to the growing mass of refugees crowding around the heliport, there were more and more soldiers waiting to get out. Some were wounded men lying on stretchers; others still wore their body armor, even though they had discarded their guns. They may have deserted, but they were still faced with the same problem the civilians had in abandoning the town: the only way out was up.

"They're coming, they're coming!" cried one soldier from his litter as his friends carried him by. "Get out while you can!"

The man looked yellow and tired but had no obvious wounds, and urging everyone to flee seemed gratuitous if only because there was nowhere to flee to. The young man squatting next to him had only a stump for a right hand and was bleeding from his boots but was quiet aside from some shock-moans. I took a lump of chewing tobacco and stuffed it in his mouth and told him it would take the pain away if he didn't get sick. Fifteen minutes later an old woman came up and told me the soldier wanted to see me. I went.

"More," he said, yawning his mouth open. I stuffed in another plug.

It had been hours and hours since the last helicopter had come and gone, although when the GRADs weren't exploding, waiting was less desperate than boring. More people came, bringing their mundane collection of belongings: cheap suitcases, bulging with old clothes; blankets and sheets that had been converted into pack bundles, cinched shut with rope or twine; some had brought pots and pans and even plates, hoping to take the proverbial kitchen sink with them into exile.

That really was not too far off the mark. Some people actually had hauled televisions, refrigerators, and even a primitive washing machine to the airfield, hoping to save the bulky junk from looters. The larger items had been hauled to the periphery by pack animals, and a small herd of horses and donkeys stood grazing on garbage and weeds that had sprung up on the edge of the tarmac. Maybe the owners thought they could get the animals out, too.

Then we heard it again: the distant droning of a motor and the sort of flutter-whoosh of rotor wings beating back gravity, the sort of sound a doe-deer makes when jumping from the yellow reeds of autumn, or a sudden covey of Hungarian partridge blowing out of a ditch. *Whoosh-Whoosh-Whoosh.* . . . Hunting in Montana, home.

The Mi-8 came in on a zig-zag course, sometimes flying below the ledge of the gorge, sometimes above, and then below again, disappearing from view, although the droning motor noise kept on getting louder. Then, with a rush, it climbed out of the gorge and hovered like a big black fly over the strip, its rotor blades blowing back everything loose beneath it: dirt and rocks and hats and scarves and even the suitcases scattered around the tarmac that had not been immediately seized and dragged out to the center of the pad.

As the throng shielded their eyes against the blow-back, the chopper touched down and a short, thick-set man with no neck jumped out. He was wearing khaki fatigues and a khaki cap and had a pistol strapped to his side. Despite the desert *purdah*, I recognized him—or thought I did. *No it couldn't be!* The man turned; it was indeed he—the erstwhile watermelon merchant, the unspeakable State Secretary, Panakh Husseinov.

"What are you doing here?" I yelled over the helicopter roar.

Panakh skewed his nose and gestured at the human mess seething all around us. He was going down with the ship. Whatever else they say about Panakh Husseinov, I will grant him this: he was the only ranking member of government to go to Kelbajar on what seemed a suicide mission.

"Where is Iskender?" I screamed.*

"Sleeping," shouted Panakh.

---

*Iskender Hamidov, the 'Bozkurt' and native son of Kelbajar, had apparently gone into a state of shock. He certainly was never quite the same after the events of March 31–April 1, 1993.

Then he was off, waving his pistol at the crowd to force them back, while some men behind him in the helicopter began throwing out bread, shoveling the loaves out the door like coal. The loaves blew this way and that under the force of the idling rotor blades. It was pretty stupid, I considered, dumping out bread like that when the only ones likely to eat it would be the approaching enemy. They were probably traveling light and would be hungry once they got into town, if their forward spotters had not already penetrated the periphery and started looting the pantries of the outlying houses. The fresh bread would probably be a welcome addition to their diet.

A man tried to force his way by Panakh to get on the helicopter before all the bread had been dumped. Panakh pistol-whipped him, and the man fell down. Then Panakh fired a few rounds into the air. Shooting in the air did not seem a very good idea, because that was where the rotors were. I had several questions: How many holes could propellers take? How well could wounded pilots fly?

The pistol reports stopped the crowd until the bread was off-loaded. Then the people surged forward again, clawing at the door, while Panakh screamed at the pilot to lift off. The rotors tilted and the chopper lurched upward ten feet off the ground, revealing two men hanging from the bottom. One was doing a pull-up on the bottom of the door frame, while the other had latched onto one of the chopper's wheels. They dangled there while the pilot rocked the hovering bird back and forth with the use of the back rotor blade to make the men fall back to earth. When they fell, or dropped off while the chopper was still low enough to do so without killing themselves, the Mi-8 seemed to jump a few feet, as if relieved of a tether. The straggling crowd surged beneath while the pilot coyly shuttled above the landing strip, looking for an empty place to land. Luggage heaved and skidded under the gale; anything light enough to get blown around got blown around, children included.

The chopper put down again near the soldiers, at the far end of the field, and the crowd of civilians ran after it. Some soldiers held back civilians while others hauled wounded soldiers aboard. Then the soldiers doing the loading got in themselves, followed by the soldiers holding back the crowds. Then the helicopter rose and started to bank away to take its dive through the gorge.

I was furious and shaking my fist at the chopper and the men aboard. The unwritten rule of refugee operations is that women and children get out first, followed by the wounded, the elderly, village idiots—and then stranded journalists. The armed men are supposed to go last. But here, the men with guns were saving themselves first.

"I hope you crash!!" someone screamed at the departing helicopter, and I realized with a jolt that it was me shouting. I wanted to be on that helicopter very, very badly.

esSKREEEeee! . . . another GRAD crashed into the eastern slope of the gorge, and everyone was down on the asphalt again.

KRVROM! VROM VROm VRom Vrom vrom vro. . . .

Once again, the missile echoed its impact in sharp, undulating waves up and down the valley.

KRRBRAAM!!! . . .

Another explosion rippled through the chasm. But it was too loud, too big for an impacting GRAD to make. And there hadn't been any preliminary scream: it was the chopper that had just disappeared over the rim.

It seemed incredible that the Armenians were shooting at helicopters with GRAD missiles, and even more incredible that they had been able to hit one. It was kind of like throwing a rock at a distant crow on the wing: a lucky shot.

I walked—why run?—over toward the cliff edge to see. Maybe the helicopter had just crashed and exploded because it hadn't been able to regain altitude due to its load and had hit an outcropping; maybe it had just continued its downward dive and crashed at the bottom of the gorge because it was overweight. The choppers were designed to carry two dozen people, maybe three, but all those flying out of the field were carrying two or three times that load, so it wouldn't be too surprising if this one hadn't been able to clear a bluff or outcropping in the canyon. It was a miracle that any of them could make it at all.

A long, gray plume of smoke was snaking over the ledge when I arrived, but another bluff at a bend in the river below blocked the view of the area from where the smoke was rising. Without getting around it and how many other bluffs that also might be between, there was nothing to see but the plume of smoke, and it was impossible to tell what caused it.

Maybe it was the smoke from the missile, or a house or barn it had destroyed. Maybe the chopper hadn't crashed at all but was whirling its way north through the canyon like helicopters do in films, skimming near but never hitting the rocky outcroppings or trees or telephone wires along the way. I wanted to think it was so and kept on waiting for the chopper to appear from beneath the canyon walls as a distant speck. It never did and there was no motor sound or even the flutter-whoosh of the blades beating back anything anymore.

I picked up one of the bread loaves that Panakh Husseinov's chopper had dumped on the landing pad and started to chew it. Someone saw me and invited me to eat some eggs and cucumber they had brought with them from home. Mustafa appeared with the Turkish correspondent, and we all hunkered down for a picnic lunch, right there on the landing pad, waiting to get saved. A few more missiles crashed into the town, but we were getting used to it by now. I even took off my shirt to catch a few rays of sun on my chest, and napped a few hours. There wasn't much else to do.

When I woke, the sun had shifted west and people now had shadows. And there were many more people camped on the landing pad than before my nap. And still more were arriving. A trickle of folks were coming from the east, mainly in ones and twos, while from the south, along a trail by the river, we could see an animal caravan of donkeys and mules piled high with bedding and sundry possessions, snaking its way toward us.

The caravan arrived. A few more missiles crashed into the town. Gunfire sputtered in the distance, closer now.

Then an old man got to his feet, hoisted his fat old wife on his back and started walking north toward the mountains. Then another man grabbed his suitcase and a single-barrel shotgun and joined the couple. The three were then followed by a group of five, then ten, then twenty others, and the entire field began to stir. Men lifted bundles on their backs and mothers cinched infants to their chests. Younger men went over to the pack animals and began strapping bundles on or taking them off, it wasn't clear which. Soldiers stripped off their uniforms, pulling on civilian clothes that didn't fit, and joined the exodus.

So it had come to this. We were going to hoof it out over the enemy lines, over the mountains, maybe. The prospect was not appealing. All of us, I am sure, could only think of one word and were praying that it did not apply to us: *Xodjali*. Would the Armenians massacre another batch of pathetic refugees? Why not?

"What do we do?" asked the Turkish reporter whom Mustafa and I had started calling 'Zaman' because that was the name of his newspaper.

"I guess we join them," I said.

"But . . . but. . . ."

I understood what Zaman was trying to say. As a Turk, he was a little apprehensive about falling into Armenian hands. Word was they had a penchant for 'doing an Andranik' on certain types of prisoners, which meant cutting off ears and things like that.[1] I tried to be helpful.

"Do you speak any languages other than Turkish?" I asked Zaman.

"Some Quranic Arabic and a bit of French," he replied.

"If we are captured, you are my photographer, from Algeria," I said. "Just do not speak Turkish."

"Okay," said Zaman, relieved to be in the possession of the fiction. I didn't want to remind him that many Armenians spoke both French and

Arabic; he might have flipped. Mustafa was going to be a different story, however. He would be dead meat if captured, and there was nothing I could think of to prevent it and live to tell the tale myself.

We picked up a couple of the loaves of bread still lying on the tarmac and walked across the field, passing the old man carrying the old woman on his back. He was already tired and had placed his wife on the ground while he caught his breath. He looked at us, and we looked at him. There was no way he was going to make it 30 miles over a mountain with his wife on his back. He wasn't going to make it one mile down the road. I would like to claim that I selflessly shouldered the old lady, but that is not true. Neither did Mustafa or Zaman. We passed them by. I know this for a fact because about a minute later we were running back past them toward the heliport. We had heard the distant buzz of a chopper—*another chopper!*

Others heard it, too. A huge, throbbing melee greeted us on the heliport pad, as panicked people sprinted across the field toward two helicopters, leaving a wake of material detritus behind them for others to stumble over.

This time, however, I was not taking pictures of the crush around the choppers—I was in the middle of it. Mustafa, Zaman, and I arrived before most others. But in a bruising instant, there were forty people between me and the door, fighting and scratching and shoving to be the first aboard.

"Let's go!!" It was Mustafa, near enough to the door to force his way aboard.

But I couldn't do it. I could not be part of the mad-dog crowd, fighting with each other for a berth.

"Women and children first," I shouted at him, and shouldered my way free of the crowd. The truth of the matter was that I was more frightened about getting aboard one of the overloaded choppers than I was concerned about the fate of the women and children at this point, but it sounded good and brave.

Then I saw Mustafa struggling to get back off the helicopter. The stupid shit, I said to myself. I was ready to abandon him to the wrath of the Armenians if caught going over the mountains, but here he is refusing to abandon dumb-shit me.

"We can still walk out," I shouted as he approached. He was furious.

"Your job is to get the news out," he slowly shouted back, looking me in the eye. "The only way you can do that is by getting out of here—and you have just thrown away our last chance."

Indeed, the second helicopter was revving its engines for takeoff, and then struggling into the air, massively overloaded.

"Where's Zaman?" I asked.

"I don't know . . . maybe up there," said Mustafa, referring to the choppers.

Silently, we watched the rescue vehicles become receding dots in the sky, and then disappear altogether. More gunfire crackled in the near distance. I felt awful. I was a captive, maybe; Mustafa was dead.

We took a step or two and then froze. Once again, there was the telltale droning of a distant helicopter that grew louder by the second. Two more choppers were coming in.

"Let's get going," said Mustafa, in a tone somewhere between an order and a plea.

The two choppers landed at different ends of the field, and Mustafa chose the one furthest away, near the edge of the gorge. Rather than trying to compete with the mass of people clawing at each other to be first in through the single door, we went around to the far side of the chopper and found ourselves staring at five porthole windows above the fuel tanks.

"This is it," said Mustafa, hoisting himself up. With a swift kick, he forced one of the windows open, and then slithered through the porthole, disappearing inside.

The pilot was gunning the engine and the rotors had begun to whirl. The machine began to lift off its springs, blowing back every piece of loose rubble beneath it with the force of the rotor-induced gale. The back wheel that was sunk in a divot in the tarmac began to rise. The moment had come.

"Lord in Heaven," I breathed a prayer, not sure if I believed in anything.

Maybe I was trying to get aboard, maybe I was trying to avoid being crushed—I don't know. But suddenly I was up on the fuselage, stripping off my jacket and stuffing it and my camera through to Mustafa. I shot my elbows through the porthole, clawing at the arms and legs and clothes of those inside to pull my way through, completing the maneuver with a sort of somersault and clear a path inside—and then I was in there, sprawling next to Mustafa on the floor. I looked at him, and he looked back at me, but there was no need to say the words on both our minds: *there was no way out of this one anymore.*

A pair of kicking feet were coming through the porthole, and a voice outside was shouting my name. It was Zaman. We grabbed him by the legs and yanked him inside; his face was about to explode with terror. The other portholes were being smashed in by others trying to flee, but there was no more room at all, so those who were already inside began pushing out the heads and feet of those trying to get in. Hands were still clawing at the open cargo door across the corridor, and a man who looked like the navigator or copilot was kicking at the fingers to pry them free.

The rotors began to turn faster, and the chopper lurched upward, with every stomach aboard sinking an inch for every twelve inches climbed. When we were hovering about ten feet off the ground, the pilot started the shaking routine in order to jostle a few extra hundred kilos of humanity off the landing gear before putting the bird in forward motion. I couldn't see the extra passengers, but I knew they were there and knew what would happen to them. They would fall and maybe die or at least get broken bones and then maybe die anyway. I felt bad for them, but the pilots had a point. There was no point in killing one hundred people, yourself included, when you had the option of abandoning only twenty to their doom. Someone had to decide and effect the triage, and it was just too bad that it was the pilots who had to be the ones to do so.

They were brave guys, the pilots, because no one in his right mind would be here now, by choice. The pilots had chosen to fly in repeatedly, which meant they were either incredibly brave and dedicated or just dedicated and courageous in the sense that animals are when they walk wires and jump through flames. That was what they called training. And if commendable, the question remained whether it was courageous or brave or just plain stupid.

I thought about that for awhile because thinking such thoughts kept my mind off the fact that I was about to die. We were all dead, I said to myself—and felt an awful tingle of adrenaline rush from my toes to my eyes. Then I told myself there was no point in being afraid of that fact because we were dead. The people who were afraid were afraid because they feared dying and the brave were only so because they were crazy enough not to fear death. But if you were dead already, why care? Everybody on the chopper was dead until proven otherwise, so it seemed stupid to get upset or worry about things like personal safety. Yes, we are all dead until proven otherwise, I said to myself, and found solace in that notion. *Dead, dead, dead*, I said, and then I smiled.

I wanted to share this insight with Zaman. He was a sight: squeezed between six or eight people, he was sweating as if he had just emerged from a Turkish bath. His lips were moving with what must have been a prayer. Others, too, appeared to lack a philosophical approach to the moment, and were suffering accordingly. An old woman squatting near my left was gasping for breath, her eyes rolling about their sockets, moaning as if she were in labor for her first child, even though she wasn't pregnant, or at least didn't look as though she was or could be because she looked too old to be so. Then she started vomiting over an old man sitting next to her, who was trying to hold her up and stay clear at the same time. It looked like Shamil, the librarian, but I couldn't be sure. A couple of other people joined in with their own retching, and the cabin quickly took on an odor of puke and sweat and filthy bodies and wounds. *What a way to die.*

I forced my way to the cockpit to say a voiceless hello to the pilot, who leaned back to give me a thumbs-up sign. From his green eyes and blondish hair, he looked like he was a Russian. He also looked familiar from some-place—the flight into Xodjali the year before? A Baku bar? It was difficult to place him, but it didn't matter. Whatever context it had been, we were in a different world now.

The chopper was way off the ground by now and still climbing in the way that helicopters make their impossible climbs, groaning and shuddering as they defy gravity and common sense. Just that one little piece of metal, holding on the rotors, and should that snap. . . .

Count the passengers, the pilot instructed me with hand signals, inter-rupting my terror-thought.

I turned around and tried to make the assessment he had asked for by twos, threes, and then fives. I got up to 75 before I stopped. The Mi-8 was designed to hold 24 people and their luggage, if fitted out for passenger service. We were at least three times that number, maybe four. The thought was about to fill me with fear until I remembered my vow of indifference and the fact that I was dead until I was alive again but this time it did not help at all.

How in God's name are we going to make it over the pass?

The blue-white mass of the Murov Mountains was coming ever closer, ridges now distinguishable by individual patches of blue and white and now blue and black and gray and white. Below, through the Plexiglas of the cockpit, I could see people, folks on foot and leading horses or donkeys or mules, all slogging upward toward some unseen pass. Just as the cliché has it, they looked like ants. Actually, they looked like people and animals the way people and animals look when you look down at them from a tall building and say that they look like ants because you don't know what else to say.

Then the ants who were people and animals started to get bigger, grow-ing to the point where you couldn't say they looked like ants anymore. They looked like tiny people. And the blue and gray and white blur of the snow field was coming into sharper focus, too. The rocks and boulders and sharp crags extended like stiff fingers from the bottom of a deep break in the mountain ridge: the pass.

Altitude, I said aloud, although no one could hear or understand me. The pilot was talking in his head set to the copilot or engineer, or whoever the other guy in the uniform looking at the dials in the cockpit was. Both sets of lips were moving, anyway, although the gauges seemed to stay the same.

Altitude, I repeated, tapping the pilot on the shoulder. It would only take a few more inches to clear the ridge, and wishing might be the way to climb up that last few feet.

An ominous clicking sound filled the cockpit over the motor roar as the chopper clawed for more sky. The pilot turned to me, trying to shout over the noise. Maybe he was telling me to jump, bravely saving the rest by removing my own body weight, allowing the chopper to soar. Or maybe he was telling me to jump and land miraculously on a deep pile of snow while everyone else smashed into the rock-face and died. I could not understand his instructions, so I stayed where I was. The dials remained frozen in place, the clicking in the cabin grated like a high-pitched rattle. The rocks and crags were so close I could have reached out and touched them. I closed my eyes.

You have had a good ride on this thing called life; you have no right to complain. . . .

The helicopter lurched forward and down, and my gut smashed through my brain. But there was no impact, and the clicking noise diminished by the second.

I opened my eyes and looked at the green-eyed pilot, and he looked at me. Sweat was pouring down his face, but he was smiling, and the copilot was reaching for a cigarette.

I looked back. The distance between us and the black crags and rocks of the Murov pass was growing, second by second.

We had cleared the pass by five feet.

The chopper after ours didn't.

* * *

We landed at Yevlak, giddy for the fact of being alive. The evening flight to Baku was ready to leave, and we 'liberated' some seats with the help of Mustafa's Defense Ministry credentials and his gun.

But the closer we got to Baku, the more we sank into a collective, evil mood. First it was listening to the idle chitchat of the other passengers on the plane. Then it was the taxi driver, who thought it a fine time to lecture us about a war he had never seen. It got worse as we drove through downtown, watching young bucks and snazzy gals on parade, poking in and out of the myriad 'commercial shops.'

I hit the outside of toleration when I got home to discover our new landlord, a former Komsomol leader who was using our $400 a month in rental money to bribe his way clear of the draft, perched in the living room, anxious that I pay a $5 electricity bill that had built up over two months. It seemed he was afraid I might die and leave him holding the tab.

I kicked him out, poured myself a long drink, and sat down to write the Kelbajar story. And that is when I started to go crazy. Not one editor I worked with was interested in Kelbajar, because it was not on the AP or Reuters wire.

"Not on the wires!" I shouted down the international telephone line. "Of course it is not on the wires! No one else was there!"

"Okay, okay," came the response. "File away."

I did so. But the story did not run that night nor the next day. Nor the next. I called to find out why.

"We were tight for space," said a subeditor.

"Well, what about an update?"

"We have already done that here," said the sub. "We topped off your material with some wire copy coming out of Moscow."

"Wire copy from Moscow? That said what?"

"Well, the Armenians are denying there was any attack on that place you said you were," said the desk man. "In fact, they say they were being attacked. So we are using that instead."

I went ballistic. I said things that I almost regret having said, but not quite. I spoke about attaching my gonads to the bottom of helicopters to get a better view of things than any motherfucker sitting in Moscow was able to get. I said I was an idiot because I was risking my fucking life for original material that no one wanted because they preferred quoting official sources and western observers and other fakes and frauds. I slammed down the phone. I had had it, I was through, finito, done, cooked, finished, fucked. It was a real déjà vu of the Xodjali Massacre story of a year before, but with a twist. Then, I had been under the erroneous impression that copy was being spiked because it went against the grain. I had been so, so wrong then: the paper that I had so publicly maligned—the *Washington Post* and its foreign editor, David Ignatius—had in fact run all the copy I sent them.

But now the newspaper in question was openly admitting to stalling and then spiking material. I have never been so disappointed in the concept of 'news' and the fecklessness of editors, before or since. *Disappointed?* Utterly aghast, amazed, driven into despair is more like it.

You don't give a fuck about the fact that I nearly died to report about 60,000 hapless souls who you won't report about because it does not suit your interests?

I have never been the same since.

* * *

But news of Kelbajar was beginning to trickle out.

One of the first things I did upon returning to Baku was to book a call to Alexis Rowell in Tbilisi to brief him on the situation in Azerbaijan. He was at a late-night party, but I left a detailed note on his answering machine. I told him to get his ass in his car and drive south until he was at the top of the Murov mountain pass. If he got there—and if he got my note—I promised him he would be the first correspondent to report on a replay of the Great Kurdish Exodus from northern Iraq in 1991. People cared about that one, then; maybe they would care about this one, too.

Around nine or ten o'clock the next morning, still sleeping off the exhaustion of Kelbajar and the drunk that had followed my fight with the editors, I was awakened by the insistent ringing of the phone. It was Alexis, speaking broken Russian.

"Alexis, cut the crap and speak English to me."

A bitter laugh greeted me, and then a burst of words.

"I can't because I'm in jail in Ganje and they will only let me speak in a language they can understand!"

"What?"

"Get me out so I can file this fucking story!!"

A man interrupted us. He was a cop, he said, and would not allow us to pass secrets in the secret language. . . .

"Give me the foreigner's assistant, you idiot!" I screamed in Azeri.

"There is no need to talk like that."

"Put the woman on the phone!"

"*Kak delo, Tomas*," came a female voice, sounding totally drained.

"Nino, what the hell is going on?"

"This is Nana."

"Sorry—which one?"

"Little."*

In obligatory Russian, Little Nana related the following: after driving all night and up the northern slope of the Murov range, Alexis had found tens of thousands of half-frozen and utterly exhausted people stumbling over the pass. Then he had turned around and sped to Ganje to file his report—only to be arrested by some policeman walking by the telephone booth because he was speaking English. The government had issued a proclamation for a state of emergency the night before, and the local authorities thought that meant censoring news reports and conversations in languages they did not understand. Aside from the one telephone call to me, Alexis was being held incommunicado.

I went into action immediately to free him. It required the personal intervention of President Abulfez Elchibey himself, although Alexis re-

---

*It was often a little confusing figuring out which of the three great Georgian translators Alexis was traveling with at any given time—Nino, 'Big' Nana, or 'Little' Nana. They all seemed to shift between Reuters, the Associated Press, and the BBC. All were and are wonderful.

mained in jail for some six hours more. In the interim, the only news out of Azerbaijan was about the government cracking down on dissent with its new emergency powers, and when he finally filed his story, it was the state of emergency that was the news, and not the bitter fall of Kelbajar.

* * *

But Alexis was not finished. The relentless Rowell got back to Tbilisi, changed translators, and then turned the corner and high-tailed it down to Armenia. There, he managed to infiltrate his way to the border facing Kelbajar, and recorded impressions about the state of the roads in the area—such as the fact that they had been recently gouged with the sort of tracks usually associated with armored vehicles working through mud. From there, he pushed into Karabakh, where in addition to being given a tour of depots filled with televisions, refrigerators, and rugs looted from Kelbajar, he was introduced to the Armenian commander who had spear-headed the Kelbajar expedition. The commander, a French national, said he had taken his Karabakh-based command—about half Karabakh Armenians and half Armenia Armenians—and the necessary equipment through the Lachin corridor into Armenia, traveled back up north to a parallel with Kelbajar, and then punched in from the west, where terrain was more suit-able for an assault.

Once more, this was news that no one wanted. Armenia still was not officially involved in the conflict—and allowing their territory to be used even by a purely 'Karabakh' force could only be regarded as involvement.* But the Armenians got away with it again because no one wanted to know—not Washington, the United Nations, or even Ankara. The weirdest and most shameless indifference to the plight of the victims, who were primarily Azeri Kurds, was displayed by international Kurdish organizations. Despite an appeal by Kurdish societies in Azerbaijan to 'The Kurds of the World' for aid and assistance or at least condemnation of the Armenian assault, the ethnic cleansing of Kelbajar, like Lachin before it, remained a taboo subject.[2]

* * *

Meanwhile, on the northern slopes of the Murov range, units of the ex-hausted and defeated Azerbaijani army, some of which had been on the

---

*A year later, in Yerevan, I met an Armenian correspondent who was with the assault group. We determined that he entered Kelbajar at around the same hour I left it. And of course, he and the assault force had entered the outlying precincts of the town from the west, from Armenia.

road for ten days, were preparing to launch a last, desperate thrust over the crest in order to save the remaining refugees trapped on the far side. It had been several days since my own helicopter escape. Now it was time to go back and cover the aftermath. With me were Hugh Pope and Laura LeCornu.

We started in Baku, flew to Ganje on a death-plane, landed, got picked up in a taxi driven by a man who was incredibly heroic until he saw a few wounded soldiers, and ended at a road sign announcing it was 36 kilometers to Kelbajar. Lined up behind the sign were nine mountain howitzers, a chuck wagon, and a white NEVA jeep, the personal property of a colonel who commanded the howitzers. He told us he had spent 25 years in the Soviet Army as an artillery specialist, and had returned to his homeland to take command of the Shemker Mobile Artillery Brigade and lead it up and over a very bad and snow-clogged dirt road into enemy turf, but he refused to tell us his name.

Perhaps he was embarrassed. His men had received two months of training and were as green as spring grass; their equipment, in contrast, was almost ancient—and of the nine 120mm howitzer units, only two had radios that functioned.

"Army, they call this an army," he muttered as the tankers checked their ordinance and waited for the orders.

Finally, it was time to climb.

"SHEMKERCILAR!" bellowed the colonel.

"XADIR!" shouted his adolescent troops, "Ready!"

"Fire your engines, and move out!"

The nine motors rumbled to life, and the kid drivers flipped open their steering hatches.

"Colonel," I said, "I want to go up with you."

He looked at me for awhile and smiled. It was against the rules and regulations, but he had already violated quite a few by allowing us to get this far.

"Get in," he said, gesturing at the white NEVA. Hugh and Laura waved goodbye.

The colonel gunned the car to the front of the line, and proceeded to lead his men up-mountain. We ground our way through a mixture of mud-ice, dead sheep, and household junk discarded by thousands of people too weak to carry even those pathetic possessions they had tried to salvage any further. Finally, in a bowl-shaped valley tucked beneath the last snowbound ridge on the north slope of the Murov Mountains, the commander ordered his men to halt and set up firing positions.

"Are you familiar with this equipment?" he asked.

"No," I admitted.

"Well, let me give you a little lesson in modern war," he said with a sardonic smile. "These machines are mountain howitzers. They have a range of five kilometers, because their shells go up and down."

"So how do you aim them?"

"With spotters, of course. But that is where we have a big problem."

"No spotters?"

"No, we have plenty of spotters—although I can't vouch for how good they are. The problem is that when we received the machines from the Russians, we discovered that they had stripped the radio equipment out of most of them."

"So?"

"So when a radio man sends down the coordinates of a target, we have to run them from one vehicle to the next."

"I see. . . ."

"No, you don't. Because if you are giving fire, you are usually under fire and when you are under fire—especially if you are a young, untrained soldier like all these kids under my command—you like to fire back, even if you don't have coordinates."

"Meaning. . . ."

"Meaning a lot of wasted ammunition, as well as a lot of self-inflicted deaths among our own front-line men when we bomb them instead of the enemy."

"In English, we call that friendly fire."

"Funny name for it."

We stood there looking at the guns crank up and down, and then the commander turned to me.

"Well, do you want to go on up and take a look at the rest of the mess?"

"Sure."

So we proceeded upward along the gouged and battered road. One strange sight was a Red Cross ambulance, shoved halfway off a ledge because it had been blocking the road. What was it doing up here? Another sad sight was that of a fresh helicopter wreck; clothes, twisted steel, and bits of mangled body lay strewn across the snow: the chopper that crashed after ours had cleared the pass.

Near the summit, we ran into a ragged company of ten soldiers collapsed on the ice.

"You cowards! Off your asses when you see an officer, or I will have you shot!" screamed the colonel, ordering them to march through the snowfields to higher positions.

The weary grunts got up and muttered among themselves. I thought for a moment that they might turn on us—it was only their commanding officer and his pistol against the bunch of them. But when he ordered them to march through the snowfields to higher positions to deploy, they shuffled upward and onward toward the Murov Mountain pass, and the lost town of Kelbajar on the far side. The last of the lot was a young man on a crutch, limping up-mountain behind his comrades.

"We are being sent to die," he said, and then clumped onward and upward. It was almost the saddest sight I have seen.

"They are only kids, I know," said the colonel. "Everyone else has run away."

The condemned soldiers moved off, turning into black dots in the glistening snowfield. Then above them, moving toward us, came three figures. Reaching the track that served as a sort of logging road, the three turned out to be five—an exhausted man in his early thirties, and two women in their twenties, carrying their infant children, aged three and six months. All were snow-burned and in semi-shock after their six-day trek through forests and 9,000-foot mountain passes.

"When we left, we were about thirty people," said Settar Tagiev, the male in the group. "But we got split up during the journey and now we don't know what happened to the others. Maybe they are all dead." I thought I recognized him from the Kelbajar heliport, but could not be sure.

The Tagiev band were probably the last Azeri refugees to make it over the main, eastern pass from Kelbajar to the refugee collection center at Hanlar, which had already processed some 30,000. Another center at Yevlak had processed the 3,000 lucky souls who had flown out by chopper, while another center at the town of Dashkesen had processed around 6,000. Although Baku said that the normal population of the region was 60,000, local officials said that the real number was closer to 45,000—which still made for some 5,000 people unaccounted for—lost, dead or captured as hostages on the south side of the pass. Those left behind were the most vulnerable—the old, women and children. Even among those who had made it across a day or two before, there were numerous cases of severe frostbite and more than 40 exposure deaths. With each day, the chances of survival for those stuck in the snow on the far side of the range dimmed—and even for those who made it across the snowfields into friendly hands. Before my eyes, the Tagiev group was reduced from five, to four, and then to three: the children the parents had carried in their arms over the pass were unwrapped from their protective bundles. They were all dead—and no one, not even the parents, knew when they had expired. In fact, the woman appeared to still think her children were alive and merely sleeping.

"Had enough?" the colonel asked me.

"Yeah," I said.

We drove in silence down through the mixture of refugee detritus, passed the mountain guns with no radios manned by soldiers who were kids and then finally arrived at the head of the valley where our journey had begun. Hugh and Laura were long gone.

"Tell me," I said. "What's your name."

"Rahim," said the colonel. "Rahim Guliyev."

"Thanks," I replied, grateful for the front-line trust.

I walked down the road from Hanlar and managed to hitchhike a ride with a truck full of sheep and refugees from Kelbajar. The Young Pioneer camps I recalled from 1991 were now filled with refugees. Four T-72 tanks and a couple of GRAD launchers with accompanying fuel and ammunition trucks rumbled by, moving up. A man's name had been stenciled on the side of the tanks, advertising the loyalty of the men inside: *SURAT.*

I quivered with anger. Husseinov's 709th division was based less than 50 miles away—but it had taken him two weeks to send the equipment. Even more flabbergasting were the people who cheered as the armor rolled by, applauding dereliction of duty that bordered on treason.

Stranger was the atmosphere at the nearby army HQ. While wounded men who hadn't slept in days were being sent over the Murov mountain pass to their doom, their comrades who had done so little to defend Kelbajar were sitting around, smoking, chatting and playing cards. I asked for the *stab*, or staff office, and was directed over to a guesthouse among the trees. A man in uniform was polishing a black Volga in front. Suddenly, everyone snapped to attention: the regional commander, General Nejmettin Sadikov, was striding down the steps of the villa. He was dressed in his parade togs, replete with a red sash running down each pant leg, and carrying a snazzy cap with the Azeri star and crescent on the brim.

"Hello, General," I said. "Got time to talk?"

"*Nyet,*" he snapped.

An aide opened the door to the back seat of the Volga, the general got in and the car roared off.

"Where is he going?" I asked one of the staff officers.

"To see Surat," replied the officer.

To see Surat, wool-merchant, descendant of the Prophet, mafia don, traitor. Surat, whose armor had been two weeks too late in moving up to save the Tagiev family, Shamil's library, and whatever and whoever else was lost in the course of the sell-out of Kelbajar. I thought of the kids on the mountain pass and wanted to puke.

These people didn't need the Armenians for enemies.

They had themselves.

Notes

1. Andranik Ozaniyan was an Armenian carpenter-cum-revolutionary who struck terror in the heart of the Ottoman authorities in the late nineteenth and early twentieth centuries. His name is usually associated with the sustained Sasun revolt of 1899 in the district of Mush, in today's eastern Turkey. Thereafter, he escaped to Russian Armenia and from there to Europe, only to reappear at the head of Armenian partisans fighting with the Bulgarians against the Ottoman Turks in 1912. Following World War I, he continued his activities in and around Karabakh and developed the art of keeping ears as proof of the number of enemy he killed. Not surprisingly, the Azeris also developed a taste for this sort of mutilation. Both sides maintain that the other started collecting ears first.

2. Appeal of the Kurds Living in Azerbaijan to the Kurds of the World. Baku, April 2, 1993: "We, the thousands of Kurds of Azerbaijan, have lived for centuries in peace and friendship with the Azerbaijanis. As regards the development of democracy in Azerbaijan, there is respect for our language, customs, and practices. We print newspapers and books in our language, and have radio broadcasts as well. There is even a Kurdish cultural center. But during the past five years, the Kurdish people, like the other peoples of Azerbaijan, have suffered greatly due to continued Armenian aggression. The Kurds of Lachin were subjected to genocidal politics: hundreds of the elderly, women, and children were killed or taken as prisoners and the honor of the Kurds grossly violated. Twelve Kurdish villages were erased from the face of the earth.

The politics that led to the expulsion of the Kurds from their lands at the hands of the Armenians continues to this day. The population of 60,000 civilians in Kelbajar have now been surrounded, and an even greater disaster than the Xodjali Massacre is now at hand. The Kurds of the region are now being slaughtered along with the Azerbaijanis who live there. Houses are being looted and then razed, and the people destroyed.

History cannot be allowed to repeat itself! Up until today, tens of thousands of Kurds have been repeatedly dislodged and hounded out of Armenia—1905, 1908, 1937, 1947–1948. In 1988–1989, over 20,000 Muslim Kurds were driven out of their ancestral homes in Armenia, of which 12,000 chose to settle in Azerbaijan. Now, once more, due to the unfounded territorial claims of Armenia against Azerbaijan, all the peoples living in Azerbaijan are bleeding as the result of yet another expulsion from their homes. We, in the name of the Kurdish community, wish to reiterate that Azerbaijan is our country, and that the Azerbaijanis are our closest friends.

Dearest kinsmen! Please inform all comrades of the disaster visited upon us by the Armenians! Accept the disaster visited upon the Kurdish men and women of Azerbaijan as your own! Let them know that the Lachin and Kelbajar disasters are merely a continuation of the Xodjali Massacre!

We call on the world Kurdish community to join us, the Kurds of Azerbaijan, to start a massive, international campaign of solidarity to free our country from aggression and occupation! We call on you to help us save our ancient homeland in Azerbaijan in the name of justice and peace!

Signed: 'Ronayi' Kurdish Cultural Center

To my knowledge, the document has never seen the light of day in any international human-rights publication because it goes so much against the grain of conventional wisdom about the Kurds and the Armenians. The one exception to this conspiracy of silence is the (Iranian) Kurdish scholar Mehrda Izadi. Having surveyed the various Armenian sources about the Lachin and Kelbajar Kurdish 'revolts,' including estimates of the numbers of oppressed Kurds living in the area, he asked the simple question of why it was that there were no Kurds to be seen in those regions today. The heart-wrenching title of his article says it all: '*You Too, Armenia?*' Cf. *Kurdish Life*, Spring 1994.

21

The Lull Before the Storm

"Tell me about the future," asked Vafa Gulizade. "The Armenians have reconquered Karabakh and taken Kelbajar, the country is filled with refugees, economic production is down by 40 percent, the government is filled with thieves, and all our neighbors hate us. I am not asking if there will be a coup. I just want to know when, and by whom."

A man known for his ability to survive every political maelstrom over the past decade, Vafa was looking uniquely depressed. We were sitting in his new eleventh-floor office in the presidential apparatus, with both the television and radios turned up full blast. The reason for this was to create static and disguise our conversation from whoever might take an interest in it.

And it was of interest. As a last-ditch measure to establish some outside contacts they could count on, the Elchibey government had taken the radical step of approving a proposal from the Central Intelligence Agency to use Azerbaijan as a 'listening post' for developments in Iran. The tradeoff would be some sort of protection from Russia.

"It's on," Vafa had told me over the telephone a few hours before our meeting.

"What's on?" I replied.

"The council of ministers has passed the John Doe proposal, that's what," said Vafa.

"Who is John Doe and what is his proposal?" I asked.

"Stop playing dumb. This is serious."

"Vafa, I don't know what the hell you are talking about."

"Maybe you had better come over here for a little chat," said Vafa after a pregnant pause. "My car will collect you in ten minutes."

The black Volga duly arrived, and I was whisked away to the presidential building, ushered through security with not even a perfunctory check, and immediately shuttled upstairs via a special elevator.

"My dear, it is so good to see you!" exclaimed Vafa, as if my visit were a surprise. Then, after an appropriate period of time chatting about his growing collection of spy books and the memoirs of statesmen, Vafa asked me if I had seen the news. No, I had not, I said on cue. Then he turned on his television full blast to mess up the reception of hidden microphones, and spilled the beans.

It appeared that some American super-spook had come through town in 1992 and floated an interesting idea: if the Azeris would allow their country to become a giant spy base to monitor developments in Iran, Langley would provide them 'protection' from certain parties in Russia. The government was initially very suspicious, Vafa said. But given present realities, Baku had warmed to the idea and (secretly) endorsed it.

But repeated attempts to message Langley through the embassy had met with no response—so Vafa had decided to take the indiscreet if direct approach, and contact the local representative of the Company—me.

"I guess it should be flattering," I said. "But Vafa, my dear, the biggest symbol of your isolation is that you continue to imagine that I am the biggest spook in town. Either I am the world's greatest fake, or you (collectively, my dear!) are attributing intelligence, insight, and activities to me that I would like to claim but that I do not deserve."

"I don't understand."

"I mean if you are depending on *me*, you are really *alone*. . . ."

Vafa put his head in his hands; he seemed to be on the verge of tears.

* * *

Others tried to put on a braver face. The Kelbajar disaster could be made into something positive—sympathy. Had not the press ink generated by yet another batch of pathetic refugees, coupled with the UN Security Council condemnations of 'local Armenians' for conquering Kelbajar succeeded in internationalizing the plight of Azerbaijan? Then there was the idea that a disaster of magnitude was exactly what the country needed to shake it out of its slumber.

"Let every family have a martyr!" Elchibey told Mehmet Ali Bayar. "It is the only way to have this war touch the entire nation, and change it through the loss of blood!"

Still others were becoming increasingly desperate to buoy the tottering Elchibey regime, lest their hopes and dreams go down with it. Chief among this category were the Turks—and especially the Turkish President, Turgut Özal.

"Let's lob a few shells across the border and wake them (the Armenians) up a little bit," Özal was quoted as saying at the time of the Kelbajar debacle. "Turkey needs to show its teeth."

But it was only a verbal bluff, and one seemingly designed more for internal political consumption than to put fear into the hearts of the Armenians. If Turkey were to 'lob a few shells' at Armenia, it was highly likely that Russia would lob a few shells right back.

Özal made his remarks during the course of a tour of the 'Turkic' states of Central Asia, generally designed to encourage pan-Turkic solidarity in the realm of economics, and specifically, to get the leaders of Kazakhstan, Kyrgyzstan, Uzbekistan, and Turkmenistan to support Azerbaijan in its period of post-Soviet trauma. All were reluctant to do so. There were even those who thought that the Armenian assault on Kelbajar had been specifically timed to underline Moscow's displeasure with Turkish meddling in Russia's back yard—and to remind the Central Asian leaders what might befall their countries, if they did not mind their place.

For Turkey and Özal, this was a disaster of the greatest magnitude. The dawning of the 'Turkish century,' the age of influence for Ankara 'from the Adriatic Sea to the Wall of China,' seemed to have gone up in smoke.

Özal arrived in Baku on April 12, determined to shore up the one government in the region that continued to share the pan-Turkish dream, even if it seemed to be entering a phase of terminal collapse. But he made it clear that Turkey could help Azerbaijan only to the extent that Azerbaijan helped itself. These were the main themes of his address to the Azerbaijan parliament, on April 14th. Speaking in a highly Ottomanized Turkish, he drew repeated applause and ovations when he berated the Armenian foe. Armenia, he said, had to be 'made to understand' that seizing territory by force was totally unacceptable, and that the 'patience of the Turkic Nation' was worn to the breaking point.

"It is impossible to regard the conflict between Armenia and Azerbaijan as limited to Karabakh," he intoned. "Rather, it is perfectly clear that the Armenian aggression is part of a design to create a 'Greater Armenia' out of Azeri lands."

But the applause was lackluster when Özal began sounding on other sensitive subjects. One was making an analogy between the current situation in Azerbaijan and Turkey's own war of independence following the First World War.

"It was not ten or twenty percent of our land, but half of it, and occupied not by one enemy, but by four—England, France, Italy, and Greece," Özal pointed out. "To secure our independence, the people of Anatolia donated 30 percent of every household's resources to the effort to expel the enemy. And more: every household had its martyr."

The message was lost on no one: the Azeri defeats were the result of general corruption and cupidity in high places and because their soldiers shamelessly ran away.

Finally, Özal rolled up his sleeves and got into his favorite subject—economics. The Azeris in the audience liked these remarks least of all.

"In Turkey, we talk about the 'curse of oil,' " he said. "The reason is simple. It makes people lazy. Thank God we have none. The result is our success in creating a new image for our own people both at home and abroad: *To Work Like A Turk!*

Polite applause met Özal at the end of his remarks; the standing ovation was proforma. The Turkish president had hit too many nails on the head. It was a brilliant speech—and his last.

That night, at the banquet held in his honor, Özal called me over to his table for a chat about Kelbajar. The music was too loud and there were other distractions, but Özal was focused and direct. Among other comments he made was the charge that Turkish military intelligence had noted many 'extra flights' arriving in Yerevan immediately before the Kelbajar invasion.

"I can assure you that not all of them were filled with humanitarian aid," Özal said.

I wanted details, but the situation made it impossible to pursue the subject. Seated to Özal's left was his wife, Semra; to her left was Elchibey, who was already swaying with too much drink. Abulfez saw me leaning over Özal, and raised a shotglass filled with vodka in a toast. Then he got to his feet and launched into a long, incoherent speech about eternal brotherhood and Turkishness and other similar themes. I looked at Özal. The contrast between the abstinent guest and his inebriated host could not have been greater.

The next day, the two presidents held a joint press conference. Özal was focused and Elchibey incoherent. After the presser, I asked Özal's spokesman Kaya Toperi if the president could meet with a smaller group of Western journalists. A date was set for the following morning, but then canceled at the last moment. Özal was simply too tired to meet with anyone.

It was not a brush-off. A day later, after returning to Ankara, Turgut Özal was dead of a massive heart attack.*

---

*One wild idea was that Özal had been somehow killed by Iskender Hamidov, who had been removed as Minister of the Interior, allegedly at Özal's behest. Others suggested that Özal, after seeing the state of affairs in Azerbaijan, had died of a broken heart. Still others have hinted darkly that his peace-feelers toward the Kurdish Workers Party (PKK) fighting in the Turkish southeast sufficiently alienated the Turkish military that they had him knocked off.

The world, I thought, had lost a statesman—and Azerbaijan a friend. The Özal era, in any case, was at an end.

* * *

I hitched a ride on Elchibey's presidential jet to attend Özal's funeral. My motivation was to pay my last respects to a man I greatly admired, but I soon discovered that there were plenty of other reasons to be there, too— like to see the other mourners.

The first head of state we met was waiting for us in the lobby of the Grand Ankara Hotel with his delegation: Heydar Aliyev. He would share the protocol honors with Elchibey of being the first foreign mourners to be brought to the grieving widow to issue condolences. The Turks had elevated Heydar to the level of 'head of state'—Naxjivan, in this case, which had apparently been put on a par with Azerbaijan itself.

The other official mourners were a mixed bag, coming, in the main, from Islamic, Third World, and former communist countries, and cut quite a picture as they registered their presence in front of the flag-draped coffin in the Great Hall of the Turkish Parliament, and then marched as a phalanx behind the coffin as it was brought to the main mosque in the capital. The western democracies, in contrast, showed surprisingly little interest in attending last rites for the man who had come to symbolize 'the Turkish Model' of economic change, cultural balance, and political progress for emerging democracies in the world. Particularly scandalous was the absence of Özal's 'good friend' George Bush, who was too busy with his presidential library in Houston to come pay his respects to the man who had risked so much in bringing his country into the anti-Saddam alliance during the Gulf War.

The strangest mourner was from a little country with which Turkey—or at least President Özal—had a big problem: the president of Armenia, Levon Ter-Petrossian. Had he been invited, or had he simply arrived to sour the occasion? It was not clear until a 'gala' reception thrown by Özal's great political rival Süleyman Demirel at the Turkish Parliament for the collected mourners. There, as cameras clicked and whirred, Demirel forced the first of three meetings with the Armenian leader on Abulfez Elchibey.

But while the meeting provided a fine photo opportunity, the reality was that the forced meeting with Ter-Petrossian destroyed whatever prestige Elchibey had left at home. He had been forced to drink from a tainted chalice of peace, and he knew it. I knew it. His entourage knew it. In Baku, people reacted to the meeting with outrage and shame. Typical of public sentiment was self-styled labor leader Nimet Panakhov, who cited the meeting as evidence that Elchibey was secretly an Armenian agent. The only people who didn't seem to know about the impact on Elchibey seemed to be the Turks.

The second meeting between Ter-Petrossian and Elchibey was in the latter's hotel room. It was a private chat that left Elchibey shattered. Vugar, our former *Spetsznaz* 'kid' was traveling with the delegation as a translator/bodyguard, and was the first in the room after Ter-Petrossian departed.

"Elchibey was holding his head in his hands," Vugar told me. "I don't know what Ter-Petrossian told him, but I had never seen him like that before—and I have seen him in a lot of different circumstances. He was crushed."

A third meeting was held at the VIP lounge at Ankara's Esenboga Airport, this time including Heydar Aliyev and Etibar Mamedov. This was "to show the Armenians the sort of solidarity that could be mustered by the Azeris, if need be," a member of the Turkish parliament's foreign relations desk told me—thus revealing a stunning, if typical amount of ignorance about the political cesspool in Baku. There was no content to the meeting; it merely slammed another nail into Elchibey's political coffin, and I know he knew it, too.

The state burial was held in Istanbul, and I flew with Elchibey and Aliyev and the rest of the Azeri delegation to attend it. Both Elchibey and Aliyev were invited to join the inner circle of close family and friends among the tens of thousands of mourners at the Mosque of Mehmed the Conqueror, and then at the graveside, where they both participated in the ritual throwing of dirt on the body.

Finally, it was time to go 'home' to Baku. I went out to the Istanbul airport VIP lounge, and was asked to board the presidential jet before the official departure ceremonial stuff began—and thus had a bird's-eye view from the top of the steps of the plane as Süleyman Demirel escorted Abulfez Elchibey and Heydar Aliyev down the red carpet to say good-bye. It was the moment when, in memory of the late Özal, hatchets were to be buried and personal vendettas forgotten. It was also the moment when Heydar Aliyev was supposed to come back to Baku and help Elchibey save the country.

Abulfez walked up the steps alone, and Heydar stayed on the tarmac.

On the way back to Baku, I wanted to ask Elchibey about this and other topics—like the content of the meetings with Ter-Petrossian.

"Abulfez Bey," I said as the president wandered back through the jet to the toilet I already knew did not flush. "Can we have a word?"

"We will have plenty of time to talk back in Baku," said Elchibey with a plastic smile.

We never did.

* * *

In May, I traveled to Tbilisi again with Hicran. The excuse was to attend Alexis Rowell's birthday bash, but more than anything else, we just wanted to get out of Azerbaijan.

We returned to Baku by road via Ganje in order to drop in on our old friend, Rashit Bey—the belligerent police chief whom we had met in the summer of 1991. His wife told us he was up in Chaykent, so we went up toward the Murov Mountain pass to find him there.

Rashit Bey didn't look very good. He had been wounded out of action twice over the past six months, and carried the sadness of having lost dozens of young lives who had entrusted their fate to him. Still, he was glad to see us. No, he was overwhelmed that we remembered him at all. He wept in front of his men as he embraced us.

"*You!*" cried Rashit, "You, here! *You!*"

We drove up the road to the trout farm where we had made a picnic that summer day two years before. Instead of other people picnicking, the road was now lined with a new mass of refugees. Many had turned to theft to make ends meet, Rashit told us. After the quick and nasty tour of his new beat, Rashit drove us over to a scruffy restaurant someone had set up in what had been the 'Lenin Youth Camp.'

"A year ago, we were on top of the Murov, cooking meat and breaking bread, remember?" asked Rashit Bey, after taking a long hit on the vodka. I pointed out it was almost two years, but it seemed much longer than that.

"Those were the days," he sighed. "But now the Armenians are on top of the Murov—can you imagine that?"

We admitted that it was difficult.

"We believed in him, you know," said Rashit. "That is why we voted for him—so we could be an independent country, be free."

He was speaking about the president.

We drank the bottle dry and chatted about the good old days and the bad present ones, and Rashit Bey told us a lot of stuff that he should not have, maybe. He did so because he was different, or maybe we were. All the former bravado had been whipped out of the man, or the foreign arrogance out of us. Who knew? We liked him a lot more this time, and he liked us. We went back down mountain, passing trucks filled with sacks of flour. Rashit informed us the aid was meant for refugees, but it was being removed to the 'free market' before our very eyes.

"We believed—and now this!" Rashit hissed.

There wasn't too much to say in response.

* * *

Back in Baku, our personal situation was becoming increasingly tenuous.

What I remember from the period was a series of idiotic 'press opportunities' hosted by the rapidly expanding American embassy in honor of visiting congressmen who did not know Azerbaijan from Albania, and the torrent of oilmen and oil industry hangers-on pouring into town to stake a claim. Soon, we found ourselves playing 'musical domiciles.' After leaving our first house on Akhundova Square, we moved into a second—only to be evicted by our 'good friend' Kubrah Hanim. Next, we were obliged to stay at Laura Le Cornu's place for a month before we were able to find a third abode, albeit one on temporary sufferance. Finally, we were forced to move into a one-and-one-half-room dive in a downmarket neighborhood, where the kitchen was the corridor leading into the WC. It was not prepossessing.

Vafa Gulizade offered to enlist President Elchibey as a housing reference. I tried to imagine the telephone call to Joe Real Estate Agent.

'Hello, Joe—this is Abulfez Elchibey, the president of your country. I understand that my friend Thomas is thinking of renting a property from you. I'd like you to know that we here at the executive office have no derogatory information about him. To our knowledge, he has no pets and keeps a clean yard. . . .'

We thanked Vafa for the offer, but declined.

It was high time to go. The one thing to hold out for was the second annual celebration of Azerbaijani independence, on May 28th. Accordingly, I decided to make a photo exhibition on our life in Azerbaijan, and invite the Tbilisi press corps down for a farewell bash. As part of our entertainment package for the guests, we arranged for a sailing boat cruise on Baku bay. Equipped with picnic lunchboxes, sufficient beer, and swimsuits, we set off on two sloops—but were instantly becalmed atop a shimmering, stinking sea of yellow, blue, and green: an oil slick.

"Don't throw your cigarette, or we'll go up in flames," said Alexis—and he was not joking. Two of our party became physically sick; everyone was affected by the fumes. It was our first and last cruise on the Caspian.

* * *

The misadventure on Baku bay did serve to underline a certain reality, however: if the Popular Front government—and indeed, Azerbaijan—was still afloat, it was because of oil. Only days before our outing, a 'final contract' appeared to be nearing completion. The oil companies involved— AMOCO, British Petroleum/Statoil, UNOCAL, Pennzoil, and McDermott (plus the junior partner, Turkish Petroleum) were told to form a consortium. The Azeri state oil company (SOCAR) chairman Sabit Bagirov had decided to unify the three huge offshore fields that had previously been subject to separate treatment, and for logistical ease, to deal with the foreign oil companies as one entity. Suddenly, it looked like things were going forward, fast.

Urgency was added when John Major invited Elchibey to make an official visit to London to 'discuss matters of mutual interest.' The trip was set for June 30th. It would be Elchibey's first trip to a major western country, and signaled a huge injection of moral (and financial) support for his government and country. The quid pro quo was that Azerbaijan would finally sign the long-awaited production sharing agreement on Caspian crude. Confirming this, the oil companies involved in the so-called 'Deal of the Century' were informed that an initial 'earnest money' investment of $70 million, paid in proportion to their stake in the consortium, was to be deposited into an escrow account at a German bank. Then one of the oil companies decided to curry favor by putting their share into a normal account—and all the others followed suit lest they appear not to trust their Azeri partners.

Within the blink of an eye, the Elchibey regime had a slush fund—and a new lease on life. The government would now be able to buy a few political favors—and maybe buy a few victories on the battlefield, too.

Even more important, the government had been able to erase the last vestiges of the Russian military presence in the country. Although the details remained shrouded in mystery, word had it that on May 24th or 25th, the Russian 104th Airborne Division stationed in Ganje had departed Azerbaijan—and had left their weapons behind.

This was incredible. Azerbaijan had become the first of all the fifteen former Soviet republics to actually get rid of Russian garrison troops—and almost a year ahead of schedule. Who knew what it had cost the government (it was assumed that there was a kickback somewhere along the line) but this fact, coupled with the imminent oil deal and the most recent, promising contacts with the Armenians via the Minsk Group of the OSCE suddenly, for the first time in months, seemed to augur something good for a change.

* * *

Hindsight may give 20/20 vision but it often exposes one's own blind spots. Mine began on June 5, 1993, when a friend called to tell us about an event of some importance in Ganje: the government, she said, had sent in troops against Surat Husseinov. The idea had been to disarm his rogue garrison and achieve a unified command, but the effort had ended in horrible bloodshed that now threatened to break out into civil war.

This was a mouthful for eight o'clock in the morning.

"Tell me more," I said.

"I don't know any more—only that it is important, and that you have to go to Ganje, now."

I played cool.

"Hicran can go if she wants," I said. "I have better things to do than drive across country chasing rumors."

"You must go," said Hicran, convinced that something big was afoot.

So we booked a taxi and set off on the monotonous ride to Ganje. I had traveled the road many times, and this time it was as boring as any before or after—300 miles of scrub land broken by villages and small towns with nothing to recommend them save for the occasional carp-bearing irrigation canal.

We stopped at Yevlak to check out reports that 'rebels' had seized control of the airport. Bewildered looks greeted us. Not only was there no trace of the rumored civil war, there was not a hint of civil disobedience. I began to feel duped. Sitting in a car cruising across the Azerbaijan flats for half a day was not my idea of recreation. Still, there was nothing to do but push on the last 50 miles and what passed for a decent meal in Ganje. Maybe we could make the evening flight back to Baku.

We ran into the first barricade at the crossroads of the main highway and a turnoff to the towns of Neftchalan and Geranboy.

"Are you with the government?" we asked a couple of guards.

"Who else would we be with?" came the logical response.

The next barricade was not far behind. It was manned by soldiers who recognized me from the front, and they let us through with a smile and wave. Then there was a third, a fourth, and then a fifth barricade, and tension grew with each one.

"What's happening in Ganje?" we would ask, and not receive anything more concrete than a strained and snarled response.

But that something was up was clear—and the closer we got to Ganje, the less we knew how to greet those who stuck their Kalashnikovs through the window and demanded our IDs. Then, at sunset and about 10 kilometers from Ganje, we were flagged down by men huddling by a tank with its gun barrel pointed in our direction.

"Who are you!" demanded one of the sentries.

"Reporters. . . ." responded the terrified taxi driver, speaking for us.

"Thank God! You're here at last to tell the truth!"

With that, the gunman jumped in the back seat with Hicran and Elmira, and told the driver to move.

"The villains, the traitors. . . ." he began, and did not end his hyperbolic screech until we had passed three more checkpoints and were deposited into the middle of Surat Husseinov's 709th brigade inside the erstwhile barracks of the 104th (Russian) Airborne Division, on the outskirts of Ganje.

We had jumped the lines; and it happened so quickly, it was difficult at first to comprehend that we were now with the rebels.

Rebels?

"What happened?" we asked Surat's spokesman, a local historian by the name of Aypara Aliev.

Aypara told us the following: on the morning of June 4th, government forces loyal to the traitor Abulfez Elchibey had launched a dastardly attack on the barracks of the Hero of Azerbaijan, the Generalissimo of Karabakh, the Deputy of the People, Surat Husseinov and his men of the heroic 709th regiment. But the brave men of the 709th had defended their leader with their blood and thrown the government troops out. Ganje was now a liberated city—but at the cost of 70 dead. Among the martyrs were many civilians, including women and children mowed down in the murderous fire thrown up by the government forces. The hospitals and morgues were full. And there was no telling what would happen that night. Although Surat's men had valiantly beaten off the attackers twice, there were fears that the government would mount a full-scale assault.

The only thing preventing the traitors in Baku from completing their work was the shock of its initial failure—and the fact that Surat's men had taken upwards of 1,000 POWs, including three ministers. In addition to signed confessions about their own role in the fratricidal disaster, documents captured with the ministers revealed spine-chilling operational details. The action even had a diabolical name: 'Tayfun,' or Hurricane. It had been ordered by the president himself. One of the prisoners, Ekhtiyar Shirinov, the deputy minister of justice, felt such remorse at his involvement in the sordid business—including his crime of opening a case against Surat Husseinov for refusing to obey orders and general dereliction of duty—that he had drafted an arrest warrant for the traitorous president in his own hand. Aypara showed us a copy of the document that he just happened to have in his pocket.

It was tragic and horrible—but there was also something wrong about it all.

We asked for a tour of the battleground around the 104th/709th barracks. It was a movie-set mess: while the headquarters itself was almost unscathed, the bunks to the rear of the building had been totally gutted. It was almost as if someone had burned the barracks for show.

True enough, there were prisoners all over the place. Surat's chief of staff, Colonel Eldar Aliev, attacked a few of the terrified youths for our benefit.

"How could you lift your hand against your brothers?" Colonel Aliev cried, tears streaming down his face as he slapped the distraught young soldiers around the room. Looking at our cameras, and speaking into Elmira's tape-recorder, the young recruits swore they had been duped. Their leaders had told them they were on their way to the Murov Mountains to do battle with the Armenian foe, and not to fire on the heroes of the 709th.

I asked to see the parking lot: it was literally filled with heavy equipment—dozens of tanks, APCs, GRAD missile systems—all captured from the government forces, who had no stomach for the fight, Aypara informed us. But a quick inspection of the machines revealed that few of them had government markings. Rather, most appeared to belong to the 104th (Russian) airborne division, which had supposedly effected its final evacuation some weeks before.

Yes, there were many odd elements and discrepancies of detail concerning the 'Surat' version of events, but all faded in the face of the emotive charge that the government was responsible for brother killing brother. The evil incantation was repeated again and again: the government was guilty of fratricide, the government was guilty of the murder of 70 of the most devoted nationalists in Azerbaijan. . . .

The mantra was repeated again and again by Aypara. Seventy martyrs! But where were the bodies? We scoured the hospitals and we scoured the morgues; there were no bodies in either place. The local imam at Ganje's main mosque confessed that he had only dealt with the corpses of four men known to be soldiers on June 4th.

One was that of Captain Mehman Aliekberov, a popular commander in Surat's group who had 'personally killed more than 100 Armenians,' we were informed. He had been shot down by government troops while carrying a white flag that morning, and was being buried with military honors in the Martyrs' cemetery on the edge of town. We hastened there and found an emotional funeral in progress. It culminated when Mehman's unit fell to their knees and took an oath that his 'blood would not remain on the ground.' But where were the others? There were not even any new graves next to Mehman's final resting place. Something was beginning to stink, and it was not rotting corpses—it was the lack of them.[1]

* * *

By June 6th, the first 'peace' delegation from Baku appeared at Surat's HQ. It was headed by the Sheikh ul Islam, Allahshukhur Pashazade, who arrived in a black ZIL limousine with several aids. Next came Doctor Shadman Husseinov, Etibar Mamedov's first deputy. He was followed by Deputy Prime Minister Rasul Guliyev and then Abbas Abbasov, a Mutalibov-era functionary who survived into the Elchibey era, and then the lanky, lisping image of a neo-commie creep, Rahim Isazade. Of particular note in the gallery of interlocutors were Nimet Panakhov and Rahim Gaziev.

There were others, too, but all were unified by a certain trait: rather than coming to urge restraint, most of the visitors seemed to congratulate the young warlord on his success in staving off the forces of the government they allegedly represented.

"What did Surat say? What did he say?" the growing number of journalists waiting outside would ask whenever a member of the 'peace' delegation emerged from the 709th HQ.

"It's not good," would come the standard reply. "Surat is angry. He wants Isa Gambar and Panakh Husseinov to resign."

"It's looking bad," another would add after emerging from the inner sanctum five minutes later. "Surat is demanding that the entire government resign and Elchibey be put on trial for treason."

Surat charged, Surat demanded, Surat required. But it was all second-hand information—because there was no trace of the man himself. I could not remember what he looked like, save for a vague sense that he must have been one of the jowly, neocommunist crocodiles I usually associated with the old regime. In Azerbaijan, wealth meant corruption and corruption meant corpulence, and as Surat was a man who had made his millions during the communist period, it followed that he was fat.

I was thus taken aback the first time I saw the *putschmeister* at close range. It was on the evening of the third day, and the various supplicants had decided it would be a good thing for Surat to meet the press. By then, Surat's base was swarming with journalists from Baku and elsewhere. Many of the Azeris seemed to be in a state of scarcely concealed joy, and it was not the idea of news that titillated them—it was the fact that they were part of a putsch in progress.

After repeated delays, we were finally ushered into a room within the barracks. Sitting around a large table were the usual suspects—Sheikh Pashazade, labor leader Panahkov, Abbas Abbasov, Rasul Guliyev, and Dr. Shadman, if I remember correctly. At the head of the table sat a young, dapper man dressed in a dark, double-breasted suit, freshly pressed white shirt and conservative tie. His cock's comb of blow-dried hair seemed frozen in place, as did the shy smirk on his face.

This was Surat Husseinov?

Well, Surat may have been on display for the press, but it was not much of a press conference. Surat was so inarticulate that he verged on incoherence and had to be prompted by the older and wiser men around him.

"Where does your support come from?" asked an old flunky television journalist brought in from Baku for the occasion.

"Huh?" snarled Surat.

"Your support, you know, the people who support you," the journalist began again, trying to coax the right answer from the younger conqueror's lips.

"*From the people—the people. . . .*" Doctor Shadman—or was it Abbas Abbasov?—whispered from across the table.

"The People," Surat mechanically replied on cue. "My support comes from the People."

The longest sentence he managed to utter was in response to another set question about the war.

"Every battle won for our national honor is ours, and every defeat that of the traitors in Baku," Surat announced. "The army knows this, the people know this, our enemies know this."

"And Karabakh?" asked another reporter, looking for a dramatic sound bite. "What is your position on Karabakh?"

Someone else sitting at the table leaned over and whispered something in Surat's ear, and he smiled, understanding at last.

"*Karabakh bil nashim i budet!*" he rumbled in Russian. "Karabakh was ours and will be!"

Thunderous applause erupted, and the press conference was at an end.

* * *

The picture of the shy and retiring, grievously wronged patriot cultivated at the press conference was at quite a variance with my other encounter with Surat Husseinov in Ganje. It was the next morning, and we were lurking around the entrance of the 709th barracks, when Surat's chief of staff, Colonel Eldar Aliev, strolled out and blew a whistle. Instantly, all the armed men prowling about scurried over to the parade ground and lined up into squads and units.

They were a pretty motley-looking bunch, if truth be told. The chief of Surat's security detail was wearing plastic shower shoes. Another man was sporting a ponytail.

"Attention!!" shouted Colonel Aliev in Russian. The 300 or so men tried to do just that—but looked even more ragtag than before. It was becoming ever harder to believe that these were the very men who had defeated the national army of the Republic of Azerbaijan.

"Present arms!"

Clang clang, click click and all that.

"Commander, I present you your troops!"

The men snapped their heads to the right as a knot of men emerged from the barracks, clearly protecting someone in their midst.

There was no doubt who it was. The suit was the same, as was the hairdo; I presumed he was wearing a new shirt, and his shoes were newly shined. Clutching a silver and ivory-plated automatic pistol in his right hand and poking his left toward the south, Surat began his harangue.

"Men of the 709th, you have achieved our first victory!" he snarled. "The task is now to root out the filth of the criminal, illegitimate leadership in Baku that has robbed the nation and sullied our honor by making brother shed the blood of brother!"

"Commander, *SIR* !" barked the men as one, "Command *US* !"

The young conqueror intended to do just that.

"On to Baku, and on to victory!" he snarled. "Dismissed!"

* * *

We got there first, but barely. All the way back to Baku, we were stopped repeatedly at roadblocks, although less for reasons of security than because we were purveyors of information. No one knew anything about what was happening in Ganje, but all were keen to learn. Apparently, state television had broken its silence on events the day before and issued a report about 'unidentified provocateurs' having tried to seize heavy weapons at the depot of the 709th garrison. Aside from that, there had been an absolute news blackout in Baku. Russian television, meanwhile, was beaming an unabashed pro-Surat slant to the 'events.' It was heartbreaking: after having spent so much effort at weaning the Azeri nation away from a Moscow-centric view of the world, the tottering Elchibey government was literally forcing everyone in the country to get their basic information about the most significant event in the country from an outside source, and a tainted one at that. Like the Mutalibov government before it, the Elchibey regime was sliding down the slippery slope of denial and disinformation. It didn't take a genius to see that it was only a matter of time before the nation would learn that the government was lying, if everyone had not already drawn that conclusion.

Then the usually pro-Elchibey Turan News Agency floated a government-approved story about a 'communist' insurrection in Ganje. The rebels had hoisted the 'hammer and sickle' of the old Soviet Union over Surat's headquarters, the agency reported.

Perhaps this was designed to evoke fear of the Soviet bogeyman among the population as a whole, but the only people who believed this fabrication were foreign journalists sitting in Moscow: Reuters picked up the Turan story, the *Financial Times* picked it up from Reuters—and the BBC took it from there.*

This was idle speculation and beside the main point, however: by being so late in providing any information, the government of Abulfez Elchibey had eviscerated whatever little confidence the public had left in it. Nothing coming out of the presidential apparatus was to be believed anymore.

This was apparent when the presidential spokesman, Arif Aliev, held a press conference devoted to the government's version of the Ganje events. Looking very worn, frustrated, and angry, Arif detailed the events that led up to June 4th. The Defense Ministry had warned Surat to stop recruiting criminals and foreign adventurers, Arif explained, but to no avail. Likewise, Surat had been ordered to turn over the heavy equipment he had pulled off the Karabakh line in February, as well as the armor left by the departing Russian 104th Division, which had been paid for by the government. Arif meticulously went over the deployment of the government troops in Ganje, piecing together the events of the morning of June 4th. Surat's 709th had been tipped off that they were about to be reined in. In order to prevent this, Surat had called in women and children to use as a defensive wall. It was then that the government had called on its men to retreat, at which point Surat's men had ambushed the transport, killing 20 men aboard a bus. Obliged to show force, on June 5th the government had flown in troops to Ganje airport. They were met with such a ferocious barrage of fire that they quickly surrendered. Then Surat's men went about destroying the terminal and the runways, both to make further government airborne arrivals impossible, and to 'prove' that it was they who were under attack, and not the other way around.

I sat in the conference room, stunned. Arif's version of events was in such total contradiction with the informational feed we had been given in Ganje that I didn't know whether to laugh at him or start throwing chairs. At the top of the note pad I used that day, I scribbled 'Presser at National Lie Machine.' I held my tongue until the press conference was over, when I approached Arif privately.

"I just got back from Ganje, and what you are saying is a lie, and you know it," I said.

Arif latched his eyes onto mine. "You of all people should understand

---

*The myth of the "Red Flag Flying Over Ganje" had begun. Those of us who had hung around Surat's headquarters decided that the Turan reporter must have mistaken a rapidly deteriorating wall mosaic of Lenin at the entrance to the barracks as reflecting procommunist sentiment—if the reporter had been in Ganje at all.

what this is all about," he said. "It is a coordinated campaign to destroy the government."

"Why should I believe a word you say? You've been silent for the past five days!" I said indignantly. "And now this business about the women and children—human shield my ass!"

"You really don't understand, do you?" he hissed, allowing what he clearly thought to be an important piece of information to sink in. "If you don't believe me, I'll show you the tape!"

"Tape my ass!"

"Look at it, damn it!"

"Maybe later."

"Look," said Arif with an edge of despair in his voice that I had not heard before. "They had everything down pat, even the timing, so that anyone with a brain left in this government was either out of town or taken hostage. I was in London when all this happened. It was their people in the apparatus who put out all the stupid disinformation. It was part of the plan to destroy all confidence in the government."

"It seems to be working."

"Yeah," said Arif slowly. "They even have you on the hook."

Meanwhile, Surat was on the move. A small detachment of men from the 709th—one popular number was 30, although they were probably more—flouted whatever verbal deal had been struck between their leader and the various envoys who had come to see him and hit the road toward Baku.

No one stopped them. The army, under strict command to avoid further bloodshed, fell back further and further. Surat's men 'took' Yevlak. Then they 'took' Barda. In control of something like 15 percent of the country, and with the regular army melting away before them, they next started the long haul over the quasi-desert toward the capital. They were 200 miles away one day and 150 miles away the next. Then they were within 100 miles of the capital and then they were 50 miles out. They would not stop, they said, until the government resigned and Elchibey stood trial for his crime of trying to rein in the 709th. Elchibey did nothing. Perhaps, as Vafa Gulizade suggested, he was in shock. Others suggested he was drunk or maybe even drugged.

Then one day—I believe it was June 9th or 10th, but it might have been the 11th or 12th—President Elchibey summoned the foreign diplomatic corps to explain the situation. The government was faced with an armed rebellion, he said—as if any clarification was needed. To counter this, he said, the government intended to resist, as was the right of any sovereign government to defend itself against rebels. This was a version of the old saw concerning 'the monopoly on the means of violence' enjoyed by governments since the first cave state was created by Neanderthal man, but Elchibey thought he was explaining something new. In the question-and-answer period, the German ambassador complained about the sorry state of his telephone and asked the president to look into the matter. Still, a position had been established at last. The government was going to defend itself! Vafa Gulizade waxed almost ecstatic.

"Finally!" crowed Vafa. "Let them come on! Civil wars can be cleansing for societies—and ours needs cleansing badly! We have allowed ourselves to sink into the slime of criminals! No longer! I myself am ready to strap on my gun and go for it!"

Surat's 'rogue' battalion (or company or maybe just platoon) kept on marching closer—and when they arrived at a dump town called Gazi-Muhammad, the government struck.

At last! But of the three attack helicopters sent to deal with the advancing column, none returned to their base. They had all gone over to the "Surats."

It was incredible: 30 men (or maybe 100) were marching across totally denuded countryside to topple a regime that allegedly represented seven million people—and were succeeding. There was little wonder about why the Karabakh Armenians (and their cohorts) were so massively successful against the governments of both Mutalibov and Elchibey.

No one was willing to fight for the survival of the state.

Note

1. It took almost a year for the official report on the 'Ganje Affair' to come out, and when it was finally released in April 1994, even the head of the commission of investigation preferred not to sign it. In essence, it whitewashed Surat and the 709th for refusing to obey the elected government and found guilt in the government for trying to rein in Surat, thus establishing, once and for all, the legal right of any disgruntled military commander to rebel and discard the existing government by force. But when it came to the numbers of those killed during the black days of June 4th and 5th, the official research could not hide a central fact: *the dead did not exceed two dozen*, and almost all were government troops—including the head of the presidential guard—who had been killed in an ambush as their bus was *leaving* Ganje on June 5th in an effort to defuse tensions. And the funerals we witnessed at the Ganje Martyrs' Lane? With the exception of Commander Mehman, the few burials there appear to have been those of soldiers killed weeks before but whose bodies had been kept on ice awaiting an appropriate moment to 'die.'

22

The Crowbar—Or Heydar Comes Home

With rebels marching on the capital, his army deserting him, and the Armenians taking advantage of all, President Abulfez Elchibey was faced with an extreme situation that called for extreme measures. Accordingly, he called on a man of great experience and wisdom and asked him to end his years of self-exile and return to the capital to mediate an end to the crisis. In other words, he called on Heydar Aliyev. It was like inviting a crocodile into the goat-pen.

The 70-year-old Aliyev was a man of many hats, and people called him many names. The most gentle was 'autocrat'; the most common was 'old, unrepentant commie.'

True, his C.V. gave cause for concern. But Heydar was no longer KGB general, Azerbaijan Communist Party leader, or even Politburo member. That was the past. Heydar was now a believer in the concepts of pluralism, universal human rights, and the free market economy. Heydar had become a democrat. This expressed itself in his total and categorical refusal to take on any new position in government anywhere, anytime, unless it was through the will of the people. And on June 9th, the people of Azerbaijan beseeched Heydar to come and save them from themselves. Their collective voice was heard through that of President Abulfez Elchibey.

Actually, it was not Elchibey himself, but the Turks who asked Heydar to suspend his self-exile and return to Baku. Specifically, it was the new Turkish President (and old political warhorse) Süleyman Demirel who did the arm-twisting on Elchibey to invite Heydar to board the sinking ship of state.

To be perfectly frank, Demirel and many others in official Ankara never really felt at home with Elchibey. Part of it was his erratic behavior, which rumors linked to heavy drinking. A month earlier, Elchibey had traveled to Ganje for an inspection. Then, on a whim, he decided to find an old girlfriend from his university days—an ethnic Georgian named Tamara. In a warped, modern version of the Caucasus classic, *Ali and Nino*, the inebriated president ordered the official caravan of cars to prowl the streets of Ganje while security guards banged on doors looking for the woman, who was now 50 years old, and married. . . .*

But in Turkish eyes, Elchibey's greatest crime was to balk when it came to defending his government. It was, after all, almost Ankara's regime—and its fall would mean the dashing of dreams of economic expansion into the Caucasus and Central Asia. Accordingly, Ankara started looking around for alternative horses to back. That is where Heydar came in.

To the Turks, Heydar was everything that Abulfez was not. For starters, Heydar was an ascetic. He didn't smoke and he didn't drink anything stronger than tea. His once notorious womanizing ways were behind him. Most importantly, Heydar understood power. He was a man with a long track record of Soviet-style organization and authority. So Demirel picked up the hotline to Naxjivan and asked his old friend Heydar to return to Baku and straighten out the Surat mess before it was too late. Leave Elchibey as a figurehead while you go about the day-to-day business of running the state, he implied.

Heydar, however, was reluctant to become associated with Elchibey and his crumbling regime. He had declined the honor on at least three prior occasions. There had been the offer of the post of prime minister in February, which Heydar had rejected 'on democratic grounds.' The subject had come up again with greater urgency during Turgut Özal's funeral in late April. Once again, Heydar managed to stay on the tarmac and not board Elchibey's presidential plane.

But the Turks were persistent. On the night of April 25–26, it appeared Demirel had finally succeeded in getting Aliyev to throw pride to the wind in the name of the greater good and go back to Baku and give Abulfez a hand. The details are obscure, but a weird fact remains: Mehmet Ali Bayar of the Turkish embassy was awakened by an urgent call and instructed to secure landing rights for GAP—the name of the prime minister's Gulf Stream jet. Was Demirel coming to Baku in the middle of the night? Bayar was instructed not to ask questions, and just to attend to the matter of getting the landing rights: Heydar was on his way, at last. . . .

Bayar secured the requisite permissions, and waited. But at the last minute before entering Azeri airspace, the Gulf Stream jet veered away—and put down in Kars. The cause for aborting the flight had nothing to do with

---

*It is possible that the Tamara story might have been propaganda churned out by Surat's people, but it was told repeatedly by the people of Ganje—and was believed.

technical problems: Kars was the closest Turkish airport to Naxjivan. Having finally accepted the Turkish invitation to return to Baku, the Grand Old Man had changed his mind at the last moment—and decided to take a ride home.

Then in early June, Demirel called his old friend again. This time, the plea was more urgent and the cause more specific: Surat Husseinov was marching on Baku and the Elchibey government was collapsing. There was no time to delay or dally over principle—you, Heydar, are the only one who can save the situation!

"What can I do? He is mad, mad!" Heydar reportedly told Demirel, referring to Surat.

"Go and use your authority," came the request.

Heydar played hard to get. His main concern was that his mission should end in failure. He then would be faced with a future he would wish on no man—that of exile.

"Don't worry," Demirel reportedly said. "We will provide."

By that, Demirel meant that the Turkish state would provide a luxury flat on the Bosphorus. A backup *dacha* in the city of the sultans secured, Heydar then told the Turks that Elchibey would have to call him—and beg. Still trying to delude themselves that a pro-Turkish 'condominium' government could be set up, and that Heydar Aliyev really meant all he had been saying about pan-Turkism, democracy, and the free market, Ankara cranked up the pressure on Elchibey until he finally consented and picked up the telephone. The putsch had just been put into high gear, and through the agency of friends.

* * *

Thus, Heydar Aliyev arrived in Baku as the 'guest' of the beleaguered president; but he kept his distance from his host. Once again, he demurred accepting any and all appointments to any and all of the offices Elchibey offered him, ranging from prime minister to chief of security. Heydar had selflessly returned to help his country as a private citizen, and had no intention to take advantage of the crisis for political gain.

But as a private citizen, he wanted to learn what the problems facing the country really were. Accordingly, he set up shop in the regal building of the Academy of Sciences in central Baku. Summoning ambassadors and oilmen as well as old loyalists and the odd opposition party representative, he began holding court. But before they arrived to be debriefed, he called on me.

It happened like this. I was fresh back from Ganje when the telephone rang. On the other end of the line was a long-time Heydar loyalist who had an urgent message: although back in town less than twenty-four hours, the *Seder*, or 'Leader,' wanted to see me—and now.

This put me in a bit of a bind. Anatol Lieven of the London *Times* was over, and I tried to be as diplomatic as possible about the appointment.

"Aliyev wants to see me," I told Anatol as I hung up the phone. "You can tag along, but if it doesn't look right for you to stay, piss off, and I will fill you in."

"Sure," said Anatol. He seemed a little sour about it, but I thought he would be grateful to be allowed to come along.

We zipped down to the Academy building, where we were met by a security guard. I knew him from Naxjivan, and managed to get Anatol through due to my high-level connections. There were more guards at a second doorway, and my connections got us through that one, too. Up the stairs—by God, I was almost late!—and through the last series of security checks, performed by a guy I knew as Heydar's personal bodyguard. He winked at me, and opened the door to the inner chamber. I walked with Anatol tagging along close behind—and we found ourselves in a room filled with Baku's sycophant press.

"Great exclusive!" smirked Anatol. "Sure you want to share the interview?"

I would have blushed, but at that moment the doors to the real inner chamber swung open and the press pack swarmed in. There, sitting alone at a long table in the middle of the room, was the man himself—Heydar Aliyev. He did not even look up when we entered and seemed oblivious to our presence. No one moved. Then I broke ranks and walked up to my old pal from Naxjivan. The Baku hack-pack literally held their breath. Such things were not done in the capital, and not with The Old Man.

"Heydar Bey," I said. "How are you?"

"Fine, fine," he replied, surprised that I didn't know the new protocols.

"I brought you a gift," I said, reaching into my bag. A security man standing by the wall flinched and brought his hand toward the revolver under his coat.

"What?" said Heydar, confused.

"This," said I, producing a photograph of the putsch in progress: a young man, a snarl frozen on his face. He clutched a silver and ivory-plated pistol in one hand while pointing the other toward Baku.

"Who is this?" Heydar asked with a queer grin on his face.

"Surat Husseinov," I said.

Heydar stared at me for a moment. He had not expected this.

"Believe me," he said in a theatrical voice. "This is the first time I have ever seen this man!"

"What do you intend to do to about him?" I asked.

Heydar seemed to be on the verge of saying something of importance. But just then the other gathered reporters, emboldened by my audacity, closed in on us—and the moment was lost. Heydar had slipped back into a defensive mode—smiling, cajoling, charming.

"I would dearly love to answer all your questions at length, and I will," he smiled. "But now I must attend to business—the French ambassador is waiting to see me."

Indeed, at that moment, the outer door opened to reveal Heydar's guest. We all fell back as Heydar rose from his chair, moved to embrace the ambassador, and ushered him to a seat on the far side of the table, smiling all the way. Flash bulbs popped and video cameras whirred.

"There was civil war, but we have managed to put a temporary stop to it," purred Aliyev in remarks we were meant to hear and record. "We now must consider how to end the crisis of government in Azerbaijan." The French ambassador nodded sagely.

The photo opportunity was over after exactly one minute. Then the security guards pushed us out of the room. It was to be the first of many 'press conferences' of the kind that the former Soviet Union was famous for: journalists scribbled notes while dignitaries smiled and chatted about nothing. Newcomers soon learned the ropes.

* * *

The conventional wisdom was that Heydar Aliyev was the mastermind behind Surat's uprising and putsch against Elchibey, and that all this was supported by the Russians.

The circumstantial evidence certainly pointed in this direction, but even from the start there seemed to be a much murkier picture, mainly because most aspects of Heydar's return simply did not fit the grand conspiracy theme—especially all the talk about the 'Russian' connection.

If the Russians had a preferred regent for wayward Azerbaijan, it was the ousted first president and last local Communist Party First Secretary, Ayaz Mutalibov. You didn't have to look any further than where Mutalibov resided—a Moscow dacha belonging to KGB chief Yuri Barannikov. And the idea that Heydar would work with Mutalibov toward any mutual goal was, frankly, insane.

The reason was rather simple. If Heydar Aliyev regarded Elchibey as an incompetent dissident who had somehow stumbled into the position of president of Azerbaijan, he did not hate him. Rather, he held him in that special sort of contempt reserved by prison wardens for former inmates.

Mutalibov, however, was a different story altogether. Not only was he a usurper but he was also the man who had tried to prevent Heydar from returning to Azerbaijan in 1990 and had heaped calumny upon him when he did. 'Traitor' was one of the kinder words in Heydar's vocabulary when referring to Mutalibov.

Making the 'Russian' connection even more dubious was the Surat factor. At the time of the June putsch, Husseinov was 34 years old—i.e., his entire career as 'wool merchant,' mafia man and deputy of the people had taken place when Heydar was in exile and out of favor and when Mutalibov was either the first or second man in Azerbaijani politics. Thus, if one threw out all the conventional wisdom about Heydar Aliyev based on his former titles and occupations (KGB general, Politburo member, etc.) and looked exclusively at his personality, one was left with the following: in June of 1993, Heydar Aliyev was a one-man band who saw his last, best chance at restoring himself to power, and rolled the dice.

Unlike Surat, Heydar had no army. He did not even have a position in government to legitimate his presence for the first few, critical days. His only real power was his reputation as the autocratic leader of a one-party state where all the shelves of state stores were full of subsidized goods, a place where people were happy because they were officially supposed to be so and where the bureaucrats made enough out of kickbacks and corruption to keep things running.

But those were the good old days, and they were long gone. So Heydar had to develop a different technique in securing power. One way was to seek new alliances—and often in the most unlikely places.

The Turkish connection was straightforward; Heydar had Ankara eating out of his hand. He also played the Iranian card well, announcing himself to be a Muslim (as opposed to a 'Turk'). Nor was he above a little groveling before the Russians as part of his policy of realpolitik: Azerbaijan, after all, had not only been part of the Soviet Union for 70 years but a Russian colony for 100 years before that. It was completely natural to cultivate the best possible relations with the behemoth to the north. . . .

The most interesting relations Heydar tried to cultivate, however, were with a distant country with little direct political clout in Azerbaijan—the United States of America. And in cultivating Washington so early on, Heydar gave the lie to anyone who said he was part of a Moscow-based conspiracy against Elchibey. This ran in the face of all the conventional wisdom then and now, but it was there for anyone with eyes to see.

The beginning of the 'special relationship,' however, was a little rocky. One night shortly after his return, Heydar asked to see representatives of the American embassy to feel out Washington's take on the brewing coup. The request placed the embassy in a diplomatic quandary. Heydar was certainly a 'political personality,' but he was not a 'leader' per se—and hardly someone to summon the ambassador. Accordingly, the embassy arrived at the following protocol decision: Neither Ambassador Dick Miles (who was conveniently out of town) nor chargé d'affaires Robert Finn would be sent. Rather, the embassy would deliver a message to Heydar through the agency of Philip Remler, the first secretary. The point was not lost on Heydar, who understood the slight instantly.

"He didn't like seeing me at all," said Philip. "He even referred to me as Robert (Finn's) lackey."

But Heydar liked the message Philip had been sent to deliver even less. That was that the government of the United States of America continued to support the concepts of democratic pluralism, universal human rights, and the transition to an economic system based on the principles of the free market in the sovereign republic of Azerbaijan, as well as the legitimately elected president of the country, Abulfez Elchibey.

Heydar, seething with humiliation and rage, said he agreed with every detail.

"Tell your government that I, too, support the concepts of the rule of law, democratic pluralism, the principle of universal human rights and—what else—oh, yes, the transition to an economic system based on the principles of the free market. And democratic legitimacy, too."

Harmony achieved, Heydar evicted Philip, commanding him to close the door on his way out.

"He had a hard time getting his tongue around some of the words, but he was a pretty quick study, all in all," said a rather battered Philip the next day.

What did it mean? If Heydar were really Russia's man, as commonly believed, why not just call up Moscow and have them send down a *spetsnaz* hit team to bump off Abulfez and establish a dictatorship with himself at the head? No one (not even the Americans) would have thought the worse of him for doing so. In fact, that is exactly what people expected him to do. But he didn't. He preferred reciting the Gospel according to Thomas Jefferson. Something did not quite fit.

* * *

Many things about Heydar didn't fit: first, the contradictions between his public and private personas; then his balancing act between the Russians, Turks, Iranians, and Americans, mixed with his attempts to recreate the past by evoking the future and vice versa. And although Elchibey's ardent loyalists never lost an opportunity to try and convince anyone who would listen that Heydar was the head of a neocommunist plot, his return was hardly a cause for celebration among the former communists associated with Mutalibov.

Slowly at first, but then with gathering momentum, Heydar began a very public campaign against corrupt factory directors, cowardly commanders, and other riffraff that managed to get in his way. The only people spared were those who showed absolute, fawning loyalty to him, the *Seder*.

As Vafa Gulizade explained one night over a diminishing bottle of bourbon, Heydar's problem—or genius—was to believe himself identical with the state. What was good for him was, by definition, good for Azerbaijan: *L'état—c'est moi!*

Vafa himself was soon pulled in. Sitting in a meeting between Heydar and the Americans in his capacity of chief advisor on foreign affairs to the (acting) president of the republic, Vafa was asked by Heydar why Gulizade was sitting on the opposite side of the table, with the Americans, and not with him.

"You see this man?" Heydar asked, referring to Vafa and displaying his phenomenal memory at work. "I first saw him at the Soviet embassy in Cairo on July 27, 1968, during the Gromyko visit! It was in the afternoon—at three forty-three. . . ."

Vafa was immediately suborned and quickly disqualified himself as a source for solid news. I did not think less of him because of the crazy about-faces and twists and turns of loyalty required of him. We were and remain good friends. But I am absolutely sure that much of what Vafa shared with me—and other old friends—was total bullshit, designed to confuse and amaze not just his interlocutors, but himself, too. One day he would tell me that Aliyev was indeed 'Moscow's man,' sent into Azerbaijan to destroy its independence from within. The next day, Vafa would be the firmest believer in Heydar's historic mission to save the country. A third day, he would open the subject of seeking political asylum to escape from the madman who had seized power. His reading of Surat Husseinov was equally contradictory. Surat was variously a GRU general (or colonel) whose task was to restore Mutalibov, or Aliyev's agent whose task was to act as a lighting rod to attract those with questionable loyalty to Heydar (and thus allow Heydar to know who his real enemies were). Some of Vafa's conspiratorial yarns became fabulously complex. One of my favorites was the suggestion that Heydar had recruited Süleyman Demirel as a KGB agent way back in the 1950s or 1960s, and was still acting as his 'minder' for the greater good of a future, KGB-led, restored USSR. . . .

And Vafa was not alone in his sudden devotion to Heydar. Many people I had long thought 'independent'—academics, reporters, and even lackeys from the Popular Front who had acquired a taste for employment in the presidential apparatus—soon turned out to have been closet Aliyevists all along.

Were they hypocrites? Not really; they simply had that almost ineffable 'Soviet' sixth sense about survival, and meant to look out for themselves. The best explanation of the Heydar phenomenon was given to me by an old-time Popular Front booster whom I ran into one day outside of parliament.

"Well," I asked, "what do you think of Heydar so far?"

He thought for a while, and then asked me if I spoke Russian.

"*Poidët*," I said. "It's okay. Why?"

"The Russians have a saying that sums up the situation rather well," he said. "I am trying to think of a way to say it in Azeri but there is no equivalent."

"Well, say it in Russian," I said.

"*Protiv loma nyet prioma*," he said. "Do you understand?"

"There is no *what* against a *what*?" I asked, stumped.

He tried to explain, but failed.

"There is no equivalent," he said sadly. "Too bad."

The phrase stuck in my mind and imagination, though, so I asked my local encyclopedia and linguist, Philip Remler, what it meant. He, too, was stumped. "Are you sure you got it right?" he asked, not wanting to admit he didn't know. None of the other Russian-speaking foreigners I knew had heard the phrase, either, although when I repeated it to ethnic Russian friends and Russian-speaking Azeris, they would either chuckle or nod profoundly in agreement. And I was getting closer. '*Prioma*' could be loosely translated as 'defense,' but as for '*Loma*' the nearest equivalent was 'stick' or maybe 'spear.' Neither quite fit the bill. 'There is no defense against a spear.' Sure there was, a shield. What was so profound about that? I had tried my Russian/English pocket dictionary, but there was no entry for '*loma*.' I got a bigger dictionary, but there was no entry there, either. Then one day, by chance, I found myself looking at a huge Russian-to-Russian monster dictionary. I flipped it open to the letter L and began running my finger down the lists of words until I found it.

Loma: An ancient agricultural instrument used for uprooting trees, shrubs and rocks. A hoe? Not quite. A pike? Possibly. Then I had it: There is no defense against a *crowbar. . . .*

Sometimes it was the slightly tapered, blunt end of the shaft, punching, wrenching, wrecking. Sometimes it was the clawed head, reaching in from behind to rip, tear, and sunder. And sometimes it was the bar itself, smashing, battering, whacking. And the man behind the instrument was Heydar Aliyev, pulling apart first the superstructure and then the foundation of the state as effectively as if he were smashing through the rotting boards and beams of an outhouse. It was not subtle, it was not artistic—but it was brutally effective and inevitable.

Protiv loma nyet prioma. . . .

It sounded better in the original, but its meaning in English was perfectly clear.

* * *

The venue Heydar chose for his demolition work was parliament. I had spent a great deal of time in the chamber prior to the June 1993 putsch. I had been there when Mutalibov was the king and when Mutalibov had been the dog. I had been there when Yaqub ('Dollar') Mamedov had reigned and when he had resigned. There had been the fight on the floor when Isa Gambar had been elected chairman, and now there were the fights on the floor demanding his demise. There would be more fights, resignations, and humiliations in the future to look forward to as well.

By June 10, 1993, the hall had been ringing for two stormy days devoted to a discussion of the Ganje events. Neocommunist deputies who had not come to the building for over a year crowded the corridors, taunting and mocking deputies from the ruling Popular Front, who in turn hurled invective at each other for handing the country back to the communists due to their own incompetence, cupidity, and cowardice. It was a sad period to chronicle. Among other things, it invited the writer to question his original analysis of earlier alliances and assessment of individuals who exposed themselves as being far less idealistic than I had allowed myself to believe.

The rogues' gallery was large, but the most distressing figure was Etibar Mamedov, arguably Azerbaijan's best-known dissident during the late 1980s. After a falling-out with Elchibey's Popular Front in May 1992, he began playing the role of 'opposition leader' with such gusto that one was tempted to call him irresponsible. There were plenty of examples of this before the putsch, but the revolt-cum-coup brought everything into very sharp focus. And on June 9th, Etibar was once again banging the drum of failed democracy, and blaming Isa Gambar as the cause.

Isa, Etibar intoned in his nasal voice, was a 'criminal' and thus incompetent to lead debate about the Ganje events in which he was so heavily implicated. Then he gratuitously threw in the idea that the whole Ganje affair was a 'plot' by the government to mount a 'coup'—against itself, I guess. Isa tried to restore reason to the chamber.

"Everyone knows that the Ganje battalion has been out of control for at least two months," he said. "It has attracted criminal elements and deserters, and it has refused to obey commands. Is Ganje a separate state? Has the government no right to rein in armed criminal elements wherever they may be?"

Then Isa invited Panakh Husseinov to the podium—despite the fact that he had already resigned 'in principle' as the first victim of the putsch. Panakh ranted, raved, and flailed his stubby arms in the air, setting off peals of nasty laughter from the assembly. But what he said was of interest.

"Don't you worry! Don't you worry about that, that—*thing*, that resignation thing, no, don't worry about that at all!" he spat. "I am finished, through! But I want to take this occasion to ask you a question that I know you do not want to answer: why is it that Poland and even Germany have had such trouble negotiating and effecting a withdrawal of the Russian garrisons there, while we had such ease removing the 104th Division from Azerbaijan? Why is Azerbaijan unique? *Might it have something to do with leaving weapons for Surat?* And I want to ask you this—how could such an undermanned regiment of several hundred take over 1,000 prisoners? Answer me this, and I will tell you the truth about the Ganje events! . . ."

The speech was interrupted by the lisping voice of Rahim Isazade, who wanted to know why Panakh, who was not even a deputy and who claimed to already have resigned from his august office, and who was a man facing criminal charges that amounted to treason and murder, was allowed into parliament at all—much less given the right to slander the duly elected deputies of the people. . . .

Hurrah! Hurrah! came the thunderous applause, and Panakh was forced to leave the podium, the hall, and public life.

An ashen-faced Isa Gambar, knowing full well that his head was next on the block, still tried to preserve his dignity, and in a sense, the dignity of the government.

"You say that it is strange that Panakh Husseinov was invited to address you, the people who have been demanding his head for weeks now," said Isa, his usual monotone disturbed by a trace of passion. "I think it would have been much stranger if the state secretary did not address you for the record."

Next, the ministers of the interior, defense, and security (KGB) were invited to give testimony about the botched Ganje operation. Rather than banging fists on the podium and demanding that their assistants be released—they were still under Surat's lock and key—the security men meekly answered the most outrageous taunts and stains against their honor. One of them, General Dadash Rizayev, of Defense, explained his failure by confessing that he could not order his men to fire on other Azeris—no matter who they were. If it had not been perfectly clear before, it was now: the Ganje operation had been sabotaged from within, and at a very high level.

Then Tahir Kerimli, the roly-poly head of the judiciary committee, asked for the floor and began to speak. He was rational enough at first, pointing out the inadequacies of debate and the fact that the parliament was filled with old communists who had not been there in a year. Gathering steam, he apportioned blame to members of the Popular Front, the government, and himself, too. He paused for a moment—and then flipped out. Jabbing his finger, then waving his hand, then flapping his arms, Kerimli was smashing water glasses and crying real tears as he vented his bitter disappointment with the world at large.

"For shame, Isa Gambar, for shame!" he wailed, "I do not know where this filthy game began or where it will end, but before the nation, I hold you responsible for it all!"

The hall was stunned, and security had to be called in to drag Kerimli away before he started ripping out microphones and bashing people over their heads.

Isa looked ashen, and tried to call for a break. But a communist deputy wanted to vote on extending an amnesty to those involved in the Ganje affair.

"The government cannot be put on trial for defending the state!" Gambar shouted, refusing to table the measure for the tenth time. But it was on trial for exactly that, and Surat Husseinov's men were marching on the capital to give witness to the crime.

* * *

On Sunday, June 13th, Citizen Heydar Aliyev called for a special session of the parliament. Parliament complied. Something was up. The hall was soon brimming with excitement and rumor: Isa Gambar had resigned! This was confirmed when the electronic voting screens flashed and deputy chairman Tamerlan Garayev, sitting in Isa's place, asked for a roll call to establish if there was a quorum. Then the doors swung open to reveal a latecomer—Heydar Aliyev.

Never one to miss a theatrical moment, Heydar had timed his arrival for maximum attention on his presence—and made damn sure that it was all broadcast live on TV. As he stiffly walked across the hall to take his seat in front of the dais, a muscular roar of applause flooded the chamber, and the deputies and observers rose to their feet. Heydar had come home!

"Order, order!" said Tamerlan Garayev, tapping his microphone.

"Speech, speech! Let our Leader speak!" cried some flunky.

"Thank God you have returned to save us!" wailed another.

"Yooouuu WORMS!!!!" thundered Heydar from his seat. "YOU FAWNING FALSE DOGS AND SELFISH SELLOUTS!"

Silence reigned, and Heydar continued.

"The President of Azerbaijan has asked me to come to Baku in order to determine if there is any possible solution to the well-known problems that beset our country. IT IS A QUAGMIRE CREATED BY YOU, THE PO-LITICAL DILETTANTES AND DWARFS IN THIS HALL! But here you are again, in this lofty parliament, fawning on me and attempting to play political games! I WILL NOT HAVE IT! I AM NOT HERE TO PLAY! Now it is not time for words. ACTION IS LONG OVERDUE! . . .

"To begin with, I will repair to the city of Ganje within the hour. Alone! I ask the deputy chairman of parliament to provide the necessary transportation for all members of the press who wish to accompany me. Accordingly, I advise you to suspend this session of parliament until my return, at which point I will be able to comment on the Ganje disaster in an informed and reasonable manner. I have had my say."

Perhaps there was a vote to suspend the session until Heydar's return, but it is also possible that there was not. It didn't really matter: Heydar had put everybody on notice that nothing was going to happen without him. An hour later, the gleaming black Mercedes usually used by the chairman of parliament, but now free for Heydar's use, stood purring outside the deputies' entrance in the parliamentary parking lot. The exterior doors opened, and Heydar walked out. Next to him was Rahim Gaziev, whispering in Heydar's ear. An aid opened the back door of the Mercedes for Heydar. Then Rahim Gaziev jumped around to the far side and slid inside the car. Strange traveling companion for a man who had just declared that he would go to Ganje alone, but no matter.

I tapped on the window, and Heydar rolled it down an inch.

"What do you want?" he frowned.

"Just wanted to offer you a cold soda," I said, forgetting he only drank tea.

"Keep it," said Heydar. "You'll need it on the road."

Then the Mercedes was speeding toward Ganje—a five- or six-hour trip on an empty road in a car like that, a ten-hour trip for your basic Soviet machine. Then the press bus rolled up. It was a rickety piece of junk blowing blue exhaust. I got on with the other members of the hack-pack, but after about a kilometer or two, I made a calculation: Heydar would be back in Baku before the bus made it to Ganje; so I got off.

As it turned out, the only thing I missed was the long, excruciating ride and the look of outrage on Heydar's face when Surat kept him waiting outside a security door for 15 minutes. I got this interesting detail from Hicran, who happened to be in Ganje with a Turkish television crew when Heydar's Mercedes arrived. It was the first hint of a very worrisome notion that could be summed up like this: at first, many people were afraid of the implication of Surat being Heydar's man. Increasingly, the same people were terrified of the implications if he was not.

* * *

Heydar's absence from Baku was like a period of grace—two blissful days and a night without parliamentary sessions and accompanying press conferences. But once Heydar was back in Baku, the process began again. A new session was called for the 15th to pick up where the session of the 13th had left off—namely, discussion of the situation in Ganje. Heydar was to provide the assembled with his impressions. But there was also something more.

"We've got a deal!" crowed Mehmet Ali Bayar of the Turkish embassy when I got into his car for the drive up to the parliament.

"What's that?"

"Heydar—he has agreed to work with Abulfez. He was not impressed with Surat at all—he thinks he is a madman who must be stopped. So he has agreed to form a 'condominium' government!"

Abulfez stays as a sort of castrated president, and Heydar takes over day-to-day affairs? I didn't want to spoil Mehmet Ali's day by pointing out that the chairman of parliament was in effect vice president—and the next man in line, should something befall the president.

The gallery was overflowing and the floor filled with deputies and special friends with connections—like me and Mehmet Ali and Philip. We sat together toward the back of the hall in the VIP section, and surveyed the swamp. Every crocodile I had ever seen in Azerbaijan was there. Today was going to be very special day.

A beeper sounded in the corridor outside to call in stragglers; the registration and voting screens glowed. The steward tapped microphones and encouraged deputies to take their seats. Tamerlan Garayev, sitting in the place reserved for the chairman, adjusted his tie and cleared his throat. Next to him was the other deputy chairman, Afiyaddin Jalilov. Finally, in the position reserved for the chairman of the Naxjivan Assembly, or second deputy chairman, sat Heydar Aliyev.

Then, to the surprise of all and the consternation of many, a door opened behind the dais to reveal a lanky, almost bent figure hobbling toward the chair reserved for the head of state. It was Abulfez Elchibey. He sat down and stared over a sea of enemies in the parliament. He was so immobile, he almost looked doped.

Tamerlan took roll call and established the fact that there was indeed a quorum. Then he went over the agenda of the day. Not surprisingly, it started right where it had left off before Heydar's trip to Ganje—that is, with the selection of a new chairman of parliament due to Isa Gambar's sudden resignation.

"But what about discussion of the Ganje events and the criminal action of the government?! You are to give us nothing but poetry and lies!" shouted Yaqub ('Dollar') Mamedov. It was the first time he had been seen in parliament since May 14, 1992, and his presence suggested a last-ditch effort to scuttle the proceedings before Heydar's election. His next remark confirmed that suspicion. "I demand the convening of the full Supreme Soviet, the congress duly and democratically elected by the people of Azerbaijan!"

Rahim Gaziev seconded Mamedov's motion. Apparently, his ride with Heydar to Ganje and back had not gone well. There were some other procedural fights as well, but Heydar cut them all short.

"You ask for my impressions of my recent meeting with Surat Husseinov in Ganje," he began, his voice slowly rising into a roar. "But I did not go to collect information for discussion. You have already discussed for two days and created a commission of investigation! THE EVENTS HAPPENED ON THE FOURTH AND NOW IT HAS BEEN TEN DAYS YOU HAVE BEEN SITTING HERE, CHATTERING LIKE MONKEYS, WHILE THE COUNTRY FALLS APART!!

"I don't understand," he began again, modulating his voice. "If you want to choose a new speaker, I will stay; if you want to talk about Ganje, I will go. What can any of you say? You are all sitting here, none of you have gone to Ganje; how can you discuss anything? And now you expect me to announce a way out of the mess you have created! If the deputies want my help, I will help—if not, not! Action, not discussion! That is why I was invited here as the guest of the President of Azerbaijan."

Tamerlan Garayev waited until Heydar had said his piece, and then called for a vote about the 'need for more information through discussion.' The electronic response was a resounding No. Then he called for the second vote—whether the assembled deputies wanted to elect a new chairman. The answer was Yes, by a vote of 36 against two.

Even before Tamerlan could announce the official results, Bakhtiyar Vahabzade, poet laureate and unofficial nominator of many a chairman, spontaneously leapt to his feet—knowing full well he was being screened across the nation on TV.

"Colleagues, countrymen! Let us speak openly for once! We need an elder, not a child! The whole nation is waiting for Him! Let us not delay or sully our names by further discussion that can only weary the man who is, himself, the very essence and personification of this country, our beloved

Azerbaijan! Please accept my nomination, O! Heydar Alirizaovich, and lead us to peace, prosperity, and the happiness we deserve!!"

Vahabzade's use of Heydar's Russian patronymic was potentially embarrassing, but no matter.

Heydar was asked if he assented to being a candidate for the office, and he nodded that this was fine.

Proceedings were halted for another moment when Rahim Gaziev asked about Heydar's legal status—was he, as chairman of the Naxjivan Assembly, the deputy chairman of the 50-member National Parliament or of the prorogued 350-member Supreme Soviet? Although it was a good point and it could not have been asked by a better man, something must have really gone wrong in that car ride, because Rahim was virtually digging his own grave by questioning Heydar's credentials.

Tamerlan Garayev admitted that this was potentially a divisive issue. So that future generations would not quibble about the legality of Aliyev's election as chairman of the 50-member Milli Mejlis, the expeditious thing to do would be to expand the Mejlis by one member to 51, with a one-time rider to the bill that the new member be Heydar Aliyev.

"This is a disgrace!" declared another Mutalibov supporter. "Today it is 51. Why not make it 52 tomorrow and 53 the day after? Change the law every day, if you want!"

Yaqub ('Dollar') Mamedov then repeated his demand that the Mejlis be dissolved and the full Supreme Soviet restored—could not the deputies remember his fate? He was shouted down, and the deputies voted by 34 against 2, with 1 abstention, to expand their group by one member—Heydar.

Next it was time to vote for a new chairman. There were no surprises. Vahabzade once more nominated Heydar Alirizaogli Aliyev, and the candidate was asked if he accepted the nomination. He did. Were there any other nominees? There were not. Accordingly, Heydar was then asked to stand at the podium to deliver some general remarks about his vision of the future, and to allow his colleagues to publicly scrutinize him before casting their votes, Yea or Nay. He rose, walked over, and waited, but there were no questions, and so he sat back down. Then Tamerlan Garayev called for the voting. Of the 38 registered deputies, 34 voted for, three against, and one abstained. A great wave of applause rolled across the chamber as Heydar Aliyev stiffly made his way to the podium to give his acceptance speech.

"I think it appropriate that all stand and be silent in respect for our soldiers, dead and dying, on the field of conflict near Agdam," intoned Heydar for his opening words.

The hall and gallery complied, and when they sat down, Heydar began his remarks.

"I am here as the guest of the president of Azerbaijan to try and determine the causes of the Ganje events and the parties who were guilty in that criminal act. And I will—I promise you with a sacred oath that no matter who is found guilty, I will make them pay!

"In this sad and desperate situation, when our beloved country is falling into the vortex of civil war, I appeal to all Azerbaijani citizens, irrespective of ethnic origin, language, or religion, to cleave together for the sake of our common country and to pull back from the disaster of the internecine conflict we are now facing.

"Unlike others in this assembly, I have no ulterior motives. I am a slave of the people and totally disgusted with your childish political games that have resulted in so much blood.

"I call on Surat Husseinov and the men of the 709th and all the citizens of Ganje to listen to me. Cease and desist! Discontinue all further progress toward Baku! I ask you to hear me again: all those responsible for the Ganje disaster will be punished, no matter who they are."

So much was expected. What was not were Aliyev's references to Abulfez Elchibey as his 'host.' Nor Heydar's next barb: a sharp cut at the Mutalibov crowd.

"The last time I spoke in this august chamber, this living emblem of the will of the people, to offer my assistance for a way out of the horrible events of January 1990, I was spurned. My efforts were denied by the traitor Mutalibov and those associated with Moscow. Many of you here were there then, and will remember, and I would remind you to dwell on the results of that spurning—since then, our beloved country has devolved into war, with thousands of martyrs. . . ."

But Heydar was forgiving.

"Many things are said of me," he growled from the podium. "But I can say this from the bottom of my heart: vengeance is not in my character. If I have been wronged by anyone in this room, I have forgiven and forgotten long ago. . . ."

The speech went on for 30 minutes, as Heydar touched on virtually every aspect of Azerbaijani society. It was not boring; and unlike that of many Azeri speakers, his language was crisp and concise and easily understood by all. Finally, he summoned up his rhetoric toward a finale, and announced his undying devotion to Azerbaijan.

"Let there be no doubt about my purpose," he orated. "I will devote the time God has left me on this earth to protect the independence of Azerbaijan and promote the rule of law, democratic pluralism, the principles of universal human rights, and the development of a market economy!"

Philip Remler nudged me and winked.*

A great roar filled the hall, rising to a crescendo as Heydar returned to his seat. It was Mehmet Ali's 'Done Deal', and it had been an impressive performance.

"See how he slammed those commies? Comeback kid, my man!" said Mehmet Ali.

"Yeah," I said.

There was a short break, and so we made our way outside for some fresh air. Then, near the deputies' entrance, I noticed some activity. Heydar was escorting his host, Abulfez Elchibey, from the parliament to the awaiting presidential Mercedes. I rushed over to capture the moment on film, and was distressed but not surprised with what I found: a confused Abulfez, looking like a rabbit in a trap, and a very impatient Heydar, looking like a fox grown old on anger. No words were exchanged; the moment 'Fez was in the car, Heydar returned to the building, surrounded by a crowd of adoring deputies and a bank of cameras.

I knocked on the bullet-proof window of the Mercedes, startling Elchibey, who looked utterly lost and alone. Abulfez looked up and recognized me and Mehmet Ali Bayar. He smiled a strained smile and clasped his hands into a sort of victory salute. It was the sort of look a prisoner shoots the press as he drives off to the gallows. He had become so utterly marginalized that no one was even interested in his going.

"Some 'condominium' government," I said to Mehmet Ali.

He did not have a ready reply.

* * *

Two days after Heydar's election as chairman, Surat's rebels were within 30 kilometers of Baku—and nothing Heydar said seemed to stop their further advance. Surat was angry, Heydar would explain in live press conferences or from his new podium in parliament, Surat was not satisfied with the heads that had rolled thus far and was still insistent that Elchibey resign—or else.

The caravan of cars continued shuttling between Baku and Ganje, bearing the regular political personalities to Surat's court to plead, admonish, or beg him to stop his mutineers to desist from marching on Baku. And all of

---

*After the session, Philip ran into Heydar on the floor. 'Ty . . . ty!' he growled in Russian, shaking a finger in Philip's face. 'You—you are responsible!' It was not clear if he was being playful or deadly serious.

the missions always achieved the same result: agreement to desist, followed by noncompliance.

The most 'successful' of the emissaries was Etibar Mamedov, who got Surat to agree to stop his men marching on Baku for one week while a parliamentary commission of inquiry concluded a report about Elchibey's 'personal guilt' in the Ganje affair. At a press conference held to announce the deal, Mamedov said that Elchibey had agreed to resign if found guilty. Then he was obliged to admit that Surat had not agreed to accept a 'not guilty' verdict. The president was guilty of trying to disarm rebels in the land, or he was guilty of trying to disarm patriots who chose to disagree with the elected government with guns. Either way, he was guilty; there was no other verdict to be had.

My wickedly intelligent diplomat pal Philip Remler, chatting with Etibar's chief aide, suggested that by logical extrapolation, all the Azeri soldiers involved in Karabakh should stand trial for trying to disarm unruly Armenians. The man was not amused.

And Surat's unruly men just kept on humping toward the capital. By the 16th, they were right outside the city. More ominous still was that what passed for loyalist troops had begun openly fraternizing with the rebels. How many were already inside the city? When would the blood-bath begin?

Responding to the potential for violence and sending a very clear signal to Heydar that the Americans were not fools, Robert Finn floated a travel advisory for American citizens in Baku. Most were oilmen or their dependents, and there was an immediate exodus to Istanbul, Moscow, and even Kazakhstan.

The price of everything seemed to drop overnight—apartments, taxies, translators, and of course, women.

"What are we to do now?" cried Myra, the geologist-turned-whore one night to Philip, Robert, and me, the only men in the bar. I quoted her in a *Business Week* story about the putsch in progress, and she later thanked me for my attention to detail.

The girls of the Old Intourist bar may have been dancing alone, but their distress about the precipitous departure of the oilmen was shared by others. Heydar Aliyev took the security exodus as a personal affront, and demanded that Finn rescind the advisory.

"Nothing will happen to you here!" raged Heydar Aliyev to Robert Finn. "I am in complete control! I give you my guarantee!"

"Better safe than sorry," said Robert.

"Get those oilmen back!"

"Get the rebels out of the capital."

* * *

I was with a small group of foreign correspondents at a table at the Caravansaray restaurant, sipping warm champagne and eating crushed caviar, when Philip Remler finally arrived for a briefing.

"Tonight's the night," said Philip with a smirk.

"What do you mean?"

"I mean I am willing to take bets that there will be a coup d'état tonight."

"Got some inside information, do you?" one of the other journalists asked.

"No, just a report that the heads of the security ministries informed Elchibey that they would not stop Surat's advance."

"We have known that for the past week."

"Yes, but they have never said it officially before."

It was Thursday, June 17th. I went to bed wondering what would happen that night. An assassination? Suicide? What? In the morning, I called Philip.

"Good thing you didn't bet any money," he said.

Elchibey was gone. It was the day before the one-year anniversary of his inauguration as president.*

Aliyev's response to Elchibey's egress was quick—too quick, perhaps. At noon on Friday, June 18th, using his favorite medium, the television, Aliyev announced to the nation in a live broadcast that due to the 'sudden, inexplicable absence of President Abulfez Elchibey,' whose whereabouts he did not know, Heydar, as chairman of parliament, was obliged to assume all duties and responsibilities connected with the presidency of the republic, in accordance with the constitution of Azerbaijan.

The announcement may have been Aliyev's only slip. Within an hour of the declaration of Elchibey's flight from Baku, the president had been located. He may have become a fugitive, but he was still in Azerbaijan—and in the same obscure corner of the country which had served as Heydar's place of exile during his years of political occlusion: deepest, darkest Naxjivan.

"The president of the United States does not stop being the president when he travels to Alaska," said Foreign Minister Towfiq Gasimov in the emergency parliamentary debate later that same day. Robert Finn took the paradigm, and then went further.

"Forget about Alaska or even Hawaii," he said, "Bill Clinton is still the president if he goes to France or China—and the United States will regard

---

*Call it a hunch or call it paranoia, but I am convinced that the timing was hardly a coincidence. Given the obsession with symbolic dates in the neo-Soviet mind, Elchibey was not going to be allowed to celebrate his first year in office.

Elchibey as the president of Azerbaijan until he is unelected, wherever he may be."

Within hours, Heydar first retracted his claim to complete power and then renounced it entirely.

"The people elected Abulfez Elchibey president of Azerbaijan," he said. "I have nothing but the highest respect for their decision, and nothing but the highest respect for President Elchibey. But in return, the president must respect the people!"

By this Heydar meant that Abulfez had to return to Baku and assume his role as leader of the nation and commander in chief of the armed forces—or possibly face impeachment for dereliction of duty. The fact that Aliyev had been unable to halt the rebel advance on the capital by force of personality was never mentioned. The president must return, Heydar said. Our leader must come back.

This became Heydar's mantra, repeated ad nauseam in live broadcasts of the daily emergency sessions in parliament as well the daily, live press conferences that followed those sessions. It seemed to me that Heydar's technique was based on some previously unknown KGB brainwashing program inspired by the famous Chinese Water Torture, designed to exhaust the nation into accepting a coup by fait accompli, or maybe 'fait d'ennui'.

Each time the cameras came on, Heydar would reiterate the litany of events that led up to the current crisis. This was followed by his detailing his most recent contacts with Elchibey and Surat as well as his meetings with concerned foreign dignitaries. Inevitably, he would conclude with dire warnings about the deteriorating security situation in the land: there was a fresh Armenian attack in or around Karabakh, a new separatist movement brewing among the Talish, or political murders among the Lezgins. Heydar, of course, was not responsible for any of this—or for solving any of the sundry threats facing the state. It was the responsibility of the fugitive president to return to the capital and deal with the situation. Let Elchibey return and lead as he was elected to do.

The weirdest moment in this context was Heydar's announcement that Surat had laid claim to the power and authority of the presidential office itself. Heydar spelled out the logic of this for those who could not think for themselves: Heydar's reluctance to assume the prerogatives of the presidency had created a power vacuum that needed filling—and Surat would do so if Heydar would not. Heydar's response? If Elchibey did not want his powers usurped, then let him return and lead the country in its hour of need.

In retrospect, this little blip on the political polygraph may have been the first real indication that Surat was not Heydar's tool at all but belonged exclusively to Mutalibov and his supporters. At the time, however, Surat's claim to the presidency and Heydar's dodging the issue seemed to be just another part of the plan to debase and discredit Elchibey. The reason for this suspicion was due to Heydar's reluctance to say anything untoward about Surat Husseinov. Notably, he only used the word 'military putsch' once during the entire process—and then after I managed to drag it out of his mouth by a journalistic trick. The venue was parliament, and the occasion yet another press conference. As was the norm, local journalists were broadcasting their undying love and loyalty to Heydar, expressed in the form of spontaneous 'questions.'

Journalist from *Vyska* ('The Mirror'): "Oh Heydar Alirizaovich, is it true that your only reason for returning to the sacred motherland during its moment of greatest need is your selfless, undying devotion to our beloved nation now faced with the greatest crisis since the demise of our first republic, when our freedom and independence were crushed by Lenin, Stalin, and Beria?"

Heydar: "Well, I'm glad you asked that question, because in fact the only reason that I chose to return at this moment of greatest crisis (etc., etc.). . . ."

After the fifth or sixth question along these lines, I decided to liven up the session a bit. Specifically, I asked Heydar why he had labeled an attempt by the government to install its minister of the interior in Naxjivan in October 1992 a 'coup,' when he had consistently avoided using that word in connection with Surat Husseinov's march on Baku in 1993. It may sound pretty oblique to the average reader, but it created deafening silence in the chamber.

"I don't understand your question, Thomas," said a smiling Heydar, setting off a wave of nervous laughter through the room.

"Why have you not once used the word 'coup' in connection with Surat Husseinov and the Ganje affair?" I repeated.

"I still don't understand," he chuckled.

"*Coup*, you know, *coup*," I repeated.

"Well all right then," he said at last. "I stopped a coup in Naxjivan, and now I am trying to stop a coup by Surat Husseinov."

The exchange turned me into a household name throughout the country. People stopped me in the street to thank me for 'asking the question' and began whispering my name, learned from Heydar himself, when I would get into elevators or approach newsstands. Then came the announcement that I had just won the coveted if previously unheard of Osman Mirzaev Prize as Journalist of the Year, named after a man by that name who had served as Mutalibov's press secretary until he was killed in the November 1991 helicopter crash in Karabakh. This seemed either a first effort to suborn me or a last gasp of thanks from the soon-to-be-censored Baku press, which was rapidly walking into a long, dark night.

By late June, whole pages of newspaper text were whited out by self-censors when not blackened with the most obsequious odes to Aliyev. Here is a sample front-page news item in a late June edition of the Russian-language *Bakinets* newspaper. The exclamation points and capital letters are original.

"HE'S BACK!!! HE had to come back! HE, namely HE was needed in this hardest, most difficult period of our people. Namely HE, possessed of the rich experience of a great politician and leader, can lead the people out of the difficult military and economic situation in which it finds itself. The people (for the most part! . . .) have long dreamed of the return of Gaidar Aliev to the post of head of state. But this was blocked at every turn. In the beginning by Moscow, then by 'ours.' Certainly, the war would long ago have ended, thousands of young people would not have perished, the tragedy of Xodjali would not have happened, the accursed Armenians would not have been ceded Shusha, the enemy would not have captured Lachin and Kelbajar, as well as 450 villages of Azerbaijan. If only his return had not been blocked by, in their times, Vezirov and Mutalibov, if in her time Elmira Kafarova had given him her post. . . . HE is late, although still not too late. HE is still full of strength and energy to save his people, who deserve to be happy. . . ."

Television, when not broadcasting or rebroadcasting Heydar's most recent press conference, began replaying footage celebrating Aliyev's achievements as leader of Azerbaijan in the 1970s. These consisted of happy oil workers, happy peasants, happy citizens moving into big, happy housing projects, happy shoppers among shelves full of food. Typical of the upbeat programming was a retrospective on the building of the largest air-conditioner factory in the USSR, founded by Heydar. Typical of the more insidious material was a feature on the 52nd anniversary of Nazi Germany's attack on the USSR. It had been edited into a documentary about the perils of nationalism, stressing the many parallels between Adolf Hitler and Abulfez Elchibey.

The pillorying of the fugitive president reached its logical conclusion on the night of June 24th, when parliament voted to 'temporarily' bestow presidential authority on the chairman of parliament, Heydar Aliyev, pending the parliamentary commission report on the Ganje affair.

Significantly, it was Etibar Mamedov who played Judas in the scenario, having been given the honor of making the impeachment motion. Happily, his reward was utter public humiliation. Instead of the post of prime minister or even secretary of state, with the additional portfolios of foreign affairs, foreign economic relations, and oil due to his party's 'share' in the anti-Elchibey coalition, Mamedov had to content himself with the appointment of one of his deputies to the post of director of state television—and then listen to his pretensions of being the 'main opposition' in the land be destroyed by a smiling Aliyev.

"Resolving the crisis is not a matter of dividing authority among political parties," Heydar explained on national television. "I, too, have a political party. But I came to Baku representing only myself. And when I offered Etibar Mamedov various positions, it was not as the leader of a political party, but as a political personality. He says he leads the main opposition party in our country. But no one knows who the main opposition party is, because no elections have been held to determine such things."

Left out to dry, Etibar then tried to reclaim the moral high ground by refusing to participate in government because the new masters of Azerbaijan had come to power via an unconstitutional military coup. The cows, however, had long since left the barn. Rather than appear as the bearer of the torch of democracy and legality in Azerbaijan, Etibar looked so hypocritical as to be pathetic.

"Who sows the wind reaps the whirlwind," whistled Philip Remler, quoting Hosea.

* * *

And the Popular Front? The initial shock of the Ganje rebellion, Heydar's return, the ousting of Elchibey's men in government, and finally, the president's flight into exile left even the most ardent Elchibey loyalists deeply confused.

A few pathetic attempts to stage protest meetings were dealt with in a nasty and violent manner. A demonstration at the university was broken up by gunmen. When the handful of would-be protesters announced they would resume their action in front of the PF headquarters downtown, they discovered their way blocked by hundreds of policemen and soldiers. At a signal, the security men waded into the crowd, taking an almost sadistic delight in whaling away at demonstrators and passersby with nightsticks.

I can attest to this from firsthand experience. As I snapped pictures of a couple of plainclothes cops whacking away at some elderly woman, another knot of cops came over and demanded I give them the film. I declined, and a quick discussion ensued that went something like this:

"Kick out his feet," said one cop.

"Get him on the ground," said another.

"He's the guy who asked Heydar the Question," said a third.

"Oh, shit," I said to myself, getting ready for a good series of shots to the head and groin. Then suddenly, other cops joined the party.

"I'll take care of him!" announced one of the new arrivals, grabbing me by the collar and shoving me across the street.

"Thomas Bey," he hissed. "I know you from the Front! Take all the pictures you can, but take care!"

The assault petered out when the acting Minister of the Interior, Ravshan Javadov, arrived at the Front Headquarters to apologize. He claimed that he had not given the orders to stop the meeting, much less the orders to start the beating. Still, with the confidence kicked out of the hardcore enthusiasts, the rest of Elchibey's remaining supporters were then easily eliminated in a piecemeal fashion.

There were even moments of humor, like a press conference held by Secretary of State Ali Kerimli, Foreign Minister Towfig Gasimov, and Presidential Spokesman Arif Aliev, who took the occasion to announce that they were suspending their activities until Elchibey's return.

"The Ganje affair means the end of the rule of law in Azerbaijan," Kerimli said. "Power is now achieved not by creating political parties but by creating armed groups."

This was so obviously true that it seemed pointless to ask any questions. When no one did, a man at the back of the room got to his feet and informed us all that we had been attending an illegal press conference and should vacate the presidential building immediately, before he called on the guards to throw us out.

"Who are you?" demanded Kerimli.

"The newly appointed deputy head of the Committee for State Security is who I am," smiled the interloper, spelling out the Azeri acronym for KGB.

"And I am the secretary of state," Kerimli replied.

"I am afraid not," cooed the KGB man. "You were fired an hour ago, so get out."

So, while the secretary of state, the foreign minister, and the presidential spokesman were unceremoniously thrown out on the street without so much as a 'please pack your bags,' I slipped upstairs to see what Vafa Gulizade had to say about events today. I caught him replacing the obligatory portrait of Mamed Amin Rasulzade with one bearing the likeness of Heydar Aliyev. Vafa smiled sheepishly and shrugged.

* * *

Less funny was the growing 'This Is Your Life' treatment of Surat Husseinov in both the television and press. While instructive about the great mutual respect between Aliyev and Husseinov, most of the reporting missed some of the more worrisome details about the young warlord's life and times.

Indeed, as the newest and most resonant personality in Azerbaijan, with youth, wealth, and increasingly obvious ambition, coupled with an army behind him (and even the queer, religious resonance of being a *Seyid*, or descendant of the Prophet Muhammad) many were beginning to wonder whether the real showdown was really between Surat and Abulfez or even Aliyev and Elchibey, or between Husseinov and whoever stood against him—including Heydar Aliyev.

This was, in fact, how things eventually played out. But at the time, I regarded all reports of 'tension' between the two men as just another part of the convoluted game designed to distract attention from the main issue— namely, that democracy in Azerbaijan had been flushed down the toilet.

That moment—if there is any particular moment to focus on in the litany of political indecencies and outrages in Azerbaijan during the summer of 1993— came on the 30th of June, when Surat was elected prime minister. Nominated to the post by Heydar Aliyev, and voted in by his parliamentary peers, Surat's elevation into government seemed to negate the very idea of democratic pluralism, civil society, and the hope for anything other than crudity and violence in solving political problems in Azerbaijan. It was truly a day of shame.

I remember it well. Rather than join the other journalists in the second-floor gallery, I managed to squeeze into the lower chamber with the deputies and diplomatic observers. It was clear that something big was afoot, but no one would say exactly what, aside from vague mumbling about there having been 'hard bargaining' between Surat and Heydar about the young man's reward for having driven Elchibey away.

Then the doors opened and Heydar Aliyev strode out to the dais amid great applause. So much was standard. But then another door opened, and with an even greater flourish, bodyguards and gunmen entered the hall, clearing a sanitary corridor. It could only be for one man: Surat Husseinov. Indeed, a moment later, and to sickening applause, the young warlord entered the chamber to take his seat. Accompanying him were Rahim Gaziev and Nimet Panakhov. Roll call was taken, and the Chairman of Parliament and Acting President Heydar Aliyev began to speak.

The situation in the country was grim, he said. In addition to continued losses to the Armenian foe on the front, armed elements in the country were planning a campaign of destabilization. Unconfirmed rumors suggested that 18,000 automatic rifles had disappeared from armories on the day President Elchibey fled the capital. That remained the essential problem facing the nation. The president had fled, and the country needed a leader.

"Accordingly, I, as Chairman of Parliament of the Republic of Azerbaijan, have bowed to the will of the people, who desire leadership during these dark days. I am pleased to announce I have found a leader. In recognition of his great achievements in battle and his unique qualifications in the area of economics, I wish to nominate the deputy of the Supreme

Soviet, National Hero, Colonel Surat Husseinov, for the post of Prime Minister of our nation."

The applause was deafening, nauseating. And while the deputies stood and clapped, the nominee, so emotionless and stiff that he seemed drugged, walked to the podium. When the applause died down, he stood before the deputies, ready to inform them of his views before they formally voted him their leader.

It is an understatement to suggest that Surat was not challenged on any issue. The questions were perfunctory and dumb; the longest response delivered by the nominee concerned how he, as an interested party, would evaluate the pending parliamentary report on Elchibey's responsibility in the Ganje events.

"I know the report," snorted Surat. "He's guilty and should be tried for his crimes against the state."

This was an amazing statement, should anyone have cared to listen. The report was not even finished, much less published—and Surat claimed not only to know its content but was willing to pronounce the president guilty of treason for having attempted to defend the state. Due process, habeas corpus and all that be damned. Given all that had come before, it was hardly surprising that no one was listening to nuance or content. Nor was it surprising when Heydar Aliyev's candidate for Prime Minister was elected by his peers some moments later. As the voting figures flashed on the two giant screens behind Heydar, a tumultuous applause filled the chamber once more. Deputies and onlookers were on their feet, cheering wildly.

Then Heydar raised his hand and asked for silence.

"I would like to take this opportunity to congratulate Surat on his election to the vital role of Prime Minister," said Heydar. "And to show my confidence in the people's choice, I would like to announce that in addition to the weighty tasks that will face him in the development of the national economy, I have entrusted him with both the ministries of defense and internal security, where his prowess as a warrior is needed."

Prime Minister, Defense Minister and Minister of the Interior—all in one shot. For the 'wool merchant', it was probably his finest moment. But I saw something else.

The grand old man from Naxjivan may have been reborn as a democrat, but he still did not tolerate rivals: Surat had just been given a long and oily rope with which to hang himself. His victorious rebel forces, so successful in toppling a government that would not fight back, had just earned the right to go up against the most battle-hardened and fanatically motivated fighting force in the former USSR—the Armenians of Mountainous Karabakh.

23

Meanwhile, Back at the Front . . .

While politicians debated events in Baku, Azeri garrisons and settlements in the Karabakh conflict zone continued to fall. The national leadership appeared to be indifferent except in the way of using the attendant misery to gain political advantage against a rival.

Once again, *satkinlig*—or 'sell-outness'—was the word of the day, only this time, there was little doubt about the accuracy of the expression.

Not surprisingly, the idea of being used as pawns in a horrible game was nowhere more widespread than among the soldiers and civilians near the front. For them, the urgent matters discussed in parliament were an obscenity. This was certainly true in the case of the city of Agdam. Situated in the flats beneath the eastern lip of Karabakh, it had seen its share of violence before. But in the summer of 1993, Agdam earned a special place in the annals of Azerbaijani disasters. It was utterly forsaken.

The process began in June, when the Armenians, taking advantage of the political chaos in the capital engendered by Surat Husseinov, launched a new offensive. It was, as a matter of course, couched in terms of being only a 'defensive action,' which was so patently false that it would have been funny had the joke not involved just more death and destruction. No, it was not funny at all. Faced with Surat's rebellion, Baku was unable to send any relief to the city, for the very good reason that such relief would have to cross Surat's lines, and the rebels were seizing all the equipment they could get their hands on. The citizens of Agdam were obliged to fend for themselves. They did so, beating off attack after attack.

Then, following Surat Husseinov's promotion to Prime Minister, they begged the new government for relief. But for weeks, none was sent. It was as if the new government wanted the place to fall in order to blame it on the previous regime.

Amazingly, Agdam still held out. Reduced to slap-dash fixing of half-destroyed armor captured from the Armenians and cadging shells off the corpses of the fallen enemy, the defenders kept fighting while waiting for supplies that never came.

"They taught us about Stalingrad during the Soviet times," said our friend Yusuf Agayev. "But we learned about the reality of encirclement and an indifferent government on our own."

Yusuf was a friend who had seen more ugly action in the war than one would wish on an enemy. Schooled in the Soviet Republic of Kazakhstan in criminology, he had hearkened to the clarion call of Azeri nationalism in 1990, and was soon posted to the most dangerous and frustrating region of all. By title, he was the 'Chief Military Prosecutor of Mountainous Karabakh.'

In practical terms that meant that he was literally the last Azeri official to set foot in Stepanakert—namely, in the autumn of 1991. Next he moved to Shusha, and in May 1992 to Agdam. Somewhere along the line, the bulk of his dossiers changed from dealing with (Armenian) 'terrorists' to (Azeri) 'deserters.' There were rather more of the latter than the former, after awhile.

It was, as might be well imagined, an unimaginably difficult job. Not only was he obliged to deal with the families of deserters trying to bribe him into 'losing' documents, but he was also forced to try and get the goods on such unsavory personalities like Yaqub Mamedov ('Katir Mamed,' the 'Mule') whom he later arrested on charges of murdering other commanders.

Yusuf also kept a discreet book on the antics of the erstwhile Minister of Defense, Rahim Gaziev, who was even then developing a reputation for playing fast and loose with government money to be devoted to munitions. He also kept a jaundiced eye pointed in the direction of Gaziev's middle-man, the 'national hero,' and now Prime Minister, Surat Husseinov.

He applied himself to the task like the a post-Soviet Elliot Ness, fully aware that his work was being torpedoed at every stage of development. He was also cogently aware of the very real danger he was putting himself in by inquiring too closely into 'affairs of state.' It was not a happy job for someone so devoted to the concept of law as Yusuf Agayev was, especially in a lawless state like Azerbaijan.

Yusuf was not there on the day I arrived in the besieged city: he had been put out of action by severe shrapnel wounds in the arms and legs several days before. Apparently, he had incurred the wounds on the very front line, while trying to show an example to others of how to defend the homeland. Somebody had to do so, and the job fell to Yusuf. Then he got wounded and the bottom fell out of the defense of Agdam. Actually, it was not even clear if the city was still there when we were going to it. It had been when we had left Baku—but that had been five hours before, and that is a lot of time in a fluid and nasty situation.

A colleague from Moscow, John Lloyd of the *Financial Times*, had popped up in Baku to do a postmortem on the putsch and had come over to my house for coffee and a chat. Then some serious news came in: according to one of the local news agencies, the Armenians were attacking Agdam with jets, fighter bombers, 'dozens' of attack helicopters, and lots and lots of armored vehicles on the ground. There had been 'hundreds' of casualties.

According to the agency, Agdam had fallen, or was falling, or was about to fall. Elements of this had crept on to the BBC via Reuters, resulting in the cancellation of the most recent OSCE/Minsk Group peace-seeking mission led by the Italian mediator Mario Rafaeli.[1]

Agdam invested? It was possible. But I did not like the sound of all the aerial weaponry the Armenians were said to be employing. They had never done so before. What was even more suspicious was Reuters' source—the local news agency. I called them and asked what *their* source was. They said it was the Defense Ministry. I called my friend Mustafa at the information section and he said he had heard the city had fallen. What was his source? The same news agency.

Smelling a rat, I called up Vafa Gulizade and told him that I was going out to Agdam, but that as he was my friend, I would appreciate a security report from the highest level before departing so I would know what I was walking into—like death.

"When are you leaving?" Vafa asked.

"Ten minutes," I replied.

He called back in five.

"It is not true that Agdam has fallen," he said. "But the situation is bad. Don't go."

"Ready?" I asked John Lloyd.

"Let's hit the road," he said in his heavy Scottish brogue.

* * *

We arrived at dusk, and approached the city through a mass of people camping along the road. Refrigerators, stoves and beds were scattered everywhere under the trees, and transportation ranging from donkey carts to road-graders was bringing up more.

Then we passed armor moving the wrong way and by the time we pulled up in front of the main mosque in the town I started to feel that familiar tug of fear on the guts that says you've gone too far. Lloyd and I were standing there in the street when two GRAD rockets slammed into a house a couple blocks away. Then a heavy machine gun opened up in the near distance.

I looked at Lloyd and he looked at me. Then we did one of those stupid things that people do in dangerous situations: we each waited for the other to suggest we get out. Neither of us did, and before we knew it, the taxi was gone. Although the driver was from Agdam and had spoken bravely and heroically all the way out from Baku, once inside his hometown, he changed his tune.

"It's not about myself that I am concerned," he pleaded. "It's the car! What if something should happen to my car? How will I live? How will I provide for my children? Let's go, please! Or you stay and let me go! I'll wait for you at the twenty-kilometer point. . . ."

"Let's take a look around," I suggested to Lloyd with a confidence I did not feel, and so the taxi left us.

We walked the few blocks to the municipal building in the center of town, pretending we were not afraid—or at least to each other. When we arrived at the mayor's office, we learned that our pretenses to one another were absurd. Everyone there was trembling.

The Armenian forces, the mayor reported, were within a kilometer of downtown. Without immediate reenforcements, there was no way the city could hold—and Baku had sent in only a couple of dozen kids without guns. Typically and pathetically, the reenforcements had immediately run away after the first GRAD had slammed in nearby—and there was no Yusuf Agayev to stop them.

Rockets were now falling in our general vicinity, and I suggested to Lloyd that we go outside: the building we were sitting in was an obvious target. Someone from the mayor's office offered us a ride to the relative safety on the eastern edge of town. We accepted. But once there, I started feeling thirsty. That is the only way I can explain it. I didn't want to run away, but I needed a drink to stay. So, rather than join the exodus and find our fearless taxi driver at the 20-kilometer mark, we asked to be dropped at an alfresco restaurant, where we ordered up some pickled food and a bottle of vodka.

Lloyd can tell his own version of what happened next, but I suspect it will conform with mine. We sat there, hands trembling a little less with every toss of the warm spirits, watching shells fall on a panorama of villages to the south and to the north of where we sat. It was abundantly clear what the Armenians were doing—enveloping the city, but leaving a last egress through which soldiers, refugees, and outside observers (Lloyd and me) might flee.*

---

*My friend Alexis Rowell of the BBC, traveling with Anatol Lieven of the *Times*, was even then recording one of his classic broadcasts. It began: 'I am walking behind an Armenian tank toward Agdam. . . .'

But Agdam had not fallen—not yet, anyway. And neither had we. Aided by the bottle of vodka we had slurped down to steady our nerves, Lloyd and I decided that there was really no reason, aside from losing our lives to a stray shell, why we should not spend the night. So we returned to city center and the mayor's office.

"Got a phone?" I asked someone. It was a slim chance, but we might get through to Baku to tell someone we were still alive.

"All the operators have run away," said our host. "But let's take a look at the exchange."

There was a blackout in the city, but we managed to find our way to the telephone exchange and then broke in, entering a room covered with a mass of sparking, tingling wires. Despite taking a hit in the roof earlier in the day, the place was still on-line.

"What the hell," said Lloyd. "Let's try Moscow."

Our man managed to procure an operator's head-gear and a dial box. Selecting a couple of likely looking wires, he pinched the alligator clips open and locked them into place. Blue sparks flew. A dial tone sounded. Then, with a pleasant, if distant click, John Lloyd was on line with his Moscow office and I got to listen to one side of an amazing conversation.

"Hello? *FT?*" he asked nonchalantly, referring to the *Financial Times*. "This is Lloyd with a dictation. In Agdam. Yes, Agdam. No, no—it has not fallen, at least not yet. Yes, Agdam—that is where I am. I don't care what others are reporting. So please take this down, now, because we don't know when they will blow up this building. . . ."

He then dictated a comprehensive story about the immediate situation, including excellent background information on the crisis in Azerbaijan. I think he paused once to check the spelling of the name of the Agdam mayor with me; he did not have a note in front of him, although he dictated for half an hour.

* * *

We wore our boots to bed that night. Our abode was that of a young man who was once a international sailor who had come back home to defend his city. I forget his name. But I do remember that he complained bitterly about the lack of any sort of government aid, reiterating the familiar charge that Baku actually wanted Agdam to fall to the Armenians as 'evidence' of the incompetence of the Elchibey government.

It was an interesting argument based in real-life conspiracy. But that government was already gone—and Surat appeared to have little interest in saving a place that had shown loyalty to the previous regime. Agdam, like so many Azeri places before it, was doomed.

In the morning, we woke to a breakfast of tea and fresh eggs. Tuning in to the BBC, Lloyd and I learned that Agdam had fallen. We thought we might take a poke around before it really did.

Agdam might not have fallen, but it sure was a ghost town. The guest-house I had stayed in before was vacant, as was the hospital that had borne the burden of the Xodjali survivors 18 months before. Aside from a few wailing women, the mosque was empty and the morgue unattended. Near the old Popular Front headquarters, long since abandoned, sheep were feeding on the fresh leaves of a large tree smashed down by a rocket the night before. The only real resident we encountered was a babbling madman. He said he would never leave. As I say, he was mad. I was tempted to suggest a jaunt out to the old cemetery and Post 19 for memories' sake, but upon reflection that did not seem like a very good idea. There was still a war on, and not very far away.

One thing was perfectly clear, however: the Armenians might be half a kilometer from city center, but they would never get any closer if anyone actually put their mind to defense. With a little help from Lloyd, I could have held the place myself. There were simply too many trees, gardens, and walled compounds from which a handful of defenders could wreak havoc on the advancing force. But there was no organization to speak of.

"Well, do you want to wait around for the evening assault?" I asked Lloyd.

"I think the evening flight back to Baku sounds like a better idea," he said.

* * *

It was a long, sad summer. First Agdam fell, then Fizuli, then Jibrail and Gubatli. Again, the Armenians claimed they were merely responding to 'massive Azeri offensives.' The only Azeris I saw massing for attacks were refugees, assaulting boxes and bags of international aid. There were lots of them. By late August, the total number of displaced people in Azerbaijan was close to one million.

Then, the new government managed to outdo itself in the way of Milo-style, *Catch 22* corruption. Encouraged by yet another United Nations Resolution condemning 'local Armenian aggression,' Baku decided to take its begging bowl to New York to ask for additional aid.

The request, made by former Premier and future Foreign Minister Hasan Hasanov, was personally presented to the UN Secretary-General, Boutros Boutros-Ghali. It contained the following list of items for the 200,000 displaced persons from the Agdam region: 40,000 tents; 200,000 blankets; 200,000 sheets; 200,000 pillow slips; 200,000 bedspreads; 200,000 towels; 59,000 sleeping-bags; 60,000 mattresses; 100,000 items of 'children's clothing'; 100,000 items of 'adult clothing'; 200,000 pairs of footwear; 40,000 heaters and 40,000 electric irons. There were also line items for forks, knives, and spoons (80,000 apiece), as well as thousands of tons of flour, milk powder, meat, and macaroni.

"Forty thousand electric irons for refugees living in tents?" said the UN representative in Baku, showing me the list. "Maybe they should have specified that the pillow slips be pink and embroidered! I have never seen such audacity and gall!"

* * *

While the Azeri leadership could be mean and cheap and nasty, the real audacity and gall was to be found thriving among the Armenians. Time and again, defense was the argument put forth to justify offense. It was transparent but it worked, and the pattern was almost always the same: the OSCE/Minsk group would call a meeting; the Karabakh Armenians would declare themselves to be under massive attack. Then, remarkably, the Armenians would turn the tables on the Azeri 'aggressors' and expand their 'defensive' perimeter. This was always into areas well outside the official frontiers of Mountainous Karabakh—and ever closer to the red line on Armenian maps that defined areas of 'traditional Armenian settlement.' The problem was that however traditionally Armenian the areas may have been in a historic sense, they had been inhabited by others, who were now obliged to clear out or die. 'Ethnic cleansing' is the word usually used for this sort of activity elsewhere, and I see no reason not to use it here. I saw enough of it on the hoof, anyway. And it was always the same.

From a distance, they looked like a caravan of Gypsies on the move to a rural flea market or county fair. Beat-up cars, piled high with rugs, pots and pans, clanking down the road on wheels with no rubber on the rims. Smoke-belching trucks overloaded with mattresses and steel bed frames, trying to pass tractors pulling wagons designed to contain tons of cotton but filled with clothes, dirty children, and squawking ducks. The rear was usually brought up by men riding donkeys or leading mule-drawn carts, while on the shoulder of the road, barefoot shepherds were to be seen, dodging in and out of the traffic to keep sheep and cows and oxen out of harm's way. The only thing disturbing the image of a Gypsy caravan on the move was the heavy construction equipment, such as cranes and road-graders, enlisted to carry refrigerators and stoves.

It was an Azeri exodus, another one.

All along the 100-mile stretch of highway along the Iranian border, from the town of Imishli to Zengelan on the Armenian frontier, tens of thousands of people were on the move.

"What did we do to deserve this?!" wailed a 55-year-old shepherd named Bakish Kerimov, describing how an armored column of two tanks and an APC backed by scores of soldiers attacked his village in Gubatli province while a cease-fire was allegedly in effect. The Armenian forces then began looting and burning what they had captured: black plumes of smoke threaded up through the distant sky, denoting an obscure place-name on a map that had become a charred cinder.

"We had little before, but now we have nothing but the animals we got out and the clothes on our backs."

Bakish Kerimov did not leave his village until the day it was attacked and was thus unable to collect his belongings and secure transport away. But other internal refugees were wiser and evacuated early because they had been told to clear out by units that were planning to retreat or desert.

The result was a strange leapfrog movement that gathered momentum and mass at each stage of displacement. Typically, the locals would try and stay about 15 miles from their last camp, always hoping that the next day they might return. But by late August, the leapfrog movement had turned into a panicked exodus as previously displaced people were joined by tens of thousands of others who had remained in their homes until the last minute. Now all were refugees. In one settlement I visited, pitched up along a miasmic, brown irrigation canal just north of the Araxes River, an angry crowd of around 300 people told me what had happened.

"The soldiers came around and told us we had to leave!" wailed Nigal Shirinova, a mother of five. "We didn't know if the Armenians were coming or whether the soldiers just wanted us to go so they wouldn't have to defend us."

Another resident, a welder on a collective farm, expressed his rage and frustration with the government by suggesting that everyone in parliament should be shot—a sentiment with which I generally agreed.

"We have been utterly sold out by the thieves and scoundrels in Baku," he shouted. "I no longer believe in anyone or anything in this godforsaken country!"

The camp, already redolent with the odor of human excrement, had been in existence for a week. Residents were quickly going through the food-stuffs they had managed to salvage. The government had sent nothing in the way of relief; all the displaced folks I spoke with told me that any interna-tional aid would be or already had been diverted into the shops owned by officials in Baku.

I got pretty tired of the road south.

First it was on my own, then it was with a junket arranged by the foreign ministry to show foreign dignitaries the plight of the refugees. Then it was to check out the Armenian-sponsored rumor that Iranian soldiers were massing on the frontier, and then again to determine the truth about the claim of yet another Azeri news agency that the critical town of Huradiz (Guradiz) had fallen. So I went there and discovered that the town had not fallen (yet), and reported it as such. It was almost a matter of indifference, because no one cared what the truth was about Azerbaijan, not even the Azeris themselves.

My traveling companion on the last trip was Captain Tom Moody, the new American defense attaché at the US embassy. He called me one day, expressing frustration that the government was not giving him permission to travel to the sort of places military-like guys like to go—like the collapsing front.

"So, what do you want from me?" I asked.

"Please, take me with you the next time you go."

This was a change—the diplomat asking the journalist for a little tag-along action. Usually, the roles were reversed, with the lowly journalist having to beg for a quote or off-the-record reference to hang a story on, as if we hacks had no brains or eyes or ears ourselves: 'Western sources, however, suggest that the offensive. . . .'

As chance would have it, I did have a little trip planned. More to the point, the usual minders from the Defense Ministry Information Department, while keen on having the most recent Armenian assault reported, were reluctant to accompany me due to the level of threat. They phrased this a little differently, of course: they 'trusted' me to go where I wanted, and on my own—and gave me generic permission papers should anyone bother to ask who I was. Because it could get a little lonely in hell, I thought that Captain Moody's presence might break the monotony of my pending trip to the nasty places. Also, I thought he might be able to give me a few military-style insights along the way.

"Moody," I said, returning his call. "Be ready to travel in half an hour."

"Where are we going?"

"Zengelan," I replied.

It was a dumpy little town near Zangezur, the Armenian salient that separated Azerbaijan proper from Naxjivan. Baku had announced that it had fallen that same day.

"Shit," said Moody upon hearing the name.

"It's your big chance to get shot at, soldier boy."

"Pick me up, could you?"

* * *

There was chaos up and down the road. Some things, like the first group of 50 deserters we ran into, spoke for themselves.

"Where are you going?" I asked a guy who seemed to speak for the rest.

"Baku!"

"Why?"

"To throw these useless weapons on the steps of the defense ministry!" he cried. "We can't fight tanks with Kalashnikovs!"

That was outside Huradiz, the town that had reportedly fallen three days before. It was pretty empty, all right, but still in Azeri hands—though not for long.

Chatting our way beyond the main sentry post on the trunk road, we sought out the commanding officer of the Huradiz region to get travel permission or at least to register ourselves as something other than spies. We found him in a fly-infested room in a building that once had been the local hospital. I either did not note the commander's name or he was unable to pronounce it, because he was dead drunk. It was his birthday, and the commander and all his NCOs were knocking back shot after shot of vodka.

"A toast, a toast! To the bravest and most intelligent commanding officer in our national war against the loathsome Armenians. . . ," cried one junior officer.

"Hrpmph. . . ," belched the boss.

It was not a pretty sight.

Meanwhile, back on the front—meaning about a mile away—the men who had not deserted remained hunkered down in shallow trenches, hungry and cold. I know this because after getting drunk with the officers, we asked and received permission to visit the front lines with the brigade's political officer. After he lectured them about bravery and commitment and love of motherland and all that, the PolOf let me ask the boys a generic question.

"Who are you?" I asked each and every one.

Most were local farmers or the sons of farmers, with the odd mechanic thrown in for vocational spice. None had any body armor or radio gear, and bullets for their Kalashnikovs seemed in short supply.

Then a couple of GRADs flashed through the sky, and we decided it was best to let the lads fend for themselves, and we returned to the headquarters again to find all the other officers completely zonked on birthday vodka, including the commander.

"This is insane," said Captain Moody, summing up the situation. He was less and less happy about having come along for the ride to nowhere.

We slept in a dumpy room in the headquarters that night and woke up before any of the other officers. While I made coffee, Moody wrote his notes about the disposition of the Azeri forces we had seen the night before. How he could write more than 'the situation is chaotic' I do not know, but as an artillery specialist, presumably he had seen things that I had not.

Then, around eight o'clock, a number of APCs rumbled toward the HQ building, and Moody went to work again, scribbling away. I asked him what was so interesting about four or five APCs under a tree. His comments were of interest.

The drivers of the APCs had parked their vehicles in one solid bunch, he explained. Doing so may have made for easier conversation among the drivers—but one well-placed rocket could have destroyed them all.

Moody gave me some other tips about weaponry. One was about the accuracy and destructive power of the GRAD versus normal field artillery. I'll take the latter. Next he took me on a tour of Soviet armor, and explained the nuanced differences between different types of BTRs, BMPs, and tanks. One thing I remember quite clearly was his warning to watch out should I ever try and load a shell in a T-72. The loading mechanisms were tricky and resulted in a lot of lost fingers, hands, and even arms. Also, the Soviet war industry believed in lots of forward gears, but only one reverse. If you wanted to retreat, he advised, turn the tank around and then flee. Paging through one of his NATO-issue guidebooks to Warsaw Pact equipment, I was surprised to learn that all the heavy armor was supposed to be able to swim across rivers and lakes like hippopotami, with a snorkel stuck above the surface for air. Once again, Moody advised me against trying the amphibious trick, because the sink-rate was unacceptably high. . . .

It was just starting to get fun and interesting when Moody announced his intention to return to Baku. He had seen enough, he said, and his brief did not include getting shot at. I tricked him into going ever further down the road, to Zengelan, by swearing to him that I had been told the place was still in Azeri hands. Actually, no one had told me that, but what the hell. . . . I also neglected to tell him that everything west of Imishli was a 'Phase Four' area in UN security jargon, which is why we had seen a few international refugee watchers to the east of that line, but not west of it—UN personnel and those working under UN contract were barred from Phase Four zones due to the level of danger.

I don't think Captain Moody begrudged me my misrepresentations. It was an interesting trip for him. He kept on scratching down notes for his Department of Defense super secret report, anyway. he saw what i saw, so here is my super secret report written especially for you, dear reader.

We crossed the invisible security line and moved up the Araxes Valley toward Zengelan, about fifty miles away at the very end of a long, narrow salient of territory. To the south and across the river was Iran, usually about a mile or two away. To the north were the Armenian lines, usually about three to five miles away. We were like steers in a chute, should anyone have wanted to brand us.

And there didn't seem to be anyone defending the front. We saw plenty of artillery pieces standing around, but without shells. A vital crossroads was being protected by a huge and almost immobile 180mm field gun—a great weapon for lobbing big shells on a distant enemy, but not exactly what you wanted in an up-close brawl with a mobile foe. The only soldiers we saw were trundling up and down the main highway in the backs of trucks, and going in both directions. We suspected that those trucks driving toward us were filled with deserters, but could not be sure.

"This is not a national army but a national flock," said the self-deprecating NCO tasked with driving us halfway down the road to Zengelan. He was playing with the words *ordu* and *ord*, which are the Turkic and Russian words meaning 'army' and 'large number of sheep'. The English word 'horde' (as in the 'Golden Horde') derives from both.

It was true. There was no army here, only knots of frightened and frustrated men with guns. The Armenians could have severed the road in a thousand places, any time they pleased. My suspicion for the reason they did not was the same logic that applied to Kelbajar, Agdam, and elsewhere: they wanted to flush the region of civilians by timely pressure, thus avoiding the need for another unnecessary Xodjali-style massacre. Once it was emptied of people, they could just walk in.

That strategy appeared to be working. Most of the civilian population in the area had fled, leaving behind the familiar detritus of refugees everywhere: empty houses, abandoned cats and dogs, broken televisions and busted suitcases discarded along the roadside; socks and underwear and shirts blown into bushes and the branches of trees, and then just lots and lots of dented pots and pans and other instant debris. Of the refugees themselves, there was scarcely a trace: a thin stream of sheep and shepherds trudging toward us were the only human beings to be seen, apparently the last to leave their homes and farms, or at least the slowest, due to the livestock. Bloated carcasses lined both sides of the road, left where they had been hit by vehicles. Some sheep (or dogs or cows or cats, it was not readily clear) had been reduced to thick patches of hair on the pavement, crushed into paste by retreating wheels.

Yes, the Armenians had managed to flush another corner of Azerbaijan clean of Azeris. With one exception: the plucky residents of Zengelan. They refused to budge, although everyone around them had fled. The result was that the 5,000 or so citizens of the town found themselves at the far end of a reverse cul-de-sac that was closing at the open end.

Upon our arrival, we asked for directions to the mayor's office both to announce ourselves and to try and get some hard information about the situation. To my surprise, I discovered the mayor's office occupied by Abbas Abbasov, the deputy prime minister. He was a man I associated more with shady dealings in Central Asian agricultural products than frontline war work.

"Abbas Bey," I exclaimed. "What the hell are you doing here?"

"I might ask the same question of you, Thomas Bey," he replied. "And who is your companion?"

"Captain Moody of the United States Army," replied the defense attaché.

"Good, good," said Abbas. "At least there will be a record of this disaster somewhere."

As for his presence in Zengelan, Abbas explained that Heydar Aliyev had gathered his ministers and asked for a volunteer to go make an assessment of the situation. Not one hand was raised. Then the new Secretary of State, Lale Hadjieva (reportedly Heydar's former mistress), announced that she would go if the men were too afraid.

"This, of course, was unacceptable to my honor, so I volunteered instead," said Abbas.

And he had made his assessment: immediate evacuation of the town. But no one would go.

"I even managed to bring a train through to the Iranian border and invited everyone who wanted to leave to get out," he explained. "They told me that a month from now, anyone who flees will be dying of hunger and disease in a refugee camp, and that that is just a more humiliating way of death. They all decided to stay, which means that I have to stay here, too."

The train had gone back to Baku the day before. Now, if the Armenians attacked, all those remaining in the town faced either the prospect of swimming the Araxes river to neighboring Iran or defending their town. But the townsfolk were insistent: they preferred annihilation, especially if their deaths would finally bring 'world attention' to Armenia's 'insatiable lust for more territory.'

"You have to draw a line somewhere, even if it is over your own grave," said Ms. Zoe Jebrailova, the counselor on humanitarian affairs in the Zengelan mayor's office. "To leave now is to hand our homes to the Armenians on a platter, and we have no intention of doing that. Don't the Armenians understand that there is no end to this? We are condemned to live as neighbors. We will stay until they kill us. Let them kill us! But tomorrow, next year, ten years from now, the people of Azerbaijan will be back to reclaim their own."

These were brave words from a little lady, but they didn't help much. We met in her office as a cease-fire was breaking down and the first incoming GRADs were hitting the outskirts of town.

Moody wanted to go and so did I, and so we did—traveling right back down the length of a 50-mile-long front that was five kilometers wide at its widest point. The problem was getting any transportation. We must have cut a pretty odd sight, if there had been anyone around to see and appreciate it: two Americans, one the defense attaché, trying to hitchhike on the odd car still in these parts.

Once back in Baku, I called Abbasov to see what had happened after we left. Remarkably, he was still there—and the Zengelan salient held out until October. Then, a group of Afghan mujahideen brought into the sector decided to launch a *jihad* against the Armenians. Sadly, the Azeri command—our birthday boy?—did not back them up, and the Armenians hit back hard, rolling all the way to the Iranian frontier, and pushing anyone left in the region into the river. Tens or scores or hundreds of new refugees were said to have drowned, depending on which reports you chose to believe.

I thought about Ms. Zoe Jebrailova and hoped that she was one of 100,000 Azeris being fed, clothed, and brainwashed in refugee camps run by the Islamic Republic of Iran.

Nobody else seemed to care.

Note

1. This resulted in an 'amusing' sidebar on the trials and travails of diplomacy. After canceling his OSCE mission on the basis of the spurious Reuters report, CSCE chief Mario Rafaeli did come to Baku to pick up the pieces of the Karabakh 'peace' negotiations. An essential part of this was contacting the authorities in Stepanakert. The usual way in was via the road from Agdam. But the Karabakh Armenians were obliged to inform the OSCE negotiator that all roads were mined, and that access via Agdam was impossible (although the mines did not seem to hinder Armenian tanks and other vehicles). Accordingly, Rafaeli asked Heydar Aliyev if it would be okay to violate protocol and fly into Karabakh via helicopter, albeit from Georgia. No problem, said Heydar. The group, now including UN special ambassador to Azerbaijan, Mahmoud Al Said, flew to Tbilisi by plane, where they picked up two military helicopters for the trip to Karabakh. Alas! the choppers 'ran low on fuel' en route to Stepanakert and were obliged to put down in Yerevan for refueling—after which they continued on their way.

Rafaeli and his party, including Al Said, were furious: they had been duped into making their visit to Karabakh via Armenia, and not Azerbaijan. This was an incredible diplomatic faux pas. Nor was the fun over. The Karabakh leadership then announced that the 'terms of disengagement' they had previously signed had to be vetted by the people of Karabakh in a referendum. Fine points like the definition of 'heavy' and 'light' weapons had to be gone over again. . . . When at last it was time to go, the diplomats got aboard their choppers—only to discover that the Russian pilots had been selling seats to locals who wanted a lift back to Yerevan. And the pilots had spent the waiting hours fraternizing and drinking booze. On takeoff, one escort helicopter plowed into a fence and crashed, forcing the entire mission to spend the night in Stepanakert.

Azerbaijani troops heading up Murov Pass, toward Kelbajar and Karabakh.
(T. Goltz)

In the rubble of Agdam High School. (O. Litvin)

Azeris abandon their homes in the Fizuli region during an Armenian counter-offensive in the summer of 1993. (T. Goltz)

Fleeing the summer 1993 Armenian counter-offensive in the Agdam/Barda region.

In Kelbajar: wounded soldiers wait for evacuation. (T. Goltz)

A helicopter resuce operation in Kelbajar. (T. Goltz)

Villagers in Geranboy/Shaumyan region attempt to save their burning homes. (O. Litvin)

A young soldier carries the body of a dead child over the Murov Pass from Kelbajar. (T. Goltz)

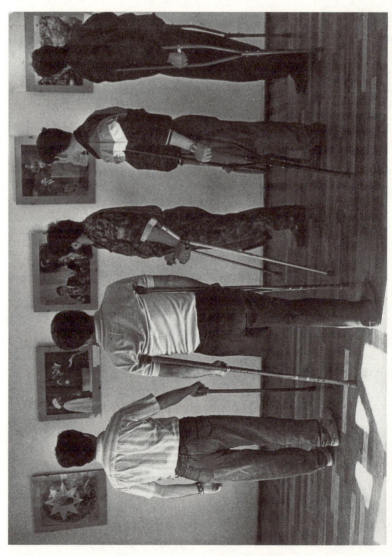

Back in Baku. Veterans at an exhibit of photographs by Goltz and Litvin on Nation Day, May 28, 1993. (O. Litvin)

24

Azerbaijan, Azerbaijan. . .

In late July, the Chairman of the National Assembly of the Republic of Azerbaijan and Reinvigorator of the Extraordinary Powers of President of the Republic* asked the Deputies to the National Assembly of the Azerbaijani Republic to call for a Popular Referendum on the Attitude of the People about the Future Status of the Self-Occluded President. Translation: Heydar Aliyev wanted parliament to give him the legal means of removing Elchibey.

Heydar himself, of course, had no position on the matter of Elchibey's future status. As a democrat, he would go along with any verdict made by the people.

He did have some commentary, however.

"If the people want Elchibey as their president, let him return. If the people do not want him, let him go!" declared Heydar from his parliamentary podium. "I have spoken with him often and begged him to come back—but he says he is afraid. I told him I guaranteed his security. He still refused. So I told him 'if you are to be killed, die like a hero,' but he has not listened. . . ."

So, Heydar floated the idea of a referendum, parliament accepted it, and the date was set for August 29, 1993. At first blink, it pleased everybody—even the American State Department. Still, while a referendum may have been democracy in action, it was instantly clear what the result would be—a popular ousting of Elchibey and an effective legitimization of the June 4th putsch, unsavory Surat Husseinov and all. Stuck with issuing vague statements of support in principle for 'democratically elected lead-

---

*In Azeri, the mouthful was: *Azerbaijan Respublikasi'nin Milli Mejlis'in Sedri ve Respublika'nin President'in Silahiyetlarini Hayata Gecerin Heydar Alirizaogli Aliyev.* Robert, Philip, and I began calling him the 'Invigorator' (*Hayata Gecerin*) for short.

ers,' most western governments got ready to hold their collective noses and accept the inevitable—although few wanted to appear to *sanction* the voting by sending observers.

"We don't like to think about our role in this business very much," admitted Robert Finn on the eve of the trust vote. "It is difficult to explain to the government why we are not sending observers to ensure a clean result, when the referendum was our idea in the first place."

* * *

Still, Finn and others had a good point: while Elchibey may not have been the most popular man in the land, there was really no need for the gratuitous humiliation he was subjected to day after day in parliament. Heydar had turned the daily sessions into a sort of real-life *David Letterman, Live!* scum-slinging forum, broadcast on prime-time television.

In addition to such regular Ed McMahon–like fences as Rasul Guliyev ("No foreign leader wanted to meet with him! He was an embarrassment to all!") and Rahim Isazade ("The people of Ganje can never forgive him chasing Tamara around all night!"), there were any number of special guests whose spontaneous remonstrations pushed things from the painful to the grotesque.

One day, Heydar recognized Nimet Panakhov, who used his five minutes of fame to accuse Abulfez Aliev (detractors studiously avoided using his taken name of Elchibey) of being an Armenian agent and the son of an Armenian agent. Another time, Heydar recognized a man by the name of Nadir Agayev, who hust 'happened' to be sitting in the visitor's gallery.

"Ah, Nadir Bey! What are you doing here? Want to have a word or two to the nation? Come on up!" said Heydar. A shabbily dressed and nervous little man stepped forward toward the podium, and as he advanced, Heydar continued his introduction in a public aside.

"*He he*," he chuckled into the microphone, as if it were not there. "This is a *real* dissident. I know because I locked him up for anti-Soviet crimes in my day as party boss in the 1970s! Let's see what he has to say. . . ."

Nadir was the chairman of something called the Azerbaijan Human Rights Defense Committee, an organization I had never heard of before. From the dais, he detailed his sufferings for Azerbaijani nationalism and human rights through the years. He shared his views with the deputies and the television audience, finishing his performance with the confession that real dissidents like himself had always regarded Elchibey as a KGB plant in the dissident movement, sent in to destroy it from within. . . .

Heydar Aliyev smirked knowingly, as if confirming the notion that he had been Elchibey's KGB handler in the bad old days. It was so disgusting, it was almost delicious. It also was more than a little odd. While everyone in the country floated the KGB charge at each other, the only person who was never accused of working with the Russians was Heydar Aliyev himself.

With one exception. One day, the former Justice Minister, Tahir Kerimli—the same roly-poly character with bad breath who had to be dragged from the chamber in June during the course of a nervous breakdown while haranguing Isa Gambar—began another, equally incoherent tirade against Heydar. The essence was that Kerimli accused Aliyev of being at the bottom of a horrible KGB plot designed to destroy his beloved Azerbaijan. Heydar let Kerimli bark and howl until he was blue in the face, and then shut him up forever.

"Tahir Kerimli," intoned Heydar, "I have let you empty your heart for the nation to hear. In fact, I have allowed you to speak for ten minutes over your allotted time, because this is democracy and everyone has a right to speak their own opinions. Do you have anything else to say? If not, let us move on."

Then there were the notes. They always appeared when an opposition deputy was discoursing on some point about the putsch. With the voice of the deputy droning away in the background, the cameras would train on Heydar as an aide approached and slipped him a piece of paper. Heydar would take out his glasses, adjust them on his nose, tap the microphone, and announce that he was about to read a crucially important piece of news—and thus totally change the subject at hand.

"I have just received this message from citizen Abdul Rahmanov via the executive committee chairman of the Qusar prefecture, who claims that unknown elements in military uniforms staged a demonstration in Dilber village calling for the return of Ayaz Mutalibov," Heydar would read. "Does the deputy from Qusar have any information on this undesirable development?"

"This telegram from citizen Mahir Tagaev of the Terter prefecture claims that Serdar Hamidov, the brother of Iskender Hamidov, has used the garden of the state guesthouse to grow marijuana—can you comment on this, Iskender Bey?"

Another Heydar technique was the apparent planting of 'spontaneous' questions from the floor, most of which easily fit into the interrogational style of the classic 'when did you stop beating your wife?'

Did Heydar Bey have any information on the whereabouts of the $70 million deposited by the western oil firms in the Frankfurt Branch of the Deutsche Bank set up by Sabit Bagirov, former chairman of the State Oil Concern as 'honest money' in the pending Guneshli/Azeri/Chirag offshore deal?

Could the Leader enlighten the deputies about the reasons why Isa Gambar's Musavat Party had not paid the rent of 4,567 manats or electricity bill of 432 manats to the relevant authorities for use of its headquarters for the past two months, and was living at the expense of the people?

My favorite piece of news that demanded the Invigorator's immediate attention came when a deputy (or someone from the gallery, it was not clear) asked Heydar about the details of the recent assassination attempt fomented by members of the Popular Front and a Turk against him.

"How did you know?" Heydar asked rhetorically, surprised that the issue of someone planning to kill him was of interest to anyone. "While it is true that we have arrested several men who had a plan to assassinate me, I personally did not give it much thought. My life, after all, is in God's hands. and He will be the One to decide the When and Where. But as you have asked, let me tell you about it. . . ."

Those few individuals who dared defend Elchibey were dealt with in a slightly less polite manner. One was Isa Gambar, the former chairman of parliament.

"Abulfez Elchibey may have made mistakes, but we all must admit that at the very least, Abulfez was a humanist," said Isa at another Elchibey slam-session. His reward was to be bundled off to a Ganje prison for a few weeks until international pressure forced Heydar to seek his release. Heydar, of course, knew nothing about the arrest.

Another target was Towfig Gasimov, the Front-era foreign minister who was trying to convince himself (and Elchibey) of the delights of being in the opposition for a spell. Heydar let him know the new limits the old-fashioned way: by public humiliation and the destruction of Towfig's reputation by Trial-by-Television.

The reader will forgive me for working the clock forward a few months to late March 1994. I had been out of the country and just returned to my dumpy office/abode, and turned on the TV out of idle habit.

There it was, another live, parliamentary session, almost as if I had not been out of the country at all. But this one was special. It was a session devoted to the final report about the January 20, 1990 Baku Massacre. The commission of investigation had found a number of guilty parties: Mikhail Gorbachev topped the list; Ayaz Mutalibov came next, along with Abdulrahman Vezirov. The late Elmira Kafarova also caught some flak.

None of this was surprising. What was of interest was that the rank and file of the Communist Party of Azerbaijan was exonerated, while the Popular Front was implicated and shared collective blame with the Russians and their stooges.

Towfig Gasimov then rose and walked to a floor microphone to launch a long-winded and generally incoherent defense of the Front—and the new authorities were waiting for him. The new Chairman of Parliament, Rasul Guliyev, let Gasimov ramble on about the unfairness of it all for almost a half hour, and then lowered the boom.

"Towfig Bey—you have been speaking for ten minutes more than your allotted time. . . ," said Guliyev as Gasimov hit the thirty-minute mark, without really having said anything.

"I am nearly finished—"

"You may be nearly finished, but you have not said anything for half an hour!"

Guffaws erupted from the audience, and then came a new voice. The camera shifted upward to reveal Aliyev, sitting in the chair reserved for him.

"Towfig Bey," said Heydar, tapping his microphone. "You have been at this for more than half an hour—I have been listening to your babble for a year now. What is it with you, Towfig Gasimov? Who are you? What right do you have to question the findings of the Parliament of the People, the Highest Authority in the Land, about the most serious and important report ever delivered?"

The camera now focused on tiny Towfig, frozen behind the podium, caught like a baby deer on the highway in the headlights of an oncoming truck, while the disembodied voice of Heydar droned on and on.

"You try to defend the Popular Front, and say the leadership was not involved—or at least not *all* the leadership!" Heydar continued. "Do you mean to imply once again that Nimet Panahli (Panakhov) was the exception, that everyone else was pure and good, while he was evil and bad? Look, Towfig the Teacher, I was there with you then. I made a speech in this very parliament, defending you against the traitor Mutalibov. But your Popular Front was in power for one year—a year!—and you still could not complete the parliamentary report on *the single most important event in the history of Azerbaijan!*

"Why? What did you have to hide? January 20th was the most important event in the history of the former Soviet Union, and for one year you did nothing!!

"I do not know who was responsible for the scheming and plotting of the tragedy—Gorbachev, Mutalibov, Gasimov—but I do know that it *happened* and that for one year the *Government* that you represented as foreign minister did *nothing* to establish the *truth.*

"Why? Towfig Bey? Do you have something to hide? I think the time has come to distinguish between the *Popular Front* of Azerbaijan (Xalg Jephesi) and the *Popular Movement* of Azerbaijan (Xalg Hariketi).

"There has always been a Popular Movement in Azerbaijan—and one I am honored to represent! But the Popular Front of Azerbaijan has proven itself to be more a selfish political party than a movement per se; and your reluctance to accept minimal *blame in the greatest tragedy our people have ever experienced* proves the point *beyond the shadow of a doubt.*

"Do you have more to say, Towfig Bey? Why not confess your guilt now, before the nation, instead of continuing your campaign of calumny and filthy insinuation against the heroes of this noble land!"

The Bukharin-style trial did not end with a bullet in the base of the brain. But it might as well have ended like that: according to the new history, the Popular Front was as much to blame for January 20th as the other demons—Gorbachev, Mutalibov, and the rest. There was only one hero of the people, then and forever more: Heydar Aliyev.

* * *

It was less a question of how Heydar managed to stage-manage such nonsense than why he bothered. Who believed in the theatrics? What was the point? If anything, all the spontaneous remonstrations and staged debates on the *Leader, Live!* network only alienated borderline supporters who felt they were being taken for idiots. It also served to undermine Heydar's sincerity the few times that he appeared to be truly addressing the nation.

The credibility gap came into sharp focus in late July, when a militia leader named Aliekber Humbatov declared the region along the southern Caspian littoral to be the 'Talish Mugam Republic,' and independent from the rest of Azerbaijan. Actually, it was the second such announcement of secession, the first having been at the time that Surat was marching on Baku. Then, Humbatov's action seemed to fit into the 'create chaos' model designed to send Elchibey packing and open up the gates for Heydar's return.

At first glance, Humbatov's biography fit perfectly into the Aliyev deep mole–mold. Starting out as a Popular Front man in the late 1980s, he had shifted into association with the Social Democrats of the Alizade brothers in 1991, and finally had been built up into a military commander by Rahim Gaziev. Like Surat Husseinov's 709th based in Ganje, Humbatov's Lenkoran Battalion showed a marked unwillingness to fight in Karabakh. And now, like Surat Husseinov before him, Humbatov was threatening to march on the capital unless Elchibey resigned.

Elchibey? He was already gone and almost forgotten. Heydar was in power, de facto if not de jure—and it was time for the game of circles within circles within circles to begin again.

Through that convoluted kaleidoscope, what some observers saw was this: Humbatov, Husseinov, and Gaziev were not playing their games to promote the career of Heydar Aliyev. Rather, they were busy trying to hoist him by his own petard in order to pave the way for the triumphant return of Heydar's old nemesis and the only other rival for power in Azerbaijan, Ayaz Mutalibov. The deposed president was featured prominently on Moscow television and radio, announcing his readiness to serve the people if and when they called upon him to do so. One rumor suggested that Mutalibov was already back in Baku, gathering his forces in his support base out in Mashtagah.

Everything snapped into place. The June putsch had not been designed to remove Elchibey in favor of Aliyev, but for Mutalibov. Heydar had thrown a wrench in the works by coming back as Elchibey's 'guest,' and one that the planners in Kremlin were now trying to extract.

It was here that Heydar showed his genius at the game of manipulation. Faced with a rebellion and with no army of his own, he chose to dispatch exactly those people he suspected of being behind the new 'rebellion' to go and reason with the rebels: he sent Rahim Gaziev and Surat Husseinov. Not surprisingly, when they returned, the emissaries were unable to give any coherent answer as to why Humbatov would not lay down his arms, aside from echoing the lame tune about Elchibey's immediate resignation.

It was then that Heydar struck a great preemptive blow. He called on the people of Lenkoran to rise and put down the rebellion themselves.

"There are rumors about a new armed rebellion, backed by the traitors Mutalibov and Rahim Gaziev and those who resemble them against our country," said an exhausted-looking Heydar on noontime TV. "I asked the Prime Minister, Surat Husseinov, to deal with the matter. But he seems incapable or disinterested. I therefore call on the source of my support, the people, to rise against the traitors. People of Lenkoran! Rise and show your courage! No one is greater than the people! Rise and defend the independence of Azerbaijan! On your feet!"

And the people of Lenkoran responded. They surrounded Humbatov's headquarters and demanded that he submit. When he did not, they chased him out. There was violence, there were deaths. We received the status report that evening on the *Leader, Live!* show—and this time it did not seem staged.

"I have received word from Lenkoran," intoned a solemn Heydar Aliyev. "The people have crushed the rebellion of the traitor Humbatov, but at the cost of three martyrs. They will live in our hearts forever. I have already issued a decree proclaiming them National Heroes of Azerbaijan and that their families be maintained by the state. I now request a moment of silence for the martyrs who put Azerbaijan before their own lives."

The deputies stood as commanded, and then sat down when Heydar motioned to them that they could. Then he began his real address. I called it 'The Dacha Speech.'

It started with the familiar rehash of the Ganje events, but ended with the surprise announcement that the cities of Jibrail and Fizuli had just fallen to the Armenians. Then Heydar changed his tone.

"Yes, two more cities have fallen. But this time, the disaster is of our own making. Yes! I am ashamed before the nation to tell you that not one soldier was killed defending Jibrail or Fizuli! Not one!! They all just ran away! And do you know why? Because their commanders had already run away, and are back in Baku making money to pretty up their dachas!!"

He let the pregnant inference hang: Surat Husseinov, deputy of the people, Hero of Karabakh, Prime Minister with responsibility for the war effort, was not in the chamber.

"Humbatov, Gaziev, Mutalibov—traitors all! And others, too!" thundered Heydar. "It is an outrage, an outrage! How can such people be allowed to rise to the positions of highest responsibility in the land?

"And no one seems to care. Here, in this room, half the deputies elected by the people are absent because they are at their dachas! Their dachas! *This is no time for dachas!* I beg of you, please think about something larger than yourselves for once in your lives! The nation is being destroyed by the enemy within and the enemy without, and yet no one does anything but fill their pockets with government looting! Our main problem is not about losing land or occupation, it is the moral disintegration in our country!

"It is time to return to basics, to faith, to religion! But look at you all! The level of corruption breaks my heart! Even now, many of you are only waiting to return to your dachas! You are all responsible, all of you! All of you!"

He was speaking Truth and looking very much alone. I almost felt sorry for him.

* * *

In striking contrast to this sort of passion were the endless setups Heydar held for the press with heads of diplomatic missions and visiting dignitaries, ranging from Russia's Vladimir Kazimirov to Strobe Talbott. Typically, the press opportunities were called for ten o'clock at night but were conducted past midnight. They began to resemble one another after awhile.

The telephone would ring around nine and we would be invited 'up the hill.' After frisking and other generally rude treatment at the hands of the parliamentary guards, we would be shuffled up to the fifth floor and camp in the antechamber until called for. Then we would go through another security door and be squeezed into Heydar's room, where his bodyguards would insure that we were all in a proper line that would allow Heydar, now scowling at his desk at the far end of the room, to rise, paint a smile on his face, and then stride over to meet his guests in such a way as to allow the television cameras to catch host and guests chatting amiably about nothing in particular. Then they would sit, and a number of set questions and repartees would be uttered, after which we would be escorted out and sent home. It was ridiculous and insulting, although the Azeri press always went along with the game, scribbling away in their notebooks and burning up perfectly good film.

The Strobe Talbott 'opportunity' was particularly ironic, because he had been obliged to stand through many similar photo opportunities during his days as a *Time* correspondent in Moscow, before being elevated by his old dorm-mate Bill Clinton to the withering heights of Deputy Assistant Secretary of State for Post-Soviet Affairs. Standing next to him in the parliamentary elevator, I was tempted to ask him about this but then thought better of it, and remained an anonymous passenger at his side.

There was one exception to these nonproductive press encounters. On the eve of the August 29th referendum, the protocol people at parliament announced a press conference in which Heydar would introduce the international observers who had come to insure that the polls were free and fair. This was curious, because to my knowledge, few if any western countries had shown any interesting in sending monitors.

Still, I went up the hill to parliament, was processed through to the fifth-floor waiting room and joined a large group of local and foreign correspondents who also had been invited to attend. Once again, we waited for an hour before being ushered into the Invigorator's inner sanctum, where we formed the obligatory line, cameras up front and print journalists in back.

The door opened again, and in walked Heydar and his entourage: State Secretary Lale Hadjieva, Foreign Minister Hasan Hasanov, and even Prime Minister Surat Husseinov. Vafa Gulizade and a handful of advisors and translators also were in attendance.

The government people sat down around a long table, chatting with one another and pretending we did not exist. Then the door opened again, and in marched the international observers.

I blinked. One of them was Robert Finn. Another was Richard Miles, the American ambassador. Next to him was Harold Formstone, the British representative. There was Altan Kahramanoglu, the Turkish ambassador, and Special Ambassador Mahmoud Al Said, head of the United Nations office, too. All looked as surprised to see us as we were them. At first, it seemed like Heydar had slipped and was violating an unspoken protocol—

namely, that diplomatic and press briefings were to be handled separately. But no. . . .

"Honored members of the international monitoring, members, please be seated!" said Heydar, indicating that the diplomats were to sit at the empty places around the table.

Looks of consternation passed from face to face among the diplomats. They had not been called to a joint briefing with the press. *They were the subject of the press conference themselves.* In a bold, even brazen move, Heydar had decided to beef up the paltry number of international monitors covering the referendum by including the diplomatic corps as observers, whether they accepted their enhanced status or not.

The Invigorator called the meeting to order and began his usual summation of the litany of events that had begun two months before. It started with the 'criminal attack' on the Ganje garrison on June 4th; hooked in his return to Baku as the president's guest on June 9th; touched on Elchibey's flight from Baku on June 17th; detailed the repeated appeals to the fugitive president to come back and lead the nation; and highlighted the parliamentary decision of June 24th that declared Heydar the Invigorator of the Extraordinary Powers of Acting President. He ended this first sentence by noting the parliamentary decision to hold the referendum on Elchibey's continued status. He spoke about the cost of the referendum and the difficulties involved in effecting it in a country at war, swamped by refugees and occupying forces, but reiterated his belief as a democrat and a believer in pluralism and the rule of law, that the people had to have the final say in the matter of the 'Elchibey issue.'

He ended his remarks by lavishing thanks on the international observers who had come from so far away to monitor the process, and lastly, on the members of the international press who were likewise in Azerbaijan to perform their crucial duty to record the Truth. True, he had expected more interest in the process of democratization in Azerbaijan; but be that as it may, the monitors had shouldered a great and profound burden as the guardians of the democratic process, and he, as the Invigorator, wished to personally thank them from the bottom of his heart.

Silence reigned supreme. Then Robert Finn raised his hand.

"Mister Chairman, Heydar Bey," said Robert, careful not to use the word 'president' or even 'acting president.' "I thank you for inviting us here to meet those observers who have come to monitor the referendum, and truly regret that there are no American observers present. . . ."

"But you are here, Robert," smiled Heydar.

"I am not an observer," said Robert, distancing himself publicly from monitorship in the blink of an eye. "The official delegation of observers from the United States who were to have come informed us of their concern about the continuation of the state of emergency, the reality of the war and the fact that President Elchibey has not felt secure enough to return to Baku to take advantage of state media. They think a free and fair referendum is impossible in the present atmosphere."

Heydar tried to smile, but there was anger in his eyes. This had not been part of the scenario.

"What other way is there, Robert?" said Heydar, his voice rising. "I asked you to show me another way, but you couldn't! If Abulfez Elchibey stayed in Baku and continued to act as president, there would have been no need for this referendum."

"This may be true, but it is difficult for many people outside Azerbaijan to understand," said Finn.

"It may be difficult for them to understand, Robert, but not for you. You are here! And that is why I ask you to explain the truth to those who do not know or care to see!"

What most of us saw was Surat Husseinov, sitting at Heydar's right like a Doberman Pinscher. The man who had led the putsch had given a press conference earlier in the day at which he had declared himself so disinterested in politics that he did not even believe in political parties. In fact, 'as a soldier,' he was against them.

Quoting back Surat's remarks about his principled opposition to political parties, one of the foreign journalists in the room asked Heydar to comment on how Surat's remarks jived with the picture of democratic pluralism the Invigorator had spoken so passionately about. Heydar looked at the smirking prime minister in the way an indulgent father might smile at a favorite son when informed of the latter's mischievous if macho doings.

"Surat Husseinov may be a soldier, but soldiers can also make good democrats," he said. "Look at the American president, Eisenhower, for example."

The Azeri press joined their political leadership in a good chortle over this reply.

"Perhaps there has been a bad translation," snapped the journalist. "That is not an answer to my question."

Heydar was startled. No one talked back to him like that!

"Well," he said at last. "I was not there and do not know what the Prime Minister said. But as the leader of Azerbaijan, I can assure you that the democratic principle will prevail. We are for democratic pluralism, freedom of thought, and internationally accepted human rights—and that means political parties!"

I decided to try a trick question myself.

"If the people find it in their hearts to express a lack of faith in the President of Azerbaijan, Abulfez Elchibey, and parliament votes to remove him from office on the basis of the popular will, the office of the president will be vacant." I said. "The constitution specifies that new elections for the office be held within three months. My question is this: will you, as chairman of parliament, recommend changes in the constitution concerning qualifications for presidential candidates or any other amendments to the basic law?"

"You are not asking a question, Tomas, you are stating a position," snapped Heydar.

I admit that my query was a little long and certainly too oblique for most of the foreigners in the room to understand, but all the Azeris knew perfectly well what I was referring to: the no-older-than-65-years-of-age clause in the constitution. Heydar had been too old to run for the executive office in September 1991 and he had been too old in June 1992, and he would not be any younger in the autumn of 1993. So I rephrased the question and asked if he wanted to change the age clause in the constitution. Heydar was not amused.

"You ask too many questions," he said.

"Well, will you seek to change it?"

"No, there will be no changes to the constitution."

"So you will not become a candidate if the office of president is vacated?"

"I do not think we should anticipate tomorrow's results."

The tone of the press conference was not what Heydar had hoped for. Then, happily, an Azeri journalist helped restore the chipper mood by asking Surat if he had any problems with Elchibey's coming to Baku for the referendum.

"Sure, he can come back and vote," Surat replied. "Won't be too many others voting for him."

All the Azeris in the room chuckled and guffawed at the young man's humor. He was learning from the master himself.

* * *

There were no surprises the next day. Out of a random poll of the first 100 people I met between my door and the voting station I meant to cover, 77 said they had voted against Elchibey, while only two had voiced support for him. Five more said their vote was secret. Nine others said they were specifically not voting, in order to register their protests about the polls being held at all. Two more said they had been refused voting rights because of a lack of identification. Three others didn't know where to vote because they were refugees. Two expressed ignorance about the fact that there were polls at all.

Altogether, that gave a straw poll participation quota of 83 percent, with a whopping 92-percent *no confidence* vote. It seemed a pretty representative cross section of the population, and reflected the other numbers I came up with when I actually started taking exit polls at Baku #7 at the Academy of Sciences and Baku # 8 at School 190—the same stations that I had concentrated on when Elchibey had been elected president.

Once again, the voting system was 'negative': voters were obliged to scratch out what they did not want on the ballot and leave their choice unmolested. In the June 1992 elections, it had been the names of four candidates. Now, if they wished to show their support for the refugee president, they were to scratch out the *No, I Do Not Trust Elchibey* slot and leave the *Yes, I Trust Elchibey* slot blank. Those who wished to show no support were obliged to scratch out the *Yes* and leave the *No* clean and exposed. Once again, any additional marks or remarks would invalidate the ballot.

Standing in front of the station with a clipboard in hand, I began soliciting sentiment. The number of people voting against Elchibey was hardly a surprise. But what I had not been prepared for was the staggering passion with which people, especially those who had voted for Elchibey on June 7, 1992, expressed their lack of confidence in him.

"Yes, yes, I voted for him last year," said a retired professor, Abdulhamid Bagirov, as he emerged from Baku #8. "But today I not only voted 'no confidence,' I voted *No Confidence With Hatred!*"

When the boxes were opened at Station Number #8 that evening, I was there to monitor the process. Of 2,792 possible votes, 2,392 had been cast, for an 85 percent participation rate. Of these, 2,178 voiced 'no confidence' while a mere 142 voiced 'confidence'—or 91 percent negative and 6 percent positive. It was a landslide rejection of Elchibey, and no one could paper over the fact.

It was the remaining three percent, however, that said it all. These were the 72 ballots that had been disqualified, mainly because voters had scribbled epithets across them. 'No with hatred' was mild. Voters had written things like 'A coward cannot be president,' 'Sellout!' 'Thief!' 'Asshole' 'S.O.B.!' and 'You Goat!' with an accompanying picture of a horned animal scrawled over the *Yes* slot on the ballot.* Other ballots were disqualified because voters had written things like 'I love Heydar Aliyev!' One simply admitted 'This is the first time I have ever voted.' That, too, was thrown in the trash.

---

*A play on the similarity between 'Elchibey ' and 'Keçibey,' or 'Mr. Goat'.

I was tired and sick and hardly in a mood to celebrate anything, even closure—so I decided to go home right after the ballot counting was over. Some guy picked me up, and I thought I might as well ask the taxi driver how he had voted. He said he had not. I asked him why. He said he did not believe in anyone anymore and never would again. Again, I asked him why.

"My brother was killed in Karabakh two days ago," he said. "Today they came to tell me that I must go next, and I know that I will die there, too. For what? For these political whores?"

* * *

This time, there was no waiting around for ten days for the official results. They came in quickly and with finality. Speaking to local and foreign reporters the day after the polls, State Secretary Lale Hadjieva announced that fully 92 percent of the 4,097,000 eligible voters had gone to the polls. Of those who voted, 97.5 declared that they had no confidence in Elchibey, with only two percent expressing support. The remaining ballots cast were invalid. And if anyone could not interpret the results for themselves, Lale Hanim provided one:

"There is no question that both the high participation figures and the results reflect the people's faith in Heydar Aliyev," she explained. "When election committees in the provinces called to give their results, there was usually no mention of having confidence or a lack of confidence in Elchibey. What they told us was '96 percent for Aliyev' or '95 percent to Aliyev.'"

The opposition challenged this, claiming that less than 50 percent of the population had voted—thus disqualifying the referendum, which they said was illegal anyway. Nonofficial observers put the participation at more like 80 percent, and criticized the figure of 92 percent participation as unrealistically high.

"Uncle Bob gets to break his leg and Aunt Nancy calls the doctor and the relatives, and so the Joneses don't vote today—that's reality," said Robert Finn. "You simply do not get 92 percent in an election, anywhere."

Some Azeri officials tacitly admitted that the numbers were at least malleable.

"We still have time to change it," suggested a concerned Vafa Gulizade, after a conversation with a western diplomat who had expressed concern over the official number of participants.

Few observers, official or nonofficial, however, quibbled with the percentage of those who expressed a lack of faith in Elchibey. Robert Finn summed it up best.

"It is not a matter of the referendum being rigged, which it probably will be," he said. "The sad truth is that Elchibey's standing is so low that he would probably receive more support votes in a rigged referendum than one held in the most pristine circumstances."

It was true. If the government was capable of goosing participation numbers up to an acceptable, Soviet-style 92 percent, why not toss cynical foreign observers a consolation prize by announcing Elchibey's support in low double digit figures, like 10.3 percent? In a warped way, it would have been the decent thing to do. But that was not Heydar Aliyev's style. Elchibey had to be crushed and the real leader of Azerbaijan exalted. There was only one such: Heydar Alirizaogli Aliyev.

* * *

There were still some technicalities in effecting Heydar's democratic deification. The people had announced their lack of confidence in Abulfez Elchibey as their president, and thus tacitly gave a mandate to the parliament to impeach him.

To my recollection, parliament neglected to effect the impeachment part and went straight to the business of calling new presidential elections. The 'hitch' of the age limit for candidates (65 years) was removed from the constitution by an obliging parliament, in the spirit of universal suffrage. Anyone of any age could contest elections for the highest office in the land.

Only three did—two in order to provide token competition for the third. They are not even deserving of becoming footnotes in history by giving their names here. The third candidate, of course, was Heydar Aliyev.

I missed the October 3rd election. I had planned on acting as a self-appointed monitor at my usual polling stations, Baku #7 and #8, but I got caught outside the country and was unable to return in time for the voting. I had a pretty good excuse: I was trapped in the besieged western Georgian city of Sukhumi with Eduard Shevardnadze in a little adventure many took to calling 'Shevy's Last Stand.' It was not pretty, and I was very lucky to get out of the burning city alive. Russian television had announced me missing and presumed dead.

There were other, much larger events turning in the world, too. Specifically, the weekend of October 3rd and 4th, Boris Yeltsin ordered the army to attack the Russian parliament, or White House. Some 160 people were killed, one being my good friend Rory Peck, whom I had seen just days before.

No, neither the reader nor the writer should feel robbed of the news of the nonevent in Azerbaijan on October 3rd—the election of Heydar Aliyev to the position of president of Azerbaijan.

A few notes, culled from those who were there, should fill in the picture. First, it was the sort of election that would have made Leonid Brezhnev proud of his protégé. In an election where no doctoring at all was necessary, the official result showed that 96 percent of the electorate had participated, and that 98.8 percent of them had voted for Heydar Aliyev. The other 1.2 percent was split between the other two candidates and invalidated ballots, probably thrown out for overenthusiasm.

And enthusiasm was the word of the day. A member of the UK foreign observer team was invited to cast a ballot for Aliyev by voting station workers. The observer noted the impropriety of doing so, and declined. The ballot was cast for him anyway.

This time, the high participation figures drew more scorn than suspicion. 96 percent? It was, frankly, impossible to believe. The only question that remained was *why Heydar felt the need to have it so.*

Mehmet Ali Bayar of the Turkish embassy explained it in the following manner.

"It might seem ridiculous, but Heydar could not bear to have history record that he was less popular than Ayaz Mutalibov," he said. "Legitimacy in the eyes of the world was sacrificed to his ego."

I hauled out the book on the elections that brought Mutalibov to power in September 1991. The numbers jived with Bayar's theory: 92 percent of the population had 'voted,' and of their ballots, the former president had received 98 percent. Heydar had to do better, and had done so. Incredible? Yes. But in the Republic of Aliyevistan—err, Azerbaijan—it fit like a glove.

* * *

The public celebrations of the official return of the Leader, now relieved of the demeaning title of mere 'Invigorator,' culminated on Sunday, October 10th. That was the day when Heydar Alirizaogli Aliyev was sworn in as president of Azerbaijan.

The venue of the elaborate oath-taking ceremony was the Republican Theater, and it was packed with everyone from ancient loyalists to the diplomatic corps, and even Hicran and me. Our designated places were in the third row, seats 35 and 36.

A symphony orchestra, replete with choir, opened the show with a choral number from the Azerbaijani composer, Uzeyir Hajibekov. Then came the speeches.

The first was delivered by State Secretary Lale Hadjieva, who was dressed in a sparkling white dress and wearing white-rimmed glasses. Lale detailed Heydar's achievements in the past and anticipated his accomplishments in the future.

The second speaker was Foreign Minister Hasan Hasanov, who described Heydar's current international status as a world leader. Heydar, intoned Hasanov, was a man greeted by presidents, prime ministers and kings and queens as kin. As evidence for this truth, Hasanov flashed a wad of telegrams and telefaxes of congratulations from world leaders, then read them one by one: John Major, Boris Yeltsin, Süleyman Demirel . . . One was strange because Hasanov did not pronounce the name of the sender, identified merely as "the president of Armenia." Another was just wrong. It allegedly came from Bill Clinton, who had not sent his congratulations at all.

Lastly, the leaders of the Muslim, Christian and Jewish communities in Azerbaijan trotted out on stage. They were all dressed in their religious-cum-tribal best, and sung their individual praises of the Leader Restored.

The moment had arrived for Heydar Aliyev to be invited to the podium. He rose from his seat in the gallery—and was instantly lost from view as everyone else rose to deliver a five-minute standing ovation. When he re-emerged, it was on the stage. He was beaming eye to eye. He strode to the podium and microphone to take his oath of office.

It took him long enough to get around to it because his inaugural address lasted a good hour. Most of it was a review of Heydar's Greatest Hits, so I will not repeat all the rhetoric about democracy, pluralism and the free market again.

He presented his audience with a tour of the horizon, and what the future held: developing relations with the West, particularly the United States and England, and reaffirming Azerbaijan's love and respect for Turkey. Iran, too, was held in esteem. But the relations with the other new nations of the CIS had to be invigorated as well. That was why he had recently gone to Moscow to sign a treaty that brought Azerbaijan into the Commonwealth of Independent States. There was no onus in doing so, he said. The only thing stranger than Azerbaijan belonging to a political and economic union would be its continued isolation as a member of none.

Heydar paused—and everyone in attendance knew what was coming next: Karabakh. The audience almost held its collective breath.

"Rise, please rise, and join with me in a moment of silent respect to our fallen martyrs, who will live forever in the hearts of the nation," said Heydar as the audience complied. Then Heydar began again.

A national disaster had been visited upon the country by the series of incompetent and possibly treasonous administrations that had preceded his. The precious lives of too many, far too many, had been squandered in a senseless war that was bleeding the nation of its resources and mortgaging the future to the mistakes of the past.

"We want peace! Peace!" Heydar declared, dumping the failure of all previous attempts to mediate a way out of the crisis on the Elchibey and Mutalibov governments.

It was painful, and much of it untrue—but as I listened, a thin flame of hope began to grow within me. Heydar was dumping now and would continue to dump all the horrible losses on the previous regimes, and then seize the moment and declare what everyone in the audience and the country was so desperate to hear—that the loss of 20 percent of the country, the one million refugees and the deaths of some 15,000 people was not his fault, and that it was time to acknowledge the bitter truth: Karabakh was gone, forever, and that it was time to start rebuilding the new Azerbaijan of the future.

Heydar did not even hint at this.

"The five-year war with Armenia has been a catastrophe," Aliyev intoned. "But it has shown the courage and determination of our people. The fallen will serve as examples for future generations—their courageous deaths will not be in vain! But if peaceful discussions fail and the Armenian army of occupation does not withdraw, we will be forced to answer fire with fire, and expel them all!"

No, Heydar, no, I wanted to cry. He was committing future generations to a war without end, and at the very moment the nation had found the excuse to cut away the cancer, and live.

No, Heydar, no, I wanted to shout—but the bellicose words were still ringing in the air, and the audience was on its feet cheering and applauding the idea of more war.

Then, with the deafening applause rolling over him, face beaming and perspiring, Heydar Aliyev rested his hand on the Azerbaijani constitution, sucked in a deep breath, and swore to devote the rest of his life to the service of the people of Azerbaijan and to the independence, territorial integrity, and constitution of the Republic of Azerbaijan.

Nor was it over. The Sheikh-ul Islam appeared from the stage wings bearing a Quran for the new president to kiss and swear fealty to. Another volcano of joyous noise erupted and reverberated through the chamber. I wondered how one could notch it any higher, and the answer was soon at hand.

The music swelled as the orchestra and chorus worked through the opening bars of the national anthem. Then, with an earsplitting crash of cymbals, two soldiers marched out on the stage, bearing the red, green, and blue banner of the nation. If anyone had sat down, they were now back on their feet again as the new president dropped to one knee before the flag, seized it with both hands, and planted his lips on a fold.

Everyone, everyone now joined in the glory of the moment with a deafening, delirious rendition of the chorus of the national anthem, welcoming Heydar Aliyev back home.

Azaerbaycan, Azaerbaycan!
Ey Gaehraeman övladin, Shanli Vaetaeni . . .
Minlaerlae can gurban oldu!
Sinen haerbi meydan oldu! . . .
Shanli Vaetaen! Shanli Vaetaen!
Azaerbaycan, Azaerbaycan!

Azerbaijan, Azerbaijan!
Oh, heroic youth, oh glorious land! . . .
Thousands of martyrs have you seen!
A battleground have you been!
Glorious land, glorious land!
Azerbaijan, Azerbaijan!

25

Scars on the Soul

The white horse, draped with a purple Georgian flag, walked gingerly, its hoofs slipping on the thin layer of ice covering the streets. Behind the riderless horse rumbled an older Soviet-style armored personnel carrier, towing a casket on a gun caisson. Behind it walked a priest bearing an Orthodox cross made of wood. Behind the priest came a wall of women, all dressed in black. They wept as they walked, each holding a candle in one hand and clenching the other into a fist.

The venue was Grozny, capital of the breakaway republic of Chechnya in southern Russia, and the date, February 24, 1994. The public passion play was the burial of Zviad Gamsakhurdia, ousted president of post-Soviet Georgia. He died or had been killed or committed suicide two months before, in the lonely mountains of the Georgian province of Svanetia. Disinterred, Zviad was now making his final journey—to a cold hole carved in the courtyard of his residence-in-exile in Grozny, seat of his government in exile for two years. The state funeral and Orthodox last rites were provided by Gamsakhurdia's Muslim host-in-exile and friend-in-revolution, Chechen president Djokhar Dudayev.

"We are gathered here today to give back to the earth a brave son of the Caucasus, a man who believed in freedom. . . ," intoned Dudayev, eulogizing his late guest at the graveside.

"I stand before you in shame," said a Russian woman from St. Petersburg. "Shame, because it is my nation, Russia, that has brought so much misery to you peace-loving peoples of the Caucasus. . . ."

Indeed. The whole region had become an alphabet soup of ethnic conflict, with Moscow throwing in the spice—usually saltpeter—to set one group off against another in a classic game of divide and rule.

And it was only going to get worse. The day before Gamsakhurdia's funeral was the 50th anniversary of the 'Chechen Genocide'—February 23, 1944. That was the day Stalin deported the entire Chechen population to

Central Asia on the collective charge of collaboration with the Nazis. Half died on the way, and the survivors had become a scarred, bitter nation. Our funeral host, General Dudayev, was a former Soviet Strategic Air Command bomber pilot and real-life Dr. Strangelove who had declared Chechnya free and independent of the Russian Federation in September 1991. To give his decision some teeth, he built an army ready to commit national suicide should the opportunity avail itself. The 50th anniversary of Stalin's attempted destruction of the Chechens seemed like a fine occasion to put these forces on display, and in addition to the funeral dirge, those in attendance had been treated to a military parade replete with tanks and missiles. The bellicose show culminated with the smashing of flaming bricks against heads and a jujitsu performed with long Chechen daggers, *kinjali,* in the streets of Grozny. This was followed by a fashion show, in which male models pranced down a catwalk to martial music, showing off the new uniforms of the Chechen armed services—including the dress togs of the landlocked country's 'navy.' At a press conference that evening, General Dudayev topped the day by reiterating his threat to detonate a nuclear device in a Moscow subway if the Kremlin tried circumventing Chechen independence. Meanwhile, the Grozny bazaar had become an alfresco arms market where one could buy anything from hand grenades to APCs.

It was kind of funny, but any fool could see it was only a matter of time before Moscow cracked down. When it did, in November 1994, Grozny was flattened and more than 50,000 were killed—but that is another story.

* * *

The priest was now droning an incantation, sprinkling holy water on the sarcophagus, and a woman from the crowd had broken loose to launch herself over its lid, digging her nails into the wooden coffin like a cat.

"*Oh, Zvi-ad, Zvi-ad, Zvi-ad!!*" she wailed.

It was Gamsakhurdia's widow, Manana, and a dozen cameras clicked and video cameras whirred, capturing the moment.

"*Zvi-ad, Zvi-ad, Zvi-ad!!*"

At the edge of the mourners, I noticed a man lighting a cigarette. It was Merab Kiknadze, chairman of Gamsakhurdia's parliament, who had followed his leader into exile and was now bidding him a final good-bye. We had met two years earlier in Sukhumi, capital of the Georgian autonomous republic of Abkhazia before it broke away from Georgia and declared itself an independent state in the summer of 1993. Merab and I had met in winter 1992. We had shivered in the cold then, and were both shivering now. We had also seen much during the interim, most of it bad.

"I heard you were dead," said Merab.

"I heard you were, too," I replied.

Then we went through a list of people we knew who had been killed, and then a second list of other people we knew who had become refugees, rather like two old friends discussing what other old friends were up to, only that the only up-to to be talked about was misery and death.

"How are our friends, the two sisters?" Merab asked, rasping over the droning voice of the Orthodox priest and the wailing voice of Manana.

"Nana is in Tbilisi living in a refugee hotel, but I think Nunu got killed when the Abkhaz took the city," I replied, referring to the family that had taken care of me during the worst of the Sukhumi siege. "I tried to get her to come out with me on the last day, on a ship the Russians had sent to pick up refugees, but she refused."

"Too bad," said Merab. "She was pretty tough."

"Yeah."

"How are things in Baku?"·

"The same."

"Well, try and take care that you don't get killed."

"You too."

We embraced and kissed each other's cheeks in what we both knew was probably a final farewell.

* * *

I had flown into Chechnya from Baku aboard an illegal flight in order to avoid Russian customs. Some people said I hijacked the plane, but that is not true. I merely paid fifty dollars to get aboard an empty Tupolev jet that was flying to Dubai via Grozny and Istanbul. There was no return flight. But getting out was not a big problem. My friend Alexis Rowell agreed to smuggle me into Georgia in the back seat of his NEVA, on the understanding that he would abandon me on the Russian border if I got caught. I said OK.

The road south was lined with the burnt-out remnants of Ingush homes attacked by Ossetians in 1992, although to read reports on that conflict one might believe that the Ingush had done the attacking. The 'victors as victims' theme was familar. The main point was to have the local Russian garrison on your side.

After lunch in the Ossetian capital of Vladikavkaz, we picked up the Russian Military Highway south over the great, natural barrier of snow-capped mountains that separates the North Caucasus from the Trans-caucasus, meaning Georgia, Armenia, and Azerbaijan. The route had once been traveled by the likes of Tolstoy, Turgenev, and Lermontov. It was now empty aside from our NEVA and Russian patrols. At the Ossetian/Georgian border post that now represented Russia's southern frontier, I fell into conversation with a man who claimed to be the head of the local society for orphans. He had taught himself English and had a pen-pal in Chicago, although he had never actually met an American before. He was thrilled to meet me because it allowed him to chat. This was good, because he was also the official responsible for checking documents, and was more interested in seeing what an American passport looked like than whether I had a visa. Alexis was furious.

"You saunter up to the most sensitive border in the former Soviet Union without a visa and just chat up the guards and walk through? Do you know how many times they have picked apart my entire car? It's not fair!"

"Luck, I guess."

This was true in far too many ways to mention.

* * *

Our first stop in Georgia was the famous Marco Polo Gudauri ski resort, where Alexis promised that we would be welcomed with open arms for the night. Georgia's multiple civil wars had scared off all tourists who might have been interested in skiing the higher ranges of the Caucasus mountains, he assured me. The place would be all ours.

We were lucky to get a room: Tbilisi, Georgia's capital, had been without electricity for a week, and anyone with money—meaning *Mkhedrioni,* 'Knight Horseman' militiamen-cum-mafia hoods—had beaten a hasty retreat to the mountain resort to wait out the power crisis. We left in the early afternoon, missing a shootout in the restaurant. A Mkhedrioni chief had complained about the food, and the Svanetian cook had taken umbrage, emerging from the kitchen with a butcher knife.

Tbilisi was very cold and thoroughly miserable. The gas-producing former Soviet republic of Turkmenistan had turned off the tap because Georgia had not paid its bills for several years. Compounding this state of affairs was a lack of electricity: the Abkhaz, who had conquered the country's largest hydroelectric station the year before, made sure that the supply was erratic. Power would come on in the middle of the night, and televisions and radios would start to blare, waking everyone. This was good, because water pumps also would start and you had to turn off them off before precious water gushed over the floor after filling the bathtub, which served as the drinking water reservoir in each and every home.

The only building in town to have a constant power supply was parliament, and it was there that I found Eduard Shevardnadze. We had seen quite a bit of each other under fire in Sukhumi—and even had time for the occasional macabre joke. On the night before the city had fallen, I was badly bitten by a stray dog that left a gaping, bleeding wound on my leg. In the morning of the last day, I ran into Shevardnadze at Stalin's dacha. He was looking particularly haggard, but asked after my health.

"I was wounded last night," I said, pulling up my dirty pant leg to show the oozing slash on my calf.

"Wounded!" said Shevardnadze with true concern.

"Yes," I replied with a grin. "By a dog."

Shevardnadze's lips drew back into a smile, and then he laughed. "By a dog. . . ." Then he went away to plan his escape.

Aides rushed to tell me that it was the first time he had smiled in two weeks. Now, meeting in Tbilisi some six months later, he asked me about the dog bite.

"I guess I am okay, because if the cur had been rabid, I'd be dead."

"Don't be so sure," he warned me. "The incubation period of Georgian rabies is longer than in your country."

* * *

Our next stop on the Caucasus-disasterland tour was the place that was always referred to as the biggest disaster of them all: Armenia. We took the 'bandit highway' south to the capital city, Yerevan. Thanks to the guarded columns of Russian Army fuel trucks churning down the road, we encountered no problems. Moscow would take care of its own.

Armenia was different than the last time I had been there, during the awful winter of 1992–1993. Due to a mixture of warmer weather, native ability at organization, and lots of international aid, Armenia was almost livable. Food was expensive but plentiful. The handful of downmarket kebab restaurants open a year before had grown like mushrooms. There were even bananas and grapefruit imported from Iran, which, if theoretically far too expensive for anyone in the country to eat—a month's salary for a piece of citrus?—were selling like hotcakes at street-side stands. No, Armenia was not starving, although that was the way it was usually represented. Power was still a major problem: most homes only had two hours a day. But unlike in Georgia, you could count on when it would come on. You could also buy a supply if you had money and influence. The friends, family and colleagues of a recently deceased mafia chief named Svoi Raf had 'requested' a week of light from the Ministry of Energy and received it.

No, Armenia was no longer a country facing national catastrophe, if it ever had been: it was a country on war footing—for a war that did not exist.

Black banners hung over streets in every Armenian town we passed through, announcing the funeral of a local boy who had recently come back from Nagorno Karabakh in a body bag. Similarly, posters noting the names and birth and death dates of other 'volunteers' from various cities were plastered on restaurant walls and telephone poles. Perhaps the most dramatic example of the growing number of Armenian dead in Karabakh came during the course of a visit to the Yeriblur Martyrs' Cemetery, near Yerevan airport. Some 500 graves dated to 1992 and 1993, but I counted over 100 freshly dug ones for those fallen in early 1994 alone—although to believe Armenian officials and even foreign diplomats stationed in Yerevan, Armenia was not involved in the war.

Two burials were in progress when I arrived on the scene—and the nature of the funerals was a stark contradiction to all the official claims about Armenian non-involvement in a war that had already taken 20,000 lives. The reason for this was that the funerals were conducted according to military last rites. The reason for this was that the youths whose deaths were being mourned were soldiers from the Armenian national army—and Special Forces members at that. According to their commander, the two had been killed 'outside Fizuli,' that is, outside the burnt-out shell of the Azeri city that had once carried that name. The two military funerals were proof positive of this, and utterly refuted the standard Armenian claims that only 'volunteers' over whom the Yerevan government had no control were engaged in the conflict with Azerbaijan in Karabakh.

Volunteers, indeed. After the last pieces of rock and dirt were thrown on the graves, a row of men in the uniforms of the Armenian National Army stood at attention, cocked their rifles—and then ejected the bullets without firing, in a silent salute. I felt like a voyeur in an ethereal realm of pregnant silence: funerals for the fallen in a war that was not.

When I asked a high-level Armenian official about our visit to the cemetery, and how it could be that no one in the country was talking about so many casualties, his way-off-the-record reply was simple and poignant.

"Maybe it is just too painful to talk about," he said. Then he went back to the official on-the-record chatter about non-involvement of Armenian citizens in Karabakh aside from 'volunteers.' He knew that I knew it was a lie, and I that knew he knew I knew—but we also both knew it was policy and I could not expect him to come clean on an issue as sensitive and vital as the myth of volunteerism.

I could respect this effort of dissembling by Armenian officials. It was their job, and they did it very well. I had much less respect for the international diplomats and journalists who continued to go along with the fiction of non-involvement. At the home of a best-nameless diplomat in Yerevan, I was shown a horrific video shot by a frontline correspondent who took his job very seriously. Truckloads of soldiers spilled out into a forest with bullets flying all around. Then a tank appeared with Armenian markings on the side.

"See that?" said my host. "That tank was donated by Armenia to Karabakh."

'Donated?' Perhaps like the mercenary soldiers and equipment from the Russian garrison in Yerevan that periodically fell into the hands of the Azeris.

The film continued. In the post-firefight sequence, a line of Azeri kids lay in a perfect row along a forest path, ready for ear-cutting. Too green to know better, they had huddled together and had been cut down like ducks.

* * *

The reason so many Armenian soldiers had 'volunteered' to fight the good fight in and outside Karabakh was because Heydar Aliyev had been true to his word. On the day of his inauguration on October 10, 1993, Heydar had announced that he would succeed where others had failed—namely, he would be the one to drive the Armenian foe from occupied Azeri lands.

The offensive began in late November 1993, and sputtered on for about four months. It was spearheaded by Afghan mercenaries and Azeri commandos trained by retired American Special Forces members. The former had been brought in by the plane-load from Kabul at the price of about ten dollars a mujahideen per month, while the latter had been brought into Azerbaijan as part of the MEGA Oil arms deal run by the rogue American merchant of death and destruction, Gary Best. Like Armenian fighters and Russian mercenaries in Karabakh, the Afghanis did not officially exist, although one could see them strutting around Baku in their tribal regalia. In any case, the 'revitalized' Azeri army, which had experienced nothing but defeat and desertion for two years, had launched a massive offensive against entrenched Armenian positions in the south, east, and north of Karabakh, and only a timely intervention of men and material from Armenia (and Russia) had stanched the lines and then stemmed the tide. The cost to Armenia was high—around 500 dead, before the Azeri offensive burnt itself out in early February. The cost to the Azeris, meanwhile, was staggering: 5,000 dead—maybe twice that number.

But you would not have known this from Baku, where the physical and psychological contrast with Yerevan was mind-boggling. To the untrained eye, it was almost impossible to tell that Azerbaijan was a country at war for its very survival. Heydar's meat grinder may have cost thousands of young men their lives, but not too many seemed to come from Baku.

That was my impression, anyway. Sitting around the bar of Club Universal, a sort of super-smoky, 1990s version of Ric's Bar of Casablanca fame, one heard or saw or seemed to learn many interesting things. Tonight's interlocutor might be one of the young, well-heeled Azeri bucks who worked as a translator for a foreign embassy, or one of the new businessmen who excelled in moving in electronic goods from Dubai. They all shared one characteristic: they were brave young souls who made enough money on the quick to be able to volunteer some of it to someone in the Defense Ministry to avoid the draft, and kept on paying to maintain that status quo. I often wondered what the cut was, and decided that the fee extracted by the Defense Ministry was in direct proportion to the amount of the country then under occupation. Thus, if the Armenians were in possession of 15 percent of the country, then the well-heeled draft-dodgers had 15 percent of their earnings and wages garnished. In fact, the Armenians had recently topped the 20-percent occupation mark, but the brave lads at the Club Universal kept on paying.

* * *

One day, Alexis came to town with his bride-to-be, Natalie, and we made a little outing to a prison south of Baku, where the Azeris kept their Armenian POWs. We were given a tour of the model facility and allowed to interview about two dozen captives without any Azeri officials hanging around. All categorically rejected the idea that they were 'volunteers.' They all said they were soldiers following orders when they were sent into Azerbaijan. The exception was a 30-year-old burglar named Aram. He called himself an 'obligatory mercenary.' In July 1993, after serving three years in prison on conviction for theft, he had been released from jail in Yerevan. But almost immediately, he was picked up by the police again. They gave him a stark choice: 'volunteer' for service in Karabakh, or else . . . After incidental training, he was shipped off to the Fizuli front, got lost, and was captured by the Azeris. He saw little chance of being included in a Red Cross exchange because no one in Yerevan wanted him, and the Azeris were in the habit of demanding disproportionate numbers of their POWs for any given Armenian. "That is my sour story," sighed Aram.

No newspapers that we worked for were interested in the story—despite the fact that it was the first hard evidence of direct Armenian involvement in the conflict. Nor were any newspapers interested in the gruesome story of eight Azeri POWs under Red Cross protection, who had been executed in an Armenian jail. Our source for this information was one Dr. Derrick Ponder, an English forensic expert who had flown to Baku to inspect the corpses.

He described his findings to us as 'the clearest violation of the Geneva Conventions' that he had seen. Six of the corpses had been shot in the head at point-blank range. In three instances, the muzzle was in contact with the head when fired; in the other three, the removal of bone and tissue fragments from the wound made it impossible to determine whether the muzzle was resting on the skull or merely an inch away. Of the other two bodies, one had been shot through the chest and the other had its throat slashed. The official Armenian version of events was that the men had been killed while trying to escape. When Dr. Ponder blew the whistle on that as a possibility, Yerevan changed its story: the eight had committed mass suicide—including the man with the slashed throat. But no one was interested in the story—and I was getting a little tired of that.

Then another paroxysm of violence started brewing along the Karabakh front. The Armenians had launched yet another 'defensive' retaliation for an alleged Azeri air attack on the Karabakh capital, Stepanakert. Perhaps the Azerbaijani air force had, as reported, dropped a few bombs. The pilots, after all, were all Russian mercenaries, who also had the nasty habit of dropping bombs on Azeri cities just when peace seemed to breaking out. And for those given to watching patterns, there were a number of familiar elements about the timing of the terror bombing and attendant 'counteroffensive': it began on the day of peace negotiations between the two sides in Prague, and on the eve of a summit meeting in Moscow designed to encourage 'military cooperation' among members of the Commonwealth of Independent States, that is, the re-establishment of Russian military bases in the states of the former Soviet Union.

Most telling were the off-the-cuff remarks by the chief Russian negotiator assigned to the Minsk Group, Vladimir Kazimirov, to my friend Araz Azimov of the Azerbaijani Foreign Ministry, when the latter reiterated his country's reluctance to allow Russian 'peacekeepers' to deploy in Azerbaijan.

"Who knows, you might lose Ganje next," the Russian had quipped.

So the Armenian armored thrust that was called a counter offensive masked as legitimate retaliation rolled forward, and I felt I had to do something about it.

"Why?" Alexis Rowell demanded on the telephone from Tbilisi. "What can you write that anyone wants to know, that is worth getting killed for? Seeing a bunch of Azeri refugees living by the side of the road in our little Bosnia-That-No-One-Wants-To-Know-About? Let me give you the lead, and you can write the story right now: 'In the face of an Armenian counterattack, thousands of Azeri civilians streamed out of their houses to take up life along the roadside—again.' "

* * *

Actually, the reason that Alexis did not want me to go to the front was because I would miss his good-bye party. He had been running on adrenaline for two years, and was burnt out and wanted to return to London while he was still sane.

I told him I would try and make it to Tbilisi in time for his party. Then I called Mustafa, my old pal, official guide, and comrade in insanity and survival over at the Analytical and Informational Department of the National Ministry of Defense and Security to ask him about getting official permission to go to 'the zone of conflict.'

"We are not allowed to give out any passes," said Mustafa. "Please go, now."

That meant it was bad. It also meant I was being called on. So I got dressed in my black undertaker's suit that I always wore when I went to war, stuffing a titanium plate in my left breast pocket as a charm, in case the snipers were aiming for the heart and not the head. I had never been wounded when I wore it, so that meant it worked—kind of like wearing a saint's tooth around your neck to fend off the plague. The idea is ridiculous, but the moment you remove the tooth, you shrivel and die.

I hailed a taxi to take me out to a heliport where they were bringing in the dead and wounded I knew would never be mentioned in any official reports. The driver was belligerently nationalistic. He trotted out all the rhetorical questions about who was in the right and who was in the wrong in the Karabakh conflict, and demanded my response.

"Have you served?" I asked, interrupting the driver in mid-screed.

"Well, not exactly," he sheepishly replied.

"Then shut up," I said. "Not only do you have no idea what you are talking about, you have no right to talk at all."

The driver sullenly held his tongue until we got out to the heliport to meet the wounded coming in: kids without feet, a guy without a jaw—just a few of the 100 wounded flown in that day.

"I had no idea," babbled the driver. "I have never seen anything like this."

The choppers were working the southern front and I wanted to go north, so I had the driver bring me to the airport just in time to catch a plane to Ganje. The taxi ride cost about ten dollars, but the air ticket cost less than a tenth of that. The taxi was cleaner, though: the airplane reeked of urine and dripped oil everywhere. Another death plane, ready to fall out of the sky. At Ganje airport, I caught a different car driven by some unlucky saps who lived in Terter, a little burg situated smack-dab on ground zero. We picked up a couple of hitchhiking soldiers who were coming back from a body-bag detail.

"How's the situation?" I asked the grunts.

"We are getting shot to shit," came the reply.

Terter was a frontline town, and knew it. The difference between it and all other frontline towns in Azerbaijan I had stayed in was that no one seemed to be running away. Women wearing too much makeup and men in ratty three-piece suits strolled down one side of the main street while missiles fell on the other.

I followed the sound of a couple of incoming GRAD missiles that had just screeched overhead and exploded somewhere nearby. One had come in on the house of Mrs. Mesnuma Pashayeva. She had been sweeping out her courtyard when the missiles starting falling into her neighborhood and decided to go back inside the kitchen and wait out the attack. Three missiles flew over, but the fourth crashed through the roof of her two-story house, passing through a wall and ceiling of the first floor and exploding within inches of where she had been standing outside, near the back steps, moments before.

"We waited until we felt sure there were no more rockets coming in, and then went out and put out the fire with the dish water," said Mrs. Pashayeva.

Next, I wandered over to the hospital to check on the wounded. The wards were full, mainly of soldiers with sniper wounds to the head. This suggested the presence on the other side of one of the notorious if almost certainly apocryphal 'Latvian Ladies' sniper units. The ladies, or the rumor of them, always seemed to show up on the winning side of a battle, thus conveniently giving the losers an excuse for losing. How could one be expected to do battle with eagle-eyed Amazons who killed you from miles away? Still, it was reassuring after a fashion to note that there did not seem to be an inordinate number of foot and leg wounds—a dead giveaway that soldiers were self-inflicting injuries just to get away. There were also a number of really lucky young men. One had been shot through the arm— the bullet had entered small but departed large, although it had apparently missed the bone.

"They are all Russians, and they won't fall when you shoot them!" wailed the man, as a doctor cleaned out the wound. Maybe the rumor of Russian 'supermen' in lightweight, flexible body armor was true. Maybe the man was just a bad shot.

* * *

My destination for the evening was the nearby town of Barda, where my old friend Yusuf Agayev, the regional military prosecutor, was the local authority. Yusuf's aide told me he was at the front. I suggested we go to find him. The aide said okay, and found a car. This was good, because traveling with military police in a war has a certain advantage: other military police do not stop you. As usual, I was illegal, and I had not even bothered to apply for permission to enter 'the zone.'

Soon, we were driving by miles of newly displaced refugees, squatting in makeshift tents. Those who had been displaced previously lived in boxcars. In and among the vineyards and laundry lines, artillery pieces let loose a terrific fire against the approaching foe. Then the refugees fell away, and we were within two miles of the front, and then right up against the fighting. Exhausted Azeri kids squatted atop heaps of ammunition, almost begging for a well-placed spark to blow them to kingdomcome. One accused me of spying.

"A foreign reporter shows up, takes pictures—and the next day we get bombed!"

"Russian satellites have photographs of every bottle cap around here," I replied. "Don't blame me."

Our conversation was interrupted by a large explosion about a mile away. We did not so much hear it as see it: a piece of Azeri armor, a tank probably, had just been hit by a high incendiary shell and was burning hot white. No chance for anyone in it: cinders.

"Aren't you afraid?" asked one of the MPs.

"Sure I am," I said. Then I thought about it. The truth was that I was just used to this shit, and almost felt at home.

Nearby was the almost deserted town of Kervant. I started taking some pictures of refugees hoisting tables and chairs on trucks, and asked them why they were leaving.

"We trust our army, but the Armenians are only one mile away!" said some character named Ayaz Humbatov.

Down the street a knot of Afghan muj were packing up to leave as well.

"Don't take pictures of them, because they do not exist," said Yusuf's aide.

Kervant was still the HQ of the Azerbaijani general staff, so I suggested we go look for Yusuf over at the farmhouse that served as the military nerve center of the Azeri forces in the area. What I really wanted to do was see the chief of the general staff, General Nejmettin Sadikov. We had met before on several occasions, most recently during the evacuation of Kelbajar in April 1993, when some 40 Armenians had sent some 40,000 Azeris scurrying over the mountains. I think I embarrassed the good general then, because at the height of the chaotic retreat I caught Sadikov dolled up in his spit-and-polish best, gingerly climbing into his staff car lest he get mud on his freshly pressed pants, replete with red bunting down the leg.

Now we would get to meet at another retreat, and I could ask him why he always seemed to get promoted after each defeat.

We found the farmhouse HQ after five minutes. Sadikov was standing outside. I got out of the car and waved to him. He recognized me, but did not seem pleased. Nor did the man at his side, who quickly walked up to the barricade and demanded my papers. By his markings, he was a KGB colonel.

"*Bumaga,*" he said, speaking Russian.

"*Pozhaluista,*" I replied, handing him my press card, #00001—the first accreditation ever bestowed upon a foreigner in Azerbaijan.

"This document is issued by the Foreign Ministry," the man said with contempt. "I want to see your permission to be here, on the front."

"I applied for one—," I gamely tried, speaking Azeri.

"Don't even bother giving me lip," said the colonel. "I know you don't have one because I am the man who issues all such passes. And I know I did not issue one for you because I did not issue one for anyone."

"Okay," I confessed. "I am here illegally. Just like I have been the illegal witness of every one of your disasters—Xodjali, Kelbajar, Agdam, Fizuli, and Zengelan." Then I detailed where I had been in the last few days.

"God," said the colonel, rolling his eyes and smiling in spite of himself. "You have violated everything, every rule we have!"

"That's right," I said, returning the KGB colonel's stare. "Someone has to write your history."

Then Yusuf Agayev appeared from behind a box of ammunition and did a double-take when he saw me. He hurried over to have a quick word with the KGB man. After a moment, the KGB colonel returned to me.

"Aside from arresting you and having you shot for espionage, the only thing I can suggest is that you leave this sector, immediately," the colonel said with finality.

"Okay," I said. "I'll go."

We drove back to Barda in silence, worried about what would happen to Yusuf. Rather than hang around his headquarters, I went around to the house occupied by the Red Cross. The chief of mission was Feri Alami, a half-Swiss/half-Iranian guy who had fled Iran when the Ayatullah Khomeini had taken power, and moved to southern California. Then something snapped, and he left his wife and his job and joined the ICRC, leading a Gypsy life of mercy that brought him to all the hot-spots of the 1990s: Afghanistan, Tajikistan, and now, Azerbaijan. Later, he would work in Rwanda and Burundi, and then in Grozny.

"Good to see you again," said Feri when I knocked on the door. "How is the situation on the front?"

"Give me a drink," I said, and he did so.

Yusuf joined us for dinner that night. Feri wanted to get to know him through me because he was working on some prisoner-of-war exchanges, and needed Yusuf's cooperation.

"They are not taking prisoners and neither are we," said Yusuf.

When we went back over to his HQ, Yusuf turned on the television and watched cartoons in Russian.

"The situation is very grave," he said. "They may even capture Barda—but we are making them pay for every inch they take."

"What are the casualties today?"

"Hundreds dead, thousands wounded."

Artillery pounded on through the night, but it no longer prevented me from sleeping. In the morning, I packed my bags and left for Baku. The road was clogged with buses carrying soldiers: young meat for the front. There would be a big battle that day, and I wanted to stay, but my job was to try and report the last one .

Once back in Baku, I checked into the Universal Club to use its new international telephone, to tell my news desk I had something to file.

"But has anything fundamentally changed?" the editor asked.

There were only a few more hundred dead and a lot more wounded and there would be more dead and wounded tomorrow, adding to the previous 20,000 killed and maybe 100,000 wounded to date. Oh, and Mrs. Pashayeva's roof had been blown in, but she had not been hurt, because she put out the fire with dishwater. The Mujahideen had been spotted again, this time in retreat, and Mr. Humbatov still trusted the army to defend him even as he liquidated his home for flight. No, nothing had changed, really, ergo, it was all the same and thus was not news until someone else flew into Baku and spoke with Western observers or sources or whomever and declared things to be different, although all those observers and sources or whoever never spent any time at the front because they were not allowed to go or because they were too afraid to push beyond Ganje when the fighting was at Terter and Barda, two dump towns that no one has ever heard of before or since but where I had friends who were getting shelled and shot and dying.

"No," I told the editor. "Nothing has changed in the way you mean it."

"Then why did you call us? We're pretty busy here, you know."

"OK, then I won't any more."

"Good."

Click.

* * *

That night there was a diplomatic party at Philip Remler's place. There were oilmen and government people and opposition people and intellectuals and all the rest. I couldn't stand the asinine conversation, so I went out on the steps to smoke. I also brought a bottle of my host's single malt Scotch. I thought it was a fine opportunity to find solace in sauce. *Glug glug.*

I was soon joined by Asim Mullahzade. A psychologist for cosmonauts in the good old days of the bad old Sov You, he was now one of the leading members of the rump Popular Front, and an old friend to boot.

"Thomas," he said. "You look depressed."

"Yeah," I replied, sucking down a hit of Islay. "Maybe I am."

"Drinking won't help," said Asim, clinically.

"Oh, no?" I countered. "Watch this."

I took another long pull, directly off the bottle.

"Seriously, it won't," said Asim. "Scientifically speaking, there is only one antidote for depression, be it compulsive, manic, or other forms of the disorder."

"Like what?"

"Danger."

I almost dropped the glass.

"You mean, I just have to drive fast or get shot at, and I will feel better?"

"In a manner of speaking, yes," said Dr. Asim, shrink for the likes of Cosmonaut Yuri Gagarin and subsequent Soviet space-walkers. "Think about it."

He was right. Increasingly, the only times I was not maniacally depressed by everything was when I was getting shot at on the front or walking through minefields at midnight, sneaking over some contested border or other. I thought of my friends, the handful of other 'informational shock-troops' who had tried to cover the 'Caucasus Cauldron' that had blown up after the collapse of the Soviet Union in 1991. Most of us were utterly burnt out. Some of us, like the late, great Rory Peck and Alexandra Tuttle, were just plain dead.

Who had we been before we had become war correspondents? Scholars, researchers, musicians, poets—I don't know. But war correspondents we all had become, and now we all thrived on it, courting death just to try and keep feeling a little bit alive. We had been pretty damn lucky—unlike some of the other long-gone pals on the bloody highways and byways of the region. My old pal Freddy Woodruff had been shot in the head the year before; Fred Cuny would disappear in Chechnya a year later. And the list of Azeri, Georgian, and Chechen friends and confidants and drinking buddies who had bit the big-one during the hurly-burly in the post-Soviet Caucasus was long and still growing: Jenghiz, Adil, Farhad, Alef, Merdad, and Zurab, just to name a few.

Danger as the antidote for depression. It said it all. I had been dancing with death for three long years. It was high time to take a cure, if there was one.

* * *

The next week was *Ashura,* or the period of self-mortification and vicarious martyrdom associated with the death of Imam Hussein, the effective founder of Shi'ite Islam. I had 'covered' the event before, but now I felt compelled to study the week of passion from the inside. Old friends were distressed when they learned what I was doing. One was Vafa Gulizade.

"You are going to tell the world that we have become a bunch of fundamentalist fanatics, like in Iran," said Vafa.

How could I explain that I only wanted to be among people who believed in something, anything?

I checked out of my hovel-house and moved into a mosque in the religious neighborhood of Mashtagah, which was sufficiently close to the Nadiran cemetery where flagellants gathered in the evening after prayers. I had some problems at first. The staff of the Iranian embassy were friendly enough to 'tip' my hosts that I was really a secret agent of the CIA, sent in to spy on Ashura-style activities, such as marching through the midnight streets with swishing steel whip in hand, lacerating oneself, while waking whole neighborhoods with plaintive dirge-chanting.

"Ay, Hussein, Vay Hussein!" (Oh, Hussein, Woe Hussein!)

"Al-em-dar! Al-em-dar!" (Standard Bearer, Standard Bearer!)

"Mus-ul-man! Shi-a-lar!" (Muslim Man, Shi'ite!)

For relief, I traveled to the shrine of Saint Khizir, the Muslim version of the Prophet Elijah, atop a mountain overlooking the Caspian Sea. Appropriately enough, Khizir is the Muslim patron saint of lost causes.

On the morning of the Ashura itself, I joined the flagellants gathering at the Taze Pir Mosque—the headquarters of the Religious Directorate of the Caucasus Muslims. The courtyard began filling up with penitents at six, and by nine o'clock it was packed. Joining the spiritual elite were thousands of ordinary citizens, and the crowds spilled out into the streets and adjoining avenues. Around eleven o'clock, men wearing ties and suit coats began cutting through the crowd. I recognized several: bodyguards, and presidential ones at that. Heydar Aliyev, former KGB general, former Communist Party First Secretary, former Politburo Member, former dissident-cum-Azeri nationalist-cum-Pan Turkist-cum-Appreciator of Islam was on his way to the mosque to bask in the glow of Ashura-association.

"Allah ul Akbar!" the crowd cried as Heydar entered the mosque. 'God

is the Greatest!' When he reemerged, the cry of *Allah ul Akbar!* was raised once more. I am not sure if he took off his shoes.

It was almost noon, and the *Qattal,* or 'killing hour' of Hussein was drawing near—and I wanted to capture the moment in the Shehidler Xiyabani, or national Martyrs' Lane Cemetery, in the heights above the city. About 10,000 others had the same idea, and progress was difficult. About halfway up the hill, I ran into a long line of penitents marching in formation: soldiers, but dressed in black.

Ay Hussein! cried the leader, *Vay Hussein!*

Mu-sul-man! the troops responded, *Shi-a-lar!*

One of the soldiers recognized me from the front, and put down his steel whip long enough to sidle over to me.

"You have been with us throughout our period of grief and mourning," he said, extending his hand. "Please stay with us until the end."

I said I would be honored to do so.

The last 200 yards took us about half an hour, but we finally arrived at the entrance to the Shehidler Xiyabani—arguably the most resonant place in the short, brief history of the new Azerbaijani Republic. It is a beautiful if infinitely sad place, a place of dreams and death. There is only one other venue in the world that I have seen like it: the *Behesht-e Zahra*, the Martyrs' Cemetery in Tehran, where some one million Iranians killed in the eight-year Gulf War with Iraq lie buried. The scale of the two cemeteries, of course, is quite different. But the sentiment pulsing through the two is exactly the same: both are dedicated to those who gave final witness in the style of Imam Hussein, making self-sacrifice a standard to emulate in the wicked, modern world.

"Here, today, the day of the Martyr Hussein, let our soldiers learn what real martyrdom is all about!" croaked the leader of the Islamic party to a wall of avid listeners. Then, fists bouncing off of breast and chains pumping into backs, groups of ten, twenty, one hundred, and more began their march among the graves.

"Alemdar! Mu-sul-man! Shi-a-lar!"

Here, we descended on the last resting place of my old Post 19 pal, Nurjahan Husseinova's son Yevlakh, who had been declared a national hero because his friends had accidentally shot him in the back of the head on his first mission; there, we passed by the grave of Alef Khadjiev, who died defending the women and children of the forsaken town of Xodjali. As we worked our way through the rows and rows of graves, we finally came to and hovered above that of another old friend: Jenghiz Mustafaev, ace cameraman, producer, and womanizer, killed when a scrap of shrapnel crept between his shirt and flak jacket and severed a vital artery in the summer of

1992. For reasons I cannot quite fathom but by no means mock, judging by the intensity of feeling of those gathered around his grave and by the sheer number of votive ribbons attached to it, Jenghiz seemed well on his way to becoming a Shi'ite Saint-Of-Something—that is, he was on his way to immortality, as real as it gets.

Then, as the moment of the Killing Hour arrived, we descended on a grave among the graves. I did not note the name. A woman, a mother, was on her knees, leaning over the canopy and weeping, remembering the things only mothers can. A man, a father, tried to remain stoic but rested his hand and then his head on the steel bars of the tombstone, blinking his eyes to hold back the flood of tears behind the should-haves and could-haves but did-nots. A girl, most likely a younger sister who had never really known her older and now dead brother, stood to the side, unsure of what to do. There might have been a fourth or a fifth member of the family at the graveside, but if they were there, they were soon lost in the crunch as two score and then more penitents arrived and turned a private remembrance into a very public lament. The hand-like Alam standard was thrust over the grave, and the penitents surrounded it, chanting and beating themselves in remorse for not having been given the chance to join the lost son in eternity.

"Mu-sul-man! Alemdar! Shi-a-lar!"

The sound of the martyrs' dirge was muffled by the canopy provided by olive trees and dwarf pine, but seemed to seep into the marble graves set in the earth. While the father began to move his lips in sync with the dirge-chant, his wife's plaintive sob took on a counterpoint, and she began tapping her thigh in time with the blows of the flagellants. I pretended to take pictures to conceal the fact that I, too, was crying.

Epilogue

I avoided Azerbaijan for almost two years, an absence that spawned a number of different rumors among my friends and foes. The Iranian ambassador said I had fled the country after having been exposed as the CIA station chief for the entire Caucasus. Another version was that I had been declared persona non grata by Heydar Aliyev. Still another, promoted by people in the Popular Front, said I had left in disgust and had taken a solemn vow not to return until Elchibey was restored to power.

The truth was far more prosaic. Hicran and I had moved back to Istanbul to try and to stitch back together some semblance of a normal existence. We failed. First we were unable to talk about anything but Azerbaijan to other people, and then we were unable to talk about anything else between ourselves. We began living separately in the summer of 1994 when I moved back to Montana and began to face the fact that no one knew where Azerbaijan was, or really cared.

But , in fact, others were starting to discover Azerbaijan—namely, the authors of the first rash of articles and instant books about the post-Soviet meltdown, often based on or referring to my published material, which was deeply irritating.* But I remained in possession of scores of notebooks recording the ins and outs of parliamentary debate over the years and pounds of paper scraps—bar and restaurant napkins, address books, calen-

---

*I guess becoming a footnote in someone else's published work should be flattering. But making an actual appearance is something else. In one book I was 'revealed' as a fake journalist and probable spy. In another, the writer set up her chapter on Baku in my apartment, and grossly distorted what a 'senior official' (who just happened to be Vafa Gulizade) had to say about Aliyev. The most egregious example of shoddy journalism and downright plagiarism, however, occurred in a book written by a man who used my early interviews with Elchibey as his own. He had been a guest in my house, and he used the occasion to surreptitiously copy my files.

dars, official invitations—on which I had scrawled down essential notes. I preserved them all for the day when I would actually sit down and write *my* book.

A first try was published by an obscure publishing house in Istanbul in 1994, and word began filtering out that Goltz had published an account of life in post-Soviet Azerbaijan. But due to the publisher's unfamiliarity with the concept of distribution, no one could find the book. One day, while working in my Montana garden, I heard the telephone ring and rushed in to grab it before the answering machine clicked on.

"Hello?"

"Mister Goltz, this is Xxx from the Central Intelligence Agency," said the voice on the other end of the line. "We met at the American Association for the Advancement of Slavic Studies conference in 1993. Do you remember?"

"Yes."

"Well, we have a slight problem that I thought you might help solve."

"Shoot."

"We can't find your damn book!"

The attention was both flattering and frustrating. Flattering, because at least there was some resonance out there; frustrating because day by day and then week by week and then month by month, I found myself becoming more alienated from my subject matter—and things were starting to change in and around Azerbaijan.

The chief symbol of this problem was the person of Heydar Aliyev, who seemed always to be described in the Western media as an unrepentant, unreconstructed 'former, former, former'—Communist Party boss, KGB general, and Politburo member. The implication was that he was 'Moscow's Man' in Baku, and that the events of the summer of 1993 were all designed to rein Azerbaijan back into the post-Soviet fold.

But even from the distant vantage point of Montana, there seemed to be something fundamentally flawed about that interpretation. From his first days in power, Heydar gave lip service to Moscow's interests in Azerbaijan and the Caucasus, but little more. Yes, he had led his little country into the CIS, the Moscow-dominated Commonwealth of Independent States, and had signed on to the various protocols referring to common defense and economic space, but he obstinately refused to implement any of the agreements in any meaningful way. And on the most crucial issue of control, that of common border defense and allowing Russian army bases in Azerbaijan, Heydar was as uncompromising as Abulfez Elchibey, the man who had managed to get the Russians removed some two weeks before Surat Husseinov's June 1993 putsch. Whoever else Heydar Aliyev was, he was not Moscow's Man.

Indeed, as the spring of 1994 turned to summer and then into fall, it looked like the anticipated showdown over power in Baku would be between the increasingly independent Heydar and Moscow's real agent in Azerbaijan—prime minister and Hero of Karabakh, Surat Husseinov. The denouement came in October 1994, just after Heydar Aliyev signed the document now referred to as the 'deal of the century'—a $7.4-billion project outlay for the development of the three main off-shore oil fields in the Caspian Sea (Guneshli, Chirag, and Azeri). The contract included terms for a $500-million signing bonus to be paid out in three installments, to help the cash-strapped government of Azerbaijan get over a fiscal hump. The first $150 million was payable as soon as the Azeri parliament confirmed the deal as legally binding.

But by mid-1994, the post-Soviet Russian bear had begun to awaken, and was demanding at least a piece of the oil action. Hard questions were being asked, the most basic of which was this: By what right did Azerbaijan claim off-shore fields that were not only well outside its twelve-mile sea-shelf, but were closer to Turkmenistan than Azerbaijan? The answer was framed in geographical terms: the Caspian, Moscow claimed, was not a sea but a lake.

The true measure of Moscow's interest in the oil deal, however, was to stir up new trouble in the form of Surat Husseinov. With Heydar away at the annual opening meeting of the United Nations in New York, Surat announced that he had problems with the 'deal of the century.' In its present structure, he said, it would only enrich Heydar Aliyev and his family but not Azerbaijan. . . .

The prime minister's words were interpreted as being a call for insurrection, and a truly convoluted series of events ensued. First, assassins killed Afyettin Jalilov, the deputy speaker of parliament (and Heydar's rumored bastard son). The Surat-friendly minister of justice, Ali Osmanov, pointed the finger at the head of the OMON para-military police forces, Ravshan Javadov, as being responsible for the murder. Javadov responded by having his men beat up and kidnap Osmanov. A large OMON force then occupied the Shaumiyan barracks on the edge of Baku, and declared themselves to be in rebellion. But against what and whom was not clear: the government of President Heydar Aliyev or that of Prime Minister Husseinov? Robert Finn decided to pay Javadov a visit to find out.

"Javadov said he had no intention to call for a revolt against Aliyev," Robert later told me. "The man was nearly beside himself trying to explain that he wanted nothing to do with Surat Husseinov and had no intention of bringing further sorrow to Azerbaijan."

Word was passed along to Heydar, who seemed to be on the verge of collapse. Now, with his flank protected, he called on the people of Azerbaijan to gather at Freedom Square for a huge rally, and there Heydar spoke.

"There are those in this government who wish to destroy our land!" he thundered into a bank of microphones. "And one of them is the prime minister, Surat Husseinov!"

More extraordinary than the public denunciation was the fact that Surat was standing next to Heydar at that very instant. Pictures taken at the moment reveal a dumbstruck Husseinov—another deer caught in the head-lights of Heydar's on-rushing truck. Within days, or maybe hours—I was not there—Surat was stripped of his titles and honors and then had calumny dumped upon him like a bucket of manure. All his efforts to exculpate himself from the charge of treason were in vain. It was Surat who had lost the war in Karabakh; Surat who had brought the economy to its knees; Surat who had isolated Azerbaijan from the rest of the world. . . .

Surat was placed under house arrest while his supporters were hounded down. Several, including his erstwhile spokesman during the Ganje Events, Aypara Aliev, began turning up dead in the streets. Another victim was my old nemesis at the time of the Xodjali Massacre, Rasim Agayev, Ayaz Mutalibov's press secretary. He was picked up and thrown into some awful prison, where he remains to this day. Meanwhile, about a week after his arrest, Surat managed to give his minders the slip and escape (or was allowed to escape) to Moscow. Another man who managed to get away from the wrath of Heydar was Rahim Gaziev. When the pair reappeared in Moscow, they were met by none other than Ayaz Mutalibov, thus proving beyond a shadow of a doubt where their loyalties lay all along.

The ultimate irony, of course—and if there is a moment to use the word *Schadenfreude* in its true sense, this was one—was that in addition to being charged with planning a coup against the legitimate government of Azerbaijan (of which, as prime minister, he was nominally the head) Surat was charged with having attempted to overthrow the legitimate state author-ity in June 1993. The Ganje Events were finally called a 'coup,' and one that Heydar, true to his word to me that fine day on live television when I had asked him 'The Question,' had finally stopped—even if a year too late to do Elchibey any good.*

---

*Baku then invoked an extradition treaty between Russia and Azerbaijan, but had to be satisfied with a piecemeal return of the three conspirators, usually in association with an attempt by the Kremlin to woo Baku into establishing closer ties. Rahim Gaziev was the first to be sent back, in the spring of 1996. Charged with treason, he was condemned to death, a sentence that has not been effected as of this writing, in late 1997. Surat

Meanwhile, back in Baku, the 'deal of the century' oil contract was duly ratified by parliament in November 1994. In order to mollify Russia, the Azerbaijani national oil company SOCAR offered half of its 20 percent share in the consortium to the Russian energy giant, LukOil. Similarly, the national oil company of the Islamic Republic of Iran, excluded from the deal due to Washington's refusal to allow American oil companies to do any sort of business with Tehran, was deftly invited to join a new consortium to explore and exploit another promising off-shore field. In the words of a Japanese executive from the giant Itochi enterprise, this 'internationalization' of the oil patch was ultimately aimed at garnering 'international insurance' by balancing state and corporate interests in the future of Azerbaijan.

Behind the glad-handing and passing of pens as each deal was signed, however, there was still plenty of doom and gloom in the oil patch. For example, the little matter of how to export the oil was left unresolved—that is, the routing of the pipeline. The logical route out of the Caspian basin was to the Gulf or the Indian Ocean via Iran. But due to Washington's prohibition about doing business with the Islamic Republic, this was a non-starter so long as American companies were involved in the pipeline project. And, so long as Armenia continued to occupy much of western Azerbaijan, the idea of building the so-called 'Peace Pipeline' favored by Washington and Ankara was likewise an impossibility. Accordingly, discussion began to focus on repairing two existing lines to the Black Sea coast: the first north through Daghestan and then Chechnya to the Russian terminal of Novorossiisk, and the second west through Georgia to the port of Supsa/Batumi.

Neither of these schemes pleased Turkey at all. Not only would such routings rob Ankara of billions of dollars in construction and transport fees if the new pipelines were instead built to its eastern Mediterranean port of Ceyhan, but every tanker passing through the Istanbul Bosphorus represented an ecological disaster waiting to happen.

* * *

While Ankara fretted about lost revenues and oil slicks in the Bosphorus, there was a bigger problem brewing. After turning a blind eye for three

remained at large until March 1997, when he was arrested in the Russian weapons-making city of Tula, and extradited to Baku just before a meeting of the CIS member heads of state. Ayaz Mutalibov, said to be resident in a Moscow dacha owned by former KGB director Yurii Barannikov, may well be next, should the authorities in Moscow want to tempt Azerbaijan to enter more deeply into its neo-imperial embrace.

years to the pretensions of the Chechen president Djokhar Dudayev to independence from the Russian Federation, Moscow decided it was time to rein in the rogue republic and put paid to Dudayev's 'criminal' regime. Whatever the real reason, there are not too many observers of the Caucasus willing to posit that Caspian oil and the politics of pipelines had nothing to do with Moscow's belligerent stance on Chechnya.

At first, efforts to overthrow Dudayev were made under the guise of an armed revolt by 'the opposition,' which resembled very much the Surat Husseinov putsch in Azerbaijan in 1993 (and, for that matter, the anti-Gamsakhurdia putsch in Georgia in 1992). The difference was that unlike Elchibey and Gamsakhurdia, Djokhar Dudayev did not run away. He ordered his security forces to crush the revolt, and they did so, capturing scores of Russian mercenaries and parading them through the streets.

By late December 1994, Moscow was obliged to admit the failure of getting rid of Dudayev through subversion. The time had come to 'restore constitutional authority' in Chechnya by other means. On New Year's Day, 1995, Boris Yeltsin ordered his tanks to roll on the breakaway mini-republic while his air force began bombing Grozny.

The immediate impact of the Chechen war on Azerbaijan was dramatic and traumatic. In real terms, this meant that Heydar Aliyev had become president of a country that had all the accouterments of being a oil-rich state but none of the substance: while private jets bearing oil executives landed at the airport and billion dollar contracts were bandied about in the press, the stark reality was that Azerbaijan would not make any significant money from its oil resources for at least a decade—and a stable decade at that. In the words of the out-going British Ambassador to Baku, Tom Young, Azerbaijan had entered a 'trough of social discontent, cut between rising expectations and falling revenues.'

I got a small taste of this atmosphere in January 1995, when I made a quick jaunt through the country, traveling incognito on my way into Chechnya over the Daghestan frontier. On my way back out of Chechnya in late February, burnt and bruised from the appalling spectacle of that war, I stopped in to see Robert Finn.

"There is something bad in the air," said Robert, a diplomat famous for his good nose. "I think we are warming up for another coup."

The moment came in mid-March 1995. Under circumstances that were even more convoluted than the abortive so-called Surat coup, Ravshan Javadov lurched back into the news, openly accusing Heydar, his family, and the so-called 'Naxjivan Clan' of plundering the oil wealth of Azerbaijan, and demanding Heydar's immediate resignation. To give some muscle to his argument, Javadov marched his men from the northern

Azerbaijani town of Gazakh to Baku and reoccupied the Shaumiyan barracks. Once again, the cards seemed to add up to a Moscow-based conspiracy designed to terminate Azerbaijani independence—or so all the pundits thought.

But this time around, there was something definitely wrong with that analysis. Ravshan Javadov hardly fit the profile of pro-Moscow putschist. Nor did any of the men who answered his call: either by direct participation or by default, they included former ministers in the Elchibey government, Iskender Hamidov and Towfig Gasimov. Indeed, Javadov was appealing to the Popular Front to urge the people to rise and dispose of Aliyev. He also called on those Chechen fighters in Baku to join in the fray. Given the personalities and politics involved, it looked less like a pro-Russian coup attempt than one with distinct *Turkish* underpinnings.

I was in Moscow when news of the new coup-in-progress was broadcast, and immediately went out to Vnukovo airport to get back to Baku. All flights had been canceled and the airport was packed with anxiously waiting Azeris. There was a flight the next day to Daghestan. I booked a seat on it, figuring that I could bribe my way across the border somehow or other. Then I went back to my abode to listen to the radio and try to keep abreast of events. News was patchy at best, but the essence seemed to be this: Heydar had called on the rebels to cease and desist, announcing that negotiations were the only way to solve the crisis. To that end, he declared a two day cool-down period to allow representatives of both sides time to talk. . . .

Less than twenty-four hours into the forty-eight-hour moratorium, Heydar ordered his men to attack. The Shaumiyan barracks were surrounded on all sides by loyalist troops. Their attack was short and it was bloody, and when it was over, some eighty OMON men were dead on the ground. Javadov died from a loss of blood while on the way to a hospital (others said while he lay in the hospital).

The mop-up operation seemed to confirm the pro-Turkish slant to the revolt. No sooner had the dust settled than scores of Turkish advisors, students, businessmen, and even the ambassador, my old friend Altan Kahramanoglu, departed the capital with their collective tails between their legs. The 'pan-Turkish' honeymoon that had begun under Elchibey was over; although the 'special relationship' between Baku and Ankara would eventually be salvaged in part, the glow was gone forever.

Although the conclusive evidence will probably never be available, the insider take on the abortive 'Turkish coup' in Baku was the following: Rogue elements in the Turkish security services who were connected with the Turkish Bozkurt movement felt they were losing the commercial presence—smuggling oil, metals, and, allegedly, drugs—they had previously enjoyed in Azerbaijan during the salad days of the Popular Front, and had decided to take extreme measures to preserve what they had left. The most efficacious way of doing so was to join forces with the Azeri Bozkurts and oust Heydar Aliyev; presumably, they hoped to restore Elchibey and the Popular Front to power.

But the leadership of the rump Popular Front did not respond. Rather than call upon its membership and supporters to take the streets, Elchibey's deputies begged people to stay home. Even more crucially, Djokhar Dudayev issued word to his men in Baku that no organized Chechen aid to the rebels would be tolerated. Individual Chechens might do what they wanted in accordance with their beliefs, but the government of 'Ichkeria' (Chechnya) would not align itself with the putchists. The Chechens stayed home.

Accordingly, Heydar Aliyev found himself confronted with two curious sets of allies by default: the 'responsible' leadership of the Popular Front, who were grateful for not being arrested and thrown into prison for crimes against the state they had indeed not committed, and the battle-hardened followers of Djokhar Dudayev, who were able to continue to use Azerbaijan as a deep base—and tacitly offer Heydar Aliyev muscle on demand, should the necessity ever arise.

The primary development to follow from the abortive Javadov putsch was stranger still. Having confronted pretenders from both Moscow and Ankara, Heydar Aliyev was obliged to look elsewhere for the sort of friends he could call on in time of need. This meant the West, and specifically, the United States of America. The means to attract that support was oil.

And at a gasping pace, Heydar Aliyev began signing multi-billion-dollar deals. In addition to the immediate impact of the signing bonuses on the national exchequer, of course, there was another element of keen interest to Azeri-watchers: every one of the production sharing or exploration deals was tacitly designed to increase outside interest in the survival of both the regime and the country. The result was that, in a very short time, my little backwater called Baku had become a hydrocarbon boomtown.

I was not prepared for the changes when I first encountered them. The first inkling came not in Azerbaijan, but in Washington, D.C.

* * *

The venue was the Great Hall of the National Building Museum, the guest list read like a Who's Who of Washington insiders, and the occasion for the regal banquet was an 'official working visit' to the United States of America by the President of the Azerbaijan Republic, His Excellency Heydar Aliyev.

"Today, looking at our two flags standing side by side in this beautiful building, I nearly weep for joy!" intoned Heydar. "Let the cooperation between the United States of America and independent Azerbaijan be the legacy that I leave for future generations!"

The crowd, as they say, went wild—and continued to do so as the Old Man and his entourage took Washington (and New York and Chicago and Houston) by storm. The only people left out seemed to be the knots of diaspora Armenian protesters, who, having failed to get U.S. President Bill Clinton to cancel the visit, had to content themselves with waving black banners outside the various venues where Heydar appeared: the Willard Hotel, Georgetown University, the National Building Museum, and, of course, the White House (where I succeeded in breaching White House security with the aid of an out-of-date Azerbaijan press pass, a passport, and my Montana driver's license).

Yes, by August 1997, Azerbaijan had been discovered by the Washington establishment and officially added to the map of American interests. A veritable telephone book of johnny-come-lately pundits and geo-strategic thinkers were all trying to get in on the act, adding their names to the growing list of 'Eurasia' experts writing for or being quoted in OpEd pieces in the *Washington Post, New York Times,* and *Wall Street Journal.* They were men like John Sununu, Lloyd Bentsen, James Baker III, and Caspar Weinberger, all of whom had taken up the Azerbaijani 'cause' (and had thus begun to attract the ire of the Armenian diaspora) in hopes of getting a piece of the oily action. I doubt if any knew about me or my experience in the bad-old-days in Baku, although there were some old timers around who seemed to appreciate my obsession. One was the president of the country.

"Tomas Bey, *khow arre yooo?*" a pleasantly surprised Heydar asked me in his best three words of English, after his security guards had dragged me through the throng during the first grand reception in the Willard Hotel.

"Welcome to America, Heydar *Muallim,*" I replied in Azeri. "I couldn't stay away on this historic occasion."

"Where are you living now?" Heydar asked. "We have not seen or heard of you in Baku for some time."

"I have been in my little town in Montana, working in my garden."

Heydar seemed to consider this for a moment, and then became aware again that the Azeri television cameras were recording every nuance of our little tête-à-tête.

"This man was the FIRST JOURNALIST to seek me out in Naxjivan before my return to Baku!" bellowed Heydar. "He followed the entire process of my return to power! You must now return to Baku to see how things have changed!"

I told him I would try.

* * *

"I'd issue you one of our new passports but the French company made too many printing errors for them to be acceptable," chortled Fahrettin Kurbanov as he stamped a complimentary year-long, multiple-entry visa in my passport later that week. It had been Fahrettin who had taken the decision to issue me the first foreign press accreditation way back in the autumn of 1991; he was now working as the chief consul of the Azerbaijani Embassy in Washington, wading through a pile of visa applications every day.

It was the start of an extraordinary return journey to Baku, lasting from September to November 1997, that might be summarized as 'we remember you; do you remember us?' every step along the way.

The first shock was that there were now direct flights to Azerbaijan from London, Frankfurt, and Amsterdam aboard British Airways, Lufthansa, and KLM. For personal reasons, however, I chose to fly via Istanbul and was thus obliged to take the Azerbaijan Airlines flight into Baku that Hicran and I had flown on in the summer of 1991.

The second shock was that this time it was a normal flight aboard a normal Boeing jet with good food and friendly service.

I had heard of nasty experiences at customs, but I experienced none of that.

"*Tomas—you!*" trilled a man wearing three stars on the epaulets of the Azeri equivalent of the old Soviet border guards uniform.

It was Asif, one of the fourteen survivors of the Xodjali garrison under the command of Alef Khadjiev, now risen to the position of security boss at Baku International airport. I soon found myself not only rushed through whatever existing procedures applied to arriving foreigners, but led arm in arm by Asif through all the security check points and out into the parking lot, while Asif's men bowed and scraped and swore eternal oaths to aid me in any way should I ever need them.

My taxi driver remembered me too, although it was a rather different context—the famous, live press conference in the summer of 1993 when I asked Heydar Aliyev what he intended to do about Surat Husseinov.

"Aren't you that foreign journalist who asked The Question?" the driver asked. (It readily became apparent that his memory did not extend to what the question had been, or the answer, for that matter.)

More remarkable than this was that, rather than roaring down the airport road in a beat-up Lada or Volga, the driver was at the wheel of a brand-new Turkish-made Fiat, one painted yellow with the familiar checker-box on top. It even had a meter. The driver explained that he was one of hundreds of new entrepreneurs who leased the cars from the government for a period of four years, after which the car would become his private property.

"Sorry, I forgot to fill up on the way out," said the driver, pulling into—once again, I could scarcely believe my eyes—a gleaming, clean gas station, replete with a huge marquee sign identifying it as being part of the LukOil chain. Immediately, a uniformed attendant came running out to stick the nozzle in the tank, and then went about washing the windows and mirrors. I strolled into the mini-mart attached to the station; shelves were sagging with cigarettes, chilled beer, snacks, and diverse lubricants and oils.

The road into town was likewise both familiar and strange. The nasty old oil fields of Sarakhan were still marked by forests of rusted derricks and not one pothole seemed to have been repaired during my absence. But the road was also lined with wholesale warehouses, bulging with all manner of goods: lightbulbs, kitchen appliances, bathroom tiles, bedroom furniture, televisions and audio equipment, and Goodyear and Firestone tires. The closer we got to Baku proper, the more crowded things became: construction sites for new buildings, billboards advertising the charms of a dozen casinos as well as the delights of a score or more restaurants and bars I had never heard of before. Competing with the entertainment facilities were other huge signs urging consumers to buy this or that cooking oil, drink this or that soft drink, or use one of four or five different brands of cell phones. Judging by the occupied ears of drivers of the Mercedes sedans and Jeep Cherokees whizzing by us, business in the communications sector was hot.

I had heard the old oil patch formula: that for every dollar of direct investment in the petroleum, another three or four dollars of direct investment is attracted to the peripheral economy, but I had never actually seen the process in action. And the commercial activity lining the airport road was merely the tip of the iceberg. Over the next few days and weeks I would come to understand much more of the dynamic at play: hot on the heels of the oil companies, with their requisite hirings of secretaries, translators, drivers, experts and such like (not to speak about apartment and office rentals required for their expatriate staff), were coming scores of other service and commercial companies from as far afield as Pakistan and Brazil. They were less interested in seeing Azerbaijan as a new Kuwait than as a new Dubai—as the commercial hub for not only the Caucasus and Central Asia, but southern Russia and maybe even Iran.

I was flabbergasted by it all—and the journey 'home' had scarcely begun.

* * *

I was tempted to check into the new Hyatt Regency hotel but did not. Even if I had had the $250 a night, the place was fully booked—and had been since its opening two years before, with the happy result for the investors that the hotel had recouped their $20 million in lightning time. I did stop in for a beer at the English Pub to gawk at the British Airway hostesses chugging down pints at $5 each, and then ran into former Texas senator Lloyd Bentsen in the lobby.

My alternative abode was *Chez le Cornu,* the one-and-a-half room apartment maintained by my old side-kick Laura Le Cornu, who was back in Baku working on a Ph.D. thesis for Oxford.

"How much do you pay for this place?" I asked her.

"Five hundred bucks a month," sighed Laura. "All the foreigners in town have driven prices through the roof."

As payment for the place on her couch, Laura insisted that I be her escort to explore the 'new' Baku swirling all around.

The tour started at Fountain Square, just outside the double gate in the Old City walls. That it was lined with shops and haberdasheries and restaurants and bars was pretty surprising in itself; more astonishing were the people strolling in and out of the stores or simply strutting their stuff up and down the pavement: well dressed matrons and their daughters, utterly beautiful Azeri women and handsome young men, all sporting designer clothes (and usually with cell phones glued to their ears), and kids roaring over the cobblestones on in-line roller skates.

"Where were all these people way back when?" I asked Laura.

"Hiding, I guess," she replied.

Needing to replenish her refrigerator, we stopped into one of several supermarkets just off the square. It was packed with everything from Single Malt Scotch to half-kilo tins of caviar and all the canned goods, tennis balls, and neatly wrapped hamburger you could ever dream of. Customers calmly wheeled carts between the aisles, while tidy clerks glided scanners over bar codes, adding up sums that people were paying for with credit cards.

A supermarket? Credit cards?

But this was Baku, my Baku. . . .

The material tour went on and on.

Up and down Neftjilar Prospekti, or Oilmen's Boulevard, shops, cafes, and Western-style bars were springing up like so many hydrocarbon-fed mushrooms. Most, like the Ragin' Cajun bistro (run by Charlie Schroeder, an American from Louisiana who, in addition to making a killing with his three world-class restaurants, was rapidly replacing me in the media's imagination as the 'first' American to have set up shop in Baku) and the Sine Klub (owned by the two Turkish entrepreneurs, Eyup and Ercan, who had previously created the old Club Universal), catered to foreigners and locals associated with the infant oil industry or the growing international community of diplomats, aid workers, and businessmen. All were pumping money into the local economy in the way of rents and salaries.

Then there were the various expenses associated with roustabouts and roughnecks looking for a little R&R in the rash of new bars and brothels scattered around town.

"Sad to say it but Baku has become a classic oil town, just like you said it would," sighed Ed Lake, who had just moved his wife and two children back from Houston to work in Amoco's newly refurbished office in the old city. Apparently there had been a corporate decision to promote the presence of stable family men in the oil patch. The first spate of broken marriages were already cropping up, and the medical team shared by all the oil companies had started to register clients according to different bars: there was the syphilis bar, the gonorrhea bar, and the herpes bar, and probably some more exotic places I never wanted to find.

Indeed, from the days of the ten o'clock curfew imposed by the Popular Front (and then maintained in the first days of Heydar's rule), Baku had become a town that did not sleep. After drinks (tequila, of course) at Schroeder's Margaritaville establishment, Laura and I sallied forth to check out several of the new bars in town that she had heard of but was reluctant to visit alone.

The first of these was the Lord Nelson, which claimed the honor of being the first 'British Pub' in Baku, replete with Guinness on tap, fish and chips, and a dart contest every Monday night. It was pretty quiet the night we stopped in, although worthwhile in that I found myself in conversation with some guy whose line of business was pest control for the new apartments and offices in town.

"It is the kind of job that if you do it too well you put yourself out of work," said the rat slayer. "There are forty firms like ours in Dubai, but we are the first to set up shop here."

Down the street was the much livelier Winston's, where clients were greeted by a blowup, life-size, anatomically correct girlie doll. The sign around the doll's neck asked visiting roughnecks off the rigs the succinct question: 'How long has it been?'

The doll, apparently, was just a joke. But after engaging in conversation with a Pakistani businessman (who had decided to come north from Dubai to seek his fortune selling office furniture) about the intricacies of the pre-tax bribe, said businessman decided to show Laura and me several establishments that might gently be referred to as down-market service centers for the oilman who has spent too much time off shore. Laura was appalled, but not in danger: the ratio of women to men was such that if she declined offers many times the per diem her research grant allowed, the suitor was able to turn his libidinous attentions elsewhere with ease. To me, more remarkable than the very existence of such places was the fact that they appeared to be staffed mostly by Azeri women, who were drinking beer and smoking cigarettes in public. I could not help thinking that their number probably drew heavily on refugee daughters and war widows. I even thought I recognized Nurjahan Husseinova. I was tempted to walk over to say hello, but then thought better of it. What would I say if it were indeed her?

* * *

After the night of sin it was time to repent, so the next morning I slogged up the hill toward parliament to pay my respects to my friends and acquaintances who people the Shehidler Xiyabani. I dropped red carnations on the graves of Nurjahan Husseinova's son Yevlakh, Commander Alef Khadjiev, cameraman Jenghiz Mustafayev, and on all those others I knew and many of those I didn't. The *Akhund,* or prayer-singer, accompanied me through the rows of graves and provided commentary on the life and times of the heroes. We were the only ones there.

Martyrs' Lane had also seen its own share of change. During my absence, the cemetery had been standardized. The personalized portraits of the dead had been converted into etchings on uniform granite slabs, and all the sundry elements that had made the cemetery so strange, if homey, had been removed: there were no longer any broken guitars, water-stained books, baby dolls, or any of the other personalized, funerary bric-a-brac that had graced and individualized each grave a few years before.

The visit also braced me for a series of meetings I knew I had to make. The first was a courtesy call on Asim Mullahzade, now deputy chairman of the Popular Front, which had managed to change itself from a 'mass' organization of the streets into a proper political party.

"Thomas," breathed Asim after a hearty embrace. "You are back!"

He quickly brought me up to date with recent events, even if his interpretation had a clear Popular Front–like spin: Heydar Aliyev was an autocrat, the leader of a rapacious clan, and a megalomaniac of the first order—but not the national traitor or Russian stooge that he had been made out to be by many in the Popular Front in 1993, including Asim himself.

"Perhaps he has changed or perhaps we never really knew who he was and what he stood for, but today Heydar Aliyev has effectively adopted all of our positions on independence, economic development, and even Iran," chortled Asim. "Rather than closing down the Popular Front, he closed down the Islamic Party and jailed all their leaders! And because of his anti-Russian bias, which really means pro-West, he has been forced to pay lip service to our concept of democratization! Sure, the last parliamentary elections were called 'neither free nor fair' by the monitors who came to control them, and yes the parliament is packed with his people, but he realizes that he cannot govern without us. We are on the right road."

It was not exactly a love-fest between 'the clan' (as everyone described Heydar's political entourage from Naxjivan) and the Popular Front, however. Asim showed me a letter inadvertently sent to his address: a complaint from the Ministry of Communications to the MTN, or Azerbaijani equivalent of the KGB, noting that as per the latter's request, the former had duly put a wire tap on Asim's home telephone for such and such a period and monitored so and so many calls, incoming and outgoing, but that the bill for having done so was still outstanding and that unless the MTN coughed up the money, the telephone company would be obliged to cease this special service. . . .

Next, Asim took me to see Ali Kerimov, who had been the last secretary of state of the Elchibey government. He was now acting head of the Popular Front Party and a deputy in the new parliament. The office was a lot smaller than his room over at the presidential apparatus had been, but one detail was still the same: a portrait of Abulfez Elchibey hung on the wall.

Our discussion focused on the fate of all the old players, ranging from Towfig Gasimov to Iskender Hamidov. The former had recently been released from a psychiatric hospital where he had been sent following the Javadov coup attempt, while the latter remained buried in the basement of some horrible jail, a broken man.

"They have our deepest sympathies and their contribution to independent Azerbaijan was great, but they were fools to have gotten involved in the Turkish coup," said Kerimov. Neither was expected to play any political role in the future, even if restored to health.

A much more sensitive subject was Rahim Gaziev, who had been condemned to death for treason after his extradition from Moscow.

"When did you know that Rahim was really a Russian agent?" I asked.

"All along," Kerimov replied with a weak smile. "But we were unable to act against Gaziev for more than a year because of the successful effort of his minders to create the legend of Rahim the Hero."

Even Gaziev's gimpy wounded-hero's leg, allegedly incurred when he tried to seize weapons from departing Russian soldiers in 1991, was apparently self-inflicted in order to win him sympathy and fame.

"So why didn't you get rid of Rahim before he destroyed the army?"

"We were still too weak to do so. We had to reduce his stature as a war hero first."

"At the cost of defeat on the battlefield?"

"Yes," Kerimov admitted slowly and sadly.

"Heydar used the same technique to get rid of Surat Husseinov," said Asim, as if that could somehow ameliorate the loss of thousands of young lives. "First he brought him into the government, and then let him hang himself."

"And Elchibey?" I asked after a pause. "How is he?"

Asim smiled.

"He is coming back next week."

"Asim," I said as gently as I could. "I have been hearing about Abulfez's homecoming next week for the last four years."

* * *

There were other meetings, so many others. My old Russian teacher, Elfrieda, complained bitterly about life, as ever, and worried about whether she or her estranged husband Valeri would get the rights to their apartment when privatization of property finally got pushed through parliament. Meanwhile, they continued to live in the same two-room flat, down the street from Laura's apartment.

A slightly different situation pertained in the household of one of our oldest friends in Azerbaijan—that of Kubrah Hanim, the director of the sanatorium that specialized in the petroleum baths that allegedly resulted in so many pairs of (Soviet) twins. The sanatorium now housed some 500 refugees, just one of the many temporary depots scattered around the country containing the human detritus of the war over Karabakh. Her husband Rauf, the all-Soviet martial arts instructor, had suffered a stroke and had been reduced to pacing the worn parquet floor in their flat. Their first son and our first guide to Baku, Kamran, had married and was living elsewhere, while the second son, Farid, was adding to the family budget by working for chump-change over at the Foreign Ministry.

"Ah, *Tomas Bey,* what can I say, things are bad and they are getting worse," said Kubrah the night I stopped over to see her. "Things may look pretty good if you are walking down the main boulevard, but the policies of this government have destroyed the intellectual class in this country. I do not say this lightly. All the doctors, lawyers, and academics in Azerbaijan have been reduced to utter penury, while the new business class, who only represent maybe 10 percent of the population, lord it over everyone. It has gotten to the point where I am considering renting out my apartment to foreigners, because it is the only resource we have left. But then what are we supposed to do? Rent a one-room hovel on the edge of town and call that home?"

A certain amount of family tension existed between Kubrah Hanim and her new neighbor in our second apartment in Baku, currently occupied by none other than my old friend Yalchin Alizade, formerly the chief correspondent in Turkey for the Soviet news agency TASS, and now a real-estate speculator in his homeland.

Yalchin stared at me in amazement when he opened the door.

"I heard you had been thrown out of the country!" he said, dragging me in. It was not clear whether he was teasing or not.

We spent a pleasant two or three hours together, Yalchin speaking Turkish to me and I speaking his native Azeri back to him. We spoke about everything, from his belief that I was CIA and my belief that he was KGB, to what happened to whom and why way back then in our common Turkey of the mid-1980s, and contemporary Turkish policy toward the former Soviet Union, and what role Azerbaijan and Karabakh (and Georgia and Armenia and Chechnya) had played in the process of disintegration, and what the CIS represented, and the impact of oil and the politics of pipelines, and the personality and phenomenon of Heydar Aliyev.

The insider shop-talk made for fascinating conversation, but left me with the larger question of why Yalchin, an Azeri with such insider knowledge of the process of policy not only in the Big Country to the North but also Turkey and the region, was content to sit at home and watch his satellite television, utterly removed from the hurly burly of political life in his homeland.

"Because I have gone into business," he replied with a sly smile.

Hawking his various cars, clothes, and even his wife Zinfiray's jewels, Yalchin had shrewdly bought up apparent junk property in the old city, and embarked on a major refurbishment project in anticipation of renting out office space to oil companies.

"The going price per square meter in Baku now is higher than in Tokyo," he smugly related. "You should really think about getting together some investors and doing some business here."

I could only think of that 'first Western-style' bar I had almost opened up, that first news agency for embassies and oilmen I had almost begun, and the dry-cleaning franchise I had almost established.

* * *

The reason I had not become rich in Baku was because the war kept getting in the way. It was still a reality, and on the lips of all. Although a ceasefire had been in place since May 1994, no real movement had been achieved in bringing about a lasting political solution to the conflict between Azerbaijan and Armenia over the Black Garden, Mountainous Karabakh.

It was time to take a walk on the other side of 'booming Baku,' namely, to visit the refugee settlements along the front, which just happened to coincide with the routing of the so-called 'Western' export pipeline up through Georgia to the Black Sea.

The occasion and motivation to do so came through the agency of a young Azeri whom I had heard much of over the years, but never had a chance to meet because he was studying in the United States all the time I had lived in Baku. His name was Elin Suleymanov, and he had just recently quit his job in Prague to return to serve his homeland—and not as an overpaid consultant or translator for the AIOC or some other Western business venture, but as a locally hired field worker for the United Nations High Commission for Refugees (UNHCR), responsible for the one million internally displaced persons (IDPs) in Azerbaijan.

"You can see just how intimately connected are the issues of refugees and oil," said Elin as we rolled along the dreary Baku–Ganje highway on a tour of his various camps. "It is the aching wound of this country and the one thing that gives the lie to hydrocarbon happiness in the new Azerbaijan."

We made numerous stops at camps and settlements along the refugee line, and then stopped for the night in Barda, where my old friend Yusuf Agayev had once held sway as the chief military prosecutor after having been ejected first from Karabakh and then from Agdam. Discreet inquiries as to his whereabouts, however, led nowhere. All along the front with the Armenian lines, those Azeri soldiers and commanders we encountered exercised extreme caution in conversation with outsiders.

"I do not know what it was like before," said Elin as we checked into the UNHCR bunkhouse. "But my impression is that there actually *is* an army out there now."

In the morning we went over to the house and office complex of the International Committee of the Red Cross, where I had stayed with Feri Alemi back in the last shooting days of April 1994, and spoke with his replacement about conditions. The situation was stable, we were told, but rivalries and jealousies were growing between different refugee groups and certainly between the IDPs and the townspeople. In Ganje, for example, the main hotel had opened up a for-dollars-only casino, replete with an English manager, that was doing a booming business among the local elite. The allegation was that many seemed to specialize in 'privatizing' international aid, and were making their money by hawking donated food that had been intended for the refugees. In the refugee relief trade, this is called 'leakage,' but in the refugee regions of Azerbaijan, it might better have been described as a flood.

Tension was immediately apparent when we stopped in to visit the so-called 'train people' on the outskirts of Barda to see what they thought about life, the leadership, and the prospects for peace.

* * *

The children and the geese were competing for space in the green, miasmic pool of drainage water while mothers scrubbed laundry or made thin porridge for lunch—hopefully not from the same water source. I declined the traditional offer of communal tea, deciding it best to stay thirsty as I prowled in and out of the hundreds of decaying boxcars that made up a veritable small city on train tracks, 'home' for thousands of IDPs.

"Look at the way we live!" cried a woman who identified herself as Mrs. Shariah Hashimova and gave her age as 60, while waving a withered hand at the drainage ditch next to her boxcar home. "This is worse than a jail! The children get sick and there is no medicine. The locals call us cowards for having fled our homes in the first place, and refuse to help us. The government keeps on saying that we will be going home soon, but they have said that for the past four years. . . ."

Mrs. Hashimova was a native of Agdam, located about thirty miles west of Barda, and had been living in her boxcar since the summer of 1993 when the city fell to the Armenians. Her husband, Handi, was killed there by shrapnel from a GRAD rocket. He had been buried by my old friend Imam Sadik Sadikov, the *Akhund* of the Agdam mosque, who had washed and buried all the bodies from Xodjali. Sadikov himself had died the previous year while living in a tent.

"It is not the Armenians who forced us into this pit of misery, but the Muslims!" said Mrs. Hashimova, referring to her fellow Azeri countrymen by their religious, not national, designation. "It was the treason of Surat Husseinov, Rahim Gaziev, and the *Satgins* (Sell-outers) that did this to us!"

Up and down the line, the story was always the same: On such and such a date in 1992 or 1993 or 1994, the Armenians had come and the people had fled, usually leaving behind a body or two: a husband, a brother, a child. Sometimes the IDPs listed several previous addresses before their arrival at their current domiciles. At one stop Elin was assaulted by an elderly woman who accused him and the UNHCR and all the other refugee-relief organizations of selling better dwellings to preferred customers. At another filthy camp another elderly woman assaulted me when I got out of the car with my video camera.

"Stop! Stop!" she screamed. "We do not want another journalist or foreigner to come in here and take our pictures! Nothing ever changes! Stop!"

A nasty incident was averted when Elin intervened and started shouting back at the woman, evoking my experience.

"Do you know who this is!" he demanded. "This is the man who reported on Xodjali and Kelbajar and the fall of Agdam!"

It was not pretty—and the contrast between Baku and the refugee-filled hinterland could not have been greater or more heart-breaking. While the newly well-heeled elite in Baku were reveling in their new homes, clothes, cars, and cellular telephones, nearly a million, mainly rural Azerbaijani citizens were still living like animals in a variety of tent cities, boxcar towns, and the basements of bombed-out buildings. Pushing our luck, we tried and succeeded in entering one of these no-go zones—the former Armenian town of Shariar, situated just outside Terter in the one tiny corner of Karabakh still under Azerbaijani control—and thus still claimed by the Armenians.

"We were here during all of the shelling and the assaults in 1993 and 1994, hiding in the basement," said Japarna Miruzeva, 26, who arrived in Shariar along with her four children and a hundred or so other ethnic Kurdish refugee families after the fall of Kelbajar in April of 1993. "We only came out to bury my father, who died of fright during the shelling. We had and have no place else to go."

I asked if they knew my host Shamil Askerov, the Kelbajar librarian, in whose house I stayed that awful night before my even more awful helicopter ride over the Murov Mountain pass. Of course they did. The showcase resettlement project, however, was in the Fizuli region, south and east of Karabakh, where the government was shoveling tens of millions of dollars to reconstruct homes in the one area 'liberated' from Armenian occupation by the Azeri forces in the spring of 1994. That project had come under criticism because many of the reconstructed homes were actually larger and fancier than those destroyed, leading to charges of preference among refugee groups for political reasons and wholesale corruption among the Azeri officials associated with the reconstruction project.

"The UNHCR is considering a general pull-out from the Fizuli region because the temporary homes we build are regarded as inadequate when compared to the permanent structures being built with World Bank money," said Elin. "The point is we are not tasked to build permanent settlements. The houses we build are four walls and a roof, and even the mortar for the joints is designed to be of such a low grade that the bricks can be disassembled quickly to move all the parts back to the refugees' real homes, if and when there is a permanent settlement to the Karabakh conflict. Explaining this to people who have been living like animals for the past four years is not easy."

Our last stop was another showcase settlement of an entirely different kind—a nameless tent city in the Barda region that was set up by the Turkish Red Crescent society in the summer of 1993. The Turks abandoned its maintenance after two years in circumstances that were not at all clear, leaving it to other international relief groups to pick up the task of looking after an estimated 10,000 people. Although visited by the UNHCR and several relief-oriented Non-Governmental Organizations, no group claimed the camp as an area of its direct responsibility, and conditions had continually deteriorated. Open sewers leading from outhouses ran parallel to a line of spigots used for drinking water; the local 'school' consisted of five canvas tents set up at the far end of the encampment in a swamp. Disease among the children was rife.

Sadder than the filthy state of the camp, however, was the notion that the government in Baku had identified it as one of the worst temporary settlements—and used it as a showcase of misery for visiting foreign dignitaries as a means of securing more foreign aid. Former American national security advisor Zbigniew Brzezinski was shown around the site, Elin related, and then refused to eat the caviar and sturgeon steak offered to him by his hosts at a luncheon following the tour, and told them to give it to the refugees instead.

"The Azeris are starting to learn from the Armenians how to suffer publicly to gain international sympathy," said Elin. "We have not got it perfected yet, but we are rapidly moving to create a national identity based on misery, sorrow, and perceived persecution—and it is a very sad thing to see. The refugees have become a pawn in the political game of getting outside forces to resolve the Karabakh crisis."

* * *

When I got back to Baku, I found that two old friends of mine, Philip Remler and Vafa Gulizade, were fully engaged in trying to find a lasting solution to the Karabakh conflict. The idea was to get beyond the seemingly intractable problem of giving preference to either the concept of 'territorial integrity of existing states' or the equally hallowed notion of 'self-determination' of local minorities.

Vafa had spent much of the past two years meeting with his Armenian counterpart, Gerard Libaridian, to talk about Karabakh, and looked ten years older for his efforts. Libaridian, for his part, had just resigned from said duty, citing his wife's health as the reason he quit. Others suggested that he was fed up serving the foreign policy objectives of Russia. Still others said he was tired of getting targeted by the Dashnaks as being the man negotiating away at the table what had been gained by force of arms.

Perhaps the truest indication of the real Armenian position on Karabakh was the new superhighway being built across the Lachin corridor, permanently connecting Karabakh to Armenia. The funds for the project came from the Armenian diaspora. More ominously, a scandal had recently erupted in Moscow when the head of the Russian Duma committee on defense had revealed that a billion dollars worth of military equipment had gone missing between 1993 and 1996, and all indications were that it had been shipped, for free, to Armenia—apparently in anticipation of the 'final battle' to be launched before Azerbaijan could spend some of its future oil revenues on the tools of war.

Philip, meanwhile, had effectively become the Number Two American diplomat in the so-called Minsk Group of the Organization for Security and Cooperation in Europe, headed by a joint U.S., Russian, and French delegation, which was trying to get Armenia and Azerbaijan to agree to a 'staged' peace plan for Karabakh. He had spent much of the past two years winging between endless negotiating sessions in Vienna, Prague, Paris, London, Lisbon—and now, once again, Baku, to present the Azeri authorities with details about the OSCE's most recent contacts in Yerevan and Stepanakert. After his official meetings—including, of course, with Vafa—Philip was supposed to go off to some official reception with the various members of the various delegations, and then link up with me for drinks and a debriefing of sorts. At the last moment, Vafa called to announce that he had no intention of going to the reception and that he wanted to take me to dinner. Hearing of my previous plans with Philip, he then proceeded to hijack the entire evening and was so insistent that both Philip and I go to dinner with him that I suspected he wanted a witness for something of importance he wanted to tell Philip in less than complete diplomatic privacy.

"Meet me in ten minutes in front of your old house, and I will pick you up with my car," said Vafa, leaving no room for argument. "We will pick Philip up at the embassy."

I could hear him talking on his cell phone to Philip before he hung up on me.

Ten minutes later Laura and I were packed into Vafa's private car and whizzing through traffic over to the new American embassy, a place that reminded me just how much Azerbaijan had changed in a few short years: I had been obliged to renew my passport there once, and had been amazed at the level of scrutiny and security imposed on every visitor. Happily, Philip was waiting in the reception area so I did not have to go through the trying rigmarole of showing identification and acquiring a clearance pass.

"Philipino," I said, giving him a quick embrace, "I'm really sorry about this change of plans but Vafa seemed so insistent. . . ."

"Fine by me," said Philip, throwing on his coat. "I'd rather spend an evening with Vafa on the town than at another reception over at the Gulistan."

Vafa, for his part, had already made out a schedule for the evening.

"Philip, my dear!" he said, acting as if the two had not seen each other in months, when in fact they had just been through a long negotiating session that afternoon. "In the new and modern Baku, we can eat at any restaurant we like—Chinese, Turkish, Indian, American steak house—but tonight I want to take you to a place where we can eat the very best national Azerbaijani cuisine! Do you agree?"

We were soon ensconced in a room at the Zirk restaurant, an obscure club so far off the beaten track that when I later went back to find it and book a table for twelve I had difficulty locating it, although it was a mere stone's throw away from the American embassy. The walls were hung with red velvet, and guests were sequestered away in private rooms waited on by tuxedoed attendants who fairly scurried in and out, delivering plates of gray caviar, salmon eggs, *dushberry* soup (miniature ravioli), quail breasts, and the most delicious sturgeon steak I have ever had. At least that was the level of service and selection of food we received.

"It is so wonderful to see you all back in Azerbaijan!" cried Vafa, raising one of the first toasts of the evening. "What changes have you noticed since your last visit so many, too many years ago?"

The small talk and general catch-up chatter continued for some time until slowly but surely, Vafa began broaching the subject he wanted to talk about: the real state of negotiations. Philip bantered back and forth diplomatically, until I decided I had to wade in and reassure him that tonight I was not a journalist, that nothing said at the table would ever leave my lips, and that indeed, we had never been at the Zirk restaurant at all. In fact, the only reason I feel that I can share these notes is that within a few days I saw a press report quoting Vafa on exactly the same items I had sworn never to repeat. They concerned Azerbaijan's changing position on having direct contacts with the authorities of Karabakh. Vafa was there to tell Philip privately that he had received permission from The Boss to tell the Americans and the Minsk group that Baku was ready to do so. It was, in its way, the equivalent of Israel and the PLO announcing that they were willing to recognize one another.

In a word, *breakthrough!**

---

*We in the news business call that news—but once again it was a story I could not write. I was too close to the coal-face of real-time diplomacy to do anything about it but

In essence, Philip and his OSCE delegation had come up with a plan that called for the Armenian forces occupying the six Azerbaijani districts around Karabakh to make a staged withdrawal in exchange for Azerbaijan (and Turkey) lifting the economic embargo against both Karabakh and Armenia itself. The final status of Karabakh, meanwhile, along with that of Susha and the so-called Lachin Corridor connecting Karabakh to Armenia, was to be left up to decisions made during the second stage of negotiations—that is, the direct talks between Baku and Stepanakert. Previously, the Armenian side had skirted around the issue of withdrawal for tacit Azeri recognition of the 'Karabakh authorities,' setting up last-minute qualifications that always scuttled the OSCE plans. But in early October, following the most recent round of OSCE/Minsk group shuttle diplomacy, Armenian president Levon Ter-Petrossian had held a rare press conference in which he effectively warned his countrymen of the growing cost of regional isolation, and that Armenia could never prosper without making some concessions along the lines of OSCE suggestions. Even more encouraging was the subsequent announcement by the leadership of the self-styled 'Republic of Mountainous Garabagh' that they were willing to talk about 'concessions in the direction of the Azerbaijani position' that would possibly establish a 'horizontal relationship' between Baku and Stepanakert that would ensure Karabakh's security while (somehow) maintaining the territorial integrity of Azerbaijan.*

"What we need is someone in the closest proximity to the president to take personal responsibility to sign off on this," said Philip.

"My dear Philip—I am that man!" cried Vafa.

I would like to share more with reader, but at this stage in the conversation I looked at Vafa, looked at Philip, looked at Laura—and told her that for the sake of security and the peace of mind of both Philip and Vafa, it was best that we call it a night and leave the two alone to hash out the last details of their semi-secret protocols away from our ears.

---

record the moment here for some eventual posterity. It was, in effect, the outline for what many in Yerevan and Moscow would subsequently refer to as the 'Daytonization' of the Karabakh conflict, meaning the imposition of an American-generated 'international' peace settlement to the detriment of the perceived interests of Moscow's allies—the Serbs in Bosnia, and the Armenians of Karabakh.

*If this was Washington's idea, it was in vain: in February 1998, Armenia's Ter-Petrossian would be forced to resign along with all the 'realist' (I am reluctant to say 'liberal') members of his government. The new interim president was none other than Robert Kocharian, Ter-Petrossian's hard-line prime minister, who also happened to be the former president of the Republic of Mountainous Garabagh—and thus technically a citizen of Azerbaijan. The entire OSCE negotiations package was back to square one.

"Thank you, Thomas," said Philip.

A month or two later, I called Philip in Washington.

"The Karabakh Armenians basically told us to take a walk," said Philip, who was packing his bags for yet another Minsk Group/OSCE trip, this time to Copenhagen.

"Back to square one?" I asked.

"In diplomacy, you never return to square one," he said diplomatically.

But it sure sounded like it to me. Mrs. Hashimova and all the rest of the 800,000 internal refugees would be spending another cold winter in their boxcars, forgotten by a world that had begun to believe that Azerbaijan equaled oil, equaled wealth, equaled happiness.

* * *

Technically, I was back in Baku to conduct research for a documentary on the 'Great Game,' meaning the new and highly convoluted politics of Caspian oil, and specifically, what role Azerbaijan played in the new, global energy sweepstakes. In real terms, that meant I was obliged to do a lot of sitting around, waiting for the film crew to set up, shoot, and then pack up before going off to the next venue. On November 3rd, I was sitting on a stone that looked like a seat in the labyrinth of the Old City, waiting for the crew to shoot an interview with a local guide, when down one of the cobblestone streets I saw a familiar figure running toward me: Asim Mullahzade.

"He is coming!" said Asim, rushing up to give me the news.

"Who is coming?"

"Elchibey!" he crowed. "He will be in Baku today!"

"Asim," I said. "You have told me that before."

"Didn't you read or hear about Aliyev's speech at the Union of Azerbaijani Writers yesterday?" hissed Asim. "He was speaking about the need for freedom of speech—he even went so far as to say that he was against the people who are trying to create a cult of personality around his person! He spoke about the need for constructive opposition—don't you understand what that means?"

I confessed I did not.

"And you, the would-be expert on reading between the lines!" cackled Asim. "It means that all obstacles for Elchibey's return have been removed! He will be back tonight!"

Yeah, yeah, Asim, I wanted to say, but politely buttoned my lip.

The film shoot in the old city was followed by lunch and then by the obligatory shopping for carpets, and I was not able to confirm Asim's heady prediction. If truth be told, I was not particularly active in trying to do so.

Asim (and the rest of the leadership of the Popular Front) had cried 'wolf' too many times before. Elchibey returning to Baku? Why?

Then, toward seven o'clock in the evening, my cell phone rang.

"Where are you?"

It was Laura Le Cornu, announcing the fact that the Popular Front headquarters was a sea of people, all waiting in anticipation of the arrival of the leader, Abulfez Elchibey.

Still not satisfied, I called Lawrence Sheets of Reuters. After a dozen or more busy signals, the line finally rang through.

"Can't talk now," said Uncle Larry. "My stringer tells me the Naxjivan plane has landed, that Elchibey is on the ground, and that there is chaos at the airport. Bye."

* * *

Elchibey! Elchibey! That was the mantra the crowd outside the headquarters of the Popular Front were chanting, and from a distance, it almost seemed like Friday Night on Freedom Square all over again. *Elchibey!*

But November 1997 was not November 1991, and it did not even require 'closer inspection' to discern that the howling, joyous crowd of Elchibey loyalists barely spilled out into the side street, much less blocked traffic on the main artery leading uptown. The crowd consisted of perhaps 500 people—and I seemed to know most of them, or at least most of them knew me.

"*Tomas* is here, *Tomas!*" crowed an unshaven guy I vaguely remembered as being one of the primary pan-Turkic howlers from the past, lurching forward to embrace me and plant a kiss on my cheek.

I guess I should have been grateful for the name recognition, because it was the only thing that seemed to propel me forward through the jostling crowd toward the main door. Still, although it may seem churlish, I have to admit that the wild-eyed faces, raised fists, elbows and knees, and total lack of crowd-control of the grand homecoming reception seemed to underline the difference between Heydar's and Elchibey's styles of leadership more than any other single event I could recall. I was getting mauled by friends, who thought they were doing me a favor by twisting their fellows' arms and necks to inch me along through the great unshaven throng.

I was in front of the main door, and then I was shoved through it. The crowd in the foyer was more of the same mass of humanity: giddy with excitement and joy, everyone lurching and pushing and sticking fingers in eyes and elbows in ears. And once more, in between the delirious repetition of the leader's name, I could hear people evoking my own, while scores of scruffy men embraced me. I could not remember who half of them were—

but I greeted each and every one as an old and dear friend, for which favor they then shoved me in front of them toward yet another internal door leading to the vestibule of Ali Kerimov's office, now blocked by security guards.

From a corner of my eye, I saw poor Laura pinned against a wall, unable or unwilling to fight her way any further forward or even back out the main door. I reached over to grab her and dragged her along as the crowd continued to push now the two of us forward until finally, blissfully, we found ourselves nose to nose with the sweat-stained security men guarding access to Ali Kerimov's ante-chamber.

"It is Tomas, Tomas!" the people behind us were shouting, as if the crowd might decide who had access and who did not. And then suddenly, one of the bulls shouldered the door open just enough for first me and then Laura to be sucked through into the ante-chamber. A select crowd of maybe a dozen local journalists were already there, waiting for the last door to be opened and to be led into the inner sanctum.

"Where's Reuters?" I asked, surprised to see that Lawrence Sheets was not present. I pulled out my cell phone and dialed his office and got the answering machine. That meant he was probably somewhere out there in the crush of humanity and trying to speak Russian, which was never a very good idea among the Popular Front crowd.

"There is a tall blonde guy from Reuters who should be here," I said to the security guard. "Pass the word back and get him in here, pronto!"

My special request got the response I wanted. Within about five minutes, the ante-chamber door was pried open a crack, and a very battered Lawrence Sheets propelled through to join us.

"Thanks," said Uncle Larry. "What a scene!"

Then suddenly, the door to the inner chamber opened, a huge billow of accumulated cigarette smoke coughed out as if from a stale lung, and the assembled journalists poured through the gap and into Ali Kerimov's office.

It, too, was jammed—but this time by a wall of very familiar faces from the dais of the Friday night rallies of the past, the opposition benches of parliament, and of course the halls of power at the executive building during the heady days of Front power between June 1992 and June 1993: Arif Xadjiev, Isa Gambar, and—I could not believe my eyes at first—Panakh Husseinov, the 'watermelon merchant'-cum-secretary of state. Standing like a proud father against the far wall was Ali Kerimov. Next to him was the stout but muscular figure of Asim Mullahzade, flush with joy. The only folks missing from the grand reunion seemed to be Towfig Gasimov and Iskender Hamidov, absent by dint of the psych ward and jail, and uninvited opposition characters like Etibar Mamadov, Leila Yunusova, and the brothers Araz and Zardusht Alizade. And in the center of the room stood a tall, lean, bearded, and ultimately dignified figure with silver-capped teeth flashing behind a broad and welcoming smile.

"*Tomas Goltz!*" said Abulfez Elchibey, extending his hands.

I could not resist. I stepped forward and kissed him on both cheeks.

"It is so good to see you in Baku, Abulfez Bey," I said.

"And where is Hicran Hanim?" he asked.

"Istanbul," I replied, surprised by the hitch in my voice.

* * *

The question of the moment, of course, was not so much why Elchibey had returned to Baku after four years of self-exile in Kelekekoy village in Naxjivan as how he had been allowed to return, and by whom.

The identity of the agent, no matter how many times denied, was there for all to see: Heydar Aliyev. Clearly, some sort of deal had been struck, although both that first night back in Baku and on all subsequent occasions when the question arose, Abulfez insisted that his return was not predicated on anyone's permission, but was a direct, democratic challenge to the strong-armed rule of the man who succeeded him.

"There are some Soviet-era communist leaders in the Caucasus who are trying to convince the West that the people of the region are not ready for democracy," Elchibey said after we had moved from personal greetings to the level of obligatory interview that first night back (I acted as Lawrence Sheets's translator, having nowhere to file the story myself). "This is totally false. Azerbaijan, Georgia, and Armenia are at the door of democracy. If we succeed here, with the support of the West, the democratic movement will roll on next to the authoritarian states of former Soviet Central Asia."

The staccato delivery, sprinkled with all the right words (democracy, freedom, human rights, and secular values), was all classic 'Fez. So, too, were his harshly critical words about the continued Armenian occupation of 20 percent of the country, diatribe against neo-imperial Russia, and blasting of the Islamic Republic of Iran for trampling on the unalienable rights of the ethnic Azeris living there. Democracy would triumph!

But somehow, the words rang hollow. Perhaps it was the presence of people like Isa Gambar, the man who, as chairman of parliament, could have called for new elections and really created a democratic basis for Azerbaijan, but never did for fear of losing his own seat. Perhaps it was Elchibey's criticism of the government's 'concessions' to the OSCE/Minsk Group Karabakh peace plan, with the tacit threat of using force if the wayward Armenians did not cease their claim to unique status inside or outside a unitary Azerbaijan: that was the position that had ultimately claimed 30,000 lives and brought the country to its knees. Indeed, most of the big questions about the use of authority and responsibility went unanswered, with the exception of one. At a press conference the next day, in which Abulfez finally had to ask the assembled journalists to stop referring to him as the 'ex-president' and to please just call him Professor Abulfez, one of the local journalists finally asked point blank the question all had been dancing around: why he had run away.

"You all know the situation in the summer of 1993," Elchibey replied. "The government was crumbling, the land was filled with traitors like Surat Husseinov and Rahim Gaziev. Had I stayed in office, there would have been civil war, and our Azerbaijan would have become a second Tajikistan or Afghanistan."

And why had he returned now?

"According to the constitution of the Republic of Azerbaijan, my five-year term in the office of President of the Republic expired on June 7, 1997," Elchibey explained. "I did not wish to return before then because I never resigned my office, and remained the legal president until that date. My returning before my term expired could have led to confusion, and I thought it best to just stay away."

I thought about that for a long time, and I still think about it now. By abandoning his office in the summer of 1993, Abulfez Elchibey had indeed saved his country from pitching into the paroxysm of a civil war sponsored by the dark forces in Moscow, but at the cost of his reputation. Yet, one could argue that in doing so, he had forced Heydar Aliyev to pick up where he had left off in the larger project of securing Azerbaijan's independence. That was the argument being made by the Popular Front in any case, that they were somehow Heydar's teachers and mentors in the ways of democratic development and national sovereignty. It sounded good, even if it was self-serving in the extreme: *We made Heydar come to heel!*

So what did the man who succeeded him make of all the fuss surrounding the return of his rival?

Nothing. And I do not think that Heydar Aliyev was silent because he was worried or scheming. Some observers around town (and many with no direct experience in Azerbaijan) chose to interpret Elchibey's return as a result of Aliyev's caving in to Western and particularly American pressure to loosen his tight rein on power and, at the very least, to give Azerbaijan a veneer of multi-party democracy. Others, without contradicting the former opinion, speculated that Heydar had decided that a little vocal, nationalist hard-line opposition on the question of the OSCE/Minsk Group proposals to settle the Karabakh conflict could serve well to make him look decidedly moderate—as well as give him an excuse to stand firm on certain points. 'Look, you keep on telling me that you cannot push Levon Ter-Petrossian too far because he has the Dashnaks to worry about, but I have got my own bunch of Popular Front hot-heads here in Azerbaijan to think about, too.'

Without rejecting either of these theories as motivating factors in Heydar's allowing Elchibey to return to Baku, I think the primary reason was simple indifference. Letting the largely discredited Elchibey walk and talk and even rant and rave about Karabakh, Russia, Iran, oil-pipelines, and anything else he wanted to address, including on state television, was a very low-risk proposition for Heydar. He simply did not care.

"Elchibey is a little like Rip Van Winkle," I quoted a close Western observer of Azerbaijani affairs as saying at the time. "He fled in the midst of a chaotic power struggle when it was difficult to buy a light bulb or toilet seat, and has returned to a new Baku that is in the middle of an oil boom."

I have to admit that I was quoting myself anonymously, and giving myself the fullest advantage of wisdom acquired through hindsight.

* * *

I had asked Vafa to tell Heydar that I was in town and wanted to chat, but the promised 'tomorrow' never seemed to come.

At first I thought Heydar was avoiding me because of all the old-boy glad-handing I had enjoyed over at the Popular Front the night Elchibey returned (and the fact that Abulfez began his press conference the next day by singling me out for thanks). But Heydar was not being elusive; he was merely being presidential, winging his way at the head of delegations to Italy (including a stop off to see Pope John Paul II, whom Heydar must have known and maybe persecuted in the bad old days of the Politburo and KGB), Moldova (for a CIS summit and meeting of the so-called GUAM-group), Poland (to promote yet a further counterbalance to Russia), as well as Paris and London, if I am not mistaken, thus making Heydar one of the most peripatetic presidents to emerge from the lands of the former USSR. When back in Baku, the list of visiting dignitaries, high-level businessmen, and diverse negotiators kept his staff working late into the night nearly every night, and in the priority pecking order men like Richard Matzke of Chevron, John Ilme of UNOCAL, and Terry Adams of the AIOC had clear preference over someone like me.

The real reason for Heydar's remoteness, however, was that he was working out the finishing details of what I referred to as 'the Heydar Hour,' namely the ceremonies surrounding Constitution Day on November 12th—which just happened to have been selected as the official lifting of the first 'early oil' from the AIOC's offshore platform known as Chirag-1. In addition to the presidents and CEOs from every major oil company in the world, the guest list included a regional Who's Who of heads of state, prime ministers, and deputy prime ministers—and Heydar was always a stickler for protocol when it came to regulating the affairs of state. No, Heydar was not avoiding me; he was just plain busy, and thriving on it.

"The amazing thing is that while people like Vafa Gulizade are visibly aging under the stress of working for him, Heydar looks younger and healthier by the day," said a best nameless friend. "Sometimes I think that Heydar is like a vampire for power: he literally thrives on it, like Dracula on blood."

Finally, I got a chance to make a personal request for an interview—or at least to pay my respects. The occasion was Turkish National Day, and the venue the Gulistan Palace and everyone who was anyone in the pan-Turkic or pro-Turkey club was there, applauding madly when Heydar noted that Turkey was the first country to recognize Azerbaijani independence, that the Azeris and Turks were eternal brothers in language, culture, and blood, and that the secular, independent Republic of Turkey as established by the Great Leader Mustafa Kemal Ataturk remained the model for development and independence not only for Azerbaijan, but for all the other Turkic states in formerly Soviet Central Asia and indeed, the entire Caucasus. This had been Elchibey's rhetorical turf, but Heydar had usurped it entirely, down to the ending flourish about the road to independence being long and difficult but that there was never, ever any possibility of going back on the hard-won independence achieved by the second Azerbaijani Republic, just as there was never, ever any going back on the hard-won independence of brotherly, fraternal, and magnificent Turkey. . . .

After the applause had died down and Heydar, accompanied by the new Turkish ambassador, had begun the protocol-perfect process of shaking hands with diverse dignitaries, I sidled over toward the inner phalanx of bodyguards to wait for an opportune moment to say hello.

". . . and the President has specifically asked Secretary Pena to drop all his other plans and commitments to be here for the great day!" I heard the American chargé d'affaires explain through a translator (Robert Finn never used one, I recalled), referring to Bill Clinton's dispatching of Energy Secretary Federico Pena to Baku for the November 12th 'Early Oil'/Constitution Day ceremonies.

"Tell him that I am grateful and look forward with great anticipation to the arrival of the Secretary and remain most eager to meet him again," Heydar responded, and then turned to the next supplicant waiting to meet him—me.

"Tomas Bey," said Heydar, perhaps a little surprised but not unpleased that I had managed to get through the phalanx of guards to join the line of ambassadors. "How very good to see you. When did you arrive?"

"About a month or so ago," I said, explaining my activities in a nutshell, and in the casual tone of voice that one speaks to an old friend. Hassan Hassanov, the Foreign Minister always loitering at Heydar's elbow, seemed to have been struck by an acute case of ague.

"So, how can I help you?" Heydar asked.

"Well, frankly, you could grant me an interview," I replied. "I am working with a major American network on a special project on Azerbaijan and I think the program could be vastly improved and enhanced if you would share with us your wisdom and insight."

"Vafa!" barked Heydar, and Gulizade was instantly by our side. "Look at my schedule and see what you can arrange in the way of an interview!"

"Heydar Muallim," I said. "Friday is not good because we are going to be out and among the refugees."

"That is a very important subject," said Heydar. "Let's try for Saturday or Sunday."

"Perfect," said I, and shook hands in agreement.

* * *

The formal, on-camera interview itself was mainly interesting for how little of it got used and that what did get used got distorted in the editing room. It was conducted in the fifth-floor 'guest' room attached to the presidential office where I had previously interviewed Ayaz Mutalibov, Isa Gambar, and Abulfez Elchibey. This time around, however, security was tight and all the protocols of the pecking order rigorously adhered to; the television team was lined up in order of rank to await Heydar's arrival: the correspondent, the producer, myself (in my role as unofficial simultaneous translator), the cameraman, and then the soundman. The state television and presidential archivist's cameras whirled and flash bulbs popped as Heydar made his way down the line, greeting all of us by name. Then Heydar sat down for fitting of the button microphone and sound test, while I hunched behind the correspondent to give him a running essence of what Heydar had to say from Azeri to English while the official translator got ready to translate from English into Azeri.

I had tried to prep the correspondent on the most salient points, and he certainly had his own questions to ask. But he also had received a batch of subjects to address from the home office, such as asking Aliyev if he planned on following the example of the Islamic Republic of Iran if the United States did not lift Article 907, the rider to the Freedom Support Act that prohibited direct American aid to Azerbaijan so long as it continued to 'blockade' Armenia and Karabakh. To me, it was a ridiculous question, but I guess the viewers back home worry about such things, if they think about Azerbaijan at all.

"No, our path is clear," replied Heydar curtly and clearly. "The system of government and style of society we are developing in Azerbaijan is based on Western values, including democratic pluralism, the free market economy, and a secular republic that respect universal human rights. That is not an American system to accept or reject. But certainly, if the unjust sanctions imposed by Article 907 continue, it will have an impact on our relations, and we will look toward other Western democracies to assist us in our development."

The correspondent then went on to ask Heydar how he countered the charge that he was a relic from the Soviet past, a former communist given to dictatorial behavior who suppressed the opposition and censored newspapers.

Heydar laughed out loud. Virtually all the leaders of all post-Soviet states had been very high up in the Communist Party of the Soviet Union, he said. The list included not only himself but Georgia's Shevardnadze, Kazakhstan's Nazarabayev, Ukraine's Kuchma, Uzbekistan's Karimov, and, of course, Russia's Boris Yeltsin. And as for the charge that he was an unrepentant dictator, Heydar patiently replied that democracy was not something 'one bought off the shelf' but was a continual learning process that had yet to be perfected everywhere, including the United States, where certain ethnic groups put their own perceived self-interest above that of the American nation as a whole by buying off congressmen through lobby groups, and what did the correspondent think about that?

"I am Canadian," the correspondent replied, ducking the question.

Heydar then launched into a precise and highly accurate critique of the history and significance of Article 907.

"That unjust piece of legislation is a scandal and shame and a blight on the record of the democratic process within the United States," he said. "But I want you to be perfectly clear on this point. Article 907 is not directed against me, although certain lobby groups in the United States would like to make people think so. I was not here in power when it was passed in 1992, nor was I responsible for the situation that led up to its getting passed in the American Congress. That was when . . . when *those people* were in power, and as the incompetent fools that they were, they did nothing to prevent 907 becoming law. But let me say this very clearly: I do not hold them responsible for the creation of disaster in Karabakh; it was the Armenians who started and waged war there, not Azerbaijan. And let me also make this very clear: as president of Azerbaijan, I take full responsibility for the removal of that unjust law, and will use every means to do so—including the use of oil."

By the time the program was aired, this last response was spliced into some commentary on Iran, with the inference that Heydar Aliyev would lead his country down the Islamic path unless the Congress of the United States of America got with the program and rescinded 907, when Heydar had never said or implied anything of the kind.

There was one other interesting moment, which Heydar Aliyev should be glad did not make the air. The correspondent, noting that Heydar had managed to establish 'excellent relations' with Bill Clinton and the executive branch of the American government, expressed interest in Heydar's opinion about his 'bad' relations with Congress, and what might be done to improve them.

"Well, young man, you have clearly not familiarized yourself with the issue that your question concerns," said Heydar, a slightly patronizing, grandfatherly tone matching the pleasant mien on his face, as he prepared to show off his prodigious memory. "In fact, I have excellent relations with many members of Congress. Indeed, during my official visit to the United States of American and its capital city of Washington this past August, I met with the Speaker of the House, His Excellency Newt Gingrich, who expressed a keen interest in developments in Azerbaijan and the Caucasus, as well as the Minority Leader, His Excellency Richard Gephardt, the Leader of the Senate Committee on Foreign Relations, His Excellency Jesse Helms, and a wide variety of congressmen and senators from both sides of the aisle, as they say in Washington parlance. I had breakfast with (naming about ten senators) and lunch with (naming about ten congressmen). Indeed, I even had a pleasant and highly productive meeting with precisely those senators and congressmen who are known to be subject to the influence of the Armenian lobby groups, including the Congressman from Illinois, His Excellency John Porter. No, it is incorrect to say that I neither know nor have good relations with the elected representatives of the Congress of the United States of America. There was only one exception, a Congressman from New Jersey who actually joined in the lines of Armenians protesting and trying to ruin the success of my visit to the United States. Yes, that Congressman from New Jersey . . . it was an Italian name, and I can't think of what it is right now. . . . What was his name? New Jersey. . . ."

A frown appeared at the edges of Heydar's grandfatherly smile and it continued to grow and grow.

"It is not important," said the correspondent. "We can pick up the name later."

But Heydar had changed his focus. There no longer was an interview, interviewer, camera, or anything else in the room.

The name, the name!

"What was his name!" Heydar shouted at the official translator.

"Your Excellency Mister President I was not in Washington at that—"

"WHAT WAS HIS NAME!"

"Sir I do not know your Excellency Mister President—"

"VAFA!!" Heydar screamed across the room at Gulizade. "WHAT WAS THAT NAME!!!"

"Your Excellency Mister President it was an Italian name—" said Vafa, rushing up to the table.

"I KNOW HE WAS AN ITALIAN AMERICAN, I ALREADY SAID THAT, BUT WHAT WAS HIS NAME!!!!"

"Your Excellency Mister President it is escaping me for a moment and—"

"WHAT DO I HIRE YOU WORTHLESS PEOPLE FOR IF YOU CANNOT EVEN REMEMBER A NAME!!! CALL HASSANOV AT THE FOREIGN MINISTRY!! I HAVE TWO WORTHLESS ADVISORS HERE AND I WILL KNOW THAT NAME!!!!"

"Yes sir your Excellency Mister President and his name is. . . ."

Vafa was so terrified his leg was shaking against my chair; I reached down a hand and grabbed the calf to let him know he was not alone. He had often joked about seeking political asylum in Montana but now it seemed like he was really thinking about it.

"THE NAME, WHAT IS HIS NAME!"

"Pallone!" cried the translator. "His name was Pallone your excellency the president, Frank Pallone was his name, Frank Pallone, Congressman Pallone from the state of New Jersey! . . ."

"Pallone, yes!" reiterated Vafa. "His name was Frank Pallone, of course, Pallone. . . ."

"Yes, Pallone, Frank Pallone," said Heydar, as suddenly calm and grandfatherly again as he had been explosive and seething with rage a moment before, and picking up the interview from the moment of self-interruption as if nothing had happened. "The Congressman from New Jersey, Frank Pallone, had the audacity to join the lines of Armenian trouble makers seeking to protest my otherwise highly successful visit. . . ."

A palpable burden had just been lifted from Vafa's shoulders, and indeed from all the shoulders in the room.

"Time to think about Montana?" I teased Vafa after Heydar had concluded the interview and left the room.

"I think I need a drink," said Vafa.

* * *

To be generous to a man who has never sought or given much of the same,
at the time of our little interview about American policy toward Azerbaijan,
Heydar was a man under extreme pressure, and might be forgiven a few
explosions.

For example, I rather doubt that Congressman Frank Pallone, Democrat
from New Jersey, would really have liked to be in Heydar's shoes during
the run up to 'Constitution Day' on November 12, 1997. That was the day
that Heydar Aliyev effectively threw the big dice and staked a $30 billion
dollar bet in the great petroleum sweepstakes of the late twentieth century.
No, he was actually playing for much higher stakes. The thirty billion bucks
in promised investment in the oil sector was really only chump change.
November 12th was the day that Heydar Aliyev bet his reputation as a
modern statesman, master manipulator, and ultimately major player on the
international scene. Heydar was betting his country.

The poker table, to strain the gambling man's metaphor, was the Chirag-
1 platform in the middle of the Caspian Sea, and the moment was the
official tap-turning ceremony marking the start of the modern journey for
Azeri crude on its way to world markets—and the real start of the convoluted politics of pipelines, spheres of influence, and international energy
corridors that pundits the world over now refer to as the new version of
Rudyard Kipling's Great Game.

My problem was that the government had restricted access to the platform
to a discrete number of cameras, theoretically corresponding to different audi-
ences. Thus, the BBC had a place on board thanks to the weight of British
Petroleum in the AIOC consortium, Reuters had a place because they represented an international news agency, and Azerbaijan was represented by several state television and presidential archivist shooters. The public relations
people traveling with American Secretary of Energy Federico Pena ('Front-
Page Freddy,' I liked to call him, due to his seemingly obsessive need for
publicity) had been given a choice of which organization they wanted to record
the event for the American viewing public—and they had chosen CNN over
the network I was working for, preferring, it seemed, to have Secretary Pena's
image and pithy words rolled over on the half-hour on Ted Turner's station
rather than be included in an actual issue-oriented, big-picture documentary on
Caspian oil narrated by Ted Koppel.

I discovered this change in plans on two hours sleep, when the taxi pulled up in front of the *Deputatski* lounge at Baku airport to go through the various security-clearance procedures before boarding the helicopters.

"We are so sorry Mister Goltz but your name seems to have been removed from the list in favor of the local stringer for CNN," said the man dishing out the security passes.

I hadn't hung around Azerbaijan for six years to be cut off the guest list to this particular party at the last minute. The only thing to do was to let everyone present understand how I felt about it. You might say I used the sort of persuasion techniques learned at the knee of the Old Man himself when he wanted to get something done, and I think the message got across: I threw a screaming fit that lasted until the head of presidential security finally decided to invite me aboard the chopper. The other option was to shoot me. The MI-8 helicopter was an exact copy of the bird I had flown over the Murov Pass in and out of Kelbajar, except that instead of carrying 100 terrified refugees the MI-8 was carrying twelve security guards with their weapons and six cameramen with their Betacam recorders. Also, no one was dangling from the wheels, aside from myself, in a manner of speaking.

We flew out over the beak of the Apsheron peninsula, gawking down at the private lives of the Baku rich. The new dacha compounds under construction, many with swimming pools, may have been hidden from prying eyes behind compound walls, but not from us. I thought of my host Kazanfer and his carnation-growing estate in Mashtagah, and wondered if I was actually looking down at it. Next, the squarish grid of *dachastan* gave way to beige and yellow sandland where ancient oil derricks took the place of houses, and black, ugly oil-swamps replaced gardens—the sad remnants of the oil-boom in Baku at the turn of the century, mixed with the Soviet legacy of on-shore drilling: it was not a pretty sight.

The reality of total exploitation followed by utter criminal neglect was further marked when our chopper passed from land to the eggshell blue water of the Caspian, and followed the battered and broken causeways leading to the Oily Rocks City on Stilts. Long lines of shimmering yellow and green traced their way through the waves, marking an oil and gas leak trail back toward underwater pipes or the scores of rust-encrusted drilling platforms we flew over, further poisoning an already poisoned sea. I thought about Mustafah, my guide and friend from the Analytical and Information Department of the Ministry of Defense, who, prior to taking me around by overloaded helicopter to places like Kelbajar, in a previous incarnation had been an environmental specialist who dealt with Caspian Sea issues. Where was he? I had heard he had been kicked out or left the army, but I did not know his last name and had been unable to find him.

We were soon out of sight of land and flying over deep water, so deep that the Soviet engineers responsible for the shallow-water carnage lacked the means to drill and destroy. The symbol of their failure was also the new symbol of the success of others. It first appeared as a distant black speck on the eastern horizon, and gained detail as we drew nearer: the AIOC's Chirag-1 Platform. It looked like nothing so much as a huge, spectacular, gleaming white spider dancing on the sea. The pilot took several long turns around the rig for the benefit of the video cameras; I noted several gunships prowling the watery periphery.

We landed at the helipad attached to the platform, and were ushered down a series of metal stairs to the reception room to be issued the requisite hard hats and told about the dos and don'ts of oil platforms. The list was long, but two commands stand out in my memory: hold on to rails from the bottom and do not smoke. Then, while the security men fanned out, the cameramen were taken on a preliminary tour of the structure.

It was then that I began to realize just how big was the platform and rig: Chirag was like a vertical factory city on stilts stuck in the sea bed. I have to say right now that I have no technical or engineering background to really appreciate what I was seeing, but it seemed mighty impressive to me. Miles of pipe twisted and turned around the platform, apparently starting at the elevated drilling station, utterly free of mud and crude on this special day, and ending in a massive 24-inch tube that snaked over the edge of the platform, the last visible portion of the 120-mile line leading along the seabed to the shore. Banks of dials and taps and gizmos and gears greeted one around every corner, inviting one to fiddle until one thought better of that bad idea. At a slight remove, a smoke stack was spewing flame: the blow-off of associated gas, which would continue until yet another 30-mile pipe connected Chirag to the gas condensation system built at Oily Rocks by Pennzoil back in 1993. It, too, was now on-line.

Then there was a living module for the hundred-odd, all-male workers aboard Chirag. Sure, it was Spartan, and no, I would personally prefer to work on shore. But for those roustabouts and roughnecks who chose to earn the premium salaries paid the men who work at sea, one month on and one month off, Chirag was Home Sweet Home: there were cabins and work rooms and offices and a world-class mess hall and a library and even a weight-room on the upper deck. Being a trained observer and curious by nature, I was soon able to ferret out the greatest secret aboard Chirag: the Level Four locker room doubled as the smoking room, a habit shared by virtually all the roughnecks on the platform. They seemed to be drawn from most of the petroleum-producing nations on earth: Scots, Welsh, English, Norwegians, Canadians, Americans, Australians, New Zealanders, Russians, Indonesians, and even the odd Azeri. The last group seemed to be wearing color-coded jackets for some reason, but all had been put on notice not to talk to strangers, so I was unable to determine if this was so and why. One thing remained very clear, however: the grand opening of Chirag-1 by Heydar Aliyev was to be a very well choreographed event indeed.

After about an hour, we were alerted that another chopper was arriving, and we went up to the helipad deck to greet it and watch a delegation of high-level oil executives and officials be ushered off and then down into the meeting room for their hard hats and safety and security lecture. I recognized one of the newcomers: Barry Halton, the public relations point man of British Petroleum.

"Hi," said Barry, whom I had last seen in London a few years before at a lecture he had organized for me at the BP headquarters. "I knew you were aboard from the list!"

"I had to fight my way on."

"I heard about that, too."

It seems that there were two guest lists—one made by the AIOC, in Barry's possession, and a second, more authoritative one, vetted at the last minute by the foreign minister, Hassan Hassanov. I was beginning to understand how that old fox exacted his revenge. . . .

Another hour passed, mainly in boredom. The VIPs had their lounge, but we press plebeians were not allowed to enter. I wandered around the rig to the extent possible, namely, by trying to locate the strange miniature seals that swam around the platform, or shunting up and down the metal stairway between the mess hall and the locker room/smoking lounge, trying to eavesdrop on conversations and even engaging in a few with the less taciturn roughnecks.

"Damn rig has never been so clean nor will it ever be again," said a long-haired, wild-eyed character named Rusty. He was from northern Canada.

"Did you see that bunny in the white helmet?" asked another gent dressed in an orange all-weather jump suit. His name was Bob and he was from Scotland.

"A woman?" said Rusty, jumping to his feet with lust in his eyes.

"Better stay away from Rusty," chuckled Bob. "He's at the end of his month on."

I asked Bob and Rusty what old-hand experts like themselves made working off-shore and they told me that figure was around five hundred dollars a day. A senior engineer might clear a thousand. The color-coated Azeri worms in training (as they say in oil-patch parlance) made two hundred dollars a month.

"Because they don't know how to run the high tech stuff?" I asked.

"High tech my ass," said Bob. "This equipment is almost twenty years old. If this were the North Sea we would have half as many men aboard, and work it all by remote control."

"You mean to say that a lot of this is job creation?" I asked.

"You with the press?" asked Bob.

"Yeah," I replied.

"Ooops," said Bob. "Better button your lip, Rus."

Both did so and we continued chain-smoking in silence until a loud beeper sounded.

"Show time," said Bob, stubbing out his cigarette. "That buzzer means the president's helicopter is approaching. You'd better get upstairs."

* * *

The presidential helicopter duly arrived, the door opened, and Heydar Aliyev and his personal guests hunched down under the blow-back and then scuttled down the metal staircase for their safety and security briefing. The inner circle consisted of Heydar himself, his son Ilhami, Russian Deputy Premier and (then) Minister for Oil, Gas and Energy Boris Nemtsov, American Secretary for Energy Federico Pena, SOCAR boss Natik Aliyev, the new Turkish Minister for Energy, Cuma Ersumer, and a host of other international VIPs representing the various oil companies in the AIOC consortium, ranging from the Japanese Itochi to the Saudi Delta Nimeri. The only person who dared violate the mandatory hard-hat helmet rule, of course, was the man of the moment himself—Heydar Alirzaoglu Aliyev.

It was a formal tour, a slower reenactment of the one the press had been ushered on a few hours before, and because I was not really shooting camera I stayed out of the way of the hack-pack as they scurried in front of the presidential delegation to record the event: Heydar gesturing toward the natural gas blow-off platform, and being informed that said wasted gas would soon be piped into the natural gas system; Heydar standing back from the stack of 30-foot drill bits that ground away at the floor of the Caspian, while listening to a technical lecture about depths and mud and viscosity levels; Heydar taking a tour of the computer room and chatting with the technicians; Heydar standing mid-platform among the baffling array of pipes that led from the well head to the spigot to the main pipeline diving overboard into the sea, and asking Boris Nemtsov how long it would take the oil to travel from here to the lifting station at Novorossiisk; Heydar congratulating the Azeri engineer who had been the one to turn the valve a few days before, initiating that same flow (and watching said engineer recreate the turning of that tap for the cameras.) There was loud chatter and talk and much stumbling of the cameramen as they tried to race down the narrow, yellow walkways after having shot the last sequence, in order to get ahead of Heydar and his security men and delegation and set up for the next stop on the tour.

"This is a technological miracle!" Heydar proclaimed loudly and for the cameras, after emerging from an area of the platform that was studded by a hundred dials and levers.

As the security men cleared the narrow path for Heydar to proceed, I found myself smack-dab in his path. Heydar, trailed by Nemtsov, Pena, and the rest of the VIPs, was nodding and smiling and muttering praise. It was all very theatrical and programmed, and I expected him to just walk on through the view-finder of the video camera I was operating. Then he caught my eye, slowed, stopped—and reached out a hand to squeeze my arm. It was a totally unexpected, grandfatherly, and gratuitous gesture.

"You doubted, didn't you?" he seemed to say with that squeeze.

"Yes, I did and I was wrong," I wanted to say or squeeze back or something, but just kept on filming.

The tour continued and there were no more surprises. It culminated with Heydar's arrival at the ceremonial spigot leading from ceremonial glass piping to a ceremonial silver bucket where the ceremonial first drops of oil would drop before being ceremoniously smeared on the cheeks of those involved with the ceremony. There were more speeches about oil, development, thanks, gratitude, the future, the past, et cetera, and then Heydar was invited to turn the tap. He did so. The oil drooled through the glass tube and then splattered in the silver bucket to much applause. Then, reluctant at first, but bowing to the words of encouragement from those gathered there on Chirag-1, Heydar Aliyev performed the traditional ritual associated with all new wells in the Azerbaijani oil patch dating to the turn of the century: he reached a few fingers into the bucket and cautiously daubed a bit of the black gold on one cheek. The crowd burst into more applause. Then, after wiping his cheeks clean, Heydar invited first his son Ilhami, then SOCAR boss Natik Aliyev, and finally each and every one of the politicians and oil executives associated with the AIOC up to the platform to daub the early oil on their own faces while the workers and lesser VIPs applauded vigorously.

Azerbaijan had just entered the modern energy age.

A caviar and champagne reception in the boardroom followed, after which we were all shunted by helicopter back to Baku to attend an even larger gala ceremony held at the Republican Palace Theater in celebration of Constitution Day. Once again, it was Heydar's moment of glory.

Standing in front of the packed auditorium of special guests, with presidents and prime ministers and diverse luminaries from across the globe lined up on either side, and speaking, as ever, with no notes, Heydar delivered a 50-minute *tour d' horizon* about everything from the pathetic state of the old Soviet-style oil wells polluting the Caspian that he had flown over on his way to the Chirag-1 platform to how Azerbaijan was willing to share its experience with all its riparian neighbors for the general good and regional development. He spun off the names of the twenty major oil firms associated with twelve countries and the level of investment each had made and then went on to the length and bore and diameter of the various pipeline routes under consideration, breaking now and again to lavish praise on the personal courage of people like AIOC president Terry Adams for having persevered in actually making the 'deal of the century' happen. He related how Chevron had recently come knocking to see about transporting Kazakh oil through Azerbaijan by rail to Georgia, and how he supported this idea, as well as an eventual undersea pipeline linking the Kazakh fields to the pipeline system in Azerbaijan, and that Kazakh president Nursultan Nazarbayev was keen on the idea, and that a similar plan was being developed for Turkmenistan.

"Today is not only a day of great significance for Azerbaijan and the riparian states of the Caspian Sea, but a wonderful economic development for the entire world," intoned Heydar. "I see with pleasure that work is starting in the other Caspian states such as Russia, Kazakhstan, Turkmenistan, and Iran. . . . Let the Chirag-1 platform serve as an example for future platforms. It is a tremendous site, an industry, truly a city at sea, a miracle at sea! . . .

"Today, when flying out to the platform by helicopter, we flew over a number of deserted platforms and deserted causeways, some collapsing into the sea. This was a disaster for Azerbaijan! A disaster that will not be repeated, thanks to the technology we are now bringing in to the country and the region. . . .

"We have laid the foundation and it will be the inheritance for future generations not only of Azeris but other littoral states and countries. And I would like to stress again and again—that all contracts signed were signed by the independent state of Azerbaijan, which is and will remain eternally independent!"

Heydar spoke and spoke, revealing himself to be not only an Azerbaijani patriot, but an internationalist, a man of vision and detail, and a retooled free-marketeer economist to boot: he took particular delight in describing how the raging 160 percent inflation in Azerbaijan in 1995 had been reduced to 6 percent in 1996 and was expected to be negative inflation this year, tacitly confirming the reports I had been hearing from moneymen in

Baku, who told me that Azerbaijan was unique among the lands of the former Soviet Union in the sense that the Central Bank was actually propping up the dollar artificially against the formerly worthless Azeri manat.

Then others spoke—Boris Nemtsov, Federico Pena, Turkish premier Mesut Yilmaz, Georgian president Eduard Shevardnadze—all heaping praise on Heydar Aliyev and his accomplishment of bringing Azerbaijan and the Caspian and the Caucasus into the new energy age and indeed the world economy.

And every word he said and they said was true.

But for me there was something else and something vastly more important. Heydar Aliyev was speaking about change, and convincing even a convinced cynic like myself that hope does indeed spring eternal and that people and countries are indeed capable of adapting themselves to new circumstances and that policy that affects millions does not get made in a day, and that sometimes it requires reaching down into oneself and bringing forth the scheming demon in order to survive. And Heydar Aliyev had done exactly that for himself and his country: he had schemed like a demon and had survived, and with him, his country. Azerbaijan.

Against all the nay-sayers and doubters, the Old Man had actually pulled it off: after a five-year period marked by arduous negotiations, revolution, war, unexpected viscosity levels, and such a maze of international intrigue that many close observers, myself included, wondered if any oil would ever be lifted at all, Caspian oil was flowing. And if there were still thousands of questions about how it would get to market, there were now thousands of parties with a vested interest in the continued existence of the producing state, the Republic of Azerbaijan.

It was Heydar's hour, and I was glad I was there to record it.

Index

Thomas Goltz is a writer and lecturer on Turkic/Post-Soviet affairs. An M.A. graduate of New York University's Middle East Department with an emphasis on Arabic and Turkish, he worked as a journalist for various U.S. and U.K. publications in Turkey during the 1980s and then received a fellowship from the Institute of Current World Affairs to visit the 'Turkic' republics of Soviet Central Asia in 1991, just before the August 19th putsch. He landed instead in the Caucasus, where he became a war correspondent, tracking the diverse ethnic conflicts of the region for such publications as the *New York Times*, the *Los Angeles Times, Foreign Policy,* the *National Interest, The Nation,* and others. He also made video documentaries for PBS and the BBC. Since 1992, he has lectured widely on ethnic conflict, Caspian oil, and other subjects. Venues have ranged from Berkeley to Harvard to Oxford to the several universities of Montana, which he calls home.